Public Administration

Approaches and Applications

Public Administration

Approaches and Applications

Edited by

Alka Dhameja

Sweta Mishra

Pearson

Editor—Acquisitions: Kaushal Kumar Jajware
Editor—Production: M. Balakrishnan

ISBN 978-93-325-5507-5

First Impression, 2016

Published by Pearson India Education Services Pvt. Ltd, CIN: U72200TN2005PTC057128, formerly known as TutorVista Global Pvt. Ltd, licensee of Pearson Education in South Asia.

Head Office: 15th Floor, Tower-B, World Trade Tower, Plot No. 1, Block-C, Sector 16, Noida 201 301, Uttar Pradesh, India.

Registered Office: 7th Floor, SDB2, ODC 7, 8 & 9, Survey No.01 ELCOT IT/ ITES SEZ, Sholinganallur, Chennai – 600119, Tamil Nadu, India.
Phone: 044-66540100
Website: in.pearson.com, Email: companysecretary.india@pearson.com

Compositor: MAP Systems, Bengaluru
Digitally printed in India by Manipal Technologies Limited. in the year of 2022

Dedicated to our loved ones who have always contributed invaluably, abundantly and selflessly to each of our endeavour

Brief Contents

Contents

Preface

This volume is a response to a long-standing demand for comprehensive textbooks on public administration. Though it is tough to encapsulate the rivers and the tributaries of an oceanic subject like public administration in one volume, we do intend to quench the curiosity of all those who want to decipher the multi-faceted nature of the discipline through this. The volume is meant for the undergraduate students of public administration in India. However, because of its multi-disciplinary focus and orientation, it may also be useful for postgraduates and civil services aspirants. The Introduction to this volume has been therefore written with a wider clientele in mind. The quality of the chapters included is also pitched in this direction.

We have tried to deal with all topics that are taught at different universities at the under-graduate levels. For the benefit of the readers, a chapter on Post-New Public Management and another one on Historical Antecedents of Civil Society have been added to broaden their knowledge base in the subject. A detailed bibliography has also been prepared for the readers. The objective of this volume is to provide them with an insight into the key concepts and concerns of public administration, especially in the changing Neo-liberal context.

Though there are many textbooks on the subject that deal with these issues, there are certain *features,* which make this volume *different* from those that are generally studied. These are as follows:

- The format of this volume is on the lines of a textbook, however, its style and design is very different from most of them.
- The volume goes beyond the scope of textbooks on public administration by dealing with concerns and approaches quite analytically.
- The volume uses boxes, tables and questions to highlight the important information to enhance recall and recapitulation for preparation of exams.
- Being an edited work, each topic covered in the volume carries the perspective and erudition of its author, making the volume an interesting read.
- The authors of the volume are from different disciplines of social sciences like public administration, political science, economics and sociology. This has given the volume the necessary interdisciplinary dimension.
- Even though the focus in the volume appears to be more on concepts or approaches, eleven full-fledged chapters of this volume explicitly deal with the specific themes in the application of public administration.

Alka Dhameja
Sweta Mishra

Acknowledgements

Writing a textbook in public administration is a task that is even more difficult than it appears. We acknowledge all those who have encouraged us to go ahead with this project. The present volume is the result of sustained and collective efforts of a team of intellectually spirited scholars, friends, colleagues and well-wishers. We record our gratitude to all of them. If some names have been unintentionally missed, we sincerely apologize for our oversight.

We are profoundly thankful to Prof. Uma Medury for her unceasing support in more ways than one in this endeavour. She has been helpful in providing reference books, and paraphrasing many sections of the chapters in this volume. We are eternally grateful to Prof. Anurag Joshi for his help with language editing of ten chapters. Mr. Saugato Sen's significant comments on some of the chapters as well as on the Introduction to this volume are highly appreciated. Dr. Sandhya Chopra Verma who has proof read all chapters of this volume deserves a huge round of applause. We are also thankful to Prof. Nita Mathur and Dr. Smita Chaturvedi who have patiently put up with our whimsical behaviour and nudged us along the entire course of editing. We thank Prof. Pardeep Sahni for his constant encouragement and his noteworthy feedback on the Introduction to this volume.

We also acknowledge the valuable comments and suggestions of our umpteen friends on this volume, of which Prof. Sushma Yadav, Dr. Rekha Saxena, Dr. Anuradha Sharma and Dr. G. N. Trivedi deserve special mention. Words of gratitude will not be adequate to express our indebtedness to them. They have been very encouraging and supportive of us all along. We specially thank Prof. Amita Singh for providing us with her views on importance of textbooks, a part of which now adorns the back cover of this volume. We owe our immense gratitude to Prof. S. N. Mishra, who has remained an iconic figure in our intellectual journey.

All our erudite contributors deserve our special thanks for making time for us and enriching this volume with their noteworthy inputs. Needless to say, their scholarly chapters have immensely added value to the volume. We are thankful for their constant support and encouragement.

We extend our sincere thanks to Ms. Yogita Vasandani for helping us with word processing and corrections. We thank the publisher, Pearson Education, from the bottom of our hearts, for bringing out the volume in a systematic format and within a record time.

Last but not the least, all our family members, who have ungrudgingly endured our dereliction of family obligations during the course of this volume.

Alka Dhameja
Sweta Mishra

About the Editors

Alka Dhameja is a Professor with the Faculty of Public Administration, School of Social Sciences, Indira Gandhi National Open University. She has twenty-five years of experience in teaching public administration through open and distance learning mode. She has to her credit an edited book on 'Contemporary Debates in Public Administration' and two co-edited books. She has also contributed more than twenty articles in reputed journals and books. Her areas of specialization are administrative theory, disaster management, administrative ethics and public policy.

Sweta Mishra is a Senior Assistant Professor, Department of Political Science, Gargi College, University of Delhi. She has been teaching public administration and political science for the last 14 years. Her areas of specialization include decentralization, governance and empowerment. She has also authored six books and has contributed several articles to various journals and edited volumes.

List of Contributors

- Alka Dhameja, Professor, Faculty of Public Administration, Indira Gandhi National Open University (IGNOU), New Delhi.
- Anil Dutta Mishra, Deputy Director, National Gandhi Museum, Rajghat, New Delhi.
- Anita Bagai, Associate Professor, Department of Political Science, Lady Shri Ram College, University of Delhi, South Campus, New Delhi.
- Anurag Joshi, Professor, Faculty of Political Science, IGNOU, New Delhi.
- Kiran Bhushi, Senior Associate Professor, Faculty of Sociology, School of Social Sciences, IGNOU, New Delhi.
- Kopal Chaube, Academic Fellow, School of Human Ecology, Ambedkar University, Delhi.
- Maneesha Pandey, Associate Professor, Department of Political Science, Hindu College, University of Delhi, North Campus, Delhi.
- Poornima M., Consultant, Associate Fellow, Council for Social Development, New Delhi.
- Roopinder Oberoi, Associate Professor, Kirori Mal College, University of Delhi, North Campus, Delhi.
- Sachin Choudhary, Associate Professor of Public Administration, IIPA, Indraprastha Estate, Ring Road, New Delhi.
- Sanghamitra Nath, PhD Scholar, Centre for the Study of Law and Governance, Jawaharlal Nehru University, New Delhi.
- Saugato Sen, Senior Associate Professor, Faculty of Economics, School of Social Sciences, IGNOU, New Delhi.
- Shubhra Pant Kothari, Assistant Professor, Department of Political Science, Zakir Hussain PG Evening College, University of Delhi, South Campus, New Delhi.
- Surendra Kumar, Assistant Professor, Department of Political Science, B.S. College, Danapur, Patna, Bihar.
- Sweta Mishra, Senior Assistant Professor, Department of Political Science, Gargi College, Siri Fort Road, New Delhi.
- Uma Medury, Professor, Faculty of Public Administration, IGNOU, New Delhi.
- Vaishali Narula, Assistant Professor, Department of Political Science, Kamla Nehru College, University of Delhi, Siri Fort Road, New Delhi.

Abbreviations

AAP	Aam Aadmi Party
ACGA	Asian Corporate Governance Association
AGM	Annual General Meeting
APSA	American Political Science Association
ARC	Administrative Reforms Commission
ASPA	American Society for Public Administration
ASX	Australian Securities Exchange
CAI	Chartered Accountants of India
CAARD	Committee on Administrative Arrangements for Rural Development
CAG	Comparative Administration Group
CAG India	Comptroller and Auditor General of India
CalPERS	California Public Employees' Retirement System
CDF	Comprehensive Development Framework
CDPC	Constitution of District Planning Committee
CII	Confederation of Indian Industries
CPA	Comparative Public Administration
CSOs	Civil Society Organizations
CSR	Corporate Social Responsibility
CVC	Central Vigilance Commission
DRDA	District Rural Development Agency
DVO	District Vigilance Officer
FDI	Foreign Direct Investment
FOI	Freedom of Information
HDI	Human Development Index
IBRD	International Bank for Reconstruction and Development
ICDS	Integrated Child Development Services
ICPS	Integrated Child Protection Scheme
ICT	Information Communication Technology
IEDC	Indian Economy Documents Compendium
ILO	International Labour Organization
IMF	International Monetary Fund
IRDP	Integrated Rural Development Programme
ITDPs	Integrated Tribal Development Projects
JNNURM	Jawaharlal Nehru National Urban Renewal Mission
JRY	Jawahar Rozgar Yojna
KMBC	Kumar Mangalam Birla Committee
LPG	Liberalization, Privatization and Globalization
MADA	Modified Area Development Approach
MCA	Ministry of Corporate Affairs
MKSS	Mazdoor Kisan Shakti Sangathan
MPC	Metropolitan Planning Committee

MSJE	Ministry of Social Justice and Empowerment
MTA	Ministry of Tribal Affairs
NDA	National Democratic Alliance
NDC	National Development Council
NGOs	Non-Governmental Organizations
NPA	New Public Administration
NPE	New Political Economy
NPG	New Public Governance
NPM	New Public Management
NPR	National Performance Review
NRCW	National Resource Centre for Women
NREGA	National Rural Employment Guarantee Act
NSTFDC	National Scheduled Tribes Finance and Development Corporation
NWS	Neo-Weberian State
OBC	Other Backward Class
OD	Organization Development
OECD	Organization for Economic Co-operation and Development
PCT	Public Choice Theory
PFI	Private Finance Initiative
PMO	Prime Minister's Office
PPBS	Programme Planning and Budgeting System
PRIs	Panchayati Raj Institutions
PTGs	Primitive Tribal Groups
RBI	Reserve Bank of India
RE	Revised Estimate
RTI	Right to Information
SA & SP	Structural Adjustment and Stabilization Programme
SAP	Structural Adjustment Programme
SCA	Special Central Assistance
SCDCs	Scheduled Castes Development Corporations
SCSP	Scheduled Caste Sub-Plan
SEBI	Securities and Exchange Board of India
SFIO	Serious Fraud Investigation Office
SHGs	Self-Help Groups
SICA	Section on International and Comparative Administration
SMART	Simple, Moral, Accountable, Responsive and Transparent
SVC	State Vigilance Commission
UDHR	Universal Declaration of Human Rights
UN	United Nations
UNCHS	United Nations Centre for Human Settlements
UNCRPD	United Nations Convention on the Rights of People with Disabilities
UNCTAD	United Nations Conference on Trade and Development
UNDP	United Nations Development Programme
UPA	United Progressive Alliance
VOs	Voluntary Organizations
WHO	World Health Organization

Understanding Public Administration: An Introduction

Alka Dhameja

LEARNING OBJECTIVES

After completing this Introduction, you should be able to:

- Understand the nature of politics–administration dichotomy
- Bring out the reasons for the rise of organizational management theories
- Appreciate the relationship among politics, entrepreneurialism, new–managerialism and public administration
- Describe the nature of organization–centric and State–embedded approaches; and
- Examine the various themes in public administration

Public administration, simply speaking is the policy or programme in public or governmental domain; its announcement, formulation, delivery and evaluation. However, when we talk of public administration, we generally cannot pinpoint on a few details, descriptions or explanations. Notwithstanding the fact that so many functions in public sector are now being privatized, outsourced and deregulated, the vision that still engulfs our minds when we think of public administration is that of schools we attend, the colleges we study at, the institutions we serve, the offices we pay our utility bills at, the hospitals we visit and so on. We witness these activities of public administration and are dependent on it, as is often quoted, 'from cradle to grave.' We perceive so much of public administration around us that we forget that it is also a discipline or an area of study with its own epistemological framework and *not* merely a field of practice or operation that we encounter every day. Public administration involves organizations – their structures, processes, behaviour and their interactions with the milieu or environment.

The environment or milieu of public administration in any country is the Constitution, the branches of government and the nature of polity. This makes the boundaries of public administration extremely fluid, its domain quite wide and its scope very vast; making it tough to constrict it in a few definitions. We may say that public administration is one of the most fluctuating disciplines of the social sciences. With its roots in the discipline of political science, it borrows and assimilates immensely from other disciplines as well, so much so that we are unable to draw out its exact precincts. For Nicholas Henry (1995), the discipline of political science is the *mother discipline* and management is the *alter ego* of public administration. This is the reason that as a discipline, it tends to define itself by the practices of management and the demands of the global political scenario. Sociology, economics and law are some other disciplines that provide inputs to the theoreticians and practitioners of public administration.

The introductory chapter of this volume on 'Concept and Significance of Public Administration' by Sweta Mishra familiarizes us with the different facets of public administration by describing its meaning, features, importance and outreach. She makes a distinction between 'administration' and 'public administration', 'private administration' and 'public administration', and 'managerial' and 'integral' viewpoints of public administration to focus on the 'public' aspect of administration, which is its very essence and makes the discipline special and distinct.

Regardless of the scope of public administration today, it continues to function through its agencies with the chief executive at the helm of affairs. Conventionally, the chief executive enjoys administrative and political powers of governance and is assisted by its agencies in execution of functions. In the changed scenario even though the nature of functions and the scenario in which the chief executive operates have changed, it continues to perform its tasks through its trusted line, staff and auxiliary agencies.

The chapter on 'Interdisciplinary Nature of Public Administration and the Changing Role of the Chief Executive' by Kopal Chaube brings out the relationship of public administration with other disciplines such as political science, economics, sociology, management and law. In fact, it discusses the role of the chief executive in the context of this very inter-relationship. It describes the significance and need for the chief executive to work in tandem with labour policies, legal framework and Constitutional guidelines. The chapter also examines the role of the chief executive and its line and staff agencies in the changing context of globalization and good governance.

So what is public administration? Is it government or governance; bureaucracy or partnership in service delivery; an implementing agency or a monitoring mechanism? What is it that comes under the *purview* of public administration? What is it that does not? Is it integral to political science or is it separate from it in nature and approach? What is so special about public administration that many universities have set up independent departments around it? Likewise, why is it that at most places, it is still taught under the department of political science? Why is it that universities abroad have combined departments of public administration with either policy sciences or public affairs or law? These *queries* need to be addressed if we want to understand the nature of the discipline.

To comprehend these questions further, it could be useful if we envisage public administration from three dimensions. These are its: Trajectory, Theories and Themes; or we can call it the 3 'T's, in line with the discipline's recent emphasis on the 3 'E's (Efficiency, Economy and Effectiveness). Note that we cannot strictly put the *trajectory* and *theories* of public administration in two different water-tight compartments. Within the framework of a particular trajectory or context, certain specific theories make an appearance and get defined in the process. The same applies to the *themes*, which also emerge from the trajectory of the discipline. We have merely used these terms as open or pragmatic categories in order to comprehend the multifaceted nature of public administration. In this Introduction to the volume, we look at public administration through these ocular lenses. Let us start with the trajectory of the discipline now.

TRAJECTORY OF PUBLIC ADMINISTRATION

Starting with the 'trajectory', it is important to understand public administration through the course it has travelled over the years. When we describe its route, we do so from the context of the times through which it has evolved. As a field of operation or action, we all know, public administration has been in existence ever since human beings formed their first civilized settlements. Greek, Roman, Indus Valley civilizations are famous for their administrative structures and activities. In India, the great epics of *Ramayana* and *Mahabharata* are replete with stories of administrative competence. Like the Machiavellian 'Prince', Kautilya's *Arthshastra* is a political and an administrative treatise.

As a field of activity, administration in India in the Mauryan, Gupta, pre-colonial and colonial periods excelled in revenue, law and order and judicial arenas. As a field of disciplinary study, however, it is relatively a new discipline and cannot be compared with the other social sciences. It is traced to Woodrow Wilson's essay of 1887 on 'The Study of Administration', which appeared in the Political Science Quarterly. Wilson strongly believed in the efficacy of a trained bureaucracy for administration. The formal recognition of the discipline is although mapped out to the establishment of American Society of Public Administration (ASPA) in 1939 (Henry, 1995), which, if we may say, was instrumental in erecting a separate identity of public administration, quite distinct from political science.

In the West, two traditions of governance have been visible, one is *Anglo-American* (Anglophone), which has believed in self-government, participation and dispersal of authority, and the other is *French* (Saxophone) that has espoused concentration of administrative power. The distinction between the two has, however, blurred over time. The disciplinary growth of public administration has been influenced by these traditions in the US, the UK, France and many parts of Europe. In India, the genesis of public administration as a *separate* discipline is directly linked with its emergence in 1937, when Madras University introduced a diploma in public administration. In 1949, Nagpur University set up a separate department of public administration and local self-government, followed by universities such as Osmania, Lucknow, Jaipur and so on. As a separate identity, public administration got a major boost with the establishment of the Indian Institute of Public Administration in 1954 in Delhi. Later, in 1986, the Union Public Service Commission (UPSC) introduced public administration as one of the optional papers in civil services examination. Since then, the growth of the discipline has not looked back, even though it has not reached where it should have.

We can try to understand the trajectory of the discipline by going through its different *evolutionary* phases at the global level (*coinciding in time and not necessarily emerging one after the other*). We have divided them into the following four sections:

- Politics–Administration Dichotomy
- Rise of Organizational Management Theories
- Coming together of Public Administration and Politics
- Emergence of Entrepreneurialism and Neo-managerialism

Politics–Administration Dichotomy

One of the most important theoretical constructs in public administration is the politics–administration dichotomy. It is central to the understanding of the nature of public administration. Even though Alexander Hamilton was the first to have used the term 'public administration' to describe the nature of his duties as cabinet secretary in George Washington's (First President of the US) regime, public administration as a discipline took birth only through the famous Wilsonian essay. After this, it took its baby steps towards developing a separate personality in the late 1880s. Wilson believed that the field of administration was a field of business and rested outside the sphere of politics.

Wilson's distinction was practical in nature, as he intended to shield administration from partisan and manipulative politics. Administration was treated as the *means* to achieve the political *ends* or policy goals. However, later theorists such as Frank J. Goodnow in 'Politics and Administration' (1900) attributed *distinct* functions to the government and its administration; making the *latter* responsible for enforcement of policies and *former* for making of policies/decisions. Goodnow spoke about the legal approach by envisioning administrative law as a separate stream of administration. In his view 'administrative law is that part of law, which fixes the organization and determines the competence of the authorities that execute the law and indicates remedies for the violation of his rights' (cited in Rosenbloom, 2013).

Max Weber carried the legacy of politics–administration dichotomy forward by creating an ideal bureaucratic framework that was separate from the political arena and exuded *specific* characteristics of impartiality, impersonality, work specialization and personal honesty. Many scholars feel that in Weber, this dichotomy is in a sense *reversed,* as Wilson and Goodnow only spoke of taking politics out of administration, while Weber proposed to take administration out of politics by elevating it to a status of technical and functional superiority over other organizations and politics.

L. D White's 'Introduction to the Study of Public Administration' in 1926 and F. W. Willoughby's book on 'Principles of Public Administration' in 1927 were the first few texts devoted fully to public administration. In 1938, Chester I. Barnard's Functions of the Executive was published. This was the time when 'focus' on *principles* of administration prevailed as the 'locus' on *institutions* of policy formulation and execution did not receive adequate attention ('Locus and Focus' is a terminology used by Robert T. Golembiewski in his Essay 'Public Administration as a Field: Four Developmental Phases' in 1974; cited in Henry, 1995). Even the locus of underlying dichotomy was perceived differently for administration and politics in this period. The institutional locus of administration included the formalized executive branch of government, while the institutional locus of politics rested in the legislature, political parties and pressure groups. Thus, this was the time when the efficiency driven 'focus' on scientific management and various managerial principles came to dominate the space in public administration. All theories that emanated within this context were related to internal functioning of organizations, thereby propelling public administration towards approaches in private sector management.

This was also the period (1890s to 1950s) when the *fact–value dichotomy* got strengthened. In an attempt to make organizations appear effective, scientific management techniques were used liberally. As a result, too much came to be made of the 'facts' at the cost of 'values'. Based on the politics/administration distinction, facts came to be associated with administration, as it was in command of policy enforcement. The values were assigned to the political domain, as they were needed to formulate policies in accordance with ethical norms of equality, impartiality and social justice. This kind of outlook further distanced public administration, at least theoretically, from the gamut of values that ideally should have been a part of its operations.

'Phases in Evolution of Public Administration', is the chapter by Shubhra Pant Kothari, which takes us through the long journey of evolution of the discipline through eight separate paradigms. Some paradigms concur in time of occurrence, but have been dealt with separately because of the distinctness of their focus. The paradigms are: Politics and Administration Dichotomy (1900–1926), Principles of Administration (1927–1937), An Era of Challenges (1938–1947), Crisis of Identity (1948–1970), Public Administration as Management (1956–1970), Public Administration as Public Administration (1965–1970), Public Policy Perspective (1970–1990) and Good Governance (1990s–Present).

Rise of Organizational Management Theories

The organization-centric approaches were a direct consequence of the politics–administration dichotomy context. The policy process was clearly segregated, with policy formulation and adjudication falling in the domain of legislature and judiciary (polity), and the executive (administration) getting all the implementation tasks. Thus, speaking in terms of the impact of this segregation on the discipline of public administration, we can say that a science of administration was visualized on the premise that the autonomous nature of administration could serve as a tool for translating policy objectives into action.

As a result, various scientific principles were developed. In the post-1887 period, the focus was to draw out scientific principles and standardized strategies to make management of organizations effective. Writers such as F.W Taylor, Henry Fayol, Luther Gulick, Lyndal Urwick, Mary Parker Follet, Max Weber, Herbert Simon and so on coined various concepts to make organizations efficiency driven. Elton Mayo's experiments on relationship between workers' psychology, working conditions and work output endeavoured to give a fresh lease of life to the classical organization theories by viewing the workers beyond the *mechanistic persona* that they had acquired. Elton Mayo, F. J. Roethlisberger, William J. Dickson also dealt with issues of workers' unrest and shortage of labour.

Alka Dhameja in her chapter on 'The Classical Approach to Organizations' explains the meaning, focus and characteristics of the approach. She talks of the contributions of the proponents of the classical approach such as F. W. Taylor, Henri Fayol, Luther Gulick, Lyndal Urwick, Mary Parker

Follett, and James Mooney among others. She examines the scientific management stream by looking into Taylor's views on development of a true science of work, division of work and responsibility, time and motion studies, differential piece rate system, functional foremanship and mental revolution. Classical approach of Fayol and his principles, Gulick and Urwick's POSDCORB principles of organization, span of control, and Mary Parker Follett's resolution of conflict in organizations form a crucial part of the chapter.

Uma Medury in her chapter on 'The Human Relations Approach' comprehensively illustrates all experiments that took place under the rubric of the Hawthorne studies by Elton Mayo and his team. She provides a critical appraisal of the approach by contrasting it with the closed classical organizations. All early experiments of Elton Mayo and the ones at the Hawthorne plant, such as bank wiring, relay assembly and illumination are described in detail.

The intent of classical and human relations scholars was to streamline processes in organizations, but the entire focus on organizational principles was rebutted as contradictory and termed as 'proverbs' by behaviouralists such as Herbert Simon. Drawing on the perspectives and methodology of 'behaviour' in psychology, the theory of administrative behaviour called for raising of scientific rigour in public administration. For Simon, decision making was at the heart of administration. Drawing on logical positivism (*based on verification and empiricism*), he worked out prescriptions for public policy and pure science of administration.

In the chapter on 'The Rational Choice Approach', Saugato Sen discusses the methodological and philosophical aspects of the approach. Different strands in rational choice approach such as those of Adam Smith, Jeremy Bentham and Max Weber are also discussed. The relevance of rational decision making in public administration is brought out by discussing Herbert Simon's intelligence, design and choice activities in decision making. Simon's views on bounded rationality form an important part of the chapter. Another focal point of the chapter is the further extensions of rational choice approach in the contemporary scenario.

The classical organizational concept was also criticized by Robert Dahl, who in his paper 'The Science of Public Administration: Three Problems' in 1947 laid down obstruction of values, differences in individual personalities and varied social frameworks as major bottlenecks in developing universal principles of administration. So were Elton Mayo's experiments, (considered to be too few and superficial for the purpose of generalizations, among various other issues), by later scholars such as Chris Argyris and Frederick Herzberg. Max Weber's ideal bureaucracy was critiqued by scholars such as Robert Merton, Peter Selznick, Alvin Gouldner *et al.* It was also called the machine model of organization, which was rigid, inhuman, impersonal and hierarchical. Warren Bennis predicted the eclipse of such bureaucratic organizations, as he foresaw their replacement by temporary and flexible work systems.

Roopinder Oberoi, in her chapter on 'Max Weber's Theory of Bureaucracy', carries forward the threads of the classical approach by delving deeper into it and examining its different characteristics. For Weber, bureaucracy was the most superior form of organization. He attributed it to bureaucratic features of rationality (legal–rational), impersonality, technicality and working capacity among others. A rather descriptive account of the bureaucratic characteristics, as identified by Weber, is given in the chapter. The focus is on the appraisal of bureaucracy, which exhaustively deals with the post-Weberian critique by different scholars.

Public administration and management interface was at a pinnacle in this phase. This was the time when sociopsychological approach drew out certain very pertinent features of organization related to an individual's psychology in an organization and their impact on organizational outcome.

The focus of all these approaches was either on individual needs, group behaviour, rational decision making or organizational design and environment or context of organizations. Chester Barnard, Abraham Maslow, Chris Argyris, Rensis Likert and Victor Vroom are some of the organizational thinkers who have contributed towards this approach.

Alka Dhameja, in her chapter on 'The Systems and Sociopsychological Approaches' speaks of the sociopsychological perspective to organizations that believed that all individuals had certain specific needs, which they expressed through their attitude towards work. These needs acted as driving forces in their work lives. Motivating factors were the ones that targeted and addressed these needs. This approach transformed the individual from a passive being who was worked upon by the organizations to an active being whose feelings and desires determined the complexion of organizations. The chapter also discusses the systems approach to organizations as a precursor approach that laid the foundation of the sociopsychological approach by talking about inducements and contributions in an organization.

These approaches are very important, as they led to many other participatory management approaches. William Ouchi through his Theory 'Z' reiterated the significance of Douglas McGregor's Theory 'X' and Theory 'Y'. This later culminated in management techniques such as organization development (OD), which came to be used in amplifying organizational behaviour. OD was a deliberately planned, organization-wide effort directed from the top to increase the effectiveness, efficiency and viability of an organization. Chris Argyris also used OD techniques in his work on senior executives. Organization theory that developed in this phase (early 1960s onwards) was administrative theory under the pretext of 'management theory'. In an attempt to strengthen its identity, public administration had further started drawing from management principles and theories.

The administrative practitioners (*administrators*) and the business schools joined hands to emphasize the mechanistic aspect of management, giving a go by to public administrationists (*those involved with the academia*). To make it more knotty, even the business firms came to be regarded as separate entities thereby strengthening the divide between public and business. Many scholars feel that this hampered the organizational growth in public sector as the area of exploratory research became a part of private organizations rather than public ones. In a sense, it was natural for public organizations to borrow from private sector as it understood the connect between processes and output for fulfilment of goals. The issue, however, was of context or environment. Public administration had to fulfil its objectives in terms of the goals of welfare and equity, whereas private administration was ruled by markets and its demands. This dichotomy stalled the disciplinary growth of public administration to some extent, as it could not develop theories that were value–laden, State–centric and citizen–oriented.

Coming Together of Public Administration and Politics

With the locus of institutions in the background, no clarity on the domain of public administration could emerge. This post-1950s period could be called the period of *intellectual predicaments* for the discipline. This is evident from the fact that in 1962, public administration was not included even as a sub-field of political science in the report of 'Committee on Political Science as a Discipline' set up by ASPA (Henry, 1995). Swimming in the whirlpool of the so called value-free organizations, which were rigidly following the scientific managerial principles, scholars in public administration thirsted to bring standards such as ethics, equity, responsiveness, participation and citizenship back into the folds of public administration. The *interface* between political science and public administration that remained unplugged from the 1890s to 1930s was revived in the late 1940s and early 1950s by scholars who understood its relevance.

F. M. Marx (*Elements of Public Administration,* 1946) questioned the politics–administration dichotomy and averred that public administration was value laden. 'Administrators could be actually working in highly political and preferential environment'. L. D. White commented that 'study of public administration…needed to be related to the broad generalizations of political theory concerned with such matters as justice, liberty, obedience, and role of the State in human affairs' (cited in Denhardt and Denhardt, 2009). In 'policy and administration' (1949), Paul Appleby 'identified politics as everything having to do with the government and everything that government does…Thus, whether an issue is policy or administration becomes completely relative; policy and administration are only two sides of the same coin' (cited in Tahmasebi and Musavi, 2011).

Dwight Waldo (*Administrative State: A Study of the Political Theory of American Public Administration,* 1948) criticized the notion of unchanging principles, as methodologies determining them were inconsistent, plus values of economy and efficiency played a substantive role in the field of administration. This concern manifested in the Minnowbrook Conference I, which gave birth to New Public Administration (NPA) movement. In the view of Ramesh K. Arora (2004), NPA focussed on 'organizational interests, everyday social experience, empirical concerns, theory building and autonomous action'. Thus, there was ample emphasis on the intricate relationship between public administration and polity from the early 1950s to 1970s.

In the chapter on 'New Public Administration', Uma Medury takes us through all the three Minnowbrook Conferences that have taken place till now. She outlines the key factors behind these Conferences and describes their thrust areas. All the goals and anti-goals of the NPA movement that came about after the first Minnowbrook Conference have been highlighted by her. The major objectives of all the three Minnowbrook Conferences have been brought out in detail. The focus of the chapter is on comparison of the three Minnowbrook Conferences and an evaluation of NPA.

Public administration got strengthened in this phase with the formation of Comparative Administration Group (CAG) in 1962. This was the period that saw the blossoming of theoretical writings on empirical, nomothetic and ecological issues in public administration (*Fred W. Riggs' contribution to comparative administration and development administration in the developing countries is pertinent in this regard*). This phase was marked by tremendous interest on the part of the multinational corporations of US and other developed countries in the developing and underdeveloped countries; their resources and markets (Farazmand, 1996). Transitional or developing societies thus became the focus of research and analysis.

The chapter on 'Ecological Approach to Public Administration' by Surendra Kumar focuses on the Riggsian approach to understanding the nature of public administration in the developing societies. He discusses the features, scope and relevance of the ecological approach. Surendra Kumar describes the fused, diffracted and prismatic models of Riggs, in the context of relationship between administration and its political, economic and sociocultural environment. The characteristics of prismatic or transitional societies such as formalism, heterogeneity and overlapping are discussed in detail along with their administrative and economic sub-systems.

Maneesha Pandey in her chapter on 'Fundamentals of Development Administration' delves into the evolution of the concepts of 'development' and 'development administration'. She describes the concept of development administration in detail and brings forth its important tools. The various characteristics of development administration such as change orientation, goal orientation, time orientation and innovation orientation are explained by her. Social justice, participation, self-reliance and equality as fundamentals of development have also been discussed.

Many scholars such as Mohit Bhattacharya (2002) have observed that this momentum on development approach could not last long as the differentiation between 'development' and 'non-development' administration was highly artificial. In his view, 'there is no development administration as a special administrative terrain'. Riggs' analysis of prismatic societies has also been critically appraised. Ramesh K. Arora (2003) has averred that 'Riggs chose to study only those actions of a prismatic society, which appeared to violate ideal standards of economy, efficiency and morality of the West. He did not make complementary efforts to compare these standards in transitional societies with those of immorality, bad economics and inefficiency in the developed nations'.

This entire phase was influenced by the US aid agencies and its programmes for developing societies, with funds and personnel for study and practice of public administration coming largely from US sources. As soon as the funding from Ford Foundation was withdrawn, the work on development administration and comparative public administration came to a halt. Moreover the CAG was also wound up. In the late 1970's and early 1980's, theoretical developments in the discipline were few and far between. This period has been broadly termed as 'End of History' by Francis Fukuyama (1989). The crisis of economy in the West manifested at this stage. In 1980's, the US and UK economies entered into deep recession. Keynesian welfare economics made way for neo-classical economics. Public administration scholars began to direct their criticism against bureaucracy. The monolith of State came under attack. It was presumed that State could no longer manage conflict and encourage participation.

The search for anti-state and anti-bureaucracy theories once again brought the scholars in public administration at the doorsteps of the managerial principles of the private sector. These were sought to improve efficiency in the government sector. The phase was marked by Thatcherism (Margaret Thatcher's line of politics with focus on low inflation, small State, free markets and privatization of public sector), as well as Reaganomics (Ronald Reagan's policies on reduction of growth of government spending, federal taxes and government regulation). The impact of recession was felt all over the globe. In India, the Fifth Pay Commission went in for public sector management type of reforms in a full-fledged manner. A call was made for pro-market reforms by way of deregulation, privatization, downsizing and contracting out of public services. This had an impact on the theoretical framework of the discipline as the approaches that emerged were once again managerial in tone and complexion.

Emergence of Entrepreneurialism and Neo-Managerialism

With house all set for opening up of economy, it was not strange to see public administration take a circular turn towards private-sector models. In 1992, David Osborne and Ted Gaebler published their famous work on 'Reinventing Government' proposing a new theory of governance using organizational ideas and values to improve the efficiency and service orientation of the public sector. The focus was on result orientation, entrepreneurialism, catalytic government, mission-driven administration, consumer orientation, innovation and so on. Encapsulating these features, the term New Public Management or NPM emerged as the 'panacea' for administrative ills. During the Clinton Administration, drawing from NPM, Vice President Al Gore adopted and reformed federal agencies through his National Performance Review (NPR) Project.

In the chapter on 'The Concept of New Public Management' by Uma Medury, all aspects of this new approach such as evolution, conceptual framework and key components have been put forth. The concept of reinventing government is described in detail. The appraisal of NPM is clearly brought out by highlighting almost all factors that have impacted the clear understanding of the concept. The chapter also deals with impact of public choice, transaction costs and principal–agent theories on the evolution of NPM.

The World Bank soon after added a political dimension to the neo-liberal reforms induced NPM approach by laying down four pre-conditions for governance, namely public sector management, accountability, information and transparency, as well as legal framework in its 1992 report. The good governance agenda was hurriedly lapped up by the developing countries, who themselves were enveloped in economic crisis and faced a dearth of theoretical approaches to deal with it.

In the chapter on 'Understanding Good Governance', Anil Dutta Mishra brings out the relationship between 'governance' and 'good governance'. He explains why it is important to understand the prefix 'good' that has been added to 'governance' by describing the inclusion of key elements of equity, participation, transparency and competence in 'governance', as these provide an extra edge to the concept. The good governance initiatives have been highlighted in the chapter, which also gives a neat appraisal of the concept, weighing its pros and cons in developing countries such as India.

The 'good governance' approach added a new dimension to the managerial theories in public sector. Many new concepts such as New Public Service and New Public Governance attempted to add a human face to the managerial form. The concept called the Public Administration Global Perspective (PAGP) that has recently emerged takes a leap beyond good governance. Its objectives are to 'advance knowledge building, address practical issues, improve public administration education and ultimately increase the relevance of the field. PAGP emphasizes theory building that bridges particularism and universalism attending to observations in specific ethnic, cultural and political contexts, while at the same time looking for greater explanatory power, wider practical implications, informed policy learning and transfer' (Hou, 2011).

The chapter on 'Significance of e-Governance' by Sanghamitra Nath speaks about digital governance to improve the system of governance that has been put in place to provide better services to the citizens. She describes the application of electronic means in the interaction between government and citizen, government and business as well as in internal government operations to simplify and improve democratic government and business aspects of governance. She also makes a case for using e–governance strategies to improve the efficiency or effectiveness of the executive function of government including the delivery of public services.

The chapter on 'Towards Post-New Public Management' by Uma Medury raises many issues that have arisen as a consequence of NPM reforms, and thus takes us beyond NPM. She talks of re-establishing the public sector ethos, building human capabilities, enlarging human choices and provisioning dignity and equality. She brings out the different concepts of post-NPM approach such as neo-Weberian State, digital-era governance, public value management, New Public Governance and New Public Service. An exhaustive account of post-NPM changes aimed at fostering cooperation; establishing linkages; coordinating policy making; ensuring cohesiveness, re-regulation and recollaboration and enhancing public service delivery has been provided. The focus is also on global initiatives in governance for striking a right kind of balance among social, political, civic and economic governance.

This entire phase (1980s to 1990s), notwithstanding the good governance approach, was marked by organization-centric theories and we can say that the dichotomy between politics and administration was back with a vengeance. Christopher Pollitt has termed this phase as 'neo-Taylorism'. The concepts of NPM, good governance and post-NPM can be viewed in a linear way with more concerns like accountability, transparency, human capabilities, value-laden management and participation being added with each approach to make it appear more relevant and citizen centric. However, none of these approaches exudes any State-embedded features. This makes it easy for us to categorize the theories in public administration till date. In the following section, we mention all these theories and concepts under two straight categories. Again these are not watertight as all approaches in public administration have State-centric features. The moment we say public, we mean State. Nevertheless when we say State-embedded, we mean drawing more from the State (its nature, functions, objectives, institutions). The trajectory outlined has given an idea of the 'context' in which these theories emerged. This would help us in understanding the impact of the political–economic setting on the disciplinary status of public administration.

THEORIES IN PUBLIC ADMINISTRATION

Every discipline has a set of *models/approaches/perspectives* through which it is studied. We desist from using the term 'paradigm', as theories or approaches in public administration do not fulfil the qualifying parameters of the term. Public administration has a rich repository of theories that make the comprehension of the discipline a bit complex. The trajectory of public administration depicts that the path travelled in its disciplinary growth has given shape to various pertinent theories. Some are internal organization centric (organization-embedded), in which organization is central and some deal with organization–environment relationship (State-embedded), in which society is integral. The organization management theories were applied to both private and public organizations and all these were totally context specific. When Wilson, Goodnow and Weber spoke of a separate identity for public administration, the approaches that emerged were more centred on organizations, public institutions and bureaucracy. Likewise, when scholars in public administration sensed a vacuum of politics–administration connect, the approaches that emerged were more environment (politico–economic) centric.

In the chapter titled 'Approaches to the Study of Public Administration' by Anita Bagai, an attempt has been made to present an outline of some of the important approaches that provide theoretical directions to administrative inquiry. These approaches are categorized into traditional, modern and contemporary. Under the traditional approaches, Bagai talks of historical, legal, institutional and case methods. Under modern approaches, she describes behavioural, systems, structural–functional and ecological approaches. She clearly explains the contemporary approaches as public choice and comparative public administration and deals with the range and type of comparative studies in detail, highlighting the inter-institutional, intra-national, cross-national, cross-cultural and cross-temporal studies. Theoretical models of comparison like the behavioural, systems and development administration also form a part of the chapter.

Bhattacharya (2001) has observed that even though there is *no* theory of public administration, there are certainly many valuable theories/concepts/models *in* public administration. This makes the discipline, in his view, rather 'poly-paradigmatic'. We can understand the concept of public administration by glancing over its major theories or approaches. On the basis of the trajectory that we have outlined, two types of approaches stand strong, one is organization centric or public systems management and the other is State-embeddedness. They both are governance theories, which aspire to make public institutions efficient and answerable to its people. What differentiates them from one another is their respective viewpoint on the 'association' of public institutions with its environment and context. We will see why a division of theories in these categories can be defended in understanding the subject of public administration.

Organization-Centric Approaches

The disciplinary progression of public administration started off on the premise that it was different and separate from political science. Initial models were *closed or universal design models* that dealt with the internal functioning and structuring of organizations, generally in the private sector. Among these were mechanical approaches like the *classical* (Taylor's Scientific Management, Weber's Bureaucracy) and *human relations* (Elton Mayo's Hawthorne Experiments). These models were criticized by the *behaviouralists* such as Herbert Simon and Robert Dahl who, however, could not offer answers to many issues pertaining to organizations such as top-down hierarchy, process of change and pertinence of negotiation. It was nevertheless felt that organizational environment that provided *inputs* to the structures/processes of organization was more important than the internal activities of the organizations.

Thus emerged the *open models* such as the systems, sociopsychological, cybernetic and network. Systems theory suggested that organizations, both public and private, could be viewed in the same way as biological or physical systems (*whole organisms independent of their parts and pursuing specific purposes*) within a complex environment. 'The organization receives from its environment the human and material resources and directives it requires to operate. These are transformed by organizations as outputs and transmitted again into the environment. The focus is on systems' energy transformation capacity, and the relationship between structures and functions of the system' (Denhardt and Denhardt, 2009).

This was not a new approach as strands of this had originated in Biology (Ludwig von Bertalanffy in 1940s) and were evident in administration (*Mary Parker Follet's Conflict Resolution*), sociology (*Talcott Parsons's Structural-Functional Approach*) and psychology (*Kurt Lewin's Gestalt Psychology*). General systems approach was an attempt to join up different approaches in science and social sciences and give a broad macroscopic view of different types of systems. Bhattacharya (2002, 2001) has pointed out that systems approach facilitated the 'contingency' or situational view of structuring organizations (*through technology and environment*), rather than concentrating on the earlier view of one best way of doing a job.

The sociopsychologists such as Chester L. Barnard defined efficiency on the basis of human behaviour and propounded a cooperative systemic approach, with focus on motivation. Simon worked on Barnard's thoughts and introduced the concept of *satisfycing* behaviour and bounded rationality in decision making. Peter Selzick later developed a cultural–institutional theory of organizational sociology parallel to the works of bounded rationality. Chris Argyris (*Organization Learning*), Abraham Maslow (*Hierarchy of Needs*), Douglas McGregor (*Theory X and Theory Y*), Rensis Likert (*Systems of Management and Leadership Styles*) and Frederick Herzberg (*Hygiene – Motivation Two Factor Approach*) attach great significance to human behaviour in organizations and institutions, and the psychological character of such grouping form the foundation of their theories.

The organization-centric theories (*closed and open*) nevertheless do not view organizations in the context of the State. In fact, they do not even essentially focus on management of public sector organizations. They talk of concepts which are presumed to be 'standard' and can be applied on both private and public sectors. The public systems management theories are all organization theories, but we sometimes call them public systems, as in public administration, focus of concern is on the term 'public' in organizations. When we apply private management concepts on the public sector, we must remember that public sector not only consists of bureaucratic organizations involved in carrying out certain governmental functions through some specific processes. but also the public sector functions within the political, economic and social context of the State. This brings us to the issue we raised earlier on in this 'Introduction', that is the issue of differing 'locus'.

The open models use an input–throughput–output analysis whereby the public sector's environment includes the executive branch of government, the rules and regulations that govern its organizations and demands of the market. For closed organizations, environment is not very important as they are concentrated on making the organizational process effective and output efficient. However, this does not mean that organizational theories are not valuable for public administration. They have immensely contributed to the growth of the discipline. We cannot overlook the fact that in the post-World War I context, their focus on technical efficiency and organizational streamlining brought respite from industrial unrest. Not to forget that scientific management of Taylor culminated in the constitution of Taft Committee on Economy and Efficiency in the US.

Weber's theory is still regarded as the most comprehensive theory of bureaucracy in public administration. All post-Weberian theories have merely been a critique or an endorsement of Weber. Barnard's concepts on acceptance of authority (*Zone of Indifference*) and leadership as a process of fulfilling the purposes of organization and management by consent have an enormous contemporary value. Besides, there are theories/concepts of group behaviour, communication, leadership, motivation, work specialization, which even though borrowed from the private sector management, have systemetized the internal functioning of organizations in the public sector.

NPM has emerged combining the features of both closed and open systems. Borrowing vastly from corporate management and neo-institutional economics (*user-pay, cost-cutting, output targets*) as observed by Jan-Erik Lane (2000), the NPM does not describe what goes on in terms of public sector reforms but recommends a new approach. The major objective of NPM is to make public administration more businesslike. It is based on the critique of Weberian theory and its claim to bureaucracy as the most efficient structure running a country. It aims to bring back the managerial values of efficiency and effectiveness in public sector. In intent, it is a pertinent approach, as it provides various alternatives to public sector delivery of goods and services and also provisions mechanisms to hold public sector organizations accountable for their actions.

The NPM approach has, however, been termed 'generic' by B. Guy Peters and Jon Pierre (2003). Its 'one size fits all' may not solve the problems of developing countries, where autonomous self-regulated networks and domination of managers instead of bureaucrats may add to the woes of the State, which has to operate in the environment, where public service provision has to tackle with issues of poverty, unemployment, inequity and human rights violation. NPM exhibits a forceful promulgation of neo-liberal ideology of the international financial institutions and transnational business for which 'Foreign Direct Investment or FDIs remain forces of public sector reforms. The interpretations of good governance are construed as the freedom to invest and de-invest to achieve the agenda of donor programmes' (Singh, 2005). Wamsley (1996) calls the National Performance Review (NPR) exercise on reorganizing the government, which draws from reinventing government and NPM, 'a futile exercise of rearranging the boxes on executive branch organization chart'. Some also feel that NPM has created artificial divisions between 'efficiency' and 'effectiveness' as well as 'output' and 'outcome'.

The strong political imperatives in the good governance theory prevent us from bracketing it strictly under the organization-centric approaches. Its emphasis on the form of political regime, the process by which authority is exercised and the capacity of governments to design, formulate and implement policies provides it a certain tilt towards State-embeddedness. However, it also has traces of anti-bureaucratic sentiments and a strong focus on non-state institutions. Scholars like

George Frederickson have called 'good governance' fashionable, imprecise, complex and broad. Frederickson has suggested a broad theory of government comprising inter-jurisdictional governance, third-party policy area-specific governance and public-non-governmental governance (cited in Medury, 2010). Now let us see how the other set of approaches is different but relevant.

State-Embedded Approaches

By now we know that public administration is not all about internal functioning of public organizations. It works in an environment that is highly political and not just executive centric. It works within the broad framework of the State and its Constitution. It means that the wax and wane tendencies witnessed in the polity are bound to cause ripples in the growth of the discipline. Although organizations are integral to public administration, they do not wholly make it. The complexion of the State determines the nature of its public administration. If the State is democratic, so will be its administration. Public administration has to look beyond the organizations and address questions of 'power', 'interests', 'conflict' and 'negotiation' in society.

Mainstream administrative theory is majorly bureaucratic or public organization theory. However, public administration is essentially State-centric governance. The bureaucracy-led public sector is merely one of the actors in governance. The sustenance of public administration fundamentally comes from two sources: *Institutions* (legislature, judiciary, executive and other representative bodies) and *people* (civil society and its constituents, interest groups, media). Joachim Ahrens et al. (2011) have observed that 'governance is not a synonym for government. Rather, it relates to institutions and processes associated with governability and accounts for institutional variety as well as its importance for State capacity in conducting policy reform'.

In its disciplinary growth route, the focus on comparative as well as development administration was the first brush of public administration with 'Beyond Organizations' or 'Beyond Public Sector' approach. It was only when public administration was seen as a sub-field of polity and society and restructuring of organizations was seen within the context of the larger environment that the objectives like change, goal, client, participation orientation were brought under the purview of administrative objectives. Ferrel Heady and Fred Riggs believed that bureaucracies were sub-systems within the political, economic and social contexts. Fred Riggs felt that 'bureaucratic expansion at the expense of political institutions tended to inhibit the development of effective politics…Lack of extra-bureaucratic institutions hampered development' (cited in Bhattacharya, 2002, 2001).

The approaches facilitated the understanding of public administration in developing countries till late 1970's but were criticized for being re-colonization approaches promoting the agenda of the developed world (Gunder Frank's Dependency Theory, Gunnar Myrdal's Asian Drama, Samir Amin's views on agrarian capitalism and monopoly of technology in his work on 'Imperialism and Unequal Development' and 'Obsolescent Capitalism…', Hamza Alavi's work on Pakistan's Political Economy and many Post-development theorists hold this view). Political economy approach is yet another perspective that emphasized the State-embedded approach to public organizations. Wamsley and Zald (1976) suggest that 'public organizations could be best understood in terms of the conjunction of political and economic factors influencing their operation. Externally, the organizations are influenced by the *interplay* of interest groups and market exchanges. Internally, they are affected by distribution of power and authority' (Denhardt and Denhardt, 2009).

We could also categorize the three Minnowbrook Conferences that were instrumental in the spread of the NPA movement as a State-embedded perspective or approach. Since the object was to bring back the values of governance into the folds of public administration, it challenged the givens of both orthodox public administration and pluralist political science. Minnowbrook II also had a strong State-orientation and so did Minnowbrook III. Minnowbrook II stressed on interdisciplinary approach, leadership, Constitutional and legal perspective, technology policy, pragmatic long-term reforms, confluence of public and business systems, innovative personnel systems and so on. Minnowbrook III dealt with comparative public administration, public policy research, role of international organizations in governance, new forms of governance and reformulation of public administration as a socially embedded process.

Immediately after the NPA, the public policy approach gained pre-eminence. This perspective is also integral to the State-embedded approaches. Public policy analysis is concerned with governmental structures and behaviour. What governments actually choose to do or not to do forms the core of Yehezkel Dror's policy science perspective, which has strengthened the public policy approach. Dror has observed that the use of extra-rational information like intuition, value preferences, extraordinary leadership and acute reality perceptions could enhance policy analyses. Incremental (*Partisan Mutual Adjustment and Marginal Incrementalism*) and rationalist approaches have added value to the public policy approach.

Saugato Sen in his chapter on 'Public Policy: Concept and Approaches' defines policy and brings out the importance of the term 'public policy'. He examines the theoretical dimensions of public policy. The various approaches to public policy such as institutional, group, systems, elite, rational choice, game theoretic and incremental are discussed by him. The purpose, significance and variations in public policy are clearly brought out. The necessary relationship between public policy and public interest is also discussed in the chapter.

We could enlist public choice approach under the category of the State-embedded approach, as it, in a way, endorsed the neo-liberal ideology by providing a theoretical framework to it (*as discussed later in this Introduction*). The legal and political approaches to public administration that many scholars talk about are State-centric approaches. Reiterating the concern of Minnowbrook I on institutional structures and values, the *Blacksburg Manifesto scholars*, in 1994, focussed on collective behaviour and completely rejected the view that 'authority and participation were antithetical and mutually exclusive in institutional or organizational life'. Their viewpoint of organizations was post-behavioural, post-empirical and post-positivist (*They called for a place for values and conjectures of the researchers in the discipline*). Blacksburg scholars called their manifesto as institutionally grounded Minnowbrook (Wamsley, 1990). John A. Rohr (1990) has observed that the most prominent claim of the manifesto is that 'public administration should take its rightful place in governance'.

As we mentioned earlier, good governance is also a State-embedded theory. One substantive development that took place as a result of the approach in 1992 is the importance that it gave to institutions. After a long time, public administration got back its 'locus' that is its institutions (*political and executive*). The normative use of the term 'good governance' emphasizes the indispensability of participatory development, human rights and democratization to governance. Strong focus on an endogenous good governance approach aiming at policy reforms as well as institutional restructuring has helped the discipline's theoretical bases as well as its field of implementation. If restructuring organizations fall in the domain of public administration, so does the restructuring of State in the interests of its people, keeping in view conditions of political instability, fragile democracy and unsteady electoral practices. In the words of Haque (2013), the mismatch between politics and administration and society and administration has to be addressed to deal with issues of public administration.

Although there are many State theories (*Anarchist, Pluralist, Institutional, Marxist, Liberal, Neo-liberal*), researchers in public administration could study those that are relevant to the discipline. The Marxist viewpoint makes place for two theories of State – fundamentalist and relative autonomy. 'If the fundamentalist class State concept gives us a reductionist idea of bureaucracy being an appendage of the dominant class, the relative autonomy theory on the other hand situationally lifts the State above societal interests and enables it to play an adjudicator positioning one interest against the other. Till 1970's the research in administration was more in terms of its relationship with society. Scholars such as Theda Skocpol "brought the State in" through her writings, recognizing the role of State in instituting comprehensive political reforms' (Haque, 2013).

A balanced blend of both types of theories (Organization/Public Systems and State/Polity) would help the growth of public administration as a discipline. A *complementarity* model has been proposed which 'recognized the interdependence, reciprocal influence and mutual deference between elected officials and administrators, proposing low political control as well as low administrative independence of administrators' (Svara, 2001). However, a theory that enables public administration to tighten its edges with the State is somehow not in sight. It is because the hangover of the dichotomy continues to linger.

Allen Schick has stated that abandonment of politics/administration dichotomy in 1940s is overstated (Henry, 1995). As Ramesh K. Arora (2004, 2003) has pointed out that although Minnowbrook II in 1988 accepted the imperatives of administrative control over policy agenda, the politics and administration dichotomy appeared to have survived. It has been rightly observed that 'this dichotomy expands and contracts, rises and falls, but never to go away'. Weber's and Wilson's views on administration and politics have not been adequately debated. Weber also viewed bureaucracy as a vast base of social power. Bureaucracy for him had to serve the State and so its goals were to fulfil State's policy goals. Wilson in 1966 had observed that politics and administration interact to improve the organic State. He believed that the administrators would always have to directly interpret and respond to public opinion. Therefore, they should be involved in the policy process and elected officials should be involved in the administrative process (cited in Tahmasebi and Musavi, 2011).

THEMES IN PUBLIC ADMINISTRATION

Now moving on to the themes in public administration, we should be very clear as to what public administration entails. What are its defining issues? What is 'publicness'? What is so special about public administration? What differentiates it from the private sector and non-state organizations? We have tried to address these issues under the following four themes (*which encompass a wide range of sub-themes*) in order to examine the relationship between public administration and the State. These are:

- Development and Democracy
- Accountability and Administrative Reforms
- Bureaucracy and Public Interest
- Research and Theory Building

Development and Democracy

The development process has to be rooted in the democratic setup of the country. Participatory democracy is a precondition to development. In context of the developing societies, this is more relevant as the development process has to address issues of regional development, minorities, social welfare and equality. Thus, development is not merely economic growth or increase in gross national product and per capita income; it also involves sensitive issues pertaining to quality of life, human rights, sustainable environmental change and gender equity. This is achievable only if policymakers address the issues of people by treating them as active and aware citizens (*not clients, consumers or beneficiaries*) and also involve them in governance processes.

India's tryst with participatory development began with the implementation of its Constitution; the Fundamental Rights and Directive Principles of State Policy enshrined in it speak of citizens' rights and duties, as well as State's obligations towards them. Participatory planning has been a part of all our Five Year Plans; it finds reflection in the number of anti-poverty programmes and development schemes for the disadvantaged, minorities, children and women. Decentralization in India (*73rd and 74th Constitutional Amendments*) is an attempt to design a new form of administration to match the needs of development at the grassroots; meeting local needs, reducing conflict, satisfying local sub-groups, supporting community and encouraging participation.

Sweta Mishra's chapter on 'Decentralization and Local Governance' gives an exhaustive account of decentralization in India; its content and implementation. The chapter, on the one hand, provides the concept, significance, dimensions and approaches to decentralization, and on the other, examines the system of decentralization in India. The highlight of the chapter is its focus on financial decentralization and the functioning of rural and urban local bodies.

Democratic participation for development cannot take place without the existence of the 'public sphere' as a mediating factor between the individual and the State. This sphere is occupied by the non-state actors (*civil society groups, social movements, social networks and media*). Robert Putnam's theory of Social Capital (1995) and Amitai Etzioni's work on Communitarianism (2003) are pertinent in this regard. Communitarianism regards community as a third way between Statism and individualism. 'The philosophy combines moral, social and civil agendas in its focus on the need to build consensus, foster trust and strengthen mutual ties of reciprocity and obligation' (Newman, 2001). The social capital approach refers to the capacity of States or societies to establish a sense of community. This accumulated social capital is integral to the efficacy of the development process. There are four views on social capital – communitarian (community groups, voluntary organizations), network (business groups), institutional (private and public) and synergy (community groups). Power does not only rest with the State or bureaucracy; it rests with, as has been observed by Michael Foucault, 'hundreds of micro-processes defining various currents coming from multitude of different sources' (cited in Bhattacharya, 2002, 2001).

Amita Singh (2005) has averred that 'real policies are made in the micro-policies or good practices at grassroots level. This diminishes the role of the traditional bureaucracy and gives enhanced role to the organs of government such as judiciary, election commission, panchayats and development agencies including civil society groups. This makes for governance'. Thus, governments in today's neo-liberal context need to build partnerships with the private sector, NGOs, assistance agencies and civil society organizations to identify the channels for democratic participation and implement the development programmes.

'Historical Antecedents of Civil Society' is the chapter by Kiran Bhushi, where she tries to explain the meaning of the term 'civil society' by looking at its evolution. Civil society appears to be an amorphous term, which is rarely explained properly to provide its true constituents. Anything that is non-state is put under the category of civil society. She gives an exhaustive account of the evolution of the concept in four different sections, namely Classical Political Thinkers; Enlightenment Thinkers; 19th Century Thinkers and Modern Thinkers. The highlight of the chapter is the views of Locke, Hegel, Gramsci and Habermas. Through their lens, the elements of civil society of today have been examined.

Poornima M. in her chapter on 'Role of Non-Governmental Organizations' clearly brings out the changing role of public administration and the role of Non-Governmental Organizations or NGOs in it. She discusses the role, significance, characteristics and evolution of NGOs in India. The nature of NGOs and their different types or variations are clearly brought out by her. The section on role of NGOs in public administration is lucidly compiled by her, as she examines their various advantages and disadvantages.

The development paradigm in India has been, for a very long time, driven by the developed countries (*Ford Foundation, Washington Consensus, Structural Adjustment*). Mohit Bhattacharya (2002, 2001) has suggested that 'endogenous development must be built around politico-administrative systems, which have roots in the soil and psyche of the local communities in the developing world coupled with responsive administrative system'. He has cautioned, however, that approaches of the State towards community participation may not always be encouraging, as they range from being anti-participatory, manipulative, incremental and participative.

The recent NPM and good governance development agenda also emanates from the structural adjustment programme of the West. This is not suggest that Western approaches have no relevance for developing countries, but these often falter when implemented out of context. Even due to global economic compulsions, as Neerja Jayal (2003) has averred, the idea of governance in the developing societies cannot be reduced to that of technical facilitator of development, delinked from conception of democracy and welfare. Jayal has therefore called it a 'highly impoverished notion'. In her view this has led to the 'application of a different set of standards for the latter, whereby democracy and development are seen as possibly incompatible, and democracy is substituted by governance'. Where, on the one hand, scholars such as Adrian Leftwich have privileged development above any other goal – democracy or welfare – there are on the other hand, the post-development theorists like Wolfgang Sachs and Arturo Escobar who have urged for a complete break with the idea of development. The word 'development' has been criticized by radicals such as Wolfgang Sachs as 'the outdated monument to an immodest era…' (Turner, 1997).

The central argument of post-development theory is that development constitutes a specific way of thinking about societal change. They look at the development discourse as a very real historical formation, articulated around an artificial construct of underdevelopment. Thus, if the power of development discourse has to be challenged or displaced, what is needed is a radical reconceptualization of 'underdevelopment' itself. 'Structural and social concerns should be treated equally with macro-economic and financial concerns. The comprehensive development framework or CDF is an acknowledgement of the complex nature of development. It is an attempt to operationalize a holistic approach to development. It focuses on non-assistance agencies and partnership with non-state actors to define development needs and implement programmes' (Bhattacharya, 2002, 2001).

It has been put forth that 'public administration has not been treated as a creator of positive political culture even though it is best positioned to effect major democratic change. It has the ability to connect social, economic and political areas and it can blend the tasks of running a Constitution with democratically organizing principles in a way that both maintains the society and achieves its human aspirations…'(Denhardt, 1996). This relationship between development and democracy is an area of pertinence and concern for public administration, as it covers sub-themes such as delegation of authority, people's movements, democratic institutions, governance by non-state actors and implementation of developmental schemes.

Accountability and Administrative Reforms

Administrative accountability seeks to ensure optimization of the available resources and at the same time to realize the organizational goals. Various expressions like responsiveness, responsibility, accountability and control are used to ensure the adherence of public officials to the standards and rules of service as well as the goals of organization. It denotes the specific methods and procedures, which help to enforce the responsibility of civil servants. Four areas of interaction between policy making and policy implementation (*politicians and bureaucracy*) have been identified by Peter Self (1972). These are policy making, arbitration of interests, treatment of individual and localized claims and balance between political accountability and administrative discretion on organizational arrangements. These areas define the contours of accountability.

Accountability is a tool of evaluation of administrators' performance. There are two types of control that ensure accountability, one is internal (*budgetary control, personnel management, professional standards and ethics*) and the other is external (*executive, legislative and judicial control; media and social audit*). Blessan (2010) has identified three types of accountability, namely responsive (*responsiveness of lower rungs of administration*), retrospective (*reviewing past performance of representatives*) and hierarchical (*improving top echelons*).

Uma Medury and Sweta Mishra have brought out the fundamentals of financial administration in their chapter called 'Nature of Financial Administration'. The chapter defines financial administration by highlighting its nature and scope. The interdependency between administration and finance is clearly brought out. The chapter discusses the nature, functions and types of budget in detail. The focus is on new types of budgets like participatory, gender and green budgets. It also examines the budgetary process in India; whereby the formulation, enactment and execution of the budget is brought out.

In the chapter on 'Forms of Public Accountability', Vaishali Narula examines the concept and types of accountability by highlighting bureaucratic answerability, political responsibility and economic conscientiousness. The traditional model of accountability is contrasted with the contemporary and changing notion of accountability. The recent focus on NPM reforms has brought the issue of accountability into prominence. Narula therefore looks at the initiatives towards ensuring accountability. Instruments of accountability such as Central Vigilance Commission, Citizen's Charters, Right to Information, Lokayukta and Lokpal are thoroughly looked at.

The most pertinent way of ensuring accountability is through continuous administrative reforms. Diverse development contexts of the countries call for an assortment of administrative reforms. Caiden (cited in Bhattacharya, 2001, 2002) has talked of four types of reforms, namely political (*through political revolution*), organizational (*targeting organizational rigidity*), legal (*bringing about reforms and enactments*) and attitudinal (*creating change in mindsets*). India has had a long history of administrative reforms in the form of Santhanam Commission on Prevention of Corruption 1966, Administrative Reforms Commission (1966 and 2005) and so on. The Department of Administrative Reforms and Public Grievances has initiated a Sevottam Model that focuses on citizens' charter implementation, good grievance redressal system and excellence in service delivery. The objective is to make way for governance and application of Information and Communications Technology (ICT) to transform the governmental functioning into 'Simple, Moral, Accountable, Responsive and Transparent'(SMART) governance.

In the chapter on 'Redressal of Grievances and Right to Information', Sweta Mishra describes the machinery for the redressal of citizens' grievances. She talks of Department of Administrative Reforms and Public Grievances, Ministry of Personnel, Public Grievances and Pensions, Directorate of Public Grievances, Cabinet Secretariat and Central Vigilance Commission as major redressal agencies in India. She specifically takes us through the passage of implementation of RTI Act by underlining its definition, significance and practice at the grassroots level. She brings out the provisions of RTI Act and also discusses the accountability tools for RTI.

The recent NPM model is an instrumental reform agenda targeting public systems in the country. It has addressed some common complaints against governments related to their size, productivity, accountability, transparency and integrity. Political and institutional reforms are the need of the hour. The most fundamental step towards which is the establishment of an appropriate policy framework, which means that right policies and political will have to be behind implementation and constant monitoring of policies (*revision, renewal and redressal*). Commenting on the classic debate between Friedrich and Finer, which is a very accurate representation of the politics–administration relationship, Peters and Pierre (2003) have observed that 'policies are implemented when they are formulated and formulated when they are implemented'. Administrative reforms get conceived and implemented through a systematic policy process. The sub-themes under this broad theme comprise policy process, policy sciences, redressal mechanism, people's movements, role of media, ICT/ e – governance initiatives and so on.

Anurag Joshi in his chapter on 'Policy Formulation, Implementation and Evaluation' coins a new acronym 'FIE' to explain the formulation, implementation and evaluation phases in the policy process in India. He provides an explicit description of all activities/actors/procedures under the 'FIE' and examines the significance of each stage under it, especially policy evaluation by distinguishing between policy output and policy outcome.

It is felt that public sector reform is not simply a technical matter of introducing private sector management to the ailing public sector. Shirley and Nellis (cited in Turner, 1997) suggest four essential elements that define the relationship between the government (State) and public sector:

1. Set clear and obtainable objectives that are attuned to commercial operation of the firms.
2. Give management greater autonomy.
3. Establish clear rules, procedures and limits for governmental participation in decision making.
4. Hold managers accountable by negotiating targets, monitoring and evaluating results and rewarding managers and staff on the basis of their performance.

Administrative reforms through state minimization are possible only if we have a systematic legal framework and policy structure to support them. The contention is, as has been observed, that 'we will not reach the "minimal" state of Neo-liberal theorizing ever. There will be cyclical patterns of State intervention in the economy, and each new cycle would bring a new mode of State intervention' (cited in Turner, 1997). The issue is not the size of bureaucracy or even hierarchy of bureaucracy. As

Anthony Giddens has stated, 'the process of how structures come into being is more important than the structures themselves' (cited in Wesley, 1996).

Amita Singh (1996) has observed that even though the Tenth Five Year Plan in India has given credence to good governance as a tool for ensuring human wellbeing and sustained development, community institutions and their accessibility to institutions of governance have not been properly recognized under the NPM and good governance approaches. The outcome of reforms has taken precedence over processes of reforms. The approach paper to the Twelfth Five Year Plan provides ample place to accountability. It has a visible focus on inclusive growth, expanding livelihood options, better implementation and improved accountability. It regards inclusive growth as a multi-dimensional concept, which has room for social welfare of SC/ST, OBC, women, children, differently-abled and other disadvantaged sections of society, but systematic and holistic reforms have a long way to go.

Sachin Chowdhry in his chapter on 'Social Welfare Administration and Protection of Weaker Sections' discusses the concept of social welfare in general and welfare administration in India in particular. For clarity and comprehension, he divides the chapter into five sections, each dealing with a specific aspect of welfare. These sections are welfare administration, social welfare under Five Year Plans, protective measures for disadvantaged sections, development strategy for weaker sections and administrative arrangements. He also provides an exhaustive list of legal enactments in the area of social welfare as well as of major guidelines for the disadvantaged groups.

As public administration today is merely one of the multiple actors engaged in delivery of goods and services, newer values of competition, conflict, negotiation and bargaining have entered its domain. It has moved on from the era of 'State monopoly' to 'State competition'. New values mean more accountability, propelling a need to embrace a broader definition of accountability, which speaks of not merely compliance but an inter-organizational culture that can be understood by all stakeholders in governance. Thus, along with the government, other non-state actors as well as the corporate sector must be held responsible for its actions. Service ethos is no longer unique to government; private businesses are increasingly being roped in to provide public services. Corporate social responsibility is one such development. Corporate governance implies that management assumes the role of trusteeship with all the attendant checks and balances, which creates an effective organizational performance, customer satisfaction, high employee morale and enhanced stakeholder value.

Roopinder Oberoi in her chapter on 'Concept of Corporate Governance' underlines a very important dimension of governance, which in the post-NPM context has become very pertinent. This is corporate governance and its impact on sustainability of business. She examines the importance of corporate governance by discussing its meaning, nature and characteristics. She also describes in detail the six principles of corporate governance. The developments in India in terms of committees and guidelines on corporate governance are neatly put forth.

Bureaucracy and Public Interest

The issue of reforms brings us to the question of public interest. All reforms must aim at fulfilling the larger interests of citizens. Provisioning public interest is the crux of reforms. Weber's bureaucracy was all about technically adept organizations, superior to all other forms. The issue of public interest did not figure in Weber's impeccably idealistic structure with all the features and processes for efficiency in order. It was, however, criticized by many scholars including the Marxists for being self-serving, self-aggrandizing and self-referential. According to them, it changed knowledge into secrecy and competence into mystery. As observed by Roberto Michels, big organizations tended to rule out internal democracy (cited in Bhattacharya, 2001, 2002).

Even post-Weber, for a very long time, public interest and neutrality of bureaucracy, including the frontline personnel (*street bureaucrats*) were considered to be contradictory to each other. Bureaucracy is generally expected to be committed to party ideology and programmes. If elected representatives implement programmes for the disadvantaged impartially under the veil of anonymity, then the purpose of public interest is defeated. Bureaucracy is involved as much in policy making as implementation. Public choice theorist Gordon Tullock finds the Wilsonian division of policy formulation and implementation rather 'dangerous'. The notion of 'public interest' of bureaucrats came under the microscope when the Weberian bureaucracy was juxtaposed with the public choice approach. Economic logic of methodological individualism and rational self-interested decision making came to be used to understand administrative behaviour in the 1960s. Scholars like William A. Niskanan (*relevance of individual preferences in bureaucrats and budget maximization*), Patrick Dunleavy (*bureau reshaping*) and Vincent Ostrom (*allocation of decision-making capabilities and utility maximization)* came to influence public policy.

The bureaucrat, for the first time, was described as a self-interested utility maximizer and budget maximizer. The public choice theorists felt that bureaucracies tend to accumulate tasks and resources and therefore checks have to come in the form of decentralization, deconcentration, multiple organizational arrangements, transparency, etc. Public choice approach is categorical about the fact that firms maximize profits, consumers maximize utility and bureaucrats maximize self-interest and political support. Taking its cue from the public choice approach, the NPM scores a point in bringing the ills or pathologies of bureaucracy into the domain of public administration debate. Management principles of efficiency and effectiveness are proposed to professionalize public service. However, alongside this efficiency approach, it has been observed, there are issues of growing 'morality' or 'ethics' in public administration. It is against this background that Mohit Bhattacharya (2001, 2002) has observed that a theory of public interest in public administration has emerged.

Public interest is not an easy concept to define. It is an evolving notion, as it represents the interests of diverse groups of people who could even be in conflict. The mitigation of conflicts is constant and contextual for public administration. This is the role which is often overlooked, but this is what that adds 'publicness' to public administration. P. Guy Peters and Jon Pierre have observed that there is a distinct theory of 'public interest' in public administration, which revolves around the concepts of institution, perfectionism, utilitarianism and social justice (cited in Bhattacharya, 2001,2002).

In the case of public organizations, public interest also takes into account the issues of minority and their work experiences in the organization. The classic study by Camilla Stivers (*Gender Images in Public Administration: Legitimacy and Administrative State,* 2002) has introduced the feminist issue in public administration. Bhattacharya (2001, 2002) points out that far from being rational organizations, bureaucracies have been found to be mirroring the prejudices of the larger society. There is an unequal distribution of power in the organization and a general trend towards restricting women to the lower rungs. In his view, there exists an 'opportunity structure' in the organization, which serves to signal women that they are not fully valued organizational members.

Anita Bagai in the chapter titled 'Feminist Perspective of Public Administration' deals with issues concerning the role of gender in governance. She talks of various parameters of gender analysis used by administrators which are by and large male centric. Women in administration, she discusses, are subjected to discrimination because of the prevalent stereotypes, male sub-texts and myths against women. She makes a comparison between 'gender of governance' and 'governance of gender' to put her point across.

Normative considerations are integral to public administration, but in the changing scenario, bureaucracy has to be more committed than neutral; more representative than impartial. There needs to be a balance between bureaucratic neutrality and responsiveness to citizens. It is a bit strange that whenever we do any impact study of developmental programmes, the most critical line of lapse is found in bureaucracy (*its structure, attitude and behaviour*). Everything is blamed on bureaucracy and private or unconventional or matrix organizations are sought after for the delivery of goods and services, not realizing that all organizations – even the non-formal and private ones – could develop bureaucratic pathologies if not managed systematically. In the view of Fredericksson (2014), downsizing shifts policy implementation to 'hidden bureaucracy' Besides, the issues of accountability and responsiveness plague the non-bureaucratic organizations too.

Levine (1988) has observed that there are genuine dangers in the impulse to denigrate government in general and bureaucracy in particular. The danger is that oversimplifications, myths, stereotypes and assumptions generally distort decisions about the proper role of bureaucracy. Certain demystification of myths pertaining to bureaucracy has to be done. These myths relate to: bureaucracy is always wasteful; business is always better than bureaucracy; government should act like business; bureaucracy is the major cause of governmental malpractices and bureaucracies are poor at goods and services delivery.

A strong bureaucracy is critical to sustain core values of equality, legal security and equal treatment, especially when newer actors have entered the domain of public administration. Pai Panandiker and E. A. Kshirsagar (conducted in 1978) has shown that bureaucracy engaged with developmental tasks at field level was less rigid and behaviourally more flexible than headquarter or secretariat bureaucracy engaged with non-development tasks (cited in Bhattacharya, 2001, 2002). Not many studies have been taken up in this area since then. All types of reforms and ethical training should now attempt at making public servants identify decision making rules, project positive and negative consequences, understand the appropriateness of ethical principles and their underlying value assumptions and moral bases (Dhameja, 2003). Role of ethics, bureaucratic functioning and restructuring, citizens' rights, pressure/interest groups, lobbying – all form the sub-themes of this broad theme.

Research and Theory Building

Research in public administration has treaded a path which, as Kettle (2014) has put it, made it sit in disciplinary backwaters. Bureaucratic politics has focussed on explaining the basic behaviour of key agency officials instead of its structure. Public management has struggled to find the sources of leverage on government's outcomes instead of designing its processes. Economic theories of bureaucracy have simply swept away the century's detritus and replaced it with simple assumptions of self-interest and deductive models of the results these assumptions produce. Thus, focus has shifted away from administrative processes, bureaucratic behaviour and public interest.

As Daneke (1994) has averred, the research in the areas that discuss or illustrate broad issues, trends or ideas in public administration as well as areas that highlight survey problems/questions of professional practice is wanting on many counts. White and Adams (1994) have also pointed out that 'much of the research in public administration does not culminate in hypothesis testing, nor does it add to existing body of knowledge. It is wanting on scientific enquiry. The issues related to relationship among public administration, State, market, non-state groups have not been sufficiently analysed.

Research is borrowed heavily from private sector reforms, instead of being defined by 'what is truly public'. We have delved a lot on descriptive and instrumental theories instead of normative dimensions to strengthen theory building'.

Now, when the research in social sciences is undergoing an unusual phase due to the emergence of the post-modern narrative, we can use a different approach to explore public administration. Post-modern approach questions the notion of singular or unifying concepts in social sciences. It argues against the building up of cumulative scientific knowledge with one theory building on the other in a linear manner. It builds on phenomenology and critical theory, which respectively focus on qualitative and interpretative methods of studying social reality, as well as distorted patterns of communication in an organization. The narrative device deployed by post-modernists is discourse analyses (Charles J. Fox and Hugh T. Miller) by deconstructing the narratives to reveal assumptions underlying the content, giving way to hitherto-neglected diverse voices.

As has been observed by Abel and Sementelli (2004), development of an evolutionary critical theory for public administration could provide opportunities to address a number of the disciplinary questions ontologically. Critical theory could address the subject matter of public administration by highlighting its inter-subjective experience of good governance; its identity crisis, its legitimacy and its proper place in governance.

Scholars like Shamshul Haque (2013) have made a case for Asian perspective of public administration. Haque has observed that 'it is imperative to launch comprehensive genealogical studies on pre-colonial to colonial and to post-colonial public administration. Their underlying causes and consequences need to be explored and possibilities of revival of relevant tenets of pre-colonial administration need to be highlighted. It is necessary to carefully identify and prioritize the critical domains of administrative activities. The administrative factors in Asia are considerably affected by social norms, political tradition, State formation and cultural values, which need to be researched'.

It has been observed that there is nothing like private being bad and public being good. Reforms have to be *objective* about borrowing from the private or the public. Both sectors have their distinct problems and operate in different environs. Society, State and organizations are enmeshed in political relationships of power and authority (Turner, 1997). Thus, as has been pointed out, the tensions between 'politicians decide', 'managers manage', 'customers choose' and 'stakeholders participate' cannot be wished away, but the solution lies in recognition of the tensions first (Colin, 2004).

Growth/status/nature of the discipline of public administration, good practices, case studies – all form the sub-themes of this broad theme. The answer to the issues in public administration will always be sought from its interface with the environment – bureaucratic organizations, legislative policies, governance partnerships, judiciary and civil society networks. These will have to work within the larger framework of the State. What is missing is the political approach to analyse their roles, processes and behaviour. Public administration cannot divorce itself from politics. It defines itself through political processes and structures. Without them it is a vacuous field with little purpose and goal.

The dichotomy between administration and politics has somehow been stretched too far. Researchers in public administration hesitate to look at the State theories and their impact on administration. Likewise, political scientists have left the study of bureaucracy, public sector reforms and decentralization completely to the domain of public administration. Administrative problems are appraised in an insular manner. Their relationship with the nature of polity and working of the State goes mostly unexamined.

Programmes and policies of the government are not merely driven by the successes and failures of bureaucracy; they are conditioned more by political will, electoral prospects, Constitutional enactments, politician–industrialist nexus, legal hurdles, social movements, co-optation by power lobbies, class conflicts, global environmental and economic concerns and so on. A multi-disciplinary approach would strengthen the study of public administration. Inputs from various social sciences have to be woven and adopted by the scholars and practitioners in public administration. Core areas can be easily sieved and operationalized. Unless this is done, Waldo's *identity* crisis (1948) and Ostrom's *intellectual crisis* in the discipline (1974) would persist. Public administration *emerged* from the womb of political science, it is important that it starts recognizing the *merger points* with it.

REFERENCES

Abel, C. F. (2004) *Evolutionary Critical Theory and its Role in Public Affairs*. New York: M. E. Sharpe.

Ahrens, J., Caspers, R. and Weingarth, J. (eds.) (2011) *Good Governance in* 21st *Century: Conflict, Institutional Change, and Development in the Era of Globalization*. UK: Edward Elgar.

Arora, R. K. (2003) 'Riggs' Administrative Ecology' in Chakraborty, B. and Bhattacharya, M. (eds.). *Public Administration: A Reader*. New Delhi: Oxford.

Arora, R. K. (2004) 'Public Administration: Resilience and Rejuvination' in Arora, R. K. (ed.). *Public Administration: Fresh Perspectives*. Jaipur: Aalekh.

Bhattacharya, M. (2001) *Public Administration: New Horizons*. New Delhi: Jawahar.

Bhattacharya, M. (2002) *Social Theory and Development Administration*. 3rd ed. New Delhi: Jawahar.

Boyne, G. and Ashworth, R. (eds.) (2010) *Organizing Government*. Vol. 1. Los Angeles: Sage.

Colin, T. (2004) 'Paradoxes of Human Nature and Public Management Reform' in Jabes, J. (ed.). 'The Role of Public Administration in Alleviating Poverty and Improving Governance' in *Selected Papers from Launching Conference of the Network of Asia-Pacific Schools and Institutions of Public Administration and Governance (NEPSIPAG)*. Asia Development Bank, Kuala Lumpur.

Cox III, R. W., Buch, S. J. and Morgan, B. N. (2005) *Public Administration in Theory and Practice*. 2nd reprint. New Delhi: Pearson.

Daneke, G. A. (1994) 'A Science of Public Administration' in White, J. D. and Adams, G. B. (eds.). *Research in Public Administration: Reflections on Theory and Practice*. UK: Sage.

Denhardt, R. B. and Denhardt, J. V. (2009) *Public Administration: An Action Orientation*. 6th ed. US: Thomson Wadsworth.

Dennard, L. F. (1996) 'The Maturation of Public Administration: The Search for a Democratic Identity' in Wamsley, G. L., Wolf, J. F. et al. (eds.). *Refounding Democratic Public Administration: Modern Paradoxes, Post-modern Challenges*. London: Sage.

Dhameja, A. (2003) 'Role of Ethics in Public Administration' in Arora, R. K. and Saxena, T. (eds.). *Ethics and Accountability in Government and Business*. Jaipur: Aalekh.

Dhameja, A. (2010) 'Introduction' in Dhameja, A. (ed.). *Contemporary Debates in Public Administration*. 3rd ed. New Delhi: Prentice Hall.

Farazmand, A. (1996) 'Development and Comparative Public Administration: Past, Present and Future.' *Public Administration Quarterly*. 20(3).

Frederickson H. George and Richard K. Ghere (eds.) 2014 *Public Management*, New Delhi: PHI.

Golembiewski, R. T. (1977) *Public Administration as a Developing Discipline: Perspectives on Past and Present*. New York: Marcel Dekker.

Golembiewski, R. T. (1995) *Practical Public Management*. New York: Marcel Dekker. pp. 20–25.

Goodsell, C. T. (1990) 'Public Administration and Public Interest' in Wamsley, G. L. and Bacher, R. N. et al. (eds.). *Refounding Public Administration*. London: Sage.

Haque, M. S. (2013) 'Public Administration in a Globalized Asia: Intellectual Identities, Challenges and Prospects.' *Public Administration and Development*. 33(4).

Henry, N. (1995) *Public Administration and Public Affairs*. New Delhi: PHI.

Hou, Y., Ni, A. Y., Ora-orn Poocharoen, et al. (2011) 'The Case for Public Administration with a Global Perspective, (Minowbrook III: A Special Issue).' *Journal of Public Administration Research and Theory* (JPART).

Jann, W. (2007) 'Public Administration under Pressure: The Search for New Forms of Public Governance' in Bertucci, G. and Rosenbaum, A. (eds.). *Implementing the Millennium Development Goals: Challenges and Responses for Public Administration.* New York: The United Nations Committee of Experts on Public Administration.

Jayal, N. G. (2003) 'The Governance Agenda: Making Democratic Development Dispensable' in Chakraborty, B. and Bhattacharya, M (eds.) *Public Administration: A Reader* New Delhi Oxford.

Lane, J. E. (2000) *New Public Management*. London: Routledge.

Levine, H. M. (1988) *Public Administration Debated.* Englewood Cliffs (NJ): Prentice Hall.

Medury, U. (2010) *Public Administration in the Globalization Era: The New Public Management Perspective.* New Delhi: Orient BlackSwan.

Moynihan, D. P. and Thomas, J. C. (2013) 'Citizen, Customer Partner: Rethinking the Place of the Public in Public Management.' *Public Administration Review.* 73(6).

Newman, J. (2001) *Modernizing Governance: New Labour Policy and Society*. London: Sage.

Peters, B. G. (2011) 'Theoretical Debates in Public Administration in the Past 50 Years.' *HKJU-CCPA*. 11.

Peters, B. G. and Pierre, J. (2003) *Handbook of Public Administration*. London: Sage.

Rhodes, R. A. W. (1994) 'The Hallowing out of the State: The Changing Nature of Public Service in Britain.' *The Political Quarterly*. 65(2).

Rhodes, R. A. W. (1996) 'The New Governance: Governing without Government' in *Political Studies* Vol 44, Issue 4, Sept. Wiley Online Library. (Accessed 22nd Sept 2014)

Rohr, J. A. (1990) 'The Constitutional Case for Public Administration' in Wamsley, G. L. and Bacher R. N et al. (eds.) Refounding Public Administration. London Sage.

Rosenbloom, D. V. S. (2013) 'Public Administration Theory and Separation of Powers' in *Administrative Change*. XL(2) and XLI(1).

Sabarwal, M. (ed.) (2013) *Public Administration in South Asia, Bangladesh and Pakistan.* CRS Press.

Self, P. (1972) *Administrative Theories and Politics: An Enquiry into the Structure and Processes of Modern Government*. London: Allen & Unwin.

Singh, A. (ed.) (2005) 'Introduction: Exploring Dimensions of Sustainability in Administrative Reforms' in Singh, A. (ed.). *Administrative Reforms: Towards Sustainable Practices*. New Delhi: Sage.

Singh, H. and Sachdeva, P. (2005) *Administrative Theory*. Allahabad: Kitab Mahal.

Stoker, G. (2002) 'Governance as Theory: Five Propositions' in Chakraborty, B. and Bhattacharya, M. (eds.). Public Administration: A Reader. New Delhi. Oxford.

Svara, J. H. (2001) 'The Myth of the Dichotomy: Complemantarity of Politics and Administration' in the Past and Future of Public Administration. *Public Administration Review.* 61. pp. 176–184.

Tahmasebi, R. and Seyyed, M. M. M. (2011) 'Politics-Administration Dichotomy: A Century Debate.' *Administration and Public Management Review*. 17(2011).

Turner, M. and Hume, D. (1997) *Governance, Administration and Development: Making the State Work*. London: Macmillan.

United Nations Document. (1995) 'Rethinking Public Administration: An Overview.' Government and Public Administration Branch, Division of Public and Development Management, Department of Economic and Social Affairs.

Wamsley, G. L. and Wolf, J. F. (1996) 'Introduction: Can a High Modern Project Find Happiness in Post-modern Era' in Wamsley, G. L. and Bacher, R. N. et al. (eds.). *Refounding Public Administration.* London: Sage.

Wamsley, G. L. and Bacher, R. N. (1990) 'Agency Perspective' in Wamsley, G. H. and Bacher, R. N. et al. (eds.). *Refounding Public Administration.* London: Sage.

White, J. D. and Adams, G. B. (1994) 'Making Sense with Diversity: The Context of Research, Theory and Knowledge Development in Public Administration' in White, J. D. and Adams, G. B. (eds.). *Research in Public Administration: Reflections in Theory and Practice.* UK: Sage.

Wolff, R. (2012) 'In Capitalist Crisis, Rediscovering Marx' cited in Musto, M. (ed.). *Marx for Today.* London: Routledge.

Websites:

Amy, D. J. Government is Good: An Unapologetic Defense of a Vital Institution. A Web Project of Amy, D. J., Professor of Politics at Mount Holyoke College [Accessed: 27th January 2014].

Blessan Available from: http:// blessan. Wordpress.com/2010

Boudreau, A. J. (1950) 'Public Administration and the Public Interest.' [Online] Available from: www.jstor.org/stable/137809

Kettl, D. F. The Future of Public Administration. [Online] Available from: www2.h-net.msu.edu/~pubadmin/tfreport/kettl.pdf [Accessed: 20th January 2014].

Francis Fukuyama, 1989-Endpoint of Humanity's Socio 'http://en.wikipedia.org/wiki/Sociocultural_evolution' Cultural evolution. (Accessed 20th Oct 2013)

Win, Dream Dare. Accountability and Control. [Online] Available from: www.jeywin.com [Accessed: 27th January, 2014].

Chapter One

Concept and Significance of Public Administration

Sweta Mishra

LEARNING OBJECTIVES

After completing this chapter, you should be able to:

- Explain the concepts of administration and public administration
- Discuss the nature of public administration
- Bring out the scope of public administration underlining the POSDCORB and subject-matter views
- Identify the differences and similarities between public and private administration; and
- Describe the significance of public administration.

INTRODUCTION

Public administration is vital to the efficient running of the government. As a specialized academic field, it deals essentially with the machinery and procedures of government. It is the *action* part of the government. It is both an *institution* of public service and a *centre of power*. As an institution of public service, it provides services to the people and promotes public interest. As a centre of power, public bureaucracy tends to be concerned with its own privileges. In recent years, the discipline of public administration has been undergoing rapid changes and has vastly expanded its frontiers. As a discipline, it has evolved and is still evolving to respond to the challenges of changing times.

The onset of liberalization, privatization and globalization (LPG) has led to significant changes in the roles of individuals and institutions, and public administration is no exception. It represents a *paradigm shift* from the traditional model of public administration to New Public Management (NPM) model, which favours a dominant presence of market forces over the State, for effective governance and efficient delivery of goods and services.

Concepts such as competition State, managerial orientation, contracting out, debureaucratization and downsizing have started gaining prominence in many countries. The new perspective has emerged as a *management tool* for achieving developmental goals. It has brought in reforms, which have attempted to create a new entrepreneurial, user-oriented culture in public organizations, with focus on performance measurement and autonomy to the organizations and individuals, in contrast to the traditional model. In fact, *managerialism* is a 'determined effort to implement the "3Es" of economy, efficiency and effectiveness at all levels of government activities'.

Public administration, in present times, has thus become complex and is slowly moving towards enlightened public governance. In the light of these introductory remarks, this chapter, in the succeeding pages, makes an attempt to *define* the terms 'administration' and 'public administration'. Subsequently, it discusses the nature, scope and significance of public administration. Finally, it analyses the *relationship* between public and private administration.

MEANING OF PUBLIC ADMINISTRATION

Public administration is an aspect of a more *generic* concept of administration. Therefore, before understanding the meaning of public administration, it is necessary to understand the meaning of the word 'administration'.

Defining Administration

The English word 'administer' is derived from Latin word *ad + ministrare*, which means 'to care for or to look after people, to manage affairs'. In its literal sense, the term 'administration' means 'management of affairs' – public or private affairs. Administration is a process *permeating* all collective efforts, be it public or private, civil or military, large scale or otherwise, and is thus of *universal* nature. Administration is a cooperative effort through which the laid down goals and objectives are fulfilled. Gladden, in his book *An Introduction to Public Administration*, has defined administration as a long and slightly pompous word, but it has a humble meaning, for it means, to care for or look after people, to manage affairs . . . it is determined action taken in pursuit of a conscious purpose' (Gladden, 1952, p. 18).

Administration means organizing and using men and materials to accomplish a purpose or a goal. Administration joins groups of people who coordinate and cooperate so that the desired goals are achieved. In other words, in order to achieve the desired goals and objectives, we need to organize and direct human and material resources. It is a universal process and occurs in diverse institutional settings. Based on these settings, administration is divided into public administration and private administration. The former refers to the administration, which operates in a governmental setting, whereas the latter refers to the administration, which operates in a non-governmental setting, that is, business enterprises.

In short, administration, thus, means a cooperative effort by a group of people to achieve a common objective. It is the specialized vocation of managers who have skills of organizing and directing men and materials just as definitely as an engineer has the skill of building structures or a doctor has the skill of understanding human ailments (Sharma and Sadana, 1998, p. 5). In other words, it is a goal-oriented, purposive, coordinative and cooperative activity, which is undertaken by a group of people in pursuit of some common goal or goals.

Features of administration

- Goal-oriented activity
- Pursuit of conscious purpose
- Direction of human and material resources
- Determined action
- Cooperation for accomplishment of common goals
- Systematic ordering of affairs
- Calculated use of resources
- Coordination and control of persons
- Getting things done

Defining Public Administration

Public administration is a segment of the larger field of administration. It is simply regarded as bureaucracy, heedless to the fact that bureaucracy as a particular organizational form is not only found in the government, but also in private and third-sector organizations (Dhameja, 2003, p. 2). Public administration is a discipline which is concerned with the organization and the formulation and implementation of public policies for the welfare of the people. It functions in a political setting to accomplish the goals and objectives, which are formulated by the political decision makers. It is also called governmental administration as the adjective 'public' in the word 'public administration' means 'government'. The focus of public administration, thus, is on public bureaucracy, that is, bureaucratic or *administrative organization* of the government.

There are *different* definitions of public administration given by different scholars, which needs to be discussed here to get a clear picture as to what actually is meant by public administration. Some of these definitions are as follows:

- Woodrow Wilson, the father of public administration, has defined it as 'detailed and systematic execution of law. Every particular application of law is an act of administration' (Wilson, 1953, pp. 65–75).
- L.D.White, in his book, has defined public administration as a discipline which 'consists of all those operations having for their purpose the fulfilment or enforcement of public policy' (White, 1958, p. 1).

- According to Corson and Harris, 'public administration is decision making, planning the work to be done, formulating objectives and goals, working with the legislature and citizen organizations to gain public support and funds for government programmes, establishing and revising organization, directing and supervising employees, providing leadership, communicating and receiving communications, determining work methods and procedures, appraising performance, exercising controls, and other functions performed by government executives and supervisors. It is the action part of the government, the means by which the purposes and goals of the government are realized' (Corson and Harris, 1963, p. 12).
- Like Corson and Harris, Pfiffner too gives a very comprehensive definition of public administration. According to him, 'public administration consists of doing the work of the government whether it be running an X-ray machine in a health laboratory or coining money in the mint... Public Administration consists of getting the work of government done by coordinating the efforts of the people so that they can work together to accomplish their set tasks. . . . It also involves managing, directing and supervising the activities of thousands, even millions of workers so that some order and efficiency may result from their efforts. . .' (Pfiffner, 1946, p. 6).
- In the words of Dimock, 'administration is concerned with "what" and "how" of the government. The "what" is the subject matter, the technical knowledge of a field which enables the administrator to perform his tasks. The "how" is the technique of management, the principles according to which cooperative programmes are carried to success. Each is indispensable; together they form the synthesis called administration' (quoted in Sharma and Sadana, 1998, pp. 6–7).
- According to Luther Gulick, 'public administration is that part of the science of administration, which has to do with government and thus concerns itself primarily with the executive branch where the work of government is done, though there are obviously problems in connection with the legislative and judicial branches' (Gulick, 1937, p. 191).
- Similarly, Herbert Simon too defines 'public administration as concerning the activities of the executive branches of the national, State and local governments' (quoted in Sharma and Sadana, 1998, p. 6).
- Nigro has defined public administration in the following words: '(a) it is a cooperative group effort in a public setting; (b) covers all the three branches – executive, legislative and judicial, and their inter-relationship; (c) has an important role in the formulation of public policy and is thus part of the political process; (d) is different in significant ways from private administration; and (e) is closely associated with numerous private groups and individuals in providing services to the community' (Nigro, 1971, p. 21).
- Nicholas Henry defines public administration as 'a device used to reconcile bureaucracy with democracy. It is a broad-ranging and amorphous combination of theory and practice; its purpose is to promote a superior understanding of government and its relationship with the society it governs, as well as to encourage public policies more responsive to social needs and to institute managerial practices attuned to effectiveness, efficiency, and the deeper human requisites of the citizenry' (Henry, 2007, p. 17).

Thus, on the basis of the above definitions, it can be said that public administration is concerned with the determination, formulation and implementation of public policies for the welfare of the people.

It is the principal agency of the State which delivers the public goods and services in an efficient and economical manner as also provides continuity to the policies of the government.

Features of public administration

- Bureaucratic decision making
- Organization and procedures of policy process
- Detailed/systematic execution of law
- Enforcement of public policy
- Performance of civilian functions
- Operation of administrative branch
- Art and science of management as applied to State affairs
- 'What' and 'how' of government

On the whole, it can be said that public administration is nothing less than the whole government in action. It is an instrument through which the goals and objectives of the government are fulfilled. In other words, it is 'the action part of government, the means by which the purposes and goals of government are realized' (Chakraborty and Bhattacharya, 2003, p. 2). In fact, public administration lends itself to two usages: it is an activity; and it also refers to the discipline (*or subject*) of intellectual inquiry and study. Before proceeding to the nature of public administration, it becomes pertinent to define the three terms, namely, administration, organization and management, which are used interchangeably. Although the *three* terms are used interchangeably, there is a specific difference in their meanings.

This *distinction* is made clear by William Schultz (2010). According to him, 'administration is the force which lays down the object for which an organization and its management are to strive and the broad policies under which they are to operate. An organization is a combination of the necessary human beings, materials, tools, equipment, working space and appurtenances brought together in systematic and effective co-relation to accomplish some desired object. Management is that which leads, guides and directs an organization for the accomplishment of a pre-determined object'. Administration, thus, is a broader concept and includes within its fold both organization and management.

NATURE OF PUBLIC ADMINISTRATION

There are two broad views with regard to the nature of public administration, namely, (a) *the managerial view*, and (b) *the integral view*.

The Managerial View

Public administration, in this context, *encompasses* only the managerial activities and not the technical, clerical and manual activities, which are non-managerial in nature. Thus, administration, according to this view, constitutes the activities of only the top persons. Simon, Smithburg, Thompson and Gulick support this view. Administration, according to this view, is same in *all* the spheres just as the managerial techniques are same in all the fields of activities. Administration has to do with getting things done with the accomplishment of defined objectives.

The Integral View

According to this view, public administration encompasses within its fold all the activities, which are undertaken to accomplish the given objective. In other words, public administration is the sum total of managerial, technical, clerical and manual activities. Thus, administration, according to this view, constitutes the activities of all persons from top to bottom. Thinkers such as White and Dimock subscribe to this view. Administration, according to this view, depends on the subject matter of the concerned agency, that is, it differs from one sphere to another.

SCOPE OF PUBLIC ADMINISTRATION

There are two views regarding the scope of public administration, namely (a) *POSDCORB view,* and (b) *subject-matter view*.

The POSDCORB View

This view of the scope of public administration was advocated by Luther Gulick. He believed that administration consisted of seven elements. He summed up these elements in the acronym 'POSDCORB', each letter of which implies one element of administration. Luther Gulick explained these *seven* elements of administration (or functions of the chief executive) in the following way:

P – Planning: working out in broad outline, the things that need to be done and the methods to be adopted for accomplishing the purpose in hand

O – Organizing: building up the structure of authority through which the entire work to be done, is arranged into well-defined subdivisions and coordination

S – Staffing: appointing suitable persons to the various posts under the organization, and the whole of personnel management

D – Directing: making decisions and issuing orders and instructions embodying them for the guidance of the staff

Co – Coordinating: interrelating the various parts of the work and eliminating overlapping and conflict

R – Reporting: keeping superiors and subordinates informed of what is going on, and arranging for the collection of such information through inspection, research and records

B – Budgeting: all that goes with budgeting in the form of fiscal planning, accounting and control (Sharma and Sadana, 1998, p. 14. These activities under 'POSDCORB' are also explained in chapter 4 of this volume).

The Subject-Matter View

Though the POSDCORB view of scope of public administration was acceptable for quite a long time, there arose a reaction, in the course of time, against this view. It was then realized that the POSDCORB activities (techniques) can neither be the whole of public administration nor even the significant part of it. This view advocates that the problems of administration are same in all the agencies regardless of the peculiar nature of the functions they perform. Thus, it overlooks the fact that different administrative agencies are faced with different problems.

Moreover, the POSDCORB represents only the *tools* of administration whereas the *substance* of administration is something different. The real core of administration consists of the various services performed for the people, such as defence, health, agriculture, education, social security etc. These services have their own specialized techniques which are not covered by the common POSDCORB techniques. In other words, each administrative agency has its own 'local POSDCORB' because of the subject matter with which it is concerned. Further, Gulick's common POSDCORB techniques are also influenced by the subject matter of the administration (i.e. *services and activities in which they function*).

Thus, the POSDCORB view is 'technique oriented' rather than 'subject oriented'. It ignores the essential element involved in public administration, namely, 'knowledge of the subject matter'. This is the reason why the subject-matter view of the scope of public administration arose. It lays emphasis on the services rendered and the functions performed by an administrative agency. It advocates that the substantive problems of an agency depend upon the subject matter (i.e. *services and functions*) with which it is concerned.

Therefore, the study of public administration does not only include the techniques of administration but also the substantive concerns of administration. However, the POSDCORB view and subject-matter view are not mutually exclusive, but *complement* each other. Together, they *constitute* the proper scope of the study of public administration. It has been observed that POSDCORB and subject matter are two important components of the instrument called public administration.

Nature of public administration	Scope of public administration
• Managerial view	• POSDCORB view
• Integral view	• Subject-Matter view

PUBLIC AND PRIVATE ADMINISTRATION

Public administration refers to the business of the State and is concerned with the ends and strategies of government policies, programmes and decisions. It operates in a political/governmental setting. Private administration, on the other hand, refers to the management of business owned and operated by private individuals. It operates in the non-governmental setting, that is, business enterprises. Hence, they are also known as governmental administration and business administration respectively.

Differences between Public and Private Administration

Paul H. Appleby, Sir Josia Stamp, Herbert A. Simon and Peter Drucker are of the view that public and private administrations are two different things. The *two* types of administration can be differentiated on the following grounds:

- Public administration is public in nature. Hence the main aim of public administration is to serve the public and to promote community welfare. It is characterized by a *service motive*. Private administration, in contrast, is characterized by a *profit motive*, not social service. Its objective is to maximize profit. All their efforts are directed to this end. In addition, public administration carries a greater social prestige than private administration because of its social role.
- Public administration operates strictly according to *laws, rules and regulations*. The administrators cannot do anything contrary to, or in excess of legal power. In private administration, there are *general laws*, which regulate the business. Individual business firms have considerable flexibility.

- Public administration is subjected to political direction in most *policy matters*. It is the minister who lays down the broad policy outlines under which the bureaucrats have to implement the policy. In private administration, there is no such political direction. Any such political direction can be exercised only in emergency situations. The ends that it pursues are its own and its objectives *do not* depend upon political decisions.
- Public administration has to be consistent in its treatment. In other words, the principle of *consistency of treatment* is the watch word of public administration. Its acts and decisions are regulated by uniform laws, rules and regulations. It means that in public administration any show of discrimination, bias or partiality will evoke public censure or legislative commotion. Administrators have to be very consistent and impartial while dealing with the public. They must treat all the citizens equally, without any favour or prejudice. Private administration, on the other hand, can practice *preferential treatment*. In private administration, it is common to discriminate with regard to choice of products, selling of products and in fixing product prices.
- Being public in nature, public administration is open to constant public scrutiny. The actions of the administrators are much more exposed to the *public gaze*. The achievements of administrators rarely get publicity but a minute fault makes newspaper headlines in no time. A public administrator is accountable for all the acts and the decisions through legislative oversight and judicial review. In other words, the moral and *ethical standards* in public administration are much higher as compared with private administration. Public gaze is absent in private administration and it is *not* so closely watched by the public and publicity media.
- The tenure of the administrators is quite *secure* as compared with the private sector employees. Apart from this, they enjoy many benefits and privileges while in job and even after retirement. This kind of privilege is *not* available to the private sector employees.
- In public administration there is *monopoly* of government and it does not allow private parties to compete. Services such as post and telegraph, railways, currency and coinage are exclusively provided by the government. Monopolism in private sector is missing. Several organizations *compete* with each other to supply the same commodity and service in the private sector domain.
- Public administration is subjected to *external financial control*. It means that finances of public administration are controlled by the legislature. In other words, legislature authorizes the income and expenditure of the executive branch. The executive cannot collect or spend money out of its own will. Thus, we see that the administration and finance are separated in public administration. Private administration, on the other hand, is not subject to the principle of external financial control. It is free to manage its finances as it likes.
- The nature of functions performed by public and private administration are also different. Public administration is more *comprehensive*. It deals with the various types of needs of the people. It carries out functions, which are more urgent and vital for the very existence of the society; for example, defence and maintenance of law and order. Private administration, on the other hand, carries out less vital functions, such as manufacture of cloth, supply of sugar, etc.
- Public administrators function *anonymously*. In other words, the functioning of civil service in government is characterized by the doctrine of anonymity which is the counterpart of the principle of ministerial responsibility. Thus, the minister assumes *responsibility* for the actions of the civil servants working under him or her. This is not so in private administration.

- Public administration differs from private administration in the *measurement of efficiency* as well. Private administration functions on a level of efficiency superior to that of public administration. Since the motive is to make profit, individuals are wholeheartedly devoted to their work and business. In other words, the resource use or profit earning (i.e. input–output relationship) is the criterion of measuring efficiency in private administration. However, the same criterion cannot be applied while measuring efficiency in public administration.

Thus, public administration has acquired certain distinctive features which distinguish it from private administration. Public accountability is its hallmark; consistency of treatment its watchword; and consciousness of community service, its ideal.

Similarities between Public and Private Administration

Even though, they differ in certain respects, there are many *similarities* between public and private administration. In fact, a group of administrative thinkers such as Henry Fayol, M.P. Follet, Luther Gulick and Lyndall Urwick do not make a distinction between public and private administration. They are of the view that administration, whether public or private, is one and possesses the same basic features and it is *undesirable* to separate public from private administration. There is much in common between the *two* and the difference is only of degree, not of kind.

The specific *similarities* between public and private administration are as follows:

- The *managerial techniques* and skills of planning, organizing, coordinating, controlling and so on are same in both.
- Both are organized on the basis of the principles of *hierarchy.*
- Both have *uniformity in accounting*, office management and procedures, purchases, disposals, statistics, stocking and so on.
- Both are being influenced by the *practices and standards of each other*. Thus, Pfeiffer and Presthus have described the emergence of public corporation as 'a halfway house between its commercial prototype and the traditional governmental department' (Pfiffner and Presthus, 1953, p. 4).
- Both have similarities so far as the *problems of organization*, personnel and finance are concerned. The similarity between them is demonstrated by the fact that there is a mutual exchange and rotation of personnel between the two. In India, we have seen that the Administrative Staff College of India located at Hyderabad organizes common training programmes for the personnel of both public and private sectors.

With the onset of globalization and the new management perspective, the boundaries between public and private administration are getting blurred. The public sector is expected to work on the lines of the private sector. In other words, it is expected to follow the principles of three E's, that is, efficiency, economy and effectiveness along with profitability. The informal organs such as people's associations, community-based organizations along with formal organs of the State, participate and discharge activities that were earlier in the public domain.

Apart from this, the private sector, functioning along market lines and the regulatory framework of government, undertakes functions that have been the prerogative of the public sector (Medury, 2010, p. 193). We can, thus, conclude that in many ways, the differences between public and private administration are diminishing. They complement and supplement each other.

SIGNIFICANCE OF PUBLIC ADMINISTRATION

Public administration has become an essential segment of modern society, which has witnessed the emergence of what administrative thinkers call the 'Administrative State'. This means that every activity of individuals from 'womb to tomb' is regulated and controlled by the State agencies, that is, administrative agencies. The significance of public administration is expanding day by day. The functions which it performs have expanded in scale, range and nature and are still increasing. It is necessary not only for maintaining public order, social security, welfare and economic infrastructure, but also for the delivery of services such as safety, utilities and enforcement of contractual obligations, as also for ensuring the rule of law and treating all the citizens equally. Its nature, contents and scope – all go to make it the 'heart of the problem of modern governments' (White, 1958, p. xvi).

Public administration is of utmost importance in developing countries with numerous plans and programmes of social and economic development. In a developing democracy such as India, which is striving hard to provide happiness and prosperity to its grieving and impoverished population, public administration has become the instrument of *change and development* and a powerful agency for achieving national integration.

As an instrument of change, especially in countries such as India, public administration has successfully implemented various development programmes such as community development, poverty eradication, employment guarantee schemes, housing schemes, rural connectivity, rural electrification, health care schemes and so on. As a result, 'public administration has definitely changed the face of rural India by providing the basic minimum facilities to the rural poor and improving their living conditions. As an instrument of national integration, it has played a very important role in rehabilitating the refugees after partition as also integrating the princely states with the Indian territory' (Chakraborty and Chand, 2012, p. 9).

Public administration is a great stabilizing force in a society. Governments come and go but administration does not change. In this way, it provides *continuity and linkage* between the old and new programmes. In a diverse country such as India, public administration becomes all the more important because it acts as a harmonizing and integrating force. It has brought the people of different castes, classes, communities and religions on a common platform. In other words, it has created an environment where people with varied backgrounds can live together. In a way, it has also provided stability and strength to the Indian democracy.

Public administration is all about *governance*. It is the heart of development. It is the interface between the market and the civil society. In the words of Frederickson, public administration is moving towards theories of cooperation, networking, governance and institution – building and maintenance in response to the declining relationship between jurisdiction and public management in a 'fragmented and disarticulated State' (Frederickson, 1999, pp. 701–711).

CONCLUSION

The 21st century has ushered in a major transformation in the role of the State. The Welfare State has been transformed to a Corporatist State. The market forces have entered in the domain which was earlier the exclusive jurisdiction of the State, bringing about a change in the role of the State. From a doer, it has become a facilitator and a regulator. To sum up, public administration plays a very important role in modern society.

Public administration is the basis of government whether in a monarchy, democracy or in a dictatorship. It is the instrument for executing the laws, policies and programmes formulated by the State. It is the instrument of social change and economic development, especially in the so-called 'third world' (i.e. developing countries), which are engaged in the process of social-welding and nation-building. It is also an instrument of national integration, particularly in the developing countries which are facing the challenges of sub-nationalism, secessionism, class wars and so on. This chapter has discussed the significance of public administration by contrasting it with private administration. It has also described the various perspectives/viewpoints on its meaning, nature and scope.

Preparatory Questions

- Discuss the nature, scope and significance of public administration.
- 'The meaning of public administration has changed since its evolution'. Comment.
- Examine the relationship between public administration and private administration.
- Describe the changing role of public administration in the context of globalization.
- Bring out the managerial and integral views of public administration.

REFERENCES

Chakraborty, B. and Chand, P. (2012) *Public Administration in a Globalizing World*. New Delhi: Sage.

Chakraborty, B. and Bhattacharya, M. (eds.) (2003) *Public Administration A Reader*. New Delhi: Oxford University Press.

Corson, J. and Harris, J. (1963) *Public Administration in Modern Society*. New York: McGraw-Hill.

Dhameja, A. (ed.) (2003) *Contemporary Debates in Public Administration*. New Delhi: PHI.

Frederickson, H. G. (1999) 'The Repositioning of American Public Administration', *Political Science* and *Politics*. 32 (4). p. 701–711.

Gladden, E. N. (1952) *An Introduction to Public Administration*. 2nd ed. London: Staples Press.

Gulick, L. (1937) 'Science Values and Public Administration' in Luther G. and L. Urwick (eds.). *Papers on the Science of Administration*. New York: Institute of Public Administration.

Henry, N. (2007) *Public Administration and Public Affairs*. 10th ed. New Delhi: Pearson.

Medury, U. (2010) *Public Administration in the Globalization Era*. New Delhi: Orient BlackSwan.

Mishra, S. (2010) 'Book Review of Public Administration' in Globalization Era. *The Indian Journal of Public Administration*. LVI (4).

Nigro, F. A. (1971) *Modern Public Administration*. 2nd ed. New York: Harper International.

Pfiffner, J. M. (1946) *Public Administration*. New York: The Ronald Press Company p. 6.

Pfiffner, J. M. and Presthus, R. V. (1953) *Public Administration*. 3rd ed. New York: The Ronald Press Company.

Schultz, W. (2010) 'Administrative Theory.' *MPA-012, IGNOU Course Material* p. 4.

Sharma, M. P. and Sadana, B. L. (1998) *Public Administration in Theory and Practice*. 37th ed. Allahabad: Kitab Mahal.

White, L. D. (1958) *Introduction to the Study of Public Administration*. 4th ed. New York: Macmillan Company.

Wilson, W. (1953) 'The Study of Administration' in Waldo, D. (ed.). *Ideas and Issues in Public Administration*. New York: McGraw-Hill.

Chapter Two

Phases in Evolution of Public Administration

Shubhra Pant Kothari

LEARNING OBJECTIVES

After completing this chapter, you should be able to:

- Trace the growth of the discipline of public administration through various temporal dimensions
- Describe the various phases that have been crucial in the discipline's growth
- Analyse the changing complexion of the discipline since its evolution; and
- Examine the future prospects of the discipline

INTRODUCTION

Public administration as an activity consists of actions that affect the purpose or aspiration of a government. It works through the system of organization and management. Therefore, it is both an activity and a discipline for systematic study. Public administration, since its inception, has been primarily concerned with problems of how to validate law qualitatively, honestly and efficiently. Today, public administration has become more concerned with the processes by which it participates in formulating and interpreting law to make it more correct with reference to public interest.

As a practice, public administration has always helped the governments to carry out actions on the basis of validated laws. The objectives of public administration in a simple society are limited, but in a large and complex society, institutions and their processes become more specialized and differentiated leading to the creation of new organizations, departments, councils, commissions, agencies and so on, especially for the administrative tasks.

As a structure of government or element of political system, public administration has been an established institution since time immemorial. Even the earliest framers of the U.S. Constitution and leaders and scholars such as Thomas Jefferson recognized the problems of public administration and inscribed its developmental path. However, the major turning point in the history of public administration came with an essay written by a young and dynamic leader, Woodrow Wilson (1887), which became symbolic in the evolution of public administration. Wilson's essay, 'The Study of Administration', published in the *Political Science Quarterly* was written at such a juncture, when there was an urgent need for restructuring the institution in quest of public interest, in order to eradicate corruption, cleanse the system and improve the efficiency of the government.

Wilson observed that till the 19th century, the major concerns of the study of politics were political philosophy, Constitutional arrangements and law-making. However, the rising complexities in society and an associated increase in governmental size and activity demanded a change. He suggested that European countries had accepted the change and were seriously working on training civil servants and expressing concern for the scientific study of administration. This chapter will trace the evolution of public administration through eight distinct paradigms. It will also try to examine the future prospects of the discipline.

Paradigms of public administration

- Politics and Administration (1900–1926)
- Principles of Administration (1927–1938)
- Era of Challenges (1938–1947)
- Crisis of Identity (1948–1970)
- Public Administration as Management (1956–1970)
- Public Administration as Public Administration (1965–1970)
- Public Policy Perspective (1970–1990)
- Good Governance (1990s to present)

THE FIRST PARADIGM: POLITICS AND ADMINISTRATION DICHOTOMY (1900–1926)

Reviews in the discipline of public administration more often recognize that the practice of public administration is as historical as society itself (Appleby, 1952). Public administration attained a distinct characteristic in the beginning of the 20th century and later, became an instrument for governmental reforms and institutionalization of management in the mid-1920s. *Three* major developments took place during these times. Firstly, the government needed reforms to improve the conditions of institutions of the government. Secondly, the 'management movement' emerged as an attempt to apply the techniques of science to improve the efficiency and to make private administration more organized. Thirdly, public administration evolved itself as a new discipline out of political science. Let us discuss them one by one:

Goodnow, in his book, 'Politics and Administration', published in the year 1900, recommended various reforms to realize the necessary and desirable, but limited control of politics over administration. Goodnow gave momentum to the discipline's evolutionary progress. He sketched a clear functional *distinction* between politics and administration. In his view, 'the former having to do with the politics or expression of the State's will, the latter with the execution of the policies' (cited in Thomas, 1962). It was Goodnow who actually conceived the politics-administration dichotomy.

> The dichotomy of politics and administration is attributed to Wilson's historical essay; but the most influential book was Frank Goodnow's *Politics and Administration* (1900). In its expression, Goodnow spoke of the 'will of the State' and identified politics with the 'expression' and administration with the 'execution' of this will. The problem of government, as he viewed it, was to achieve harmony between the expression of the will and its execution, the alternative being conflict or paralysis. But while politics should have certain control over administration, it should not extend to certain levels and aspects thereof, which embrace 'fields of semi-scientific, quasi-judicial and quasi-business or commercial activity – work which has little, if any, influence on the expression of the true State's will' (De Grazia, 1960)

In the beginning of the 1920s, public administration came to be recognized as an important sub-area of political science. Public administration started gaining recognition in the American universities and its study began to widen. This period is also referred to as a period of orthodoxy, as it was the time of general agreement and self-assurance. There were differences among scholars, but the general beliefs prevailed.

In this direction, the earlier books gave only non-concrete views of the interests of the newly founded discipline. The most widely used textbook in the period that focussed exclusively on the discipline was White's *Introduction to the Study of Public Administration* (1926). This book reflected the dominant theme of that era. Its main focus was the importance of administration in an increasingly complex and interdependent society, the necessity for *efficiency*, the possibility and desirability of approaching administration scientifically, and so forth. According to White, efficiency and economy were the main ethos of public administration. Thus, the main attribute of the first paradigm was the *clear division* of the functional areas of government between administration and politics. However, the focus on efficiency and economy provided a new perspective of the subsequent paradigm that focussed on the principles of administration.

SECOND PARADIGM: PRINCIPLES OF ADMINISTRATION (1927–1937)

The second paradigm in the evolution of public administration had its main focal point on the theme of principles of administration. In 1927, Willoughby's *Principles of Public Administration* emerged as the second textbook in the field of public administration that echoed the new thrust of the discipline, which laid focus on certain scientific principles of administration to make public administration effective and efficient. Public administration emerged as a new science, where questions based on *values* were no longer problematic for administration. The principles of management rather became an important tool for the practitioners of administration. During this time, that is, between 1927 and 1936, the number of universities offering public administration courses multiplied. The growth was immense enough to give anxious moments to the academicians.

This paradigm reached its *zenith* with the invention of Luther Gulick's and Lyndall Urwick's *seven* principles of administration under the famous acronym POSDCORB in 1937, in their paper, 'The Science of Administration' (you will read more on it in chapter 4 on Classical Approach in this volume). While economy and efficiency still remained the main idea of the administrative system, the central focus of this paradigm was on the principles of administration; their evolution and practice. These changes helped to further strengthen the politics-administration dichotomy.

THIRD PARADIGM: AN ERA OF CHALLENGES (1938–1947)

During this period, new changes were seen in the nature of public administration. Due to the devastating effects of World War II, many of the classical theories of administration came under attack. Taking quick and validated decisions in a war situation required flexibility, creativity and also discretion in decision making. The dissent from mainstream public administration accelerated in the 1940s. This dissent, it has been observed, was evident in two directions; '*one* was that the dichotomy of politics and administration came under sharp criticism, and *second* was about principles being less than final expression of managerial rationality' (Henry, 2002).

The main emphasis shifted towards social, moral and political values that became a challenge to the tenets of managerial value. The pioneering work, which became a movement challenging the earlier studies in administration, was the *human relations* approach. It was a culmination of the experiments at the Hawthorne Plant in the 1920s. In the post-World War II phase, these studies of human behaviour laid stress on the human aspects of administration. As has been observed, 'they also focussed on the importance of social recognition, credit to the employees, ego satisfaction, security of employees and employees' group attitudes. These studies brought out the lapses of machine based concepts of organization by focussing on the social and psychological aspect of work situation' (Bhattacharya, 2001).

In the year following the publication of Gulick's and Urwick's major work, Chester Barnard's *The Functions of the Executive* in 1938, challenged the politics-administration dichotomy. Their work had a major impact on Herbert Simon, when he was writing his volume on *Administrative Behaviour* that got published in 1947. Simon questioned the managerial principles and claimed that there is no such thing as principles of administration. He averred that what are postured as 'principles' are in truth no better than 'proverbs'. Simon recommended a new science of administration having a methodology based on logical positivism and social psychology.

Robert Dahl challenged the claim of public administration as a science in his book 'The Science of Public Administration: Three Problems' published in 1947. He argued that there was lack of scientific validity and universal relevancy in public administration. Robert Dahl emphasized the need to take into account *normative* considerations, human behaviour and sociological factors, while defining and broadening the parameters of public administration. He brought an element of *behaviouralism* in public administration. Dahl argued that the science of administration can only emerge by emphasizing on comparative public administration. Thus, this phase can be called the 'phase of *demurring* to the dichotomy and puncturing the principles' (Henry, 2002).

FOURTH PARADIGM: CRISIS OF IDENTITY (1948–1970)

The fourth paradigm re-initiated the linkages between public administration and political science, owing to the challenge posed by the behaviouralists. This was the phase that can be called *crisis of identity* phase for the discipline of public administration. The public administrators were unsure about further developments in the field. Waldo, in his *Administrative State* (1948), widened the orientation of public administration to include policy issues and decision-making processes. On the other hand, many political scientists began to argue that the true objective of public administration was 'intellectualized understanding' of the executive. There was also a talk of continued 'dominion of political science over public administration'.

In short, this period witnessed the spectacle of political science not letting public administration separate itself from it, and at the same time not encouraging its growth and development within its own field. Therefore, in the post-World War II period, the credentials of public administration as a science and a distinct discipline in its own right were questioned. This led to the *twin* development of *public administration being viewed as political science* and also as an administrative science.

Henry (2002) observes that writings on public administration in the 1950s spoke of the field as an 'emphasis, an 'area of interest', or even as a 'synonym'. As a result, public administration came to be identified as a discipline without a fully comprehensible intellectual framework. The emergence of new nations in the post-World War times (*as a result of the process of decolonization*) gave a new dimension to the study of public administration. Many scholars began to portray their interest in the study of the decaying administrative patterns of the newly independent countries. This period saw the tilt towards importance and relevance of environmental factors, out of which evolved the new concepts of *ecological, comparative* and *development* administration in the study of public administration. This was also the time when *case studies* came to be used as epistemological tools.

By the 1950s, new courses on comparative administration began to be taught in American universities, but the real thrust came in 1962, when the Comparative Administration Group (CAG), which was formed in 1960, got a massive financial aid from the Ford Foundation. Academicians of the *comparative public administration* threw light on the question of administrative development in the newly evolved states to direct socio-economic change in cross-cultural perspectives. This immensely helped in the creation of the sub-field of *development administration*.

In his article 'Trends in Comparative Study of Public Administration', Fred Riggs (1962) emphasized the need to study politico-administrative institutions in their social settings. Thus, comparative public administration became a focussed, cross-cultural and cross-national study of public administration. The contribution of Dwight Waldo, F. W. Riggs, Edward Weidner and Ferrel Heady (1966) is significant in this regard, as they gave *impetus* to the scope of public administration.

> Public administration has two differences with its comparative sub-field. One is that public administration is forthrightly culture-bound and second is the question of action versus theory, with comparative administration being more into theory-building.
>
> Henry (2002)

FIFTH PARADIGM: PUBLIC ADMINISTRATION AS MANAGEMENT (1956–1970)

In both paradigms, public administration as political science and public administration as management (*both paradigms also coincide in time of occurrence*), the casualty was the discipline of public administration; its identity and distinctness. Henry (2002) points out that in 1956, the journal *Administrative*

Science Quarterly was founded by public administrationists on the premise that public, business and institutional administration were *false* distinctions, and that administration was administration. Writings of James March, Herbert Simon (1961) and James D. Thompson (1959) on organizations and their behaviour justified the *tilt* towards management with organization theory. In the 1960s, 'Organization Development' (OD) began as a specialized field of management. Management was considered as a logical successor to the traditional paradigms of public administration. The university curricula in the US had a management overtone, where public and private administration began to be taught together. Some management texts started referring to 'government' as a constraint in the organizational environment of the corporation (Henry, 2002).

SIXTH PARADIGM: PUBLIC ADMINISTRATION AS PUBLIC ADMINISTRATION (1965–1970)

During the late 1960s, an alternative perspective towards public administration was generated. This was the *New Public Administration* (NPA) based on 'public' perspective. Now, the public administrators were re-evaluating the linkages of the discipline with political science and management. In 1968, Minnowbrook Conference I, based on the theme of NPA was convened, where a group of young scholars showed their resentment for the traditional instrumentalities in public administration and displayed their preferences towards normative theory, focussing on subjects relevant to the emerging society such as *ethics, urbanism, technology and public policy*.

The NPA demanded *autonomy* from both politics and management. This Conference concluded that public administration needed to be viewed as an academic discipline, as a field exercise and as administration in public interest. The Conference focussed on different ecological settings, which operate in order to achieve a set of social goals. The protagonists of NPA declared that the main concern should be on the distributive functions and impact of governmental institutions. The rationale of public action ought to be the reduction of economic and social disparities and the enhancement of life opportunities for all social groups. Accordingly, NPA's thrust on the importance to resolve contemporary issues and problems with a rationale towards their solution, and to have organizational change to suit the changing times became pertinent.

SEVENTH PARADIGM: PUBLIC POLICY PERSPECTIVE (1970–1990)

From the early 1970s, increasing analysis of the way government policies affected the public resulted in a concept called the 'public policy approach' to administration. Public choice school became one of the major paradigms in the evolution of public administration. This school gave impetus to the 'extent to which stage in devising and executing a policy affects the overall shape and impact of the policy'. The scholars of this approach failed to accept bureaucracy as rational and efficient, as they were doubtful about its operational quality and the structure itself.

The concept of public policy focussed on the way a problem is conceived in the first place and how it influences a range of remedies. The nature of the decision-making process may determine whether a course of action is merely incremental or truly radical. It has been argued that the nature of the decision-making process shapes the outcome of the decision itself, particularly when the process is dominated by powerful groups. Moreover, the willingness of the government to evaluate programmes, and modify them if necessary, affects the outcome.

Many supporters of the public policy approach regard the concept as an important tool for constructing a body of knowledge on which recommendations can be based. It has successfully provided possibilities of citizen-friendly organizational alternatives. In this paradigm, another great achievement for public administration took place in the form of Minnowbrook Conference II held in 1988, as it gave birth to the *New Public Management* (NPM) approach towards governance.

The Conference produced several academic papers based on NPM. The debates in the Conference continued to challenge the status quo of public administration in theory and practice. The Conference was held against the backdrop of the changing role of the State and government, privatization and enlarging the role for non-state actors in the process of governance. The driving force of NPM or market-driven administration was towards implementing the 3E's (efficiency, economy and effectiveness) in administration.

The NPM, with its increased focus on market and over-dependence on private sector, got a *mixed* response from many countries. Most of the countries adopted policies that supported private sector initiatives such as deregulation, cost cutting, price controls, layoffs and so on. In the 1990s, decentralization and privatization of administration was adopted as an official policy by many countries. NPM emerged as a method of management to reach set goals of the State, ensuring transparency and accountability in bureaucracy. NPM has been viewed by many scholars as the reconstruction of the discipline of public administration by changing its dynamics. However, it cannot be forgotten that this refreshing perspective has its roots in the earlier research in classical theory.

EIGHTH PARADIGM: GOOD GOVERNANCE (1990s–PRESENT)

Enormous changes in many sectors and the development of technology, communication, global economy and most importantly, the power and role of government has led to self- analysis of business and government sectors. These changes have influenced the dynamics of government facilitating its entrepreneurial growth. In 1992, with the publication of 'Reinventing Government', Osborne and Gaebler reconstructed the functions of government. They argued that as governments have become entrepreneurial (*Birth of Entrepreneurial Government*), various radical changes can be witnessed. Changes such as improvement of public management by performance; reduction of budgets; downsizing of government; contracting out in selective areas were being observed. Thus, the major thrust was on decentralization, de-bureaucratization and democratization of administration, largely taking into account citizens' interests.

The 1990s also saw a moving away from *government* towards *governance* by creating laws, policies, organizations, institutions, cooperative arrangements and agreements that control citizens and deliver public benefits; government being institutional and governance institutional and networked (Henry, 2002). In the process of assisting the developing countries to achieve their developmental path, a new tool of *Good Governance* was adopted by the World Bank that was based on neo-liberal attributes. The concept of *Good Governance* was first highlighted in the World Bank document on Sub-Sahara Africa in 1989. The document gave a comprehensible meaning to the concept.

> It incorporated *four* major facets to the context, namely (a) public sector management; (b) accountability; (c) legal framework for development and (d) information and transparency.
>
> Bhattacharya and Chakraborty (1999)

The political and economic development in the West in the 1990s, gave a boost to certain developmental policies that incorporated features such as *Good Governance* and democratization. According to Adrian Leftwich (2008), contemporary western aid and overseas development has defined three major features of governance; firstly, the *use of aid* to support and promote market friendly and competitive economies, and the other two are support for *democratization* and insistence on *good governance* (all these concepts such as NPA, NPM and good governance are discussed in detail in different chapters of this volume).

Good governance was defined at three levels – simplistic, political and administrative. In the administrative context, *good governance* means an efficient, independent, accountable and an open public service. The concept could also be related with the emergence of a new world order. United Nation's Economic and Social Commission for Asia and the Pacific has provided eight major characteristics related to *good governance*: (i) participatory, (ii) consensus oriented, (iii) accountable, (iv) transparent, (v) responsive, (vi) effective and efficient, (vii) equitable and inclusive, and (viii) rule of law. It also pledges to eradicate, or at least minimize, corruption. It also assures to take into account the views of minorities and voices of the most vulnerable of society in decision making.

Since its origin, public administration as a discipline of academic study has evolved through several paradigms. *Globalization* is another phenomenon that has created unprecedented challenges for the discipline. It is moving away from the rigid traditional structures to more flexible, accommodative and less-hierarchical ones in the backdrop of networks, collaboration and information. Also, it is not an overstatement that globalization has led to radical changes in public administration with increased researches in comparative public management and public policy across international boundaries, and an enhanced role of international organizations in governance.

Therefore, in the era of globalization, the role of public administration has become more responsive – that of being a *facilitator* or *catalyst* towards enabling public–private partnerships for delivering public goods and welfare functions.

> 'Globalization has transformed the nature and character of State from a traditional administrative welfare State to a corporate welfare State with the corresponding changes in the nature of public administration'.
>
> Farazmand (1991)

Features of good governance

- Public sector management
- Accountability
- Legal framework for development
- Consensus-orientation
- Information and transparency
- Participation
- Equity and inclusiveness

The latest paradigm becomes incomplete without analysing Minnowbrook III, which was as important a Conference as its earlier counterparts – Minnowbrook Conferences I (1968) and II (1988). It was organized in two phases on the theme 'The Future of Public Administration, Public Management and Public Service around the World'. A total number of 200 scholars and practitioners from 13 countries participated in Minnowbrook III, including the veterans of Minnowbrook I and II. The Minnowbrook III was the most demographically and internationally diverse congregation of public administration scholars of the three Conferences, over the past 40 years.

The result of the two phases of Minnowbrook III involved analysis of the current state and future direction of the discipline. The themes that were investigated and debated included: making public administration scholarship relevant; academic–practitioner relations; collaborative governance; democratic performance management; financial management; globalization/comparative perspectives; information technology and management; law, politics and public administration; leadership and so on.

The two phases of Minnowbrook III experience provided a useful analytical understanding for the evolution of the discipline as well as a set of yardsticks against which to measure the relevance of public administration scholarship in the future. The participants of Minnowbrook III recognized a need to assess before offering broad and untested theories and recommendations. As represented by Minnowbrook III participants, the future evidently lies in a more global approach to thinking about the institutions and work of public administrators.

The most ubiquitous and highly important issue addressed at Minnowbrook III was the impact of globalization. This is the most important change since Minnowbrook II that focussed on NPM, and certainly since Minnowbrook I that focussed on NPA approach towards public administration. Minnowbrook III participants demonstrated *tangible* examples concerning how comparative public administration research and practice have responded, and continue to respond, to the challenges of globalization. Some authors even proposed the integration of a global perspective with public administration studies. Many others contributed to the discipline by analysing a growing number of international organizations and regional networks of public administration. The insights and analysis presented by these academicians endeavoured to provide a global perspective of public administration.

The scholars took a call on public administration's ability to connect to a critical dialogue on agendas concerning the development of rigorous research methods for comparative studies with a global perspective. Issues such as authority and responsibility, the rule of law and citizens' engagement with administration were probed and debated. This new perspective on governance recommended that collaboration was the required norm and that power was getting diffused through a number of institutional mechanisms and policy instruments. As a result, 'new' managerial tools such as facilitation, negotiation and collaborative problem solving and dispute resolution have assumed heightened prominence.

CONCLUSION

If we talk of the prospects of public administration, we can observe that all the paradigms of administration have not only added quality to the evolution of public administration, but also strengthened its future prospects. Today, public administration *oscillates* between two theories. The first theory is based on its independence as a discipline of study and the second theory rests on its dominant purpose of formulating and implementing social change and social welfare. These theories actually complement each other, as one is irrelevant without the other.

Public administration is striving for a right combination of theory and practice. The promotion of better understanding of the government and its focus on the relationship with society has enormously defined its purpose. However, to reinforce its domain, it will have to inculcate a different type of professional training and education to prepare public administrators to work with a range of institutions and individual actors, across governance domains and sectoral boundaries. These emergent changes in governance have made the field of public administration more specialized than in the earlier paradigms. However, specialization does not signify greater democratization, even though governance is modifying itself across political structures, philosophies, cultures and citizenship.

Many of these political and administrative structures are demanding more active citizens' engagement and participation, while some other structures are evolving well. It is a clear indication that while governance has become more global, deep-rooted, diverse and represented by intricate governing arrangements and ethics, it is also a departure from the long dominant standards entrenched in the western approach towards democratic governance. Finally, these transformations will definitely necessitate more research and interaction between scholars and administrators. It will also lead to essential changes in teaching prospects of public administration for the next generation. The future public administration conferences such as Minnowbrook IV will have several new challenges to mull over.

Preparatory Questions

- 'The growth of the discipline of public administration has travelled through various temporal paradigms'. Discuss.
- Examine the paradigm of 'crisis of identity' in the post-World War II period.
- 'The paradigm on "principles of administration" is very important as it echoed the new thrust of the discipline'. Comment.
- Describe the 'public policy' paradigm of public administration.
- Write a note on 'good governance' paradigm of the 1990s.

REFERENCES

Appleby, P. H. (1952) *Morality and Administration in Democratic Government.* Baton Rouge (LA): State Univ. Press.

Bhattacharya, M. and Chakraborty, B. (eds.) (2006) *Public Administration: A Reader*. New Delhi: Oxford University Press.

Bhattacharya, M. (2001) *New Horizons of Public Administration*. New Delhi: Jawahar Publisher and Distributors.

Dahl, R. A. (1947) 'The Science of Public Administration: Three Problems, a Brief, Incisive Critique of "Orthodoxy."' *Public Administration Review.* 7. pp. 1–11.

Davy, T. J. (1962) 'Public Administration as a Field of Study in the United States.' *International Review of Administrative Sciences.* 28. pp. 63–78.

Grazia, A. D. (1960) 'The Science and Values of Administration.' *Administrative Science Quarterly*. 5. pp. 363–397; 557–582.

Farazmand, A. (ed.) (1991) *Handbook of Comparative and Development Administration*. New York: Marcel Dekker.

Gaus, J. M., White, L. D. and Dimock, M. E. (1936) *The Frontiers of Public Administration.* Chicago (IL): University of Chicago Press.

Goodnow, F. J. (1900) *Politics and Administration: A Study in Government.* New York: Macmillan.

Gulick, L. H. and Urwick, L. (eds.) (1937) *Papers on the Science of Administration.* New York: Institute of Public Administration (*Reprinted 1954*).

Heady, F. (1996) *Public Administration: A Comparative Perspective.* Englewood-Cliffs (NJ): Prentice-Hall.

Henry, N. (2002) *Public Administration and Public Affairs*. New Delhi: PHI.

Landau, M. (1962) 'The Concept of Decision-Making in the 'Field' of Public Administration' in Malick, S. and Van Ness, E. H. (eds.). *Concepts and Issues in Administrative Behaviour.* Englewood-Cliffs (NJ): Prentice-Hall. pp. 1–28.

Leftwich, A. (2008) 'Governance, the State and the Politics of Development.' *Wiley Online Library* [Accessed: 22 October. 2013].

Long, N. E. (1962) *The Polity.* Chicago (IL): Rand Mc-Nally.

Molitor, A. (1959) *The University Teaching of Social Sciences: Public Administration.* Paris: UNESCO.

Molitor, A. (1961) 'Public Administration towards the Future'. *International Review of Administrative Sciences.* 27. pp. 375–384.

Mosher, F. C. (1956) 'Research in Public Administration: Some Notes and Suggestions.' *Public Administration Review.* 16. pp. 169–178.

Redford, E. S. (1958) *Ideal and Practice in Public Administration.* Alabama (AL): Univ. of Alabama Press.

Riggs, F. (1962) 'Trends in Comparative Study of Public Administration.' *International Review of Administrative Sciences.*

Robson, W. A. (1961) 'The Present State of Teaching and Research' in Public Administration. *Public Administration.* 39. pp. 217–222.

Roethlisberger, F. J. and Dickson, W. J. (1964) 'Management and the Worker:' An Account of a Research Programme Conducted by the Western Electric Company, Hawthorne Works, Chicago (Paperback Edition). Harvard: Harvard Univ. Press.'

Sayre, W. S. (1958) 'Premises of Public Administration: Past and Emerging.' *Public Administration Review.* 18. pp. 102–105.

Simon, H. A. (1961) *Administrative Behaviour: A Study of Decision-making Processes in Administrative Organization.* 2nd ed. New York: Macmillan.

Thompson, J. D. (1959) *Comparative Studies in Administration.* Pittsburgh (PA): University of Administrative Science Centre.

Waldo, D. (1948) *The Administrative State: A Study of the Political Theory of American Public Administration.* New York: Ronald Press.

Waldo, D. (1955) *The Study of Public Administration.* Garden City (NY): Random House.

Waldo, D. (1965) 'The Administrative State Revisited.' *Public Administration Review.* 25(1). pp. 5–30.

White, L. D. (1955) *Introduction to the Study of Public Administration.* 4th ed. New York: Macmillan.

Willoughby, W. F. (1927) *Principles of Public Administration: With Special Reference to the National and State Governments of the United States.* Baltimore (MD): Johns Hopkins Press.

Wilson, W. (1953) 'The Study of Administration' in Waldo, D. (ed.). *Ideas and Issues in Public Administration.* New York: McGraw-Hill. pp. 65–75.

Chapter Three

Approaches to the Study of Public Administration

Anita Bagai

LEARNING OBJECTIVES

After completing this chapter, you should be able to:

- Describe the traditional, modern and contemporary approaches to the study of public administration
- Distinguish between the traditional and modern approaches to the study of public administration
- Understand the nature of institutional, natural, cultural and temporal dimensions of comparative studies
- Comprehend the theoretical models of comparison; and
- Explain the significance, nature and range of comprehensive public administration

INTRODUCTION

For a realistic understanding and analysis of the administrative system and processes, scholars have been using numerous devices and methodological techniques. Many changes have taken place in the approaches, methods and content of the discipline of public administration since its inception. As the convictions, values and beliefs of an era undergo change and transform the political system, they get reflected in the method of investigation and analysis of the political and administrative reality too. In this chapter, an attempt has been made to present an outline of some of the important approaches that guide us and provide theoretical directions in administrative inquiry.

STUDY OF PUBLIC ADMINISTRATION: MAJOR APPROACHES

Major approaches can be clubbed under three categories:

1. Traditional
2. Modern
3. Contemporary

• Traditional approaches	Historical Legal Institutional Case method
• Modern approaches	Behavioural Systems Structural–functional Ecological
• Contemporary approaches	Public choice Comparative

1. **Traditional Approaches**

   Traditional approaches include historical approach, legal approach, institutional approach and case method approach.

   - *Historical approach*: The historical approach treats the knowledge of history as absolutely essential for a clear perspective of public administration of a country. It lays emphasis on the historical examination of institutions from the earliest to modern times. According to this approach, history unfolds to unravel the origin and evolution of administrative systems (e.g. tracing the origin of the British *Parliamentary System* to the Magna Carta). This information provides a beginning or a base to understand the contemporary institutions. The focus of historical approach on chronology and time span of developments also facilitates a grasp over the uniqueness, and also the elements of 'continuity and change' in administrative institutions. For example, understanding the colonial legacy of the Indian administrative system is necessary to appreciate the nature of the post-independence administrative apparatus.

   - *Legal approach*: The roots of the legal approach go back to the European tradition of defining public administration in legal terms. Taking note of the importance of sovereignty,

Constitution and regulation in public administration, the advocates of the approach view public administration as a distinctly legal matter. According to them, public administration is concerned with the application and enforcement of law. It is infused with legal and adjudicating concerns (Rosenbloom and Kravchuk, 2002).

Scholars such as Frank Goodnow and Woodrow Wilson subscribed to this approach. Their attention was directed towards a formal legal study of governmental institutions. The concern was with legal forms and prescriptions; the study of various branches of government, for instance, referred to Constitutional and legal provisions.

- *Institutional approach*: The focus of this approach was on institutional analysis. It paid attention to legal and formal governmental institutions such as various organs of the State – the executive, the legislature, departments, corporations and commissions, and considered the study of their structures an essential element in political analysis. Among others, L.D.White, Woodrow Wilson and Luther Gulick were protagonists of this approach. Their research centred around the description of institutions as they were supposed to be. In keeping with this hypothesis, they argued for politics-administration dichotomy.
- *Case method approach*: This approach to the study of public administration developed in the 1930s. According to Nicholas Henry, cases were reports written by practising public administrators as managerial problems and their solutions. This approach enhances the understanding of the administrative system by in-depth case studies, based on theory and empirical inquiry. These studies are usually grounded in field work, archival investigation, interviewing or scholarly monographers. Waldo welcomed the case method as a means of being empirical and behavioural (Henry, 1995). However, one needs to keep in mind that case studies were essentially configurative or constructive, and each system was treated as a unique entity.

A brief account of these traditional approaches is sufficient enough to reveal that these approaches were essentially formal, parochial, static and monographic. They merely provided a superficial and mechanistic interpretation of administration and politics. They were limited in their explanation and analysis of political institutions and were predominantly descriptive rather than problem solving in their method. In other words, the emphasis was on 'pure description in terms of endless piling of fact on fact'. There was little attempt to develop a general theory by verification of hypotheses and compilation of significant data. Dissatisfaction with subjectivism, formalism and empirical deficiency of traditional approaches provided an impetus for the emergence of the behavioural approach to public administration, what Robert Dahl has called 'empirical theory' in contemporary studies (Bertalanffy in Ray, 1999).

2. Modern Approaches

- *Behavioural approach*: Dissatisfaction with the existing conceptual and technical equipment, which placed excessive emphasis on formal and judicial structures, slowly gave way to function-oriented research. Behavioural approach was a novel method of analysing administrative problems because it stressed the study of behaviour of persons or groups rather than the structure, institutions or events. It favoured the application of proper scientific methods of research, focussing attention on actual behaviour. 'Behaviour' being something that could be observed and objectively studied was becoming more and more the focus of all 'scientifically' inclined scholars of public administration. In an effort to differentiate between the behavioural and traditional modes of inquiry, David Easton (cited in Chilcote, 1994) identified the major tenets of 'behavioural credo'.

The tenets of the 'behavioural credo' include the following:

- Regularities or uniformities in political behaviour, which can be expressed in generalizations or theory
- Verification or testing of validity of each generalization
- Techniques for seeking and interpreting data
- Quantification and measurement in the recording of data
- Values as distinguished between propositions relating to ethical evaluation and those relating to empirical explanation
- Systematization of research
- Pure science or the seeking of understanding and explanation of behaviour before utilization of knowledge for solution of societal problems
- Integration of political research with that of other social sciences

The behavioural approach was widely accepted and integrated into the discipline of public administration by the contributions of renowned sociologists and psychologists such as Herbert Simon, Chester Barnard, Abraham Maslow and Douglas McGregor.

- *Systems approach*: The emphasis on empirical theory by the behavioural school encouraged some theoretical innovations such as the systems approach. This approach stems from the general systems theory that crystallized around the concept of systems which Von Bertalanffy, the German biologist, defined as a set of 'elements standing in interaction' (cited in Ray, 1999).

  A system is an entity composed of various sub-systems in which everything relates to everything else, that is, a change in one sub-system inevitably produces change in other parts. According to Nicholas Henry, 'systems are composed of components that work together for the objectives of the whole and the systems approach is merely a way of thinking about these components and their relationships' (Henry, cited in Ray, 1999).

  In the systems approach, the focus is on the whole of the system rather than merely on its parts. There is also a strong awareness of environmental influences upon the system. The systems approach introduced a new trend in public administration. It suggested that equilibrium or disequilibrium in political life was the outcome of the interaction of many variables such as the personality and motivation of participants and environmental influences.

  The usefulness of the systems approach can be attributed largely to 'the compulsion to predict correctly and thereby be able to change things for the better' (Chilcote, 1994). Scholars such as David Easton, Herbert Simon, Chester Barnard and Mary Parker Follett made use of the systems approach in their organizational analysis. This approach laid the foundation for the development of new techniques of political analysis such as structural–functional approach and ecological approach.

- *Structural–functional approach*: This approach is an offshoot of the systems approach. It begins its inquiry into public administration within a systems framework. Basic to this approach are the twin concepts of structure and function. Inhe c crent in the structural functional analysis is the technique to analyse the administrative system, which is to locate the structures first and then analyse the functions they perform. It believes that an administrative system, which aims at the provision of services to individuals and groups, requires organizational structures, whereby it can channel its efforts to achieve the desired ends.

Administrative systems, however, are not a set of fixed patterns. They are neither uniform nor static in terms of their structure or the functions they perform. For instance, one structure may perform multiple functions or many structures may perform similar functions. According to the different forms the structures assume and the functions they perform, they maximize diverse values and serve different needs.

These structural patterns and functional processes clearly have a deep impact on the members of the society. The protagonists of this approach such as Gabriel Almond, David Apter, Talcott Parsons and Fred Riggs, therefore, rank structural–functional analysis as their primary concern and consider it to be a useful conceptual framework for administrative analysis.

- *Ecological approach*: The systems approach enhanced the analysis of administrative systems by seeking to probe the internal dynamics of organization. There was an increasing attempt to view the larger administrative system in terms of 'sub-systems' and their interaction with the environment. This led to the genesis of the ecological approach. This perspective in public administration was introduced by John Gaus in 'Reflections of Public Administration' (1945). This approach considers *environment* to be of crucial importance to organizations. It treats people, their ideas, wishes and values, situations, science and technology etc., as part of the environment that affects the nature and scope of public administrator's activity.

  In simple words, the crux of the ecological approach is that administrative behaviour is moulded by the culture and social system as a whole (we will discuss this approach in a chapter 9 of this volume. In fact, some of the approaches discussed in this chapter will be discussed in detail in this volume). Both Riggs and Robert Dahl, the major exponents of this approach, agreed that one could not afford to ignore the relationship between public administration and its social setting because public administration cannot escape the effects of this conditioning.

3. Contemporary Approaches

- *Public choice approach*: The contemporary 'public choice' approach provides a political economy perspective to administrative analysis by emphasizing economic considerations, conspicuously overlooked by the earlier approaches (political economy approach experiments with the application of economic methods/models to solve political problems).

  Renowned economists Buchanan and Tullock, Ostrom and Niskanen have largely contributed to the development of this approach. This approach critiques the Weberian paradigm, which invested full faith in bureaucracy as the most efficient form of organization. In contrast, it doubts the legitimacy of bureaucratic organization as the promoter of public interest and depicts bureaucracy as inefficient, unresponsive, self-aggrandizing and self-seeking. This approach assimilates the market friendliness and State minimalism arguments. Basis of the public choice approach is the idea central to modern economic theory that 'individual is a utility maximizer who is always in search of increasing net benefits' (Bhattacharya, 1999).

  It proposes a recipe that dismantles government monopoly as the supplier of public services and introduces competition in public administration to improve the standard of services. In the opinion of Buchanan and Tullock, 'decentralization creates opportunity for the promotion of competition among government agencies and in the process the individual choice increases' (Bhattacharya, 1999).

- *Comparative approach*: The approach which made the best known contribution in the direction of expanding the scale or spectrum of public administration in the post-World War II period is none other than 'Comparative Public Administration' (CPA). Put simply, CPA is the study of public administration on a comparative basis. The comparative approach observes the differences in form and processes within varying contexts and identifies the range across which administrative phenomena vary. Hence it is also called 'cross-cultural' public administration.

According to Moshe Maor and Jan-Erik Lane (1999), however, CPA is 'more than simply the accumulation of descriptive material about public sectors and policy attributes in different countries'. They define it as 'the construction of explanatory generalizations that are logically applicable to administrative system and policy-making processes and outcomes in different countries and hence, different cultural settings'.

Rise of comparative administration as a distinct approach is a post-World War II development, but the tradition of comparing administrative systems is an old one. Woodrow Wilson's essay 'The Study of Administration (1887)' provides a standard account of comparing administrative systems. The spirit of Wilson's essay was that 'comparisons with other countries could yield suggestions for improvement in one's own', because he saw the process as relatively constant (Dunsire, 1973).

Comparative studies received a further boost with Robert Dahl's article, 'The Science of Public Administration: Three Problems' in 1947, wherein the *third* problem that we cannot afford to ignore is the relationship between public administration and its social setting. He was clearly highlighting the differentiating effects of social settings upon public administration. Special mention must be made of Fred Riggs who also played a leading and creative role in the endeavour. Riggs' essay 'Agraria and Industria' (1957) is universally accepted as the key work in CPA.

However, as mentioned earlier, it was a chain of events after the World War II that completely transformed the scene and there was a renewed interest in comparative studies. Some of the prominent reasons contributing to the change in environment were as follows:

1. *The behavioural revolution*: Prior to the behavioural revolution, comparison was largely *pedagogical* or theoretical, rather than scientific, relevant or meaningful. The behavioural revolution rescued the comparative studies from its parochial clutches and injected them with scientific methods of study. Comparative administration with its cross-cultural orientation was essentially an outgrowth of the behavioural science movement after the World War II.
2. *Emergence of the third-world countries*: Earlier, the study of public administration was confined to the study of selected foreign governments. They provided a laboratory for comparative analysis. The process of decolonization after the World War II and the resultant turmoil of independence in the third world influenced the scholars of public administration to turn their attention to these new nations. They realized the intellectual bankruptcy of their techniques in analysing administrative practices in these third world countries. They became aware of the deviations from the standard pattern of the 'American experience'. It convinced them of the need to analyse and compare different administrative systems, since administration was culture bound.
3. *Cold war and the technical assistance programme*: Interest in comparative studies can also be attributed to the emergence of cold war and the American strategy to contain the Soviet Union, which incorporated launching of the Marshall Plan for economic recovery of Europe and the Point Four Programme for developing nations. These programmes widened the web of American commitments around the world. One of the assumptions underlying the American

foreign policy was that development would lessen the chance of 'communist takeovers' and hence development in the third world was in the national interest of the US. It was further believed that development could be facilitated by the transfer of resources and technologies from advanced to underdeveloped countries.

This necessitated an understanding of the administrative institutions and practices in the recipient countries. It provided curricula through which public administration experts and advisers were placed in more than 50 countries, undertaking several hundred projects in administrative improvement. Paul Appleby's consultancy in India in 1951 was among several such placements supported by the Ford Foundation. Therefore, the study of CPA was prompted by the increasing stake of the US in other countries of the world.

4. *Comparative Administration Group and the Ford Foundation*: The initiatives in comparative administration crystallized with the formal institutionalization of the Comparative Administration Group (CAG) in 1960. The CAG brought together a mass of scholars from the American Society for Public Administration (ASPA) and the American Political Science Association (APSA). Riggs was the chairman of the CAG since its inception. The ambition of Riggs and of the CAG was to develop a science of comparative administration based on empirically derived set of generalizations about administration (Lynn and Wildavsky, 1990).

Supplementing the intellectual resources of the CAG was the enormous financial aid and the assistance provided by the Ford Foundation. The generous financial support for academic research devoted to the understanding of non-western countries went a long way in creating a favourable and optimistic environment for comparative research possibilities.

The factors precipitating comparative studies were as follows:

- Behavioural revolution
- Emergence of third world countries
- Cold war and technical assistance programme
- CAG and Ford Foundation

SIGNIFICANCE OF COMPARISON

The need for comparison has been widely acknowledged. Comparison by itself was considered by many scholars, including Robert Dahl, as the road to true and scientific theory of administration. It was believed that comparative analysis of administrative structures and behaviour in different countries could provide a breakthrough in formulating generalizations and theories which provide a scientific basis to the study of public administration. The goal of CPA movement, to be precise, was also the development of a science of administration comprising general propositions of universal applicability (Jackson, 1996).

Comparative approach provided a more acceptable alternative to the devalued traditional approaches, which viewed organization as a closed system separated from the complex influences of its environment. It facilitated cross-cultural comparisons by being concerned with the interdependence of administrative behaviour and institutions with culture and sought to explain how a great variety of non-American forms, institutions and practices worked in other countries (Jreisat, 1975).

It facilitated objective and rational judgement about the success or failure of particular structures and practices in different ecological settings. This knowledge was particularly useful to the newly emerging countries which could benefit from the administrative experience of older States. According to Ferrel Heady (1979), another persuasive reason for the understanding of public administration across national boundaries was the increasing interdependence of nations and regions. In his view 'the comprehension of the conduct of administration in different countries was no longer just a matter of intellectual curiosity. Various administrative devices developed abroad might prove worthy of consideration for adoption or adaptation at home'.

He gave the example of the Scandinavian institution of Ombudsman, which had been adopted in numerous countries including the US, Britain, France and India for the redressal of citizens' grievances. In other words, a comparative study sought to dispel the dangerously misleading form of ethnocentrism that one's own country was superior to any other (Bertalanffy, cited in Ray, 1999). Due to these perceived advantages, the comparative method of research became popular and truly dominated the post-war period.

(a) *Range and scope of comparative studies*: Since the early 1960s, the engagement of comparative administration has been with the identification of universals or regularities in different administrative systems. It raises questions that are relevant across societies. The subject matter, range and scope of analysis in the published writings on CPA however, varied and assumed a variety of forms. It was observed that comparative studies handled the complex variables at three analytical levels – macro-level, middle-range level and micro-level.

Macro-studies undertook the comparison of entire systems of administration within the natural and social setting. Comparison of administrative systems of the US and India is an example of macro-study. A micro-study, on the contrary, dealt with a small variable of the administrative system, for example, the recruitment practice of civil services in India and Bangladesh. Middle-range studies handled standard administrative sub-topics, that is, those parts of administrative systems that were significant and comprehensive; for instance, the comparison of monarchy in Britain, Japan and Nepal, or the study of the role of bureaucracy in two or more countries. In other words, in comparative studies, the unit of analysis may be a part or the whole of the administrative system.

The types of comparative studies are as follows:

- Inter-institutional
- Intra-national
- Cross-national
- Cross-cultural
- Cross-temporal

The *range* of the phenomena that can be compared is also very wide. One can conveniently say that anything that is 'administrative' can be compared. Broadly speaking, types of comparative studies can be classified as follows:

- *Inter-institutional*: The categories of comparison here are the structures and processes involved in the activity of administering public affairs in a country. For instance, comparison of the structure and functioning of Ministry of Finance with the Ministry of Railways.
- *Intra-national*: When the focus of comparison is the administrative institutions within a country, such as the functioning of Panchayati Raj institutions in West Bengal and Bihar, it is called intra-national comparison.
- *Cross-national*: Cross-national comparative studies draw comparison between administrative systems of different countries. Such studies usually select variables common to a large number of countries, for example, comparing the upper house of the Parliament, such as the House of Lords in Britain with the Senate in the US.
- *Cross-cultural*: The base of comparison in cross-cultural analysis is the administrative institutions in areas with different cultural experience; for instance, a study of interaction between the bureaucracy and the political system in western democracies, the communist world and the third world countries.
- *Cross-temporal*: Such studies are oriented to comparison of administrative institutions and practices in different historical periods or timeframes; for example, a comparison of administrative system in pre-independence and post-independence India. Likewise, a comparison of the role of bureaucracy in policy formulation before and after liberalization and globalization would be categorized as cross-temporal analysis.

Thus, we find that the scope of comparison may be narrow or broad. Comparisons may be made within the framework of a society or culture or cross-culturally between societies.

(b) *How to compare techniques of comparison*: Just as the scope of comparative analysis may vary, according to Robert H. Jackson, the rigour with which comparisons are made is also subject to some variations, that is, comparisons may be made in a relatively loose or precise manner (Jackson, 1996). The nature of comparative studies has been changing since its inception in the early 1960s. This transition has resulted from the 'dramatic expansion of the range of coverage of the subject and a drastic re-orientation of approach' (Heady, 1979). In order to approach the study of public administration from a broad perspective, the comparative administration movement found it necessary to develop new methods and techniques of analysis.

Riggs, in his presentation, has successfully tried to capture the three emerging trends in the comparative study of public administration – shifts in approaches from 'normative' towards 'empirical', from 'ideographic' towards 'nomothetic' and from 'non-ecological' towards 'ecological'. Some elaboration on these trends is in the following order:

- *Normative to empirical*: Traditional literature on CPA was normative. It was dominated for a long time by political philosophy. It was pre-occupied with prescribing ideal or better patterns of administration. In fact, the normative flavour of comparative studies must be viewed as a response to the liberal-democratic environment in which they developed. In other words, they were normative because of their commitment to the values of constitutionalism and western liberal democracy and their belief in unidirectional development of political and administrative system on the western pattern (Arora, 1972).

Selected concepts based on western administrative systems were assumed as the most efficient elements of administration. It lacked the concepts to cope with the complexity of organization of governmental institutions in emerging non-western developing nations. The behavioural science movement in the post-World War II period heralded a shift in the approach. It stimulated interest of the scholars in descriptive and analytical information for its own sake. The empirical studies began to concentrate on the actual behaviour of human beings in administrative organization. Scholars such as Monroe Berger, Robert Presthus, Michael Crozier conducted empirical studies of bureaucratic behaviour in different cross-cultural settings (Arora, 1972).

- *Ideographic to nomothetic*: The second trend was a movement from what Riggs called ideographic towards nomothetic approaches. Ideographic approach can also be called a case study approach. Such studies were essentially 'non-comparative in nature' for despite the study of governments of several nations within a single volume, cross-cultural and cross-temporal analysis and explanations were rare (Arora, 1972). They treated administrative systems in isolation as unique cases without making an attempt to ascertain similarities and differences in their administrative behaviour and practices.

  Edward Shils (1960), however, feels, an 'inquiry can be considered comparative only if it uses a single set of categories to compare different societies so that their identities and uniqueness may be disclosed and explained'. Nomothetic approach shares a similar concern. By 'nomothetic', Riggs means an approach primarily concerned with the formulation of laws and general propositions (Shils, 1960). These studies were different from the ideographic studies because they sought 'generalizations, laws, hypotheses that assert regularities of behaviour correlation between variables' (Heady, 1979). Thus, the trend was to arrive at universal generalizations and put them together in a general theory.
- *Non-ecological to ecological*: The third trend was a shift from non-ecological to ecological studies. Traditional studies overlooked the importance of cultural, social, economic and political environment which embraced the administrative structure. The study of administration was divorced from the social and cultural order. Fred Riggs and Robert Dahl among others stressed that cross-cultural administrative analysis 'should focus upon the interaction between an administrative system and its external environment and also study the dynamics of socio-administrative change in the context of such interaction' (Arora, 1972).

The thrust of the argument of these scholars is that the best way to understand an administrative system is to place it in the context of its surrounding conditions, influences and forces that shape and mould them, because the two are inextricably bound. Although Riggs had stated his preference to consider as 'truly' comparative only those studies 'that are empirical, nomothetic and ecological', one must recognize the fact that today all these approaches co-exist in the literature of CPA.

THEORETICAL MODELS FOR COMPARISON

Comparative analysis necessitates the development of analytical tools upon which rigorous comparison can be made. It requires a theoretical framework or a model as a common denominator within which administrative phenomena can be compared. The lack of an identifiable core in the field of public administration, however, has made it difficult for the researchers to select a model which in the words of Waldo is 'large enough to embrace all the phenomena that should be embraced without being, by virtue of its large dimensions, too coarse-textured and clumsy to grasp and manipulate administration' (Jreisat, 1975).

Scholars of CPA use various models and theories to describe a reality and hypothesize about it. Selection of a particular model or a framework determines what type of variable will be compared. Among the important models that developed in comparative analysis, the bureaucratic model, the systems model and the development administration model deserve special mention.

Bureaucratic model: Bureaucratic model is a middle-range construct with bureaucracy as the chosen means of comparison. The focus on bureaucracy becomes understandable in view of the fact that it is common to all contemporary nation-states and is a universally existing structure (Heady, 1979). Dwight Waldo, Max Weber, Jong Jun, Lee Sigelman and many others recognized bureaucracy as the most manageable and appropriate basis for comparative studies. Dwight Waldo, for instance, said that the bureaucratic model was useful, stimulating and provocative (Heady, 1979). Some scholars focus on the structural profile of bureaucracy; some define it in behavioural terms and some others in terms of its goals and purposes.

However, Max Weber's treatment of bureaucracy as an 'ideal type' remains, till date, the most dominant conceptual model. He described bureaucracy as the rational and most efficient form of organization. Enumerating the structural and behavioural characteristics of the 'ideal type', he said it was characterized by hierarchy, specialization, role-specificity, recruitment by merit, career development, anonymity, impersonality and political neutrality.

The Weberian model has been criticized for ignoring the other side of the bureaucratic picture. Critics take Weber to task for his oversight of the dysfunctional aspects of bureaucracy. They also question the relevance of the Weberian model in meeting the needs of the third world countries. Despite the attacks, the bureaucratic model is still helpful for the purposes of comparing not only structural variations but also behavioural patterns among bureaucracies.

Systems model: As comparative studies grew in rigour and vitality, a new set of scholars, inspired by the sociological tenets of Talcott Parsons and Marion Levy, 'began to study not only political institutions but societies or cultures – wholes made up of parts kept together by mutually beneficial interaction' (Dunsire, 1973). Talcott Parson's development of structural functionalism had a lasting impact on comparative analysis. 'The twin assumptions of structural functionalism are: (a) the involvement of the concept of "social system" as a given and (b) the discussion of that society in terms of that society's structures and functions' (Jun, 1976).

Riggs, one of the earliest system theorists, applied this theoretical construct in his 'agraria–industria' typology. A purely traditional society was called 'agraria', an industrialized, modern society was called 'industria' and a society in the phase of transition from agraria to industria was labelled as 'transitia'. Later, Riggs came up with another construct in which he designates the models of modern, traditional and developing societies as diffracted, fused and prismatic societies respectively.

This typology based on structural–functional approach ranks the societies on the scale of functional differentiation of social structures. Of greatest interest to Riggs, however, was the developing society, which was half way between a fused society (*with no specialization of roles*) and a diffracted society (*with high degree of structural differentiation*) (Riggs, 1964). Viewing diverse societies with this frame of reference created new vistas of comparative research.

Development administration model: Development administration approach/model represents a bold attempt at conceptualizing the transitional societies and the role of administration therein. The weakness of the western-centric approach had been exposed. For instance, the hierarchically organized and functionally specialized bureaucratic model seemed heavily loaded with western presuppositions and was therefore ill-suited for catering to the needs of the developing countries. Further, it was not comprehensive enough to explain the social phenomena in the developing countries – Neither the complexity of their regimes nor the multiplicity of their goals. This stimulated the search for an alternative paradigm.

Theoretical models for comparision are as follows:

- Bureaucratic
- Systems
- Development administration

To cover up the lacunae in administrative theory, the concept of development administration was introduced by Edward Weidner and stressed by Riggs, among others (Arora, 1972). The followers of this approach were interested in explaining the dynamism of administration in developing countries in a changing environment. They devoted their attention to the problems of administrative adjustment which these developing countries faced in achieving their goals of nation building and rapid socio-economic and political change. In simple words, they grappled with the issues of 'administrative development' and 'development administration' (Riggs, 1964).

In the words of Weidner, 'the study of development administration can help identify the conditions under which a maximum rate of development is sought and the conditions under which it has been obtained' (Heady and Stokes, cited in Ramesh K. Arora, 1972). This approach continued to be dominant for about a quarter of a century until the mid-70s, and almost became synonymous with CPA.

The decade of 1960s was described as the heyday of comparative administration by Ferrel Heady, but soon the euphoria subsided, and by 1970s, the CPA movement slid down an inclined plane. This was partly because of the drop in the funding of such projects by the US government and partly because the CAG went into oblivion following its merger with the International Committee of the ASPA to form the new Section on International and Comparative Administration (SICA) (Heady, 1979). The legacy of the CAG came to be questioned. Doubts were raised regarding its relevance. One of the complaints was that CPA had 'failed to establish itself as a field of study with a generally accepted restricted range of topics to be addressed' (Heady, 1978).

It was felt that the diversity of concerns of CPA made it difficult to sift and distinguish the substantive issues from the peripheral ones. Perplexed by the wide range of seemingly independent concerns, Jreisat (1975) lamented 'the absence of integrative concepts and central foci in comparative research and analysis'. Keith Henderson even wondered 'what was not within the scope of Comparative Public Administration' (Jreisat, 1975).

The CPA movement's obsession with model construction and theory building was another target of attack. Although a concern with methodology was considered a healthy trend per se, the critics targeted CPA's pre-occupation with theorizing on the ground that they 'were often not so much theories, in any scientific sense of the word, as they were fantasies' (Heady, 1978).

According to Jreisat (1975), another factor contributing to the non-relevance of CPA was its 'pre-occupation with ecology of administration', which marginalized and subordinated the crucial administrative questions themselves. He felt 'the studies of political, economic, cultural and educational forces often appear as ends in themselves and not as means to discover those environmental influences which shape or affect administrative actions, processes and institutions'.

Echoing the same argument, Ramesh K. Arora said that Riggs' model makes more extensive analysis of the structure of social environment of the administrative systems than of the administrative systems themselves (Arora, 1972). Another charge against CPA is levelled against its intimate concern of development administration. Garth Jones, in unequivocal terms, criticizes the CAG for appropriating the concept of development administration for ulterior motives, calling it a 'device to secure money for research'. By changing the name of the 'game' to development administration, the CAG seized upon a term more marketable to the Ford Foundation, without actually contributing much to the solution of development administration problems (Heady, 1978). In simple words, it had limited significance to the experience of the developing countries.

Despite its faults and weaknesses Jun (1976) says that CPA deserves praise for having placed the field of public administration in a global context (Riggs, 1976). It also deserves appreciation for its bold assertion that crucial issues of contemporary times have become global and that their solution requires a global framework. Therefore, the new paradigm for public administration must be comparative (Riggs, 1976).

CONCLUSION

A plethora of approaches discussed in this chapter clearly points out that our understanding of public administration is undergoing considerable rethinking. There has been a decline of institution dominated, historical approach and scholars are delving into unexplored areas seeking a critical understanding and alternative explanations of the administrative reality. Each of these approaches highlights a relevant aspect of the political process. For instance, despite its deficiencies, the traditional approaches still provide the base or starting point of administrative analysis. With the behavioural and systems approaches, one observes a shift in the focus to methodology and quantitative techniques.

The contemporary approach, on the other hand, offers a new framework based on institutional pluralism and social democracy. However, the point to be noted here is that no single approach or perspective on public administration comprehensively 'explains it'. The administrative reality is much too complex and diverse to be viewed through the prism of one approach. A judicious combination of these approaches alone can provide insights into the richness of the discipline.

Preparatory Questions

- What are the major approaches to the study of public administration?
- Discuss the traditional approaches to the study of public administration, bringing out their limitations.
- Distinguish between traditional and modern approaches to the study of public administration.
- How do modern approaches help in the analysis of public administration?
- Explain the significance, nature and range of CPA.
- 'Public choice approach' has made substantial contribution to administrative analyses. Discuss.

REFERENCES

Arora, R. K. (1972) *Comparative Public Administration: An Ecological Perspective.* New Delhi: Associated Publishing House. p. 10.

Bertalanffy, L. V. (1999) 'General Systems Theory Foundation, Development, Applications' in Ray, S. N. (ed.). *Modern Comparative Politics: Approaches Methods and Issues.* New Delhi: Prentice Hall of India Private Ltd. p. 8.

Bhattacharya, M. (1999) *Restructuring Public Administration; Essays in Rehabilitation.* New Delhi: Jawahar Publishers. p. 17.

Chilcote, R. H. (2000) *The Political Economy of Imperialism: Critical Appraisals.* Maryland: Rowman and Littlefield.

Dunsire, A. (1973) *Administration: The Word and the Science.* London: Martin Robertson and Co. Ltd. p. 137.

Easton, D. (1965/1994) 'A Framework for Political Analysis' in Chilcote, R. H. (ed.). *Theories of Comparative Politics: The Search for a Paradigm Reconsidered.* 2nd ed. US: Westview Press. p. 57.

Fried, R. C. (1990) 'Comparative Public Administration: The Search for Theories' in Lynn, N. B. and Wildavsky, A. (eds.). *Public Administration: The State of the Discipline.* Chatham House Publication. p. 320.

Heady, F. and Stokes, S. L. (eds.) (1962) *Papers in Comparative Public Administration.* Ann Arbor (MI): Michigan Institute of Public Administration, The University of Michigan (quoted in Arora, R. K. p. 12).

Heady, F. (1978) 'Comparative Administration: A Sojourners Outlook' *Public Administration Review.* 38. p. 359.

Heady, F. (1979) *Public Administration: A Comparative Perspective.* 2nd ed. New York: Marcel Dekker. p. 5.

Henry, N. (1995) *Public Administration and Public Affairs.* US: Prentice-Hall. p. 32.

Jackson, R. H. (1996) 'An Analysis of the Comparative Public Administration Movement' in Canadian public administration. *The Journal of the Institute of Public Administration of Canada.* IX(1). p. 108.

Jreisat, J. E. (Nov/Dec, 1975) 'Synthesis and Relevance of Comparative Public Administration' *Public Administration Review.* p. 663.

Jun, J. S. (1976) 'Renewing the Study of Comparative Administration' *Public Administration Review.* 36. p. 643.

Kousoulas, G. D. (2003) 'On Government and Politics' in Ray, S. N. (ed.). *Modern Comparative Politics: Approaches Methods and Issues.* p. 1.

Maor, M. and Jan-Erik Lane, J. E. (eds.) (1999) *Comparative Public Administration.* Vol. II. Dartmouth, Brookfield (VA): Ashgate.

Ray, S. N. (1999) *Modern Comparative Politics Approaches, Methods and Issues.* New Delhi: Prentice Hall of India. p. 6.

Riggs, F. W. (1962) 'Trends in Comparative Study of Public Administration.' *International Review of Administrative Sciences.* 281(1). pp. 9–15, cited in Jun, J. S. (1976) Renewing the Study of Comparative Administration: Some Reflections on the Current Possibilities. *Public Administration Review.* 36. p. 642.

Riggs, F. W. (1964) *Administration in Developing Countries: The Theory of Prismatic Society.* Boston (MA): Houghton Mifflin Company.

Riggs, F. W. (ed.) (1964) *Frontiers of Development Administration.* Durham (NC): Duke University Press.

Riggs, F. W. (Nov/Dec, 1976) 'The Group and the Movement: Notes on Comparative and Development Administration.' *Public Administration Review.* p. 652.

Rosenbloom, D. H. and Kravchuk, R. S. *Public Administration: Understanding Management, Politics and Law in the Public Sector.* 5th ed. New York: McGraw Hill. p. 15.

Shils, E. (1960) 'Political Development in the New States.' *Comparative Studies in Society and History.* 2(3).

Chapter Four

The Classical Approach to Organizations

Alka Dhameja

Scientific Management Approach to Organizations
Scientific Management of Taylor: An Evaluation
Classical Approach of Henri Fayol
Views of Luther Gulick and Lyndall Urwick
Views of Mary Parker Follett
Appraisal of Classical Approach
Conclusion
References

LEARNING OBJECTIVES

***After completing this chapter, you should be able to*:**

- **Discuss the philosophy of F.W. Taylor's scientific management approach to organizations**
- **Describe the tenets of the classical approach as propagated by Henri Fayol**
- **Understand the principles of organization as espoused by Luther Gulick and Lyndall Urwick**
- **Examine the views of Mary Parker Follett on conflict management; and**
- **Make an appraisal of the classical approach to the study of organization**

INTRODUCTION

The classical approach of administration belongs to the era when industrialization was well into its own, but industrial processes remained haphazard and unsystematic. It was a time when processes and functions in industries were not keenly studied to improve efficiency, productivity, profits and workers' welfare. The classical theorists aimed to streamline these very processes to achieve the objectives of maximum production at effective costs. The classical theory or approach is also known by various other names such as traditional theory, formal organizational theory, structural theory, management process theory and mechanistic theory. We will be using the terms theory and approach interchangeably in this chapter.

On the one stream of classical theory are F. W. Taylor and his associates Henry L. Gantt and the Gilbreth couple, Frank and Lillian, who have propagated, what is famously called, the 'scientific management' perspective of organization, whereas on the other stream are theorists such as Henri Fayol, Luther Gulick, Lyndall Urwick, Mary Parker Follett, James Mooney and A. C. Reiley. There are, however, *essential differences* in the two streams, as far as their approach to the organization is concerned. While Taylor focussed on shop floor management and believed in one best way of doing a job after delineation of tasks through time and motion studies, Fayol, Mooney and the others spoke of managerial level staff in an organization. For them, organizational structure was foremost and efficiency was possible through implementation of certain specific principles that they outlined.

Henri Fayol was among the first to write on industrial efficiency. In fact, his works preceded that of Taylor's. However, the import of his works was realized only when they were translated into English from French much later. This explains why we talk of Taylor first in our discussions on the classical approach. This chapter will make an attempt to explain the meaning, focus and characteristics of the classical approach by underlining the contributions of its major proponents.

SCIENTIFIC MANAGEMENT APPROACH TO ORGANIZATIONS

Before we study Taylor's stream of classical approach, let us be clear about the main concerns of the approach. The basic focus of classical approach is on structure and within the structure, the spotlight is on efficiency and communication. The assumptions of classical approach relate to the following:

- Relationship between employees and management, which is defined by means of formal structured communication process.
- Laid down rules, defined tasks, delineated accountability, formalized procedures and practices.
- Incentive-driven management strategies that satiate the economic side of the workers.
- Workers being cogs in the process of production.

Scientific management is a crucial component of this approach. Scientific management lays accent on efficiency in organizational work. The command structure is designed to highlight both – the overall objectives of the organization and the specific purposes of the functional units. When we talk of scientific management, the first name that crosses our mind is that of Frederick Winslow Taylor. Since Fayol's works remained untranslated for long, it can be observed that the scientific way of analysing management practices began with Taylor.

Famously known as the 'Father of Scientific Management,' Taylor has many firsts to his credit. He was the first management consultant – first to invent industrial equipment such as cutting tools, steel hammer, hydraulic power-loading machine and tool feeding mechanism, which aimed to increase efficiency levels of the workers; first to find 'one best way of doing a job'; and first to lay down the principles of scientific management. From a mere labourer to a general manager, every stage/phase/process of product manufacturing passed through his penetrating gaze (Singh, 2002).

Taylor observed that management had no clear understanding of its responsibilities, effective work standards, designing of jobs, division of work, placement of workers, incentive schemes and scientific decision making. As a result, productivity remained low, and management, workers and consumers *all* suffered in the process. Taylor firmly believed that management principles were actually scientific in nature and could be applied to all social activities. To him, best results could be achieved through a cooperative partnership among trained staff, qualified management and supportive labour.

Frederick Winslow Taylor was born in German town, Philadelphia, Pennsylvania, in 1856. He, joined the Enterprise Hydraulic Works of Philadelphia as an apprentice. After that he joined the Midvale Steel Company. He worked as a labourer, gang-boss, research director and even chief engineer in the company. He received his degree in mechanical engineering in 1884. Consequently, in 1890, he became General Manager of the Manufacturing Investment Company in Philadelphia. Later, he joined Bethlehem Steel and also worked as a Professor at the Tuck School of Business at Dartmouth College. He published very pertinent research papers and became the President of the American Society of Mechanical Engineers in 1906

In the early 1890s, Taylor observed that various managerial practices were slowing down managerial procedures. Workers, he felt, were deliberately slow and displayed delaying tactics, as they perceived over-productivity to be a threat to their well-being in the organization. Taylor coined different terms for this behaviour such as 'soldiering' and 'skiving'. In his view, workers exhibited this behaviour due to following reasons:

- Workers showed sheer casualness about their work.
- Workers believed that if they became productive, they would be eliminated by the management.
- Non-productive wage system encouraged low productivity by workers.
- Workers feared that high pace of work would become the standard norm, bringing down their wage levels.
- Too much reliance on rule of thumb and unscientific methods and practices led to wastage of time by workers.

Papers published by Taylor are as follows:

- Piece Rate System, 1895
- Shop Management, 1903
- Art of Cutting Metals, 1906
- Principles of Scientific Management, 1909

F. W. Taylor believed in the following:

- Applying scientific methods of research and experiments to the management problems.
- Standardizing working conditions and placing the workers on the basis of scientific criteria.
- Imparting formal training and specific instructions to workers to perform the prescribed motions with standardized tools and materials.
- Promoting cooperation between workers and management.

Taylor envisioned a philosophy of management, which focused on higher productivity, so that certain work conditions could be achieved. His vision encompassed the following:

- Science, not rule-of-thumb.
- Harmony, not discord.
- Cooperation, not individualism.
- Maximum output instead of a restricted one.
- Development of worker to highest level of efficiency and prosperity.
- Maximum prosperity to the employer.
- Higher wages to workers.
- Lower priced goods for the customers.

These goals, he thought, would be attainable if four basic principles of scientific management were followed. For Taylor, these principles were integrated and cohesive for achieving the objectives of productivity and efficiency:

1. *Development of a true science of work*: Replacing the old rule of thumb and encouraging an understanding of true nature of a fair day's work through a scientific investigation of daily tasks. Classification and tabulation of the tasks by understanding the traditional role of workers and division of the tasks into rules and work methods to arrive at 'one best way of doing a job' to increase productivity.
2. *Scientific selection and progressive development of the worker*: Including scientific selection of workers and placing them in jobs that do justice to their knowledge, skills and attitudes. This, he felt, was possible through effective training to tap the potential and aptitude of the workers to enable them to enthusiastically adapt to new methods, tools and conditions.
3. *Bringing together science of work and scientifically selected and trained men*: Involving constant motivation of the workers by the management. Dealing with management resistance to motivate and inspire workers, so that they produce to their highest capacity. Promoting cooperation of management and labour to accomplish the goals of organization, in line with the scientific methods.
4. *Division of work and responsibility between management and workers*: Calling upon workers and management to share equal responsibility for their work. This, he thought, was possible through division of work based on a feeling of understanding and mutual dependence on the part of both workers and management.

Taylor argued that even the most basic, mindless tasks could be planned in a way that would dramatically increase productivity. He propagated the scientific way of doing work as a motivator for the worker, instead of the 'initiative and incentive' stimuli, suggested by the later classical theorists and human relationists. To scientifically determine the optimal way to perform a job, Taylor performed experiments, which he called the 'Time and Motion Studies'. These studies were characterized by the use of stop watches to time a worker's sequence of motions.

Taylor studied the amount of time taken to complete a particular task. He believed that every technique comprised several motions such as digging earth, carrying load, cutting metals and lifting coal as different tools and equipment such as shovels or pulleys were required to perform a particular motion. Taylor believed that these motions could be studied to determine the amount of time required to finish a motion using a specific equipment. The objective was to determine standardized methods as per the capability of workers towards higher work productivity and efficiency.

Taylor found that the floor or the lowest level in the shop or factory was the most neglected part and that there was no motivation for higher performance at this level. In his 'Art of Cutting Metals', he suggested devices such as machine improvement, instruction card and time savers to differentiate lower performance workers from higher performance ones. The *standardized* system worked on its own methods, and the manager did not have to bother too much about it. Items that were *not* standard or exceptional were to be dealt by the manager separately. This was called 'Exceptional Principle' by Taylor, which he introduced in *Shop Management* (Singh, 2002).

Differential piece rate system was Taylor's wage payment plan for the workers. On the basis of time and motion studies, tasks were scientifically analysed, divided and executed. A standard classification of tasks (*below, up to and above standard*) was arrived at and rates were fixed for different pieces. Taylor was of the view that payment should be made on the basis of the number of pieces that workers make and *not* on the basis of positions.

Taylor demonstrated his views through case studies conducted by him over time which were as follows:

- Moving Pig Iron at the Bethlehem Steel Company to recommend resting periods and lifting of iron as per capability
- Studying the science of shovelling through time studies to determine the optimal weight that a worker should lift in a shovel
- Bricklaying, as studied by his associate Frank B. Gilbreth through motion studies to reduce the motions for laying bricks
- Inspecting small polished steel balls for bicycle bearings
- Introducing slide rules to run a machine shop well

Taylor suggested that workers should be controlled, not only by giving of orders and maintenance of discipline, but also by taking away from them any decisions about the manner in which their work was to be carried out. By division of labour and by determining each and every stage of work performance, management could control the actual process of work.

Two concepts are specific to Taylor, which also make his contribution to management rather unique. These are his concepts of 'functional foremanship' and 'mental revolution'. Functional foremanship advocates division of work in an organization, not just between workers, but also the management. Taylor believed in sharing of responsibility between workers and management. He divided work under *four* heads at the supervisory level called planning bosses and four heads at the execution level called execution bosses.

Planning bosses	Execution bosses
• Order of work and route clerk	• Gang-boss
• Instruction card clerk	• Repair-boss
• Time and cost clerk	• Speed-boss
• Shop disciplinarian	• Inspector

Scientific management, according to Taylor, primarily involved a complete 'mental revolution' on the part of workers and the management, as to their duties, work, fellow workers and daily difficulties. It demanded a realization of the fact that mutual interests of management and workers were not antagonistic, and could be sorted out through cooperation and prosperity. Taylor believed that management and workers should *both* take their eyes off their immediate interests and concentrate only on *increasing* the surplus of the organization. This way surplus would increase to such an enormous extent that workers would be ensured of *higher wages* and management of *greater profits*. This type of change in mental attitudes would lead to a revolution in surplus production, rendering division of output a non-issue between the management and workers.

SCIENTIFIC MANAGEMENT OF TAYLOR: AN EVALUATION

Initially, Taylor was very successful at improving production processes. His methods involved getting the best equipment and people, and then carefully scrutinizing each component of the production process. By analysing each task individually, Taylor was able to find the right combinations of factors that yielded large and increased production. After a while, scientific management principles, which improved productivity and had a positive impact on industry, began to increase the monotony of work. According to many critics, scientific management ignored psychological and sociological variables within an organization, as Taylor neglected individual differences and perceptions of efficiency, which varied from worker to worker.

Taylor did lay emphasis on the economic nature of people in the organization, but overlooked the fact that economic interests of workers and management often clashed. The idea of disregarding the 'initiative and incentive' stimuli has also been criticized by many, as a worker's individual creativity never found its due place in Taylor's work place. While Taylor's scientific management theory proved successful in the simple industrialized companies at the turn of the 18th century, it did not fare well in modern companies.

The philosophy of 'production first, people second' has been criticized by the later human relations and sociopsychological theorists, as they believed that neglect of human element in scientific management led to a decline in production and quality, dissatisfaction with work, and loss of pride in workmanship as well as organizational pride. Managers were opposed to Taylor's focus on skills, qualification and training. Those who reached top positions without appropriate qualification were averse to Taylor's emphasis on higher education and training.

Taylor's dichotomy of work between planning and execution has also been criticized. Trade unions criticized him for destroying the practice of collective bargaining and unity of labour unions. They also feared that scientific management would cause extensive unemployment. Use of stop watches was seen as looking at management from a 'mechanical or automaton', rather than human point of view. The agitations by trade unions led the American Congress to amend the Army Appropriation Act in 1915, which put a stop on the use of stop watches and the payment of bonuses in army arsenals.

Later, Elton Mayo, through his Hawthorne Experiments, proved that the emotional attitude of the workers towards work was more important for increased productivity than organizational arrangements. Behaviouralists have also criticized Taylor's attempt to underplay the initiative of workers. Subsequent chapters will deal with these concerns in detail. March and Simon observed that 'Taylor's contribution was not a set of general principles for organizing work effectively, but a set of operating procedures that could be employed in each concrete situation to discover the methods that would be efficient in that situation to secure their application. They described it as physiological organization theory' (Sahni and Etakula, 2010).

Taylor's 'functional foremanship' was considered to be confusing for the workers, as they would put them under the control of eight supervisors. According to Peter Drucker, the central theme of Taylor's work was not 'inefficiency' but the need to substitute industrial warfare by 'industrial harmony'. He remarked that under Taylorism, organization became a piece of poor engineering judged by the standards of human relations, as well as those of productive efficiency and output (Sahni and Etakula, 2010).

Even though Taylor saw organizations in isolation of their immediate environment, or as closed systems, it does not take away from him the fact that he was a pioneer in the application of *quantitative techniques* to the study of industrial management. His theory of management analysed and synthesized *workflows* and had a huge impact on the industrial practice in countries such as the US, erstwhile USSR, Germany, France and England. In fact, it became a movement, as scholars such as Henry Gantt, Frank Gilbreth, Lillian Gilbreth, Henri Fayol, Luther Gulick and Lyndall Urwick went on to do a systematic study of industrial management and organizational principles.

The concepts given by Taylor speak immensely about his insight into managerial methods and techniques. He wrote at a time when industries worked without any laid down rules and scientific standards of job definition and analyses. He believed that a free market would strive to achieve maximum profit and efficiency, and what is called the *Protestant work ethic* would make workers work harder and behave rationally, putting the organizational goals at the top.

> The Protestant work ethic is a concept, which lays premium on hard work, frugality and prosperity as a display of a person's salvation in the Christian faith. The phrase was initially coined in 1904 by Max Weber in his book 'The Protestant Ethic and the Spirit of Capitalism'.

Taylor earnestly intended to give the worker the necessary skill and training to live up to an optimum work potential in a suitable work environment. So those who criticize Taylor of propagating impersonal rules and inhuman standardization of jobs, forget the context in which he practiced his ideas. His approach to the study of work settings and procedures is still valuable to organizational functioning.

CLASSICAL APPROACH OF HENRI FAYOL

Now, moving over to the other important classical theorists of the second stream, we may say, as also mentioned earlier on in this chapter, that their approach to organization was somewhat different from that of Taylor. These theorists namely Henri Fayol, Luther Gulick, Lyndall Urwick, Mary Parker Follett and James Mooney went a little beyond Taylorism in terms of management concepts and theories. For them, each organization had its special needs depending on the situation and demand of the job.

Henri Fayol, who is called the Father of *Management Process School*, did not make a distinction between public and private organizations (administration and management), and approached both through certain general principles. To him, management as a science could be developed, studied and applied, both to public and to private organizations. Fayol's principles were not rigid, as he never propagated 'one best way of doing things'. Fayol's 14 principles include the following:

1. Division of work: Specialization of labour.
2. Commensurate relationship between authority and responsibility.
3. Discipline or obedience.
4. Unity of command: One boss for an employee.
5. Unity of direction: One head and one plan for every activity.
6. Subordination of individual to general interest of the total organization.
7. Remuneration of personnel, based on fairness and satisfaction to both personnel and the firm.
8. Centralization, based on the degree of initiative, which varies, depending on top managers, subordinates and business conditions.
9. Scalar chain or hierarchy/line of authority.
10. Order or placement of personnel.
11. Equity, based on kindness and justice in employer–employee relations.
12. Stability of tenure, to minimize employee turnover.
13. Initiative or ability to think afresh.
14. Espirit de corps or harmony and unity among personnel (Prasad and Prasad, 2010).

> Henri Fayol (1841–1925) was a prolific writer. His most outstanding work on management writings is 'General and Industrial Management', first published in 1916. His paper on the 'Theory of Administration of State' presented at the Second International Congress of Administrative Sciences is considered to be his major contribution to the theory of public administration

Fayol divided managerial activity into six groups or categories, namely technical (production, manufacture, adaptation), commercial (buying, selling, exchange), financial (optimum use of capital), security (protection of property and persons), accounting (stocktaking, balance sheets, costs) and managerial (planning, organizing, commanding, coordinating, controlling). These managerial activities are famously known by the acronym POCCC, which denotes the following:

- *Planning*: Fayol believed that plan of action was the crux of administration. He treated it as the most effective instrument of providing unity, continuity, flexibility and precision to organizational processes and actions. Planning, he believed, was an effective way of segregating short-term plans from long-term considerations.
- *Organizing*: Fayol called for organizing goals, activities and efforts in an organization through adequate plan of action, coordination, selection of employees, motivation, reward, pay structure,

supervision and decision making. He made a distinction between material organization and human organization, and included personnel, leadership and structure in his organization.

- *Commanding*: Fayol's manager in command was a person with certain personal qualities and knowledge. He felt that the manager could control effectively if he had the qualities of competence, integrity, auditing, attention to detail and omniscience.
- *Coordinating*: Fayol advocated harmonization of the activities of the organization's departments to ensure that efforts of one department are in harmony with the other.
- *Controlling*: Fayol advocated strict conformity to plan, instructions and principles. In the process, weaknesses and errors had to be rectified and their recurrence prevented (Prasad and Prasad, 2010).

While Taylor propagated a bottom-up approach, Fayol was in favour of top-down. He also found Taylor's eight bosses to be unworkable. He suggested that it was important to have unity of command; that is, only one supervisor for each person in an organization. The most famous concept given by Fayol is that of *gangplank*. It refers to level jumping in a hierarchical organization. To guard against red tape and formalism, Fayol felt that in an emergency or in urgent need, the hierarchy in an organization could be jumped and lateral relationships could be established. He cautioned, though, that 'gangplank' was possible only if immediate supervisors permit the juniors to jump levels in a clear line of authority.

Fayol believed that management theories could be developed, rather than actually taught. However, like other classical theorists, he has been criticized for imposing a *mechanistic* model on a live organization. The fact that he gave more importance to the functions than the structure has also been criticized. His theory was said to be very formal, superficial, simple and unrealistic. It was considered to be more relevant in stable and predictable environments.

VIEWS OF LUTHER GULICK AND LYNDALL URWICK

Other theorists such as Luther Gulick and Lyndall Urwick sought to create an organizational science. Called the 'machine model' of organization, this science underlying organizations, believed that authority rested in positions, not people. Gulick gave seven principles of organization, famously known by the acronym POSDCORB, published in their 'Papers on Science of Administration', where 'P' stands for planning, 'O' for organizing, 'S' for staffing, 'D' for directing, 'Co' for coordinating, 'R' for reporting and 'B' for budgeting. These principles were meant to give a status to organizations, independent of people.

> Luther Halsey Gulick III (1892–1993) was born in Japan and shifted to the US later, where he did his graduation, post-graduation, PhD and Litt. D. His major publications include 'Metropolitan Problems and American Ideas', 'Modern Management for the City of New York' and 'Papers on Science of Administration'

Gulick and Urwick synthesized the organizational or management theories as applicable to public organizations. 'The Papers on Science of Administration'; their edited work published in 1937, contributed significantly to the science of administration. Gulick laid emphasis on decentralization and timing in an organization. To him, human welfare and survival should be regarded central to any organization. His ten principles of organization are as follows:

1. Division of work or space.
2. Bases of departmental organization.

3. Coordination through hierarchy.
4. Deliberate coordination.
5. Coordination through Committees.
6. Decentralization.
7. Unity of command.
8. Staff and line.
9. Delegation.
10. Span of control.

For Gulick, 'division of work' was the most important principle, falling under design of organization. It is based on 'purpose', 'place', 'process' and 'people', commonly known as the four P's:

- *Purpose* or function is important to an organization, as its work is organized on the basis of major functions and goals. The advantage of this basis is that the whole job comes under one director, with control of all those required in the performance of work. However, Gulick felt that if purpose became the sole basis, then many types of technical work would not fit in.
- *Place* or area as a basis is suited to activities that follow nature of work under a single systematic umbrella of organization.
- *Process* or skill means that the work based on similar process should be grouped together. If process is the basis, then division of work and specialization are in place. It would also use labour to the maximum extent and save machinery and mass production.
- *Persons* or clientele basis makes use of specialized skills in running a particular group. It produces area specialists, but this principle as a sole basis is also difficult, as there could be overlapping and duplication of work efforts. Thus, according to him, organizations would have to generally use a combination of bases to divide work and fix responsibility.

> Lyndall Fownes Urwick (1891–1983), born and raised in the UK, was an outstanding management consultant. He was instrumental in the establishment of the Administrative Staff College at Henley-on-Thames. His important books include 'Management of Tomorrow', 'The Making of Scientific Management', 'Elements of Administration' and 'Dynamic Administration'. With Luther Gulick, he founded the academic journal, the Administrative Science Quarterly

Urwick gave utmost priority to the structure of organization, urging managers to start on the assumption of 'clean slate', that is, design first, determine positions, qualifications and division of work and then allocate functions. He felt that lack of design was illogical, cruel, wasteful and inefficient.

He identified eight principles of organization which are as follows:

1. Principle of objective.
2. Division of work or specialization.
3. Scalar principle.
4. Principle of responsibility.
5. Span of control.

6. Unity of command.
7. Principle of coordination.
8. Line and staff.

Three of these principles, namely, scalar, unity of command and span of control have been prominent in Urwick's writings. 'Scalar principle' refers to hierarchical or graded organization comprising several levels, where duties are graded not as per functions, but as per the degree of authority and responsibility, and authority equates the capacity of people performing duties.

Urwick was one of the first writers to apply the concept of 'span of control' formally to business. He has also addressed the reasons for leaders ignoring the principle of span of control. He wrote about the problems of managing a large number of employees, identified multiple levels of supervisory management and used a formula to determine minimum and maximum number of subordinates a manager can effectively supervise. His work was an important step in blending the principles of scientific management and the views of Weber and Fayol.

In fact, Gulick and Urwick, together coined the principle of 'span of control'. The principle is based on the assumption that an official cannot effectively control more than a certain number of subordinates at a given time. This, they based on the lines of *Graicunas' formula* according to which, in any organization, if there are three subordinates, direct single relationships would be three, cross relationships six and direct group relationships nine. If more members are added, specialized work may get affected, necessitating a change in span of control, rather than routine work.

As per Graicunas' formula, in any group, the relations between an executive and his subordinates cannot just be calculated on the basis of a single relationship alone. The direct single relationship always increases in the same proportion as the number of subordinates, but there also exist direct group and cross relationships, which increase very rapidly in mathematical proportion

Unlike Taylor, Gulick and Urwick have followed Fayol and focused on single executive and unity of command. They both felt that subordinates should receive orders from only one superior. For them, advantages of following this principle negate inefficiency or confusion.

Major contributions of Gulick and Urwick are as follows:

- Division of labour
- Scalar principle
- Span of control
- Line and staff

Borrowing from the military context, Gulick and Urwick also adopted the principle of 'line and staff'. They believed that an executive in an organization functions well with the help of staff agencies, responsible for advice and technical expertise – knowing, thinking and planning.

They also believed that administrators should keep the requisite authority with them and delegate the rest to their subordinates. Authority and responsibility were treated as being coterminous and the executive was supposed to know how to delegate.

VIEWS OF MARY PARKER FOLLETT

Mary Parker Follett pioneered the understanding of *lateral* processes within hierarchical organizations (*this recognition later led to the formation of matrix-style organizations*). She analysed organizations from the point of view of *conflict and coordination*, giving it a human dimension altogether. For her, conflict is unavoidable in an organization, as it involves different human perspectives that often clash; conflict is neither good nor bad, it simply exists and there is no need to be judgemental about it. In fact, she felt that conflict could turn out to be healthy for an organization, as she calls it *constructive conflict*. Organizations need to recognize these conflicts and arrive at acceptable solutions. She suggested the following three ways of resolving conflict:

1. Domination
2. Compromise
3. Integration

Domination, she felt, is a victory of one side over the other. This is the easiest way of dealing with conflict, but not necessarily the best one. People resolve conflict, only for the time being because of fear or sheer passive obedience to the dominator. After some time, the dormant desires of the dominated may resurface and give rise to fresh conflict.

Under *compromise* too, conflict resolution is temporary as both parties give up some desire of theirs to reach a compromise and resolve the conflict. This is not very easy to achieve as everyone has to give up a little to achieve conflict resolution.

Follett advocated the principle of what she termed 'integration', or non-coercive power sharing based on the use of her concept of 'power with' rather than 'power over'. *Integration* means the creation of a novel solution that is not punitive for anyone, and ideal for democracy. When two desires are *integrated*, conflict gets resolved. It means that a solution has been reached in which both desires have found a place that neither side has had to sacrifice anything. However, there could be desires which are so variant and antagonistic that they *cannot* be integrated.

> Mary Parker Follett (1868–1933) was an American social worker, management consultant and pioneer in the fields of organizational theory and organizational behaviour. She admonished over-managing of employees, a process now known as micro-managing, as 'bossism'. She is regarded by some writers as the 'mother' of scientific management. Follett published many works, including The Speaker of the House of Representatives (1896), The New State (1918), Creative Experience (1924) and Dynamic Administration (1942)

So, in Follett's view, integration, though desirable, is not always possible and requires a *change in attitude* on the part of parties involved. Moreover, mindsets need suitable training for the principle of integration to be successful. There has to be total transparency, issues have to be discussed threadbare and broken into clear constituent parts. Follett talked of *anticipation* of conflict and *response* to the conflict, if integration has to be reached. She spoke of various obstacles to integration, such as faulty language of communication, needless theorizing, external influences and habit of domination, which required to be kept in check. Thus, to her, integration is a complex process, but can lead to 'constructive conflict resolution', which is permanent and lasting. Coordination is the first step towards this.

Mary Parker Follett believed in the following:

- Three ways of resolving conflict, namely, dominance, compromise and integration
- Four dimensions of coordination, namely, direct contact among managers, expression of diverse views, understanding decisions in relation to situations and change orientation

Mary Parker Follett gave four dimensions to the principle of coordination. She viewed coordination as follows:

1. As a direct contact among managers, somewhat on the lines of *gangplank* of Fayol.
2. As a way of including the viewpoints by all managers and taking into view their divergence of opinion towards integration of differences or conflict through reconciliation.
3. As a manner of relating managerial decisions to situations, clearly indicating that authority is connected to the job and not people or situations.
4. As a continuous process, hinting at the need for organizations to change along with the changing situation.

Follett encouraged people to be active as citizens and learn their lessons on democracy by participating in group and community activities. She believed in the concept of self-governance as she felt it was important for the growth of individuals and their groups. Besides, her ideas on negotiation, power and employee participation have been highly influential in the areas of organizational studies, alternative dispute resolution and the human relations movement.

Other classical theorists such as James D. Mooney and Alan Reiley elaborated the principles raised by Follett a little further by giving the following four principles:

1. Coordinating principle.
2. Scalar principle based on delegation and chain of command.
3. Functional principle based on specialization.
4. Line and staff based on the need for specialized advice and support to line agencies.

The emphasis was on establishing a *universal* set of management principles that could be applied to all organizations. Urwick later clubbed the principles given by classical theorists, namely Fayol's 14 principles, Mooney and Reiley's principles of process and effect, Taylor's management principles, Follett's viewpoints and Graicunas' ideas. These got reflected in the 29 principles that Urwick compiled. Some of them are investigation, forecasting, planning, appropriateness, organization, coordination, order, command, control, authority, leadership, initiative, equity, discipline and so on.

APPRAISAL OF CLASSICAL APPROACH

Although the pertinence of the classical approach to the study of organization cannot be belittled, we have to say that it was in fact rigid and mechanistic in nature. Its major deficiency was that it attempted to explain peoples' motivation to work, strictly as a function of economic reward. Workers were treated as mere inert biological machines engaged in work processes.

According to L. D. White, while the terms line, staff and auxiliary agencies; hierarchy' authority; centralization etc., are useful terms for describing or classifying administrative situations, they are no more than that. They provide no guidance as to whether a given system, more or less, should be highly centralized or as to whether auxiliary agencies should be given more or fewer duties or authority. They are not rules. They suggest only working rules of conduct, which wide experience seems to have validated (cited in Sahni and Etakula, 2010).

Many feel that the classical approach did not have a base in empirical research and scientific methods. The administrative principles were based on personal experiences and limited observations. They lacked uniformity and did not have merit of being put to verification. The classical principles of division of work, hierarchy, coordination, supervision and unity of command were in nature of *postulates*, not universally applicable and even mutually contradictory. Herbert Simon has called these principles 'Proverbs', as they appear in the nature of mutually contradictory pairs.

For every principle, Simon observed, there is a counter principle. If there is a proverb 'look before you leap', there is another contrary proverb – 'he who hesitates is lost'. Although the two principles of the pair will lead to exactly opposite organizational recommendations, there is nothing in the theory to indicate which one is the proper one to apply. For example, the principle of unity of command implies that in an organization, the employee should receive orders from only one superior but it contradicts another principle, that is, the principle of specialization. The present organizations are highly complex and due to reasons of specialization, the specialist would receive orders from technical as well as general supervisors. Through his attacks, Simon points to 'the yawing gulf, between the principles and practice' (cited in Sahni and Etakula, 2010).

Some scholars such as C. Pollitt have termed the new public management or the NPM paradigm of late 1990s as nothing but 'Neo-Taylorism' because of its renewed focus on efficiency, cost-effectiveness, economy and rule-orientation (Singh, 2010). As per Simon and March, inadequate focus on concepts such as motivational assumptions, intra-organizational conflict, role of cognition and complex information processing system was a serious drawback of the classical approach (cited in Prasad and Prasad, 2010).

The classical approach has been criticized on following counts:

- Propagation of contradictory principles
- Gap between principles and practice
- Lack of focus on intra-organizational conflict
- Absence of role of cognition in task identification and classification
- Inadequate attention on programme evaluation
- Oversimplified human motivational assumptions
- No place for relationship between organization and environment

CONCLUSION

The classical approach has been criticized from various quarters, be it industrialists, trade unionists, human relationists, behaviouralists, sociopsychologists and so on. However, the relevance of the classical approach cannot be depreciated. It did try to create a science of administration in the turbulent industrial era. Even after it fell into the oblivion in the 1930s, most of its themes such as rationality, empiricism, work ethic, efficiency and elimination of waste continue to influence industrial engineering and management in today's changing scenario of organizations against the backdrop of liberalization and privatization.

Thus, criticism of the classical approach notwithstanding, it is still the managerial or classical administrative principles that we are revisiting again. The following specific ideas of practical value emerged from the contribution of the classical school:

- The identification of 'economic man' in an organization.
- Clear definition of organizational tasks based on set basic principles.
- Description of time and motion studies as well as many strategic and planned processes such as decentralization, coordination, authority, responsibility, command and control, to streamline work in organizations.
- Recognition of goals of efficiency, economy and productivity.

Preparatory Questions

- Explain the philosophy of management as envisioned by F. W. Taylor.
- Describe Henry Fayol's views on managerial activities.
- Enlist the ten principles of organization as laid down by Luther Gulick.
- Discuss the views of Mary Parker Follett on conflict resolution.
- List Lyndall Urwick's eight principles of organization.

REFERENCES

Prasad, R., Prasad, V. S. et al. (2002) *Administrative Thinkers*. New Delhi: Sterling.

Sahni, P. and Etakula, V. (2010) *Administrative Theory*. New Delhi: PHI Learning.

Singh, A. (2002) *Public Administration: Roots and Wings*. New Delhi: Galgotia.

Singh, A. (2010) 'Marketing Public Administration: The New Public Management Approach' in Dhameja A. (ed.) *Contemporary Debates in Public Administration*. 3rd ed. New Delhi: PHI Learning.

Wikipedia information for biographical details of thinkers such as F. W Taylor, Lyndall Urwick, Luther Gulick Henry Fayol and Mary Parker Follet.

Chapter Five

The Human Relations Approach

Uma Medury

LEARNING OBJECTIVES

After completing this chapter, you should be able to:

- Explain the concept of human relations approach
- Describe the features of the closed and open models of organization
- Examine the important phases of Hawthorne Experiments
- Make a comparison between human relations and classical approaches; and
- Provide a critical assessment of the human relations approach

INTRODUCTION

The classical approach to management prescribed a set of pre-determined principles for organizations, functioning in a hierarchical structure and in a logical and systematic manner. The main emphasis of the classical theorists has been on the formal structure of an organization. However, during the 1920s, the years of Great Depression, some sort of rethinking on organizational functioning was observed; social factors at work and behaviour of employees within an organization started getting importance. The basic *distinction* between the classical and human relations approaches lies in the *way* a worker has been viewed in an organization. Talyorism sought to apply the basics of science to management of employees at the workplace. Focus was on increased productivity to achieve economic efficiency.

Elton Mayo viewed the worker as a 'social person' rather than a robot working towards industrial productivity. This perspective, he believed, could facilitate the workers in gaining an identity and stability within the job, and the satisfaction they derived could make them more willing to cooperate and contribute to the efforts towards accomplishing goals. He examined the relationship between employers and employees from a humanistic perspective. This chapter will discuss the meaning of human relations approach to organizations. Bringing forth the features of closed and open systems, it will try to explain the importance of human relations in an organization. It will examine the major experiments conducted by Elton Mayo and provide a critical appraisal of the approach.

THE HUMAN RELATIONS APPROACH

The human relations approach focussed on the human aspects of the organization, emotions, feelings, personal motivation and informal norms. This was in contrast to the classical approach that laid emphasis on the structural aspects of the organization. It brought to fore the fact that physiological or mechanical variables at work place *do not* contribute to increased productivity. Understanding the human psyche was very essential to the human relations approach. It gave primacy to natural human groupings, communication and leadership in an organization.

> The human relations approach was an outcome of the human relations movement. It refers to studies made to understand/analyse the effects of social relations, motivation and employee satisfaction on industrial productivity

Elton Mayo, the pioneer of the human relations approach, published his first book titled 'Social Problems of an Industrialized Civilization' in 1933. He was of the opinion that even though industrialization initiated an upward economic growth and solved the problem of production, it did not pay attention to *improving* the social status of the worker. There were constant and frequent tensions/conflicts between the workers and the employees and these needed to be resolved through psychological insights. This thinking formed the basis of his Hawthorne studies.

> George Elton Mayo, born in 1880, was an Australian psychologist, sociologist and organization theorist. He formulated a humanistic view of industry drawing ideas from anthropology, psychology and physiology. He was of the opinion that unlocking the psyche of the worker is the key to understanding industrial unrest at home and abroad

Unlike the classical approach, Mayo primarily viewed industrial organization as a sociopsychological system with importance assigned to human resources – their behaviour, emotions, sentiments and satisfaction. Mayo termed this approach of examining the behaviour of workers and production capacity from the physiological, psychological and economical perspectives as 'clinical method'. He believed that unlocking the psyche of the worker was very important to understand the industrial unrest.

Before we shift our focus on Mayo's experiments to determine the impact of sociopsycho environment on worker's productivity, we must understand the nature of organizational system in which we position the human relations approach. The term *Organization* – be it government, private, non-governmental or community-based – has different connotations. Its definition varies according to its context and perspective. An organization is basically a structure with people working across various levels. Its framework varies depending on the form, bases of division of work and the type of interactions it has with the people. Chester I. Barnard has defined an organization as a 'system of consciously coordinated personal activities of two or more persons'.

In general, there are certain distinct characteristics of organizations. The organizations are considered to be the following:

- Purposeful and complex human collectivities characterized by impersonal relationships
- Specialized and having limited goals
- Involved in sustained cooperative activity
- Integrated within a larger social system
- Providing services and products to their environment
- Dependent on exchanges within their environment

On the basis of these characteristics, organization theorists such as Burns and Stalker (1961) have laid down the principal features of closed and open systems. The closed model of organization, also termed as bureaucratic, hierarchical and formal, is said to exist in a routine and stable environment and has certain *distinct* features.

Closed Model

A closed model has the following characteristics:

- This model of organization is based on the principle of hierarchy.
- Specialization of tasks based on division of labour is at the core.
- Vertical interactions between people in the organization are directed towards securing obedience and command.
- Loyalty and obedience to one's superior is stressed.
- Emphasis is on means employed rather than on ends desired.

Open Model

An open model of organization has the following characteristics:

- Interactions between different parts and also with external environment, which are based on cooperation.
- Focus on variables such as sentiments, emotions and informal norms.

- Specialized knowledge contributing to common tasks in the organization.
- The style of interaction is directed towards accomplishments and advice rather than command.
- Interaction between people in the organization is majorly across horizontal levels.
- Emphasis on shedding of responsibility.
- Importance assigned to the ends or goals rather than the means.

While the classical approach falls under the closed model, human relations borders on the open model and systems approach completely comes in the domain of open model. In an attempt to study the human side of organizations, Elton Mayo and his team including F. J. Roethlisberger and Dickinson undertook several studies between 1920 and 1930 to examine the attitudes of workers in an industrial organization and establish a relationship between workers' attitudes and organizational productivity.

ELTON MAYO'S EARLY EXPERIMENTS

The early research conducted by Elton Mayo in 1923 in a textile mill near Philadelphia came to be known as the *First Enquiry*. In this, Mayo attempted to study the impact of fatigue and working conditions on production levels. He conducted work at the spinning department of a textile mill. This mill provided all the facilities to the workers and yet the mule spinning department of the mill had the problem of labour turnover to the tune of nearly 250 per cent. Despite several incentives provided to the workers in this unit, the turnover assumed huge proportions. The financial incentives also did not provide any respite or solution to the problem. Elton Mayo examined this problem intensively from physical, social and psychological aspects and put forth the following observations:

- The *physical discomfort* being faced by the worker in operating the spinning machine, in terms of covering a long distance to watch the working of the machine when the frames moved back and forth.
- The number of machines under the control of each worker were *large*, ranging from 10 to 14.
- *Lack of communication* between the workers due to the noise emanating from the machine.

On the basis of the study conducted, Mayo came to the conclusion that *physical fatigue* was the key demotivating factor for the workers that contributed to the fall in industrial productivity. He experimented with giving two *rest periods* of 10 minutes each, twice a day – in the morning and evening – to each team of workers. This had a remarkable impact on the workers. This rest period scheme found favour with the workers and led to a gradual decline in the labour turnover, facilitated increase in production and brought about an improvement in morale.

Another measure that Mayo suggested was related to the workers' earning the *bonus*. Under this scheme, those workers producing more than a certain percentage were to be given bonus in proportion to the extra production. Elton Mayo attempted to establish a link between the worker turnover and the emotional response of workers to work performance. More than the monotony involved in doing the tasks, he believed that repetitive work done under conditions of isolation leads to abnormal preoccupations.

HAWTHORNE EXPERIMENTS

The turning point in the development of the human relations theory came with the well-known experiments conducted at the Hawthorne Plant of the Western Electric Company near Chicago in the US between 1924 and 1932. The Hawthorne plant had nearly 29,000 employees and it manufactured telephones and telephone equipment. The Hawthorne studies were funded by the National Research Council of the National Academy of Science at the behest of the General Electric Company, the largest manufacturer of electric bulbs in the US. The major objective was to establish the relationship between workplace, lighting condition and individual efficiency.

The Hawthorne experiments are categorized into the following four phases:

- Illumination experiments
- Relay assembly test rooms
- Interviewing programme
- Bank wiring observation room

1. *Illumination experiments*: During the period of two and a half years from 1924 to 1927, a series of illumination level studies were conducted by the industrial engineers of Western Electric Company Works in Cicero, Illinois.
   - In the first experiment, the experiments were conducted by the researchers on three different departments. Irrespective of increasing or decreasing levels of illumination, an increase in productivity was witnessed. The illumination levels did not impact the productivity.
   - In another study, two groups were formed – *control* and *experimental*. The 'control' group continued to work with constant illumination – the level and the type with which the groups started working in the department. The 'experimental' group was subjected to a series of increasing light levels. Both the groups showed increased productivity, despite variations in illumination levels provided to the two groups.
   - The researchers experimented with decreased lighting on the same groups. The control group received stable illumination, whereas the other experimental group got decreasing levels of illumination. Yet, both the groups steadily increased production, but finally when the experimental group got very low illumination, they protested and production decreased.
   - The illumination experiments were gradually abandoned by the researchers and other incentives in the form of increased wage payments, rest periods, duration of working hours and so on were introduced. These measures also increased the production. Later, these privileges were withdrawn and the initial conditions were restored. This led to fall in production levels initially, but later it increased to levels higher than the original, which surprised the research team. No conclusive relationship could be established between illumination levels, incentive schemes and productivity levels. The research team observed that increase in productivity could have been due to interest shown by the research team in the workers or retention of incentive wage plan.

In 1927, Elton Mayo was invited to the Hawthorne plant to examine the problem encountered by the research team. Mayo and Roethlisberger analysed the results of the experiments and made the following observations:

- Change in the mental attitude of the group
- The feeling of being a 'social unit' experienced by the girls in the test room
- A sense of participation in the project among the workers

Mayo and his team, based on the observations, further conducted a series of other experiments to investigate the factors behind worker productivity.

2. *Relay assembly test rooms*: These experiments were conducted to examine the impact of other variables on productivity. Two women were chosen as best subjects and they were asked to choose four other workers to join the test group. The two groups worked in separate rooms over a period of five years (1927–1932) assembling telephone relays. It involved putting together a number of small telephone parts. The output was measured mechanically through counting the number of finished relays. They were later moved to the experiment room and there they interacted with a supervisor, who discussed changes with them and at times also put their suggestions into practice.

   The researchers measured the impact of different variables such as payments, breaks, refreshments and shortening the work duration on the group and individual productivity. In general, it was observed that changing a variable increased productivity. They came to the conclusion that there were certain significant factors impacting the productivity. These included extra attention given to the worker, having a sympathetic supervisor and the apparent interest shown towards them by the management. These were the main reasons contributing to higher productivity. The six individuals constituted a team and the team's participation in the experiment was wholehearted as they were working without coercion from above or limitations from below.

   In fact, regular medical checkups indicated no signs of cumulative fatigue and labour turnover declined by 80 per cent. Another significant observation was the innovativeness exhibited by each girl in putting the component parts of telephone relays together. They experimented with varied techniques to deal with work-related monotony. The experimental group developed a sense of responsibility and the discipline came from within the group itself. The outcome resulting from the experiment is referred to as the Hawthorne effect. It established a *link* between supervision, morale and productivity. The researchers hypothesized that choosing one's co-workers, working as a group, being treated as special and having a sympathetic supervisor were the actual reasons for increase in the productivity. It was interpreted that the six individuals became a team and the team gave itself completely to cooperate in the experiment.

3. *Interviewing programme* (1928–1931): Interviewing was another significant phase of the Hawthorne experiments. This was done with the basic objective of studying the human attitudes and sentiments and their relationship to the productivity. The illumination experiment and relay assembly test room studies brought to fore the form of supervision as a contributory factor to the workers' levels of production. In order to gauge workers' feelings towards general working conditions and supervisors, a large interviewing programme was undertaken, wherein nearly

20,000 workers were interviewed. Initially, the workers were asked a specific set of questions by the interviewers. This method did not yield results, as the workers' responses to the questions were vague, subjective and to some extent even irrelevant.

It was perceived that the workers intended to discuss issues other than mere supervision and working conditions. Hence, the style of interviewing was modified to a non-directive and open-ended form with no set list of questions and workers were given the freedom to discuss about any aspect of their work. The *approach* of the interviewers was quite friendly and sympathetic. It was also impartial and non-judgemental.

This methodology was quite successful as the workers' true feelings and attitudes could be assessed by the researchers. They could secure information not just about supervision and working conditions, but also about the company itself, its management and society in general. This also provided an opportunity to the workers to come out openly and freely express their feelings and problems and be able to 'let off steam' in a friendly atmosphere.

This experiment was significant in the following aspects:

- The workers being treated on par with the management in soliciting their views too about the problems of the company.
- The significance given to human attitudes and sentiments as these play an important role in work situation.
- Change in the attitude of the supervisor too, as their feelings were being observed by the research team.
- The significance of informal social forces at work place which makes an organization not just an economic and technological structure, but also as a network of human relations that are held together by a system of sentiments.

The interviewing programme focussed on the following aspects:

- Workers being at par with management
- Significance of human attitudes
- Change in attitudes of supervisor
- Pertinence of informal social forces at the workplace

4. *Bank wiring observation room*: This was the last study undertaken by Elton Mayo and his team in Western Electric Company to observe a group of 14 people performing a task in a bank wiring room. It was observed that they formed their own informal organization with subgroups of *cliques* and with natural leaders emerging with the consent of the members. In this experiment, wages were paid on the basis of a group incentive plan and each member got his or her share on the basis of the total output of the group. Despite a financial incentive scheme, where the workers would be receiving more money with more work produced, they decided on a level of output well below the level they were capable of producing. This resulted in the following observations:
   - The output was restricted – the group had a standard for output which was respected by the individuals in the group.
   - The group was indifferent to the employer's financial incentive scheme.

- The group had developed a behavioural code of its own based on solidarity in opposition to the management.
- The output was determined by informal social groups rather than by the management.

Elton Mayo, on the basis of these Hawthorne experiments, concluded that workers had been unable to find suitable outlets for expressing their personal problems and dissatisfaction in the work life. He felt that the basic answer to industrial problems resided not in technical efficiency but taking into cognizance the human and social attitudes and sentiments. Mayo's experiments stressed the importance of the need for informal approaches and groups based in human emotions, sentiments and interactions. The management should strive for establishing equilibrium between the technical and human organization and develop skills in handling human relations and situations. These can take the form of developing skills in understanding human behaviour and interpersonal skills in counselling, motivating, leading and communicating.

The bank wiring observation room made the following observations of the study group:

- The group had a set standard for output
- It was indifferent to employer's financial incentive scheme
- It followed a distinct behavioural code
- It was influenced by informal social groups that determined the standards and behavioural code

SIGNIFICANCE OF HAWTHORNE STUDIES

The human relations theory which grew out of the Hawthorne experiments emphasized the emotional aspects in human behaviour. The research conducted showed the impact of groups on the behaviour of individuals at work. These studies brought out that work satisfaction depended to a large extent on the informal social pattern of the work group. Once the feeling of 'being important' is instilled among the workers and norms of cooperation and higher output are established, the physical conditions or financial incentives cease to have high motivational value. People's work performance, he concluded, is dependent on both social issues and job context. Elton Mayo arrived at the following conclusions:

- Job satisfaction increased as workers were given more *freedom* to determine the conditions of their working environment and to set their own standards of output.
- Intensified interaction and cooperation created a high level of group *cohesion.*
- Job satisfaction and output depended more on *cooperation* and a feeling of self-worth than on physical working conditions.

The most important discovery of the Hawthorne experiments was that the workers felt a strong need to *cooperate* and *communicate* with fellow workers. The *basic* tenets of the human relations approach emanating from Elton Mayo's experiments are as follows:

- Individual workers cannot be treated in isolation as they are social beings.
- Informal groups formed at work have a strong influence on the behaviour of workers.

- Productivity to a large extent is influenced by social and psychological factors.
- Conditions within the organization exercise strong social control over the work habits and attitudes.
- Managers must be aware of the social needs and cater to them to ensure that employees collaborate with the official organization, rather than work against it.

The Hawthorne experiments were the emotional and intellectual source of the organizational behaviour perspective and modern theories of motivation. The experiments showed that complex, interactional variables such as attention paid to the workers as individuals, control of workers over their own work, differences between individuals' needs, management's willingness to listen, group norms and direct feedback, all play an important role in motivating people in organizations. Elton Mayo concluded that at work, the worker–management adversarial relationship stemmed from workers' misunderstanding and distrust of management. The management contributed to this situation by giving attention only to economic efficiency and not to social cohesion. Hence, workers felt alienated.

A clash between a worker's 'logic of sentiment' and a manager's 'logic of cost and efficiency' could lead to conflict within an organization. A worker's performance is dependent on both social issues and job content. It is the responsibility of management, according to Mayo, to align workers' interest with that of the organization and also acquire the necessary social skills to secure workers' participation.

HUMAN RELATIONS AND CLASSICAL APPROACH: A COMPARISON

As you have read in the previous chapter, the classical approach laid down the fundamentals for a comprehensive theory of management. F. W. Taylor's scientific management emphasized the need for increased productivity from each worker through structuring the technical work in the organization and provisioning of monetary incentives for better productivity.

The classical theory or approach associated with the works of Taylor, Fayol and Weber focussed primarily on the design of a coherent organization structure, which promotes efficiency. It prescribed a set of pre-determined principles underlining the basis of management. The classical approach focussed mainly on the jobs and structure within the organization and viewed workers as cogs in the machine. The human relations approach, on the other hand, introduced the significance of informal organization within the formal structure of organization that influences employee behaviour and also fulfils employees' social and emotional needs, which in turn increase performance and social harmony within the organization. The basic premise of human relations was that people formed the bases of an organization. An organization is to be looked at as a 'social function' focussing on people's needs, emotions, sentiments and relationships that would foster organizational performance.

The classical approach gave primacy to fulfilment of economic needs of workers, whereas the human relations approach considered social and personal needs as the key motivators for performance. The role of management under the classical approach was to create job specification, rules, procedures, etc, and make workers adhere to them. On the contrary, the human relations approach viewed the management's role as that of soliciting cooperation and coordination within the organization.

While the classical approach, especially Taylorism, sought to apply principles of science to management of employees at the work place to gain economic efficiency and labour productivity, Mayo's work led to the discovery of the 'social person', facilitating workers to be seen as individuals, rather than mere robots designed to work towards industrial productivity. The concern of advocates of both the approaches was to rationalize management to increase workers' productivity but the *basic* difference lied in the underlying assumptions. Taylor believed that the best way to induce workers to work harder was through monetary incentives. The human relations theory emphasized power, status and group coherence as determinants of worker performance. In short, we can say that Taylor's economic individual gave way to the social being/individual in the human relations approach.

AN APPRAISAL OF HUMAN RELATIONS APPROACH

The Hawthorne studies, which formed the basis of human relations approach, have been subjected to criticism by several scholars. Some of the points of criticism are as follows:

- The Hawthorne experiments have been questioned on *methodological* basis. Carey (1967) viewed the studies as scientifically worthless. Several scholars identified some of its methodological limitations such as theoretical constraints, situational bias and paucity of evidence regarding workers' home life.
- In terms of research methodology, several scholars including Carey (1967) considered that the sample of five to six women chosen for the experiments could not be considered a reliable sample to make *generalizations*. For example, Briefs (1940) questioned the external validity of the sample as the women formed relationships that they might not have formed if the sample size had been larger. Moore's (1947) observation related to non-inclusion of African–Americans in the study, though some consider that the large-scale migration of African–Americans to the north of USA had not yet taken place at that time.
- It is also said that the human relationists did not sufficiently appreciate the *complexity* of human nature and humans' relationship to their work environment. Their experiments were conducted under controlled situations and the workers were fully aware throughout the period that they were being observed.
- The Hawthorne studies did not take cognizance of the *impact of technological factors* in enhancing productivity.
- The emphasis was more on group rather than individual decision making.
- Etzioni (1964) observed that human relationists tended to devote more attention to informal relations among workers and between workers and supervisors but little to formal ones.
- Marxists considered Mayo's methodologies as techniques to exploit workers as they *de-emphasized* the economic factors in the organization.
- Carey (1967) opined that material, especially the financial rewards, were the principal influence on the workers' morale and behaviour. He considered that incentives that were provided to the workers caused an increase in productivity.
- Daniel Bell (1976) criticized Mayo and other industrial sociologists for *adjusting* 'men to machines rather than enlarging human capacity or human freedom'. He termed the work of Elton Mayo and the human relations school as 'cow sociology', as it aimed to make the workers content and satisfied so that they could produce more.

The United Automobile Workers' publication 'Ammunition' (1949) labelled the Hawthorne researchers as 'cow sociologists' – as according to them, contented cows give more milk. Bell focussed on the exclusion of union workers in the Hawthorne studies. Loren Baritz has also criticized the human relations theory as being pro-management and anti-unionist

- Contemporary scholars have also noted that economic benefits perhaps motivated the Hawthorne workers more than the social benefits (Viteles, 1941). According to another critic (Roy, 1952), 'workers did not care about money, because the workers whom Mayo studied functioned like "calculating machines" in determining output and daily pay'.
- A few critics opined that the underlying assumptions of a conflict-free state and workers' contentment were *Utopian* and not practical. Tensions and conflicts in organizations were inevitable and there was a need for healthy outlets to enable the employees to air their problems. Hawthorne experiments, in view of some critics, were manipulative in nature as workers knew they were being controlled.
- The human relations approach has been challenged and extended later by scholars by classifying different groups' behaviour into different types. Sayles (1958) looked at 300 work groups in 30 plants in the US through interviews and observation and found that group cohesion and behaviour depended on technology and work organization rather than by management abilities. He categorized group behaviour into four categories – apathetic, erratic, strategic and conservative.

Basically, the brickbats that the human relations approach got from several quarters rested on the fact that this approach could not decipher the multi-dimensionality of motivation; it could not understand human relationships in totality. The generalizations drawn were based on too small a sample. However, despite varying viewpoints regarding the authenticity and interpretation of Hawthorne experiments, they can be considered a turning point in management thinking. It generated new ideas regarding work groups, informal organization, motivation and so on. It was a significant milestone in providing insight into human behaviour at work and laid a strong base for the development of organizational behaviour.

The approach brought to fore the significance of humanizing the work organization. It gave primacy to groups, group values and norms in influencing individuals' behaviour at work. It emphasized the importance of wider social needs to individuals and the work organization as a social organization. The human relations approach paved the way for generation of new ideas on group relationships and leadership styles. Subsequent theorists such as Maslow, Herzberg, McGregor and others examined the factors affecting the motivation of individuals working in an organization. These have been termed as 'neo-human relations' approaches.

Abraham Maslow's (1943) work presents a theoretical framework of individual personality development and motivation based on a hierarchy of needs. Maslow's fivefold classification of needs – physiological, safety, social, esteem and self-actualization acted as a link between the human relations and neo-human relations approaches. Later, Herzberg put forth two different sets of factors affecting motivation, namely, hygiene and growth factors. He was of the view that proper attention needed to be given to growth factors in the organization to motivate the employees to give their best.

Douglas McGregor's Theory X and Theory Y made certain assumptions about people and work, which had wider implications for leadership and management. McGregor suggested that the links between organizational design, motivation and productivity were more complex than thought of by

Mayo. His ideas on emergence of informal organization were further researched by Chris Argyris and other management thinkers. The major contributors to neo-human relations approach include Rensis Likert, David McClelland and Chris Argyris. The neo-human relations (*also called sociopsychological approach*) generated new ideas about organization structuring, group dynamics, job satisfaction, communication and leadership styles.

CONCLUSION

The conclusions drawn by Mayo from the Hawthorne studies marked the emergence of management style which aimed at contributing to industrial productivity, the interpersonal skills that were as important as monetary incentives and a more humanistic approach that was a means of satisfying the organization's economic needs and human social skills. The human relations approach, the foundation of which was laid several decades ago, is more relevant in contemporary times as the significance of team work, motivation, and leadership assumed more prominence. In present times too, as we see in multinational companies, the concepts of team work, incentives and group work have a positive impact on organizational productivity.

The current perspectives on organizational working focus on the importance of needs and values of people and their integration with the goals of the organization. Thus, we can conclude by stating that the torch of human relations, which was a trail blazer of an *interface* between human social skills and industrial output, has been carried forward by later theorists with precision. In fact, humanizing workplaces remains the utmost objective of organizational behaviour studies till date.

Preparatory Questions

- Describe the characteristics of open and closed models of organization.
- Write a note on illumination studies and bring out their objectives.
- What was the outcome of relay assembly experiments?
- 'The interviewing programme experiment was significant in certain aspects'. Elaborate.
- In what respects are the Hawthorne experiments significant?
- Make a comparison between the human relations and classical approaches.
- 'The Hawthorne studies which formed the basis of human relations approach have been subjected to criticism by several scholars'. Discuss.

REFERENCES

Bell, D. (1976) *The Coming of Post-Industrial Society.* New York: Basic Books.

Briefs, G. A. (1940) 'Book Review of the Industrial Worker.' *American Sociological Review*. 5(1).

Burns, T. E. and Stalker, G. M. (1961) *The Management of Innovation*. Urbana (IL): University of Illinois.

Carey, A. (1967) 'The Hawthorne Studies as Radical Criticism.' *American Sociological Review*. 32(3).

Etzioni, A. (1964) *Modern Organizations*. New Jersey: Prentice Hall.

Herzberg-Motivation-Hygiene Theory www.net mba.com/mamt/ob/motivation/Rerzbeng, [accessed July 27, 2015]

Maslow, A. (1943) 'A Theory of Human Motivation', http/docs/google.com/field [accessed July 27, 2015]

Moore, L. E. (1974) 'Current issues in Industrial Sociology.' *American Sociological Review*. 12(6).

Roy, D. F. (1952) 'Quota Restrictions and Gold-bricking in a Machine Shop.' *American Journal of Sociology*. 57.

Sayles, L. R. (1958) *Behaviour of Industrial Work Groups*. Newyork, Wiley.
Viteles, M. S. (1941) 'The Role of Industrial Psychology in Defending the Future of America.' *Annals of the American Academy of Political and Social Science*. 216.

Websites:

Approaches to Organization and Management. Available from: Pearson ed.co.UK/assets/hip pdf. [access date June 10_2014]
Human Relations findings of Elton Mayo. Available from: http:/www.change.freeUK.com/learning/business/mayo. [access date June 15_2014]
Available from: http.www.acel-team.com/motivation/hawthorne. [access date June 20_2014]
Elton Mayo and the HRM Movement. Available from: apps.business.ualberta.ca. [access date June 15_2014]
Available from: http://en.wikipedia.org/wiki/Elton_Mayowww.vectorstudies.com/management.
Available from: gurus www.mbsportal:bl.UK. [access date June 25_2014]
Available from: Wikipedia.org/wiki/human relations movement

Chapter Six

Max Weber's Theory of Bureaucracy

Roopinder Oberoi

LEARNING OBJECTIVES

After completing this chapter, you should be able to:

- Define the term 'bureaucracy'
- Discuss Max Weber's views on bureaucracy
- Explain the typology and nature of authority
- Summarize the characteristics of bureaucracy; and
- Examine the limitations and strengths of Weber's theory of bureaucracy as put forth by other theorists

INTRODUCTION

One of the other prominent classical theorists is Karl Emil Maximilian Weber (1864–1920). Max Weber, as he is more commonly known, is conventionally described as a sociologist who rose above politics. As a much celebrated economist and sociologist, Weber altered the understanding and approach towards organizational studies. Weber's empirical and moral diagnosis of modern society remains a compelling one till date. Preoccupied with understanding the distinctively individual or unique character of the historical phase, Weber was convinced that modern bourgeois reality is marked by a predominant 'passion for bureaucracy'. It does not mean that Weber went beyond the other classical theorists in giving organization a somewhat human dimension, which was found wanting in the traditional classical approach. He evidently viewed organizational structure from two key parameters, namely 'rationality' and 'efficiency'. His work focussed on the methodological precision of organizational studies. The object was to establish clear-cut lines of authority and control in an organization.

It is Weber's focus on *rationality* that makes him different from other classical theorists. Weber believed that in the backdrop of capitalism, bureaucratic organizations were a superior form of organization, as their form of domination was legal and their legitimacy legal–rational. His derivatives of organization were domination, legitimacy and leadership. Separating domination into *patrimonial* and *legal–rational,* he suggested that bureaucratic organizations were capable of achieving their goals more efficiently, as they were driven by rational principles of written rules, impersonality, division of work, hierarchy, merit recruitment, systematic career advancement and judicious use of public resources. This chapter shall make an attempt to describe the different features of bureaucracy, as given by Weber. It will provide an insight into the Weberian ideal of bureaucracy, focussing on authority, rationality and efficiency, and also give an evaluation of Weber's views.

MEANING OF BUREAUCRACY

The term bureaucracy is often attributed to Max Weber, although he did not coin the term. It was actually done by a French economist, Vincent de Gourney (1712–1759), who observed: 'We have an illness in France, which bids fair to play havoc with us; this illness is called bureaumania'. However, the lineage of the term 'bureaucracy' is not quite clear. Fritz Morstein Marx (1957) has pointed out, 'it was first used in the French form 'bureaucratie' by a French Minister of Commerce, it then spread to Germany during the 19th century as 'burokratie' and has since found its way into English and many other languages'. The word 'bureaucracy' is frequently used in a pejorative sense, that is, to characterize organizations loaded by formalities, burdened by red-tape and fraught with inefficiencies.

Merriam Webster lists the following definitions of bureaucracy:

- A body of non-elective government officials; an administrative policy-making group
- Government characterized by specialization of functions, adherence to fixed rules and a hierarchy of authority
- A system of administration marked by officialism, red tape and proliferation

Weber defined bureaucracy as a rational ideal and a logical organization. In fact, to begin with,while speaking on bureaucracy, Weber made a distinction between authority and 'domination'.

Authority or domination in his view, is instrumental in the materialization of 'organization' or (*Verband*). An essential attribute of an administration is that it resolves *who gives directives and to whom*. Consequently, 'each kind of authority articulates and operates like administration'. J. S. Mill applied the term bureaucracy to characterize the specialized governors of the government in a society. For Laski, bureaucracy is a 'rule of the officials'. Mosca depicted it as 'one class of ruling elites', whereas Dimock and Michels branded bureaucracy with large-scale organizations and inevitably subjected to 'iron law of oligarchy'. By 1944, the Austrian economist Ludwig von Mises noticed that the phraseology bureaucracy was 'always equated with an opprobrious connotation', and the American sociologist Robert Merton (1952) pointed that the word 'bureaucrat' had become 'an epithet'. Bureaucracy is, additionally, distinct in its one-dimensional structure as 'a body of non-elective government officials' and/or 'an administrative policy-making group'.

MAX WEBER'S VIEWS ON BUREAUCRACY

Coming to the specific idea of bureaucracy, as propounded by Weber, we should know that the most systematic study of bureaucratic phenomena is traced back to Max Weber (1864–1920). Weber's major works deal with rationalization in sociology of religion and government. His most famous work is his essay *The Protestant Ethic and the Spirit of Capitalism*. Weber created and worked in the anti-positivist, hermeneutic or experience-oriented tradition, and his interpretative sociology gave equal weight to irrationality and rationality.

> Carl Emil Maximilian Weber was born in 1864 in Germany. He studied law and then did his doctoral on history of medieval trading companies. In 1891, he worked on the significance of agrarian history for public and private law, followed by several papers on law. He became a professor of political economy in 1894. His range of writings was very broad, as he laid focus on subjects such as sociology, economics, religion, history and politics

Weber's analysis of bureaucracy was first published in 1922, *albeit,* after his death. He analysed the ancient administrative systems of Egypt, China and the Byzantine Empire and studied them in the light of the modern European systems of the 18th and 19th centuries. The context was advancing capitalism and industrial State, which somehow looked at bureaucracy as a social instrument against feudalism and catholicism. Max Weber's *Sociology of Religion* incorporates a description of the emergence and progress of modern western culture. This description interprets the commentary of the West in terms of two interrelated progressions: the rise and spread of occidental (instrumental) rationalism (*the process of rationalization*) and the associated *disenchantment* (*Entzauberung*) of religious superstition and parable.

The sociological judgement of Weber's theory is that the processes of *cultural* rationalization occasionally transform the establishment and nature of *social* life. Undeniably, this is the fundamental point of the *Protestant Ethic*: that reallocates the background, principles and beliefs (*or culture*) of a population. When coupled with approving material situation, it can provoke deep alteration in the nature of societal organization, for example, the rise of modern capitalist structures.

> What Weber depicted was not only the secularization of western culture, but also the development of modern societies from the point of view of rationalization.
>
> Habermas (1971, pp. 143–278) and Schluchter (1981)

According to Weber, the emergence of bureaucracy fits into this process of rationalization for several reasons. First, bureaucracy itself is a rational or logical event. Second, bureaucracy is the principal organization for the application of official law, which is an additional critical element of rationalization. Third, bureaucracy as an essential constituent of the public sphere is requisite for the implementation of the capitalist economy because the capitalist firm is based internally on specific computation and accounting.

> For bureaucracy, the very component of calculability of its rules has been in actuality of key implication. The nature of the modern civilization, especially its technical economic structure, requires calculability of consequences. For ascetic Protestantism, not only provided the 'spirit', which facilitates the progress of advanced capitalism in the West, but also contributed, *albeit* indirectly, to the 'rational' forms of ordering life, which lie at the centre of the 'godless' new world (*Modernity*).
>
> Weber (1966, p. 350)

Weber's analysis was not an extensive depiction of the dynamics of the bureaucratization process. It did not assert to represent or reproduce theoretically the 'really real' content and form of modern bureaucratic reality. Weber's concern was not to elucidate and comprehend this actuality; instead he methodically relied upon *ideal-typical* grouping.

For Weber (1930, 1947), bureaucracy was a superior form of organization. It was technically superior to any other form of organization. He felt that precision, speed, unambiguity, knowledge of the files, continuity, discretion, unity, strict subordination, reduction of friction and material and personal costs are raised to the optimum point in the strictly bureaucratic administration, and especially in its monocratic form

According to Weber, the scheme of free enterprise and moneyed economy were the mainstay of capitalism, which helped inspire the institution of bureaucracy. To begin with, exchange in the market, the basis of the capitalist economic order, is 'the archetype of all rational social action'. Unhampered by sacred taboos, by traditional status-group privileges or by any 'obligations of brotherliness or reverence', market transactions are determined solely by the 'purposeful pursuit of interests' by an 'orientation to the commodity and only to that' (*Economy and Society*, 1968a, pp. 635–636). Rogers Brubaker quotes in his book *The Limits of Rationality* (1991) that modern capitalism, which Weber argues, presupposes this calculability: The modern capitalist enterprise presupposes a legal and administrative system, whose functioning can be rationally predicted, at least in principle, by virtue of its fixed general norms, just like the expected performance of a machine (Weber in *Economy and Society*, 1968a, p. 1394, 1094–1095). According to Weber the rationalization of economic production, has created the 'iron cage' of capitalism, a 'tremendous cosmos' that constrains individuals from without, determining their lives 'with irresistible force' (*Economy and Society*, 1968a, p. 181).

Private enterprise necessitated strong and systematic administration in 'its own' particular interest. The bureaucratic doctrine gives the capitalist the indomitable capacity to achieve cost-effective scheduling to safeguard a steady market for goods and services. Weber's highlighting on calculability as the essential characteristic of modern capitalism involves two distinct strands of analysis. First, the production process itself – the performance of the human and non-human means of production – is *calculable*. Second, the legal and administrative environment is calculable: the actions of judges and bureaucrats, in so far as they affect economic conduct, can be reliably *predicted*.

Weber therefore presupposed that in the conditions of free enterprise, bureaucratic organizations were the most apt organizational composition, as their structure of authority was legitimately sanctioned and thus legal–rational. His derivatives of administration were power, legitimacy and leadership. By disentanglement of authority into combination of *patrimonial* and *legal–rational*, Weber advocates that bureaucratic workers become accomplished and trained to achieve their purpose professionally and specifically under legal rational unit. Bureaucrats are enthused by a consistent set of guidelines or procedure of printed rules, impersonality, distribution of work, hierarchy, merit-based staffing, meticulous career progression and thoughtful utilization of public assets. The concept of pragmatism and instrumentalism emphasized by Weber communicated the design of an organization as a device intended to seek reasonable objectives in a most efficient way – therefore the *organization's design is a means to an end.*

Weber's views on bureaucracy are as follows:

- Capitalism gives rise to the institution of bureaucracy
- In turn, bureaucracy gives capitalism the capacity to achieve cost-effective strategies to safeguard the market
- Bureaucracy fits into the process of rationalization that transforms establishment and nature of social life
- Bureaucratic structure of authority is legitimately sanctioned and legal–rational
- Bureaucratic administration is aimed at command through knowledge

RATIONALIZATION OF SOCIETAL ORGANIZATION AND TYPES OF AUTHORITY

Bureaucratic administration, to Weber (*Economy and Society*, 1968a, p. 181), aimed at 'command through knowledge. This is the characteristic, which makes it distinctively rational'. This type of *legal–rational domination* is an impersonal form of rule, founded upon the intent lack of complicatedness of the Nation–State and the rule of formal equality before the law. It gives rise to a 'distant order' of social relations or an 'external life' in which private or eventual values and beliefs are subordinated progressively more to the rational deliberation of worldly behaviour: 'It is crucial for the modern allegiance to an office that, in the pure type, does not create an association to a *person*, like the vassal's or disciple's faith under feudal or patrimonial authority, but rather is dedicated to *impersonal* and *functional* purposes'.

Weber distinguished between four types of rationality:

- Purposive
- Value-oriented
- Affectual
- Traditional

Zweckrational or purposive rationality, in Weber's view, is instrumental rationality and is related to expectations about the behaviour of other humans/objects, which serve as a means towards achievement of goals. *Wertrational* or value-oriented rationality is intrinsic to a person, as it is based on beliefs that emanate from ethical, religious or aesthetic values. These are means, which need not necessarily lead to goals. 'Affectual' or meaningfully oriented rationality is determined by a person's feelings and emotions. 'Traditional' rationality is determined by habits that are ingrained. All rationalities are applied in combinations, the first two being more imperative. Weber's interest in the nature of power and authority, plus his preoccupation with modern inclination of rationalization, make him relate with the procedure of modern large-scale enterprises in the political, managerial and financial realm.

Weber spent much of his work analysing bureaucracy. He saw it in the following ways:

- The purest type of exercise of legal authority
- The pinnacle of efficiency, superior to any other form of social organization
- Remarkably destructive of the human spirit
- Rational calculation, reducing every worker to a cog in this bureaucratic machine

TYPES OF AUTHORITY

As we mentioned, Weber believed in the legitimacy of authority in systems. He said that legitimate authority was the only accepted authority. He spoke of two types of authority, namely, traditional and charismatic, falling under *patrimonial,* and legal–rational falling under *legal* domination.

Patrimonial Authority

Weber identified the following two types of authority:

- Patrimonial (traditional and charismatic)
- Legal (legal–rational)

Traditional Authority

It includes gerontocracy, primary patriarchalism, patrimonialism and in extreme cases, *Sultanism.* This type of authority is based on obedience to tradition, the divine form of authority or inherited authority. Traditional authority is based on customs, traditional norms, precedents, usages, habits and symbols. This type of authority is unclear as use of traditional norms, etc., depends on tribal chiefs, monarchy or community leaders.

Charismatic Authority

Charismatic authority is based on the personal qualities of leaders or rulers. It could be a prophet, a community leader or a priest. It rests on the faith of the leaders in a very value-free sense. Individuals comply with the leaders, as if there are some superhuman powers attached to them, resting on loyalty to the outstanding inviolability, heroism or excellent personality of individuals and of the normative blueprint or order made known or predetermined by them. This class or sort of authority is not constant, as the moment the leaders misplace their influence due to explanations such as ascendancy of a new leader or decline of charisma or adjustment of milieu, the public may discontinue following the leader. Both these types of domination (*traditional and charismatic*) are personal rather than impersonal forms of rule, and neither is grounded in a system of rational law.

Legal Authority

Legal–Rational Authority

Legal–rational type of authority is based on legally established impersonal order. It is characterized by value–rational (*wertrational*), rather than instrumentally rational social action. That is, it is 'determined by a conscious belief in the value for its own sake of some ethical, aesthetic, religious, or other form of behaviour, independently of its prospects of success', and also by affectual action 'determined by the actor's specific affects and feeling states'. It is based on a set of abstract rules; authority is exercised on the basis of impersonal system of rules and procedures common to all and not on whimsicality of the rulers.

As we mentioned earlier on, Weber felt that in the context of industrialization, large enterprises and capitalist structures, legal–rational was the most appropriate authority. The career bureaucrat of the industrial State represents the legal–rational authority. Thus, Weber *distinguished* between power and authority or 'domination'. Authority or domination is instrumental in the emergence of *Verband*, that is, organization. The most important aspect of the administration is that it determines who is to give commands to whom. Thus, 'every form of authority expresses itself and functions as administration'.

Weber could be considered both conservative and critical due to the following reasons:

- He was critical of capitalism but emphasized gradual change
- He favoured democracy not because he believed in the masses but because he believed in its dynamism and ability to produce leaders
- He showed interest in domination, referring to the likelihood that specific commands would be obeyed
- He was inclined towards a diffused base of power

NATURE OF AUTHORITY

Weber's concept of modern (*as distinct from traditional*) bureaucracy is one example of what he called an 'ideal type', a method he used to construct a logically precise definition. He theorized that *modern bureaucracy embodied three groups of characteristics*; this formulation, though modelled largely on the German civil service, was intended to apply in general to both private institutions and government departments:

- The first group of elements relates to the *structure and function of an organization*. There exists a *hierarchy* of offices with fixed areas of jurisdiction, specified by laws or administrative regulations. It means that division of labour is acknowledged. Each official's degree of authority and amount of responsibility are clearly set forth, thus promoting functional specialization and the cultivation of expertise. Decisions are made on the basis of the *written regulations*. The files documenting these decisions, writes Weber, 'are preserved in their original or draught form' and record actions and decisions taken. These records provide a mechanism for monitoring an individual's performance and set precedents for future actions.

- A second group of characteristics deals with means of *rewarding effort*. An official receives a *fixed salary* graded by rank. The official's position should be the only occupation and needs to be accepted with the understanding that it will not be exploited for emoluments or rents (*a practice of earlier periods*). An official exercises authority by holding office but does not own the office and therefore cannot designate a successor.
- For the third group, Weber specifies *the protections accorded to the office holder*. The administrative office constitutes a *career*, with promotions granted by seniority or achievement. A clearly defined course of training with prescribed examinations is a prerequisite for merit-based appointment. The qualification for office is, therefore, ability (*presumably ratified by a credential*), rather than political or personal connections. In the modern era, the administrator is no longer the personal agent of a ruler. As a civil servant, she/he serves the State and cannot be removed at will when the political leadership changes. A bureaucrat retains her/his position as long as she satisfactorily discharges her/his duties.

According to Weber, bureaucratic organizations operate '*sineira ac studio*, meaning without a sense of bias of favour, relying solely on a professional decision-maker'. With such an emphasis on professionalism, there is a sense of a guarantee that rational objectivity is the order of the day, rather than the personal choices of an arbitrary authority.

Characteristics of Weberian bureaucracy:

- Written documents
- Impersonal rules
- Hierarchy of offices and graded line of authority
- Clear superior–subordinate relationship
- Division of labour
- Fixed areas of jurisdiction
- Laid-down qualifications
- Career advancement
- Full working capacity of officials
- Specialized office management
- Distinction between official duties/property and private sphere of life

KEY CHARACTERISTICS OF WEBERIAN BUREAUCRACY

Weber's focus was on *accountability* of bureaucrats and to check their tendency of bypassing rule application. He therefore developed the ideal type of bureaucracy with distinctive characteristics. According to Max Weber, modern officialdom functions in the following specific manner:

- There is a fixed jurisdictional area under which the officials have to function.
- This jurisdictional area is limited by rules and regulations, which are general/stable/exhaustive.

- Duties in this jurisdictional area are distributed in a fixed way.
- Authority to give commands within the jurisdictional area is also fixed.
- Provisions are made for regular fulfilment of these duties and regulation of corresponding rights.
- The office follows principles of written documents, division of work and clear superior–subordinate relationship.
- The office hierarchy is monocratically organized and centred in the bureau.
- The working of the bureau comes under the domain of public life and is strictly separated from private life of officials.
- Knowledge of these rules represents a special technical learning, which the officials possess. It involves jurisprudence or administrative or business management.

Weber regarded bureaucracies as good and efficient and held the following views on bureaucratic organizations:

- The most efficient means of controlling the work of large number of people
- Technically superior to any other type of organization in accomplishing complex goals
- Efficient in bringing about equality since civil service rules and codes of conduct reduce discrimination
- Rational, efficient and expert because they master a problem through specialized knowledge

IRRATIONALITIES AND LIMITATIONS OF BUREAUCRACY

Despite bureaucracy being constantly challenged and scrutinized from almost all quarters and repeatedly tested and negotiated by practitioners as a method of rationalizing modernity, it sure has a lasting value. By virtue of its indispensability as a technical means, bureaucracy is among those social structures, which are the hardest to destroy. Weber, of course, admits that the generalized substitution of democratic, decentralized and less formally rational organization for bureaucracy is thinkable. In Weber's view, the necessity of bureaucratic command can overcome the irrational effects of administration. The fundamental political problem posed by bureaucratic organization is how to subordinate, restrict and harness its technical expertise and proficiency. Weber is, in principle, opposed to *Beamtenherrschaft,* that is, officers' monopoly rule (*the dominating rule of senior civil servants without a calling*), precisely because their authority, in his view, must be limited to the honest execution of the orders of political leadership.

The rationalization of societal organization has often been criticized, as it leads to over enthusiasm for rationality. 'It not only strips the world of its ultimate values, but subordinates' creative action to the rational consideration of means and ends, in the course, draining social life of its vitality and humanness' (*Menschentum*). Weber himself, while discussing the flip side of bureaucracy, summarized this process as follows: 'Bureaucracy develops the more perfectly, the more it is "dehumanized", and the more completely it succeeds in eliminating from official business love, hatred, and all purely personal, irrational, and emotional elements which escape calculation'.

As Max Weber himself noted, 'real bureaucracy will be less optimal and effective than his ideal type model'. In fact, he was aware that competences could be ambiguous and could be used in contravention to the spirit of law. Decisions could become more important than their consequences, and ills such as nepotism, corruption and personal biases could creep in to mar the element of meritocracy in recruitment and promotion system. Weber seriously insists that the irrational effects generated by organized capitalist societies are symptomatic of a developing imbalance, under contemporary conditions at least, between the requirements of formal and of substantive modes of rationality.

Modern bureaucratic life, Weber proposed, is marked by definite *nihilistic* (negativistic) tendencies. The chronic incapacity of modern bureaucratic organizations to justify their *raison d' etre* to themselves and others constitutes a subsequent instance of the disequilibrium between the requirements of formal and substantive rationality under contemporary capitalist conditions. These must be viewed as the substantively irrational effect generated by the adoration of technical proficiency in all spheres of contemporary life. Precisely because of this, modern bureaucratic world is more and more often confronted with a loss of a sense of purpose. Weber felt that bureaucratic coordination of activities was the distinctive characteristic feature of the modern era. He argued that bureaucratization of the modern world has led to its depersonalization.

Gouldner's research on bureaucracy (1950s) was propelled by several unresolved tensions in Weber's theory of bureaucracy. In particular, Gouldner believed that Weber was indistinguishable of whether an employee's compliance was based on a consensual agreement about the value of rules and procedures or the authoritative command by superiors. This was a vital theme for Gouldner's analysis of bureaucracy since he believed rule compliance would depend upon the 'mode' on which rules are formulated.

The contending paradigm, the public choice or economics of bureaucracy school (Downs, 1967; Niskanen, 1971), conceives bureaucracy as the realm of individual selfishness and rent seeking at taxpayers' expense under the veil of information asymmetries and infested by principal–agent pathologies. While Weber's notion of public administration as 'bureaucracy' may appear underpoliticized, public administration presents itself as an overpoliticized phenomenon in the public choice perspective.

Theodore Lowi initiated debate by concluding in a book *The End of Liberalism: The Second Republic of United States* (1979) that the government does not exercise effective oversight of bureaucratic agencies. Instead, policies are made by 'iron triangles' consisting of interest groups, appointed bureaucrats and government subcommittees. The idea of 'iron triangles' has since evolved to 'iron hexagons' and then to a 'hollow sphere'. William Niskanen's (1971) 'budget-maximizing' model, complemented Lowi's claims that legislatures failed to exercise oversight, Niskanen argued that rational bureaucrats will always and everywhere seek to increase their budgets, thereby contributing strongly to the State's growth. Niskanen's model provided a strong underpinning for the worldwide move towards cutbacks of public spending and the introduction of privatization in the 1980s and 1990s.

For neo-classical economists, bureaucracy is a synonym for non-market. It is a system in which the *invisible hand* of market does not provide clear and immediate feedback on the efficiency of activities and outputs and in which market forces do not sort out the under performers. If market is the only mechanism that is able to provide perfect efficiency, bureaucracy as a non-market system, by definition, is inefficient for neo-classical economics (Mises, 1944/1966; Downs, 1967, pp. 29–40; Beetham, 1974, pp. 24–30). The primary reason for the existence of bureaucracy – that is, government in this context – is to correct market failures (Weimer and Vining, 1996, pp. 30–32, 41).

Some scholars point to the other inherent contradictions among certain internal features of bureaucracy. 'The most frequently mentioned contradiction is the one between *hierarchy and the rule of rules on one hand and expertise on the other*. The trade-offs between specialization and coordination, and between quick and reliable communication, and hierarchy also appear in organizational sociology' (Simon, 1946; Crozier, 1964; Etzioni, 1964; Blau and Meyer, 1987).

Bureaucracy is no longer considered as an essentially closed system since citizens can participate in the decision-making process through advisory boards, neighbourhood councils and others forms. In this vein, Wilson (1989) contends that the bureaucratic system has become irrational and inefficient. He bemoans this situation by stating that 'this popular involvement would be taken as evidence that the administrative system is no system at all, but a bungling, jerry-built contraption wallowing in efficiency and shot through with corruption and favouritism' (cited in Stillman, 2000, p. 484).

As a result of adherence to rules and openness to the public, Wilson observes that 'public bureaucracy is neither as rational nor predictable as Weber hoped nor as crushing and mechanistic as he feared. It is rule-bound without being corrupt' (1989, p. 484). However, Max Weber's notion of bureaucracy conceives public administration as the apolitical tool of government. It is, in his conception, the 'purely bureaucratic, thus bureaucratic-monocratic, document-based administration that guarantees "the highest degree of performance" as the "formally most rational type of authority"' (Weber, 1947).

Another principal question to ask is *whether bureaucracy is compatible with democracy*? There are many who say it is not. For example, Hayek (1994) in his book, *The Road to Serfdom*, argues that bureaucrats represent central planners who are interested in increasing governmental control of everyday life to the extent that every bureaucratic society runs the risk of becoming a totalitarian society.

McSwite (1997) also laments the reluctance of people within the field of public administration to resolve the question of how bureaucracy fits into democracy, they are of the view that 'keeping the question alive is essential to the identity that it wishes to maintain for the republic administrator – the power-wielding Man of Reason'. In other words, the more time we spend discussing the role of bureaucracy in the organizational development, the more the professionals or experts (bureaucrats) who dominate the decision-making process will continue to consolidate their position within the society. As bureaucracy creates more and more rules and procedures, their complexity rises and coordination diminishes, facilitating creation of contradictory and recursive rules.

Mills (1959) makes a similar point in *The Power Elite* about the kinds of expertise, power and superior technical skills, which tend to concentrate in bureaucracies. Scholars in public administration (e.g. Jreisat, 2002) usually just point out that bureaucracies represent unelected officials and to some extent are accountable to no one. Then, there are those who just dislike bureaucracies because they represent rules, regulations, hierarchy, standardization and impersonality.

The tension between bureaucracy and democracy leads the discussion towards the issues of *legitimacy* of bureaucracy, power, discretion and judgement in the field of public administration. It is averred that 'Beneath these questions is the even more fundamental issue…how to make the power exercised by career bureaucrats consistent with the democratic government. It is assumed that modern government needs the expert and efficient action that bureaucracy makes possible. How, then, does the bureaucracy make itself answerable to the people'? (Stivers, 2001, p. 159). Meier and O'Toole (2006) find that bureaucrats are fairly powerful and can alter political programmes is to reflect their own values – they are strategic agents. All these theoretical difficulties in the Weberian model and its interpretation have raised serious reservation about the general efficiency of bureaucratic organizations.

Limitations of bureaucracy are as follows:

- Concentration of means of operation
- Strict hierarchy
- Dehumanization
- Indispensability
- Loss of sense of purpose
- Rigidity, inflexibility and red tapism
- Closed structure
- Impersonality
- Lack of coordination
- Goal displacement
- Self-perpetuation
- Conflict between bureaucracy and democracy

Empirical research has, in fact, proved that bureaucracies are far from always being the most efficient organizations (Heydebrand, 1973; Blau and Meyer, 1987, pp. 79–97). The Weberian model seemed to be inapplicable for those who wanted to base their model on rationally acting individuals, bureaucrats, whose behaviour is driven by individual utility maximization principle (e.g. Crozier, 1964; Tullock, 1965). Another possible defect/pathology concerns whether a large bureaucracy actually hinders or stunts a developing country's development in other ways, such as political development. Heady (2001) calls this the 'imbalance thesis' and it argues that 'a large bureaucracy displays elements of political favouritism, and more importantly, over-participates in the political affairs of State, to the detriment of elected politicians'.

Even though if one argues that the ideal bureaucracy is only a conceptual guide for organizations to follow, it should be clear that this guide might be a misleading one because organization possesses 'patterns of activities and interactions that reveal how social conduct is organized'. Peter Blau and Marshall Meyer (1987, p. 26) assert that 'empirical studies have shown that this approach is misleading'. However, it must be emphasized that the word 'ideal' did not imply or mean 'the best' or 'what we should strive for'. Weber meant it as 'defining characteristics' – that is, when we use the word this is what is meant. It is *essentially a conceptual model of bureaucracy,* rather than something we thought that we should strive for.

Ralph P. Hummel (2007) in his classic book, *The Bureaucratic*, argues that 'bureaucracy is getting worse in spite of all efforts exerted by the theorists of quality management, corporate reengineering, and the new public management because it is still "business as usual" for bureaucracies'. He explains that 'bureaucrat becomes only a mechanistic technician, isolated from her/his emotions, society, and family. He adds that bureaucracy replaces human identity, character, and autonomous will by the organisation identity. Such a bureaucrat could be a threat to humanity' (Bodley, 2002, p. 75).

Hummel (2007) further avers that 'there is a divergence between society and bureaucracy and all attempts to humanize relationships between a bureaucracy and society must be therefore considered suicidal or window-dressing when they come from within bureaucracy itself, and as declaration of war when they originate in society'. In other words, bureaucracy is 'blind, deaf, and dumb'. James Q. Wilson (1989) argues that 'bureaucracy is laden with rules, that is a sure sign that the bureaucracy is aloof from the people, distant from their concerns, are preoccupied with the power and privileges of the bureaucrats – an elaborate, grinding machine that can crush the spirit of any who dare oppose it' (cited in Stillman, 2000, p. 484). Despite the criticism, it has to be acknowledged that even though Weber believed that rationality and efficiency can be attained through bureaucracy, he was always mindful of its shortcomings, as evidenced by the fact that he also associated it with 'an oppressive routine adverse to personal freedom' (Fry, 1989, p. 33).

CONCLUSION

The modern organization epitomizes the systematic, methodological and rational legal instrumentality of industrial society. Its central task is to stand steadfast against contrary forces of unreason, disorder and disorganization. The profound changes in recent decades have led to aggravated contest over institutional practices and assumptions of modernity and modern bureaucratic organization. It has further triggered wider debate over the birth and viability of post-modern bureaucratic organization.

In conclusion, we can say that post-Weberian theories have either confirmed Weber's analyses or outrightly refuted them. Thinkers, post-Weber, have been unsuccessful in giving a comprehensive and ample insight into bureaucratic organizations. Weber continues to be a reference point from which the good and bad effects of bureaucracies persist to be evaluated, especially, granted the implausibility of Weber's ideal–typical account of the technical superiority and disciplinary capacity of bureaucracy.

Weber's failure to recognize the reproach by scholars strengthens the broad charge proposed by many of his critics that he failed to demonstrate the impossibility of defending autonomous public life against the bureaucratic domination. This chapter has attempted to describe Weber's approach or views on bureaucracy, the ideal characteristics that he propounded for bureaucracy and the drawbacks of such an approach when translated to real situations.

Preparatory Questions

- Briefly describe Weber's views on the relationship between bureaucracy and capitalism.
- Explain the ways in which authority is legitimized in Weber's view.
- What is the function of the 'ideal-type' in Weber's study?
- Define bureaucracy and explain its characteristics.
- Explain the merits and demerits of bureaucracy.

REFERENCES

Albrow, M. (1970) *Bureaucracy*. London: Macmillan.

Barzelay, M. (1992) *Breaking through Bureaucracy*. Berkeley (CA): Cambridge University Press.

Beetham, D. (1974) *Max Weber and the Theory of Modern Politics*. London: George Allen & Unwin.

Bendix, R. (1962) *Max Weber: An Intellectual Portrait*. Garden City (NY).

Hummel, Ralph P. (2007) *The Bureaucratic Experience: The Post-modern Challenge*. 5th ed. Library of Congress Bedford.ST Martins.

Lowi, T. J. (1979) *The End of Liberalism: The Second Republic of United States*. New York: W. W. Norton and Company.

McSwite, O. C. (1997) *Legitimacy in Public Administration: A Discourse Analysis*. Portland (OR): Advances in Public Administration, Portland State University.

Meier J. K. and O'Toole, L. J. (2006) 'Political Control Versus Bureaucratic Values: Reframing the Debate' *Public Administration Review*. 66(2) pp. 177–192.

Mills, C. W. (1959) *The Power Elite*. New York: Oxford University Press.

Niskanen W. (1971) *Bureaucracy and Representative Government*. New York: Aldine Atherton.

Rhienstein, M. (1954) *Max Weber on Law in Economy and Society*. New York: Simon and Shuster.

Riggs, F. (1993) 'Fragility of the Third World's Regimes.' *International Social Science Review*. No. 136 pp. 199–243.

Riggs, F. (1994a) 'Bureaucracy: A Profound Perplexity for Presidentialism' in Farazmand, A. (ed.). *Handbook on Bureaucracy*. New York: Marcel Dekker. pp. 97–148.

Riggs, F. (1994b) 'Global Forces and the Discipline of Public Administration' in Garcia-Zamor, J. and Khator, R. (eds.). *Public Administration in the Global Village*. Westport (CT): Praeger. pp. 17–44.

Rourke, F. (1984) *Bureaucracy, Politics, and Public Policy*. New York: Harper Collins.

Rowley, C. and Schneider, F. (eds.) (2004) 'Principal Agent Relationships' in the Theory of Bureaucracy. *The Encyclopedia of Public Choice*. Vol. II. New York: Springer. pp. 758–761.

Selznick, P. (1943) An 'Approach to a Theory of Bureaucracy.' *American Sociological Review* 8(1) pp. 47–54.

Schuchter, W. (1981) *The Rise of Western Rationalism: Max Weber's Developmental History* (trans.). Berkeley (CA): University of California Press.

Shils, E. A. and Finch, H. A. (eds.) (1949) *The Methodology of the Social Sciences*. New York: Free Press.

Simon, H. (1947) 'Administrative Behaviour', London, Macmillan.

Stillman, R. J. (2000) *Public Administration: Concepts and Cases*. Boston (MA): Houghton Mifflin Company.

Stivers, C. (ed.) (2001) *Democracy, Bureaucracy and Study of Administration*. Boulder (CO): West View Press.

Tullock, G. (1965) *The Politics of Bureaucracy*. Washington, DC: Public Affairs Press.

Von Mises, L. (1944) *Bureaucracy*. New Haven (CT): Yale University Press.

Waldo, D. (1948) *The Administrative State*. New York: Ronald Press.

Weber, Max. (1947) 'From Max Weber in Gerth, H. H. and Mills, C. W.' (trans. and eds.). *Essays in Sociology*. London: Kegan Paul.

Weber, M. (1947/1966) 'Weber's Book translated A. M Henderson and Talcott Parsons in Parsons, T. (trans. and ed.).' *The Theory of Social and Economic Organizations*. New York: Free Press.

Weber, M. (1949) 'Objectivity in Social Science and Social Policy' in Shils, A. and Finch, H. A. (ed. and trans.). *The Methodology of the Social Sciences*. New York: Free Press.

Weber, M. (1966) 'In Rheinstein, M. (ed. and trans.).' *Max Weber on Law in Economy and Society*. Cambridge (MA): Harvard University Press.

Weber, M. (1930), 'Weber's Book translated by A. M Henderson and Talcott Parsons, T. (trans.) and Giddens, A. (Intro).' *The Protestant Ethic and the Spirit of Capitalism*. London: Routledge.

Weimer, D. L. and Vining, A. R. (1996) 'Economics' in Kettl, D. F. and Milward, H. B. (eds.). *The State of Public Management*. Baltimore/London: The Johns Hopkins University Press.

Wilson, J. Q. (1989) *Bureaucracy, What Government Agencies Do and Why They Do It*. 1st ed. New York: Basic Books.

Chapter Seven

The Rational-Choice Approach

Saugato Sen

LEARNING OBJECTIVES

After completing this chapter, you should be able to:

- Provide an insight into the evolution of rational-choice approach to social sciences
- Explain the important strands of thought in rational-choice approach
- Analyse the different facets of rational decision making; and
- Examine the further extensions of rational-choice approach in the contemporary context

INTRODUCTION

Organizations are run by people. The functions as well as the health of organizations depend on the choices made and decisions taken by the people who make up the organizations. This chapter discusses an approach to the study of administration that claims that in order to understand administrative systems and organizations, we should look at the decision-making processes in these organizations as well as study the outcomes resulting from these decisions. An attempt has been made to explain the decision-making process in formal bureaucratic institutions. At the heart of the discussion of decision making in administrative organizations is the issue of whether these decisions are 'rational' and if so, what constitutes 'rationality'.

In general, the write-ups on 'rationality in decision-making in organizations' focus more on Herbert Simon's viewpoint, taking it to be integral to the discussion on the said theme and less on the utility and pertinence of rationality. However, the present chapter attempts to rectify this and gives you an insight into the evolution of the concept of rationality, along with its application to the decision-making process. We begin by looking at the basic rational-choice approach to bureaucratic decision making. It is a part of the general rational-choice approach to the whole of social sciences. It has to be admitted that the rational-choice approach was adopted by and applied to public administration much later than it was in the case of other social sciences. Therefore, we begin by looking at the rational-choice approach to social sciences in general.

THE RATIONAL-CHOICE APPROACH TO SOCIAL SCIENCES

The rational-choice approach has a *methodological* aspect as well as a *philosophical* aspect. As social sciences were developing and evolving, they were doing so in an era when industrial capitalism was itself developing and evolving. It was immediately obvious to several social scientists that in capitalism not only were the different and new types of business organizations, such as the industrial firm and the joint stock company, witnessing change but even the government organizations were rapidly changing. A class of appointed officials who were entrusted with the task of administration was evolving.

Actually, as social sciences were developing, the modern era was dawning. In the modern era, one of the earliest thinkers was Adam Smith. He put forward the idea of what he called the 'invisible hand'. By this, Smith meant that each individual undertakes activities and makes choices that will bring gains to him or her. That person intends only his or her own gain, but is led 'as if by an invisible hand' to fulfil an end that was no part of the person's objective or intention. This basic insight has become the basis for understanding how a market economy functions.

Smith pointed that we do not obtain our daily supply of bread because of the benevolence of the baker; rather, the baker aims only at his own profit. Looking at the self-interest of numerous such people, we can see how at the macro-level a market economy is able to function efficiently due to the self-interest of individual persons, each of whom intends only his or her own benefit, but unwittingly ends up helping other people make gains.

Another very important strand of thinking that emerged – in a way, intellectually, from Smith – was *utilitarianism*, which posited that the aim of society should be to undertake measures that would provide the greatest good for the greatest number. In the course of providing the theory of utilitarianism, Jeremy Bentham suggested that people are engaged in computing a 'pleasure–pain calculus', by which he meant that everyone decides on courses of action by weighing the relative benefits and costs of that decision and undertakes that decision if the benefits outweigh the costs. In modern terms, it would be called cost–benefit analysis of some sort. It is quite relevant to mention the theories of Smith and Bentham because the ideas that they propounded in fact led to the development of the rational-choice approach. Indeed, this approach is a dressed-up and modern version of the ideas of these classical thinkers.

One more important strand of thought that combined with the ideas of these thinkers was that of Max Weber, about which you read in a previous chapter of this volume. Weber gave fundamental and deep ideas about the nature of rationality and also suggested that social scientists should focus on the actions and motivations of individual actors. Max Weber was one of the great theorists of the industrial era. Weber was looking for a general theory of human actions. He distinguished between affective, cultural and rational actions. Weber held the rational actions to be of two types: rational action with respect to *goals* and rational action with respect to *values*.

Strands of thought in rational-choice approach:

- Adam Smith's invisible hand (gains for individuals in choices)
- Jeremy Bentham's utilitarianism (pleasure–pain calculus; benefits outweigh costs)
- Max Weber (motivations and actions of individuals determine collectivities)

Two critical components of the rational-choice approach are 'methodological individualism' and 'atomism'. The two are not quite the same. As mentioned earlier, the rational-choice approach has two aspects, methodological and philosophical. Methodological individualism is the methodological aspect. It gives us a method that putatively gives insight and incisiveness.

Methodological individualism claims that the only gainful way in which we can understand social phenomena is by seeing how social outcomes result out of the actions and motivations of *individual* actors. Indeed, it asserts that any social phenomenon arises only from individual actions. It does not see 'wholes' as anything other than the sum of individual parts. It does not believe in the dictum 'the whole is greater than the sum of its parts'. In other words, methodological individualism rejects *holism*. By looking at the 'macro' picture, it insists on determining the 'micro-foundations'. Methodological individualism as a way to conduct the study of social phenomena was introduced in a formal way in the social sciences by Max Weber in the first chapter of his *Economy and Society*, though he did not ever use the term, and the first use of the term in German as well as in English was by Joseph Schumpeter (1908 in *German and* 1909 in *English*).

The way Weber perceived methodological individualism was to point out that we do speak of *collectivities* such as nations, organizations and associations as though these were individual entities having their own plans, goals, choices and actions. Weber suggested that apart from considering these as individual entities, we must still look at the motivations and actions of the individuals comprising these collectivities. But how can we consider the individual actions and motivations of so many people that make up these collectivities?

Here, Weber's concept of *ideal types* assumes importance. We might think that Weber's suggestions about methodological individualism are about giving importance to the individual over the whole. Actually, the crux of Weber's formulation of methodological individualism was to give pride of place to the role of actions and the motivations for these actions. Weber's assertions about using the concept of 'methodological' in social sciences are also related to his methodological concept of *verstehende* (interpretive understanding).

'Atomism', the philosophical part of methodological individualism, seeks to promote individualism as a creed. It prefers individualism over collectivism or communitarianism as an ideology and as an efficient way of organizing society. Freidrich von Hayek suggested that atomism leads to the emergence of 'spontaneous order' in society. These two concepts play a significant role in decision making. In fact, the degree of rationality in decisions is influenced by these concepts, especially by their import to 'self' and 'individual motivations'.

RATIONAL DECISION MAKING IN PUBLIC ADMINISTRATION

What are the steps in rational decision making? But before that, what are the ingredients of rational decision making? How do we recognize if a decision is rational? Rational behaviour is not only about reasoned behaviour but also about making optimal choices. First, we need to identify the decision maker. Let us, for the time being, take the bureaucratic organization to be the decision maker. In other words, we assume that the representative official in the organization has the *same* goals as the goals of the organization. Later in the chapter, we shall discuss the situation of the official's and the organization's goals not being aligned.

Organizational success depends on making decisions and solving problems. It involves choosing issues that require attention, setting goals, finding or designing suitable courses of action and evaluating and choosing among alternative actions. The first three of these activities – fixing agendas, setting goals and designing actions – are usually called *problem solving*; the last, evaluating and choosing, are usually called *decision making*.

So let us suppose we have an organization. We say that the organization is rational if its decision makers do the following: first, they identify its basic goals. This is the stage when the problem in hand needs to be explored. Now, how a decision-maker approaches the problem depends on how he or she perceives the problem as per his or her intelligence or intellectual acumen (*Intelligence Activity*). The second stage is designing the blocks to figure out the strategy of overcoming the problem. This stage focuses on alternatives that would lead to problem solving. This is when a proper *design* to overcome the bottlenecks has been worked out (*Design Activity*). How a decision maker chooses alternatives depends upon the choice he or she eventually makes. Now let the goal be quantifiable. Let us suppose that the variable that will depict the goal can be at various levels. Let some specific variable depict the goal. Now, a higher value of the variable will show that the goal has been better, or more fully, attained. Usually the higher the value of the variable, the more satisfaction the organization will obtain. That is, higher values of the variable shows better goal attainment and hence given more satisfaction. Thus, there may be *alternative* courses of action that would influence the level of goal attainment and hence, satisfaction, depending on the choice made (*Choice Activity*).

As per Simon, the decision-making process can be divided into three identifiable stages or activities:

- Intelligence activity
- Design activity
- Choice activity

We say that the organization is rational if the organization can rank the various courses of actions in terms of preference and choose the one that it most prefers (*make a choice*). This is the third stage in decision making. Moreover, rationality demands that the choices and preferences are consistent. Suppose the organization has three courses of actions: *a, b* and *c*. It prefers *a* to *b* to *c*. In another situation presented with the same three courses of action, the organization should not prefer *c* to *b* to *a*.

Rational-choice approach claims to explain outcomes by focussing on one aspect of behaviour, namely, decision making or choice. Rational-choice approach says that there is a goal that every organization has. The attainment of the goal gives utility. So the organization has an objective function with respect to the goal. The organization wants to optimize with respect to the objective function.

The organization is supposed to have certain actions as its choices which, if it chooses correctly and in a judicious way, will lead to the optimization of the objective function. These actions or choices within its control are called the control or choice variables. The control variables taken together and all the feasible values they can take make up the *opportunity set*. The variables that are part of the opportunity set are called *state variables*. The state variables are not in control of the decision maker; the decision maker cannot manipulate these. The outer limit of the opportunity set defines the constraint that the decision maker faces.

Thus, we say that the decision maker chooses from among the opportunity set the appropriate levels of the *control variables* in order to *maximize* the objective function subject to constraints. Of course, while we say that the decision-making unit has a single objective/function, it may face more than one constraint. This is for a single optimization exercise. It is possible that the decision-making unit may be engaged in different kinds of activities spread over many departments.

Now while the organization as a whole may have a single overall objective function, each of these departments may have its own objective function. Thus, there may be multiple objective functions and so we may say that rational behaviour has two interrelated characteristics: 'optimization subject to constraints' and 'consistent ranking of preferences'. Some questions may arise in your mind at this point: does rational behaviour mean selfish behaviour? How will behaviour change if the decision maker does not have enough information? What if there is uncertainty? Does rational behaviour mean calculative behaviour? What happens if the interest of some individual clashes with, or is not aligned with, the interests of the organization? When individuals interact with other individuals and when organizations interact with other organizations, and this interaction can be in terms of cooperation or conflict or a combination of the two, how do we *identify* rational behaviour?

Finally, do humans actually, in real life, engage in optimizing behaviour? Can they be so calculative? And while this can be posed as a moral issue, *should people engage in cold calculations geared towards optimization*? This can also be presented as a simple search for empirical validation: Do people and organizations optimize? Can they optimize? To take the last two questions first, the answer suggested by one of the greatest social scientists of the twentieth century is a resounding 'no'. The name of this thinker, this multifaceted genius, is Herbert Simon. After explaining his sequence of activities (*intelligence, design and choice*) in decision making, let us now discuss Simon's theory of rational decision making in administrative organizations.

HERBERT SIMON AND RATIONALITY

Simon made two kinds of statements about rationality. On the one hand, he took issue with thinkers such as Luther Gulick and advocated the logical and psychological approach to rational human behaviour in administration. He agreed with and used the definition of rationality that is used in social sciences, particularly economics. On the other hand, he also claimed that in actual life, people do not make optimal choices for the simple reason that they cannot do so. They have cognitive and other constraints.

Simon came up with the concept of *bounded rationality*. He said people and organizations seldom possess the information to optimize an objective function. People do not merely have greater constraints than we think; according to Simon, in most cases they do not even know or have a clear-cut objective function itself. So their rationality is 'bounded'.

> Simon was one of the greatest thinkers of the 20th century. He had almost a thousand publications. He was a polymath: political scientist, economist, administrative theorist and psychologist. He contributed to economics, public administration, psychology, cognitive sciences, artificial intelligence, computer sciences, management and sociology. He received the Nobel Prize in Economics in 1978

According to Simon, people, far from engaging in optimizing behaviour, are actually engaged in what he called 'satisficing' behaviour. The word 'satisficing' is constructed by a combination of two words – 'satisfying' and 'sufficing' (even though some claim that the suffix 'cing' comes from 'sacrificing' – people are willing to sacrifice some gains). According to Herbert Simon, people do not seek the best possible solutions to problems but operate within what he has called *bounded rationality*. He pointed out that human beings lack the cognitive resources to optimize. His concept of rationality was bounded on three sides – *skills, habits and reflexes*. These limitations bounded the administrator in an organization.

Herbert Simon, whose primary object of research was problem solving, coined the term 'to satisfice', which denotes the situation where people seek solutions or accept choices or judgements that are 'good enough' for their purposes but could be optimized. In the tradition of rationalistic decision making, it was conventionally assumed that individuals seek the optimal result. Instead, as Simon argues, it is often *rational* to seek to satisfice in that the process of looking for better solutions/results expends resources. A better solution would thus have to justify the extra costs carried in finding it. Thus, Simon suggested that decision makers are not entirely rational and that there are bounds to their rational (optimizing) behaviour. Thus, decision makers are only *bounded rational*.

The basic thing to understand about Simon is that he, in contrast to Weber, was not content to merely study formal organizations; he also took up with the idea of suggesting improvements in their working. Simon made a strong plea for adopting scientific logical techniques in making decisions, while at the same time pointing out that people have cognitive limitations in making rational decisions. Thus, Simon's was not merely a descriptive or even an analytical agenda about the study of organizations; it was a *prescriptive* one.

Simon's approach to the study of organizations can be appreciated if we pause for a moment to consider the nature of public administration. Public administration is not merely an academic discipline; it is also a field of practice. So students of administration analyse organizations but part of the objective is to recommend better techniques of administration to administrators. From the very beginning of the evolution of the subject, the classical thinkers in public administration have been concerned with enhancing the efficiency of the administrative organizations.

Woodrow Wilson, who is considered the Father of public administration (and who later went on to become President of the United States), wrote in a seminal article entitled 'The Study of Administration' in 1887 that 'it is the *object of administrative study* to discover, first, what government can properly and successfully do, and, secondly, *how* it can do these proper things *with the utmost possible efficiency and at the least possible cost either of money or of energy*' (Wilson, 1887, emphasis added).

Thus, searching for efficient administrative practices has been the hallmark of the study of administration. Herbert Simon's work has to be seen in this light. Hence, Weber, while pointing out that modern societies were moving towards increasing bureaucratization, felt that this injects a bit of dehumanizing of everyday life, no such view had ever been forthcoming from Simon.

> To recapitulate, we can say that Simon suggested that decision makers are unable to exercise rational choice to maximize their objectives because of the limitations of incomplete information and clarity of goals. Indeed, claimed Simon, they usually do not even intend to maximize; rather, they satisfice, to use Simon's term. He went on to suggest that since decision makers cannot, and usually do not, optimize, they undertake actions to the extent that suffice to reach the satisfactory level of the goal

Commenting on classical administrative theorists, Simon felt that traditional theory consisted of mainly *proverbs* (*often mutually contradictory*) and rule of thumb. He felt that as administration was concerned with actions towards realizing basic goals, the methods and processes had to be efficient. He felt that the earlier theorists had not placed proper emphasis on choices and decisions. Rationality is defined by Simon as 'a relation of conformance (*efficacy*) between pre-established ends and the means to reach them. To him, the specification of these ends is a question of *value* and, hence, is beyond the scope of science. However, the relation between means and ends is a question of *fact*' (Gustavo, 2010).

Simon, thus, made a distinction between 'facts' and 'values'. The objective function and the control variables we had talked of earlier were described by Simon as *values*, since the basic goals and choices that the organization made would be based on the values that the organization has. On the other hand, are what Simon called as facts. These are what we described as the state variables, which are the collection of variables that make up the opportunity set. These are facts because these cannot be altered by the organization, as it takes these 'state' variables as given.

The main contribution of Herbert Simon was that he made it possible for a dialogue to take place between public administration and bureaucracy. He gave the study of decision making in bureaux a much-needed scientific rigour. He made, as you have seen, decision making the centre of attention and looked at the behaviour of organizations in terms of their goals. He also focussed on the cognitive aspects (*emphasizing, along with his colleague James March, in* 'Organizations', 1958, *the cognitive limitations of the individuals in the organization*).

Simon and March (1958), even went on to list out the factors affecting the three stages of decision-making activities. These factors are as follows:

- Ability, predilections and inclinations of the decision maker.
- Role of inducements and incentives in selection.
- Information-processing ability of the decision-making group.
- Time and cost overruns in taking a decision.
- Structural design of the organization where the decision maker is placed.

To this list, many more impediments could be added, such as information overload, mental fatigue, group conflict, selective use of facts etc. Simon, in a sense, gave pride of place to rationality. Let us now look carefully at the main content and import of Simon's theory of decision making. Simon not only worked on the notions of rationality and the importance of studying human decision making in a scientific way, but he also applied these to the study of organizations and bureaucracies. Thus, while he exhorted the scholars who intended to study public administration to focus on decision making as a process (*and rational decision making at that*), Simon at the same time joined issue with the conventional notions of rationality as had been used in social sciences, particularly economics.

Simon's contribution, therefore, was two-fold. On the one hand, he demonstrated the importance of *studying decision making* as a way of understanding organizations and bureaucracies and emphasized the concept of rationality; on the other hand, he compelled social scientists to take a relook at the *conventional notion of rationality* and propounded a new and a more 'realistic' notion of rationality. He contended that decision makers have bounds on rationality. So, to put it more accurately, he did not question the extant notion of rationality but he merely held that this notion of rationality was too stringent and is usually not realized in practice.

This new approach, characterized by the use of *bounded rationality,* is part of a more general approach called the behavioural approach to the study of social processes. This approach studies the evolution of institutions, organizations and conventions, and as has been observed, Simon's major interest was to *study human behaviour* in organizations. 'Rationality is centrally placed in this behavioural theory: it is the main explaining element, although not the only one'. To Simon, 'the distance between rationality and behaviour is bridged by the concept of "decision". A choice is a selection of one, among numerous possible behaviour alternatives, to be carried out' (cited in Gustavo, 2010).

March and Simon in their piece on 'Organizations' (1958) observed that 'most human decision-making, whether individual or organizational, is concerned with the discovery and selection of satisfactory alternatives, only in exceptional cases is it concerned with the discovery of optional alternatives' (Singh, 2002)

FURTHER EXTENSIONS OF THE RATIONAL-CHOICE APPROACH

The rational-choice approach has been used in all social sciences to understand the decision-making processes. Political scientists have used it to explicate the theories of Hobbes and Locke. It has been used in sociology to understand people engaging in all types of social processes. It is, of course, staple fare in economics. The theory of rational-choice can be extended, and indeed has been extended, in several directions. The first was, of course, by Herbert Simon himself who questioned the notion of an omnipotent, omniscient, rational decision maker who possesses all information and is very clear about the goals.

In fact, there have been clear nuances in the theories of various theorists, of whom Simon was one. Let us review some of the important extensions. The basic rational-choice theory has been extended in a number of ways. First, the basic theory accounts only for choice at a given time – that is, the model is *static*. In contrast, a *dynamic* (*or intertemporal*) model allows the agent to plan for the future as well as make choices in the present. In a dynamic model, 'the agent is still assumed to maximize utility, but the concept of utility is generalized to include not only present satisfaction but also future satisfaction.' (Green, 2002).

To extend rational-choice approach within the purview of the *static* approach that we have discussed in this chapter, let us review its basic contents. First, rational choice requires that the decision maker knows all the alternatives from which the choice of decision has to be made. In addition, the decision maker knows the entire opportunity set, which contains all the alternatives. Further, the decision maker knows the goals or the objectives of the organization in whose name she is making the decisions. Technically, this is called the 'objective function'. Along with this, it is assumed that the decision maker has complete information related to all aspects of decision making. The decision maker, it is further assumed, is aware of all the constraints that impinge on the goal-realization process.

Later writers on decision making in the political and administrative spheres have *questioned* the idea that decision makers passively accept the constraints they face. While it is acceptable that decision makers are rational, it is not entirely clear why they should optimize, subject to the constraints. They may take steps and act to remove the constraints. For example, administrators may take the overall political scenarios and the broad policy framework as given (*these aspects that are taken as given in optimization are known as 'constraints'*) and the decision maker may strive to change other constraints so that the decision maker creates a new and a different optimization exercise.

Many scholars not only in public administration but also in other disciplines such as economics have seized upon Simon's notion of bounded rationality and have studied decision making in administrations, in business firms and so on. Over the years, the theory of rational decision making has incorporated new changes and developments in theories and concepts. One of the basic extensions has been to acknowledge that very often, the decision maker may be acting as per the *tenets* of rationality but the outcome that results is due not merely to her own action but is also influenced by the actions of *other* decision makers. For example, a government official takes actions towards implementation of a policy but other actors such as politicians also take their own action and so do the stakeholders in the policy item.

Thus, the government official has to factor in the actions of all these other decision makers. This study of rational decision making, where outcomes are determined by interdependent actions and the payoffs (*not necessarily monetary, but some gain or 'utility'*) to each person depends not only on her own action but on that of all decision makers, is called *game theory*. This theory is the study of interaction among rational decision makers. The rational actions in this context are called strategies. Game theory can deal with situations where the decision makers take actions simultaneously or with situations where one decision maker can observe the decisions of others and can choose a strategy in response to the decisions of others.

Scholars such as Douglas McGregor (*Theory X and Theory Y*), Charles Lindblom (*Incremental Approach*), Chris Argyris (*Organizational Learning and Control Systems*) and Amitai Etzioni (*Mixed Scanning*) have worked further on decision-making processes. They have taken cue from Simon's decision-making approach and have come up with many more psychological insights into these processes. They have also brought out the role of motivation, leadership and organizational interrelationship in solving problems. The main applications of rational decision making to bureaucracies are by Niskanen (1971; *budget maximization*) and Dunleavy. However, these writers did not always consider bounded rationality but the more conventional notion of rationality. These writers focussed on the object that is optimized in bureaux.

The contemporary work on decision making has distanced itself from bounded rationality or even rationality. Scholars such as Robert Audi (2007) have argued between theoretical rationality and practical irrationality and come up with a new concept of 'global rationality' that believes that 'a high degree of theoretical rationality might counterbalance some degree of practical irrationality, and no rational person need exhibit rationality all of the time. Some irrational actions, and even isolated moments of a wider irrationality (*non-rational emotions*), are compatible with the overall rationality of a person…'

Theories to understand rational decision making have neither been *homogeneous* nor have they remained *static*. Many a time, bounded rationality implies *uncertainty* in overcoming the bounds underlining the decisions. The decision maker is supposed to maximize this objective function, subject to the constraints. The theory is sometimes modified to consider situations of uncertainty or those situations where the decision maker has to make a sequence of decisions over time. Jeffery A. Weber (2003) talks of an *uncertainty constant*, which he describes as 'uncertainty that is not possible for an actor to overcome, despite advances in knowledge and technology. He has coined the term "bounded uncertainty", the boundaries being placed on uncertainty being: (a) amount of information the actor chooses to consider, (b) the length of time the actor chooses to consider; and (c) the amount of possible future interaction that are projected'. The new strategically rational actors take account of the environment and are involved in processes of learning and reflection. Scholars like James Gleick talk of 'Chaos' theory of decision-making thereby rendering many possibilities to extensions of rational-choice approach to decision-making.

CONCLUSION

Rational-choice theory is an approach used by social scientists to understand human behaviour. The approach has long been one of the major paradigms in economics but in recent decades it has become more widely used in other disciplines such as sociology, political science, anthropology and public administration. The chapter's major focus has been on bounded rationality of Herbert Simon, underlining his concept of satisficing man. The chapter has discussed the meaning and concept of rationality. It has examined the utility of rational decision making for organizations. The fact that the behaviour of an organization could be studied through rationality in decision–making has been the central point of the chapter. It has also touched upon theories that have used rational–choice approach and even extended it further.

Preparatory Questions

- Describe the rational-choice approach to social sciences.
- Explain Simon's views on rationality.
- Discuss the stages in Simon's decision making and examine the factors impeding them.
- Write a note on further extensions of rational-choice approach.

REFERENCES

March, J. G. and Simon, H. A. (1958) *Organizations*. New York: John Wiley and Sons.

Niskanen, W. A. (1971) *Bureaucracy and Representative Government.* Chicago (IL): Aldine-Atherton.

Singh, A. (2002) *Public Administration: Roots and Wings.* New Delhi: Galgotia.

Tullock, G. (1967) *The Politics of Bureaucracy.* New York: Sage.

Weber, J. A. (2003) 'Understanding the Dimensions of Uncertainty in Public Administration' in Dhameja, A. (ed.). *Contemporary Debates in Public Administration*. New Delhi: PHI.

Websites:

Audi, R. (2007) *The Architecture of Reason*: *The Structure and Substance of Rationality*, London: Oxford, 2007. Available from: http://www.oxfordscholarship.com/view/10.1093/acprof:oso/9780195158427.001.0001/acprof-9780195158427-chapter-9 [Accessed: 5th January 2014].

Green, S. L. (2002) 'Rational choice theory: An Overview.' *Baylor University Faculty Development Seminar*, May 2002. Available from: business Baylor.edu/steve_green/green/doc [Accessed: 2nd January 2014].

Gustavo, B. (2010) 'Herbert A. Simon and the Concept of Rationality: Boundaries and Procedures.' *Brazilian Journal of Political Economy.* 30(3). (119), pp. 455–472, July-September, 2010. Available from: www.scido.br/pd/rep V30n3ao6v30n3, "http://www.scido.br/pd/rep%20V30n3ao6v30n3,2010" 2010 [Accessed: 23rd December 2013].

Wilson F. W. (1887). 'The Study of Administration', www.heritage.org (Accessed 22nd January 2014).

Chapter Eight

The Systems and Sociopsychological Approaches

Alka Dhameja

LEARNING OBJECTIVES

After completing this chapter, you should be able to:

- Discuss the different types of motivation theories
- Describe Abraham Maslow's Need Hierarchy
- Explain Douglas McGregor's Theory 'X' and Theory 'Y'
- Examine the views of Chris Argyris, Frederick Herzberg and other theorists on Socio-Psychological approach

INTRODUCTION

The central point of all organizational approaches has been to enhance the achievement of organizational objectives through efficient processes and increased output. The *medium* of achieving these objectives has either been 'structures and methods' or 'people and contexts' or at times, all these factors put together. The classical, behavioural and human relations approaches to the organization have attempted to look at the processes of an organization from technical, structural and social contexts. As we all know, the classical approach treated the workers as instruments towards industries' or organizations' output. The focus of the approach was on effectively structuring organizations towards the fulfilment of the laid down goals. Scientific management and bureaucracy were its major components. The behavioural approaches, on the other hand, focussed on technology for carrying out work in the organizations.

The focus of all these approaches was either on individual needs, group behaviour, rational decision making or organizational design and context of organizations. Building on this very emphasis, the human relations approach drew attention to the impact of social factors such as group or peer pressure, informal group behaviour, physical conditions and leadership on the working of organizations. These approaches have already been explained in the preceding chapters of this volume. This chapter will deal with the sociopsychological approach to organizations. It will discuss how these approaches brought into purview the need to analyse individual psychology and its impact on organizational efficiency. The chapter will also try to examine the contribution of psychologists such as Chester Barnard, Abraham Maslow, Chris Argyris and so on. The systems approach that preceded the sociopsychological approach will also be discussed in the chapter.

TYPES OF MOTIVATION THEORIES

Taking the *medium* of 'methods and people' a bit further, the organizational thinkers in the 1950s and 1960s, focussed on specific types of behaviour related to 'motivation' in an organization. They worked on personal and professional perceptions of individuals as the driving forces for motivation. By motivation, they meant the 'will to work'. Their theories went beyond the usual capability to work, which many in an organization presumably possessed. The theories involved willingness to work, which came through motivation. These thinkers believed that individuals in an organization had certain specific needs, which they expressed through their attitude towards work. These needs acted as driving forces in their work lives. Motivating factors were the ones that targeted and addressed these needs.

These thinkers focussed on psychological orientation of individuals in an organization. Their major meeting point was the recognition of individuals' personal desires or ambitions in an organization and their effect on group relationships and leadership styles. This *shift* of emphasis was almost *paradigmatic* in nature. The centre point shifted from the individual as an inert component in an organization that could be manipulated or transformed through work processes, methods and leadership styles to the individual as an active thinking person whose psychological adjustments to processes, methods and leadership styles needed to be kept in mind for organizational outcomes. This new approach known as sociopsychological, or neo-human relations approach by some brought into the purview of organizational analysis, factors such as self-actualization, esteem, job security, content of work, belongingness and job environment.

There are various types of motivation theories such as content and process. Maslow's need hierarchy, Herzberg's Two-Factor, David McClelland's Basic Needs (Power, Affiliation and Achievement) that motivated an individual and Clayton Alderfer's ERG (Existence, Relatedness Growth) all fall under content theories. In Process theory, Victor Vroom has talked about separation of effort which arises from motivation, performance and outcome. In his view, behaviour resulted from conscious choices. For him, efforts, performance and motivation were all interlinked and based on variables of expectancy, instrumentality and valence

The major contributors to the neo-human relations approach have been Abraham Maslow, Douglas McGregor, Chris Argyris and Frederick Herzberg. These thinkers spoke of a different and wider dimension of motivation, which was multidimensional. Unlike the behaviourists and the traditional human relationists who believed in motivators such as the work environment, peer group pressure and interpersonal relationship, the human psychologists spoke of both the external and internal factors as motivators. The human psychologists were not dependent on a few factors such as group behaviour, work conditions and leadership styles. They went deep into the sources of motivation at various levels. For them, motivational factors went beyond physical conditions and economic incentives. They gave a larger basket of 'motivators' or job facilitators to choose from, be it 'extrinsic' benefits such as pay packets, career advancement, retirement plan, fringe benefits, holidays, bonus and profit sharing or 'intrinsic' benefits such as appreciation or praise, self-esteem, status, participation, delegation of authority and enriched job responsibilities.

THE SYSTEMS APPROACH

Before we discuss the sociopsychological or motivation theories, we may examine the 'precursor' theory that in a way formed the basis of all motivation theories. This theory is called the systems approach. We must remember that the vision of motivation was given first by Chester Barnard through his 'inducement–contribution' theory. Chester Barnard strongly dismissed the concept of 'economic man' and gave the theory of contribution–satisfaction equilibrium. He believed that organization should be able to give back more than the individual's contribution to the organization. This, in his view, was the major factor leading to satisfaction, as he believed that a satisfied individual could only further contribute to the organization.

Chester Irving Barnard was born in Massachusetts, USA in 1886. He majored in economics and government from Harvard in 1906. In 1909, he joined the American Telephone and Telegraph Company. He became the President of the Bell Telephone Company in 1927. He was awarded various honorary degrees throughout his career. Inspired by thinkers such as Elton Mayo and Mary Parker Follet, he published 37 papers besides his well-known classic 'Functions of the Executive'

Barnard firmly believed that besides economic material incentives such as money, things and social conditions, many other factors lead to satisfaction. As cited in Prasad et al. (2010), these are as follows:

- Personal non-material opportunities for distinction, prestige and personal power.
- Desirable physical conditions of work.
- Pride of workmanship, sense of adequacy, altruistic service for family and patriotism.
- Compatibility with associates.
- Adaptiveness to working conditions.
- Feeling of enlarged participation.
- Comradeship and mutual support in personal attitudes.

In Barnard's view, organizations came into existence and sustained themselves only if the following attributes were present:

- Communication levels on the part of individuals.
- Willingness to contribute.
- Individuals driven by a common purpose.
- Intense level of cooperation.
- Formal organizations gave way to informal organizations.
- Compatibility between personal and organizational interests.
- Unquestionable acceptability of orders by individuals in organization within a certain boundary (zone of indifference).

Barnard viewed an organization as a cooperative system; a system that understood different philosophies explaining human conduct. This type of system made space for philosophies that defined individual identity through exercise of freedom of choice. It made the individual adapt well, both physically and mentally, to the changing environment. An organization, in his view, took cognizance of available alternatives or choices, worked on them through various organizational processes and modified action in pursuance of desired goals and motives.

For Barnard, individuals in organizations needed team efforts and interpersonal relationships to achieve organizational goals that would not be possible at an individual level. He talked about incentives and persuasion to motivate/induce employees to contribute towards the organization's goals. As individuals interacted within the organizations, the organizations too, at the same time, interacted with other organizations for resources such as land, labour and capital. Thus, a system equilibrium was needed to be achieved by the organizations, which comprised equilibrium at two levels, one at the level of organizations' interaction with external organizations and two at the level of individuals' pursuance of collective purpose within the organization (which an organization encouraged through inducements or motivation).

In order to reaffirm individual compliance to authority towards system equilibrium, Barnard gave the concept of zone of indifference, which implied that individuals would comply with authority only if they could understand communication and only if they could find compatibility between their personal interests and organizational goals. Barnard was the first to realize the role of individual satisfaction in an organization's growth and the relevance of non-material incentives in increasing satisfaction. He based his concepts of organizational cooperation, communication, domain of authority, zone of indifference and effective leadership only to facilitate satisfaction levels in individuals within the organization. However, many critics felt that the very process of arriving at cooperative behaviour in an organization was not properly dealt with by Barnard. The inevitable tensions between the individual and the organization were not resolved by him. Yet, the very fact that later thinkers such as Maslow, McGregor and Argyris used Barnard's parameters to develop their own theories establishes the relevance of his systems approach once again. Hence, Barnard's contribution to organizational behaviour cannot be downplayed.

SOCIOPSYCHOLOGICAL APPROACHES

Maslow's Need Hierarchy

Now coming to the sociopsychological approaches, we all know that Abraham Maslow is called the Father of Humanistic Psychology. He published his work 'Motivation and Personality' in 1954, with which he established the general pattern of needs' recognition and satisfaction that people followed in the same sequence. Maslow divided human needs into a distinct hierarchy, which clearly put an employee's needs into five categories, encompassing self-actualization, esteem, belongingness, security and physiological needs. These, in his view, acted as major determinants in individual adjustment within an organization.

Abraham Maslow was born in 1908 in Brooklyn, US. After studying law, he did his PhD in Psychology in 1934. From 1951 to 1969, He was Professor and Chair of Psychology Department, Brandies University and then Roosevelt Fellow in California. Maslow attempted to understand human behaviour through psychoanalysis. He wrote on psychology extensively but his works became popular after people became familiar with Douglas McGregor's and other sociopsychologists' ideas. His published works include 'A Theory of Human Motivation' (1943), 'Motivation and Personality' (1954), 'Religion, Values and Peak Experiences' (1965), 'Eupsychian Management' (1965), 'Psychology of Science' (1966) and 'Towards Psychology of Being' (1971). Of these, his work on 'Motivation and Personality' became very popular, as it gave a comprehensive theory on the 'Hierarchy of Human Needs'

Maslow believed that individual behaviour was the result of the conscious and subconscious goals that the individual harboured. These goals were personal as well as organizational. He placed the personal needs at a lower level and organizational ones at a higher level. In between, the middle order needs comprised both personal and organizational or professional goals. His pyramid of needs started with physiological or primary needs such as hunger and thirst, moving up to safety needs at the second tier, which included physical security, emotional security and community security. The third tier or level was of social needs comprising belongingness and love, such as acceptance by peers, friendship and affiliation, moving up to the fourth tier of self-esteem needs. This level included needs of self-respect, autonomy, achievement, status, recognition, attention, etc. His fifth and topmost tier of pyramid was of self-actualization and self-transcendence needs such as growth, self-fulfilment and professional accomplishments. Thus, the higher order needs were that of self-actualization, whereas the middle order or level needs were that of esteem and belongingness. The lower order needs were basically the safety and physiological needs. All needs were meant to behave like a pyramid, as the satisfaction of lower needs was a precondition for fulfilment of middle order and higher order needs.

Maslow's need hierarchy pyramid

Higher level needs:

Self-actualization – Fulfilment

Middle level needs:

Self-Esteem – Self-esteem or self-respect, respect for others
Social needs of Love/Belonging – Being loved and cared for by family and friends

Lower level needs:

Security – Personal and financial security, stability, protection
Basic/Physiological – Thirst, hunger, desire

For Maslow, a need was a physiological and psychological deficiency that a person had to satisfy. The major needs at the first four levels of need hierarchy in Maslow were called 'deficiency' or 'D' needs. The last level higher needs were called 'B' or 'being' or 'progressive' needs. According to Maslow, if these needs were not met first then the individual would not feel motivated towards higher needs or, as he averred, would not reach the stage of 'meta-motivation'. So there are two principles underlying Maslow's theory: (a) deficit and (b) progression. As per the deficit principle, a satisfied need no longer motivated the behaviour and the progression principle implied that individual needs performed or functioned in a hierarchical sequence. (Prasad, et al, 2010)

In particular, Maslow's self-actualization needs have to be comprehended, as they were unique in nature. Taking inspiration from the writings of Mahatma Gandhi, Abraham Lincoln, Thomas Jefferson and Albert Einstein, Maslow propounded his self-actualization needs. He felt that these stalwarts had self-actualizing tendencies. These tendencies encompassed many characteristics such as problem-centric approach, democratic values, spontaneity, simplicity and so on. In Maslow's view, these self-actualizers were not perfect people, they simply strived towards self-actualization, which could be achieved through what Maslow called as 'peak experiences'. He, in fact, gave a list of characteristics that could be attributed to a self-actualized person. As cited in Prasad et al.(2010), these attributes are as follows:

- Lack of overriding guilt and anxiety.
- Inclination for solitude and privacy.
- Desire for autonomy and freedom.
- Derivation of ecstasy, inspiration and strength from the basic experiences of life.
- Deep feeling of identification and sympathy for humanity.
- Experiences of mystic happenings.
- Interpersonal relations with a few people.
- Ability to differentiate between ends and means, as well as right and wrong.
- Sense of humour, creativeness and originality.

It has been observed that in case of needs other than self-actualization, it is possible to predict behaviour and the accuracy of the prediction would be higher as one goes lower and lower in the hierarchy.

In the case of self-actualized persons, if the lower order needs were gratified, then their behaviour would only be influenced by self-actualization need. In this case, one might be able to predict what such people do, but such a prediction was not possible on the basis of mere motivation theory. It is even difficult to gauge if self-actualized persons were motivated or not. Maslow talked about the special and driving needs of the self-actualizers. They included truth, goodness, uniqueness, perfection, justice, self-sufficiency and so on. When self-actualizers did not get these needs fulfilled, they responded with meta-pathologies and developed despair, depression, alienation and cynicism (Prasad et al., 2010).

Thus, Maslow analysed the relationship between human beings and organizations from the standpoint of human needs. He gave a comprehensive description of each need, analysing its components and potential to motivate. However, critics have averred that each tier in the need hierarchy was not as distinct as Maslow professed; tiers overlapped and it was a little difficult to prove when the need for one motivator was over and was not required again. Moreover, whether all employees were driven by all motivators in a similar progression was not clear. Some could be merely motivated by physiological and security needs and some only by esteem and self-actualization needs. The same need, for example, the need to interact socially at work, could cause variant behaviour in different individuals. The consequences of divergent performance of the needs in individuals were not discussed by Maslow. In fact, Maslow himself gave a new conceptualization of his self-actualization concept in his later years, as he related it to altruism and spirituality. Despite these shortcomings, Maslow did provide a broad framework to study human motivation and employee attitudes towards organization.

Some other organizational theorists who wrote on human motivation were Clayton Alderfer and David McClelland. Alderfer's ERG or existence, relatedness and growth theory drew inspiration from Maslow's need hierarchy. Alderfer combined Maslow's five-level needs to give his three-level needs. In his view, existence needs were psychological and material desires. Relatedness needs referred to interpersonal relationships. This corresponded to Maslow's social needs. In Alderfer's view, growth needs implied consistent psychological growth and development. These matched with Maslow's self-actualization and esteem needs. McClelland gave an acquired needs theory including 'need for achievement' (drive to excel), 'need for power' (drive to control) and 'need for affiliation' (drive or desire for close and friendly relations)

Views of Douglas McGregor

Another thinker who had a significant impact on the concept of 'motivation' in an organization was Douglas McGregor. His work called 'The Human Side of Enterprise' differentiated between the two motivation theories as 'traditional' and 'professional'. He tried to answer the age-old question on whether managers were born or made. McGregor was the first to attribute the characteristics of individuals or the way they performed in an organization to the way they were perceived by the manager. He believed that '…the way a business was managed determined to a very large extent what people were perceived to have and how they 'developed potential…'(Prasad et al., 2010). He came up with his management theories of 'X' and 'Y' to describe human nature and based his motivators on these theories only. Theory 'X' was the traditional human behaviour theory that believed in punitive and retaliatory approach to garner results, whereas theory 'Y' described humans as malleable and believed in the inherent goodness and potential of workers in an organization. Weightage was given to a manager's attitude towards human nature and behaviour. This was considered necessary to invoke either theory 'X' or theory 'Y' to get the desired results.

Douglas McGregor was a sociopsychologists who was born in Detroit, Michigan in 1906. He obtained his Doctorate in Psychology from Harvard University in 1935. His book 'The Human Side of Enterprise' had a huge impact on management education and practice. In this book, McGregor brought out an approach to create an environment within which employees could feel motivated. He laid stress on gainful engagement of management and workers towards professional objectives. His entire work focussed on management's perceptions and attitudes towards controlling human resources in an organization. His other book 'The Professional Manager', which was published after his death in 1964, reflected his commitment to the development of professional management system through theory building

While theory 'X' was rigid, conservative and static, theory 'Y' was dynamic, optimistic and flexible in approach. The assumptions behind theory 'X' were as follows:

- People or workers in an organization were lazy and did not like work.
- Workers wanted to work as little as possible and tended to avoid it.
- Self-centred and non-committal behaviour to organizational needs was noticeable in the workers.
- Workers were not intelligent and creative. They also resisted change of all types.
- People/workers wanted security and tried to avoid responsibility; they preferred to be directed.
- Managers had to thus control, direct, coerce and threaten the workers to get them geared towards organizational goals.
- Managers following theory 'X' were intolerant, distant, short tempered, anti-social, poor listeners, vengeful, non-participatory, unhappy, unconcerned, biased and bad leaders.

The assumptions behind theory 'Y' were as follows:

- People or workers at the job treated work as natural if the environment was suitable.
- Workers or people were imaginative and creative.
- People were not passive or change resistant; they were willing to accept responsibility.
- Employees/workers/people could self-control and self-direct towards organizational goals.
- The intellectual capacity of an average human being was in fact only partially utilized in modern industrial life.
- Managers believing in the assumptions of theory 'Y' were result-oriented, even tempered, participative, effective, democratic, understanding, constructive, positive and satisfied.

Theory 'X' and theory 'Y' were not two sides of a scale but, as has been observed, two different cosmologies. Theory 'Y' was very useful for easing out the skirmishes or conflict between the line and staff agencies. McGregor also worked with Fredrick Lesiaur on the Scanlon Plan. It spoke of loss reduction sharing and effective participation. The plan did not lay down any set of procedures but envisaged a new philosophy of management. Its assumptions were in consonance with theory 'Y'. It emphasized the fact that participation, integrative management and self-control could lead to ego satisfaction and motivation and subsequently goal fulfilment.

McGregor also spoke of transactional concept of power and influence. His concept of transactional influence has been of great relevance. He emphasized on how managers, through this concept, could deal with their role, style, power, issue of control, team work and their own selves. Working through the differences is what he propagated to foster team work. McGregor's ideas were not new; he was deeply influenced by Maslow. The novelty was in his assertion that it was the managers' perceptions about workers that generated effectiveness and motivation. The manager's characteristics were secondary in motivation creation. He based his theory of motivation on what people were like and what they thought or assumed. Theory 'X' and theory 'Y' may not be very straight categories to describe human behaviour, but they are good analytical tools for predicting human behaviour in organizations. The fact that William Ouchi used it in 1981 for his analysis of human behaviour in organizations goes to show how relevant this theory is for all times.

Views of Chris Argyris and Frederick Herzberg

Later, Chris Argyris and Donald Schon undertook studies on learning processes in organizations. They believed that organizations learned through experiences and actions of individuals. It was not just the individuals who learned in organizations, even organizations did that. While responding to the changes in the environment at the workplace, individuals learned and acted as learning agents for the organization. He propagated a double-loop learning model so that errors were detected and inconsistencies were resolved. As a result, organizational theory and organizational action were both restructured.

> Chris Argyris, an American business theorist, was born in New Jersey in 1923. After serving in the US army in World War II, he studied psychology at Clark University and obtained his MA in 1947. He did his MSc. in Psychology and Economics in 1949 from Kansas University. In 1951, he received his PhD from Cornell University and in the same year he started his career in Yale University. After this, he moved to Harvard University in the 1970s, where he became Professor of Education and Organizational Behaviour. He served Harvard Business School as Professor Emeritus. Known for his seminal work of learning organizations, he authored 30 books and 300 articles. His publications include 'Personality and Organization' (1957), 'Organization and Innovation' (1965), 'Invention Theory and Method: A Behavioural Science View' (1970), 'The Applicability of Organizational Sociology' (1972) and 'Knowledge for Action: A Guide to Overcoming Barriers to Organizational Change' (1993)

Chris Argyris brought to the fore challenges and issues of incompatibility between organizational strategies and individual need fulfilment much before the works on participative management got mainstreamed. His research works focussed on the impact of organizational structures, control systems and management of individuals, organizational change and organizational learning. He recognized the tension between organizational development and individual needs of self-actualization. He believed that if these needs were properly fulfilled, the individual as well as the organization could benefit. In his view, managerial controls revolved more around financial costs than human costs.

Argyris recognized the role of informal groups in beating frustration, conflict and failure in employees. Pressure-oriented directive leadership, in his view, suffocated the employees. The solution, he felt, could be found in the maturity–immaturity theory (people mature and develop as they grow), improving interpersonal competence, innovative organizational structures, non-pyramidal and matrix organizations (division of project into temporary teams which work till the project is active) and 'T group' sensitivity training (laboratory programme to provide opportunities to employees to expose their behaviour or receive feedback, experiment with new behaviour and develop self-awareness).

Inspired by the writings of Argyris, Maslow and McGregor, Frederick Herzberg worked on the relationship between meaningful work experience and mental health. For him, needs emanated from the desire to avoid pain and grow psychologically. He identified events that led to job satisfaction and the ones that led to job reduction. Herzberg's motivation theory is called the two-factor content theory or two-need theory. Herzberg's division of factors affecting motivation and satisfaction hinged on 'maintenance' and 'growth'. These maintenance factors were the hygiene factors for Herzberg, which were concerned with job enrichment – factors that were 'extrinsic' to the work itself. The growth factors were the motivators for Herzberg, as these were concerned with job content – factors 'intrinsic' to the work itself. He believed that the hygiene factors had to be addressed or satisfied first. Once this was done, focus should revolve around growth factors which were the actual motivators.

Frederick Irving Herzberg was born in Massachusetts in 1923. After serving in the army during World War II, he joined the University of Pittsburgh as a Research Director. He went on to become a Professor of Psychology at the Case Western Reserve University in Cleveland and a Professor of Management at the University of Utah. His major contributions include his books such as 'The Motivation to Work' (1959), besides many articles of which 'One More Time, Do You Motivate Employees' sold over a million copies. By 1968, his two-factor theory had already been replicated 16 times in different types of situations. Herzberg's Two-Factor Theory of Motivation: Hygiene or Maintenance Factors and Growth or Motivating Factors towards Job Contentment and Enrichment remains invaluable till date. Herzberg expanded his hygiene theory to come up with his works on 'Work and the Nature of Man' (1966), 'The Managerial Choice' (1982) and 'Herzberg on Motivation' (1983)

In his view, hygiene factors or dissatisfiers could create job dissatisfaction but their presence did not motivate or create satisfaction. However, without them growth motivators were adversely affected. They produced only short-term changes in job attitudes and performance. These, in his view, were the company policy and administration, wages, salaries, quality of supervision, quality of interpersonal relations, working conditions and feeling of job security. Motivation factors or satisfiers were the ones that led to job satisfaction, job enrichment, achievement, recognition and challenges. The presence of these factors motivated employees but their absence did not lead to job dissatisfaction. Factors such as status, opportunity for advancement, gaining recognition, challenging or stimulating work and a sense of personal accomplishment were some of the motivators for Herzberg.

Satisfiers were related to the tasks being performed. They related to what a person did, whereas dissastisfiers related to the situation in which the persons or employees or workers did their work. Salary, as a motivator to Herzberg, worked only in a group and was not a satisfier in the true sense. For Herzberg, job satisfaction and job dissatisfaction acted independently of each other. In his view, satisfaction and dissatisfaction were not on a continuum, with one increasing and the other one decreasing. Hygiene factors caused dissatisfaction among employees in a workplace and thus had to be lessened or removed. Once this was done, motivation factors could be increased to enhance job satisfaction.

As cited in Prasad et al. (2010), the three key principles of the motivation–hygiene theory were as follows:

- The factors involved in producing job satisfaction were separate and distinct from the factors that led to job dissatisfaction. Growth occurs with achievement and achievement required a task to perform. Hygiene factors were unrelated to tasks.

- The opposite of satisfaction on the job was not dissatisfaction. It was not merely any job satisfaction. Satisfaction and dissatisfaction were discrete feelings. They were, as Herzberg described, 'unipolar traits'.
- The motivators had a long–lasting effect on sustaining dissatisfaction than hygiene factors had on preventing dissatisfaction. Motivators were self-sustaining, whereas hygiene needs could not be completely satisfied and had to be reapplied.

Herzberg suggested job enrichment and job loading to satisfy individual needs. By job enrichment, he meant that the job should be challenging enough to utilize employees' abilities. Increased ability should be adequately rewarded with higher responsibility. Through job enrichment, managers could maximize intrinsic motivation of employees. If the job could not accommodate a specific ability in an employee, then it should have the potential to provide the employees with appropriate job of their ability. Herzberg provided a different framework for understanding motivation and its impact on work environments. He spoke about horizontal loading of job instead of vertical loading. It meant challenging the employees by increasing the amount of production expected of them.

Herzberg's theory has been criticized on the grounds that factors that cause job satisfaction in one individual could cause job dissatisfaction in another. Moreover, some motivators or satisfiers are 'neutral' in character. For instance, salary or pay could be both – a satisfier and a dissatisfier. Even Herzberg's methodology drew flak from various quarters, as it was natural for people to take credit for satisfaction and to blame external environment for dissatisfaction. There was no broad measure of satisfaction that was used. The premise that satisfied workers produced more could also not be generalized on the basis of a small sample of nine companies and 200 odd engineers that Herzberg deployed. Critics felt that his theory had its limitations, as growth and hygiene factors had a tendency of interchangeability at times. It could not be proved that a hygiene-seeker employee would not be interested in substantive aspects of a job or would limit to only job environment. A motivation-seeker employee could look for challenges and be an overachiever. However, Herzberg's research method was based on open questioning and critical incident analysis, which made his work pioneering.

OTHER CONTRIBUTORS TO MOTIVATION OR SOCIOPSYCHOLOGICAL THEORY

Besides Herzberg, theories of motivation boast of many other names such as Rensis Likert and Victor Vroom. Rensis Likert believed that highly effective work groups were linked together in an overlapping pattern by other similarly effective groups. In line with theory 'Y', he too saw employees as having their own needs, value and worth, working in effective and supportive work groups and committed to the objectives of organization. He described two types of supervisors – job centred and employee centred. The job centred exerted heavy pressure on employees, had little confidence in them, exercised close supervision, allowed very little freedom to subordinates and used punitive measures of reform. On the other hand, the employee-centred supervisors exerted little pressure on subordinates, increased the achievement motivation and exercised general supervision.

As per Likert's linking-pin model, which encouraged supportive organizations, each individual had twin roles in two overlapping groups, that is, an individual was a member of higher-level group as well as a lower-level group. Group functions and processes grew upwards from organizational base as against top-down management in traditional classical organization. Likert developed a four system management order to determine motivation-friendly framework. His systems were (a) authoritarian or exploitative (the superior has no faith in the subordinate), (b) benevolent (the superior has condescending confidence and trust in subordinates leading to master–servant kind of relationship), (c) consultative (the superior has substantial but not complete confidence in subordinates), and (d) participative (the superior has a high level of confidence in his subordinates).

Victor Vroom's Expectancy Theory

Motivation = Valence × Expectancy

Motivation
↓
Action
↓
Results
↓
Satisfaction in the form of Rewards

Victor Vroom's theory of motivation is called the expectancy theory. It is based on *valence*, which refers to emotional orientations, which people hold with respect to outcomes or rewards. *Expectancy* in his theory implies different expectations of employees and levels of confidence about what they are capable of doing. Thirdly, it is based on the *instrumentality* perceptions of employees to determine whether they will actually receive what they deserve. Vroom argued that the strength of a tendency to act in a particular manner would depend on the strength of an expectation that the act is worthwhile and would lead to an attractive outcome for the individual performing it. The employees would be motivated only when they were sure that the performance would fetch personal growth and positive work appraisal. Thus, in his view, efforts were related to performance. The performance was in turn related to rewards and rewards were related to personal goals.

As mentioned, William Ouchi's theory 'Z' was inspired by McGregor's theories. It combined the features of the management styles in the US and Japan. His theory laid emphasis on workers' participation in decision-making and other productive activities in an organization. It focussed on (a) work rotation, (b) expansion of staff skills through training and personal development, (c) interpersonal relationship of workers, (d) cooperation with fellow colleagues, and (e) well-being of workers.

CONCLUSION

The motivation or sociopsychological theories hinge upon those psychological aspects of human behaviour, which emanate from personal and professional human needs. These are noteworthy in many ways despite the criticism from various quarters. The factors which put these theories on a pedestal are many. Let us attempt to figure some of these. Firstly, these theories gave predominance to individuals' preferences and desires in an organization. Secondly, an individual in an organization changed from a passive being to an active being, motivated by personal goals and got humanized under these theories. Thirdly, the compatibility between personal and organizational goals became a central concern in these theories. Fourthly, these theories gave an assortment of motivators linked with human needs at different levels of individual well-being and organizational expectations. Finally, it was through these theories that concepts such as interpersonal relationship, organizational behaviour, leadership approaches, participative management, cooperation and communication came to be debated and analysed for all future organization development approaches. This chapter has tried to examine the key features of these approaches or theories.

Preparatory Questions

- What are the different types of motivation theories?
- Examine Abraham Maslow's theory of need hierarchy.
- Why is Chester Barnard's systems approach considered a precursor approach to sociopsychological theories of organizational behaviour?
- What is the relevance of Chris Argyris' views for motivation theories?
- List the assumptions behind theory 'X' and theory 'Y'.
- Write a note on Frederick Herzberg's two-factor content theory.

REFERENCES

Dixit, M., Chaturvedi, J. and Syed, I. H. (2003) *Public Administration*. Lucknow: New Royal Book.

Prasad, D. R., Prasad, V. S., Satyanarayana, P. and Pardhasaradhi, Y. (2010) *Administrative Thinkers*. 2nd ed. New Delhi: Sterling.

Websites:

https:\\en.m.wikipedia.org>wiki>Frederck Herzberg [Acessed on August 6, 2014]

https:\\en.m.wikipedia.org>wiki>Chester Barnard [Acessed on June 6, 2014]

https:\\en.m.wikipedia.org>wiki>Abraham Maslow [Acessed on August 20, 2014]

https:\\en.m.wikipedia.org>wiki>Theory and Theory [Acessed on September 10, 2014]

Chapter Nine

Ecological Approach to Public Administration

Surendra Kumar

LEARNING OBJECTIVES

After completing this chapter, you should be able to:

- Explain the concept of ecology
- Bring out the relationship between administration and political. Economic and socio-cultural environment
- Understand the comparative perspective of public administration
- Discuss the Riggsian model of administration
- Describe the features of prismatic society; and
- Appreciate the role of 'Bazaar Canteen' and 'Sala' subsystems in administration

INTRODUCTION

The ecological perspective of public administration can be termed as one of the most pertinent perspectives to the discipline. It is a part of the comparative administration approach that ruled the roost in the late 1950s. F. W. Riggs pioneered this approach, which got strengthened with the formation of the Comparative Administration Group (CAG) in 1961. However, the dimension it gave to public administration has stayed till today, and in view of many scholars, the recent emphasis on 'one size does not fit all' has rekindled the faith in comparative approaches. The inability of Washington Consensus to impose standardized norms, principles and paradigms such as New Public Management on developing countries has also pushed the wheel back to Comparative Public Administration (CPA). This chapter will try to explain the ecological approach of F. W. Riggs and bring out its features, scope and relevance. It will bring out the comparative perspective of public administration and describe the inter-relationship between administration and the political, social, economic and cultural environment.

CONCEPT OF ECOLOGY

The word 'ecology' has been borrowed from biology, where it connotes the interdependence between the animal species and the natural environment. Sociologists used this term to mean 'a study of man's spatial relations in urban settings. In public administration, John M. Gaus stressed the need to employ the concept of ecology to study the necessary interdependence of public bureaucracy and its environment' (cited in Arora, 1984). Similarly, Robert Dahl emphasized the 'need for cross-cultural studies and laid stress on the impact of environment on administrative structure and behaviour. He observed that public administration cannot escape the effects of "national psychology" and political, social and cultural environment in which it develops. He denounced the state of total ignorance about the relationship between the so-called "principles of public administration" and their general setting' (cited in Arora, 1984, pp. 69–70).

It was in the 1950s that real and widespread interest in the study of relevance of 'ecology' to public administration was witnessed. This was also the period during which the US technical assistance programme was in its early period of growth. So, there was an emerging interest in the US in the study of administrative patterns of the newly independent countries during the post-World War II period. By 1961, Fred W. Riggs in his book called 'The Ecology of Public Administration' had, from a comparative perspective, explored the interaction between public administration and the environment in which it develops (cited in Arora, 1984, p.70).

Ramesh K. Arora and Augusto Ferreros have explained the meaning and significance of the ecological study/approach to public administration. According to them, the basic premise of the ecological approach in CPA is that public bureaucracy may be regarded as one of the several basic institutions in a society. Thus, 'in order to understand its "structures" and "functions", it must be studied in the context of inter-relationships with other institutions. In systemic terms, the bureaucratic system is continually interacting with – affected by and feeding back upon – the economic, political and socio-cultural subsystems in a society' (cited in Arora, 1984, p. 71).

Administration, thus, shapes the environment and gets affected by it in turn. It is not a closed system. It receives a feedback from the social system and responds to the demands put on it by the system. In a way, development administration is related to the environment and involves a close interaction between administration and environment. Study of ecology or environment is 'both a modifying influence on the systems as well as a system, which is modified by their activity. It has been recognized that the knowledge of the ecological dimensions of public administration in various settings can aid the "scientific" development of the study of public administration. Its practical importance lies in the insights it provides in the policy formulation process in the areas of technical assistance and administrative development' (cited in Arora, 1984, p. 71).

A useful approach in the ecological analysis of different social systems is 'structural functionalism'. Riggs has considered this framework of analysis appropriate to his ecological orientation in the study of administrative systems. He has observed that only those studies are truly comparative, which are empirical, nomothetic and ecological (Riggs, 1962). From this perspective, the administrative process may be viewed as a system having an environment with which it interacts and in which it operates (Riggs, 1962, p. 17).

According to Riggs, the nature of public administration in any country has to be examined within its larger social setting. Thus, his approach is ecological in nature, as he has attempted to analyse the interaction between the sub-systems, be it political, social, cultural, economic and administrative. In the view of Riggs, administration and environment influence each other to a great extent. They share a close relationship. If administration is influenced by environment so is environment influenced by administration, making the relationship between the two components two-pronged. He has clearly delineated the influence of administration on the political, economic and sociocultural environment and vice versa.

ADMINISTRATION AND POLITICAL ENVIRONMENT

To substantiate the relationship between administration and political environment, we can say that the nature of the administrative system during the colonial regime was centralized, authoritarian and repressive. Likewise, after independence, it was decentralized, democratic and welfare–centric. Administration is thus most immediately influenced by the political system. Administration helps formulate governmental programmes and policies. The administrators provide different types of data, information, expertise, suggestions, feedback and so on to the political executive on the basis of which pragmatic programmes and policies are formulated. Thus, administration and political system impact each other.

ADMINISTRATION AND ECONOMIC ENVIRONMENT

Administration is influenced by the economic set up. For example, in a country with limited economic resources, administrators are not in a position to implement governmental programmes and policies successfully. On the other hand, the administration of a developed country can successfully implement programmes and policies because of the abundance of resources. Further, in a country with a closed economy, the scope for administration would be wider, whereas with an open economy, administration would have less scope, as here, private entrepreneurs are the basic players. Thus, economic environment has a visible impact on administration.

In turn, public administration also influences the economy. In all countries, whether developed or developing, public administration regulates the economy. This is generally done by administering an effective license and quota regime, fixing of prices of commodities, preventing monopolies, guarding against unfair trade practices and controlling imports and exports and so on. Further, if administration is efficient and effective, development and growth will take place, and thus, overall economy will be impacted positively. Thus, administration and economy affect each other.

ADMINISTRATION AND SOCIOCULTURAL ENVIRONMENT

The sociocultural environment affects the administration. If casteism, corruption, nepotism, favouritism and other ills are prevalent in the society, these will find reflection in the attitudes and functioning of administrators. It is because the administrators operate in the same society that has raised them and they are affected by the same social disorders. Similarly, administration can also influence social environment by contributing to the formulation of policies for mitigating social evils. Thus, administration and the social environment also impact each other.

COMPARATIVE PERSPECTIVE OF PUBLIC ADMINISTRATION

In line with the ecological approach, the comparative perspective of public administration aims at comparing the administrative structures of different countries in different cultural settings. The CAG has defined it as the public administration applied to diverse cultures and national setting and the body of factual data by which it can be examined and tested. The purpose of comparison is to seek the universal elements in public administration. Woodrow Wilson is considered the founder of CPA. It was he who first of all stressed the need for a comparative study of public administration. Further, Robert Dahl also emphasized the utility of CPA to develop a science of public administration. However, CPA became popular only after the emergence of third world countries in the post-World War II period. These nations were confronting the problems of modernization and technological development. It was presumed that CPA would provide insights into their problems. The CPA was considered useful not only to strengthen the theory-building process in public administration but also to know whether the administrative practices in a particular nation could be applicable to other nations or not. On this basis, the applicability of the administrative models could be judged and practiced in other political systems. In short, CPA aimed at cross-cultural and cross-national studies of administrative systems (cited in Chakraborty and Bhattacharya, 2005). Fred Riggs' contribution to comparative approach or perspective cannot be denied, as he remained the head of CPA till it was wound up in the 1970s. In fact, he developed all his models to study administrative structures through the comparative lens.

RIGGSIAN MODEL OF ADMINISTRATION

Initially, Riggs extended two types of models, namely, 'agraria' and 'industria'. Agraria model was for traditional societies and industria was for developed societies. However, there was no place for developing societies in these models. Therefore, he coined a new model, that is, 'transitia' for developing societies. Thus, he extended the agraria–transitia–industria model. However, the transitia model was not as well–developed as the agraria and industria models. It was not in a position to adequately explain the nature of developing societies.

Therefore, Riggs abandoned this model altogether and extended a new model on the basis of structural–functional approach namely, *fused–prismatic–diffracted* model. In this model, he made an adequate handling of the prismatic model. He took up an analogy of a 'prism' to understand and analyse his models.

Fused Model

The fused model has the following characteristics:

- It represents traditional societies.
- Agriculture is the main occupation, therefore it is also known as *agraria* model.

- There prevails no differentiation of functions, that is, only one structure performs all the functions.
- Examples are Thailand, the Philippines and Imperial China.

Diffracted Model

The diffracted model has the following characteristics:

- It represents modern or developed societies.
- Industry is the main occupation, hence it is also known as *industria* model.
- Differentiation of functions is found here. Different structures perform different functions. For example, family performs social functions, market performs economic functions and political party performs political functions.
- Examples are the US and other developed countries.

Prismatic Model

The prismatic model has the following characteristics:

- It represents developing or transitional societies and is therefore also known as *transitia* model.
- The traits of both fused and diffracted societies are found here. In other words, it is neither totally fused nor totally diffracted. It is a combination of both.
- Examples are India and other developing countries.

Comparative shifts in public administration as identified by Riggs

Traditional approach	Shift	Comparative approach
Normative	⟹	Empirical
Ideographic		Nomothetic
Non-ecological		Ecological

The prismatic society of Riggs exhibited three broad features, namely, formalism, heterogeneity and overlapping:

Formalism: Formalism connotes the extent to which 'a discrepancy exists between the prescriptive and the descriptive; between formal and effective power; between the impression given by Constitution, law and regulations, organization charts and statistics and actual practices of government and society. The greater the *discrepancy* between the formal and effective, the more formalistic is a system' (Arora, 2000). Thus, formalism, according to Riggs, means the existence of *gap* between stated objectives and real performance. He says that it is comprehensively found in developing societies. Here, the goals determined are something different and the real performance is something different. In other words, formalism is nothing but a gap between theory and practice.

In a prismatic society, formalism appears in many forms and at different levels, for example, Constitutional, administrative and academic. Constitutional façade may provide for political structures like elections, parliament and cabinet. However, Riggs says that the essence of formalism lies in the inability of parliament to control the government and hence the relative indifference of the population and even the ruling group to the actual conduct of the elections (Riggs, 1961).

At the administrative level, it leads to 'intra-bureaucratic politics and ritualization of procedures. This happens because the bureaucrats have no idea about the goals and policies to be accomplished. There is no operative political control over the bureaucracy. The officials take their own decisions. The prevalence of *formalism* leads to corruption. As a result, officials develop a tendency to misuse the written law in dealing with private citizens for their personal advantage' (Riggs, 1961).

Heterogeneity: A prismatic society is characterized by a high degree of heterogeneity, which means 'the simultaneous presence, side by side, of rather different kinds of systems, practices and viewpoints'. The coexistence of the fused and the diffracted traits is an indication and consequence of incomplete and uneven social change (Riggs, 1961). In a prismatic society, there exist urban areas with a sophisticated intellectual class, western style offices and the modern gadgets of administration. In parallel, there exist rural areas possessing a traditional outlook, with village heads combining various political, administrative, religious and social roles. Heterogeneity applies not only to the society as a whole, but it applies also to public administration. The whole range from archaic to formal political structures may be found together, with numerous paradoxes and conflicts as a result (Riggs, 1961).

Overlapping: In Riggs' view, overlapping is yet another feature of a developing society. In a diffracted society, different structures perform different functions. Therefore, no overlapping prevails here. For example, as we mentioned, the family performs social functions, the market performs economic functions and the political party performs political functions. In a fused society, one structure, for instance, family, ruler or king performs every function. Therefore, no overlapping is found in this society either. However, in a prismatic society, overlapping among different structures prevails. Specialization is not found. One structure may perform the function of another structure. With the pace of development, new structures emerge alongside old ones. Therefore, overlapping between old and new structures is found here.

Riggs' administrative models are as follows:

- Agraria–transitia–industria
- Fused–prismatic–diffracted (formalism, heterogeneity and overlapping are the characteristics of the prismatic model)

SALA MODEL: PRISMATIC ADMINISTRATIVE SYSTEM

In a diffracted society, the administrative unit is known as office or bureau. Here we find efficiency and rationality in administration. In a fused society, the administrative unit is known as chamber. Here we find neither rationality nor efficiency; personal whim has the final say here. In a prismatic society, the administrative unit is known as 'sala'. It is a Spanish word which means a drawing room. Here we find the traits of administrative systems of both fused and diffracted societies. On the one hand, we have honest, efficient, effective and rational administrators (*diffracted*), and on the other hand, we also have corrupt, inefficient, ineffective and irrational administrators (*fused*). Thus, a prismatic administrative system combines the administrative traits of both fused and diffracted societies. Other administrative ills of prismatic societies are *nepotism, polycommunalism and polynormativism*. These terms are discussed below:

- *Nepotism*: In a diffracted society, the considerations of a family loyalty are divorced from official behaviour. While in a fused society, the politico-administrative system has a patrimonial character, and therefore, accords dominant importance to kinship or family. On the other hand, in a prismatic society, the new formal structures are superimposed on the family and kinship. In addition, universalistic norms in administering the laws are often disregarded, whereas the official recruitment is determined by nepotism. Thus, patrimonialism is officially proscribed and, in fact, practiced (Riggs, 1961).
- *Polycommunalism*: It means simultaneous existence in a society of various ethnic, religious and racial groups, which live in a relatively hostile interaction with each other. In such a polycommunal society, membership in various interest groups is largely community based. Riggs has called these groups 'clects' (clan + sects = clects), which have characteristics of attainment orientation, selectivism and polyfunctionalism. Clects carry out relatively diffused functions of a semi-traditional type, although they are organized in a modern associational way.

  Polycommunalism and 'clects' influence the character of the 'sala'. Public officials in a prismatic society are likely to develop a greater sense of loyalty towards the members of their own community than towards the government. In matters of recruitment to the official positions and of the administration of rules and regulations, the dominant minority community gains disproportionate representation. Sometimes, the 'sala', or one of its agencies, develops close relations with particular 'clects', or starts functioning like a 'clect' itself. As a consequence of this alliance between sala and clects, sala officials profit through kickbacks or rebates. This aspect of prismatic behaviour is closely related to the economic subsystem of prismatic society (Riggs, 1961).
- *Polynormativism*: In a prismatic society, new sets of norms and rules coexist with the traditional ways of behaviour. As a result of an overlapping of the formal and the effective standards of conduct, prismatic society's social interactions are characterized by a lack of consensus on norms of behaviour. Such a situation of 'polynormativism' or normlessness affects the 'sala', where officials, although publicly claiming to follow objective, universalistic and achievement-oriented practices, actually follow more subjective, ascription-oriented and particularistic modes of conduct. They also respect the traditional rigid hierarchy of status. These officials claim to apply Western rationalistic norms in their conduct but still continue to cling to the traditional practices. In their desire to imitate the West and their own past simultaneously, the officials develop a behaviour which involves borrowing or appropriating what others have done (Riggs, 1961).

Subsystems given by Riggs are as follows:

- 'Sala' model or administrative subsystem, characterized by nepotism, polycommunalism and polynormativism
- 'Bazaar–Canteen' or economic subsystem

PRISMATIC ECONOMY: THE 'BAZAAR–CANTEEN' MODEL – THE ECONOMIC SUBSYSTEM

In a diffracted society, the prices are determined by the market forces of demand and supply. Here, the prices are almost fixed and no bargaining takes place. In a fused society, 'arena factors' (*considerations which determine balance of power, prestige and solidarity*) dominate the economic system and the question of price hardly arises. In a prismatic society, 'market' and 'arena' factors interact with each other and produce a state of 'price indeterminacy', where it is generally impossible to determine a common price for a commodity or service.

Price indeterminacy promotes a 'bazaar'-like atmosphere in a prismatic society involving considerable bargaining on the amounts of financial dealings with regard to areas such as taxes, fees, rebates and bribes. Such practices influence considerably the whole setup of the financial administration and most particularly that of budgeting, accounting and auditing. Price indeterminacy also impairs the collection of government revenues, causing, among other things, low salaries for public officials. As a corollary to low emoluments through regular channels, public officials feel more inclined and motivated to increase their income through illegitimate means. Thus, the norms of official conduct are affected by and, in turn, affect the economic subsystem of a prismatic society (Riggs, 1961).

A prismatic society's source of potential public officials is generally restricted to certain particular groups. Even when the officials acquire rank through achievement (*via education or through a competitive examination*), the opportunities for career development and fringe benefits depend largely on ascribed means, particularly support of one's superiors and seniority, in service. Even the citizen, in his relationship with the 'sala', is polynormative – ready to disregard official rules for his or her own benefits and yet stressing the idea that governmental conduct should be of a strict legal–rational character. Thus, Riggs has provided a comprehensive treatment to his prismatic model, which gives an adequate picture of the developing countries. However, he has also been criticized for the following reasons:

- Riggs has very liberally coined new terms to explain his model.
- Riggs has also given different meanings to the words already in use.
- Free use of words and words with different meanings create confusion instead of making things clear.
- In order to provide a scientific temper to his model, Riggs has borrowed most of his terminologies from physical sciences, but by simply borrowing these words from science, administration cannot become a science.
- Riggs has highlighted only negative aspects of prismatic society. There can be many positive features as well, which he has not highlighted. For example, overlapping may be a positive feature, in the sense that it increases healthy competition among different structures and as a result efficiency and quality can increase.

CONCLUSION

Despite all the criticism, the Riggsian theory has been phenomenal in analysing the situations of developed countries in general and developing countries in particular. His theory makes it amply clear that administration is influenced by the environment in which it operates, and in turn, it also influences the environment. That is to say, there exists a *two-way* relationship between administration and its ecology. The formulation of a particular public policy is also influenced by the environment in which it has to operate. A lot of environmental factors affect formulation of governmental policies. Some of these factors are as follows:

- Geographical factors – for example, natural resources, climate and topography influence the formulation of a governmental policy.
- Demographic variables – for example, size of population, age and gender also influence formulation of governmental policies.
- Political culture of a country impacts formulation of public policies.
- Societal structure determines a governmental policy.
- Different nations themselves serve as factors for policy making in the fields of defence and foreign relations.

These are the major environmental factors, which influence the determination of governmental policies. Based on these environmental factors, government formulates policies. We cannot understand and analyse a particular policy out of context of its environment. Thus, a public policy is influenced by the environment in which it operates, making the ecological study an important approach in public administration.

Preparatory Questions

- Discuss the concept of ecology of administration.
- What do you understand by comparative perspective of public administration?
- Explain the broad features of prismatic society.
- 'Administration is influenced by the environment in which it works'. Comment.
- Describe the sala model, as propagated by Fred Riggs.
- Discuss the economic system of the prismatic societies.

REFERENCES

Arora, R. K. (ed.) (1984) *Administrative Theory*. New Delhi: Indian Institute of Public Administration (IIPA). pp. 69–71.

Arora, R. K. (2000) '*Comparative Public Administration*'. New Delhi: Associated Publishing House.

Chakraborty, B. and Bhattacharya, M. (eds.) (2005) *Public Administration: A Reader*. New Delhi: Oxford. p. 115.

Riggs, F. W. (1961) *The Ecology of Public Administration*. New Delhi: Asia Publishing House. pp. 104–121.

Riggs, F. W. (1962) 'Trends in the Comparative Study of Public Administration.' *International Review of Administrative Sciences*. XXVIII. pp. 15–17.

Chapter Ten

Fundamentals of Development Administration

Maneesha Pandey

LEARNING OBJECTIVES

After completing this chapter, you should be able to:

- Trace the evolution of development administration
- Explain the concepts of development and development administration
- Distinguish development from development administration
- Identify the characteristics of development administration; and
- Describe the fundamentals of development administration

INTRODUCTION

Development administration emerged as an instrument to develop an innovative process of change in developing countries. The postcolonial developing world realized that whatever was done in the name of development by the Imperialists or Colonialists was *not* development in the real sense of the term. The developing countries thus wanted to change the status-quoist approach into a developmental approach. The underlying purpose was to make development possible in every sense for which it was necessary to opt for innovation and creativity. Thus, a series of experiments were undertaken in order to adapt administration to the 'developmental' needs.

Development is the priority of every nation though the precise nature of problems that are faced during the developmental process differs from country to country. However, the problems of development in the developing countries are immense, ranging from promoting literacy, improving nutrition and health and increasing productivity to uplifting the disadvantaged and bringing about social justice. Development is generally termed as 'directed social change' in society. Its thrust is to bring about social and material advancement for the majority of people. This chapter will focus on the evolution, meaning and elements of development administration. It will underline the goals of development administration, and examine its salient characteristics.

EVOLUTION OF DEVELOPMENT ADMINISTRATION

The problems of administration in developing countries have always been different from those in the industrialized developed world. The diverse origins of the problems and the reasons for the differences are *pertinent* areas of study. The identification of these differences has led to the development of an *interdisciplinary* approach to the study of public administration, which could synthesize with the regional economics, history, sociology, psychology and anthropology. The influence of 'behavioural sciences' on the process of development has been observed. This has led to the idea of strengthening the development process by incorporating these insights.

This interrelation of administration and social setting was pointed out in 1947 by Robert A. Dahl in his famous article 'The Science of Public Administration: Three Problems'. However, two more books on public administration, Herbert Simon's 'Administrative Behaviour: A Study of Decision Making Processes in Administrative Organization' (1947) and Dwight Waldo's 'The Administrative States: A Study of the Political Theory of American Public Administration' (1948) evidently pointed out the dissatisfaction with the traditional approach. However, the credit of conceptualizing the idea is given to some very prominent American scholars such as George F. Gant, Fred Riggs, Edward Weidner, Milton Esman and Alfred Diamant. These scholars not only highlighted the concept of development administration but also brought to fore the issues pertaining to its relevance and feasibility in developing nations. The most important contribution was made in 1961 by the Comparative Administrative Group (CAG) under the aegis of the American Society of Public Administration (ASPA).

In the 1950s and 1960s, a general optimism about development was widespread. Many developing countries of Asia, Africa and Latin America gained their independence from Western colonial rule after the World War II. During the 1960s, the obvious way for these countries to develop was to follow the western model of development. This happened because the western theoretical models could not successfully account for the development in the third or developing world. Both internal and external forces contributed to the failure of development approaches. The major *internal* factors of underdevelopment included widespread poverty, illiteracy, inefficient and corrupt bureaucracies and lack of adequate infrastructure to utilize natural resources. On the other hand, the *external* factors revolved around multinational terms of trade, economic imperialism of multinational corporations and lack of attention towards assistance in development programmes.

Many began to believe that there was no single comprehensive theory of development. Rather the approaches to development had to be 'pluralistic' and less western in their cultural assumptions. The need for *re-conceptualizing* the problem of development was felt during 1970s and 1980s. In the 1970s, a questioning stance loomed over development. These were the times when goals of basic human needs, equitable distribution of socioeconomic benefits and people's empowerment were beginning to be treated as developmental goals.

Development administration grew as an academic discipline when western industrialized nations began to provide aid for development of developing countries, using government and public sponsored institutions as agents of social change. Earlier, development was primarily viewed as economic development and development administration was largely economic administration. However, lately, development administration is less bound by western approaches of development. Its focus is on *indigenous* development, which is *sustainable*. Development administration, it has been observed, 'focuses on planned change to meet a nation's broad political, economic, social and cultural objectives' (Wesley and Caiden, 1978).

One of the contemporary trends in development administration theory is a shift from a 'blueprint' approach to a 'learning process' approach. The 'blueprint' approach 'involves designing a specific plan of action in advance for administering a development programme' (Korten, 1984). In contrast, a 'learning-process' approach is a relatively open-ended strategy to planned social change. The learning process approach emphasizes planning with the people, with focus on flexibility and periodic adaptability.

Evolution of development administration has passed through the following phases:

- Writings of Gant, Riggs, Weidner and Esman
- Formation of CAG
- Optimism about the concept of development
- Emphasis on people-centric development
- Focus on pluralism
- Western aid for development programmes
- Shift from 'blueprint' to 'learning-process' approach
- Change from production-centred to people-centred approach
- Moving towards context-based theories

Another trend in contemporary development administration is a shift from a production-centred approach to a people-centred approach. The 'production-centred development approach emphasizes production of goods and services to maximize returns on investment' (Korten, 1984). The needs of people take precedence over the needs of production system in the *people-centred* approach. The key elements in people-oriented development are human growth and well-being, equality, self-reliance and sustainability as a measure of lasting equality in a development programme (White, 1987). In the present context, development administration is characterized by context-based theories, which incorporate indigenous social, cultural, political and economic realities of third world countries' (Bjur, 1975).

MEANING OF DEVELOPMENT ADMINISTRATION

There is no consensus on the precise meaning of the term development. It generally means growth and advancement of economic goals, social objectives and cultural equality. Concepts such as social justice, equality, freedom and ethics are at the heart of all development strategies and processes. The term 'development' includes the need and the means to provide better lives for people in poor countries. It includes not only economic growth but also human development, which means provision of health, nutrition, education and a clean environment.

Until the end of the 1960s, the modernization perspective on development held sway. Development was seen as an evolutionary process in which countries progressed through an identified series of stages to become modern. The focus was always on nation building, institutional growth and socioeconomic change. In a nutshell, administration that was concerned with development in the postcolonial developing world was called development administration.

Although widely used for more than four decades now, the word 'development administration' has not been able to acquire a consensus definition despite extended discussion and arguments on the matter. Theorists such as J.H. Kunkle have explained 'development in terms of the influence of social structure and social institution on individual personality traits' (cited in Montgomery and Siffin, 1966). Montgomery has argued that 'human behaviour could be modified and social change initiated, once a society rewards or punishes specific behaviour of its individuals. He has opined that development administration is carrying out planned change in economy or in capital infrastructure or to a lesser extent in social services, especially health and education' (cited in Kunkle, 1970).

Development administration means the following:

- Planned change in economy or infrastructure
- Influence of social structure and social institutions on individual personality
- Modification of human behaviour for social change
- Creation of improved conditions of material life
- Achievement of national development
- Distribution of social ingredient of health, education and employment equitably
- Protection of human rights and democratic values
- Fulfilment of the goal of sustainability for future generations

According to Turner and Hulme (1997), development administration today is defined as 'an economic component dealing with the creation of wealth and improved conditions of material life, equitably distributed social ingredient that is measured in terms of well-being in health, education, housing and employment. It has a political dimension including such values as human rights, political freedom, enfranchisement and some form of democracy. A cultural dimension is also there in recognition of the fact that cultures confer identity and self-worth to people, a commitment to ecologically sound and sustainable development, so that the present generation does not jeopardize the position of future generations.

Another prominent exponent of development administration, Edward Weidner (1970), defined the concept in a very scientific manner. He defined development administration as 'an action-oriented, goal-oriented and change-oriented effort. Development administration, in his view, focuses on the *results* to be achieved, rather than the traditionalist view of strict adherence to rules and hierarchy. Development, per se, is oriented towards change in a destined direction'. Thus, development administration is change oriented and rejects status quo.

In this regard, the contribution of F. W. Riggs is crucial, as he devoted almost his entire life to explore how the administrative systems in developing nations are shaped by their contexts of politics, economy and culture. According to Riggs (1962), 'development administration is the name often given to the way a country's government acts to fulfill its role in achieving development. He defines development administration as organized efforts to carry out programmes or projects thought by those involved to serve developmental objectives'.

In the view of Donald C. Stone (1963), 'Broadly, development administration is concerned with achieving national development. It is concerned with plans, policies, programmes and projects, which focus on nation-building and socio-economic development'. Administrators under this concept are supposed to be committed to the policies, plans and programmes. This commitment is not so much towards the political parties or policy makers but to the values that an administrator should sustain.

George F. Gant (1979) defines development administration as a 'complex of agencies, management systems and processes that a government establishes to achieve its developmental goals. development administration has an innovative dimension, as it is flexible enough to design new methods, procedures, policies, which could save time, increase effectiveness and quality'. The characteristic features of development administration, according to George F. Gant, can be identified by its *purposes*, *loyalties* and *attitudes*.

The purpose of development administration, he has observed, is to 'bring about socio-economic change in a destined direction. Development administration has an innovative dimension to design new methods and procedures. The purpose is to implement policies and conduct programmes of development. The loyalty in development administration must be towards the people. The attitude of development administration should be outward reaching and not inward looking'.

In a nutshell, development is ultimately aimed at the people and hence it should accord primacy to the public and be *client oriented*. Every development function has a goal to be achieved, that is, economic development has the goal to improve the quality of life such as better literacy rate, life expectancy and reduction in poverty. Development administration is also concerned with political development, which includes equality and capacity of the political systems to produce according to the demands.

For the development functions to be effective and people oriented, participation of people is emphasized in formulating plans, monitoring implementation and sharing the benefits derived. Thus, development administration should focus on 'planning with people', rather than 'planning for people'. It should be people centred rather than production centred, that is, aimed at not only maximizing production, goods and services but also addressing the needs of people and empowering them simultaneously.

Important tools of development administration include the following:

1. Administrative systems – planning commission, etc.
2. Political organizations – political parties, etc.
3. Voluntary associations – non-profit trusts/societies such as voluntary health association, etc.
4. People's organizations – non-governmental organizations, community-based organizations, etc.

DIFFERENCES BETWEEN TRADITIONAL ADMINISTRATION AND DEVELOPMENT ADMINISTRATION

Many scholars such as George Gant and Ferrel Heady feel that development administration differs from traditional administration in its objectives, scope, complexity, structure, attitudes, methods and degree of innovation. The distinction between the traditional and development administration has been presented by S. P. Verma and S. K. Sharma (1984) as follows:

Traditional administration	Development administration
• Regulatory administration	• Unpredictable new tasks or problems
• Oriented towards efficiency and economy	• Oriented towards organizational growth and effectiveness in achievement of goals
• Task orientation and conformity to rules and procedures	• Relationship oriented with emphasis on high-performance standards
• Sharp and elaborate hierarchical structure, authoritative in nature	• Structure shaped by requirements of goals – flexibility and change
• Centralized decision making	• Wide-sharing decision making – empirical approach
• Emphasis on maintaining status quo	• Continuing organizational development in response to environmental demands – dynamic, adaptive and futuristic

Traditional administration has been visualized as one that is concerned with fulfilling all the legal requirements of governmental operations and maintenance of social stability. This type of administration confines itself to the maintenance of law and order, collection of revenue and regulation in accordance with the statutory requirements. The assumption behind the differentiation between development administration and traditional administration is that administration in newly independent countries should march towards developmental values from law and order values. There is one more point of differentiation, which is the fact that development administration is oriented more towards attitudes and processes rather than procedures and structures.

However, there are some scholars who object to such a differentiation on the grounds that 'division of government servants into developers and non-developers might result in the loss of esteem to one and gain as well as over-importance to the others. This would demoralize administration'. The commonness of the two could also be observed from the following facts as presented by V. A. Pai Panandikar:

- Prevailing structure of general administration has a decisive influence on the strength and weakness of development administration.
- Both have a common source of authority within the structure of the government, for instance, a cabinet responsible to a legislature.
- A number of key officials, such as divisional commissioner and district collector, combine general and developmental functions.
- Citizens observe and judge the acts of administration, drawing no fine distinction between general and development administration (cited in Bhattacharya, 2002).

Thus, a rigid distinction cannot be made between traditional and development administration. The traditional functions of maintenance of law and order are also basic to development. Development administration has assumed the responsibility of formulating and implementing various development and welfare functions because of growing complexities of administration and aspirations of people. These functions are not absolutely separate from traditional functions. In fact, maintenance of law and order and security is a precondition for an economy to undertake developmental tasks. However, since development administration is wider, broader, participative, innovative and change oriented, the traditional administration has to create conditions for effective working of development administration. The differences of views on the question of dichotomy still persist leading to an inconclusive debate.

CHARACTERISTICS OF DEVELOPMENT ADMINISTRATION

The concern of development administration is how the ideas and mechanisms of public administration can be used as instruments of social and economic development. 'Development administration' is generally similar to the traditional 'public administration' in its concern with how a government implements its rules, policies and norms. It *differs,* however, in its objectives, scope and complexity. Development administration is more innovative, since it is concerned with the societal changes necessary for achieving developmental objectives. It is easier to understand the concerns of development administration in three parts: firstly, how to guide government action towards development objectives purposefully. Secondly, how to take account of the many and complex interdependencies of societal change and lastly, how to ensure that government administration is dynamic and innovative.

George F. Gant (1979) has rightly pointed out that the function of development administration is to ensure that appropriate congenial environment and effective administration support are provided for delivery of capital, materials and services, wherever needed in the production process-whether in public, private or mixed economies. The required inputs are skilled manpower, finances, logistics, information, participation and legitimate power. These six inputs together form the content of development action.

There is a lack of consensus on what exactly is characteristic about the administrative situation in *transitional* societies. There is even disagreement on the relationship *between* administration and culture – whether administrative behaviour is uniquely determined by particular cultures or not. Riggs presented the concept of 'prismatic society' to explain the *unique* conditions and the dynamics of politics and administration in developing countries (this has been explained in chapter 9 on Ecological Approach of this volume).

The contribution of development administration is to highlight those conditions which make it difficult for planning to be either long range, systematic or knowledge based. The problems of administration are as deep rooted as the problems of the society as a whole. Edward Weidner thus defines development administration as 'an action oriented, goal-oriented administrative system' (Waldo, 1970). On the basis of the different definitions of development, a number of characteristics of development administration can be identified, which are as follows:

- *Change orientation*: Development administration is primarily change oriented. It focuses on nation building and socioeconomic development. It aims at achieving socioeconomic goals through the talents and expertise of bureaucracy. Development administration focuses on the results to be achieved rather than the *traditionalist* view of strict adherence to rules and hierarchy, which create rigidness and delay. The main task of developing nations is to handle the problems of over population, poverty, malnutrition, underemployment to name a few. The plans taken up by administration should be constructive and, at the same time, effective.
- *Goal orientation*: Another characteristic of development administration is that it is goal oriented, which implies that it is targeted towards specific programmes and their results. It involves modernization of administrative structure, capabilities of personnel and attitudinal and behavioural changes among administrators. The goal of social justice and overall growth can be achieved through development administration.
- *Client orientation*: Development is ultimately aimed at the people. It should accord primacy to the public and hence administration should be client oriented. It is concerned with the upliftment of the poor and the downtrodden and primarily the weaker sections of the society. This is integral to administrative ethos and value. For example, in India, a number of schemes and programmes have been introduced. The 73rd and the 74th Constitutional amendments have introduced reservations for the weaker sections of society. In fact, the involvement of panchayati raj institutions (PRIs) in planning and administration has found renewed support in the development strategy of India. This is because they represent the people at grassroots.
- *Time orientation*: Time orientation is also another prominent feature of development administration. For the goals to be achieved, the means and ends need to be related, and for this, planning and temporal dimensions are *salient* features. Planning aids/helps in deciding the resource required for the goal and the time in which they need to be achieved. The timeliness of all activities assumes considerable significance in development administration.
- *Participation orientation*: Participation of people is emphasized in formulating plans and implementing and sharing the benefits derived. Planning should be people centred rather than production centred. There should be a close relationship between public and administration, without which desired socioeconomic changes cannot be achieved. The bureaucratic structures need to involve the citizens actively in the developmental strategies and not treat them as mere passive recipients of benefits of goods and services. Hence, effective formulation of programmes and their implementation with the help and association of the local people helps in giving them an increasing share in the governance and management of developmental affairs of the government. For this reason, the involvement of PRIs in planning and administration has found renewed support in the development strategy of India.

- *Environment orientation*: Development administration needs to interact and respond to its environment. It was Fred W. Riggs who explored how the administrative systems in developing nations were considerably shaped by their contexts of politics, economy, culture and environment. He had also set directions of comparative administrative studies in developing nations. He observed that administrative changes affect environment and changes in environment have an impact on administrative activities.
- *Innovation orientation*: Development administration has an innovative dimension also. It requires qualities of flexibility and responsiveness in administrative actions and methods. It designs new methods, procedures and plans to meet administrative requirements/targets. The aim of development administration is to increase effectiveness and quality at the same time. For example, in India, various development programmes such as Mahatma Gandhi National Rural Employment Guarantee Act, Integrated Rural Development Programme, Jawahar Rozgar Yojna and many others have been initiated. Broadly, these programmes aim at addressing the issues of poverty, unemployment and underemployment. The thrust or crux of development administration is to be innovative and creative.

Today, development administration focuses on indigenous development, which is sustainable. The sensitivity towards ecological factors has a clear projection. The concept of development administration, unlike industrial nations, requires a multi-dimensional approach and an interdisciplinary perspective. The developing nations are widely practising development administration in order to achieve the goal of socioeconomic change and nation building.

Economic growth does not necessarily mean economic development. Growth in investment, capital formation, industries and national income do not assure overall development and social justice. Therefore, we must view development in its totality, as one single, *unified* concept incorporating social, political, cultural and economic angles/dimensions.

Features of development administration include the following:

- Change orientation
- Client orientation
- Goal orientation
- Time orientation
- Participation orientation
- Environment orientation
- Innovation orientation

FUNDAMENTALS OF DEVELOPMENT ADMINISTRATION

The two major goals of development administration are: *administration of development and development of administration* or administrative development. Administration of development means the application of innovative tasks required to control the process of development. It is how development plans and policies are carried out or implemented at grassroots level. Development has to be a *self-reliant* process, with focus on social development and human capital. It must make effective use of scarce resources towards securing basic needs of population in order to justify itself as an ideological norm. Development of administration or *administrative development* refers to that aspect of development administration where administrative systems and capacities are developed for the purpose of effective deployment of limited resources to implement the development policies. It strives, on the one hand, to bring about political development, economic growth and social change and on the other hand, makes an attempt to bring about adaptability, autonomy and coherence in administration. As opposed to traditional administration, development administration is concerned more about social justice and holistic development. According to planners in India, the concept of development must incorporate the following elements:

- *Social justice* is basic to development, that is, it provides the base and foundation of development and works as the principle and main objective of development.
- Development has to be a *participative exercise* and not a unilateral politicizing exercise, where only those who wield power are in control of affairs.
- *Self-reliance* is a pertinent and inseparable aspect of development. It asserts that developing countries should be able to participate in the development process on the basis of complete equality in international affairs for reaching an accord, which will be mutually constructive to both parties involved.
- Scarcity of natural resources urges maintenance of a *balance* so that they are not exploited in the name of development.

Fundamentals of development administration include the following:

- Social justice
- Participation
- Self-reliance
- Fresh thinking or innovation
- Equality and equity

CONCLUSION

In conclusion, we can say that development administration is a complex concept that includes the ideals of change, participation, innovation, social justice and economic growth. Different scholars view it differently but the crux or essence of development administration in all definitions revolves around people's needs and participation. In the 1950s, developing nations, for the most part, imitated the West in administering their developmental programmes. It was only after the formation of CAG that the period of *rejection* of western ideas and prescriptions began.

In the late 1960s and 1970s, developing countries began to develop administrative practices suitable to them. The anti-development theorists suggested that the western concepts should be debunked and people should revert to their *indigenous* ways and include themselves in the administrative process. The International Labour Organization (ILO) and the World Bank were compelled to revise their approach towards the goal of 'growth with equity'.

This new approach was termed as neo-colonialism, as it was inferred that under the garb of equity, this was a new way of packaging western concepts for developing countries. The 1980s was a major turning point in the evolution of the concept of development administration, as scholars wanted administration to be flexible and inclusive of people. Towards the 1990s, the very pertinent 'new right philosophy' and public choice theory emerged as pertinent approaches (as discussed in chapter 14 of this volume). This resulted in a new paradigm of development administration. This paradigm is now commonly known as 'good governance'.

The discourse theory of development administration has been one of the latest. It asserts that development administration should have two major criteria: one is the *human needs* approach and the other is the *sustainable* approach. Thus, the issue of effective, equitable and judicious governance remains central to development administration, from whatever approach or paradigm we choose to look at.

Preparatory Questions

- What do you understand by the terms 'development' and 'development administration'?
- How has development administration evolved over the years?
- Bring out the difference between traditional administration and development administration.
- Describe the different features of development administration.
- Write a note on the fundamentals of development administration.

REFERENCES

Bhattacharya, M. (2002) *Social Theory and Development Administration*. 3rd ed. New Delhi: Jawahar.

Bjur, W. et al. (1975) *The Sociology of the Third World*. Cambridge: Cambridge University Press.

Bjur, W. and Caiden, G. (1978) 'Reforming Institutional Bureaucracies'. *Institutional Review of Administrative Sciences*. XXIV. pp. 359–365.

Dahl, R. (1947) 'The Science of Public Administration: Three Problems'. *Public Administration Review*. 7(1). pp. 1–11.

Gant, G. F. (1979) *Development Administration: Concepts, Goals, Methods*. London: The University of Wisconsin Press.

Korten, D. C. (1984) 'Rural Development Programming: The Learning Process Approach' in Korten, D. C. and Klans, R. (eds.). *People-Centred Development: Contributions Towards Theory and Planning Frameworks*. Connecticut: Kumarian Press.

Korten, C. D. and Camer, G. (1984) 'Planning Frameworks for People-centred Development' in Korten, C. D. and Klans, R. (eds.). *People-Centred Development: Contributions Towards Theory and Planning Frameworks*. Connecticut: Kumarian Press.

Kunkle, J. H. (1970) *Society and Economic Growth*. London: Oxford University Press.

Montgomery, J. D. and Siffin, W. (eds.) (1966) *Approaches to Development: Politics, Administration and Change*. New York: McGraw-Hill.

Riggs, F. W. (1962) *The Ecology of Public Administration*. Bombay: Asia Publishing House.

Riggs, F. W. (1964) *Administration in Developing Countries: Theory of the Prismatic Society*. Houghton Mifflin Company.

Stone, D. C. (1963) 'Government Machinery Necessary for Development' in Kreisberg, M. (ed.). *Public Administration in Developing Countries*, in Proceedings of an International Conference, Bogotá, Brookings Institution, Columbia, April 15–21.

Swerdlow, I. (1963) *Development Administration: Concepts and Problems.* New York: Syracuse University Press.

Turner, M. and Hulme, D. (1997) 'Development: Creator and Destroyer of Values.' *World Development.* 20(3). pp. 467–75.

Verma, S. P and S. K. Sharma (eds.) (1984) *Development Administration* . Indian Institute of Public Administration (11PA), New Delhi

Waldo, D. (ed.) (1970) *Temporal Dimensions of Development Administration*. Durham (NC): Duke University Press.

Weidner, E. W. (1970) 'Development and Innovational Roles' in Weidner, E. W. (ed.). *Development Administration in Asia.* Durham (NC): Duke University Press.

White, G. L. (1987) *Creating Opportunities for Change*. Boulder (CO): Lynne Rienner.

Websites:

Available from: http://planningcommission.nic.in/reports/articles/ncsxna/index.php?repts=irdpm.htm [Accessed: December 2013].

Available from: http://publicadministrationtheone.blogspot.in/[Accessed June 2014]

Available from: http://www.scribd.com/doc/39746885/IGNOU-s-Public-Administration-material-Part-3-Development-Administration[Accessed July 2014]

Chapter Eleven

Feminist Perspective of Public Administration

Anita Bagai

LEARNING OBJECTIVES

After completing this chapter, you should be able to:

- Provide an insight to the feminist perspective of public administration
- Discuss the basic components of feminist approach
- Focus on the parameters needed to understand the concept of gender in administration
- Appraise the administrative concepts of ethics, expertise and leadership from the feminist perspective; and
- Examine the necessity of feminist perspective to public administration.

INTRODUCTION

When we talk of feminist perspective of public administration, three factors become pertinent: first, inclusion of women-friendly policies in governance; second, participation of women in public administration and third, a change of attitude to the issue of 'gender' in administration. The third factor is the most crucial and is thus the central theme of this chapter. Change or reform can come from any direction; it can be internal from within the organization or can be externally precipitated. The last decade of the 20th century was marked by the idea that the government can be reinvented at all levels. The idea came to grip the imagination of administrators, elected officials, citizens and scholars alike as frustrations mounted over the way government delivers services, makes decisions and treats its employees and clients.

This chapter explains the feminist approach to public administration. It deals with the issues concerning the role of 'gender' in governance by highlighting the parameters of *gender analysis* in governance or administration. Finally, the chapter speculates on the direction in which the allegedly 'hostile administrative State' must head, so as to be equally hospitable to both men and women.

UNDERSTANDING THE FEMINIST APPROACH

The *reinvention project* is a multi-faceted and open-ended project, advocating a range of measures including facilitating participation, accountability, efficiency and an end to corruption to encourage good governance. Most importantly, though, it takes the market as its ideal, with bureaucratic government gradually giving way to entrepreneurial government – one that is competitive, decentralized, streamlined and performance driven, rather than regulation bound and rule driven.

The reinvention project is significant in that it challenges the Weberian model of bureaucratic organization as the taken-for-granted reality of administrative life. It further suggests that administrative structures, practices, principles and values are neither permanent nor unalterable. However, what is more significant is the fact that feminist scholars have long imagined alternatives to the bureaucratic model, much before the 'reinvention project' became fashionable, with the publication of the Report of the *National Performance Review* in 1993 under the Clinton administration.

Unfortunately, the alternative theories of power, virtue, nature of organization and of leadership and professionalism based on feminist research and women's organizational experiences failed to capture the attention of policy makers and citizens and few of these ideas made their way into conversations in public administration (Stivers, 1993).

Feminists note that thus far the project to reinvent government ignores the gender dimensions of administrative life and feel that women's experiences are no more a part of the new entrepreneurial government than were a part of the old bureaucratic government. These scholars seek to render women's experience *visible* and argue for a development of a feminist perspective to public administration, which constructs the administrative reality in *gender-inclusive* rather than *gender-neutral* terms.

In order to develop a feminist approach to public administration, it is first important to recognize that for many decades the discipline, like so many other sciences and social sciences, was rooted in an ostensibly neutral but overtly male, upper class, white mentality. Like so many other sciences and social sciences undergoing revision today, public administration too has come to be redefined in the light of explorations of feminist and other marginalized groups on the subject, resulting in an expansion of its boundaries and a reassessment of its norms.

There are several dimensions to the feminist reappraisal of public administration. While supporting the cause of a *gender-inclusive* public administration, we will first define feminist theory and then try to investigate the 'gender of governance', that is, explore the extent and the manner in which administrative power, institutions and policies are organized around femininity and masculinity, male dominance and female subordination. Attempt is also made to investigate the 'governance of gender', that is, see the extent to which administrative policies set the rules and circumstances that not only regard and reward, but also produce and position women and men as different and unequal (Brush, 2003). The crux of the argument is that gender relations cannot be understood apart from the administrative State; administrative States influence gender relations and are in turn influenced by gender relations.

Issues in feminist perspective of public administration include the following:

- Relationship between 'gender of governance' and 'governance of gender'
- Administrative policies towards women
- Impact of administrative State on gender relations
- Gender as a useful category of analysis
- Need for a change in gendered power relations

THE FEMINIST THEORY

A feminist is someone who identifies with gender as a crucially *useful* category of analysis, who takes a critical perspective on women's current status and prospects. To use Gerda Lerner's (1984) words 'feminist is the one who believes in a system of ideas and practices which assumes that men and women must share equally in the work, in the privileges, in defining and dreaming of the world'.

Feminism is not one unitary concept, but instead a *diverse* and multifaceted grouping of ideas and, indeed, actions. Despite the fact that the feminist movement encompasses different and even contradictory political viewpoints – liberal, Marxist, socialist, radical, postmodern to name a few – all have a firm faith in the equality of men and women and are committed to the elimination of 'gender-based injustice' (Freedman, 2001).

Feminism is all about creating a space for heterogeneous gendered perspective; about perceiving and working to change gendered power relations. It is like using a 'gender lens' to view things. Anyone who wears glasses knows that a lens provides a powerful corrective and can completely change the way you view things. Given the fact that *both* the theory and practice of public administration have long been notoriously masculine endeavours, such a corrective can prove to be a vital tool. Therefore, using a gender lens means 'working to make gender visible in social phenomena, asking if, how, and why social processes, standards and opportunities differ systematically for women and men' (Brush, 2003).

Gender of Governance

A mere glance at the history of social sciences would reveal that all over the world, the public political domain has been, and continues to be, defined and controlled by men. Women have been, as Sheila Rowbotham (1973) has put it, 'hidden from history' (Polity Reader, 1994). Concerned about the absence of women from established political structures, feminist scholars have tried to account for this phenomenon. In view of Bystydzienski (1992), for many the 'macho' tradition of conceptualizing politics has been responsible for the exclusion of women from politics.

The central mechanism by which this exclusion is realized is the assumption that the political is public and that the private realm of the domestic, familial and sexual relations lies outside the proper concern of the study of politics. In other words, with politics restricted to the public sphere of human life and perceived as an arena of male activity, the private or personal realm, by contrast, has come to be seen as a sphere reserved for women. Judith Squires (1999) rightly observed that 'the institutional manifestations of politics located in government have been notoriously resistant to the incorporation of women, their interests or perspectives. Women have by and large been excluded from defining their activities as political'.

Many political theories/intellectual tools people use to explain policies and processes are *androcentric* (Brush, 2003). They consider some aspects of gender – specifically male dominance – to be normal, neutral and universal, that is, they assume a masculine point of view but call it universalism or neutrality. For instance, Carole Pateman charged that liberalism's past 'is deeply and, for the most part unambiguously, patriarchal' for it assumed a natural separation between public and private (Squires, 1999). According to her, liberalism is blind to its own gendered character. Distinction between public and private is neither natural nor always good for women. In fact, making the liberal distinction between State and civil society, public and private is a *gendered* political practice.

Feminist theory in the latter half of the 20th century began to realize how potent this *duality* was, for the ways in which male and female roles are constructed and the means by which women, from the very understanding of what is 'political', may be excluded or simply made invisible (Arneil, 1999).

Thus, began a re-evaluation of many male-created theories, principles, concepts and institutions including those of politics and administration. One of the pioneers, Kate Millet in her classic work 'Sexual Politics' redefined politics from an activity taking place within established government structures to *relationships based on power,* whereby one group of people is controlled by another. Radical feminists went one step further by attacking the notion that there exists a distinct political sphere and proclaimed that 'the personal is political' (Bystydzienski, 1992).

The claim that 'the personal is political' destabilized all that had been previously presumed. Feminists rejected the conception of political as located only within the *institutional* area of government. They challenged the traditional views on family and personal life as outside the remit of 'politics' and argued that the private sphere was in fact a *primary* site of power relations and of gendered inequality. They emphasized the way in which personal circumstances are *structured* by public factors. Women's lives are regulated and conditioned, for example, by the legal status of wives by government policies on child care, by the allocation of welfare benefits, by labour laws and the sexual division of labour, and by laws on rape, abortion and sexual harassment. 'Personal' problems can thus be solved only through political means (Freedman, 2001).

They clearly adopted the instrumentalist conception of politics as power and proceeded to extend the definition of power such that power is ubiquitous and politics is all encompassing (Squires, 1999). It is apparent that gender is about power. Through gender relations, people recreate and reinforce the distinction between masculinity and femininity. Gender also organizes power at the level of complex institutions. It saturates different spaces – even the administrative State. It would not be far from truth to say that the administrative State and its policies are gendered. Power in general and the State power in particular is never neutral (Brush, 2003).

The administrative State is inflected with masculinity and femininity as different and unequal markers of power. It bestows political and economic privileges on the culturally masculine qualities at the expense of those who display culturally feminine ones. The characteristic masculinity of public administration is systemic and structural. Its coherence is sustained by women's disproportionate responsibility for domestic work (*provision of food, clothing, shelter and nurturing children*) without which life would simply not be possible and more importantly men would not have the time/energy for public pursuits. This, in turn, limits both women's opportunities to participate in public life and the time and energy they have to devote to it. The commonsense notions of administrative State are thus deeply dependent on traditions that privilege men and their pursuits and devalue women's contribution and concerns.

Governance of Gender

The universalist pretences of administrative State can make it hard to see gender and the power relations it constitutes. However, the feminist writers have shown how masculinity is the invisible, unexamined foundation of the administrative State. A gender lens reveals the male bias of public administration – how men and masculinity are considered simultaneously normative, prescriptive and objective in the definitions of administrative principles and concepts. In simple words, it contributes to feminist understanding of how male dominance organizes/constitutes the administrative State.

However, a gender lens also allows an assessment of the effect of such an administrative State and its policies on men and women. It shows that an administrative State, which is a gendered hierarchy, produces inequality and assigns different life chances to men and women and reinforces material realities that oppress women.

> A feminist approach to public administration includes calling those boundaries into question that differentiate capabilities/potential qualities on the basis of gender; giving preference to males over females. It also means exploring the implications of these attitudes in governance

In general, there is an understanding of public administration rooted in the images of expertise, leadership and a form of virtue, which can be identified as culturally masculine (*although, of course, this masculinity is not overtly acknowledged*). This peculiar nature of the public–organizational reality where links are drawn between ideas of masculinity and public administration norms of professionalism, leadership and neutrality; where working women bear the double burden of housework and paid employment; are relegated to lower bureaucratic ranks; and a glass ceiling blocks their access to the position of greatest power and monetary reward are declared misfit with organizational expectations about professional and managerial behaviour, harms women and restricts their political and social freedom (Stivers, 1993).

Culturally dominant masculine modes of thought and action privilege men and their interests by establishing boundaries that exclude all but a few exceptional women from positions of authority. A feminist approach to public administration theory entails calling off these boundaries into question and exploring their implications, which include material differences in access to resources and power that they sustain and the perceptions of self and the world they generate (Stivers, 1993).

PARAMETERS OF UNDERSTANDING GENDER IN ADMINISTRATION

The analysis of the extent to which gender is *embedded* in the very structures of organization (*gender of governance*) and the extent to which it figures in the world view/policies of administrators (*governance of gender*) has exposed the exclusion of women from the political world. The feminists, however, argue that true equality cannot be achieved by just 'adding in' women to traditional theories, but that the very basis of the theories must be challenged. Accordingly, they examine and analyse several issue areas in public administration that call for a *new* configuration and offer a new version of the spectrum of the feminist opinion, which promises to be fruitful in shaping administrative theory and practice.

There are certain parameters against which public administration and gender can be analysed and are as follows:

- Ethic of justice
- Expertise
- Leadership styles

Ethic of Justice

It has been observed that the public realm, of late, has been systematically denuded of public moral values and the public morality of justice has been overtaken by the forces of power, coercion and violence. Politics has come to be understood as power politics – conflictual rather than consensual. Not surprisingly, the ethic of justice has emerged as a significant research concern for public administration scholars. Their response is to reassert the integral relation between politics and ethics in creating an ethical polity. The ethical discourse within public administration, however, would be both broader and deeper, if ethics from a feminist perspective were to be included.

Ethical reasoning is usually equated with an 'ethic of justice'/idea of impartiality or a universalistic morality. Such a conception of moral reasoning assumes that the administrator must adopt a universal point of view, which demands that one abstracts from particular experiences, from feelings, desires and commitment and adopts a detached and dispassionate view (Squires, 1999). The 'ethic of justice' is widely criticized within the feminist political theory. It is considered a product of the male psyche and hence, intrinsically gendered and *limited*.

The feminists argue in favour of extending the range of moral reasoning so as to include another form of reasoning called an 'ethic of care', which ought also to be recognized. It is said that women are more likely to adopt this *ethic of care* than men and that to the privilege of the ethic of justice. Women's distinctive moral voice should not be silenced. It is claimed that women's experiences as mothers within private spheres provides them with certain insights and concerns, which are valuable to the public sphere of the administrative State, but are currently absent from it (Squires, 1999).

The discovery of an alternative moral orientation based on care originates in Carol Gilligan's work, 'A Different Voice'. Gilligan uncovered a *moral* orientation among women that centred on emotional relationships of attachment, interdependence, connections and networks of concrete relationships, along with a general concern that 'no one be hurt'. The justice orientation, on the other hand, focuses upon equality, universality, rules and rights.

As per Gilligan (1982), 'A justice (ethic of justice) perspective draws attention to problems of inequalities and oppression and holds up an ideal of reciprocity and equal respect, a care (ethic of care) perspective draws attention to problems of attachment and abandonment and holds up an ideal of attention and response to need'.

Gilligan's theory reflects the belief among feminist scholars that women perceive dilemmas differently and behave differently from their male counterparts. They call for a change in the way the ethical decisions are made. The insights of Gilligan and other ethicists are valuable for public administrators because many operate in this *dual ethical context* throughout their professional lives. As administrators, they are expected to apply rules fairly and equally, at the same time they are expected to help and care for citizens. The *value conflict* between rules and personal discretion is a problem area that would immensely benefit from feminist ethics analysis.

Feminist scholars such as Gilligan nowhere endorse the rejection of the ethic of justice in favour of an ethic of care. Rather, they want the ethic of justice to be *tempered* by an ethic of care. They want to incorporate an ethic of care into the political discourse along with the ethic of justice because according to them, the public administrative world, in order to flourish, must nurture and sustain a set of ethical imperatives, including a commitment to preserve, protect and defend human beings in their capacities as private persons (Lynn and Wildavsky, 1990). Their belief is based on the conviction that the recognition and acceptance of 'a different voice' is crucial to the transformation of public bureaucracies.

Expertise

Feminist theorists have drawn upon and contributed to the debates about the image of expertise in public administration. Historically, the need for expertise has been the central tenet of the Wilsonian–Weberian paradigm of public administration. Classical public administration grounded in politics–administration dichotomy was based on the assumption that public administration was legitimate because it was manned by expert professionals. The Wilsonian–Weberian model of professional expertise with an implicit emphasis on objectivity, assertion of autonomy and hierarchy is considered *inconsistent* with the widely accepted notions of womanhood.

Generally speaking, there has been a tendency to banish norms that are culturally recognized as 'feminine'– such as passivity, compliance and vulnerability – from public life, thus creating an approach wherein public administrators, both men and women, seek ways to appear technically expert, tough and heroic – in other words, to project a more masculine 'competent image'.

Camilla Stivers (1993) claims that prevailing ideas about bureaucratic competence and expertise stress a neutral objectivity that depends on a separated self-mastering nature and sees the ideal form of knowledge as hard data; this sort of objectivity supports individual liberty valued in liberal philosophy by making the State a neutral arbiter among competing claims. The feminist perspective, however, reveals this model of knowledge to be anything but neutral, because of the centuries old association between nature and women; the privileging in liberal thought of the public 'male' sphere over the private, where the State does not arbitrate – making a firm case that a *liberal State* depends on the subordination of women.

The conventional idea of expertise also privileges a notion of *autonomy* over and above the public servant's obligation to be politically responsive. From the feminist perspective, such ideas of expertise block connectivity and affiliation of the administrator with the world around him. They not only separate the individual from the field but they also raise the administrator above the field. Professional competence reduces those over whom authority is exercised to a state of dependence. Expertise *depoliticizes* the claims of clients, discounts the value of citizens' views and disassociates itself from non-professional workers.

The recognition that the perspectives of all the parties to the situation – clients, citizens and workers – are important in ascertaining genuine public interest made the feminists campaign for a form of professional competence that is non-hierarchical. They also argue for a form of competence in public administration that moves beyond the myth of a heroic male professional who sacrifices 'selfish' family concerns in a single-minded fashion to his career.

The central theme of Stivers' account is also her assertion that not only do most women find it difficult or impossible to live up to such an *ideal*, but that the ideal itself is flawed, in that it compartmentalizes life and the men and women who live it, relegating the family to a lower status and the performance of its responsibilities to lesser people.

Problems of gendered perspective are as follows:

- Masculine ethic of justice versus feminist ethic of care
- Subjectivity of liberal model
- Limited representation of women in top jobs (glass ceiling)
- Characteristics of objectivity, autonomy and hierarchy are considered inconsistent with the widely accepted notions of womanhood
- Leadership skills have a masculine subtext
- Negative stereotypes/prejudices about women
- Feminist traits regarded contrary to leadership requirements

From the feminist perspective, the legitimate public administrator will be a *whole* person, one who is understood to have developed in a family and continues to be member of a family; the work of agencies will be seen as supporting and supported by the wider dimensions of its members' lives, and agencies' personnel policies will reflect this understanding. Policies such as parental leave and on-site day-care facilities will be seen as in the public interest because they promote the development and the nurturing of children; they will not be viewed solely as meeting the needs of individual employees.

Leadership Styles

Leadership style is yet another issue area identified by Stivers that would benefit from feminist study. The feminists are disturbed by the limited representation and functioning of women in top jobs, both in business and in public administration, and believe it to be *the* crucial issue in gender inequality. They seek answers to the following questions – why are there very few women managers especially at the senior levels? Do men and women differ in their leadership abilities and style? Is there, perhaps, a specific female form of leadership that is preferred by the majority of women? Are prejudices and other obstacles preventing women from attaining leadership positions? Or do females express other value orientations than to exercise authority over others?

The feminists critique the conventional image of public sector leadership – that of a visionary, the decision maker, the symbol and definer of reality. They feel that management and leadership skills, as constituted, are *broadly* constructed with a masculine subtext because most of the public figures that fit into this category are men with a clear masculine, even heroic aura.

Dominant views on leadership are seen as difficult to integrate with femininity, that is, they conflict with the expectations about women's behaviour. Popular literature suggests that women differ from men in terms of some *orientations* and emphasizes differences in terms of leadership style which are presumably grounded in their personalities. Women are negatively stereotyped. They are perceived to be deficient in management traits, skills and behaviour required for success. Further, it is assumed that women want, first and foremost, to be womanly companions to men and to be mothers, making them *less* inclined to give priority to, and make sacrifices for holding a managerial job. Such feminine traits are seen to be contrary to the requirements of the leadership role. Thus, compared with men, women are rated as less desirable for leadership positions and are extended fewer jobs and receive lower salaries (Stewart, 1990).

Those women who move to leadership positions are often caught between contradictory ideals of being feminine and being managerial, leading to great risks of negative evaluation for being either unfeminine or unmanagerial. Such sex-role stereotype constructions, although regarded as old fashioned, still prevail. It works against them and acts as a barrier to their advancement to leadership positions.

Although the feminists are disturbed by the fact that only a very small percentage of top jobs in business and public administration are held by women in most countries, they are not sure if simply adding women in key positions will be enough to bring about a fundamental change. They also want to raise another pertinent question – whether we need leaders at all. Conventional administrative theory sees hierarchy as the inevitable 'given' in the complex organizations in post-industrial society. It appears uncomfortable with the vacuous feeling of being without a structure that a leaderless group evokes.

Feminists such as *Stivers*, however, see the perceived need for leadership as a function of hierarchy, which socializes those in lower ranks to believe that they are incapable of taking decisions or contributing to a joint effort to decide what to do. Widespread dissatisfaction with hierarchy and control led women organizations to experiment with non-hierarchical forms of organizing. Called *interactive leadership*, it draws on many of the qualities previously dismissed as 'feminine' in leadership literature (Burnier, 1994).

The ingredients of this new style of leadership/management include a more participatory, non-hierarchical, flexible, group-oriented style of management. The feminists believe that female leadership contains the seeds of connective leadership since women are seen as skilled at listening, artistic, sensitive, integrated, deep, subjective, empathetic, associative, open, personalized, receptive and nurturing.

Hence women's experiences appear to be more suited to the new organizational setup. Although such a leadership style has been associated with women, feminists are not arguing that all women are interactive leaders or that it excludes men. The feminists simply want a shift in the norms of leadership such that feminist leadership is viewed as a complement, not as a replacement, to traditional leadership forms. The new integrative model of leadership with interactive and indirect leadership styles is still evolving and awaits full acceptance, but the fact remains that the feminine perspective of administrative leadership articulates an alternative that promises to be more suitable for the dramatically changing workplace of the 21st century.

ALTERNATIVE ORGANIZATION THEORY

The feminist position on the above-mentioned themes raises questions that bear directly on organization theory. The feminists are developing *alternative* models of organization, based primarily on their experience in the women's movement. They are experimenting with new patterns of group activity, which substantially depart from the rational model of administration. They also challenge domination by superior through hierarchical patterns on the grounds that it restricts the growth of individual members. They propose the adoption of fluid, temporary, more flexible and egalitarian forms of organization. The potential impact of the feminist critique of the key concepts in public administration prompted Robert Denhardt and Jan Perkins (1976) to predict the demise of 'the administrative man' and urge the adoption of an alternative model based on the organizational values of women's movement.

An alternative perspective would entail the following:

- New integrative model of leadership with interactive and indirect leadership styles
- End of perpetuation with 'the administrative man'
- Adoption of fluid, temporary, more flexible and egalitarian forms of organization
- Need for a 'gender lens'
- Gender-inclusive policies

CONCLUSION

For long, the governance perspective has ignored the impact of the feminist approach to public administration. Always at the receiving end and subjected to various stereotypes, women have not got a fair share in governance. Women have not been generally considered for occupation of top positions, decision making or skill enhancement. It is high time that the feminist approach got its due.

The feminist perspective of public administration, till today, remains a neglected issue. Either the administrators or those studying administration are disregardful of its existence or they feel that feminism evokes certain negative connotations. We can safely conclude that this perspective has not received the attention it deserves. Unfortunately, we associate administrative traits such as decision making, team leadership and discipline enforcement as masculine. It is not appropriate to genderize or categorize on gender lines the administrative tasks and skills. A new approach to understand gender in administration is required.

This chapter has made an attempt to explore the feminist approach to specific aspects of administration – the idea of feminist ethic, expertise, leadership styles of women, organization theory and their impact on the way administration is carried out. This is by no means an exhaustive list of avenues of feminist theorizing on public administration. The effort has simply been to build a persuasive case for a feminist perspective on public administration.

Preparatory Questions

- What according to you are the special insights offered by feminist perspective of public administration?
- Examine the feminist critique of the 'administrative State'.
- What is patriarchy? Why do feminists describe the administrative State as patriarchal?
- Explain how administrative State reinforces women's subordination and marginalization.
- Bring out the feminist reappraisal of administrative concepts such as ethics, expertise and leadership.
- Write a note on 'governance of gender'.

REFERENCES

Arneil, B. Seyla Benhabib, Rosi Braidotti, Nancy Chodorow, R.W. Conwell, Cathereine Hall, Michael Stanworth, Klaus Thaveleit, Sylvia Walby and Jefferey Weeks (1999) *Politics and Feminism.* Oxford, UK: Blackwell Publishers. p. 43.

Brush, L. D. et.al (2003) *Gender and Governance*. US: Alta Mira Press. p. 19.

Burnier, De. Lysa. (1993) 'Reinventing Government from a Feminist Perspective: Women's Experience and Administrative Reality,' 4th Women's Policy Research Conference Washington DCA.

Bystydzienski, J. M. (ed.) (1992) *Women Transforming Politics*; *Worldwide Strategies for Empowerment.* Indianapolis (IN): Indiana University Press. p. 1.

Denhardt, R. B. and Perkins, J. (1976) 'The Coming Death of Administrative Man'. *Public Administration Review*. 36(4). p. 383.

Freedman, J. (2001) *Feminism*. Buckingham, UK: Open University Press. p. 5.

Gilligan, C. (1982) *A Different Voice*. US: Harvard University Press.

Hennig, M. and Jardin, A. 'The Managerial Women,' cited in Stewart, D. W. (1990) 'Women in Public Administration' in Lynn, N. B. and Wildawsky, A. (eds.). *Public Administration: The State of the Discipline.* New Delhi: Westview Press.

Lerner, G. (1984) 'The Rise of Feminist Consciousness' in Bender, E. M., Burk, B. and Walker, N. (eds.). *All of Us Are Present.* Columbia: M. O. James Madison Wood Research Institute, Stephen's College.

Lynn, Naomi B and Aaron Wildawsky (1990); Public Administrative The State of the Dicipline, Chatham House, NJ

Pateman, C. (1999) 'Feminist Critique of Public/Private Dichotomy' in Squires J. (ed.). *Gender in Political Theory*. Cambridge, UK: Polity Press. p. 1.

Rowbotham, S. (1973) *Hidden from History*. London: Pluto Press.

Squires, J. (1999) *Gender in Political Theory.* Cambridge, UK: Polity Press. p. 47.

Stewart, D. W. (1990) 'Women in Public Administration' in Lynn, N. B. and Wildavsky, A. (eds.). *Public Administration: The State of the Discipline.* New Delhi: Westview Press. p. 221.

Stivers, C. (1993) *Gender Images in Public Administration: Legitimacy in the Administrative State.* Newbury Park: Sage.

Young, I. M. (1999) 'Justice and the Politics of Difference' in Squires, J. (ed.). *Gender in Political Theory.* Cambridge, UK: Polity Press. p. 142.

Chapter Twelve

Public Policy: Concept and Approaches

Saugato Sen

LEARNING OBJECTIVES

After completing this chapter, you should be able to:

- Define the term 'public policy'
- Identify the constituent elements of public policy
- Describe the purpose and significance of public policy
- Explain the classification of public policy
- Understand the interrelationship among people, public policy, public welfare and public interest
- Examine the important approaches to public policy

INTRODUCTION

'Policy' is a word you come across often. A shop may have a policy about you being able to return a product if you do not like it; you, as an individual, may take out an insurance policy; the government may be criticized on its fiscal policy and so on. In all of these, a policy refers to a set of rules or a series of goals or a decided response to a particular situation. When the modifier 'public' is placed before the word 'policy', you can be sure that it is the government whose policy we are talking about.

A policy is termed as a public policy, only if it is formulated, implemented and enforced in true spirits by the various government institutions/agencies. Then, of course, you may immediately start to think 'should it not be *policies*'? After all, the government is engaged in a wide spectrum of activities and it must be having a lot of policies that it formulates and implements. Certainly, but when we *study* public policy, we use it as a *generic* term, a generalized concept of policy making and implementation in a sense that captures the common elements in all of the different policies. These *common* elements are not necessarily about the content. Indeed, the contents of the various government policies are necessarily at variance with each other, and yet, this common element is what makes it worthwhile as a topic of study.

So why is public policy important – and interesting? Let us begin by looking at the evolution of public policy in 'modern' times. Beginning with the end of the World War II, suddenly all across the world, national governments started to play a far greater role than they had done earlier. There were several reasons for this. One was, of course, that many countries in the so-called third world attained independence from colonial rule. So first they had sovereign independent States that soon started on the path of 'nation building'. In the economies of all these countries, there was an undeveloped capitalist class, and hence the government had to assume a huge role in economic development. In addition, for the advanced nations of the West, the World War II had been preceded by the Great Depression, beginning with financial upheaval of enormous proportions. This again meant a greater role for the State towards national growth in these western nations. It is for this reason that public policy gained so much importance or significance.

Public policy is implemented by public functionaries in administration. In the 1960s, public policy emerged as a field within political science. Analysts started giving more attention to the *content* of policy rather than the *processes* by which it was made. The study of public policy from around this time has been of two types. The first concerns the substance of the various policies, *descriptive* accounts of the *contents* of the policies and the process of their formulation. The second seeks to discuss the *theory* behind policies or the ideas behind the policies. It explicitly prescribes what kind of policies ought to be formulated and implemented and also engages in predictions about the effects and impacts of policies. In other words, this second type of studies is not primarily descriptive but *predictive* and *prescriptive*. Due to these two approaches, public policy has come to straddle both political science and public administration.

We can *thus* approach the study of public policy from two angles: one is to look at the theoretical dimensions of public policy – the concepts, the approaches, the types, the models and so on; the other is to examine the processes and stages of public policy – its formulation, implementation and finally its evaluation. This chapter, as its title suggests, limits itself only to the former of these; a later chapter in this volume will acquaint you with the processes and stages of public policy.

This chapter begins by trying to define public policy and see what its constituent elements are. Then it goes on to discuss the significance and purpose of public policy. Subsequently, the chapter discusses the various approaches to public policy. When we use the word 'approach', we do not mean different approaches to policy adopted by the makers and implementers of policy; rather, we mean the various approaches adopted by analysts and scholars to understand and explain the nature and content of public policy. Finally, the chapter discusses public policy in relation to the concept of public welfare and public interest. The focus of this chapter is on the nature and content of public policy.

NATURE OF PUBLIC POLICY

Broadly speaking, public policy is the *sum total* of the actions and broad guide to rules formulated by the government to satisfy public needs and wants. If the *end* is the welfare of the people, then public policy is the *means*. Let us elaborate on the nature and content of public policy. The word 'public' denotes the collective group of citizens in a generalized sense, and the government that is to serve this collective group. The word 'policy' can be taken to refer to all the actions that the government takes to attain a stated goal or goals.

Given specified objectives or goals, the *proposed* course of actions to attain these objectives is public policy. Thomas Dye (1978) defines policy as 'whatever governments choose to do or not to do'. Guy Peters (1996) defines public policy as the 'sum of government activities, whether acting directly through agents, as it has an influence on the lives of citizens'. James Anderson (1975) has distinguished between policy (policy in general, not only public policy), which he describes as 'a purposive course of action followed by an actor or set of actors in dealing with a problem or matter of concern', and decision, which refers to choosing between alternatives.

We must remember the following features of public policy:

- There are two ways of looking at public policy – descriptive and prescriptive
- Public policy is formulated and implemented by government institutions/agencies
- Though government has many policies, the term policy is used in a generic sense
- Study of public policy deals with theory or ideas on one hand and activities or processes on the other
- Increasing role of the State in socioeconomic growth of a country accords pertinence to public policy
- Public policy is the means for achieving the welfare ends of the State
- Public policy is the proposed course of action to attain developmental goals or stated targets
- The guidelines for action that direct towards achievement of objectives make for public policy

It is interesting to see how Yehezkel Dror (1974) has approached the definition of public policy. He observes that 'governments have to serve the *public interest* and this has to be achieved by the best possible means. The government organs have to undertake actions to achieve these. For undertaking these actions, some guidelines have to be formed. The "dynamic process" by which the guidelines for action directed at the future are decided is what Dror calls policy'. Thus, according to Dror, it is not so much the actual actions to achieve the objectives, or even the guidelines to these actions that constitute policy, but the *dynamic processes* by which the guidelines are formed that makes up policy.

Having looked at the various definitions of public policy suggested by different thinkers, we are in a position to focus on the basic *characteristics* of public policy. Basically, public policy refers to a set of *goal-oriented actions* and not *ad hoc* actions. In addition, public policy refers to a set of actions by the government to serve the *public interest.* In addition, governments search for *legitimacy* for public policy *not* only in legal and authority terms mandated by the Constitution but also in popular democratic terms, through approval/disapproval of citizens. Finally, public policy includes both the actions that governments *actually* take and the actions that the government *intends* to take. Public policy includes, along with actions, the rules as well as the programmes of the government. Public policy is a pattern of action that helps to *resolve* conflicting claims on economic and political resources or helps to provide incentives for cooperation. Thus, policy is not an isolated event but a regular action, a regular practice and hence a recurring activity.

Characteristics of public policy include the following:

- It refers to a set of goal-oriented actions
- It intends to serve the public interest through its actions
- It is legitimized in legal authority terms (as provided by the Constitution and legal framework)
- The legitimacy of public policy also comes through public opinion building and consensual public approval
- It is not only about the course of actions it actually takes, but also that it intends to take
- It is a pattern of actions aimed at resolution of conflicting claims on economic and political resources

PURPOSE AND SIGNIFICANCE OF PUBLIC POLICY

Keeping in view the objectives and characteristics of public policy that we have discussed till now, the significance of public policy becomes *apparent* in many ways. Public policy is central to governmental functioning and to give voice and shape to the government's goals and objectives. The *content* of public policy is very important, as it reflects the Constitutional ideals and the very essence of a country's polity and vision. It is a different matter that the content gets diluted or modified by political parties in power and also by regimented or prejudiced bureaucracy. However, we will not go into the issue of policy *goal displacement* here. It is sufficient to understand the fact that public policy is, in principle, the embodiment of a country's socioeconomic and cultural spirit.

Public policy is thus a significant component of a political system. It is concerned with betterment of people and society. In the words of W. Parsons, 'wider purposes of public policy relate to involving enlightenment, fuller development of individuals in society and development of consensus, social awareness, legitimacy, rather than simply the delivery of goods and services'. It means that public policies aim at bettering democratic and political capabilities of people and not merely efficiency of delivery of goods and services. According to Chakraborty and Chand (2012), public policies not only help us understand social ills but also provide mechanisms for moving a social and economic system. Public policy has a developmental role, as well-planned policies help in the socioeconomic development of a nation.

We must also remember that public policy is a specialized area in its own right. Scholars such as Yehezkel Dror have formulated a science around it called policy sciences. Policy analysis is a rigorous search for causes and consequences of public policies and therefore becomes the main dimension of policy science. It studies various policy options and helps to select an *alternative* by finding out evidence for and against the possible options. It builds up concepts and methodologies, borrowing from other sciences and focuses on the importance of decision making (Dror's views, cited in Singh, 2002).

Thomas Dye (1978) gives *three* reasons on significance of public policy – scientific, professional and political. Firstly, public policy can be studied to gain greater knowledge about its origin, processes by which it is developed and its consequences for society. Secondly, professionally, an understanding of public policy permits us to apply social science knowledge to solution of practical problems. Policy studies can produce professional advice. Thirdly, public policy ensures that the nation adopts the right policies to achieve the right goals. Political scientists have a moral obligation to undertake advanced studies on specific policy.

Public policy studies try to answer questions such as: what do governments do? Why do they choose to do what they do? How do they choose their actions and activities? How well have they done what they set out to do? Moreover, increased political participation by the public has led to *renewed* focus on the policy process and has also necessitated a fresh look at the concept as well as the content of public policy. One of the reasons for the emergence of the theoretical and analytical aspects of the study of public policy is the increasing academic awareness that traditional analyses of government have not been adequately describing the various aspects of government and political activities. It has been felt that it is important to understand the 'why' and 'how' behind the policy process.

Thus, the fundamental purposes or objectives of public policy that add to its significance are social welfare, economic development, democratic participation, public interest, delivery of public goods and services, social awareness, capability enhancement, institutional building, legitimacy and accountability. For example, in India, for several decades since 1951, central planning has played a crucial role. Public policy also has a role in instilling a sense of *political awareness* in the people simply by making them aware of their entitlements and trying to see if the government is pursuing good policies. Thus, the very formulation and implementation of policies carries the potential of analysis of these policies by the people at large. Despite being informal, this type of analysis helps people to formulate and voice their opinion on policy.

Significance/objectives of public policy include the following:

- It upholds and reflects the very ideals of Constitution
- It mirrors a country's vision, the essence of its basic polity and economy
- It helps people become aware of the 'why' and 'how' of the government's intent
- It leads to an informal analysis of policy implementation by people
- It makes clear the governmental positioning on important issues
- It aims at achieving welfare, public interest, participation, legitimacy and accountability

TYPES OF PUBLIC POLICY

Public policies are supposed to be formulated and implemented for social welfare and hence are *multifarious* in nature, touching the various areas related to the lives of citizens. This is particularly true in a democracy. Along with social welfare, a goal of public policy is also to make clear the government's stance in different areas of political, economical and social lives. Before discussing the different types of policies, we should be clear about the way policies get to the floors or are implemented. Though chapter 17, will explain the entire policy process; Gladden's four-level hierarchy of policy making explains the process very clearly.

Gladden (1964, cited in Singh, 2002) has identified following four levels of policy making.

- Political or general policy-making level (*a broad outline of policies of government in power*).
- Executive policy (*division of policy into concrete practical objectives, e.g., cabinet policies*).

- Administrative policy (*form of executive policies in operation*).
- Technical policy (*actual day-to-day implementation of policies by administrators*).

Let us now look at the various types of policies:

- *Substantive policies*: These are policies that are macro in nature and deal with the general welfare and development of society. This is not designed keeping any particular section of society in mind. Examples would be defence policy, health policy, law and order and so on.
- *Distributive and redistributive policies*: Distributive policies include all public assistance and welfare programmes for society; anti-poverty programmes and minimum needs programme are part of these. We may also include pulse polio mission, mid-day meals and old-age pension under this category. These policies are targeted at specific sections of society. Redistributive policies aim at *ethical rearrangement* of the gains of public goods and services to various sections of society.
- *Regulatory policies*: These policies are designed so that business, industry, public utilities and infrastructural facilities are regulated by the government, often through independent regulatory authorities. Regulation of telecom, insurance and stock exchanges are examples of this type of policy.
- *Capitalization policies*: Under these, no particular section of society is targeted. Neither is the whole society the recipient of welfare measures. Rather, under these policies, the central government provides financial subsidies to State and local governments and also to public enterprises at various levels.

Types of public policy include the following:

- Substantive
- Distributive and redistributive
- Regulatory
- Capitalization

APPROACHES TO PUBLIC POLICY

According to Chakraborty and Chand (2012), public policy approach is a systematic and scientific study of public policy process with the objective of improving it. The concept of policy approach was first formulated by D. Lerner and Harold Lasswell in their work, *The Policy Science* in 1951. After looking at the meaning, nature, significance and objectives of public policy, let us now see how experts have tried to explain the policy process. The approaches to public policy help us in understanding policy better. According to Thomas Dye (cited in Bhattacharya, 2001), there are four models of public policy, namely, *institutionalism, group theory, elite theory and rational models*.

In fact, scholars in the area have looked at the approaches to public policy from different standpoints. Some have categorized them into process and output approaches to policy making and implementation (Henry, 2002), whereas some have described them in terms of rational and non-rational approaches, focussing on comparative analysis of incremental and rational approaches. Some make a comparison between incrementalist and rationalist models. We must keep in mind that apart from the rational-choice approach, rest of the approaches fall under the non-rational category (systems, group, institutional, incremental, game, etc.).

Broadly, there are two major approaches to public policy, one is the *process* approach and the other is the *output* approach. We use the words approach and model interchangeably here. The 'process' approaches includes the group approach, the elite approach, the institutional model, etc. The 'output' model includes the rational-choice approach, the game-theoretic approach and the incremental approach. Each approach has a distinct focus and specific goal. Each explains some or the other aspect of political life and policy activity. Let us understand these approaches one by one.

Process Approaches

The Institutional Approach/Model

This has traditionally been the standard approach to studying not just policy but also basic government activities in the political sphere. This approach suggests that the basis of public policy lies in the various institutions and organs of the State, such as legislature, executive, judiciary, political parties and so on. For a policy to assume shape as public policy, it has to be determined in an authoritative manner by some institution of the State. The institutions of the State not only give legitimacy to the public policies but are also responsible for their formulation, enforcement and implementation.

Thus, the institutional approach helps to bring out the basic relationship between public policy and institutions of the State. However, over time, this approach has come to be seen as somewhat simplistic. Subsequently, behavioural and rational-choice approaches to social sciences, as also the systems approach, have sought to provide a richer and more nuanced analysis of public policy. Now let us consider a couple of approaches to public policy, which have in common the view that public policy is formulated not entirely by the State that only has the general public interest in mind. These approaches suggest that certain sections of the society exert pressure on the State and try to influence the institutions in making policies, which would benefit these sections.

The Neo-Institutionalist Model

The neo-institutionalists, such as institutionalists, are concerned majorly with political institutions. However, they are more concerned about how different policy types (the ones that we discussed before – distributive, redistributive, regulatory, etc.) actually relate to the branches of government.

Group Model

This model asserts that special interest groups and lobbies heavily influence the determination of public policy. For example, in the making of economic policies, Chambers of Commerce or groups of rich farmers can try to influence policies. Now, there would be several groups in society, some of which may enter into *conflict* among each other. Thus sometimes, public policy is formulated as a resulting process or outcome of *balancing* of the conflicting interests of the various pressure groups. Of the conflicting interests, the *equilibrium position* is the formulation of policy.

Elite/Mass Model

This approach suggests that public policy largely reflects the preferences, choices and values of *small* elite, which is in a position to govern. This approach or theory suggests that the majority population is somewhat passive and most people are not so well informed as to be able to influence policy. Thus, the viewpoints and preferences of the elite get reflected in public policy. Public administrators merely carry out the policies, which have been formed by the influence of the elite. Thus, the channel of public policy is, in a manner of speaking, from the elites to the state agencies and thereupon trickling down to the masses. It means policy flows downwards from the elite to the masses.

The elite theory or model has some resemblance with group model, as *both* suggest that public policy is designed under the influence of a *subset* of the whole society. Both suggest that a section of society can influence the formulation of public policy that will have an impact on the whole of society. The basic difference *between* the two is that while group theory allows for the presence of several groups who jostle with each other for influence (the resulting policy is the balancing of the positions of these contending groups), elite theory suggests the presence of a single small and powerful elite that can influence policy and have it 'imposed' on the people at large.

Systems Approach

The systems approach draws a metaphor from information theory and uses terms such as inputs, outputs, feedback and sees the policy process as essentially cyclical. David Easton in his black box model has explained the relationship between the input and output in a political system, with focus on how the input gets transformed into output due to environmental factors. This approach begins by looking at the sphere or arena of the political setup, where public policy is made and calls it the political system. This is akin to the suppliers in the supply–demand model in economics. Thus, the political system consists of all the institutions, organs and agencies which make *authoritative* decisions in a society.

Decisions in the political sphere may be seen as *allocation of values*, akin to the allocation of resources in the economic sphere. These decisions are binding on society. The political system or the policy-making arena receives inputs from various sources. These *sources* can be people who are affected by the policies or who demand efficiency from policies, or these can emanate from the support (from various quarters) that the policies receive. Those political conditions and events that are *outside* the boundary of the political sphere are called the environment.

Also, individuals and groups make claims and demands on the policy makers. The policies or the authoritative value allocations may be called the output of the system. Here the systems approach suggests that there is a feedback from the demand side to the policy-making process. These lead to a modified policy making. Thus, policy making becomes a *cyclical* process. Policy is formulated, implemented and then readjusted and modified.

This model has been criticized on two grounds. Firstly, it is somewhat simplistic. The stages of policy formulation, implementation, feedback and then modification of the policy may not always take place in this simple *linear* manner. Secondly, while this approach mentions the various stages of formulation, feedback and modification, it does not fully explain how policy is exactly formulated in the sphere of the political system.

Output Approaches

Rational-Choice Approach

This approach considers the typical policy maker as a representative individual or agency. It investigates the functioning of this representative individual. The approach suggests that the policy-maker attempts to choose 'rationally' the optimal policy from among various policy alternatives. This approach does not inherently claim that individuals in the policy-making agency follow their own interests to the detriment of the agency. Rather, the rational-choice approach considers the decision-making agency as the rational decision maker. The rational-choice approach not just claims that decision makers are rational it also asserts that being rational leads to efficiency.

Policymakers ought to choose that policy, from among alternatives, the net benefit of which is greatest. Benefits and costs are, of course, to be suitably defined. Along with the choosing of efficient policies, the rational-choice approach is concerned with the method of devising efficient rules, which would lead to choosing efficiently an efficient policy programme from among a menu of possible policies. Rational choice is concerned with positive rather than normative aspects of policy making. Hence, this approach seeks to distinguish facts from values; the values being important to devise standards by which the chosen policies are to be evaluated.

Game Theoretic Approach

This approach is closely related to the rational-choice approach. This is why we have put it under the output approach. Like the rational choice, this approach suggests that rationality *underpins* the decision making by political actors but it does not consider individual decision makers in isolation. It understands that decision-making units (*policymakers in our discussion*) form decisions through interaction with other political actors. This understanding that political outcomes result from interdependent rational decisions by political actors is at the heart of the game theoretic approach. Each decision maker makes his or her decision independently. However, each is aware that the final outcome that results is due to the *interdependence* of the decisions of all. The game theoretic approach has been seen more as an *analytic* device to understand policymaking rather than as a practical guide for policymakers.

Incremental Approach

Incrementalism views public policy as an ongoing process, with new public policies only a minor modification of the previous policies. According to this view, largely associated with Charles Lindblom, policymakers do not change or drastically revise policies regularly. Instead, they merely tinker with existing policies, which in any case have legitimacy. As regular or big-scale revision would involve large costs in terms of time and money, policymakers settle for minor alterations in existing policies wherever possible.

Moreover, the consequences and outcomes of changing policies in a big way would be uncertain, and hence policymakers are reluctant to make the changes. Besides, existing policies have already had large investments made into them. These also induce reluctance in policy makers to change existing policies in a big way. Further, incrementalism is conducive to political stability, because small changes in policies lead to smaller disagreements.

Lindblom has used two concepts to explain actual policy process in government: (1) marginal incrementalism and (2) partisan mutual adjustment, with focus on feasibility and accommodation. Thus, incrementalism reduces conflicts. According to Lindblom, public policy makers are not totally efficient or rational, but rather they are pragmatic; they 'muddle through' (*known as the muddling-through approach to decision making*). When there is an absence of unanimous societal goals and values, incrementalism gives rise to practical and acceptable decisions.

Stream and Window Approach

This model was put forward by John Kingdon. This is a pertinent approach and is often referred to as the organized anarchy model. John F. Kingdon (cited in Henry, 2002) studied the agenda setting and policy making process using the theoretical construct concerning organized anarchies (a concept that was developed by Michael Cohen, James March and Johan Olsen in 1972). According to this model, a policy 'window' opens up when three 'streams' converge. The three streams are: (1) the policy problem stream, in which there is identification of the *policy problem*. This stream calls attention to a specific problem and demands a specific solution in terms of a new policy or changes to an existing policy; (2) the political stream, in which the identified policy problem is placed on the *agenda*. Here, different political institutions and agencies interact and bring the policy problem to the centre stage. These can be the legislature, political parties, etc., and (3) the policy stream, in which a policy is chosen for implementation from a *menu* of policies. It is a very significant approach as it follows the design used for making policies more often.

Process approaches	Output approaches
• Institutional	• Rational-choice
• Neo-institutional	• Incremental
• Group	• Game Theoretic
• Elite/Mass	• Stream and Window
• Systems	

A CRITICAL REVIEW OF APPROACHES TO PUBLIC POLICY

As mentioned earlier, some experts make a *different* type of classification of the approaches to public policy. According to these experts, the approaches can be broadly divided into two categories: the 'incrementalist' model and the 'rationalist' model. Several approaches/models such as the elite/mass, the group, the systems, the institutionalist, the neo-instititionalist and the organized anarchy fall within the incrementalist model. Unlike our exposition, according to this classification, the elite and the group models are *subsumed* under the incrementalist model.

In the rationalist model or approach, there is sometimes a gap between planning and implementation. In addition, rationalists do not take into account the proper role of an entrepreneur. Kingdon (cited in Henry, 2002) claims that the 'policy entrepreneur' is crucial for the policy process. Another criticism of the rational-choice model is that often its predictions are inaccurate. A final criticism is that real-life policymaking is very complex but the rational-choice approach makes it seem mechanical.

The incremental approach has also been criticized on several grounds. First, it has been alleged that 'muddling through' is not always an efficient way of decision making. Some critics have also argued that the incrementalist approach can be seen as a 'bargaining' concept. When resources are abundant, this model can lead to efficient outcomes, but when resources are scarce, incrementalism is *not* the most efficient of methods and other ways to allocate values and resources have to be devised. To quote Dror, 'such models become continually less useful for deciding what to do next, since *incremental* changes in them cannot produce significantly better results' (cited in Bhattacharya, 2001, p. 127).

Another criticism of incrementalism can be made using game theoretic concepts. By this view, incrementalism depends on the feedback from the claimants of policy and sometimes the 'players' in the 'bargaining game' hide their true preferences and can play 'strategically'. Since incrementalism *rejects* the rational-choice approach, many useful rational models are not made use of for an efficient policy process.

Incrementalists have also been criticized for being *short sighted* and lacking in imagination and vision. Critics believe that they *overplay* pragmatism and realism. This criticism is the opposite of what is levelled on the rational-choice approach, which is not seen to consider the complexities of real-life policymaking. A related criticism of incrementalism from social scientists is that it is *not* intellectual enough in its approach to policymaking. Finally, incrementalism is seen as conservative in its approach; by tinkering with small, incremental changes and by rejecting a liberal or radical approach to policy change.

Amitai Etzioni (1964) combines the elements of *both* rational comprehensive model and disjointed incrementalism. *Two* kinds of policy processes are identified by him. These are:

- Fundamental policymaking that sets basic directions.
- Allied incremental processes that prepare fundamental decisions and develop them further.

Etzioni's method is of *mixed scanning*. It provides for scanning the entire subject area in question very broadly and not in great detail and then concentrating on those revealed aspects that call for detailed scrutiny (cited in Bhattacharya, 2001, p. 127). Some weaknesses and deficiencies of the incrementalist and rationalist approaches have led some scholars to put forward the strategic planning paradigm, which blends economic and rational analyses, political values and psychology of participants in an organization.

THE STRATEGIC PLANNING APPROACH

The strategic planning approach developed as a response to the criticisms against the rational-choice approach and the incremental approach. It seeks to combine the strengths of the two approaches while avoiding their shortcomings. This approach first emerged in corporations and was adapted to the public policy process. Both firms and policymaking agencies were, after the World War II, becoming increasingly conscious of the need for strategic long-term planning. Of course, strategic planning in public policy agencies is different than in private firms. The strategic planning approach combines short-term activities with long-term planning.

The strategic planning is neither rigid in following blueprints of a collection of unrelated plans nor is it on the whims and fancies of the top executives of the policymaking agencies. It focuses on *rational calculative strategies*, but also takes into account important *intangibles*. It combines economic and political analyses and does not neglect the psychological factors as well. Strategic planning involves the formulation, development and communication of important policy goals and *blending* these with budgeting and 'management' systems. For the success of strategic planning approach, it is necessary that it is adopted at each level of government – national, state and local.

PUBLIC POLICY AND THE PUBLIC INTEREST

We have seen that public policy is a series of regular actions that is undertaken by the government for purposes of development, distribution, regulation, etc. The central, implicit assumption about any type of public policy is that public policy is always undertaken in the public interest. Notice that 'public' in public policy stands for the State, whereas 'public' in 'public interest' stands for the nation or community or the collectivity of citizens. Hence, we implicitly assume that the State is representative of the community and is also a *benevolent* one. So not only does the State have the best interests of the community in mind, it also is supposed to represent the community.

The important question is whether this is borne out in practice. In other words, does the State invariably make public policy in the public interest? Within the rational-choice approach to the making of public policy, the public choice approach *asserts* that public policy is after all made by officials, politicians and other political actors and functionaries. Just as rational businessmen aim to maximize their own profits or rational consumers aim to maximize their own satisfaction from consumption, there is no reason why individual politicians and functionaries will not maximize their own individual and personal interests.

There may be stray individual cases, where some political actor may try to make individual gains at the cost of the organization or the State, etc.; these are cases of corruption. To give an example, the State has a policy of imposing high tariffs and custom duties on imports and suppose a customs officer takes bribes and lets some people smuggle in expensive luxury goods at an airport, this is a case of corruption and falls under the rubric of moral hazard.

The public choice approach to public policy says that we should look at the State or the government as having its own interest, rather than the interest of the people. For example, politicians would like to maximize votes, bureaux would like to maximize budgets and so on. Thus, instead of thinking of policymakers as public-spirited actors seeking to maximize societal welfare, we should think of policymakers as displaying purposive behaviour, which maximizes utility. They take constraints into consideration while maximizing utility and respond to incentives and disincentives.

CONCLUSION

In this chapter, we have provided a basic discussion of public policy – its nature, significance and objectives. We have also discussed the types of public policy and described the various approaches to public policy. The central purpose of the chapter has been to stress the fact that if we want to understand the government in action, or administration in function, we have to understand public policy. The government has to have a framework for its activities and this framework is provided by public policy. It is very important to understand this framework, this scaffolding. We have to study the basis of its formulation – who makes it and for whom?

Does the whole society have its views and desires reflected in policy formulation or is there a benevolent authority that purports to act on the behalf of society without explicitly taking society's views directly into consideration? Moreover, does the State actually act on behalf of its citizens or are there powerful groups and elites who are more vocal and have the clout to have their voices heard more and hence are able to have policies designed in a manner to benefit them disproportionately?

This chapter has looked at this issue while discussing the various approaches to public policy. This issue also came up in the discussion on public policy in relation to the public interest. This section has discussed not merely the question of whether the State acts in the public interest but whether, for certain types of problems, collective action on part of the people can lead to a solution without requiring State action. As mentioned earlier, this chapter has *not* been concerned with the process of public policy – the *how* of it; it has only been concerned with the *what* of public policy. Chapter 17 in this volume deals with the formulation, implementation and evaluation of public policy.

Preparatory Questions

- Discuss the nature of public policy, underlining its features and characteristics.
- Examine the purpose and significance of public policy.
- Explain the process approaches to public policy.
- Describe the output approaches to public policy.
- 'The incrementalist approach is generally contrasted with the rational-choice approach'. Elucidate.
- Bring out the relationship between public policy and the public interest.

REFERENCES

Anderson, J. E. (1975) *Public Policy Making.* New York: Thomas Nelson and Sons Ltd.

Bhattacharya, M. (2001) *New Horizons of Public Administration*. New Delhi: Jawahar Publisher and Distributors.

Chakraborty, B. and Chand, P. (2012) *Public Administration in a Globalizing World.* New Delhi: Sage Publications.

Dror, Y. (1974) *Public Policy Making Reexamined.* San Francisco (CA): Leonardo Hill Books.

Dye, T. R (1978) *Understanding Public Policy*, Better World Books, US.

Etzioni, A. (1964) *Modern Organizations*. New Jersey: Prentice Hall.

Henry, N. (2002) *Public Administration and Public Affairs.* 6th ed. New Delhi: Prentice-Hall.

Parsons, Wayne (1995) 'Public Policy: Theory and Practice of Policy Analysis: An Introduction' in Edward Elgar, London, Cheltenham.

Singh, Amita, (2002) *Public Administration: Roots and Wings*, Galgotia, New Delhi.

Peters, B. Guy. (1996) *American Public Policy: Promise and Performance.* 4th ed. New Jersey: Chatham House.

Chapter Thirteen

New Public Administration

Uma Medury

Introduction

Landmarks in Emergence and Growth of New Public Administration

- Honey Report on Higher Education for Public Service
- Philadelphia Conference
- Minnowbrook Conference I
- Minnowbrook Conference II
- Minnowbrook Conference III

An Evaluation of New Public Administration

Conclusion

References

LEARNING OBJECTIVES

After completing this chapter, you should be able to:

- Trace the genesis and growth of New Public Administration
- Describe the outcome of First Minnowbrook Conference
- Discuss the goals and anti-goals of New Public Administration
- Explain the features of New Public Administration
- Analyse the deliberations of Second Minnowbrook Conference
- Identify the focus areas of Third Minnowbrook Conference; and
- Relate the relevance of New Public Administration to contemporary times

INTRODUCTION

The discipline and practice of public administration, since 1987, has undergone several changes. We know how the politics–administration dichotomy, propounded by Woodrow Wilson, slowly gave way to a gradual recognition of the science of management. F. W. Taylor's scientific management movement and Elton Mayo's Hawthorne experiments in the 1920s, subjected the structures and processes of public organizations to a critical analysis, bringing in the human side of organizations to the fore and discarding the cog in the machine concept. Gradually, during the post-war period, concepts such as informal organization, work group, team work, leadership and cooperation gained prominence. The importance of the human element in the organization came to be emphasized, especially by the protagonists of the Human Relations school. Later, Herbert Simon's *Administrative Behaviour,* in the 1940s, brought to the fore the significance of facts and values in the area of decision making and established the much-needed link between the means and ends.

However, by the end of the 1950s, it was realized that public administration was becoming vacuous. The scholars started making a clamour for bringing back values, ethics, relevance and accountability within the folds of public administration. This churning culminated in the new public administration (NPA) movement that brought together young scholars around the world under the dynamic leadership of Dwight Waldo. The influence of the 'NPA' movement was a turning point in the history of public administration, as it made way for rethinking and redesigning administrative objectives and processes. This chapter will try to examine the goals and anti-goals of the NPA approach to public administration. It will discuss all the major landmarks, especially the three Minnowbrook Conferences in strengthening the NPA movement. An attempt will also be made to study its relevance in the contemporary times.

LANDMARKS IN EMERGENCE AND GROWTH OF NEW PUBLIC ADMINISTRATION

The American society, by the end of the 1960s, was confronted with a number of problems. These included the Vietnam war, population explosion, environmental problems, social conflicts and economic crisis, which made the younger generation intellectuals question the efficacy and response of the political and administrative systems to these problems. Serious concerns were raised regarding efficiency and economy in administration. It was felt that the dissatisfaction arising from the persisting turbulent environment called for restoration of values and purpose in government. There was a demand to make administration more humane and value oriented.

There was a general concern to inject the goals of responsiveness and social equity in service delivery. This thinking led to the emergence of NPA. It intended to provide a philosophical outlook to public administration. It was, however, during 1967–1968 that various efforts were initiated in the US, with the aim of providing a multidisciplinary, public policy–centred and social equity-oriented focus to public administration.

The significant landmarks in this direction include the following:

- Honey Report on Higher Education for Public Service
- Philadelphia Conference on the Theory and Practice of Public Administration
- Minnowbrook Conference I
- Minnowbrook Conference II
- Minnowbrook Conference III

Honey Report on Higher Education for Public Service

The American Society of Public Administration (ASPA), for quite some time, was concerned about the growth of public administration as a discipline with a distinct identity and enlarging its scope in the curriculum offered by university departments. In 1966, John Honey of Syracuse University undertook an evaluation of public administration as a field of study in the US universities. His Report recommended generation of resources from government and business, encouraging higher studies in public administration, interlinking university departments and government through appointment of professors to positions in government and setting up of a *National Commission on Public Service Education* to provide leadership in the field. The Report, despite its shortcomings, laid the basis for examining the role of public administration in generating social awareness.

Certain problems confronting the discipline were highlighted and included the following:

- Uncertainty and confusion over the status of the discipline
- Inadequate funds at the disposal of the university departments for promotion of the discipline
- Institutional shortcomings
- Lack of communication between the scholars and practitioners of public administration

Philadelphia Conference

In 1967, with a view to examine the developments in the discipline, the American Academy of Political and Social Sciences under the chairmanship of James C. Charlesworth, organized a Conference on 'The Theory and Practice of Public Administration'. This Conference is considered quite significant, as it provided a broad philosophical basis to the discipline of public administration. The outcome was the convening of the Minnowbrook Conference of 1968.

The major viewpoints that emerged out of the Conference include the following:

- Promoting social equity and other values such as efficiency, accountability, administrative responsiveness and people's participation in decision making
- Excessive emphasis on adherence to other internal mechanisms increases hierarchy and administrative rigidity. Hence to enhance its efficacy, there is need for management flexibility and other innovation
- Training of administrators in professional schools
- Training programmes in public administration to sharpen not just managerial abilities and skills but deepen the social sensitivity of the trainees
- Emphasis on administrative ethics in the training programmes

Minnowbrook Conference I

The 1960s in the US was marked by an optimistic view about public administration's ability to solve the country's technological as well as social problems. The social atmosphere was characterized by a steady decline in the commitment of Americans to institutions such as family, church, media, profession and government. This was due to cynicism among the younger people towards the institutions. Besides, the African Americans were denied a share in the growing prosperity of the country in the 1950s and 1960s.

It was against this backdrop that in 1968, Dwight Waldo of Syracuse University took the initiative of *examining* certain key concerns. The idea was to analyse the changing perspectives in the field of public administration, from the perspective of those who experienced the Great Depression, New Deal, World War II and those who worked in the field in the 1960s. It was intended to examine the enduring effect of varying perspectives on public administration and government. This Conference was held at Minnowbrook by the young scholars of public administration under the guidance of Dwight Waldo. The basic objective of this was to examine the ways of making public administration responsive to social concerns and assume the role of a change agent in reforming the society. The NPA was the outcome of this Conference. The Minnowbrook Conference focussed on certain important concerns of public administration, which included the following:

- The public policy approach to public administration, which has become important as it has a significant effect on the quality of government.
- In addition, for efficiency and economy in implementation of policies, social equity needs to be a key objective.
- The earlier notion of public administrators being mere implementers of fixed decisions is no longer valid. In addition, values such as ethics, honesty and responsibility in the provision of public service holds good in the practice of public administration.
- As public needs change and government agencies often outlive their purpose, wherever needed, cutback of government agencies needs to be resorted to.
- Responsive government has to manage change, not just growth.
- Active and participative citizenry needs to be a part of public administration.
- The efficacy and usefulness of the concept of hierarchy have been challenged.
- Implementation has come to occupy a significant place in the decision-making process.
- Though pluralism is accepted as a useful device for explaining the exercise of public power, it has ceased to be the standard for the practice of public administration.

The young academics who participated in the Conference were sensitive to the problems in the functioning of American democracy. Hence, they attempted to provide a new focus to public administration. One forceful view was that 'the study of administration is just another expression for the study of politics'.

Thrust areas of Minnowbrook I included the following:

- Social equity as a key objective of public administration
- Values such as ethics, honesty and responsibility in the provision of public service
- Cutback of government agencies
- Responsive government
- Active and participative citizenry
- Accent on implementation

Goals of New Public Administration

The NPA scholars emphasized *six* major goals that public administration needs to take cognisance of, namely, relevance, values, social equity, change, participation and client orientation.

1. *Relevance*: Traditionally, efficiency and economy have been the key concerns of public administration. The discipline, the Conference felt, needed to be relevant to the contemporary issues and problems. The excessive management orientation in the discipline needed to be done away with and public administration had to deal with political and administrative implications of administrative action. The scholars desired radical changes in the curriculum of the discipline to make it more relevant to the realities of public life.
2. *Values*: The earlier view regarding the value-neutral orientation of public administration was vehemently criticized and rejected. The Conference made a plea for a greater concern with values, issues of justice, freedom, equality and human ethics. It was held that commitment to values would enable the discipline to promote the cause of the disadvantaged sections in society. According to Nicholas Henry (1975) 'The focus was disinclined to examine such traditional phenomena as efficiency, effectiveness, budgeting and administrative techniques, conversely the NPA was very much aware of normative theory, philosophy and activism. The question it raised dealt with values, ethics … "if there was an overriding tone to the NPA, it was a moral tone".
3. *Social equity*: The then prevailing social unrest in the society strengthened the belief that social equity needed to be the primary aspect of administration. The Conference made a plea for distributive justice and equity to be the basic concerns of public administration. George Frederickson (1989) considered that public administration which fails to work for changes to redress the deprivation of minorities is likely to be eventually used to repress the minorities. The NPA protagonists were in favour of making the discipline proactive towards major social issues.
4. *Change*: Public administration is generally considered to be status quo oriented. The Conference attempted to make the discipline more relevant and social equity oriented through change and innovation. The administrator was considered a change agent. Hence, the discipline needed to be receptive to change.
5. *Participation*: The Conference advocated greater participation by all employees in an organization in matters of public policy formulation, implementation and revision. In addition, participation from individuals and groups from outside the organization was sought to make public administration more responsive and client oriented.
6. *Client orientation*: The Conference took the lead in identifying client orientation as a key goal of public administration. This called for a change in the attitudes of bureaucrats to be people oriented. The Minnowbrook Conference made a significant contribution in changing the complexion of public administration by advocating client orientation, social sensitivity and normative concerns. The normative approach called on the government to adopt the objective of reducing the economic and social disparities and enhancing the life opportunities for everyone in the society.

Anti-Goals of New Public Administration

Robert Golembiewski (1977) identified the following three anti-goals or situations that the NPA needs to abandon:

1. *Anti-positivism*: Positivism implies absolute uncertainty about facts, which are not definite. This makes administration more rigid. The NPA movement intended to reduce the rigidities in administration to make it more adaptable, receptive and problem solving.

2. *Anti-technology*: This implies human beings are not to be treated as cogs in the machine to foster the traditional goals of economy and efficiency.
3. *Anti-hierarchy*: Hierarchy as an organizational principle promotes bureaucracy, brings in rigidities, kills creativity and innovation and isolates the administrator from the surrounding environment. Hence, the NPA scholars condemned hierarchical structures as traditionally propagated by public administration.

Goals of NPA	Anti-goals of NPA
Relevance	Anti-positivism
Values	Anti-technology
Social equity	Anti-hierarchy
Change	
Participation	
Client orientation	

Features of New Public Administration

George Fredericksson(1989) has referred to certain *key features* of NPA and these are:

- *Change and responsiveness*: There is change all over in the social, political, economic and technological environment. This calls for administration to bring about necessary and appropriate changes both internally and externally to the environment. Necessary *flexibility* and *adaptability* also need to be introduced in the functioning of administration.
- *Rationality*: This implies judging the efficacy of administrators' actions not only from the point of view of the government but also from the citizens' perspective.
- *Structural changes*: NPA calls for experimenting with different organizational structures in tune with the relevant situation and needs of environment. There is need for small, decentralized, flexible hierarchies to facilitate citizens' interaction.
- *Emphasis on a multidisciplinary perspective*: Public administration is influenced not just by one single thought but several knowledge streams. Hence, an understanding of various approaches including political, management, human relations is essential to contribute to its growth.

NPA focussed on the prevailing societal problems and the need to make the theory and practice of public administration more relevant to the society. It made a case for abandoning value-free and value-neutral research and embarking upon an approach that emphasizes social equity, ethics, citizens' participation, change and rationality.

Minnowbrook Conference II

The second Minnowbrook Conference held on 4 September 1988, after a gap of 20 years since the first one, was attended by 68 scholars and practitioners of public administration and other disciplines such as history, economics, political science, psychology and so on. It was sponsored by the Universities of Syracuse, Kansas and Akron. It was held against the backdrop of the changing role of State and government, privatization, contracting out and involvement of non-state actors in the governance process.

The first Minnowbrook Conference held in the 1960s, as we mentioned earlier, was a period characterized by influence of public purpose, the Vietnam war, urban riots and campus unrest accompanied by growing cynicism towards all institutions, especially the government. However, the scenario in the 1980s was entirely different, as this was the time of domination of philosophy of privatization and a concern for private interest. Minnowbrook II aimed to compare and correct the changing epochs of public administration. This was attempted through a comparison of theoretical and research perspectives of the 1960s with that of the 1980s, and their respective influences on the conduct of governmental and other public affairs.

Since 1968, there was a sea change in the context of American public administration. Due to change in the nature of State, emphasis on governance, privatization and contracting out, a general preference was observed among the American public towards lesser role of government. New and improved methods of government responsiveness were inadequate at that time. Added to this were increased levels of poverty and unemployment, especially among urban areas. The discipline of public administration underwent significant changes during this phase. Its field expanded since 1960s, with many universities in the US offering programmes in public administration. In addition, it became more interdisciplinary in nature compared with the times when it was a part of political science.

The Conference, which drew participants from diverse areas such as policy sciences, economics, planning and urban studies attempted to deliberate upon wider themes such as ethics, social equity, human relations and so on, thereby ensuring continuity in intellectual interests. Due to the changing scenario, some new thrust areas such as leadership, technology, policy, legal and economic perspectives also found place in the deliberations. The Conference reiterated the necessity of government as a tool for strengthening society. Public administration, in the changing scenario, was to renew its capacity to cope with the problems of emerging future. The need to strengthen and establish linkages between the theory and practice of public administration on the one hand and amongst scholars and administrators and other officials, on the other hand, was emphasized.

Eleven themes emerged out of the deliberations of Minnowbrook II. The first five themes provided a historical perspective, which aimed at comparing the discussion at Minnowbrook II with the legacy of Minnowbrook I. The last six themes focussed on the current and future visions of the discipline. These themes were as follows:

1. Though social equity was a predominant theme at Minnowbrook I, it was felt that in the present times, it is much closer to *reality* than it was in 1968.
2. Strong concerns were expressed about *democratic values* and the centrality of public administration in promoting them. The concern was manifest in the focus on ethics, accountability and leadership in public administration.
3. The debate between the *normative and behaviourist* perspectives was reinforced.
4. Diversity in society and in the workforce was accepted as a basic value among the participants. *Diversity* was identified in three main contexts: the issue of generalists versus specialists; racial, ethnic and sexual diversity; and gender diversity. However, not much attention was given towards the reality that heterogeneity brings and also on the conflict resolution strategies, arbitration skills and values clarification.
5. The radical reforms that emerged from the discussions in the Conference were considered to be in the nature of *short-term goals*. It was felt that the environment in which public administration must perform is so complex that a meaningful long-term vision is neither reasonable nor perhaps even possible.
6. The discussions gave an impression of the prevalence of 'a professional ethnocentricity' or parochialism indicating that public administration, as a field, is not much concerned with examining interdisciplinary issues.

7. There was a strong *negative attitude towards business* as an enterprise. The deliberations exhibited a condescending acceptance of capitalism and business.
8. One of the challenges to public administration, it was felt, was to *manage the* 'seams' of society, than building on the best that business as well as public sector offer.
9. Impatience was exhibited with the constraints of public personnel systems. A need was felt for *innovative personnel practices*, to bring out the best in the employees and reinforce high productivity.
10. Unwillingness to address technological issues was evident, though some areas such as *artificial intelligence*, design science, expert systems formed part of some of the themes.
11. Unwillingness to look at the specifics of what government should do was evident. Despite the discussions focussing on the inevitability of administrators exerting control over policy agendas, the *politics–administration dichotomy* was still alive (Guy, 1989).

Themes included in Minnowbrook II deliberations were as follows:

- Emphasis on social equity
- Stress on democratic values of ethics, accountability and leadership
- Accommodating diversity in society
- Promoting professional ethnocentricity
- Condescending acceptance of capitalism
- Focus on innovative personnel practices
- Recognition of technological issues such as artificial intelligence and design science
- Inadvertent reinforcement of politics–administration dichotomy

The deliberations of Minnowbrook II Conference highlighted certain key concerns. The first was the changing nature of American public administration, the diversity in the problems faced by the government such as AIDS, nuclear waste, budget, trade deficits and so on. Hence, the environment within which the administrator worked had become substantially more complex than it used to be, and this made it essential for them to rely much more on facilitation, dialogue and negotiation. The schools teaching public administration had a key role in this context. The curricula needed to be revised with a view towards highlighting the societal as well as political context, and emphasizing interpersonal skills and techniques. Thus, the Conference made a strong case for *developing a theory* of public administration.

A second proposition emphasized the need for administrators to keep in view the requirements of democracy and employ democratic process-based methodologies in the performance of their duties. This was felt necessary due to (1) need for positive action by public officials for the fulfilment of its potential by the representative government and (2) underlying obligation to advance democracy, which was an ethical requirement of public service.

A major thrust at Minnowbrook II was on altering the imbalance between the public needs in the present times and the resources devoted to their amelioration. To maximize the value of the administrator's role in these situations, it was felt that a bureaucracy that is concerned more with dialogue and consensus was required. In the backdrop of the American system of government, the bureaucracy needed to utilize the democratic methodologies in its work. Hence, it was emphasized that practising public administrators needed to be more proactive in the performance of their duties. In addition, openness and public participation in administration needed to be encouraged. Resonating the concerns underlined by Mary Ellen Guy on Minnowbrook II, Mohit Bhattacharya (2001) observed that the distinctive character of Minnowbrook II is evident from its emphasis on certain thrust areas such as these:

- It set its vision to the near future, without trying to be radical. There was a tacit acceptance of the fact that the environment of public administration is exceedingly complex and the problems are of huge proportions. Hence, a meaningful long-term vision is neither reasonable nor feasible.
- The scholars in the discipline, being aware of their indebtedness to other disciplines, exhibited a strong sense of intellectual parochialism. The general model was not to lose disciplinary identity; rather, there was keenness to rebuild the discipline.
- Even if 'privatization' was accepted tacitly, there was a strong negative attitude towards business. The Minnowbrook II worldview was expressed in terms of a curious tension between capitalism and democracy that resulted in 'an unusual form of a truncated capitalist economy operating within a truncated democracy'. Against this backdrop, public administration has to rely on the best that business offers as well as the best that the non-profit public sector offers.
- Public personnel practices came in for closer scrutiny and the discussions underlined the need for innovative personnel practices in order to move away from public managers' current inability to hire employees on a timely basis, promote the best employees and reinforce high productivity.
- The participants had been generally unwilling to deal with the technological issues. 'Technology was faulted more than vaunted' it was said. There was general reluctance to idolize technology as a necessary tool for improving public policy.
- The specifics of what government should do were avoided.

The second Minnowbrook Conference made an attempt to examine the theory and practice of public administration in the changing scenario. It tried to project a future vision for public administration by balancing the business and public sector. The effort has been on rebuilding the discipline and not to lose its identity. It reiterated the significance of core values of public service with better-trained practitioners and a more positive image of the public service.

Minnowbrook Conference III

The third Minnowbrook Conference, attended by nearly 200 participants was held at Syracuse University in September 2008. It was more diverse and internationally representative. The Conference deliberated on *The Future of Public Administration, Public Management and Public Service.* It was held in two phases. The phase one of the Conference focussed on focal areas which included academic–practitioner relations; collaborative governance; democratic performance management; information technology and management; law, politics and public administration; networks; leadership; public administration values and theory and so on. The phase two of the Conference involved presentations relating to the identified focal areas of concern. The most prevalent and important issue addressed at the Minnowbrook III was the impact of globalization on public administration.

The outcomes of both the phases of Minnowbrook III involved analyses of the current state and future of public administration. The deliberations highlighted concrete examples concerning how public administration research and practice have responded and continue to respond to the challenges of globalization. The participants recognized the need to evaluate what works and what does not, before offering broad untested theories and recommendations. The future of the discipline, it was felt, laid in a more global approach towards examining the institutions and the work of public administrators. The insights and analyses presented by the scholars emphasized the need to engage in *critical* dialogue on issues concerning the development of rigorous research methods for comparative studies with a global perspective.

The most prevalent and important issue addressed at the Minnowbrook III was the impact of globalization on public administration, and this was related to the following:

- Comparative public administration research and practice
- Public policy research
- Role of international organizations in governance
- New forms of governance
- Methods of action research
- Reformulation of public administration as a socially embedded process

AN EVALUATION OF NEW PUBLIC ADMINISTRATION

NPA had a significant impact on the discipline and profession of public administration. In all the Conferences, an attempt was made to relate public administration with the prevailing socioeconomic scenario and the dominant philosophical concerns of the times. The second Minnowbrook Conference was held in a changed scenario, especially in context of American public administration. It was marked by cynicism towards big government and increasing public preference for less government. The State had undergone a change in nature from welfare to regulatory State. It came to be characterized by more privatization, outsourcing and predominance of private over public purpose values. In addition, a change in the nature of the discipline of public administration was being witnessed. The field, which was an *integral* part of the political science in the 1960s, had become more multidisciplinary, analytical and theoretically developed.

There were variations in the mood and tone of the three Conferences. While the 1968 Conference was contentious, confrontational and revolutionary, the 1988 Conference was more civil and practical. The 1968 dialogue was considered anti-behavioural, whereas that of the 1988 Conference was more receptive to the contributions of behavioural science to public administration. Minnowbrook Conference I, intended to redefine public administration by the then prevailing socio-political and economic scenario. During the intervening period of nearly 20 years, when the second Conference was held, the environmental setting of public administration had undergone a sea change. People's confidence in public administration, especially the bureaucracy, had decreased considerably. Managerialism and privatization had gained a respectable place on the agenda of public administration scholars. Yet, there was also a marked sense of confidence in public organizations for tackling societal problems.

The Conference of 1988, according to Marc Holzer (2011), sketched two arguments for public administration as a challenging pursuit. First was the citizen seeking a renewed sense of community and shared endeavour, emphasizing interpersonal values and de-emphasizing personal gains; and the second was to look at public administrators as an important link in the social system, since government was an inevitable tool for strengthening society. Hence, this involved adherence to two key measures; firstly, to establish a linkage between theory and practice and between public administrators and other government officials. To facilitate this, the schools of public administration need to build the theoretical capacities of the practitioners of public administration by providing a number of educational programmes and enriching communication through new techniques.

Secondly, public administration must be amenable to radical reforms. To build equitable, sensitive, open and productive organizations, some key concepts require attention, which include competitiveness not only between the sectors but also between public sector organizations, compensation systems, improved capacities, changes in recruitment practices and management–employee relations. Some scholars have opined that the NPA is nothing new except that it made a plea for making administration *responsive* to societal problems prevalent during that period. Besides, doubts were expressed whether the new thinking would sustain for long. In addition, according to Frederickson (1989), while both the Conferences were theoretical, the original one's overall perspective was decidedly 'anti-behavioural', whereas the latter was more 'receptive to contributions of behavioural science to public administration'.

NPA made a moderate impact by redefining public administration with its emphasis on key concepts such as participation, responsiveness, client orientation and so on. An attempt was made to bring administration closer to people and strengthen its capacities to solve societal problems. It stirred intellectual thinking towards democratizing public administration and building a theory of public administration in tune with its interdisciplinary nature, thereby attempting to reform public administration in its *outlook* and *functioning*.

CONCLUSION

The NPA that evolved in 1960s in the aftermath of the first Minnowbrook Conference gave primacy to key concerns that had relevance during those times. They included social equity, policy issues, change, participative citizenry and so on. The development that occurred in the 20 years since Minnowbrook I in the form of regulatory State, less government, more governance and privatization reflected public's cynicism towards government in tune with the changes in economy, technology and employment. The NPA movement had a significant influence in the process of evolution of public administration. Minnowbrook Conference I reiterated the need for a proactive public administration with regard to social issues, whereas Minnowbrook II focussed on ethics, democracy, philosophy and so on. Minnowbrook III, in step with the developments in the present times, made a strong plea to uphold and shape the culture of public administration, a culture that is open minded to and appreciative of multiple theoretical and methodological perspectives, with an emphasis on 'publicness'.

The NPA movement, thus, gave predominance to social equity, justice, responsiveness, public participation, goal orientation and so on. The emergence of new themes such as new public management, reinventing movement, good governance, new public service, public value creation and so on can be considered as antithetical reflections of the post-Minnowbrook Conferences. The process would continue, giving rise to new perspectives in the years to come, which may very well form the agenda for the fourth Minnowbrook Conference in 2028.

Preparatory Questions

- Examine the problems confronting the discipline of public administration as indicated by the Honey Report on Higher Education for Public Service.
- Bring out the major viewpoints that emerged out of the Philadelphia Conference.
- 'The first Minnowbrook Conference focussed on certain important concerns of public administration'. Elaborate.
- Discuss the goals of NPA.
- Explain the features of NPA.
- Describe the thrust areas that emerged out of the second Minnowbrook Conference.
- What were the focus areas of third Minnowbrook Conference?

REFERENCES

Bailey, M. T. (1989) 'Minnowbrook II: An End or a New Beginning.' *Public Administration Review.* March–April.
Bhattacharya, M. (2001) *New Horizons of Public Administration*. New Delhi: Jawahar Publishers.
Frederickson, G. H. (1989) 'Minnowbrook II: Changing epochs of Public Administration.' *Public Administration Review.* March–April.
Golembiwski, R. (1977), *Public Administration as a Developing Discipline*, New York, CRC Press.
Guy, M. E. (1989) 'Minnowbrook II Conclusions.' *Public Administration Review.* March–April.
Henry N. (1975) *Public Administration and Public Affairs.* New york: Prentice Hall.
Holzer, M. and Richard W. S. (2011) *Public Administration*. New York: M.E Sharpe.
Marini, F. (ed.) (1971) *Toward a New Public Administration.* Scranton (PA): Chandler.
Sahni, P. and Etakula V. (2010) *Administrative Theory.* New Delhi: PHI Learning Private Limited.

Chapter Fourteen

Concept of New Public Management

Uma Medury

LEARNING OBJECTIVES

After completing this chapter, you should be able to:

- Bring out the stages in the evolution of new public management
- Provide a conceptual framework of new public management
- Distinguish new public management from traditional public administration
- Explain Osborne and Gaebler's Reinventing Government Model; and
- Analyse the efficacy of the concept of new public management in the contemporary scenario

INTRODUCTION

Contemporary public administration is very different from what it used to be a decade ago. We are witnessing a substantial transformation in the political, social, economic and cultural spheres across the world. This, to a large extent, is due to the impact of liberalization, privatization and globalization (LPG), which has resulted in the spread of global culture characterized by global corporates, global mass media and communication technologies.

A host of factors including the development of information technology, telecommunications, computing, liberalization of trade, deregulation of financial and banking systems, and growth of transnational corporations and so on has given impetus to globalization. As a consequence, there has been a formidable spread of goods, services, technology, processes and practices across the globe. It has also led to new societal expectations and changing value systems that are altering the nature of the State and governing systems.

Globalization is affecting the public administrative system, as it is *embedded* in the framework of the State. The pressures exerted by global institutions are also immense. The aid provided by these institutions, especially to those in developing countries, has wider repercussions, as it increases the dependency (*financial, military and political*) of developing countries in the West. The developments also render the people, in these countries, without a choice; making them unable to determine their own priorities and policy preferences. The structural adjustment (SA) strategies, pursued by many of these countries, have been considered a negation of local democracy and effective governance.

Globalization, propagating economic integration and technological changes, is pushing the 'State' towards adhering to certain global standards and behaviour. On the one hand, a new paradigm called the new public management (NPM) has emerged as a result of the structural adjustment programme (SAP), followed by the UK and US to make their administration efficient and effective. Simultaneously, on the other hand, the internal social and political pressures are attempting to assert that the role of the State and its powers in protecting the interests of the governed needs to be strengthened.

The State is undergoing a transformative role and as a corollary, its impact on public administration is also multi-dimensional. This chapter will try to explain the changing role of State and public administration in the LPG context. It will examine the genesis of NPM as a new administrative model, and also critically evaluate its relevance and characteristics.

CHANGING ROLE OF THE STATE

The State has always been at the centre stage of governance. Traditionally, many countries embarked on the concept of welfare State – a political system with high degree of responsibility for the welfare of the population. The spread of globalization and its influence on various fronts in the 1980s and 1990s brought out significant transformation in this role of the State. The impact of international economic forces has changed the complexion of State, transforming it into a 'competition State' that favours deregulation, privatization, irrespective of the local political and administrative cultures.

A powerful new paradigm of limiting government action that was dominant in the western democracies held the view that government should:

- do less
- reduce or relinquish their previous overburdening responsibilities
- privatize public services or their delivery wherever practicable
- cut down expenditure
- reform their own operations in accordance with the market concepts of competition and efficiency

The belief in 'government by the market' rests upon the proposition that the market system is inherently a better method of satisfying human wants and aspirations than recourse to government. The first objective of this thinking was to slim the State and liberate the market forces in a variety of ways such as *deregulation* as well as through suitable monetary and fiscal policies. The second objective was to import *market* concepts and *incentives* into the operations of the government itself. The third objective was to take measures to *reduce* the relative size and growth of public *expenditure* and to cut down a range of functions performed by the government. The changing complexion of the State also brought in new structures and features. A pro-market and anti-state philosophy of 'private good' and 'public bad' came to prevail during 1980s and 1990s in the UK and US. It saw the rise of a new central actor, that is, the NPM.

EVOLUTION OF NEW PUBLIC MANAGEMENT

Public administration, traditionally speaking, has always had a major obligation towards promoting public interest, assuring equity, representativeness and responsiveness to the citizens. However, its excessive reliance on bureaucracy, hierarchy, rules and regulations, in course of time, put a question mark on its efficacy and effectiveness. This coupled with the dismantling of Soviet Union, increasing levels of public expenditure and taxation, and dissatisfaction with the functioning of bureaucracy strengthened the notion that the 'traditional' State model had failed to implement appropriate policies and deliver effective services. Thus, a need for an *alternative* model was strongly felt. This model, with stress on political economy of development based on 'market' instead of the 'State' as the managerial orientation, was termed as NPM.

NPM aims at making public administration market-based, committed to the three prime goals of Economy, Efficiency and Effectiveness (3 E's). NPM denounces the traditional public administration as a failure. It starts with the premise that the traditional, bureaucratically organized public administration is 'broke' and 'broken' and consequently the public has lost faith in government (Al Gore, 1993).Thus, the orthodox public administration has found a new reform replacement in the form of NPM, which has stirred intellectual debates and discussions during 1980s. The complexities and intricacies of the traditional model of public administration have paved the way for a new thinking that focuses on the following:

- The present changing scenario, which needs government reforms
- The public organizations that need to undergo a change in mindset from mere execution of tasks to performance orientation
- The need for risk-taking, mission-oriented and service-oriented public organizations

NPM has thus emerged as a major manifestation of competition State approach. This new paradigm, which gained wider usage, with varied labels – reinventing, reengineering, quality management and performance management, focuses basically on changes in the structure and processes of government. The hierarchy laden, rigidly structured and inflexible Weberian bureaucracy has given way to flexible organizational structure, decentralization, goal achievement, efficiency and effectiveness. Managerial improvements aimed at ushering in business management techniques and market mechanisms, competition and client orientation have begun to gain prominence, under the rubric of 'NPM'.

Evolution of NPM: key factors

- Increasing public expenditure
- Wastage, inordinate delays, mismanagement coupled with corruption, inefficiencies in various governmental operations
- Gradual managerial reforms
- Epistemological developments in the areas of public choice, principal–agent and transaction-cost approaches
- Lack of accountability
- General perception among citizens, of being remote from the decisions taken by the government

Even though NPM has been an outcome of a systematic and phased process of managerial reforms in public administration, certain theories or approaches such as the New Right and Public Choice have also strongly influenced it. This is, to a large extent, due to the influence of neo-institutional economics that attempted to apply market framework to institutions and organizations.

THE IMPACT OF NEW RIGHT PHILOSOPHY

The New Right, since the 1950s, attacked the welfare State and the social programmes. It propagated the cause of free markets as effective social market economy with privatization of social security system, replacing government subsidies towards education, public housing through loans and cash grants. The traditional welfare State supposedly served the interests of middle class, whereas this model was said to promote economic interests of the poor.

The proponents of New Right have observed the following:

- Markets are efficient than any other method of allocation and what could be left to the market should be left to them
- All motivations are selfish, so managers should not be allowed to make big decisions on budgets or services because they will only serve their own interests and not those of the people who they should serve
- Workers' motivations are the same and they should therefore be tightly controlled
- Self-reliance is better than other dependency, and therefore the State should do as little as possible

The New Right ideas of restricting the scope of government were propagated because the government was considered an ineffective mechanism to realize the goal of welfarism. Freidrich von

Hayek, Robert Nozick and Milton Friedman rejected the basic idea of government intervention in the economy. The group of influential neoliberal economists criticized 'big' government and was of the opinion that only free markets could put together the incongruent elements in a society.

The period during mid-1970s witnessed a favourable climate towards policies, aimed at reducing the size of the government. The influence of economic thinking was quite visible, as evident from the views put forth by conservative market economists such as Hayek and Friedman. The public choice theory (PCT) proponents such as Gordon Tullock, William Niskanen, James Buchanan and Patrick Dunleavy assumed prominence, with their propositions on the reduction of government and bureaucracy, reliance on market structures with flexible structure and incentives, reduced the role for public sector and restricted it to provision of bare minimum functions. This gave a theoretical foundation to bureaucrat bashing, reduction of government activities and designing market-based public policies. Let us now look at the approaches under New Right philosophy, which have impacted NPM.

Public Choice Approach

Public choice is considered to be an *application* of the theory of economics to understand politics. In the US and Britain, during 1940s, various writings attempted to apply economic methodology to the study of political processes and institutions. Public choice attempts to explain and predict political behaviour on the assumption that an individual is a utility maximizer. Public choice methodology basically comprises of two related elements (as you have already read in chapter 7 on Rational Choice Approach in this volume).The First is methodological individualism that considers individual instead of society as the unit of analysis. This approach does not take cognizance of the organic view of the society. The second element is application of rational choice in taking decisions from an 'individual gain maximizing' perspective rather than from public interest view.

The basic premises of the PCT are that the individuals are utility maximizers, whereas politicians are vote-maximizers and bureaucrats are *self-aggrandizing and budget maximizers*. Government tends to function not in the interests of public, as it expands to meet the preferences, interests of politicians, bureaucrats and other interest groups. PCT assumes individuals as egoistic, self-regarding and those who seek maximum possible benefits or personal gains from the decisions they take involving least costs. Their choice of decisions to a great extent depends on the consequences ensuing from the decisions.

Public choice theorists make the assumption that individuals, be the voters, politicians, bureaucrats and lobbyists are guided by 'self-interest'. The absence of appropriate rewards and incentives in public sector is said to demotivate the bureaucracy and politicians to a large extent. This often results in bureaucrats not showing any inclination to reduce costs, and regulate expenditure, thereby leading to inflated budgets.

The PCT proponents, guided by the notion of promotion of selfish interests, do not take cognizance of concepts such as public interest, public spirit and public service. They give primacy to market forces and arrogate a minimal role for government. Markets are considered to be more accountable than bureaucracy and importance is given to privatization, outsourcing of services and contracting, to free the State from fiscal burden and lessen the dependence on public provision of services.

A more sophisticated public choice model of bureaucracy has been developed by Patrick Dunleavy referred to as 'bureau shaping' model. This model refutes the earlier thinking that bureaucrats attempt to maximize budgets. On the contrary, it says that apart from them managing a large organization, bureaucrats tend to maximize their status by rendering advice to the politicians.

Principal-Agent Approach

Traditionally, economics has focussed on voluntary exchange among consenting parties, which can be individuals, organizations or even nations. The information available with different parties such as buyers and sellers about the features of transactions in a 'contract' or exchange is varying. The analysis of such situations of asymmetric or imperfect or incomplete information and situations of repeated transactions or relationships among economic agents has come to be known as economics of information. Within this format lies the principal-agent approach.

The principal-agent approach attempts to understand the *dynamics* of the relationship between the 'principal' and the employee or the 'agent'. The agent is said not to act in the best interests of the principal, especially in a situation where the employee has the advantage of possessing information and has diverse interests compared with the principal. The approach is based on the premise that there are two persons involved in provision of a service and they are not on an equal standing in legal terms. The party who is engaging the other is called the 'principal' and the party that is getting engaged is called the 'agent'. These two are involved in provision of a service, but are not on par in legal terms. This approach basically focuses on the issues that arise when the agent carries on the work on behalf of the principal and promises to deliver the services mutually agreed upon by both the parties.

The relationship between the principal and agent is said to be perfect when there is free flow of information and the principal is able to monitor the performance of the agent and design a set of sanctions and incentives. However due to lack of information, some problems of monitoring are likely to arise. An effective contract between the principal and agent needs distribution of risks between the two in an efficient and mutually acceptable manner.

Transaction-Cost Approach

The other key economic approach, which has had some influence on the current managerial changes, is transaction-cost approach. 'Transactions' include those costs that are incurred in the process of execution of transactions where there is exchange of goods and services involving payments for the performance. Transaction-cost approach outlines the need to compare the transaction costs of internal and external provision of services and then determine the necessity of outsourcing. The chief proponent of this approach is John Williamson.

In an extensive work, Williamson and Ouchi (2003) argue that the make or buy decisions should be determined by the comparison of transaction costs of internal versus external provision. According to Williamson, the firms work towards minimizing the costs of transactions, as this is essential for their efficiency and profitability. This framework is useful for evaluating the efficiency of alternate governance structures and institutional arrangements.

The application of transaction-cost framework enables the governments to minimize problems arising out of contracting. It helps in choosing the contractors, contract design and specifications determining the quantity and quality of services. The contracting process can be suitably reviewed and restructured to derive benefits of contracting and reduce the opportunistic tendencies of contractors.

NPM attempts to emphasize efficiency and uses contracts as important institutional variants in public service delivery. These models help in assessing the efficacy of use of alternate institutional arrangements, comprehending the inherent dilemmas and intricacies involved in contractual relationships and balancing the efficiency and accountability aspects of contracts.

The neoliberal ideas gained prominence because of the economic crises in the West, which followed the massive increase in oil prices in the 1970s. In 1976, the UK went ahead with the structural adjustment programme (SAP). It borrowed loan from the International Monetary Fund and had to introduce divestiture of public enterprises, public expenditure cuts and so on. Gradually, other countries followed suit. It was increasingly felt that the poverty and economic stagnation, especially in the developing countries was the result of State undermining the operation of market forces. The need for structural adjustment and reduced role of State in economic development was considered indispensable.

This led to the emergence of Washington Consensus. It basically comprised the reform measures promoted by Bretton Woods institutions, US Congress and Treasury and several think tanks, which aimed to address the economic crises, especially by Latin American countries in the 1980s. This was also termed as structural adjustment and stabilization programme. It emphasized the need for sound macro-economical and financial policies, trade and financial liberalization, privatization and deregulation of domestic markets. Gradually, this became integrated with the neoliberal policies of NPM, which emerged out of an *interplay* of several reasons – attempts to provide a mix of policy and administrative solutions. It affirms the strong feeling of several scholars and practitioners that government has to bring reform through adoption of business practices and procedures.

A *conglomeration* of managerial and economics-based precepts, techniques and practices, NPM assumed a form of administrative improvement suited to each country. In the process, it resulted in a myriad of organizational and structural changes globally. It encompassed several policy areas such as education, health and communication, making a huge impact on the complexion of the discipline and practice of public administration.

The Washington Consensus prescribed by John Williamson advocates the following measures:

- Free trade
- Capital market liberalization
- Flexible exchange rates
- Market-determined interest rates
- Deregulation of markets
- Transfer of assets from the public to the private sector
- Public expenditure on well-directional social targets
- Balanced budgets
- Tax reforms
- Property rights
- Protection of intellectual property rights (Held, et al., 2005)

CONCEPTUAL FRAMEWORK OF NEW PUBLIC MANAGEMENT

The NPM doctrine termed by Christopher Hood (1991) and labelled in various terms such as managerialism (Pollitt, 1995), market-based approach to public administration (Lan and Rosenbloom, 1992), entrepreneurial/reinventing government (Osborne and Gaebler, 1992) and post-bureaucratic paradigm (Barzelay, 1993) is marked by certain distinct features.

The features of NPM are as follows:

- Productivity: gaining more services from lesser revenues
- Marketization: Replacing traditional bureaucratic structures, mechanisms and processes with market strategies
- Service orientation: Keeping the needs of customers as a priority
- Decentralization: Transferring service delivery responsibilities to lower levels and local governments
- Distinguishing policy from execution
- Accountability for results, focussing on outputs and outcomes, instead of processes and structures

NPM broadly exhibits the following distinct characteristics:

- Complementing managerial along with policy-making skills.
- Disaggregating public organizations into separate self-contained units having their own goals, plans and requisite autonomy.
- Adopting private sector managerial practices by the public sector.
- Setting explicit measurable performance standards for public organizations.
- Controlling the performance of public organizations by pre-determined output measures.
- Contracting out, private ownership and competition in public service provision.
- Promoting competition among public sector organizations and public and private sectors.
- Making services more responsive to the needs of the customer and ensuring value for money.
- Using information technology to facilitate better service delivery.
- Focussing on achieving results rather than primarily conforming to processes.
- Introducing market principles, such as competition, and contracting out in the provision of goods and services.
- Making public administration customer driven to enhance service ethic and efficiency.
- Assigning the role of steering activities to the government rather than rowing, relying on third parties such as non-profit organizations and other levels of government in implementation of policies.
- Deregulating the government activities to make it result oriented.
- Empowering the employees to serve the customers as it promotes team work.
- Changing the overall public administration culture towards flexibility, innovation, entrepreneurship, enterprising as 'opposed to' rule bound, process orientation and focussing on inputs rather than results (*paraphrased*).

The NPM perspective has certain key components, which are as follows:

- Disaggregation of units in the public sector
- Increased managerial autonomy and efficiency with reduction of central agency controls
- Simplification of organizational structures, flattening of hierarchies and creating conditions for more positive and productive managerial leadership
- Private sector styles of managerial practices
- Rigorous performance measurement of individuals and organizations
- Ensuring transparency in budgetary transactions and determining the costs of inputs and outputs

A prominent issue is whether NPM is a distinct *variant* of public administration or are there some points of commonality between the two. There exists an academic debate on claiming NPM to be a dynamic new approach *without* sacrificing the best of the old values. It has been expressed that on the intellectual front, NPM, like traditional public administration borrows ideas from business management, and has been influenced by writings of Taylor, Fayol, Gulick and so on. Besides, both are said to share a *common* core of specialized areas such as organization theory, decision theory, financial management, systems analysis, economics and sociology. While public administration is based much more on political science and law, NPM draws heavily from economics and business administration. Since there are some core values in public organizations in contrast to other organizations, a closer look reflects these concerns as indicated in the following section.

NEW PUBLIC MANAGEMENT AND TRADITIONAL PUBLIC ADMINISTRATION

Components	NPM	Traditional public administration
Focus	Clients	Citizens and communities
Principal means	Management	Policy making
Characteristics of public servants	Entrepreneur (acting)	Analyst (thinking)
Values	Entrepreneurship, freedom for managers, flexibility, creativity, enthusiasm, risk taking	Ministerial responsibility prudence, stability, ethics, probity, fairness, transparency
Vocabulary	Service to clients, quality, skills, managerialism, empowerment, privatization	Public interest, democracy, social equity, due process
Culture	Private sector, innovation, business management, accountability by results, politics-administration dichotomy	Bureaucratic (hierarchical), functionalism, stability, process accountability, politics-administration continuum
Structures	Civil service as organizational units, simple and frugal government, introduction of quasi-market mechanisms, decentralization	Civil service as an institution, large departments, government-wide systems, central authority resource allocation

Source: Charih and Daniels (1997).

NPM is a reform strategy encompassing a series of methods and techniques that aim at government reforms. In contrast to routine tasks, functions and activities, it gives emphasis to jobs, missions and processes. It focuses at debureaucratization and delayering of levels in organization through decentralization, delegation of authority and responsibility to various teams. Its focus is on customer orientation and satisfaction. It gives primacy to identification of customers, assessing their needs, and choices and devising ways of meeting their requirements. The *distinction* between the core components of traditional public administration and NPM can be brought out as follows:

Traditional public administration	NPM
Policy-administration dichotomy	*Policy-administration confluence*
Government is the exclusive provider of public services	Network of stakeholders including government, market, civil society and so on are providers of public service
Structure oriented	People oriented
Anonymity and secrecy in operations	People friendly, responsive, transparent and accountable
Authoritative approach	Participatory approach
Public–private distinction	Public–private partnership
Emphasis on rules, structures and processes	Emphasis on performance and outcomes
Hierarchic model	Flexible model

REINVENTING GOVERNMENT

The management approach to public administration in the US assumed pace in the 1990s, with the liberalization of economies. It gained momentum due to the policies initiated in 1980s by Margaret Thatcher in the UK and Ronald Reagan in the US. The transformation of governmental systems received a new turn in 1992, with the propagation of the concept of 'Re-inventing Government' by Osborne and Gaebler. In their work *Reinventing Government, How the Entrepreneurial Spirit is Transforming the Public Sector*, they made an elaborate case for transforming the bureaucratic government into an 'entrepreneurial' one.

Their prescription is not for abolishing government but *reinventing* it. The concept of enterprising government is one which is never static, but adaptable, responsive, efficient and effective. This enables the government to produce quality goods and services and be responsive to the citizens. Osborne and Gaebler *envisaged* the need for a particular type of government, which is essential for a developed society. The enterprising government that they prescribed is not so much concerned with what government does, but how it does it. They emphasized the following:

- Government cannot run like a business 'because government and business serve different purposes, both of them valuable and necessary'.
- The question is not how much government we have, but what kind of government we have. Hence they made a case for government undergoing a change or reinventing itself.

The model, they conceptualized, has the following ten forms:

- *Catalytic government*: Providing not only services, but also catalysing all sectors into action in the solution of problems
- *Community-oriented government*: Empowering of citizens in service delivery

- *Competitive government*: Promoting competition among various service providers
- *Mission-driven government*: Driven by missions and not rules and regulations
- *Result-oriented government*: Measuring the performance of organizations on the basis of their outcomes than on inputs
- *Customer-driven government*: Redefining clients as customers and offering them choice in service delivery
- *Enterprising government*: Mobilizing efforts towards earning money instead of just spending
- *Anticipatory government*: Being proactive in the sense of preventing problems before they emerge
- *Decentralized government*: Resorting to decentralizing authority with a view to taking decision making close to the citizens
- *Market-oriented government*: Relying on market mechanisms in the provision of services rather than bureaucratic mechanisms

Osborne and Gaebler consider that these fundamental changes are *necessitated* by crisis situations, which require people with vision, leadership qualities and support of business, government as well as societal organizations. The reinventing government model presented by Osborne and Gaebler is a wider exercise in the NPM perspective. It reaffirms the reform agenda of increased efficiency, decentralization, accountability and marketization.

NEW PUBLIC MANAGEMENT: AN APPRAISAL

It is noticed that the *apolitical* dimension of NPM is gradually leading to certain downgrading of values, which occupy a key place in public administration. This has certain serious implications as discussed in the following sections.

Clash of Values between Traditional Public Administration and New Public Management

NPM promotes a new set of values that foster marketization and entrepreneurship. This includes autonomy, flexibility, performance orientation and so on. Here comes the clash between the diverse set of values. It is argued by critics that entrepreneurship places value on autonomy, personal vision, secrecy and risk-taking, which are considered to be opposed to administrative values such as democratic accountability, participation, openness and stewardship. It is assumed that entrepreneurial risk taking may conflict with the obligation to be a steward of the public good. Public policy goals might become less important due to revenue crisis in comparison with economic goals.

The market predominance in several sectors is generally considered to affect the values that public service organizations are to foster, which include equity, social justice, fairplay and so on. The orientation of NPM in promoting those values that result in benefits to people in 'economic' terms in a way is more professional and business/profit oriented.

Contradictory Nature of Reinventing Government Postulates

Some critics have pointed out to certain inconsistencies in reinventing government reform movement, which they consider is seriously flawed, providing contradictory advice, which could be harmful. Williams (2000), in a typical Simon style, terms them as *proverbs* of government as they occur in mutually contradictory pairs. In addition, the advice provided in reforming/reinventing government is considered conflicting, devoid of clear-cut guidance in choosing the right alternative.

Osborne and Gaebler advocate competition between private sector service providers, public and private sector providers, and also within government. Competition is bound to lead to duplication of activities, which is objected to by Osborne and Gaebler. It does not indicate any clear-cut ways of fostering competition between government units and programmers in providing best services or rationalizing government or promoting competition.

Sovereign State versus Supermarket State

Many democracies have parliamentary system of government with people electing their representatives to political bodies, with executive power vested in them and the presence of neutral professional civil service, which is entrusted with the formulation, and implementation of public policy. Olsen (1989) makes a distinction between two State models, namely, sovereign rationality bound State and Supermarket State. The 'sovereign rationality bound State' is considered the conventional model of governance. This *presumes* that there is a centralized State with a large public sector in which standardization and equality are prominent features. The model emphasizes the *collective* and *integrative* features of the political administrative system, the common heritage and the role of the citizens.

The other alternative model of democracy and political-administrative control is labelled as the 'Supermarket State'. This model presumes that the government and the State in general have a service-providing role with an emphasis on efficiency and good quality and views the people as consumers, users or clients. In this model, the hierarchy is in a sense turned upside down. It means rather than the State controlling the society on the basis of a democratic mandate from the people, society controls the State more directly through market mechanisms.

Taken to its extreme, this model implies that if governmental units do not produce satisfactory services at a low price, they should be abolished or downsized. The Supermarket State has economic overtones and is concerned with efficiency, quality and consumer preferences. In addition, there is ambiguity on the citizen–politician relationship.

Managerial Predominance over Policy Capacity

NPM does not accord any primacy to the strengthening of policy-making capacities. Managerial orientation receives utmost significance over public policy and political management. Hughes (1991) opines that policy analysis is absorbed into public management. It has become less relevant as policy analysis is being replaced by economics, allied with modern management as applied to the public sector.

Reinforcing the Traditional Notions of Politics-Administration Dichotomy

NPM makes a distinction between the strategic policy making and implementation, reopening the politics-administration dichotomy debate. The creation of executive agencies in Britain, where the overall policy guidelines are provided by the parent ministry and implementation is the responsibility of the specially created agencies; special operating agencies in Canada reinforces this. Earlier also, measures directed towards performance measurement, linking rewards to achievements have been propagated by the proponents of scientific management. Some consider that the dichotomy propagated by NPM is no different from the traditional paradigm.

Narrow Perspective of the Roles of Politicians and Bureaucrats

One of the key theoretical postulates of NPM is the PCT. This considers bureaucrats as budget maximizers, whereas managerialism calls for professionalism on the part of bureaucracy. These two views run contrary to each other. It is not clear as to how could selfish attitudes foster entrepreneurialism and risk-taking behaviour among bureaucrats.

Many consider that PCT provides a narrow and pessimistic perspective of the roles of politicians and bureaucrats. Questions have also been raised about the arguments on public choice validity, as they seem to lack evidence or empirical examination. The PCT models are based mostly on the US framework, which may not hold good for countries in different institutional settings.

The notion of a rational individual and the idea of a vote-catching politician and a budget-maximizing bureaucrat are not always real-life prototypes. Human beings cannot be looked upon as just economic beings, as they are influenced by social, political and cultural factors and are moulded by certain beliefs, attitudes, etc. Bureaucrats are not necessarily always self-interested. Their interests can always be influenced by other factors, organizational culture and professional values. Politicians also need not always be vote maximizers, as they can be motivated by other factors such as political ideology, ethics and so on.

Absence of Clear-Cut Concept of Accountability

The traditional public administration offers clarity about the concept of accountability, which is in the nature of democratic accountability. It provides the citizens a direct and effective means of ensuring accountability as they can vote the officials out of office. NPM propagates enhanced accountability, as one of its goals and the focus is more on results or outputs.

Citizen versus Customer Orientation

NPM emphasizes responsiveness but in a different perspective. The conventional public administration's commitment to public service has been the provision of effective and equitable public services. The concept of citizenship is a key component in public administration. It fosters concern for public interest and plays an important role in the creation of a harmonious society. It leads to developing a cooperative behaviour and involvement in public matters. But NPM provides diverse channels for articulating and aggregating their interests in a democracy. In addition, it enables them to act in different capacities as citizens, voters, consumers, clients or members of interest groups.

It calls for empowerment of customers, not citizens, increased choices for citizens and empowered government providing public choices in meeting the needs of the customer. The significance accorded to the consumer represents an economic view of human behaviour. There is a stark distinction between a citizen and a client or customer. A citizen is an individual in a Constitutional State, a repository of rights and duties endowed upon by law, rules and regulations, whereas a customer or client functions in a market atmosphere, holding certain rights and responsibilities, and is willing to pay for the services received.

In general, public services have always been associated with fair distribution, adherence to social justice, equity, the ideals also propagated by the elected representatives. There is a provision for appropriate political channels, and expression of dissatisfaction of citizens with public services. But NPM is ambiguous as to the mechanisms through which people can influence the provision of public services as the service providers or market forces are generally concerned about their profits.

The introduction of user fees for public services in developing countries works contrary to the principle of equity, ability to pay and fairness. It is bound to affect large sections of population preceding dissatisfaction and dissent among them. NPM initiatives intend to empower consumers while supposedly diluting the citizens' rights. It gives predominance to those who can pay for services and customers' claims for efficient services. The service providers also imbibe a market-oriented approach giving predominance to maximization of profit. This can affect the important aspects of equity, equality, fairness and quality of services. It could also lead to problems in ensuring fair competition among several market players.

Applicability of NPM as a Dominant Paradigm of Administrative Reforms in Developing Countries

The NPM reforms, which promote market-oriented changes, according to critics, have been partial in nature, as they are not supplemented by basic institutional and political reforms. In many African States, the impact of SAP has been minimal due to general underdevelopment, weak markets and States and limited extent of reforms in key areas such as health, education and infrastructure.

The fundamental inadequacies of the NPM paradigm of reforms for Asian countries lie in the misfit between its logic and the sociopolitical reality of Asia. NPM emphasizes the market, rather than the State as the locomotive of governance and public sector reforms. Indeed the whole logic of NPM is to downsize the public sector in favour of the 'private' market and for public sector organizations to emulate business practices and the management ethos of the private sector and to introduce market measures, which would presumably carry the virtues of the private sector. Such a paradigm does not fit in well with the East and South East Asian experience, where the State institutions have always dominated the scene and where the market for practical purposes has seldom been independent of State power, but on the contrary, has been dependent on it for patronage and support (Cheung and Scott, 2003).

IMPACT OF NEW PUBLIC MANAGEMENT REFORMS

NPM has broadened the managerial choices in the public sector. As it has not been applied extensively outside the Commonwealth countries, its impact especially in developing countries has not been adequately examined. The most comprehensive overview of NPM type of reforms has been offered by Batley (1999). Summarizing the conclusions, Batley (1999) observes that the effect of NPM reforms has been a mixed bag, at best, with some improvements in efficiency and diverse effects on equity. On the downside, he notes that the transaction costs of radical reforms to autonomies service delivery agencies have tended to outweigh the efficiency gains of unbundling, and that reforms that seek to separate purchasers from providers sometimes reduce accountability.

In addition, failure to evolve proper indicators of measurement of reforms has been another problem. Generally, the implementation of any reform is considered to be the key indicator of success. The acid test of any administrative reform programme, NPM or otherwise is the achievement of its promised outcomes. This has been a major lapse in this entire exercise. It is difficult to assess the impact of NPM in purely quantitative and qualitative terms. There are methodological problems pertaining to examining what and how to measure, especially relating to public service performance. Whether reforms in developing countries produce the desired results, it is difficult to provide a definite answer to this.

We can, however, say that these reforms have developed a new vocabulary of reform strategies such as marketization, corporatization, managerialism, privatization, emphasizing efficiency, productivity, rationality, value for money and so on. But, despite their vast reach, there appears to be inconsistency and incoherence in the reforms. It has made public sector very complex, created more hybrid structures and multi-structured public apparatus. In this process, the distinct features of public organizations seem to be fading away.

NPM attempts to create a new entrepreneurial and user-oriented culture in public organizations, with emphasis on performance measurement and autonomy to organizations and individuals. Although the focus appears to improve government functioning, doubts arise regarding the divergence between market economy's interests and pursuance of social concerns.

The process of marketization of public sector in developing countries has led to several associated problems. For example, in Cochabamba in Bolivia, owing to privatization of water, the prices have increased by nearly 200 per cent. In Peru, Sarah Grutsky found that residents paid as much as 3 per cubic metre of water. After World Bank and IMF policies have been enforced in Ghana, she pointed out 'three buckets of water cost a family almost half of the minimum wage' (Sainath, 2006). Any such effort, especially relating to key resources would result in people having limited access to the resources accompanied by high price. The government's move towards privatization of water supply in Delhi has also been met with vehement resistance.

Following are the drawbacks of NPM:

- Imposition of standardized managerial norms over governance structures
- No attention on creation of institutions and institutional values
- Lack of transparency
- Mixed impact on equity
- Relegation of social concerns to the background
- No clear-cut policy guidelines for privatization initiatives
- Methodological problems pertaining to evaluation

International experience indicates that some countries even *reversed* the process of privatization in certain areas. In California, the power sector, which was privatized into several companies, ran into problems and the government had to step in to correct the mess. The British railways, which were privatized in 1984, encountered insolvency and the government, had to again take over this sector. Similar is the case with British coal mines too. In New Zealand also, the government had to renationalize the airlines.

The focus of NPM is on efficiency we all know. However, this is considered by many as *negation* of values of social justice and equity. Some feel that the anti-state ideology the NPM pursues can lead to a decline in basic social services provision, creating a host of inequities. The reigning themes of reform are targeted towards achievement of objectives such as economy and efficiency. However, the issues of social equity, justice, accountability and participation are equally important to be taken cognizance of by any system.

The countries, which embarked upon the public management reforms since 1980s, had career-based public administration *rooted* in certain values of ethics, commitment, accountability and neutrality. In an attempt to give prominence to efficiency and economy, public management was envisaged as a way to deliver improved public services, instead of institutionalizing certain governance values, practices and strategies. Hence, some of the reforms appeared to be technical and scientific without having much of the needed impact.

The public sector enterprises, which are generally loss making, have not been able to attract private buyers, and also there has been a stiff resistance by the labour unions. The developing countries, which are already grappling with unemployment, economic inequalities and absence of a developed capital market through which funds can be mobilized, have not gained much with the privatization initiatives. The strikes that have been resorted to by trade unions in the banking and insurance sectors in India reflect their apprehensions and problems encountered with the process. There are no clear-cut policy guidelines or political will to make provisions for alternative employment opportunities.

Privatization methods are also said to have been less transparent and they appear to be an exercise in redistribution of economic power. Some enterprises have been privatized hastily under the influence of political pressures. The disinvestment process in India has also lacked a holistic perspective. Although the various committees that examined this process have recommended ways of improving the performance of public enterprises, the implementation of the strategies has been devoid of zeal and commitment. In India, the public management reforms, which were introduced as part of SAP, assumed several forms such as liberalization, deregulation, privatization and disinvestment. These were to a large extent due to aid conditionalities of the donor agencies such as World Bank and IMF. The situation on the domestic front in the 1990s was such that the country had to go in for a different economic development model. The changes had to be introduced in financial, banking and regulatory sectors, and the economy had to be opened up to the market forces.

However, we cannot make generalizations on the basis of these examples. It is because there has not been much of *research* on the impact, focussing on the successes and failures of NPM reforms. According to Pollitt (1995) much of the scholarly research till date has been at the micro-level and 'highly context specific'.

The NPM, has no doubt, triggered intellectual discourse about evolving ways of *optimizing* resources, alternative market mechanisms for delivering public services, with a focus on performance measurement, autonomy of the operating agencies and individuals. Above all, as Bhattacharya (2006) has observed, there is this thing called 'public interest' which lies at the heart of government operations and it is irreplaceable by any market philosophy.

CONCLUSION

The public sector reforms ushered in globally in the last two decades and labelled as NPM are the outcome of several changes embedded in the social as well as political context in the Western democracies. The very rationale of the public sector has been questioned and the functioning of the welfare State has come under cloud. NPM drawing on the principles of economic theories/approaches positioned itself as an alternative paradigm. It is reflected in the primacy it accorded to satisfaction of individual needs, self-actualization behaviour of bureaucracy, dismantling of public monopolies and promotion of competition.

Essentially, NPM, a reform model that originated in the West, spreads its wings to developing countries too. It did give a jolt to monolithic bureaucratic administration and propelled the State in these countries to adapt to values of marketization, competition, efficiency and productivity. However, NPM focussed more on internal organizational mechanisms and processes. Juxtaposing this type of managerial model within the framework of State and governance system has been its major flaw.

The model or paradigm, as many call it, has been rather ambiguous in its attempt towards restructuring administration. In a way, a 'borrowed' model was sought to be imposed out of context in different countries. A complete disclosure of the proposed reforms, mechanisms for evaluation, involvement of public, market mechanisms, alternative solutions for effective public service delivery and so on could never be made. It appears that to a large extent, it is the common citizen who has been the *casualty* in this entire process.

We need to look *beyond* NPM reforms to strive towards blending of economic and social values. In evolving and adapting a new administrative framework, it is necessary that each country examines its feasibility as per clearly formulated reform objectives, examine suitable prerequisites for reform and create a conducive atmosphere for its implementation. The citizens as a constituent of the democratic process have certain expectations from the state and government in the resolution of their problems.

The reforms need to fit into the apparatus of the State and its mechanisms. NPM as a framework of administrative reform can at best solve not all but a few specific problems. In the present globalization scenario, a balance needs to be maintained between managerial reform and governance challenges, as NPM can only be but one strand in the entire process of change. The feasibility of installing the reform processes, which are imposed as packages from other countries, needs to be examined in the perspective of the socioeconomic and political milieu of the recipient country.

Preparatory Questions

- What are the basic premises behind limiting government action?
- Discuss the factors that triggered the evolution of NPM.
- What are the tenets of public choice approach?
- Highlight the features of NPM.
- Distinguish NPM from traditional public administration.
- Describe the ten forms of government, as conceptualized by Osborne and Gaebler.
- Critically examine the NPM model.

REFERENCES

Al Gore. (1993) *From Red Tape to Results: Creating a Government that Works Better and Costs Less.* A Report of the National Performance Review 1, Washington, DC.

Barzelay, M. (1993) *The New Public Management.* US: Russell Sage.

Batley, R. (1999) *The Role of Government in Adjusting Economies: An Overview of Findings.* Birmingham: International Development Department.

Bhattacharya, M. (2006) *New Horizons of Public Administration.* New Delhi: Jawahar Publications.

Charih, M. and Daniels, A. F. (1997*) New Public Management and Public Administration in Canada.* Canada: Institute of Public Administration.

Cheung, A. and Scott, I. (2003) *Governance and Public Sector Reforms in Asia: Paradigms, Paradoxes and Dilemmas.* New York: Routledge. p. 12.

Hughes, O. E. (1991) *Public Management and Administration: An Introduction.* 2nd ed. New York: Palgrave. p. 36.

Held, D. et al. (2005) *Debating Globalization.* Cambridge: Polity Press.

Hood, C. (1991) 'A Public Management for all Seasons?' *Public Administration*. 69. pp. 3–19.

Lan, Z. and Rosenbloom, D. H. (1992) 'Editorial: Public Administration in Transition.' *Public Administration Review*. 52(6). pp. 535–537.

Olsen, J. P. (1989), *cited in* Christensen, T. and Laegrid, P. (2001) *New Public Management: The Transformation of Ideas and Practice*. Aldershot: Ashgate. pp. 15–17.

Osborne, D. and Gaebler, T. (1992) *Reinventing Government: How the Entrepreneurial Spirit is Transforming the Public Sector.* New York: Plume Books.

Pollitt, C. (1995) 'Justification by Works or by Faith?' 'Evaluating the new public management'. *Evaluation*. 12. pp. 133–154.

Sainath, P. (2006) 'Privatization: Come Hell or High Water'. *The Hindu*, 22nd March.

Williams, D. W. (2000) 'Reinventing the Proverbs of Government'. *Public Administration Review*. 60(6). pp. 522–526.

Williamson, O and William O. (2003), *cited in* Bovaird, T. and Loffler, E. (eds.). *Understanding Public Management and Governance.* London: Routledge.

Chapter Fifteen

Towards Post-New Public Management

Uma Medury

LEARNING OBJECTIVES

After completing this chapter, you should be able to:

- Distinguish the focus areas of the first and second generation reforms
- Analyse the major facets of transition from New Public Management to Post-New Public Management
- Discuss the important Post-New Public Management concepts; and
- Focus on the Post-New Public Management initiatives at the global level

INTRODUCTION

Public administration, as a discipline and practice, is placed in a *peculiar* position in the 21st century, which is undergoing transformation on several fronts. The discipline that has roots in political science is presently more attuned to resolving the issues pertaining to performance, efficiency and effectiveness. The globalization process is leading to reconfiguration of society, State and government, resulting in experimentation and innovations.

The reform movement, be it reinvention, New Public Management (NPM), business process engineering, gives prominence to competition, market economy, entrepreneurialism and customer orientation. The erosion of faith and trust in traditionally structured and hierarchical organizations pave the way for market-based institutions as well as new informal and network groups.

The strong neo-liberal agenda influencing the government policies (as you have already read in the earlier chapters of this volume) has gained prominence in the form of Washington Consensus. It has acquired the distinct neo-liberal and right wing connotation due to the impact of policies in the UK and US. This has raised fears that these narrow set of policy prescriptions would promote privatization, free trade and deregulation, which could undermine the governing capacities of public institutions. In addition, it is felt that these prescriptions have not paid much attention to the development of human capital, economic infrastructure, market institutions, safety nets and so on.

The pro-market ideology, which reigned supreme in the 1980s, argues that the government is less efficient than markets in providing services to individuals. Due to competition and profit motive, the market firms make a more effective use of given resources than the government agencies, which lack similar incentives. Besides, individuals can choose the services they want from the market, subject to their income, whereas provision of services by government leaves them with little or no choice.

The new political economy of development based on 'market', and not the State as the central actor, has led to a far-reaching reform movement termed as NPM about which you have read earlier in this volume. Another development in the recent times has been termed as post-NPM reforms by scholars in the discipline. There have been *myriad* factors responsible for these changes including external pressures, retaining the typical administrative features peculiar to several countries, political, social factors and so on. Several questions arise, whether the new wave of post-NPM reforms that is emerging has replaced NPM or has it only supplemented or assimilated the earlier reforms, their distinct features and complex forms. This chapter attempts to address some of these issues.

CONTEMPORARY SCENARIO

Over the last two decades there have been far-reaching modifications in the structure and dynamics of the public sector. The impact of global forces on State, polity, economy, society and administration has been phenomenal. It has drawn attention to the issues concerning the division of responsibility within and beyond government, and also to the quality of governance.

As has been observed, 'the emerging global public administration is based on a number of structural adjustments or readjustments that have been taking place around the globe. The readjustments have been in the form of redefining the scope and boundaries of public and private sectors, of administrative reforms or civil service reforms, of organizational reconfiguration and restructuring and many more' (Farazmand, 1994).

NPM reforms intended to usher in technically oriented changes with a view to redesigning the organizational framework of public sector. The measures included disaggregation, privatization, contractualization, marketization, performance assessment and so on. This has resulted in structural disintegration and fragmentation of public sector. One of the major criticisms of this reinventing reform movement has been the erosion of democratic values in administration.

Reforms at global level are as follows:

- NPM reforms with focus on 'one size fits all'
- First-generation structural adjustment reforms with focus on market
- Second-generation structural adjustment reforms with focus on State
- Good governance reforms with focus on transparency and accountability
- Post-NPM reforms with focus on public value and citizen orientation

> The basic norms of public service such as neutrality, impartiality, accountability, responsiveness, representativeness, equality, justice, integrity and commitment are being replaced by pro-market values like competitiveness, efficiency, productivity and profitability.
>
> Haque (1998)

The reforms have presented a new orientation towards State and society, *replacing* the notion of collective welfare and shared identity of citizens by a more individualistic ethos. The value of individual satisfaction is judged more than the value of achieving collective democratic consensus. The NPM's prescription which centred on 'one size fits all' has led to certain adverse effects. NPM with its basis in economic orientation considers individual actors as driven by incentives and pursuing their own interests, and civil service as structure modelled on principles of devolution, contracts and markets. In the same vein, the citizen is viewed as customer or consumer with individual rights and choices.

The Structural Adjustment Programme that was introduced as part of aid conditionalities of the World Bank and International Monetary Fund aimed at bringing about structural changes in the economies along with increasing the role of market forces, improving the efficiency of public sector and mobilizing additional resources. These reforms termed by some as *first-generation* reforms, as several studies indicate, had many repercussions, especially for developing countries. These according to critics have contributed to decline in national income, increase in unemployment and non-fulfilment of objectives of higher economic growth and poverty reduction, which has resulted in perpetuation of existing inequalities.

The first set of structural adjustment reforms, in a way, was not considered to be coherent and holistic and this was imposed top-down. Gradually, the reigning conception of State 'being an obstacle to development' began to lose ground. It was realized that the State was crucial, not only for development but also for democratization. A strong need was felt for improving the governing mechanisms and systems to protect the civil, political and social rights of individuals and communities. This realization gave rise to *second-generation* reforms with focus on State institutions, markets as well as civil society (as shown in Table 15.1).

Table 15.1 First- and second-generation reforms

	First generation	Second generation
Main objectives	Crisis management: reducing inflation and restoring growth	Improving social stability and reducing risk; maintaining macro-economic competitiveness and stability
Instruments	Drastic budget cuts, tax reform, price liberalization, trade and foreign investment liberalization, deregulation, social funds, autonomous contracting agencies, some privatization	Civil service reform, labour reform, restructuring social ministries, judicial reform, modernizing of the legislature, upgrading of regulatory capacity, improved tax collection, large-scale privatization, restructuring of central–local government relationships Presidency and cabinet, legislature, civil service, judiciary, unions, political parties, media, state and local governments, private sector, institutions Reorientation of middle and local government to apply global institutional norms in locally sustainable ways
Actors	Presidency, economic cabinet, central bank, multilateral financial institutions, private financial groups, foreign portfolio investors	
Main challenge	Macro-economics management by an insulated technocratic elite	

Source: Craig and Porter (2006).

Post-NPM reforms attempt to *take forward* these changes in a modified manner. It is not about returning to 'traditional public administration'. It entails reaching out to the society and enabling individual and organized private actors in society to be better informed about public policy and to participate in making policy more representative and implementable. There is no doubt that new forms of governance are supplementing the State. A positive aspect of this trend is the 'notion of community', which is occupying centre stage of the political spectrum. It has become a dominant force in the contemporary scenario. Social sustainability is becoming a challenging task for governance. Social democracy is being propagated with emphasis on a framework for shared values and common institutional practices. According to Held (2002), social democracy encompasses the following:

- The promotion of rule of law at the international level.
- Greater transparency, accountability and democracy in global governance.
- A deeper commitment to social justice in pursuit of a more equitable distribution of life chances.
- Protection and reinvention of community at diverse levels.
- Regulation of the global economy-through public management of global trade and financial flows and engagement of leading stakeholders in corporate governance.

TRANSITION FROM NEW PUBLIC MANAGEMENT TO POST-NEW PUBLIC MANAGEMENT

NPM reforms brought in structural devolution, which led to fragmentation of structures and activities, lack of coordination, creation of multiple levels of accountability and erosion of public service ethos. These developments, as we have mentioned earlier, paved the way for post-NPM reforms. The impact of NPM has often been a matter of debate and discussion.

No research study has been able to reach a decisive deduction on the impact of NPM. Over the last few years, a new wave of reforms, labelled as post-NPM, has emerged, which goes to show that the NPM reforms have been wanting on many fronts. Loss of political control, excessive importance to economic factors and need for better coordination have led to post-NPM reforms.

Post-NPM agenda does not mean that all the 'bread and butter' or basic issues on the NPM agenda have become irrelevant. The second-generation reforms that entail governance should not be interpreted as anti-NPM. They supplement the NPM reforms. An important characteristic of post-NPM reforms is coming together of societal forces in formation of collaborative networks and creation of new competencies. There is stronger *focus* on political steering and democracy. The reforms focus on departing from market-based solutions and focus on political steering, democracy, citizens' participation and community well-being.

The structural reforms have to be supplemented by administrative and cultural aspects and also need to be within the ambit of international environment. In post-NPM scenario, efficiency is no longer the *main* goal, but is being challenged by other public sector values and ethical questions. The focus is more on re-establishing the public sector ethos. The post-NPM agenda, with its emphasis on rule of law, human rights, empowerment and participatory development attempts to provide a countervailing force to the excessive managerial orientation.

There is an increasing realization that if development has to be sustainable, it must take cognizance of social and political development, human prosperity rather than just economic development. Under globalization, citizens' demands are more diverse and refined. They want choices, improved responsiveness and an assured quality of services. The reforms envision a diminished role for the State, and espouse a market-oriented economy supported by a democratic government with an efficient and quality-oriented public administration as a formula for both economic development and the well-being of citizens.

Privatization, deregulation, debureaucratization and decentralization are the core political issues. Performance-oriented governance and management strategies are advocated to improve responsiveness and accountability. No wonder the concept of *development management*, which has gradually expanded to encompass bureaucratic reorientation and restructuring, integration of politics and culture into management improvement, participatory and performance-based service delivery, programme management, capacity building of community and non-governmental organizations, policy reform and implementation, is increasingly gaining ground especially in the context of developing countries (views of Brinkerhoff and Coston 1999, cited in Jain, 2004).

Public administration in contemporary times is in a more humanizing environment and it is being realized that the social values inherent in public services may not be adequately addressed by economic efficiency motive of the markets. The development discourse is undergoing transformation. The concerns expressed over the neo-liberal tone of reforms have led to changing complexion of governance. It is acquiring a holistic perspective aiming not only at economic growth but also political and social transformation.

It is now being felt that the ultimate goal of development, pursued by State or market is to build human capabilities and enlarge human choices to create a safe and secure environment where citizens can live with dignity and equality. As opposed to its traditional economic orientation, it now implies promotion of all aspects of human life. The need for a comprehensive approach to development is being emphasized, with an understanding of poverty, human capital, physical capital as well as institutions, governance and participation.

Craig and Porter (2006) consider the changing complexion of neo-liberal ideas as 'inclusive neo-liberalism'. According to them, while retaining core conservative neo-liberal macro-economic and pro-market settings, 'inclusive' neo-liberalism adds positive 'liberal 'approaches emphasizing 'empowerment' to enable participation and ensure inclusion of countries and people in global and local markets. These include institution building and enabling State ensuring global market integration; building human capital via services (*health and education*); empowering and protecting the rights of the vulnerable through participatory voice and legal access; engendering moral obligations to community and work (Table 15.2).

Table 15.2 Distinction between conservative and inclusive neo-liberalism

Conservative neo-liberalism	'Inclusive' (neo) liberalism
Getting the State out of markets	State must create institutions to enable markets
Deregulated markets, a law unto themselves	Markets need to be embedded in institutions and community by 'smart' re-regulation
Countries open up and conform to global market rules 'sink or swim'	Countries 'own' reforms, commit to good governance, enable markets
People participate/are included in market	'Enabling', people to participate/be 'included' in markets and community through basic services
State/others as funder of services, market as provider	'Joined-up' co-production of services, central and local, State, markets, civil society: 'soft' institutions
Poverty reduction through market integration (structural adjustment)	Poverty reduction through markets, 'enabling' services and empowering partnerships
Market and fiscal discipline: International Financial Institutions (IFIs) loan conditionalities	Market, fiscal and moral discipline: the obligation to participate, govern through efficient incentives
'Thatcherism', neo-classical economics, structural adjustment	'Third Way' social democracy (Blair/New Labour); (IFI) International Financial Institution/multilateral-led Poverty Reduction Strategy Papers (PRSP) and poverty reduction

Source: Craig and Porter (2006).

POST-NEW PUBLIC MANAGEMENT CONCEPTS

Neo-Weberian State

The term neo-Weberian has been in use in political science, sociology, organization theory and other disciplines. The label Neo-Weberian State (NWS) was introduced by Christopher Pollitt and Geert Bouckaert in 2004 in their book *Public Management Reform: A Comparative Analysis.* In the context of public management reforms, NWS refers to traditional (Weberian) administrative systems that are in the process of modernization, but retain distinct public service qualities. This is based on centrality of State, preservation of public services and protection of individuals from unpredictable actions of State agencies by focussing on enforcement of administrative law, public consultation and citizens' involvement. It lays emphasis on result orientation and enhancement of bureaucracy's competence to meet the citizens' needs. Pollitt and Bouckaert (2004) have highlighted the following Weberian elements:

- Reaffirmation of the State as the main facilitator of solutions to the new problems of globalization, technological change, shifting demographics and environmental threat.
- Reaffirmation of the role of representative democracy.
- Reaffirmation of the role of administrative law.
- Preservation of the idea of a public service with a distinctive status, culture, terms and conditions.

Neo-elements include the following:

- Shift from an internal orientation to bureaucratic rules towards an external orientation to meeting citizen's needs.
- Supplementation (*not replacement*) of the role of representative democracy by a range of devices for consultation with, and the direct representation of citizens' views.
- Modernization of relevant laws to encourage a greater orientation on achievement of results.
- Professionalization of public service.

Digital-Era Governance

This emphasizes the use and impact of information and communication technology, social media in public service delivery and management. It focuses on reintegrating functions and providing need-oriented and holistic services to citizens. This has been discussed in detail in the chapter 25 on e-governance in this volume.

Public Value Management

Public value management is considered as 'post-competitive', which is concerned with the broader government goal of public value creation. This goes beyond the efficiency concerns and individualism of market and makes a case for searching 'public value' in government actions. Public values are basically derived from the society and in a way they provide the focus and direction for public activity. The service delivery is considered to create public value if it is based on civic engagement and exchange between government and other stakeholders.

Public value creation and its management is a multi-faceted activity involving governments, community groups and citizens. Here no one sector has monopoly towards public service and there is no specific ethos that is considered appropriate. It is based on individual and public preferences resulting from public deliberation.

Mark H. Moore (1995) is credited with the propagation of public value framework and the central tenet of this has been the utilization of public resources to increase the value in a manner analogous to value creation in private sector. Since the operations in organizations consume public resources, producing real consequences for the society – intended or not, the managers in organizations need to account for the value that is produced.

Post-NPM includes the following concepts:

- Neo-Weberian State (Pollitt and Bouckaert, 2004; Dunn and Miller, 2007)
- Public Value Management (Mark Moore, 1995)
- Digital-Era Governance (Dunleavy et al., 2006)
- New Public Governance (Osborne, 2006)

New Public Governance

This is a mode of governance that emphasizes cooperation between State and non-state actors to achieve policy objectives. It propagates networking of actors to ensure collaboration and interdependence. Stephen P. Osborne (2006) has termed these participatory, interactive and collaborative forms as New Public Governance (NPG). He uses this term to designate a new orchestration of public policy implementation and service delivery. Osborne considers this as a mode of governance within a State characterized by an interaction between a plethora of independent actors in policy delivery and a *combination* of different processes in the policy making system. NPG is based on the premise that in the present scenario no single actor has the required knowledge, capacity or the resources to manage the governance process.

> This is a polycentric form of social coordination in which actions are coordinated voluntarily by individuals and organizations with self-organizing and self-enforcing capabilities.
>
> Mcginnis and Ostrom (1996)

It encompasses network-based collaboration and coordination, public involvement and democratic participation. It is a coherent model of governance that supplements and does not replace State and the market. The second-generation reforms, which we have discussed under the broad rubric of NPG, are assuming the form of networks and partnerships. They are variedly labelled as 'whole-of-government', 'joined-up governance', and 'one-stop government'. The main thrust of these initiatives is to improve horizontal and vertical coordination between the organizations and stakeholders and simply the governance process. It encourages negotiation between public authorities at multiple levels, public–private sector collaboration, enhances shared capacity for innovative solutions and promotes use of new governing tools. Networks attempt to bridge the space between public and private sectors, bureaucracies and markets.

The key premises of NPG include the following:

- Blurring of boundaries between the State and non-state actors in public service delivery
- Collaboration between the multiple stakeholders
- Interdependence in pooling of varied types of resources in meeting the policy objectives
- Network of relationships with requisite autonomy and functioning within a framework of accountability

New Public Service

Denhardt and Denhardt (2007) assert that in the changing scenario, there is a need to evolve the concept of New Public Service, which encompasses task of public administration to:

- Serve rather than steer.
- Pursue public interest.
- Think strategically, act democratically.
- Serve citizens, not customers.
- Recognition that accountability is not a simple task and it is not just to the market, but the Constitutional law, community, citizens' interests and professional standards.
- Value people, not productivity.
- Value citizenship and public service above entrepreneurship.

The concept of 'citizenship' is reinforced in a democratic society, and values such as efficiency and productivity are to be placed in a larger context of democracy, community and public interest. Post-NPM focuses on coordination and integration strategies. It attempts to foster vertical and horizontal coordination to overcome and lessen the impact of cross-cutting of different policies and fragmented structures undermining each other, to make better use of scarce resources and to create synergy between various efforts of stakeholders in particular policy areas. It aims to provide citizens with seamless services. Post-NPM efforts aim at establishing coordination among various levels of governance and build partnerships that are based on cooperation rather than conflict. Horizontal linkages are set up and the organizational networks are made flexible rather than bureaucratic.

The post-NPM reforms are also culturally oriented governance efforts. By this we mean that 'they focus on cultivating a strong unified sense of values, cultural integration, team building, the involvement of participating organizations, trust, value-based management, collaboration and improving the training and self-development of public servants' (Ling, 2002).

Some of the postulates that we have been discussing under the rubric of NPM, governance, post-NPM reforms are not really something 'new'; they are ingrained in the sociopolitical framework of countries. However, these have remained dormant for a long time and the contemporary developments have given them the impetus and catapulted them to a prominent place in countries' democratic framework.

Post-NPM changes aim at the following:

- Fostering cooperation, coordination and integration between sectors and administrative units
- Establishing linkages across the boundaries and administrative levels to achieve shared goals
- Coordinating policy making and service delivery
- Ensuring cohesiveness of policy making in governance system
- Re-regulation to provide direction to de-regulated industries
- Re-collaboration, vertically and horizontally, across organizational and hierarchical boundaries
- Enhancing public service delivery and system responsiveness
- Improving governance through partnerships and networks
- Creation of professional and proactive bureaucracy
- Encouraging citizen orientation and participation

At the global level, currently the efforts are on to tackle the repercussions of globalization through appropriate *indigenously* developed mechanisms as well as governance values and practices. Held (2002) highlights the notion of 'cosmopolitanism' as relevant to making globalization democratic. The features of cosmopolitan democracy are as follows:

- The people govern through communities, associations, states, institutional organizations and all are subject to cosmopolitan democratic law.
- The form of global governance is *heterarchy* – a divided authority system subject to cosmopolitan democratic law.
- The key democratization instruments are Constitutional and institutional reconstruction, intensification of globalization and regionalization, new social movements and possible global crises.
- The traditions of democratic thought are liberal democratic theory, developmental democracy, participatory democracy and civic republicanism.
- The ethic of global governance is 'democratic autonomy'.
- The mode of political transformation is reconstruction of global governance.

GLOBAL INITIATIVES

Globally, initiatives are underway to bring innovations in governance processes. In the UK, in 1990s, the labour government had attempted to introduce a new political idea, that is, *third way*, bringing about a reconfiguration of relationships and a new approach to governing. This includes a harmonious and non-conflict partnership between government and health professionals in the modernization of the National Health Service, between central and local government, local governments and with local communities.

> Bhagidari, a citizen–administration partnership programme initiated in 2000 in the National Capital Territory (NCT) of Delhi is a measure towards networking in governance, wherein the citizens through Resident Welfare Associations and public utility departments collaborate to chalk out development programmes and facilitate/improve governance

The *third way* is an attempt to bring together and blend certain facts of neo-liberalism with social cohesiveness. The measures introduced by the labour government put emphasis on the significance of *collaboration* between public and private sectors, as well as between voluntary and community-based organizations functioning in collaboration with the government. Since 2000, the partnership with the private sector taking on the responsibility for provision, maintenance and building of the infrastructure has gained momentum. This includes hospitals, education, schools, roads, railways and so on, amounting to nearly 400 such initiatives.

The *Private Finance Initiative* (PFI) has been visible in the sale of equity in State-owned enterprises. The urban regeneration initiative brings together as partners in area-based programmes, central government agencies, local government agencies, community organizations and private sector companies. The PFI has stimulated the private financing of new public facilities, including transport projects, roads, prisons, hospitals and museums (McCourt and Minogue, 2000).

Australia's 'Whole of Government' concept variously termed as integrated or horizontal governance is an initiative towards collaboration and integration. The agencies working across portfolio boundaries strive to achieve a shared goal. The agencies constituted around functional hierarchies are brought together in horizontal collaboration and integration in their modes of operation. 'Whole-of-government' approach uses new coordination instruments and cross-sector programmes and projects to modify horizontal fragmentation.

CONCLUSION

Under post-NPM, what is required is reinventing or reconstructing the relations in governance mechanisms. The multiple relations between government and market, government and citizens, and government and society need to undergo a change. The present scenario has also opened up opportunities for change and reform. There are maladies and constraints in any system. However, these should not deter the transformation process.

The reform process has globally acquired significance and is gaining momentum. The crucial question is the rooting of these in the specific local/contextual milieu and ensuring its sustainability. Reforms are multi-dimensional in nature and need to be accompanied by changes in all related spheres. It requires public support, political will and a conscious attempt on the part of all concerned to innovate, create, assess, institutionalize and ensure the longevity of new institutions and practices.

To recapitulate, we must keep in mind that for the sustainability of the post-NPM model, the essential pre-requisite is achievement of public purpose efficiently and effectively; thereby, fostering a right balance among social, political, civic and economic governance. The challenges in the contemporary times require the coming together of societal forces through collaboration and cooperation. This would supplement/complement the political and bureaucratic authorities in achieving public policy goals.

This also calls for acquisition of varied creative, technical, behavioural, critical and ethical skills/attitudes for meeting the challenges of management of public affairs. This new model establishes a close relationship between the State, government, economy, citizens and civil society. The earlier neo-liberal thinking had undermined the significance of social forces. The emerging approach attempts to integrate political, economic and social dimensions and provide an answer to the negative impact of globalization. We therefore reiterate that for development to be sustainable, it has to take cognizance of social, political and human aspects to prosperity rather than focussing merely on economic development as a parameter of growth and governance.

Preparatory Questions

- Distinguish between first- and second-generation reforms.
- Examine the major facets of transition from NPM to post-NPM.
- Explain the key premises of New Public Governance or NPG.
- Discuss the concept of New Public Service.
- Write a note on post-NPM initiatives at the global level.

REFERENCES

Brinkerhoff, D. W. and Coston, J. M. (1999), *cited in* Jain, R. B. (2004), 'Sustainable Development through Good Governance in India: Challenges and Strategies' in Geden M. M. and Haque S. (eds.). *Handbook of Development Policy Studies.* New York: Marcel Dekker. p. 584.

Christensen, T. (2012) 'Post-NPM and Changing Public Governance.' *Meiji Journal of Political Science and Economics.* 12.

Christensen T. and Laegreid, P. (2011) *Ashgate Research Companion to New Public Management.* Farnham: Ashgate Publishing House.

Craig, D. and Porter, D. (2006) *Development Beyond Neo – Liberalism? Governance, Poverty Reduction and Political Economy.* New York: Routledge.

Dunleavy, Patrick et al., (2006) 'New Public Management is Dead – Long Live Digital Era Governance.' *Journal of Public Administraton Research and Theory,* Vol No3, P. 467–494.

Denhardt J. V. and Denhardt, R. B. (2007) *New Public Service.* New York: M. E. Sharpe.

Farazmand, A. (1994) 'The New World Order and Global Public Administration: A Critical Essay' in Garcia, J. E. et al. (eds.). *Public Administration in the Global Village.* West Port (CT): Praeger.

Haque, S. M. (1998) 'Legitimation Crisis: A Challenge for Public Service in the Next Century.' *International Review of Administrative Sciences.* 64(January–March)., p. 13-26.

Held, D. (2002) 'Cosmopolitanism: Ideas, Realities and Deficits' in Held D. and McGrew, A. (eds.). *Governing Globalization.* Cambridge: Polity.

Kettl, D. F. *The Future of Public Administration.* Available from: www.h-bnet.org/pubadmin/tfreport/kettle [Accessed: 5th January 2014].

Ling, T. (2002) 'Delivering joined-up Government in the UK: Dimensions, Issues and Problems.' *Public Administration.* 80(4)., p. 615-642.

McCourt, W. and Minogue, M. (2000) *The Internationalization of Public Management: Reinventing The Third World State.* UK: Edward Elgar.

Mcginnis, M. D. and Ostrom, E. (1996) 'Design Principles for Local and Global Commons' in *International Political Economy and International Institutions,* Vol. 2. UK: Edward Elgar.

Moore, M. (1995) *Creating Public Value: Strategic Management in Government.* Cambridge: Harvard University Press.

Osborne, S. P. (2006) 'The New Public Governance.' *Public Management Review* (Editorial). 8(3).

Osmani, M. (2012) 'Developing a Conceptual Framework for Evaluating post-NPM Public Sector Transformation'. *Doctoral Symposium.* Brunel Business School, London.

Pollitt, C. and Bouckaert, G. (2004) *Public Management Reform: A Comparative Analysis.* 2nd ed. Oxford: Oxford University Press.

Chapter Sixteen

Historical Antecedents of Civil Society

Kiran Bhushi

LEARNING OBJECTIVES

After completing this chapter, you should be able to:

- Trace the historical antecedents of civil society
- Explain the concept of civil society
- Analyse the intellectual climate of enlightenment period
- Discuss Hegel's and Marx's ideas on civil society; and
- Examine Gramsci's and Habermas's analysis on civil society

INTRODUCTION

The term 'civil society' has become a much used term in recent times. Politicians, citizens, government organizations, non-government organizations (NGOs), activists, advocacy groups, corporates and just about everyone is using the term. Much of the current fascination with civil society revolves around NGOs, especially those concerned with various causes involving environment, corruption, women's issues, tribal rights and such other related grounds.

Many would argue that the civil society as a concept came into prominence with the crisis in the communist State of Poland and erstwhile Soviet Russia, and Czechoslovakia. The socialist States, especially under Stalin not only came down heavily on individual rights but also collective, community initiatives. All public institutions, such as universities, scientific laboratories, hospitals, publishing houses and newspapers were under the control of the State.

The emergence of emancipatory social movements in these and other States in the form of what are also called the 'colour revolutions' (Georgia's *Rose Revolution* 2003, Ukraine's *Orange Revolution* 2004 and Iraq's *Purple Revolution* 2005), not based on traditional notions of power such as class (*which was a major preoccupation with the socialist left*), added to the interest in civil society.

Drawing upon the notion of civil society, these new social movements focussed their attention on the complexity of human experience and the limitations posed by the State. They advocated and canvassed for a range of issues related to democratic and human rights, legitimacy of government, social justice and so on. All these movements drew upon the notion of civil society. On the other hand, many who look at civil society as emanating in the larger context of liberal economies, see it as a reflection of the larger process of power structures of which both the State and market are implicated.

Concept of civil society is complex and takes a while to fathom. Different scholars have understood it differently from the vantage point of the era they lived in. NGOs, community-based organizations and social movements form a vital part of civil society. As a later chapter in this volume discusses NGOs, its meaning, nature, role and relevance, we will refrain from dealing with the issue of relationship between NGOs and civil society here. This chapter will make an attempt to trace the antecedents of the concept of civil society from ancient times. In order to make readers understand the historical antecedents of civil society, we have divided the chapter into four sections dealing with different scholars' views on civil society at different phases of time. But first, let us be clear about its concept.

CONCEPT OF CIVIL SOCIETY

The term 'civil society' loosely refers to those groups, networks and relationships that are not organized or managed by the State. The meaning of civil society organizations can be best understood in the light of the relationship of civil society with the State, as well as the market. In the present context, both State and the market determine the complexion of civil society. The viewpoints on the composition of civil society are varied and debatable in the absence of a consensus on its nature and scope. It is therefore pertinent to understand the historicity of the term to understand its scope and range.

Civil society means different things to different people. It is generally seen as a space outside the State. Civil society as a particular social form is unique to the modern world – the particular historical conditions, which led to the emergence of the modern distinction between State and civil society. As we all know, various functions of the State have now fallen into the private sphere. It is the relocation of functions between public and private institutions that civil society represents. It is a particular set of social relations, which are not necessarily opposed to the State.

Civil society is

- Space outside of the State
- Avenue for emancipatory dialogue
- Advocacy of plurality and diversity as basis of human experience
- New relationship between 'public' and 'private' institutions
- Network of social relations

'Global civil society' is a related term that is widely prevalent now. The combined words 'global' and 'civil' and what it means has many varying interpretations.

> For some, Global Civil Society refers to the protestors in Seattle and Prague or Green Peace's actions against transnational corporations; in other words, a counter-weight to global capitalism. For others, the words have something to do with the infrastructure that is needed for the spread of democracy and development; the growth of professional associations, consumer organizations, and interests groups that span many countries. Yet, others identify the phenomenon with the efforts of groups like Save the Children or *Médécinssans Frontières* to provide humanitarian assistance; global solidarity with the poor or oppressed. Or perhaps the term just refers to the growing connectedness of citizens-Internet chatrooms, networks of peace, environmental or human rights activists, student exchanges, or global media.
>
> Anheier, et al. (2001, p. 3)

The concept of civil society, as can be seen from the above interpretations, does not have single school of thought. However, some common themes are associated with the concept. Civil society often denotes a space outside of the State, where there are possibilities for democratic emancipatory dialogue. The concept also highlights plurality and diversity as being the basis of human experience.

The renaissance of interest in civil society draws strength from its European roots, which are traceable to the late 18th century and early 19th century development of the distinction between civil society and the State (Keane, 1998). During the revolutionary period 1750–1850, the traditional language of civil society (Societascivilis), which had until then referred to a peaceful political order governed by law, underwent a profound transformation. Contrasted with government, and institutionally separated from State institutions, civil society meant a realm of social life. This is the sense in which civil society is still understood today (Melucci, 1988)

Whatever may be the uses of the concept of civil society in contemporary terms, the concept has a long history. Many philosophers, thinkers and scholars have used the term in various ways through history. For instance, in the Classical Athenian usage of the term, it means a normative order that is achieved by the citizenry (*usually men*) that is reasonable and just, and aims to achieve civility.

Civil society in this conception expresses the growth of civilization to the point where society is 'civilized'. It is, as classically expressed in the Athenian *polis* or the Roman republic, 'a social order of citizenship, one where men (*rarely women*) regulate their relationships and settle their disputes according to a system of laws; where 'civility' reigns, and citizens take an active part in public life' (Kumar, 1993, p. 377).

The connection of citizenship with civil society was lost in later writings argues Keane (1998). In fact, 'the term Civil Society lay buried for a long time, but it was resurrected in 20th century public life. Keane says the present usage refers more to the late eighteenth and early nineteenth century conceptions of the term'. By the eighties, it had become apparent even to the left leaning intellectuals in the West that 'the Socialist State had taken a toll both on the individual and the institutions' (Beteille, 2000, p. 174). Not just the Socialist State, but the emancipatory possibility associated with the State even in democracies, also clouded the relationship among State, individuals and communities.

> The originally 18th century term 'civil society' has also been used to make new and different sense of contemporary social and political developments. In Poland, Czechoslovakia, Hungary and elsewhere, the complexion of civil society has been instrumental in resisting Totalitarian regimes after the crushing of the Prague Spring; and it has featured in most political efforts to overthrow dictatorship, be it in Taiwan, Brazil, South Africa or Iran (Melucci, 1988).

Clearly, there are *different* usages of term and different lineages and origins. To fully understand the theoretical scope and its translation into action, it is important to understand the history of the term. We have divided the antecedents of civil society into four sections, as mentioned earlier. First, let us start with the classical thinkers.

Concept of civil society can be understood through the writings of

- Classical thinkers – Socrates, Plato and Aristotle
- Enlightenment thinkers – Hobbes, Locke, Ferguson, Paine
- 19th century thinkers – Hegel and Marx
- Modern thinkers – Gramsci and Habermas

Classical Political Thinkers

Whenever there is reference to classical philosophers, one is essentially talking about Greek philosophers such as Socrates, Plato and Aristotle. These classical philosophers were associated with ancient City-States of Greece. The Greek term for these City-States is *polis,* which literally means a city and also refers to citizenship or body of citizens. The City-States were known for their democratic orientation, which meant that the citizens had role in governing themselves. However, one central concern for many classical philosophers was how do citizens realize and fulfil their political rights without impinging on the larger entity of society.

There are bound to be conflicts between citizens' interests and State's needs. The conflicts can be resolved through dialectics according to Socrates (one garners ideas of Socrates through the writings of Plato, particularly from his book 'The Republic'). Socrates recommends a dialogue in which propositions are tested and refuted or reasoned till resolution is achieved. Plato being an idealist thought that a person must place reason above all else in pursuit of truth; above his appetite for physical satisfaction and societal approval. For Plato, it is only then a just society is possible, a just society where common good is the guiding principle. In his view, the *Philosopher King* is ideally suited for entrusting the task of ruling a society, to achieve common good.

For Aristotle, it was not the 'Philosopher King' who is the ideal candidate, but the average man and not the expert who must deliberate upon what kind of rules should govern them. Aristotle was not in favour of *Oligopoly*, which is the rule of the wealthy few, instead he recommended democratic rule by the majority. Aristotle also believed that human being was essentially a social animal who lived in society that could be clearly determined like the natural world. So he found it unnecessary to theoretically contemplate on nature of a society including the political aspects. Thus, for Aristotle the society can be built on rational principles which are grounded in experience.

Enlightenment Thinkers and Civil Rights

The Age of Enlightenment was a period in history where reason took centre-stage. It was a movement, which emphasized individual rights over monarchy, secular and rational ideas over faith and tradition. The Roman Catholic Church and religious orders in general, which exercised considerable control and influence over the population were the favourite target of Enlightenment thinkers. It was intellectual climate, which strongly opposed oppressive rulers of all shades and advocated civil liberties. This was the period when terms such as liberty and equality were in vogue. Many philosophers of Enlightenment, such as John Locke, Adam Ferguson and Thomas Paine, among others, were deeply influential in creating *discourse* around citizenry.

This thinking echoed changing economic realities: the rise of private property, colonial mercantile interests, and the rise of new class – *the bourgeoisie*. It also grew out of the mounting popular demand for liberty, as seen in the American and French revolutions. The term 'civil society' became a part of the general political discourse in the 16th and 17th century Europe. At this time, theorists of democracy besought this concept to define a democratic form of government rooted in the rights of citizens. The concept 'societascivilis' was coined to depict a zone, which was not under the papal (*Rule of Pope*) influence, and was governed by laws other than those of divine origin. Within civil society people had the right to choose their king and be governed by laws that focussed on the minimum shared interests of the people.

Later theorists built upon this conception and by the 17th century civil society came to designate a *distinct* form of political society – one in which the rights of individuals were given primary priority (Mahajan, 1999, p. 1188). Political thinkers such as Hobbes and Locke wanted to focus on the rational positioning and pursuits of individual as the basis of political life. Hobbes and Locke underlined the co-existence of the State and civil society and argued for a political system, in which civility can prevail among human beings, and can be ensured through social pacts or contracts.

They considered civil society as a community that maintained civil life, the realm where civic virtues and rights were derived from natural laws. In the approaches of Hobbes and Locke, human beings could plan out their political order. This was not in consonance with the Divine Rights theory. This idea had a great impact on the thinkers in the Enlightenment period. Thomas Hobbes underlined the need of a powerful State to maintain civility in society. For Hobbes, human beings are motivated by self-interests (Graham, 2001, p. 23). Moreover, these self-interests are often contradictory in nature.

Therefore, in *state of nature*, there was a condition of a war of all against all. In such a situation, life was 'solitary, poor, nasty, brutish and short' (Graham, 2001, p. 25). Upon realizing the danger of anarchy, human beings became aware of the need of a mechanism to protect them. As far as Hobbes was concerned, rationality and self-interests persuaded human beings to combine in agreement, to surrender sovereignty to a common power (Kaviraj, 2001, p. 289). Hobbes called this common power *Leviathan*. While Hobbes argues for the necessary evil of enforcing authority of the State, the conception of individual rights was most forcefully brought out in the writings of John Locke, who has influenced many later political theorists.

Locke exercised a powerful influence in launching liberal philosophy and by separating the realm of the Church and the State.

> At a general level, Locke maintained that civil society comes into existence when men, possessing the natural right to life, liberty and estate, come together, sign a contract, and constitute a common public authority. The public authority, or the supreme sovereign established through voluntary contract, has the right to promulgate and administer laws that are required to exercise and enjoy rights that are given to men by nature.
>
> Kaviraj (2001)

Writing about Locke's ideas on civil society, Gurpreet Mahajan (1999) adds that 'For Locke, the presence of law and governance in accordance with law transform a collective body into a political society. However, the existence of civil society requires more than the rule of law. Civil society emerges only when the citizen's right to life, liberty and property is guaranteed by law' (1999, p. 1189). This inalienable right of individual was meant to guarantee equality before law and also check the arbitrary powers of the State. This liberal thinking heralded the birth of secular democracies.

The civil society, which brought the individual and citizenry to the forefront, was pragmatically used as a guide to achieving political goal of civic and just society. This pragmatic usage is best expressed in the revolutionary pamphlet *Common Sense* (1776) by Thomas Paine, 'Despite the pragmatic usages of the liberal theories, the idea of natural rights of Hobbes and Locke vested the State with sovereign powers, without which the society would reduce to chaos. For the Natural Law theorist, *Monarchical Absolutism* could be countered by the assertion that individuals were granted certain rights through natural laws, which at least in theory of Locke was God-given. But the theorist of natural law assumed the governess of this law. It was independent of specific society. The theory of Contractarians was arbitrary; the need for civil society and State was based upon hypothetical thought, experiment and a speculative notion of human nature which varied from theorist to theorist'.

This particular notion that rights were located in eternal universal laws of nature was questioned by later political theorists by locating the rights and notion of civility in particular society, which has reached an advanced stage. Thus, Adam Ferguson argues in his *An Essay on the History of Civil Society* (1776) that civility is an attribute of advanced, polished society as opposed a barbaric primitive society. Ferguson's conception of civil society had an emphasis which differed from Hegel. For him, the basic contrast was not between civil society and political society but between civil society and natural society. The Scottish moral philosophers were evolutionists. They treated society rather than State as a subject of science (Beteille, 2000). For the Enlightenment political economists such as Ferguson and Adam Smith, among others, the civil society is not an artificial creation but progressive evolution of society. This perspective and the historical turn to understanding progression of society were to influence subsequent thoughts and writings on civil society and State.

19th Century Thinkers: Hegel and Marx

The idea of progression of society to an advanced level finds its expression, *albeit* in different forms in the approaches of Hegel and Marx. According to Hegel, the civil society (he uses the term 'bürgerli-cheGesellschaft', which also means bourgeoisie society and is also a key word around which Marx's analysis revolves) is a separate realm, a 'system of needs', that is the, "stage of" difference, which intervenes between the family and the State' (Hegel, 1991, p. 184).

What Hegel means to say here is that the private realm of family and the public institution come together to secure freedom of the individual such that the subjective goals and objective freedom get articulated. What Hegel recognizes, like the political economist before him such as Adam Ferguson and Adam Smith, the rise of economic sphere was an outcome and aftermath of Industrial Revolution. This economic sphere which he considered private was distinguished with the public realm of the State; this view was a break from all previous notions which saw civil society *subsumed* within the political realm of the State.

In the liberal tradition and particularly the contractarians theories, the State was the result of coming together of individuals. However, for Hegel, the State was an organic outcome of evolutionary process. Hegel too, like his predecessors, felt that earlier societies did not possess civil society. For Hegel, 'the concept of State was an ethical substance rather than multitude of individuals. It is an organic ethical community in which a special class of rulers is charged with the task of maintaining independence and integrity of the ethical whole and the health of its spiritual life'(cited in Pelczynski, 1984, p. 5).

The State was more than coercive and sovereign power according to Hegel. In fact, Gurpreet Mahajan (1999, p. 1191), in her analysis of Hegel, writes 'Like many analysts of the 18th century Hegel did not view the State simply as a symbol of legitimate authority expressing the sovereignty of the ruler, or as an instrument of coercive power. For him, the State signified a structure which upholds and protects the freedom and rights of the individuals. While its law embodies the conditions of objective freedom, its institutions secure subjective freedom that allows individuals to pursue their particular ends. Consequently, for him as well as many of his immediate contemporaries, the State and civil society are closely related. In fact, one is a part of the other; and, more importantly, both are embodiments of the idea of freedom'.

For Hegel, both individual freedom and universality of State are at par and equally important. The emergence of a new class and a new sphere of social existence, a distinct and autonomous 'economy' in his view facilitated this viewpoint. It was in this new sphere that private or particular and public or universal interests could interact. This was a space which was neither household nor State, but an arbitration between the two.

Marx questions the validity of Hegelian *metaphysical* form of dialectics at a later stage when he develops his methodological understanding of society with the concept of historical materialism. However, Young Marx has expressed his views through dialogue with Hegel over the issue of individual freedom. 'On the Jewish Question', he writes 'Man, as the adherent of a *particular* religion, finds himself in conflict with his citizenship and with other men as members of the community. This conflict reduces itself to the *secular* division between the *political* State and *civil society*. For man as a *bourgeois* (i.e. as a member of civil society, "bourgeois society" in German), "life in the State" is "only a semblance or a temporary exception to the essential and the rule". The individual centred right to freedom in the civil society was seen to be "not based on union of man with man, but on separation of man from man" (Marx, 1971, p. 103).

The bourgeoisie with their right to property were seen as selfish by Marx. The civil society based on these rights was believed to lead 'man to see in other men not the realization, but the limitation of his freedom'. The political emancipation envisaged by liberalism was seen to produce a false *dichotomy* between the actual man of civil society, 'who was recognized only in the form of the egoistic individual', and the true man of community 'who was recognized only in the form of an abstract citizen' (Marx, 1971, p. 10).

> The bourgeois may have succeeded in freeing the civil society from the authority of the State, however, the civil society was not the *domain* of freedom because within it was created a new relationship of power between owners of the means of production and wage workers. civil society was the *arena* of reproduction of capitalist production relations, of continuing slavery of wage earners. Hence, as the battleground of two opposing classes, the civil society lost any unifying principle.
>
> Kumar (2000, p. 2777)

The civil society, in essence, served the interests of the bourgeoisie. The political sphere represented by the State for Marx was part of the superstructure, which reflected the interest of bourgeoisie under capitalism. Thus, for Marx, civil society did not have any emancipatory possibilities. As Beteille (2000, p. 176) observes, both Hegel and Marx believed that civil society 'is driven by private economic interests, even when they appear in the clothing of universal rights'.

> Civil society is a term that 'both describes and anticipates a complex and dynamic ensemble of legally protected non-governmental institutions that tend to be non-violent, self-organizing, self-reflexive, and permanently in tension, both with each other and with the governmental institutions that "frame, constrict and enable their activities". In the contemporary period, the term civil society has proved useful in many fields of research, including the analysis of past phenomena, such as the uneven geographic distribution of absolutist States' (Szucs, 1988), or 'the emergence of modern forms of exclusion of womenfrom public life' (Pateman, 1988), or the '"civilizing" of European manners' (Elias, 1978) (para cited from Melucci, 1988).

Modern Thinkers: Gramsci and Habermas

The term civil society lay buried for a while to resurface later in the writings of Gramsci. He saw civil society as an essential leg of the bourgeois rule in liberal States. For Gramsci, the State operated in society not only through coercive mechanisms such as police but also through consent. He uses the term hegemony (as used by Lenin, which was further refined by Gramsci) to capture the various mechanisms in society that make the individuals compliant to ruling class ideologies.

> According to Gramsci (1971), the State is not only an instrument of the ruling class, but a complex web of social, political and economic relations. The historical unity of ruling class realizes in the form of State, but there is an organic relationship between State, political society and civil society.
>
> Tas (2013, p. 1)

Traditional and orthodox Marxism has predicted that the contradictions of a capitalist society will eventually lead to a *proletarian revolution*, leading to withering away of the State. This prediction did not come true in all societies. In fact, capitalism was found to be far more entrenched than before. 'Capitalism, Gramsci (1971) suggested, maintained control not just through violence and political and economic coercion, but also through ideology. The bourgeoisie developed a hegemonic culture, which propagated its own values and norms so that they became the "common sense" values of all. People in the working-class (*also other classes*) identified their own good with the good of the bourgeoisie, and helped to maintain the *status quo* rather than revolting. To counter the notion that bourgeois values represented "natural" or "normal" values for society, the working class needed to develop a culture of its own'.

Gramsci brings to forefront the cultural aspect of hegemony and not just economic or political domination of the bourgeoisie. In a similar vein, his conception of the capitalist State extends beyond the mere political aspect. He sees the capitalist State as constituting (a) political aspect – signified by the coercive mechanisms and institutions such as the police and legal-constitutional control and (b) civil society aspect – signified by the institutions of family, unions, civil associations, education, etc. The civil society in that sense is a *private* realm and not political and it is not an economic realm either. He avers, however, that these distinctions are heuristic (*experience-based*) divides and in reality there are overlaps.

According to Gramsci, the capitalist State is a complex web and connotes an organic relation between the political, economic and civil society. The State not only exercises coercion and control but also achieves consent through its various spheres. Power, for Gramsci, is a relational concept. The social relations in a civil society are also expressions of relations of power. It is therefore not enough for the subordinate groups to seize the political power, it must extend to civil society.

He further writes, 'It is true that the State is seen as the organ of one particular group, destined to create favourable conditions for the latter's maximum expansion. But the development and expansion of the particular group are conceived of, and presented, as being the motor force of a universal expansion, of a development of all the "national" energies. In other words, the dominant group is coordinated concretely with the general interests of the subordinate groups, and the life of the State is conceived of as a continuous process of formation and superseding of unstable *equilibria* (*on the juridical plane*) between the interests of the fundamental group and those of the subordinate groups – *equilibria* in which the interests of the dominant group prevail, but only up to a certain point, that is, stopping short of narrowly corporate economic interest' (Gramsci, 1971, pp. 181–182).

The State here is complex play of classes and social forces. While the interests of the ruling class are realized through the State, he adds that the State is also subject to democratic forces from the subordinate groups. Here Gramsci brings in the arena of civil society. He does not clearly define civil society, the confusion is further exacerbated by the way he collapses civil society into the realm of the State. However, he does spell out the arenas of operation of civil society, 'civil society is the sphere where capitalists, workers and others engage in political and ideological struggles and where political parties, trade unions, religious bodies and a great variety of other organizations come into existence. It is not only the sphere of class struggles; it is also the sphere of all the popular-democratic struggles which arise out of the different ways in which people are grouped together – by sex, race, generation, local community, region, nation and so on'.

Thus, it is in civil society that the struggle for ***hegemony*** between the two fundamental classes takes place. In several passages in the *Prison Notebooks,* Gramsci says that 'civil society is ethical or moral society, because it is in civil society that the hegemony of the dominant class has been built up by means of political and ideological struggles'. Thus, for Gramsci's civil society with its complex relations the State provides a perspective for the transition from capitalism to democratic and participative forms of socialism, built from below and not imposed from above.

In fact, as has been observed, the contemporary Marxists have turned to Gramsci rather than Marx, as their source of insight into civil society (Beteille, 2000). Jurgen Habermas is another social philosopher who is known for his writings on civil society. He belongs to the Critical School of thinking, but unlike many of the Frankfurt School scholars, Habermas was not a pessimist and felt that the enlightenment project was unfinished and that it still held emancipatory potential. He saw this as a potential in the civil space of public sphere.

In *The Structural Transformation of the Public Sphere,* Habermas argues that prior to the feudalera, the European culture had been dominated by a 'representational' culture, where a monarch or single party represented itself with the intention of overwhelming its audience, through the spectacle of the State. With the coming of capitalism there has been a rationalization process which creates, according to him, a public sphere or what he calls – *Öffentlichkeit.* It is space where public exchanges views and knowledge and where there is room for dialogue. The public spaces such as coffee houses, clubs, reading clubs, masonic (*research-based*) lodges and such other spaces, and the growth of newspapers and journals in the 18th century, especially in England encouraged him to think that healthy dialogue is possible for the public outside of the realm of the State.

Locke	Hegel	Gramsci	Habermas
• Civil society emerges only when the citizen's right to life, liberty and property is guaranteed by law	• State and civil society as distinct and separate spheres	• Signified by the institutions of family, unions, civil associations, education, etc. • A private realm and not political or economic realm • Collapsed into the State	• Healthy dialogue outside the realm of State • Human emancipation in ideal speech situation in a public sphere

Habermas, inspired by Weber's understanding of rationalization process, also realized the increasing march of formal rational structures, whether it is the State structures or capitalist modes of rationality or structures seen even in the increasing commercialization of mass media. This rationalization process through its formal structures colonized the *lifeworlds* of the public (Habermas, 1983, p. 10).

Habermas (1983) believed that the 'human capacity of reason has to be resurrected, through proper communication. His "theory communicative action" rests on the understanding that all human beings communicate or have speech acts with the goal of being understood, a universal pragmatics as it were'. However, this communicative competency has been taken over, as already mentioned by the State, the market and other organizations with their instrumental rationality. Although Habermas finds communicative rationality being threatened by rationalizing modern society, he nevertheless argues that the core of communicative rationality, 'the unconstrained, unifying, consensus-bringing force of argumentative speech', is a 'central experience' in the life of a human being (Habermas, 1983, p. 10).

So, for Habermas an 'ideal speech situation' is possible if everyone has the same capacities of discourse, which are achievable if there is social equality and if the speech is not confused through the operations of ideology. Although Habermas gives us the possibility of human emancipation in ideal speech situation in a public sphere, he is not very clear how exactly this can be achieved.

> Lifeworld (Lebenswelt) means universe of what is self-evident or given. It is a sum total of experiences in everyday life (individual, social, perceptual and practical experiences)

Many of Habermas' critics say that his idealized analysis is outdated in mass-media dominated world we live in.

> The *basic* weakness of Habermas' project is its lack of agreement between ideal and reality, between intentions and their implementation. This *incongruity* pervades through both the most general as well as the most concrete phenomena of modernity and it is rooted in an insufficient conception of power. Habermas himself observes that discourse cannot by itself ensure that the conditions for discourse ethics and democracy are met. But discourse about discourse ethics is all Habermas has to offer. This is the fundamental political dilemma in Habermas' thinking: he describes to us the utopia of communicative rationality but not how to get there.
>
> Flyvbjerg (1988, p. 215)

Contemporary political scientists such as Neera Chandoke (1995, pp. 164–198) draw upon thinkers such as Hegel, Marx, Gramsci and Habermas. Chandoke observes that their works give us a more discriminating view of civil society. She speaks of civil society as 'a space for dialogue and contestation. She feels it is not something that can be constructed once and for all. It can be a source of tension, so it must constantly reenact itself and patrol its borders. For her, civil society is a public sphere, where individuals come together for various purposes, both for their self-interest and for reproduction of an entity called society. The inhabitants of this sphere are linked together by social bonds created out of new identities and new institutions'.

Thus, 'civil society is simultaneously a goal to aim for, a means to achieve it, and a framework for engaging with each other about ends and means. When these three "faces" turn towards each other and integrate their different perspectives into a mutually-supportive framework, the idea of civil society can explain a great deal about the course of politics and social change, and serve as a practical framework for organizing both resistance and alternative solutions to social, economic and political problems' (Edwards, 2005).

CONCLUSION

This chapter endeavoured to bring a succinct understanding of some of the main articulation on civil society through the history of political thought. The idea was to decipher the essence of the concept by explaining the nature and growth of civil society. As can be discerned, the early political philosophers collapsed the civil and the State together, often it meant the citizenry. For the Greek City-States, citizens were only men, not slaves and not women, so it was only a *partial* representation of society. From then on it evolved to a stage where individuals of all hues were considered equal. The ideals of French revolution – equality and freedom – were the cornerstones around which much of liberal philosophies revolved. However, this aspiration of individuals was sought to be collectively achieved through the State by agreements and contracts.

It is Hegel who first came up with a civil society concept, which has resonance with the way we use the term in contemporary contexts, as a sphere apart from the State and the market. It is here that the State and civil society were seen as distinct and separate spheres. But it took Gramsci, who gave it the context and an element of praxis by locating in the real politics of society. For him, in reality, State and civil society were not *dichotomous,* but denoted a web of relations of power. Perhaps, this analysis of Gramsci can be used to understand Habermas' quandary of how to mitigate the role of ideological structures; mass media could be one of them or even the bureaucratic structures.

As a student of political theory and public administration, it has to be borne in mind that the various strands of thinking need not be discarded but discussed upon. We can conclude by saying that the idea of civil society remains compelling, not because it provides the tidiest of explanations or the most coherent of political theories – it does not and probably never will, but it remains convincing because it speaks to the best in us – the collective, creative and values-driven core of the active citizen – calling on the best in us to respond in kind to create societies that are just, true and free.

Preparatory Questions

- What do you understand by the term 'civil society'?
- What is citizenry according to the Greek philosophers such as Plato and Aristotle?
- Describe the intellectual climate of the Enlightenment period.
- In what way are Hobbes and Locke responsible for bringing forth the 'rights' argument?
- 'The individual freedom and the absolute State were brought into a dialectic fold by political philosophers'. Discuss.
- For Gramsci, 'civil society was an essential leg of the bourgeoisie society'. Explain.
- Outline the essential features of Habermas' ideas on civil society.

REFERENCES

Anheier, H. et al. (2001) *Introducing Global Society*. UK: LSE Global Governance, London.

Beteille, A. (2000) *Antimonies of Society: Essays on Ideologies and Institutions.* New Delhi: Oxford University Press.

Chandoke, N. (1995) *State and Civil Society: Explorations in Political Theory*. New Delhi: Sage.

Flyvbjerg, B. (1998) 'Habermas and Foucault: Thinkers for Civil Society?' *British Journal of Sociology*. pp. 210–233. Volume 49

Graham, P. (2001) 'Civil Society Theory and Euro-Nationalism.' *Studies in Social and Political Thought.* (4). pp. 31–56. Issue 4

Gramsci, A. (1971) *Selections from the Prison Notebooks*. New York: International Publishers.

Habermas, J. (1983) *Theory of Communicative Action*. Vol1. Cambridge: MIT Press

Hegel, G. F. W (1991), *Philosophy of Right*, (Edited by Allen W. Wood), Cambridge University Press, Cambridge, 1991.

Kumar, K. (1993) 'Civil Society: An Inquiry into the Usefulness of an Historical Term' *British Journal of Sociology*. pp. 375–395. Vol 44, No. 3.

Kumar, S. (2000) 'Civil Society in Society.' *Economic and Political Weekly*. 35(31), pp. 2776–2779.

Mahajan, G. (1999) 'Civil Society and Its Avatars: What Happened to Freedom and Democracy?' *Economic and Political Weekly*. pp. 1188–1196.

Marx, K. (1971) *On the Jewish Question* (Karl Marx, Early Texts, Edited and Translated by David McLellan). England: Oxford.

Pelczynski, Z. A. (ed.) (1984) ,*The State and Civil Society: Studies in Hegel's Political Philosophy*. CUP Archive. London.

Wood, E. M. (1990) 'The Uses and Abuses of Civil Society'. *Socialist Register*. 26(26).

Websites:

Available from: http://www.marxists.org/archive/marx/works/1844/jewish-question/(Accessed 20th November, 2013).

Edwards, M. (2005). Available from: http://infed.org/mobi/civil-society/(Accessed 20th November, 2013).

Gramsci, A. Available from: http://en.wikipe dia.org/wiki/Antonio_Gramsci (Accessed 26th November, 2013)

Gramsci, A. Available from: https://www.academia.edu/3673738/Gramsci_political_thought (Accessed 5th January, 2014).

Kaviraj, S. (2001). *Civil Society: History and Possibilites*. U.K. Cambridge University Press.

Keane John (1998). 'Civil Society: Old Images New Visions.' Broadway St Redwood. Stanford University Press.

Melucci. (1988). Available from: http://johnkeane.info/media/pdfs/jk_civil_society_definitions_encyclopedia.pdf (Accessed 20th October, 2013).

Simon, R. *Gramsci's Political Thought: Civil Society, the State and Power.* London: Lawrence & Wishart, electronic book. Available from: https://www.academia.edu/3673738/Gramsci_political_thought (Accessed 25th October, 2013].

Tas, S. Available from: https://www.academia.edu/1619415/Civil_Society_in_Gramsci_and_Habermas [Accessed: 26th November, 2013].

Chapter Seventeen

Policy Formulation, Implementation and Evaluation

Anurag Joshi

LEARNING OBJECTIVES

After completing this chapter, you should be able to:

- Explain the core components of public policy process
- Discuss the important facets of public policy formulation
- Examine the various components of policy implementation
- Describe the agencies involved in the policy process; and
- Bring out the difficulties in policy evaluation

INTRODUCTION

Effective public policy process is the strongest *manifestation* of an efficient public administrative system. The policy process necessitates that the government has a vision, a desire or will to think, create and execute policies and decisions, which are citizen oriented, justice laden and participatory. Public policy process is tedious, yet interesting. We can say that a government gets *transformed* into governance through the public policy process.

In this chapter, we are going to discuss the formulation, implementation and evaluation (FIE; pronunciation to rhyme with 'tie') of public policy and have therefore divided this chapter into these very *sections*. Study of public policy is the core of *policy sciences* which is now a discipline in its own right. It is another matter that as a discipline it partakes of other disciplines, the most *notable* of which are political science, public administration and management.

Insofar as public policy is concerned, you have already been introduced to its meaning, nature, significance and approaches in considerable details in chapter 12 of this volume. So, we are not getting into details again. In order to *refresh* your memory, a public policy most fundamentally is a government policy, formulated and implemented *largely* by the government but – and interestingly at that – evaluated, generally by non-governmental actors/agencies, even though various other agencies are involved in the exercise (it shall become comprehensible to you later in this chapter why it is so).

The following points help recall the salient features of public policy:

- Government policy
- Formulated and implemented mainly by the government
- Evaluated generally by governmental, non-governmental actors/agencies

PUBLIC POLICY PROCESS

Policy process entails three distinct stages, that is, formulation, implementation and evaluation. In recent times, this FIE of public policy has acquired a great salience, especially in developing societies of the world. This focus on FIE, to a great extent, stems from a widespread perception – in *both* the developed and the developing world – that public policies have not been as effective as they should have been; developmental goals have *not* been fulfilled to a large extent. We use the acronym FIE, as it is also an expression of disgust and disdain. This perception may be correct or otherwise, but it is there.

Policy sciences is the term coined by Harold D. Lasswell. It combines systematic analysis and evaluation of policies. It methodically studies the nature, causes and effects of policies, keeping in view the alternatives available, to determine the policies that will achieve given goals.

The fact that we are now living in a liberalizing, privatizing and globalizing or LPG world wherein the State is supposed to be withdrawing or retreating makes the issue of FIE all the more cogent. Increasingly, the view is that the State is formulating public policies targeting *some* rather than *all* sections of society and these 'some' sections are the advantaged, rather than the disadvantaged.

Also, even vis-à-vis the relatively advantaged, the benefits of the various public policies are not reaching all the intended beneficiaries. Then, as already indicated, there is the matter of the withdrawing/retreating State washing its hands altogether of welfare measures. It is against this background that FIE of public policies has acquired a keen poignancy in our times. Let us discuss the FIE *stages* one by one.

Formulation of Public Policy

As you all know, a public policy passes through various stages. The starting or the first stage is its formulation or the 'F' of FIE. This fact is so obvious that is does not need any elaboration. Thus, the 'first stage in public policy process is policy formulation'. The formulation stage basically entails (i) taking cognizance of the demands being made on a political system and then (ii) conversion of these demands into appropriate public policies by the concerned political system. As you must have read, 'public policy is a proposed course of action dealing with public demands and problems' (Sahni and Etakula, 2010). Accordingly, as per the *input–output* model, suggested by Gabriel A. Almond, demands made on a political system are *converted* into policies.

This conversion process is either aided or based on what Almond and others such as David Easton have called 'inputs'. These inputs, basically, are grounds/bases/feedback and so on for a political system (government in lay person's language) to take note of and act (formulation of policies). Inputs, generally, cover domains such as political socialization, interest aggregation, interest articulation and political communication (Sahni and Etakula, 2010).

If one were to sum up the meaning of the various domains, it would imply the demands made on the government by a particular citizenry – a citizenry seeped in a political culture unique to itself. David Easton has talked of a *feedback* model of policy formulation, wherein 'the demands of the people, which are not converted into policies, are again fed through the same procedure till action is taken on them. At the (*stage*) of policy formulation, a close–knit relationship between the executive and the legislature, the executive and the judiciary and the judiciary and the legislature facilitate policy making' (Sahni and Etakula, 2010). What we have stated above can be represented schematically as below:

Policy formulation as envisaged by Easton

Inputs (Demands)	Outputs (Supply)
• Political socialization	• Rule making
• Interest aggregation	• Rule application
• Interest articulation	• Rule adjudication
• Political communication	• Authoritative allocation of values
• Others	

The above scheme is, in a general sense, applicable to all well-ordered, functioning societies of the world and in fact, has been followed by them. However, regarding societies which are failing or have failed, we cannot say for sure whether the above *schema* or pattern was applied and if so, why it did not work out. The scope of this chapter does not permit a detailed discussion of this; however, this points to an area of further research by scholars of policy sciences.

What we have discussed above has been lucidly explained by Hoshiar Singh in his book 'Administrative Theory' (Singh and Sachdeva, 1997). He basically elaborates on the *sources* through which the administration gathers information for the purpose of enactment of laws by the legislative arm of the government. He lists four sources which are briefly enumerated and discussed ahead:

Internal sources: Herein, he basically refers to the data collecting activities/efforts of various government departments for facilitating policy formulation. Thus, every department is a centre to which flow periodic reports and returns from various fields/establishments. These reports and other material are recorded by the department for future use, whenever the need arises.

External sources: For supplementing the data accessed through their own sources, government departments rely on various external sources as well. The main reason for this is that frequently data collected internally is not only inadequate but unreliable as well. This makes the government seek appropriate feedback and information, etc, from labour unions/chambers of commerce or other professional associations.

Special investigation: In India, as elsewhere, special investigations for specific purposes are conducted by commissions/committees of enquiry 'for finalizing facts in respect of a particular matter or field'. Such investigations are very *useful* for policy making as they provide the maximum thought in a particular field.

Research and study: Within any country, and India is not an exception, there are several research organizations/think tanks and similar bodies engaged in continuing research about various aspects of society, economy and polity. The research conducted by these organizations acts as a very rich source of information for the policymakers. What you should note also is that governments utilize records/study conducted by international organizations as well, namely, the United Nations and its various affiliates such as World Health Organization, International Labour Organization, International Bank for Reconstruction and Development and International Monetary Fund.

The above should give you a reasonably good idea of all the sources that policy makers draw upon when engaged in policy making.

Actors/Levels Involved in Policy Formulation

Gladden (cited in Singh 2002) identified the 'policy making hierarchy' as having the following four levels:

Political or the general policy: This generally refers to 'the broad outline of policies mentioned in a ruling party's manifesto'.

Executive policy: This 'is regarded as the systematic and effective reduction of the general policy into concrete practical objectives which manifest into the cabinet policy'.

Administrative policy: 'It is the form which the executive policies take when in operation through administrators'.

Technical policy: This 'is the day to day operation of the policy by administrators who actually implement the administrative policy'. This four-tier approach given by Gladden will give you a fairly good idea of policy formulation.

This is further illustrated in the box below:

Stages in policy formulation

- *Political*: Broad outline of policies mentioned in a ruling party's manifesto
- *Executive*: Systematic and effective reduction of general policy in concrete practical objectives (manifest in cabinet policy)
- *Administrative*: The form which the executive policy takes when operationalized through administrators
- *Technical*: Day-to-day operation of policy by administrators engaged with implementing the administrative policy

What we have stated above and shown in the accompanying box as well can be more clearly understood with reference to our own country. Now, let us focus on actors involved in policy formulation in India; these include (i) Constitution, (ii) Legislature, (iii) Cabinet, (iv) Planning Commission (Now nomenclatured Niti Aayog), (v) National Development Council, (vi) Bureaucracy, (vii) Cabinet Secretariat and the Prime Minister's Office (PMO) and (viii) Others (Singh and Sachdeva, 1997).

Before we get into details, you should note that (i) in any liberal democracy, not just India, actors involved in policy formulation are the actors listed here and (ii) within the context of any specific country, the legislature and the cabinet refer not only to the central (national) units, but to the provincial (state, etc.) units as well. For instance, the Indian parliament and any state legislative assembly. The reason why we are mentioning this specifically is that in a democratic form of government – unitary, federal or a mix of the two – the provincial/local units often have the exclusive right to formulate policies with regard to certain subjects (*areas of jurisdiction in Union, State and Concurrent Lists*).

Now coming to the actors engaged in policy formulation in India, let us briefly touch upon them.

Constitution: In any liberal democracy, the Constitution and its Preamble provide the basic framework for policy formulation by both the national and the provincial governments. Put differently, no policy can be framed that violates the letter and the spirit of the Constitution.

Legislature: The parliament of the country and the various state legislatures are tasked with the enactment of laws in order to give a concrete, tangible shape to broad policy directives given in the Constitution. 'The role of legislature is primarily that of vetoing and controlling policies because it itself rarely (*emphasis added*) takes the initiative in sponsoring legislation. It influences and moulds policies through general discussions, adjournment motions, interpolations, resolutions, etc.' (Singh and Sachdeva, 1997).

Cabinet: In India, the central (national) cabinet headed by the Prime Minister is the most important source of public policies (incidentally, this is the case in most democracies). Of course, the provincial (state, etc.) cabinets headed by the chief minister, too, play an overarching role as far as policy formulation is concerned.

Niti Aayog/Planning Commission: This is a non-constitutional body. It performs an advisory role to the government but even as an advisory body, it wields a tremendous influence on the governments of the day in the arena of policy formulation (it is now called Niti Aayog, the role and functions of which are yet to be thoroughly defined).

National Development Council: This is a body headed by the Prime Minister and has a *mixed* membership. Thus, it consists of some central ministers, chief ministers of all states, members of various political parties, social organizations and eminent persons drawn from various walks of life. In our country, it is the supreme policy-making organ guiding even the planning commission. Its preeminent position can be gauged from the fact that 'about 50 per cent of the public spending at *both* (*emphasis added*) the central and state levels is directed by it under the broad approval of the central government' (Singh and Sachdeva, 1997).

Bureaucracy (*Civil Services*): Strictly speaking, bureaucracy comes into the picture only when one talks of policy implementation but this scenario was the norm when there used to be a politico-administrative dichotomy in public administration (*dealt with in detail, later in this chapter*). Now, this dichotomy – which in any case was artificial – no longer exists and bureaucrats or civil servants are no more a mere implementing arm. They *participate* in policy-making in that (*emphasis added*) they advise and supply the necessary data to the minister for policy-making, give legislative form to the policies and lay down administrative rules and regulations for giving effect to approved policies.

Cabinet Secretariat and the PMO: In our country and elsewhere where liberal democracy exists, the cabinet secretariat and the PMO, (*and their counterparts elsewhere in the democratic world*) are the two key actors *vis-à-vis* policy formulation. The cabinet secretariat was meant to be the superior/dominant of the two, but over time, particularly from the time of the late Prime Minister Rajiv Gandhi, it is the PMO, which has largely been calling the shots.

Others/Miscellaneous: Apart from these major actors involved in policy making in India (*and this is representative of other democracies of the world as well*), there are other actors as well. These others include (a) Standing Committees (Estimates/Public Accounts, etc.), (b) Advisory Bodies (Central Advisory Board of Education/University Grants Commission for example), (c) Pressure Groups (Trade Unions/Chamber of Commerce), (d) Political Parties and (e) the Press. All these bodies not only 'advise, suggest but sometimes protest and demand correctives in regard to a particular policy' (Singh and Sachdeva, 1997).

At the state levels too, the same procedure of policy formulation is followed. The state governments formulate policies and make laws on items mentioned in the State and Concurrent Lists. At the State level, the state legislature and council of ministers under the leadership of the chief minister and other advisory bodies participate in the formulation of policies. Our discussion of policy formulation will not be complete without a reference to the views of Yehezkel Dror.

Dror on Policy Formulation

Yehezkel Dror has employed the terms 'megapolicy' and 'metapolicy' in the context of policy sciences. Megapolicy is a broad outline of the shape of policies to be followed in the coming years. 'It is a general direction or a blueprint or a framework of the further course of action of the government' (Amita, 2002).

To quote Dror himself 'Megapolicies involve determination of the postures, assumptions and main guidelines to be followed by specific policies. They are a kind of master policy, clearly distinct, from detailed discrete policies'. Metapolicy is the framework of policy formulation. Its importance in the context of *megapolicy* lies in that 'a *megapolicy* is of limited use unless it is supplemented by the framework within which the specific policies could be formulated'. This framework is provided by a metapolicy. Dror, in fact, has explained a metapolicy as 'a policy on how to make policy' (views of Dror, cited in Singh, 2002).

You can make out that 'metapolicy and megapolicy are interdependent and together exist and improve policy analysis'. It is important to mention here that Dror firmly believes that 'unless this policy making system is reformed very little can be done to improve policies' (views of Dror, cited in Amita, 2002). From the above exposition, you would have got a reasonably good idea of policy formulation and its various levels/stages. However, our discussion will not be complete without a mention of approaches to policy formulation. This has been dealt with very briefly in the section ahead. It will suffice over here if you have a passing acquaintance with the major approaches to policy formulation.

Approaches to Policy Formulation

Since public policies are of different types, the approaches to them also vary. According to A. Lee Fritseher and Michael C. Wilson (as cited in Singh, 2002), there are four substantive perspectives on policy formulation/analysis. These are the *Systems, Institutional, Elite and Group* approaches. The focus of these approaches is upon policy determinants. In addition to these four approaches, there are three other approaches that go by the name of the *Rationalist, Empirical and Intuitive*. These three approaches are basically concerned with the policy process or its consequences. If one were to think of 'generic' expressions, then all these approaches can be subsumed under (i) rational and

(ii) non-rational approaches (Singh, 2002.). These approaches have been already explained in detail in chapter 12 of this volume. We now move onto the next crucial part of this chapter and this itself concerns with the issue of policy implementation.

Implementation of Policy

Policy implementation or 'I' of the acronym FIE is often more important than its formulation. This stems from the fact that often well-crafted policies go haywire because of poor or ineffective implementation. This is particularly true of developing societies such as India, where the benefits of several well-meaning and well-defined public policies have often not reached the intended beneficiaries because of unimaginative, tardy, poor and corruption-laden implementation.

It may interest you to know the reason for the unsatisfactory implementation of public policies. 'The most conspicuous are said to be lack of consistency, inadequate political sense of civil servants, limited political competence, inadequate organizational capability and absence of strong policy pressure groups'. Besides, communalism, regionalism, casteism, terrorism, people's apathy and infighting within various political parties, factionalism and groupism have also been responsible for poor policy implementation' (views of S. N. Sadasiram, cited in Singh and Sachdeva, 1997).

We have the well-documented statement of the late former Prime Minister Rajiv Gandhi wherein he had, in the context of the government's anti-poverty programmes, stated that out of every one rupee meant for the selected target groups, only a measly fifteen paise reached them. The most recent debate in the Indian government and elsewhere on provision of subsidies via direct cash transfer is only a recognition and cognizance of the problems of implementation. The above should give you a really good idea of the importance of effective public policy implementation.

There are many truths, half-truths and even myths about what policy implementation actually means. Much of the confusion emanates from the dichotomy maintained between politics and administration by the scholars and practitioners of public administration for a very long time. This and allied aspects are discussed in the section below.

Some Crucial Aspects of Implementation

As we have said, what really is implementation is often steeped in a hazy mist. Thus, to start at the start, 'implementation is the *task* of putting *formulated* polices to *practice*' (Amita, 2002, emphasis added). As Sahni and Etakula (2010) aver, 'it is very rare that the policies formulated are self–executing and are executed by mere statement. Often the policies require some action.... The implementation process has certain activities working within it.....'. From what has been given above, we can say that when we talk of implementation of policy, we essentially mean its operationalization.

It has also been observed that for implementation to occur '(i) there must be an *entity* with sufficient resources assigned to carry out the implementation task, (ii) the implementing agency must be able to translate goods into operational framework, (iii) the entity assigned the implementing task must deliver its assignment and be accountable for its actions' (cited in Chakraborty and Chand, 2012, p. 202).

It is important for you to note that the implementation process involves the continuation of the political process which had actually authored the policy. This is important because 'this is the reason why governments which have formulated a particular policy find it easier to implement it rather than the governments which inherit the task of implementation from the previous governments. The task is made more difficult for new governments, which happen to be ideologically and electorally different from the previous one. The implementation process in any functioning society of the world has certain well-defined characteristics with which you should be familiar. These *characteristics* are outlined in the next section.

Characteristics of the Implementation Process

Amita Singh, (2002) has described the following features of policy implimentation.

Scope of operation: Implementation is 'within the arena of political forces'.

Collective action: A defining feature of implementation is that it *converts* policies into collective action. The idea is to bring 'beneficiaries and passive people together so that the implementation could be effectively channeled'.

Control and accountability: The process of implementation concerns itself 'with problem of control and accountability in administration'. This basically refers to the issue of *controlling* 'hierarchies in bureaucratic structures. Authority from the top is heavily exercised to the bottom and the fears and anxieties of the top are transferred to the bottom level. Also proper control through the higher level bureaucracy can make the lower level bureaucracy more accountable in implementation'.

Street-level discretion: It has been observed that the success of the implementation process greatly depends upon what has been termed 'street-level discretion'. Luther Gulick discovered that 'the actual discretion used in administration is used at the very *bottom* of the hierarchy when public servants touch the public. So it is absolutely necessary to make this bottom layer of administration or the street level bureaucrat more informed, effective and reliable so that policies are adopted without much turmoil'.

No clear-cut end point: This is a rather crucial aspect of implementation, but seldom recognized as such. The point is that 'policy implementation has no clear-cut end point, which marks the end of the implementation processes. What we should be cognizant of is that 'the implementation of a section in a policy is the starting point of the other episode or problem area. It is an ongoing process, which never ends till the policy is withdrawn or the funds end'.

Intergovernmental bargaining: This dimension of implementation concerns itself with the issue of convergence and divergence between different governmental agencies in the context of implementation. As has been stated, since every policy involves the cooperative efforts of several agencies, their mutual understanding, cooperation in policy execution, coordination among themselves and allocation of grants play a decisive role in getting the policy implemented. Moreover, in federal systems, the tough bargaining between the states and the centre on the one hand and states and local governments on the other can lead to the success and failures of the formulated policy.

Implementation as a system of games: Some scholars of policy sciences have viewed the implementation process as a system of games. As you might know, implementation concerns itself to a great extent with the aspect of bargaining, persuasion and manoeuvring. These aspects have been refined by Eugene Bardach in his idea of 'implementation games'. The main thesis of Eugene Bardach is that 'system is formed of loosely interrelated structural elements called games. The relationship and interaction among two or more players sets the conditions for the other. These games which the elements play make the implementation process difficult and complex'.

Characteristics of implementation are as follows:

- Scope of operation
- Collective action
- Control and accountability
- Intergovernmental bargaining
- No specific end goal
- Implementation as a system of games

From our discussion on the process of implementation, we can infer that it is much more than a mere carrying out of the orders of a political and/or bureaucratic authority. Just to refresh your memory and also to facilitate your understanding, the various characteristics of implementation are given in a capsule form also in the box earlier. You may be curious as to who are involved in the process of implementation. This is mentioned in the section below.

Actors/Agencies Involved in Implementation

Generally, in any reasonably well-ordered society of the world, one finds the involvement of the following in the task of implementation, namely, (i) political parties, (ii) pressure/interest groups, (iii) a wide assortment of bureaucratic outfits, (iv) judiciary and (v) civil society and NGOs. We will not get into details here as these have been discussed at length elsewhere in this volume.

Before we move onto the last section of this write-up on evaluation of public policy, a word on *politics-administration dichotomy* is necessary to fully comprehend the subtle *nuances* of implementation. If you will remember, we had mentioned this at the start of our discussion on the process of implementation. A dichotomy or a disjuncture between politics and administration has been a feature of public administration for a long time.

> There was a time when it was thought that the task of making policies is that of the legislature and the executive and the implementation of the policies made by the government is to be done by the administration. There used to be a hard and fast dichotomy between politics and administration, that is, between policy formulation and its implementation.
>
> Sahni and Etakula (2010)

However, now with the growth of liberal democracy and a considerable expansion of the State's activities, 'the politics-administration dichotomy is no longer accepted. The administration now attempts to find out the best way of implementing a policy….. to carry it out as suggested by the policy formulators. The concept of "delegated legislation" has further strengthened the ties of relationship between politics and administration' (Sahni and Etakula, 2010).

It may interest you to know that among the scholars of policy sciences, Luther Gulick was among the first to point out 'that politics-administration dichotomy cannot work and that administration cannot be completely divorced from policy making' (Singh and Sachdeva, 1997). In reality, public officialdom, in the opinion of Singh and Sachdeva, is involved in policy formulation in the following *three* crucial ways:

i) *Supply of information*: The bureaucrats or the civil servants have to provide their political bosses/legislatures with information/advice necessary for policy formulation and neither the political executive nor the legislative arm of the government can ignore the inputs thus received. The most important reason for this is that the members of the legislature or the ministers are amateurs who have risen to position because of, popular will and not because of administrative talent…'.

ii) *Initiative from the administration*: In the developing world, the initiative for policy formulation often comes from the administration. A basic reason for this could be the poor personal/professional characteristics and capabilities of the political class. Be that as it may, it is the administration which is in constant touch with the general public and is in a better position to understand the difficulties that arise in the execution of legislation'.

iii) *Time and knowledge assistance*: Since legislatures today suffer from an acute *shortage* of time and knowledge, they focus on 'skeletal acts' and leave the details to the administration. It is here that administration is most supreme in policy making. In order to execute these acts, the administration frames rules, regulations and bye-laws which are a major contribution to policy making. Clearly, the dissonance between politics and administration was always artificial and it is good for the entire gamut of FIE that this has been recognized and acted upon in an increasingly globalized world. We now move onto the last section of this chapter, namely, policy evaluation.

3) Policy Evaluation

Of the three components of FIE, evaluation or 'E' did not get much attention till recently. There are/can be different reasons for this, details of which are beyond the scope of this chapter. What is important for you to know is that comparatively recent focus on policy evaluation stems from a widespread perception among both the policy makers and the common public that various policies are not really delivering the goods. The policy makers are perplexed as to why extremely well thought out (*at least according to them*) polices are not working out, whereas the common person is aggrieved and agitated that the policy makers are not doing enough. Hence, the focus is on an exhaustive scrutiny of public policies, especially by the civil society. Naturally, since policy evaluation is gaining ground, we should be clear as to what it really means. You should also become familiar with some major problems encountered in evaluation studies. These aspects are dealt within the section that follows.

Meaning of Evaluation

A good definition of evaluation was given by Ira Sharkansky way back in the 1970s but it holds good even today. Thus, 'the evaluation of public policy is an attempt to assess the contents and effects of policy on those for whom it is intended'. Similarly, Singh (2002) states that 'Evaluation is a process through which all defects of the policies are brought out through the study of its impacts in a manner that improves upon the pre–existing policies. It is one of the most reliable and meaningful input to policy improvement'.

In so many other words, policy evaluation concerns itself with *judgement* over the *success/failure* of a policy and *suggestions/prescriptions* for its improvement. You should know that 'often policy evaluation occurs *throughout* (*emphasis ours*) the policy process, not necessarily at its termination stage'. Stated differently, 'evaluational activity may restart the policy process (problem formulation onwards) in order to continue, modify or terminate existing policy' (Basu, 1990).

Methods of Policy Evaluation

Basu (1990) mentions that generally there are three recognized methods of policy evaluation: (i) policy impact evaluation, (ii) policy strategy evaluation and (iii) policy project appraisal. These are, very briefly, discussed here.

Policy impact: Policy impact concerns itself with an overall assessment of a policy. 'The emphasis is on determining the extent to which programmes are successful in achieving basic objectives and on the comparative evaluation of national programmes'.

Policy strategy: As you can understand from the subtitle above, here 'the emphasis is on determining which strategies, methods and procedures are most productive or effective'.

Policy project: Herein, the process of evaluation concerns itself with 'an assessment of individual projects through site visits and other activities with emphasis on managerial and operation efficiency'. The techniques used in policy evaluation could be cost-benefit analysis, programme planning and budgeting system, various experimental methods and many more statistical methods and tools. However, we find that despite the elaborate and systematic evaluation procedure, policy impact is not very easy to determine.

Before we move onto a discussion of difficulties involved in evaluation, there is one more vital dimension of evaluation with which you should be familiar and that is the *distinction* between policy *output* and *outcome.*

Distinction between Policy Output and Outcome

Many students of public administration think that policy output and policy outcome are one and same and thus, often use the terms interchangeably. However, in reality, there is a fine distinction between the two terms. Thus, 'Policy output refers to the *quantifiable* actions of the government which can be measured in *concrete* terms; for instance, construction of government offices, schools.... These activities can be measured in concrete terms, but figures reveal very little about the policy *outcomes* or the *qualitative* impact of public policies on the lives of the people'. Thus, 'proving how much is spent on pupils in a school system on a per capita basis will reveal nothing concerning the effect schooling has on the *cognitive* and other abilities of students, let alone the *social* consequences of the educational system' (Basu, 1990, emphasis added).

Difficulties in Evaluation

We have mentioned that evaluation as an aspect of public policy did not receive much attention till recently. One of the most fundamental reasons for this has been that evaluation as an exercise has certain difficulties. The difficulties and complexities (Basu, 1990) involved in evaluation mainly focus on the following:

- Situation of uncertainty over policy goals.
- Problems in determining causality.
- Diffused (unclear/vague) policy impacts.
- Difficulties in acquiring data.

We feel that details insofar as the above difficulties are concerned are beyond the scope of this chapter, however, some more lacunae in policy process could be listed out as follows:

- Absence of adequate financial resources.
- Vagueness of goals.
- Intangibility of objectives.
- Lack of understanding of concepts such as monitoring, appraisal and review.
- Multiplicity of agencies involved.
- Inadequate coordination among evaluating agencies.
- Lack of political will and bureaucratic cooperation.
- Operational convenience rather than focus on public needs.
- Lack of non-governmental inputs and informed debate.
- Absence of evaluation criteria/parameters.

- Lack of systematic analysis and integration prior to policy making.
- Stress on statistics (*statistical data for outcomes*) rather than research.
- No accountability or grievance redressal.

Agencies Involved in Evaluation

Our exposition on policy evaluation will remain incomplete without some mention of the bodies involved in this exercise. We are mainly talking of India here but similar organizations, institutions and agencies are involved elsewhere in the democratic world. In India, the following are engaged in policy evaluation:

- Planning Commission (Niti Aayog).
- Parliamentary Committees.
- Comptroller and Auditor General of India.
- Political Parties.
- Non-governmental Organizations.
- Media.
- Editorials.
- Seminars and Conferences.
- Articles in Journals.
- Research Institutes.
- Reserve Bank of India.
- International and Regional Institutions.
- University Institutions.

It is evident that the bodies engaged in the evaluation exercise are *multifarious*. However, it is a matter of great concern that very often 'their evaluation findings and suggestions are not given due consideration and proper application by the government' (Singh and Sachdeva, 1997).

If we have not been able to see our policies fructify to meet their targeted goals, then as Somanathan and Agarwal (2005) put it, this could *a priori* due to the following reasons:

- Adopting the wrong public policies.
- Poorly implementing the right public policies.

However, the situation is more complex than this. We have noted down the lacunae in policy process in the earlier section. These problems/lacunae need to be recognized and worked upon if the policy process has to be made more effective. Somanathan and Agarwal (2005) lay down the following solutions:

- Reduction in fragmentation of thought and action on public policy.
- Separation of policy making from implementation and decentralizing implementation authority.
- Widening and enhancing the knowledge base used in policy making and promoting integration and synthesis.

CONCLUSION

In this chapter, you have been introduced to the salient aspects of what we have chosen to call FIE of public policy. What you should note is that the focus on FIE in recent times is essentially because of a widespread perception and mostly correct at that, that public policies are not turning out to be very effective even when well conceived. This is leading to consternation among the policy makers and discontentment and resentment among the public. A better and more nuanced understanding of FIE can help stem the rot.

Preparatory Questions

- Describe the different sources through which administration gathers information for enactment of policies.
- Explain the role of the agencies/actors involved in policy formulation.
- Write a note on the characteristics of the policy implementation process.
- Discuss the stages in policy formulation.
- Examine the difficulties in policy evaluation.

REFERENCES

Basu, R. (1990) *Public Administration: Concepts and Theories*. 2nd Revised ed. New Delhi: Sterling Publication Pvt Ltd.

Chakraborty, B. and Chand, P. (2012) *Public Administration in a Globalizing World: Theories and Practice*. New Delhi: Sage.

Sahni, P. and Vayunandan, E. (2010) *Administrative Theory*. New Delhi: PHI Learning Pvt Ltd.

Sharkansky, I. (1978) *Public Administration and Policy Making*. Harcourt: Houghton Mifflin.

Singh H. and Sachdeva, P. (1997) *AdministrativeTheory*. Allahabad: KitabMahal.

Singh A. (2002) *Public Administration: Roots and Wings*. New Delhi: Galgotia Publishing Co.

Website:

Somanathan, T. V. and Agarwal, O. P. (2005) 'Public Policy Making in India: Issues and Remedies'. Available from: *floatingsun.net/udai/files/Agarwal-Somanathan.pdf*. [Accessed: January 22nd, 2014].

Chapter Eighteen

Interdisciplinary Nature of Public Administration and the Changing Role of the Chief Executive

Kopal Chaube

LEARNING OBJECTIVES

After completing this chapter, you should be able to:

- Analyse the changing contours of public administration in the globalization era
- Examine the interdisciplinary character of public administration
- Discuss the different types of chief executives and their functions
- Explain the functions of line, staff and auxiliary agencies; and
- Assess the inter-relationship amongst these agencies

INTRODUCTION

Public administration is undergoing a significant change in the era of globalization. As a consequence, the institutions, strategies and processes of government and governance are also undergoing a sea change. This process of globalization has various facets, which mean different things to different people. It is associated with change and is often perceived as a challenge to the traditional pillars of public administration. Some of the prominent aspects of these changes such as good governance have been discussed in this chapter. The role of the chief executive and its line, staff and auxiliary agencies have also been affected in this context and are witnessing a transformation in their functions. Holding on to the traditional nature of its functions, the chief executive today has to adapt to the changes in the milieu, the rise of private sector and involvement of civil society in governance. The current chapter looks into the changing nature of organization in the era of globalization through the lens of public administration. It discusses the different types of chief executives and their changing contours. It also brings out the synergies between the chief executive's line and staff agencies in the contemporary scenario.

CHANGING CONTOURS OF PUBLIC ADMINISTRATION

Before going into the changing role of the chief executive, we need to understand the importance of globalization and how it is impacting the institutions of public administration. As we all know, private sector has come to play a very significant role in public administration. The chief executive, be it a departmental head or an organizational head in the public sector, has to work along with the different stakeholders from the private sector and civil society. There are multiple stakeholders in the arena of governance today; the ones who were hitherto not engaged with health, education, electricity supply, telecom services, manufacturing and so on. Following liberalization post the early 1980s, public administration and its agencies have had to work in an environment which is not exclusively their own. The onslaught of globalization has changed many things to a significant extent.

Let us first try to understand this changed context a bit. The scholarship on globalization is divided into three distinct leanings – those in favour of globalization (Muller, 1989; Fukuyama, 1992; Friedman, 1999, as cited in Farazmand, 2012), those totally opposed to it (R. W. Cox, S. Ellener and J. Korbin) and lastly those that tread the middle path (Theda Skocpol, Joseph Stiglitz and J. Zysman). The first perspective in some measure is deterministic because it predicted 'end of the world' (Fukuyama, 1992), and the demise of Soviet Russia was seen as a consequence of globalization and privatization (Farazmand, 2012). This approach believes that State would eventually become irrelevant in the face of globalization and privatization. Therefore, public administration would also become redundant.

The second perspective is antithetical to the first one and argues that globalization is pernicious for the 'public' because it threatens the existence of the State itself and thereby of democracy as well. Chilcote (2002) elaborates that 'The idea of globalization also implies that.... the capital flows have created a new world order with its own institutions and network of power relationships'. However, the third perspective prescribes a State that is subservient to corporate power elite. The character and behaviour of the public administration as per this perspective are transformed from an administrative welfare State to a coercive corporatist State. The primary role of the State then is no longer that of public administration and welfare, instead State is geared towards management of 'public', so as to facilitate corporate capitalism.

Predatory globalization, as Farazmand (2012) calls it, is a phenomenon where the corporations are lessening State control in search of profit through cheap labour and resources, deregulated market and environmental protection. India is closer to the third model, where government is progressively deregulating various sectors (the latest being the investment sector in the current budget year 2015–2016 where Foreign Direct Investment has been increased from 26% to 51%), promoting investments and creating a corporate-friendly regime, rolling back from the social sector, negotiating public subsidies (current budget document talks about rationalizing subsidies to prevent leakages). It is thus pertinent to understand the role of the chief executive in an administrative milieu, where the State has opened up to the non-state actors in a liberal way. For this, it is very important to understand the relationship of public administration with other social sciences, as this interrelationship significantly determines the nature of today's administration.

INTERDISCIPLINARY CHARACTER OF PUBLIC ADMINISTRATION

Public administration as an area of study emerged from the womb of political science to establish itself as a separate entity in the 1940s. In the process, it has borrowed from many social sciences, so much so that critics have questioned its separate entity and theoretical bases (already discussed in chapter 2 on 'Phases in Evolution of Public Administration' of this volume). In 1946, Herbert Simon in his essay 'The Proverbs of Administration' indicated that public administration had conflicting and contradictory theories and an absence of a knowledge base that could provide a guide to practice. He made a valid point at that time because administration has existed ever since human beings started leading an organized life. All the civilizations of the world have survived on the basis of excellent administration. However, administration has been ubiquitous and least dealt with as an area of academic enquiry.

The study of public administration is an interdisciplinary field, which derives from a variety of disciplinary approaches and values. As Rosenbloom puts it 'in addition to the traditional managerial emphasis on efficiency and effectiveness, the field of public administration is heavily influenced by the representative and responsive nature of our political system, as well as our legal system's emphasis on individual rights and social equity. Thus, public administration is an interdisciplinary field, defined by the need to address conflicting political, legal, and managerial values and processes' (cited in Wright, 2011). More so, because a social phenomenon as complex as government (*with its multiple organizations and policies as well as in its multiple relations with society*) cannot be understood within one discipline or approach. Public administration is a study that does not quite fit into the established disciplinary mould. Let us examine the relationship of public administration with these disciplines.

Relationship with Political Science

In the early life of public administration as a discipline, prominent authors such as Woodrow Wilson emphasized the dichotomy between political science and public administration. To them, political science was value loaded and public administration aspired to be value neutral. In the opinion of J. B. D. Miller and David Easton, political science dealt with ethics, values and power struggle, whereas the administration was all about facts, techniques and use of that power. However, public administration is very closely connected with political science, as it emerged as a discipline out of political science. So, in this sense, political science is the mother discipline. However, as Herbert Simon has pointed out 'public administration is concerned with how things might be as well as how things are while improving the state of administration and this led it to search for scientific quality and practical relevance' (Perry 2012, cited in Meier, 2014). Although both subjects deal with the 'political', they approach the subject of 'State' from different positions. Political science is concerned about aspiration and vision of the State, whereas public administration is concerned about what the State strives to achieve. There is, however, a lot of common concern, where the two disciplines converge, for example, Constitutional and administrative laws, local self-government, policy studies, legislation, budgeting and so on. In addition, since public administration is about government, it requires an elementary understanding of the political institutions and the politics itself. These distinctions, however, are very thin and can hold value only if we try to consider certain key factors given in the box below.

The differences between political science and public administration are as follows:

- Political science deals with the value judgements and abstract concepts. Despite the behaviourist and positivist movements in the discipline, it has retained its emphasis on value. Authors such as John Rawls have emphasized the fact that political science cannot be value neutral if it tries to understand concepts such as justice and equality. Public administration, on the other hand, has been more inclined towards value neutrality as it is about 'practice'. The emphasis has been on 'scientific enquiry' and managerial efficiency since the inception of public administration as a discipline
- Political science is much wider in scope than public administration
- Political science deals with the ethical questions of politics, whereas public administration deals with the practical aspects of it
- Since politics is about who gets what, when and how, political science deals with the question of power and the struggle to retain it, whereas public administration looks at power as a tool for realizing policy goals

Again, it has to be realized that these differences are more conventional in nature and approach. Real-life administration borrows heavily from political science and works within the boundaries set by political science. Looking at the role of the chief executive in this interdisciplinary scenario, one can say that the chief executive is not just the implementer, but also the policy maker. We cannot say that the chief executive, while taking up policy decisions, does not really indulge in ethical questions, justice-related issues or power struggle. In fact, the chief executive is very much studied by both political science and public administration, for example, study of cabinet secretary, district collector, Prime Minister (PM) and President.

Relationship with Economics

Public administration is closely related to economics. An efficient administration is fuelled by an effective budget, and an administrator is as responsible for managing money as much as for planning, coordinating and organizing budgetary provisions. Even in today's time when the forces of globalization are forcing the State to roll back and follow a non-interventionist policy in the economic domain, the administration is, more than ever, occupied in understanding the domains of market and money. To be able to make an informed choice for the citizens, public administration needs to engage closely with the discipline of economics. Whether we look at the ancient times – when Kautilya emphasized the significance of finance for administration or today – where State is playing a very vital role by striking to maintain an equilibrium between the demands of globalizing capitalism and its own agenda of a welfare and responsive State, the relationship between public administration and economics is evident.

Public administration involves taxation, industrial policy, agriculture, labour welfare – all of which entail a sound understanding of economics. Even in the domain of public goods such as water, health and education, the discourse is progressively moving towards privatization, thereby making economics relevant in this context too. Within the domain of disciplinary study, public administration now includes study of agricultural economics, economic administration and planning and labour economics, which highlights the importance of the inter-relationship between the two. In this context, we can say that the chief executive has to coordinate with private players in policy making, implementation and analysis. The chief executive, in most cases, is engaged with all issues pertaining to finance under its administrative sphere and must partner effectively with other agencies over control of the purse.

Relationship with Law

Law is responsible for maintaining order in the human society. In the earlier times, social conventions, rulings of the monarchs and traditions did this work but in due course, social conventions and norms or justice prevalent in societies got codified in the form of legal system, which we know today as the law of the land. Public administration and law share a close relationship. Administration has a two-fold job of overseeing and facilitating: (a) framing of laws and (b) adjudicating legal enactments. Let us understand this clearly. In the democratic set up, the legislature is responsible for framing of laws, whereas the judiciary is responsible for adjudicating it. Both are covered in the ambit of public administration, which is responsible for smooth running of the system. Moreover, a sound legal framework is crucial for an effective and efficient administration. Within the disciplinary domain of public administration, the study of Constitution, legal systems and tribunals are not just mandatory but are highly useful as they help in understanding issues such as accountability, governance and administrative reforms.

Relationship with Sociology

Sociology studies the structure of society in a scientific manner. There is a close relationship between public administration and sociology as social structures and governance processes are intertwined and impact each other in the process of policy making. Governance is set up in a larger social context. Without a social context or an understanding of societal processes, public policy, governance or the nature of executive functions would be completely vacuous. Not being able to understand the societal structures and processes amounts to not comprehending the full nature and extent of public administration as a discipline. The policies and their implementation in such countries need to be studied within a broad framework of class, caste and power. This is the reason why Fred Riggs' analytical work on developing societies is pertinent till date. He understood and defined administrative structures in the comparative context of poor and developing ecologies.

In this broader interdisciplinary context, the chief executive works within the interlinks of public administration with economics, political science, law and sociology. When we talk of the role of the chief executive in today's context, we cannot overlook the fact that as a head of a public organization, the executive works in a scenario that is intertwined. There are pressures from the political parties, pressure groups and lobbies. In addition, the executive also works within a legal framework. The inter-relationship of public administration with economic reforms, budgetary processes and labour movements is also pertinent. The chief executive is the head of an organization in this given context and heads the organization with the help of line, staff and auxiliary agencies. The success of an organization depends largely on the effectiveness of its chief executive.

Relationship with Management

The relationship between management and public administration is most significant, as both study organizations (internal functioning as well as their relationship with other organizations). The organization theories such as closed, open, network and cybernetic are common to both public administration and management. Both disciplines address the organizational issues of leadership, coordination, client satisfaction and conflict management rather analytically. These days, public management is the most rapidly developing sub-field of public administration. Today's chief executive is majorly a public manager trying to network with other organizations keeping in mind the organizational principles and goals. Many feel that public administration borrows heavily from management theories at the cost of developing its own theories.

TYPES OF CHIEF EXECUTIVE

There are primarily two types of executives: (1) parliamentary and (2) presidential. In the former type, usually, there are again two types of executive: 'de jure' (i.e. according to law), which is vested in the President and 'defacto' (i.e. in reality), which is vested in the PM. In the latter type, that is, presidential form, the executive is the President. Private organizations spend a great deal of time and resources in picking up their chief executive but in the public domain the executive is generally elected and her/his election depends on political, economic and social factors. Traditionally in India, the PM is chosen along the lines of his or her political party. In the parliamentary system, the chief executive is totally responsible to the legislature, while this is not the case in the presidential system.

Besides these categories, the chief executive could be categorized as real (*President in the US*), titular (*in name only such as the President in the parliamentary system)*, plural (*functioning of cabinet in parliament*), single (*PM in parliament*) and collegial (*Swiss Federal Council with shared political powers in Switzerland*). Among these categories, there are micro-level and macro-level chief executives. Heads of democratic elected bodies at the district level, chairperson of zilla parishad, head of panchayat samiti, sarpanch of gram panchayat, cabinet secretary and divisional commissioners are all examples of micro-level chief executive. Macro-level chief executive again is the president or the PM.

The following are the types of chief executive:

- Presidential/Parliamentary
- Permanent/Political
- Real/Titular
- Single/Plural
- Micro-level/Macro-level

FUNCTIONS OF CHIEF EXECUTIVE

Having emphasized the importance of this position, let us understand the functions of the executive. The functions of the chief executive are primarily political and administrative.

1. *Political*: Political functions are very crucial for a leader as s/he represents a country, so the responsibility of steering a nation, establishing its political culture and protecting its image rest on the shoulders of the executive. S/he represents the country to the world, so developing linkages through diplomacy, bilateral/multilateral ties and alliances to serve the national interest are the important political functions of the executive. At the domestic level, promoting political education and political development aimed at providing support and energy to the organization is another political function of the executive. Political function at one level involves managing the political structure. These functions include policy making, policy implementation, policy analysis and managing party functions and affiliations; basically everything that aims at facilitating the processes of governance.
2. *Administrative*: The administrative functions are majorly concerned with management of people, material and money. Gulick has prescribed the administrative functions as 'POSDCORB', which is an acronym for Planning, Organizing, Staffing, Directing, Coordinating, Reporting and Budgeting (we have read about them in chapter 4 of this volume). Apart from these primary functions, an executive is required to undertake tasks such as internal management of organization, maintaining public relations, implementation of programmes, initiation and execution of administrative and fiscal reforms and leading the organization smoothly towards the achievement of set objectives. All these functions have become very complex and specialized and the executive cannot be expected to undertake and deliver all tasks on her or his own. S/he is supported in this by the line, staff and auxiliary agencies. Thus, an executive is expected to perform an array of functions, which involves management of personnel, finance and material. The list of the functions is exhaustive but some of them are given in the box below:

Political functions of the chief executive	Administrative functions of the chief executive
• Policy making	• Planning towards achievement of organizational objectives
• Execution of governmental policies/programmes	• Organizing tasks
• Policy monitoring and evaluation	• Recruiting personnel
• Liaison with political parties and interest groups	• Undertaking training sessions
• Maintaining governmental records and statistical data	• Coordinating the work of various departments
• Facilitating governmental programmes and policies	• Reporting from the micro-level to the macro-level
• Undertaking welfare work	• Controlling and supervising subordinate agencies

CHANGING ROLE OF THE CHIEF EXECUTIVE

Whether one subscribes to the 'End of Ideology' hypothesis or not, the contemporary State is predominantly classically liberal, welfare and socialist (Joshi, 2003). Classical liberal State by definition is a minimalistic State, but even welfare States with proclaimed socialist leanings have either turned or are increasingly turning minimalist under the influence of globalization. India is a good example where the State has been progressively rolling back and the phenomenon has accelerated post the liberalization phase in 1990s. A cursory glance at the annual budget 2015–2016 reveals that the central funding in the social sector has declined, especially in the areas of health and education where State seems to have rolled back (33,150 crores from 39,238 in 2014–2015), Sarva Shiksha Abhiyan (SSA) (22,000 crores from 27,758 in 2014–2015), Integrated Child Development Services (ICDS) (8335 crores from 18,195 in 2014–2015).

Even in other sectors such as water and sanitation, labour, health and family welfare, the central plan outlay has declined, as compared to previous years (say 2013–2014). Centre expects the States to meet the shortfalls through their exchequer. It may be noted that India is a federation with a strong centre, where the States depend on the centre for fiscal allocations. The budget document pledges its continued support to SSA, Mahatma Gandhi National Rural Employment Guarantee Act (MNREGA) and social security but plans to do it with the money generated through the 'make in India' initiative. Theoretically, there is nothing wrong in attracting investments for industry but the problem arises when the 'surplus' generated does not strengthen the 'weakest link', as John Rawls (1971) says, of the society.

The changing role of chief executive include the following:

- Being accountable and transparent in policy cycle
- Promoting competition and not monopolies in key areas of governance
- Steering, not rowing, the major projects
- Facilitating, not directing, the administrators below
- Partnering with non-state actors in governance
- Encouraging participation in decision-making
- Being personally and organizationally ethical for all acts of governance

The Indian story today is a true example of the changing nature of the chief executive in a globalizing world. A chief executive is the administrative head of the country/State. Our country follows the parliamentary system of governance and although the president is the chief executive, the real executive is the cabinet headed by the PM. For a very long time, India was a one-party dominant system with a strong leader. Such political environment allowed the executive to perform its whole range of functions with complete autonomy. However, the era of coalition politics announced difficult times for the executive, as it constrained the executive from various forces which often countered each other. The era of coalition in India prevailed for almost two decades and even today we have a coalition government but with a single dominant party, which alone has the required majority. Coalition politics makes a huge demand on the functions such as planning, coordination and budgeting, whereas in a one-party dominant system, the executive assigns priority to its various functions depending on the prevailing circumstances.

We are living in times where public administration is made to work under the agenda of 'good governance', which emphasizes 'trimming' of public departments and adoption of 'management model' of organization. These factors have had a profound impact on the nature and working of public organization. If we look at the Indian scenario, two things are happening simultaneously – on the one hand, the executive is acquiring the role of a manager – steering and not rowing, facilitating rather than directing, promoting competition and leading its team in its economic policies; and on the other hand, it is transforming the role of the executive akin to the President, where s/he exercises overriding powers. India did have such practice in the past, especially during Indira Gandhi's tenure as PM, one may argue, but traditionally the PM has followed the established norm of collegiality within the cabinet and the parliament.

The norms are changing owing to huge demands on the government to create effective service delivery in an accountable and transparent manner. The executive is getting stronger by the day. An efficient administration requires delegation of administrative functions to agencies developed to perform them. There are majorly three types of agencies – line, staff and auxiliary – that have evolved to perform administrative functions of the executive so that s/he can dedicate her/his time and energy in guiding the organization towards the desired objective and planning for the future. These agencies are highly developed in a complex organization, but may be fused or simple if the organization is a small one. Let us understand the functions and nature of these agencies.

RELATIONSHIP AMONG LINE, STAFF AND AUXILIARY AGENCIES

In classical organization theory, the concept of line and staff is viewed in terms of authority and command. A line organization has the primary source of authority and it performs main organizational functions, whereas the staff agencies have an existence outside the direct chain of command. So we can understand staff organizations as those that enable goal achievement by helping the line agencies to do their work. Railways, Education, Information and Technology, Postal Services and Panchayati Raj are all examples of traditional line agencies, whereas examples of staff agencies are PM's Secretariat, Union Public Service Commission, Central Public Works Department, Directorate General of Supply and Disposal, to name a few.

The relationship between line and staff has been a tumultuous one because neither can do without the other. A staff agency engages in planning, research and advice but does not accomplish any managerial or operational tasks, which are in turn performed by the line agencies. Authority is capable of being manoeuvred by influence and as the number of staff and type of its functions increase it is capable of performing activities, which are traditionally line functions. This is one of the causes of conflict between them as staff work becomes a combination of direct and indirect activity which includes giving direction to the line officials. The demarcation between line and staff function is not water tight and is usually determined by the organizational objectives. This also explains as to why some functions are line functions in certain organizations and staff functions in certain others. For instance, there are agencies which have these structures, that is, line and staff structures but are either line agencies or staff agencies in themselves. Examples are University Grants Commission and Planning Commission/Niti Aayog. Each of these organizations will have a line and staff structure but both these organizations are staff agencies which help the executive with planning and research, whereas the district collector's office (which again will have these structures) acts as a line agency for implementation of plans (conceived by Planning Commission).

Line Functions

The term 'line' is drawn from military organization wherein line refers to command. Therefore, it can be understood as a chain of command. The hierarchy which commands the military forces in the battlefield is known as line, whereas staff agencies are the ones which help in execution of command. Let us look at the functions which are performed by line agencies to understand the concept better:

- *Chain of command*: Line is about command and hierarchy. It enables the superior to issue orders to the subordinates. The superior's orders are inviolable, and within the regulatory framework of the organization, a superior is free to issue a wide range of directives and command with a guarantee that it would be obeyed so long as it is within the prescribed limits of her/his authority.
- *Channel of communication*: Apart from being a chain of command, it is also a line of communication where information usually flows from the higher to the lower level. It follows the hierarchy. However, with changing times, information loop is preferred, where information flows as in a loop within the line authority and not necessarily in a single direction – from higher to lower levels of command chain.
- *Assignment of responsibility*: The line function also implies assignment of responsibility. By virtue of following the chain of command, each level is committed to fulfil the entrusted task, thereby accepting responsibility for it. It can be understood with the example of any national level policy. In the case of Sarva Shiksha Abhiyan for instance, the Ministry of Human Resource Development is responsible for its formulation, which then assigns the responsibility of its implementation to the state governments. The ministry at the state level in turn assigns the task of implementation to the bureaucracy, which is ultimately responsible for its successful implementation. At each stage, the responsibility and a task is assigned to each line official.

Staff Functions

Staff, as we have discussed earlier in this chapter, is primarily to aid the line agencies in the implementation of organizational objectives. Staff is mainly of three types:

- *Personal staff*: It consists of personnel attached to the line officer/executive and is responsible for advice and aid in performing their task. Their work may include preparing documents, arranging meetings and ensuring amiable working conditions for the line executives.
- *Specialized staff*: This consists of experts who have domain knowledge of the required field such as intelligence, information technology, accounts and human resource. They provide the necessary input for implementation of tasks pertaining to specific subjects.
- *General staff*: This type of staff aids and advises the higher management and also consists of experts from different fields. For example, the PM's staff would consist of several civil servants, special officers and experts from various fields who aid and advise her/him on a range of matters.

As per the nature of the staff, a range of functions are assigned to it. Pfiffner (cited in Basu, 2013) gives the following list of staff functions:

- Advising
- Coordinating
- Research
- Planning

- Assisting the line departments
- Performing delegated tasks

However, according to Mooney (cited in Goel, 2008), the following are the three major functions of staff agencies:

1. Informative
2. Advisory
3. Supervisory

These functions involve research, collection and processing of data and information to help the executives formulate a decision as well as to ensure that the decisions are duly communicated to and implemented by line agencies. So if we agree that the functions of line and staff agencies are not water-tight compartments and the boundaries between line and staff as well as among line, staff and auxiliary agencies are increasingly blurring, then the obvious question is why to have them as distinct entities at all. In order to unravel this, let us understand the rationale of these agencies.

Functions of line agencies	Functions of staff agencies
• Planning	• Advising
• Making policies/decisions	• Coordinating
• Following a chain of command	• Researching
• Facilitating channel of communication	• Assisting
• Assignment of responsibility	• Informing
	• Performing delegated tasks
	• Supervising

Staff agencies evolved because the implementing agency or the line agency cannot be expected to: (a) have the time or resource to understand or investigate pertinent questions for the purpose of decision making and (b) shift focus away from implementation. The need was therefore felt for a specialized agency to aid the executive in research and technical advice. Their function involves analysis of information, planning, decision making, coordination, policy formulation and so on. With the advent of modern technology the staff agencies have become efficient and vital. Staff has, since inception, exercised greater authority as compared to line agencies. They enjoy a higher status and usually belong to the cadre of senior management. So, other than the heads of the line agencies, most others have to succumb to the demands and direction of staff agencies. The executive also has greater interaction with staff agencies because staff agencies also oversee the working of line agencies. The executive delegates its power to staff, thereby placing it in a very powerful position many a time. Line agencies, despite being the fundamental force behind implementation of the executive's decision, are relegated to the peripheral realms.

RATIONALE FOR EXISTENCE OF LINE AND STAFF IN ANY ORGANIZATION

The nature of functions of line, staff and auxiliary agencies determine the rationale for their separate existence. The following are some of the deciding factors:

- *Scale of organization*: In smaller organizations the line and staff functions may be fused but as the organization grows, it needs a set of specialized people for fulfilling the organizational objectives. For the sake of efficiency and effectiveness in an organization, a division of roles and responsibility is needed and thus the distinction of line and staff becomes useful.
- *Maintenance of checks and balance*: These agencies ensure that the chain of command stays intact and responsibility is defined at each stage of implementation. Since the staff and line complement each other, they act as a check and balance to ensure that any particular agency is not influencing the authority in its favour and to the disadvantage of the other organization.
- *Maintenance of accountability*: Separation of roles and responsibilities provides for a system that is accountable. Concentration of authority or responsibility in fewer hands leads to a system that is vulnerable to arbitrariness of the decision maker, whereas deconcentration tends to increase the transparency and accountability. Distinction of line and staff aids in increasing the accountability of the organization. However, the perquisite is effective coordination between the two, otherwise it will add to chaos and loss of effective functioning of the organization.

Auxiliary Agencies and Functions

It is important to note that authors such as Pfiffner do not distinguish between staff and auxiliary agencies. To him staff's functions include auxiliary functions. However, auxiliary agencies are agencies that aid the line agencies in performing their tasks (*like staff*) but their nature is more like housekeeping. They serve the departments but not the public and perform functions common to all departments. In this sense, the scope of their functions is limited. However, they are different from staff agencies in the following aspects:

- Staff is involved in planning and advising, whereas the auxiliary agencies are involved in a range of operating services such as recruitment and purchase.
- Auxiliary agencies are not involved in major substantive policies unlike staff agencies (Basu, 2013).

CONTEMPORARY CHALLENGES BEFORE THE EXECUTIVE

Public organization is increasingly shifting towards corporate structure which has a teleological approach, meaning – the attainment of organizational objectives is the ultimate end. Under the influence of the governance agenda, this approach is now adopted by countries including India and we are witnessing an emergence of public–private partnership. The State is rolling back from the public sphere under various pretentions such as participatory governance, transparent system and an accountable government. The agenda now is 'less government and more governance'. This has implications for the staff agencies too. It implies decreasing their powers and augmenting the line functions.

One can understand this in the context of demise of planning commission in the present form which was more of a staff organization that advised the government on policy formulation through research and deliberation among its members (who were drawn from varied fields of knowledge based on their excellence). It has been replaced by Niti Aayog which is more akin to a line agency. As the name itself suggests, Niti Aayog is focussed more on the implementation rather than advice and assistance in policy process. Public administration is opening up to non-public sectors, its scope is expanding and so is its budget. Clearly, we see a departure from the traditional administration system to a system infused with corporate vocabulary. The planning commission, in some sense, had evolved with the Indian National Congress itself and its seeds can be traced as far back as the late 1930s. So it was organic to the country and its fallacies too were well known. However, replacing it with a new agency dipped in new ethos may create discomfort within the organization structure and its future prospects remain to be decided.

The role of the chief executive is pertinent to any organization, whether at micro or at macro levels. The role is indeed changing in the globalization context but the core role of line and staff in relation to the chief executive remains the same. Even as the chief executive has to operate in a multi-stakeholder scenario and also in a larger context of the relationship between public administration with other social sciences, the fundamental functions that underline its role remain the same. The World Bank prescribes certain parameters for measuring effective governance, which also provide the benchmarks of the chief executive's effectiveness. These are as follows:

- Measuring political, civil and human rights
- Stability and probability of violence
- Competence of bureaucracy and public service delivery
- Promoting market-friendly policies
- Quality of contract enforcement, police and justice system
- Extent of corruption

These measures call on the government for its accomplishment as they cannot be outsourced to private agencies. The need for the State and public administration is established but its complexion is different from traditional times. Talking more specifically about India, we are witnessing some emerging trends within the public administration such as the following:

- Progressive rollback of the State from the social sector
- Increasing facilitation for corporate investment and presence
- Increasing role of Line agencies
- Corporate style of governance with lean staff, fusion of functions and less permanent structures, executives as managers
- Emergence of flexible matrix of organization to suit the public–private partnership model
- Commitment of the State to deliver public goods in an accountable, effective and transparent manner

CONCLUSION

The institutions of public administration are here to stay, despite the fact that the context of globalization could shrink its budget and resources. It means that the chief executive would always work with the line and staff agencies to carry out tasks. Their functions may change a little but by and large the goal of public welfare and justice would drive them to partner with non-state actors in the same way as they have been working with the governmental agencies. However, the new developments compel us to think of two possible future courses for public administration in India, as averred by Ali

Farazmand: (a) it could become a bold State, which has institution building and capacity building as focal points, to handle operational issues of public administration and to restore the trust of the citizen in institutions or (b) as a reduced State with private players geared towards facilitating globalization through disinvestment and reduced regulations. Considering the fact that administration in contemporary India is still guided by the ethos of its founding fathers such as Gandhi, Nehru, Ambedkar, the challenge for the chief executive will be to find out an amicable solution to this dilemma and go along with the larger interests of public in mind. This chapter brought out the role of cheif executive along with its aid agencies in the concept of relationship of public administration with other social sciences and the influence of liberalization and globalization.

Preparatory Questions

- Which are the three schools of thought on globalization?
- What are the roles of executive in an organization?
- How has the role of the executive changed in the recent years?
- What do you understand by a line agency and a staff agency?
- What are the functions of line and staff agencies?
- What is the impact of globalization on the nature of public organizations?

REFERENCES

Allan, J. (ed.) (1998) *Public Enterprise in an Era of Change*. University of Regina Press.

Basu, R. (2013) *Public Administration: Concepts and Theories*. New Delhi: Sterling.

Bhattacharya, M. (2001) *New Horizons of Public Administration*. New Delhi: Jawahar Publishers.

Chakraborty, B. and Chand, P. (2012) *Public Administration in a Globalizing World: Theories and Practices*. New Delhi: Sage Publications.

Chilcote, R. H. (2002) 'Globalization or Imperialism?' *Latin American Perspectives*. 29(6).

Harris, R., *Globalization and Globalism in Latin America and the Caribbean*. Sage. 29(6). pp. 80–84.

Dhameja, A. (ed.) (2003) *Contemporary Debates in Public Administration*. New Delhi: PHI Learning.

Farazmand, A. (2012) 'The Future of Public Administration: Challenges and Opportunities: A Critical Perspective'. *Administration and Society*. 44(4). pp. 487–517.

Chapter Nineteen

Decentralization and Local Governance

Sweta Mishra

LEARNING OBJECTIVES

After completing this chapter, you should be able to:

- Conceptualise the term 'decentralization'
- Explain its significance and approaches to decentralization
- Analyse the functioning of rural and urban local bodies; and
- Critically appraise the working of these bodies

INTRODUCTION

One of the important problems of organizations, including public organizations, is the issue of centralization versus decentralization. On the one hand, the compulsions of socioeconomic planning, the requirements of national integration and the consideration of defence strategy pull the administration towards centralization (*centripetal*) and on the other hand, the political commitment for autonomy, greater participation by the people and the need to take democracy to the grassroots pull administration towards decentralization (*centrifugal*). We are thus confronted with contradictory pulls and pressures.

This chapter will first try to first provide the meaning of the term decentralization as also its significance, approaches and the various dimensions. It will then go on to discuss the system of decentralization in India. Finally, the chapter will make an attempt to analyse the functioning of rural local bodies and urban local bodies (RLBs and ULBs) in India. The latter part of the chapter is on decentralization pattern in India, which is divided into three sections for clarity and comprehension.

CONCEPT OF DECENTRALIZATION

We must be very clear about the meaning of decentralization if we have to grapple with its issues and concerns.

> The Planning Commission symbolizes the *trend* towards centralization, while Panchayati Raj epitomizes the *trend* towards decentralization
>
> Awasthi and Maheshwari (1980, p. 64)

Decentralization has emerged as a prominent issue in the literature of public administration and is regarded as one of the most important politico-administrative innovations of this century. It has been and continues to be advocated as an important component of policy packages to improve governance in developing countries, especially in the context of disillusionment, which has set in on account of central planning.

The centralist regimes find themselves overburdened with complex and widespread socioeconomic problems for which they have no answers, as the governments have sought to create more socially equitable patterns of economic growth to meet the basic needs of the poor. Decentralization has become a major element in the administrative organization of governmental services as a result of enormous increase in the variety, number and complexity of functions of the modern State (Mishra, 2003, p. 178).

Numerous countries are experimenting with decentralization initiatives to *devolve* powers and responsibilities to elected bodies at the lower *tiers* of the political and administrative system. In many countries, decentralization as a means of achieving socioeconomic goals has got the Constitutional mandate (Kueck et al., 1998).

In case of India, efforts in this direction have been made since independence. There have been strong voices in favour of decentralization and to have a *third* tier of governance where local decisions will be taken by the people. As a result, in 1992, the 73rd and 74th Constitutional Amendment Acts have been passed with an aim to provide the third tier of governance, *both* for the rural and the urban areas. These Acts have opened avenues for facilitating social mobilization process at the grassroots level.

The term decentralization is understood differently by different individuals or groups. The dictionary captures the idea of decentralization as a political phenomenon involving both administration and government (Smith, 1985, p. 1). Louis A. Allen refers to it as one of the most confused and confusing of the administrative techniques, which characterizes the art and science of professional management. According to L. D. White (1958), the progress of *transfer of administrative authority* from a lower to a higher level of government is called 'centralization', the converse, 'decentralization'.

In the words of Pfiffner and Sherwood (1960, pp. 190–191), 'in some respects decentralization has come to be a gospel of management. Firstly, it is regarded as a way of life to be adopted at least partially on faith, secondly, it is an idealistic concept, with ethical roots in democracy and thirdly, it is in the beginning a more difficult way of life because it involves a change in behaviour running counter to historically-rooted culture patterns of humankind. That is why the new literature on decentralization talks about how to bring about *change in organization behaviour*. People find it difficult to delegate, to think in terms of the abstractions required by long-term planning, to listen rather than to give orders, to evaluate other men and their work in terms of overall results instead of irritations and tensions of the moment. Yet this is the very key to the behaviour required of leaders in a decentralized organization'.

Decentralization means *dispersal of authority* among a number of individuals or units. When the central authority in any complex and large-scale organization divests itself of certain powers, which are subsequently given to the local units of the same organization and these units, as a result, become autonomous, organizational decentralization takes place (Sarkar, 2010, pp. 168–169).

Decentralization is not only a device for the delegation or dispersal of administrative authority but it is also a democratic method of devolution of political authority. Further, in a decentralized organization, it is also essential to adopt the democratic norms. Such norms help the various levels of the administrative organization to develop a reasonable capability for the exercise of authority to reach the most desired decisions. Moreover, they help to assimilate in them the virtues of greater interactions not only among the various organizational levels but also between the organization and the clientele among the general public (Mishra, 1994, p. 3).

Decentralization carries the following meanings:

- Transfer of authority from higher to lower level of government
- Dispersal/divesture/localization/development of authority
- Democratization of political power
- Mobilization of support for national development policies
- Deconcentration of responsibility
- Delegation of functions
- Change in organization behaviour

Decentralization refers to the physical location of facilities and the extent of dispersal of authority throughout an organization. Hence, it is an arrangement by which the ultimate authority to command and the ultimate responsibility for results is *localized in units* located in different parts of the country. It is argued that in assigning of functions and responsibility for their efficient and effective performance to the decentralized organization, lower levels are allowed to decide many matters and only a few cases involving major policies or interpretations are referred to the higher levels of the organization.

It is a process of *democratization of political power* and thereby aims at achieving democratic values in practice. Decentralization aims at 'widening the area of people's participation in decision making, micro-level political authority and autonomy through transfer of specific powers to people's representative institutions at the bottom' (Mishra, 1994, pp. 8–9).

In some countries, decentralization is seen as a way of mobilizing support for national development policies by making them better known at the local level. Greater political participation in development planning and management supposedly promotes national unity by giving groups in different regions in a country a greater ability to participate in planning and decision making and thus increases their stake in maintaining political stability.

In most Asian countries, decentralization has taken two major forms, one has been the *deconcentration* of responsibility for development functions to field agencies without giving them discretion or autonomy; the other has been *delegation* of functions to agencies that are outside the regular administrative system (Rondinelli and Cheema, 1983, p. 18).

The goals of decentralization are as follows:

- Self-reliance
- Mobilization for policies
- Widening of people's participation
- Strengthening local leadership
- Solidifying efforts for economic modernization
- Establishing a direct relationship between the citizens and the administration
- Ensuring accountability of public officials to citizens

The concept of decentralization, as it applies to India, presents a different approach to the decentralization of political and administrative powers. Having its mixed goals of democracy, decentralization and development, it refers to the programmes and tendencies, which implies devolution of governmental powers and responsibilities, decentralization of political institutions, development of local leadership and strengthening the efforts for economic modernization. It is the process whereby the government *divests* itself completely to certain duties and responsibilities and devolves them on some other authority (Mishra, 1989, pp. 156–157).

To be precise, decentralization is an ideological principle associated with objectives of self-reliance, democratic decision making, popular participation in government and accountability of public officials to citizens. It is a prime mechanism through which democracy becomes truly representative and responsive (Arora and Goyal, 1995, p. 285). Decentralization is a political decision and its implementation, a reflection of a country's political process. It is dispersal of authority among the lower levels of organization and its field offices. It, thus, creates a sense of responsibility in local decision-making agencies with more or less independent existence and powers. It is sharing the decision-making authority with lower levels in organizations, thereby improving their efficiency, effectiveness and responsiveness (Chakraborty and Chand, 2012, p. 256).

IMPORTANCE OF DECENTRALIZATION

Development administration is basically *oriented* towards speedy socioeconomic transformation. Hence, all throughout the developing world, there is a universal concern to design new forms of administration to match the needs of development. Decentralization has been looked at as a *singularly* useful mode of administration to deliver the public services from convenient local centres close to the clients' locality. Bringing administration to the doorsteps of the citizens and establishing a *direct* relationship between the citizens and the administration have been the driving force behind decentralization in most of the developing countries.

The clamour for decentralization has come from many sources. Firstly, it has been prompted by the need to deliver the basic public goods such as food, housing and water from local units of administration as soon as possible. Secondly, most people in the developing countries live in rural areas, which are away from the national capital. Administration has to penetrate the rural areas and link these up with the nation as a whole. Thirdly, in many countries, sociological diversities manifest themselves in ethnic, linguistic and religious differences. Administration needs to be decentralized in response to regional diversities.

Fourthly, regional and local resources can be utilized for the area development purposes, only if administration would move out to the regions and localities. Decentralization, therefore, facilitates local planning and development with the help of local responses. Fifthly, decentralization has its own value in political and administrative terms. Politically, local participation in development activities with intensive response paves the way for meaningful articulation of local demands.

Planning thus becomes much more *realistic* and receives ready political support. From the administrative point of view, local capability to govern local areas increases through sustained *participation* in local decision making. Decentralization is expected to release local energies and enlist *local support* for development activities. In the process, the local community can steadily attain political and administrative maturity. Finally, it is needed to *institutionalize* participation of citizens in development planning by creating alternative means of decision making. It can increase political stability and national unity; can deliver public goods and services at lower costs and make the administration more innovative, flexible and creative.

Some of the reasons to encourage decentralization are as follows:

- Expediting delivery of basic goods and services
- Reaching out to remote rural areas
- Utilizing regional/local resources in a better way
- Meeting the challenges of regional diversity
- Encouraging local participation in developmental activities
- Making administration more innovative, flexible and creative

Thus, we see that decentralization is needed to develop a sense of pride in one's own community and a sense of responsibility in public mind. It also enhances people's participation. In the words of Rajini Kothari, 'decentralization is an alternative system of governance based on a people centred approach to sorting out local level problems. In the entire process, people are located at the centre of power so that they become the basic engine of the development process and not, as hitherto, merely its beneficiaries' (Kothari, 1988, p. 48).

APPROACHES TO DECENTRALIZATION

The different approaches to the concept have been clearly and profoundly presented by James Fesler (1965, pp. 555–565). According to him, the approaches can be grouped into four categories: the doctrinal, the political, the administrative and the dual role.

The Doctrinal Approach

The doctrinal approach seeks to transform decentralization as an end itself through a process of 'romantic idealization'. The Gandhian concept of 'concentric circle' of power distribution and the idealization of village community in Panchayati Raj have reduced decentralization almost to a dogma and as an article of faith. Instead of treating decentralization as a means to the achievement of some end values, such idealization tends to elevate it to the status of a hardened doctrine.

The Political Approach

The political approach underscores the essentially political character of decentralization. Initiatives to decentralize and willingness to pass on powers and functions to the decentralized units and to allow these units to actually operate within a framework of autonomy are politically determined. Creation of field units of government away from central headquarters exemplifies *deconcentration*. Decentralization in the shape of devolution to local self-governing bodies marks an attempt to set up autonomous governments at the level of the locality. Field units of government, such as district administration, are the long arms of the central government. To create and maintain local government is thus a major political commitment. In the absence of such commitment, devolution to subnational governments, including self-governing bodies, will remain more in law than in practice. This leads to what Fesler has called 'illusory decentralization'. Both Panchayati Raj and municipal government in India represent to a considerable extent this so-called façade or illusory devolution.

The Administrative Approach

The administrative approach to decentralization is motivated by efficiency criterion. Enhancement of administrative rationality becomes necessary. When field administrative units are set up through a process of deconcentration, the measure is considered appropriate for field-level decision making and prompt problem solving. In this process, administrative units might come up at many levels between the locality and the central headquarters. With more and more demand for specialized functions, multiplicity of functional departments would appear at the field level.

The administrative situation gradually presents a picture of *polarization* between general area-based administrative demands and specific function-centred claims of particular functional departments. District administration in India is faced with this problem of area function duality. Decentralization in administrative terms may not therefore always guarantee clarity of authority and orderliness of operations. To promote such operational principles, conscious attempts are needed to readjust from time to time the conflicting claims of area and functions in deconcentrated field administration.

The Dual-Role Approach

Finally, the dual-role approach, according to Fesler, is a kind of a rehearsal of the area-function dichotomy in a new setting. Decentralization is placed within a larger context of development and change, as distinguished from maintenance of status quo. Conceived in administrative sense, the dual-role approach seeks to highlight the conflict in field administration between tradition and change. Most field administrative systems were evolved in an earlier era mainly to maintain the established order, to collect revenue and to keep things from going wrong. Almost all the developing countries that have inherited the colonial field system are seeking to bring about speedy social and economic change. The functions of field administration have changed radically as a consequence.

In the words of Fesler (1965 , p. 566), 'the intent is to change established ways of doing things so as to carry economic and social development forward rapidly. This contrasts with the status-quo orientation of a field system geared to maintenance of the established order and may conflict with the personal orientation to field generalists so chosen and trained as to identify themselves with the classes, families, and other groups who continue the establishment'. Resolution of conflict between two different orientations in field administration calls for adaptation of decentralization to changing circumstances. The theme is not unfamiliar to Indian administration in general and to district administration in particular.

The approaches to decentralization are as follows:

- Doctrinal
- Political
- Administrative
- Dual Role

DIMENSIONS OF DECENTRALIZATION

Decentralization, as we have seen, is an important component of policies to improve governance in the developing countries and is often regarded as a necessary precondition for social, economic and political decentralization. In this context, different dimensions of decentralization can be identified, namely, administrative, political, functional and fiscal. These dimensions reflect, in general terms, increasing and often sequential stages of progress in achieving the objectives of decentralization (Jain, 2003, p. 588). Let us now study these dimensions of decentralization.

Political Decentralization

Political decentralization refers to transfer of political powers and functions from the central levels of government to the lower levels of governments. It means that the powers and functions, which are concentrated in the hands of the higher level political organs be decentralized to the lower level political organs that have been democratically elected by their constituencies (Mishra, 2006, p. 69).

In other words, it means devolution of powers and functions to the local bodies, that is, panchayats and municipalities. Under political decentralization, people are drawn into the decision-making process through empowerment. It aims at broadening and deepening the base of democracy by involving more and more people in the decision-making process. In India, the process of political decentralization which started in 1959, on the recommendation of *Balwant Rai Mehta Committee,* finally got implemented in 1993 by way of the 73rd and 74th Constitutional Amendment Acts. As a result, now there are governments at five levels, namely, central, state, district, block and village, making the governance process more representative with locally elected representatives paving the way for greater people's participation.

Administrative Decentralization

Administrative decentralization refers to the decentralization of authority to the lower officials in the administrative hierarchy of organizations. It may also mean decentralizing powers or functions to the subordinate units. It involves placing planning and implementation responsibilities to functionaries and elected members. It aims at providing better facilities and services to the people through the local authorities.

In India, though the development process started way back in 1950 after the setting up of the Planning Commission, we could not achieve the developmental goals. The main reason for this was that the welfare policies and programmes, which were meant for the people did not fully reach them. These policies were made top down and the local people could not get any benefits of these policies and programmes as the local perspective was missing. The policies and programmes were, in a way, imposed as they were designed by officials who had no idea about the ground realities existing in the villages.

Functional Decentralization

Functional decentralization refers to transferring subject specific functions to local tiers in order to enable them to discharge their responsibilities in an effective and efficient manner. It means that the sphere of activity of each tier should be clearly specified and each tier should be allowed to function independently. Functional decentralization is an essential condition to strengthen the units of participatory development and decentralized governance.

In India, there was absence of clear-cut functional jurisdiction so far as the local tiers were concerned. With the passing of the 73rd and 74th Constitutional Amendment Acts, 1993, the issue of functional decentralization has been taken care of. The Acts under Schedule 11 and 12 of the Constitution provide for 29 and 18 subjects/functions to the panchayats and municipalities respectively on which they can make laws. However, there is still no clarity with regard to the functional jurisdiction of each local tier. In many states, the functions are delegated through executive orders rather than transferred through a piece of legislation (Mishra, 2006, pp. 72–73).

Financial Decentralization

It involves devolving powers with regard to taxation, funds and expenditure upon local bodies in order to first improve the financial position and then giving them the financial autonomy for planning and implementation as per the local needs. Devolution of funds upon the local bodies by the State is important in order to augment financial capacity of the local bodies. In order to provide the local bodies some scope to prepare plans as per local needs and then to make expenditure, financial decentralization becomes important. The local bodies in India could not function properly because of lack of funds. They had to depend on the devolutions and the grants-in-aid from the state governments. This problem has also been taken care of to some extent after the passing of 73rd and 74th Constitutional Amendment Acts.

The Acts empower the local bodies to levy and collect the taxes. In Kerala, the panchayats get around 35–40% of the total plan expenditure in the form of grant- in-aid and untied fund. Since 1996–1997, the government has taken bold steps for devolving funds upon Zilla Parishad in lump sum with a formula to further allocate them to the tiers. The general category fund is divided among the gram, taluk and zilla panchayats in the ratio of 70:15:15 respectively. In West Bengal, it is in the ratio of 50:20:30. In Karnataka, it is the opposite. The allocation is in the ratio of 25:35:40 (Status Report, 2000, pp.14–15). Thus, we see that the various dimensions of decentralization got operationalized only after the passing of 73rd and 74th Constitutional Amendment Acts.

Dimensions of decentralization are as follows:

- Political
- Administrative
- Functional
- Financial

DECENTRALIZATION PATTERN IN INDIA

Decentralization in India has historical roots dating back to 1870s. Decentralization was a practiced governance strategy of the British Empire at the urban as well as rural levels. For better understanding of decentralization pattern in India, we have divided this Section into 3 distinct parts. Let us discuss them now:

Historical Background

Decentralization and local governance has been a major concern in India since long. It goes back to Lord Mayo's Resolution of 1870, which advocated decentralization and made arrangements for strengthening the municipal institutions and involving more and more Indians in these bodies. Lord Ripon's Resolution of 1882 strongly advocated the cause of decentralization of administration through the establishment of local self-governing institutions. The British administrators were not prepared to accept the Ripon thesis as they questioned the competence of Indians to manage local administration and feared a general weakening of field administration under a local self-government regime. The Resolution of 1882 was hailed as the *Magna Carta* of local government.

The Decentralization Commission Report, 1909 and the Government of India Acts 1919 and 1935 also favoured local governance. The Government of India Act 1919 introduced 'dyarchy' in the provinces and local self-government became a transferred subject under the charge of a popular minister of the provincial legislature. The Act increased the taxation powers of the local bodies, lowered the franchise, reduced the nominated element and extended the communal electorate to a large number of municipalities. After the Act of 1919, panchayats became legal entities, losing their traditional prerogative powers. The Act of 1935, for the first time, introduced a federal form of government and conferred 'provincial autonomy' on the provinces and envisaged self-government for the country as a whole.

The second phase of the debate in post-Independence India was staged on the floor of the Constituent assembly. Panchayati Raj was an important component of Mahatma Gandhi's vision of future India in which economic and political power would be decentralized and each village would be self-reliant economically. It was in deference to the wishes of the Mahatma Gandhi that Article 40 of the Constitution of India was adopted, stipulating that 'the State shall take steps to organize village Panchayats and endow them with such powers and authority as may be necessary to enable them to function as units of self-governments'.

Rural Local Governance

After Independence, the first attempt in the direction of rural local governance was the inauguration of the Community Development Programme in 1952, followed by the National Extension Scheme in 1953. Both these programmes could not deliver goods. As a result, the *Balwant Rai Mehta Committee* was constituted to enquire into the questions of economy and efficiency and suggest other measures for the reorganization of the Community Development Programme. The Committee submitted its Report in 1958. It came out with the suggestion of a *three-tier system* of rural local government, which would be given statutory status and upon which the various developmental functions performed by blocks were to be devolved.

The first states to go for full stream with the scheme of democratic decentralization were Rajasthan and Andhra Pradesh. Late Pandit Jawaharlal Nehru inaugurated the Panchayati Raj Institution (PRI) in Nagaur district in Rajasthan on October 2, 1959. The movement rapidly spread all over the country. By the end of 1963, most of the states had enacted legislations to introduce Panchayati Raj within their jurisdiction. However, after initial enthusiasm and a promising start, the PRIs began to show signs of decay and could not function as institutions of local governance.

In 1977, another Committee popularly known as the *Asoka Mehta Committee* was appointed by the then Janata Government and was entrusted with inquiring into the sorry situation which was eating into the vitals of PRIs and suggesting measures to revivify them. The Committee outlined the reasons for the decline of PRIs, haphazard programmes, nonperformance, rise of vested interests (*sugar lobby being an example in Maharashtra*), lack of adequate financial resources and so on. The concept of Panchayati Raj itself got lost in a haze of conflicting interpretations (Mishra, 1981 p. 55). The Committee's principal thesis was the functional necessity for decentralization of administration. The Committee recommended a two-tier system of PRI.

It also recommended that the first point of decentralization below the state should be the district and the district should be the unit of planning in most of the states. On the basis of the recommendations of the Asoka Mehta Committee, a meeting of the Chief Ministers was convened by the Ministry of Rural Development in August 1979 and a Model Bill was prepared to be adopted by each and every state of the country. Meanwhile, the Janata government failed and the Bill died its unnatural death.

However, the Karnataka Government took the recommendations of the Committee seriously and adopted a new system of Panchayati Raj in 1985. The states of West Bengal and Andhra Pradesh followed suit. After publication of the Asoka Mehta Committee Report and its experimentation in states of Karnataka, West Bengal and Andhra Pradesh, hectic activities at the central level started towards strengthening grassroots democratic organizations and achieving the goals of real democratic decentralization.

Apart from the concern expressed by the central government, several state governments including Madhya Pradesh, Bihar and Rajasthan also took serious steps in this direction. Some of the Committees set up by the central government are Committee on Administrative Arrangements for Rural Development 1985, L. M. Singhvi Committee for the Concept Paper on PRIs 1986, Sarkaria Commission 1988, P. K. Thungon Committee 1988, Congress Committee on Policy and Programmes 1988, etc.

The net result of the recommendations of these Committees was that a proper environment was created in favour of giving new *thrust to the concept of democratic decentralization.* All political parties by and large arrived at the conclusion that it was high time to give Constitutional status to PRIs. The result of such consensus was the introduction of *64th Constitutional Amendment Bill* in the Parliament in July 1989. The Bill was passed in the Lok Sabha. However, it failed in Rajya Sabha due to serious apprehensions regarding the timing and the intention of the Bill and could not become a part of the Constitution. After the defeat of the 64th Amendment Bill, the National Front Government introduced in the Lok Sabha on September 4, 1990 a new Amendment Bill known as the *Constitution* (*Seventy Fourth Amendment*) Bill 1990. However, this Bill died its unnatural death, as the Janata Dal government collapsed before passing the Bill.

In June 1991, the minority Congress government with P.V. Narasimha Rao as Prime Minister came to power. It gave top priority to the PRIs and brought out the Constitution (Seventy-Second Amendment) Bill, 1991 as bill no. 158-C of 1991. After preliminary discussion on the Bill, it was referred to the select Committee of the house for detailed scrutiny. After receiving the comments of the select Committee, the Bill again came before the house for discussion and adoption in the winter session of the Parliament in December 1992.

Finally, on December 22, 1992, the Bill was passed by the Parliament and is now known as the Constitution (Seventy-Third Amendment) Act 1992. By 23 April 1994, all the states had completed the process of enacting fresh legislation on strengthening the PRIs. As many as 11 states pushed through fresh legislation in 72 hours, some of them even in the early hours of April 23, 1994 to beat the stipulated deadline of April 23, 1994, the day panchayats became part of the Indian Constitution (Mishra and Mishra, 2002, p. 18).

73rd Constitutional Amendment Act, 1992

The 73rd Amendment Act, 1992 has provided Constitutional status to the panchayats and is a step in the direction of speeding up the process of decentralization and giving strength as well as stability to local institutions. Some of the features of the Act are as follows:

- It has made mandatory for all the States to set up *three tier* (in smaller States having less than 20 lakh population – two tier) panchayats, namely, Zilla Parishad at the district level, Panchayat Samiti at the block level and Gram Panchayat at the village levels.
- Periodic elections to all the tiers at regular five-year intervals and, if dissolved earlier, fresh elections to be held within six months.
- Reservation of seats for SCs and STs in all the panchayats at all the levels in proportion to their population.
- One-third reservation of seats for women in panchayats.
- All posts at all levels (with two exceptions) to be filled by direct elections.
- Indirect elections to the post of chairperson at the intermediate and apex tiers.
- Creation of a State Election Commission to conduct elections to PRIs.
- A State Finance Commission to be set up in each state every five years in order to review the financial position of the PRIs.
- Devolution of powers to the panchayat bodies to perform 29 functions suggested in the Eleventh Schedule.
- Organization of gram sabhas.

The following are some of the committees/commissions on local governance:

- Balwant Rai Mehta
- Asoka Mehta
- Administrative Arrangements for Rural Development
- L. M. Singhvi
- Sarkaria
- P. K. Thungon
- Congress Committee on Policy and Programme

Functioning of Rural Local Bodies

Mere legislative enactments do not ensure effectiveness and viability of the PRIs in the states. What is important is their operationalization. Despite almost two decades since the passage of the 73rd Amendment Act, there exist large variations among states in the functioning of PRIs at the operational level.

In the new system, the Gram Sabha is a very important part of Panchayati Raj. It is the basic unit of Indian democracy. It is through the *Gram Sabha* that the elected representative is made accountable to the electorate. Only if Gram Sabhas are vigilant and sensitive to their own problems, can the PRIs be successful. At the same time, it has to meet periodically with maximum participation of the people. This was not the case initially and the benefits did not reach the needy. However, in some states the Gram Sabhas started meeting on a more regular basis and the benefits of the rural development programmes started reaching the common people (Sharma, 2007, p. 46).

At the same time, in some cases, increased participation of the local community is also being witnessed. In the state of Kerala, more than two million persons participated in the first Gram Sabha organized way back in 1996. In general, the Gram Sabhas were a huge success and generated public debate on development all over Kerala (Sharma, 2007, p. 46). In Madhya Pradesh, the Gram Sabhas have got a new status through a state law to ensure holistic development of villages. In West Bengal, absolute power has been given to the Gram Sansad/Gram Sabha in respect of selection of individual beneficiaries under the poverty alleviation programmes (Mathew, 2007, p. 314).

The *Eleventh Schedule*, which assigns 29 subjects to the PRIs have been added in the body of the 73rd Constitutional Amendment, The Constitution expects the State Legislature, by law, to endow the panchayat with such powers and authority as may be necessary to enable them to function as institutions of self-government and such law may contain provisions for the devolution of powers and responsibilities upon the panchayats at the appropriate level. However, the powers and functions have not been actually transferred to the PRI in the true sense of the term, as no detailed executive instructions devolving powers and responsibilities on the different tiers of the PRIs have been issued.

The sphere of activity of each tier under each item has not been defined and is left to the discretion of the concerned state governments (Mishra, 2003, p. 187). As a result, there exists variation from state to state with regard to assigning of *powers and functions* to each tier of PRIs. In the state of Karnataka, for example, the state government has retained many regulatory, controlling and supervisory powers, which in fact takes away the autonomy of the PRIs (Aziz, 2007, p. 126). The experience gained so far is that, at the district level, various departments/agencies implement programmes and function under the overall supervision and control of the district collector. The PRIs, therefore, have to be content with backseat driving (Vittal, 1998, p. 8).

Under governmental direction, each level is now conducting 'activity mapping'. The activity mapping now being undertaken by states is being done with the expectation that it will clearly identify the functions that are to be performed at each level of the panchayats. This will help in assessing the revenues required and assigning their sources. In addition, it will help in the devolution of functionaries to implement these activities (Mathur, 2013, p. 78).

The functioning of the PRIs with regard to the mandatory provision for reservation of seats for the scheduled castes (SCs), the scheduled tribes (STs) and one-third reservation for women (*including women from the SCs and the STs*) reveals that in spite of the reservation for the above categories, the problem has not been completely solved. In most states, democratic decentralization has made politics more inclusive of women, SCs and STs, but has done far less to empower them (Jayal, 2006, p. 19).

Initially, by and large only those individuals were elected from reserved constituencies, who had the patronage of the dominant sections of the society and who functioned like the mouthpiece of the affluent sections in the formal meetings of the PRIs. Women members acted on behalf of the male members of their family. However, slowly this scenario started changing and today the situation is much better. Today, the democratic base of women has been widened. Indeed, around 80% of all women elected are from reserved seats. It has also motivated many women to contest elections and participate in the political process (Mathur, 2013, p. 84). Women members have performed well in states such as Kerala, West Bengal, Karnataka and Madhya Pradesh. They have taken up many serious issues relating to the development of their areas. They have fought against odds and taken up issues, which cater to the vital needs such as children's education, safe drinking water, primary health care facilities for women and basic nutrition.

Another important issue in the functioning of panchayats is the *finance*. Though many provisions have been made in the Act with regard to improving the financial status of the panchayats, still the financial autonomy of the PRIs is restricted. Only in the state of Kerala there is a large degree of autonomy as 40% of funds under general sector are in untied form. States such as Gujarat, Karnataka, Madhya Pradesh and Maharashtra provide substantial funds to the Zilla Parishad but even they do not give much scope to PRIs in terms of autonomy, as funds are invariably tied to a particular programme or scheme (Sweta, 2006, p. 77).

PRIs do not have the incentive to raise revenues. The major proportion of the transfers is scheme based. They have to depend on the devolutions and the grants-in-aid from the state governments. Besides, most of the states have not transferred funds for the subjects transferred to the PRIs. Decentralization without a strong resource base is therefore likely to have pitfalls if not accompanied by enhanced financial capabilities. Though the fiscal capabilities of the PRIs and *nagar palikas* are expected to improve in the wake of the Finance Commission exercise, what is important is a strong fiscal base accruing from sources internal to them. Moreover, many taxing power and other financial provisions such as auctioning the Gram Panchayat *financially beneficial* properties such as fisheries, ponds, pastures and others will ultimately improve the financial position of PRIs (Mishra, 2005, pp. 74–75).

The PRIs and municipal bodies should be encouraged to take steps for innovative resource mobilization such as generation of income from entrepreneurial activities, projective loans, public contribution, tax sharing and tax assignments, matching grant incentives for tax collection instead of totally depending on the governmental grants. Besides, proper tax collection machinery at panchayat/municipal level is required. PRIs/ULBs should get a share of more elastic and productive taxes such as sales tax. They may be assigned all or part of sales tax proceeds of the area within their purview.

Another important aspect observed in the functioning of the PRIs is the problem of coordination among the three levels of PRIs on the one hand and the bureaucracy and NGOs on the other. This is giving rise to the following issues:

- Ambiguities related to the distribution of powers and functions among the three tiers of PRIs mentioned in the *eleventh schedule*.
- Lack of clarity on the role of PRIs as planning and implementing agencies.
- Absence of understanding with regard to the relationship between the PRIs and local level bureaucracy.
- Problem of open competition between the PRIs and NGOs. These factors aggravate the complexities of coordination and raise doubts with regard to the usefulness of PRIs (Mishra, 2003, p. 186).

To sort out the problem of coordination, what is required is to weave and develop a new and responsible participatory culture at the local level. Besides, there should be necessary amendment in the Panchayati Raj and Municipal Acts of various states, which is possible only if there is a strong political and administrative will. PRIs and ULBs need to be made responsible both for planning and for implementation of development programmes for the local community, and their capabilities in this regard need to be enhanced. Therefore, if the PRIs have to be made effective, the District Rural Development Agency has to be placed under the control of these institutions so that the people's representatives can be involved in the implementation of development programmes.

Many states are experimenting with innovative measures to improve the functioning of PRIs and ULBs. To maintain transparency in the implementation of rural development schemes in the state, the Assam government has ordered the constitution of vigilance and monitoring Committees in each block (Sweta, 2003, p. 188). Panchayati Raj in India has also found a special mention in the UNDP Report, 2002. It reiterates the fact that 'In principle, decentralizing power from the centre to provinces, districts or villages enable people to participate in decision-making more directly. But in reality, it simply transfers power from one set of elites to another. Democratic decentralization, could truly give voice to the people, but it requires enhancing participation, especially by the people who are often marginalized, and increases the accountability of public officials at local levels' (Panchayati Raj Update, August 2002).

The need is to appreciate the importance of making people aware and of educating them through *well-organized* educational programmes. In a way, people's participation needs to be internalized by the PRIs and ULBs. On the whole, the functioning of PRIs in various states during the last two decade presents a mixed picture. It has provided an element of continuity and enlarged the participatory process at the grassroots level. The periodic shuffling and reshuffling of leadership by way of regular elections and increase in the level of politicization of local community will certainly ensure the success of the PRI in the foreseeable future.

Urban Local Governance

After Independence, Article 40, which provided for setting up of panchayats, was inserted in the Constitution. The Article only talked about creation of panchayats and was silent on the creation of urban bodies. The only reference to urban self-government was made in two entries, namely, Entry 5 of List 11 of the *Seventh Schedule* and Entry 20 of the Concurrent List. Apart from this, the central government appointed several Committees and Commissions from time to time in order to improve the ULBs. Some of these Committees are as follows:

- The *Local Finance Enquiry Committee* (1949–1951), which mainly recommended the widening of the sphere of taxation of urban bodies.
- The *Taxation Enquiry Committee* (1953–1954), which recommended that certain taxes be segregated so that it can be exclusively utilized by or for local government.
- The Committee on the *Training of Municipal Employees* (1963), which emphasized the fact that training institutes be set up both at the central and the state levels so that they can provide training to the municipal personnel.
- The *Rural–Urban Relationship Committee* (1963–1966), which enquired into all the aspects of municipal administration from personnel, planning and taxation to interdependence between the town and its surrounding villages.
- The *Committee of Ministers on Augmentation of Financial Resources of ULBs* (1963), which highlighted the fact that the ULBs were not levying taxes even in the fields earmarked for them and urged the local bodies to set up statutory urban development boards to undertake town development.
- The *Committee on Service Conditions of Municipal Employees* (1965–1968), which suggested the constitution of a state-wide cadre of municipal employees.
- The *National Commission on Urbanization* (1988), which recommended the revitalizing of the urban government.

In 1989, the Constitution 65th Amendment Bill was introduced in the Parliament, which aimed at providing Constitutional status to the ULBs. The Bill was passed in the Lok Sabha but was defeated in the Rajya Sabha. Once again a similar effort was made in the year 1990, when the National Front government headed by Shri V. P. Singh, introduced the Constitution 65th Amendment Bill in the Parliament. However, this Bill too met the same fate. Finally, in 1991, the Congress-led government headed by Shri P. V. Narasimha Rao introduced a new Bill which was passed by the Parliament and is now popularly known as 74th Constitutional Amendment Act.

74th Constitutional Amendment Act, 1992

The 74th Amendment Act ushered in a new era in urban local governance in India. It has institutionalized the municipal local bodies by providing them a Constitutional status as also making it mandatory for the government to constitute them. Some of the important *features* of the Act are as follows:

- The Act inserted a new part in the Constitution, namely, *Part IXA,* which deals with issues relating to municipalities such as their structure and composition, elections, powers and functions, finances and reservation of seats.
- A uniform *three-tier structure* of ULBs, namely, Municipal Corporation, Municipal Councils and Nagar Panchayats.
- One-third *reservation* of seats for women in all the three ULBs.
- Reservation of seats for *SCs and STs* in proportion to their population.

- A uniform *tenure* of five years for all the three ULBs and in case of dissolution, elections to be held within six months.
- The *twelfth schedule* provides 18 *subjects* on which the municipal bodies can make laws and implement schemes for economic development and social justice.
- Each state shall constitute a *State Finance Commission* to look into the financial position of the ULBs.
- Constitution of *District Planning Committee* (*DPC*) and Metropolitan Planning Committee (MPC) to prepare a development plan.
- Constitution of a State Election Commission to conduct *elections* to the ULBs.
- Provision of *ward Committees* for better proximity with the citizens.

Evaluation of the Urban Local Bodies

So far as the functioning of ULBs is concerned, it presents a similar picture as that of the Rural Local Bodies or RLBs. Although two decades have passed since they have been granted Constitutional status, there is lack of uniformity with regard to the functioning of the ULBs. the 74th Amendment Act has undoubtedly revived them but the actual situation is that they still face a number of problems.

With regard to *functional devolution* of the ULBs, we see that there is absence of clear-cut functional jurisdiction. The 18 subjects, as mentioned in the *twelfth schedule*, on which the ULBs are to make laws have not been devolved uniformly. States such as Himachal Pradesh, Haryana, Rajasthan and Chhatisgarh on an average have devolved sixteen functions to ULBs out of eighteen listed in the *twelfth schedule* but some key functions such as roads, regulation of slaughterhouses, water supply and sewerage and urban planning including town planning are yet to be devolved to ULBs.

It is also worth noting that though the 16 functions are devolved to ULBs, very little is actually in the hands of municipalities, as the core decision-making power rests with the state government or district administration. At the same time, overlapping of functions between various departments is also a reality (Occasional Paper Series, No. 4, 2008, p. 8).

In many states, the functions are delegated through executive orders rather than transferred through a piece of legislation so that, it is apprehended, they can be withdrawn easily. Some of the states have transferred their schemes of local nature along with funds and functionaries. They have adopted a *pragmatic* approach of giving supervisory and controlling power to local bodies while retaining the power of appointment/dismissal and promotion/demotion with them. Kerala has shared its plan budget with its local bodies to the extent of 40% (Chaubey, 2004, p. 39).

Devolution of funds upon municipalities by the state is important in order to augment the *financial capacity* of the municipalities. The functioning of ULBs reveals a different picture. The ULBs still have to depend on grants from states and central governments. Municipalities are not able to raise sufficient resources on their own to be able to cover their costs and are therefore increasingly dependent on state transfers for financial sustenance. Octroi or in lieu/octroi compensation is the major untied grant which all municipalities get from the state government. However, it is also not completely untied. A portion of the grant is tied – to be used by ULBs only for meeting establishment/administration expenditure, whereas the remaining amount can be used for other purposes. The poor financial situation in turn affects adversely the expenditure priorities of the municipality (Occasional Paper Series, 2008, p. 18).

The financial position of the ULBs has been very well presented in the *Twelfth Finance Commission* Report. It has summed up the financial problems of the ULBs in the various states as follows:

- Poor revenue realization by municipalities – negligible tax and non-tax revenue.
- Excess dependence on state transfers, even for day-to-day expenses.
- Excess expenditure on establishment.
- Irregular disbursement of octroi compensation grant which also adversely affects the day-to-day functioning of municipalities.
- Poor accounting practices leading to lack of clarity on financial situation.
- Mounting arrears of payments such as pension and provident funds (Occasional Paper Series, 2008, p. 18).

If one has an overview of the working of the ULB's, attention is automatically attracted towards the non-functional character of the DPC. For the first time, the DPCs, under Article 243Z(d), received Constitutional status by way of 74th Constitutional Amendment Act. Unfortunately, however, the DPCs have been made ineffective. Though most states have taken the steps to constitute the DPCs, there are variations in their composition and functioning. For example, the (MLAs) or Member of Legislative Assembly and (MPs) or Member of Parliament are either the members or special invitees of DPC in all the states except Kerala (Sweta, 2006, p. 111).

In states such as Rajasthan, Tamil Nadu and Uttar Pradesh, they have been given voting rights. in still some other states such as West Bengal, MLAs and MPs can become members of the DPC and have voting rights by the special government order. Yet another variation is visible in Tamil Nadu where one-fifth of total block chairpersons in the district are the members of DPC by rotation. In no other State are the chairpersons of Gram Panchayats and Block Panchayats members of the DPC (Mishra, 2006, p. 111). In Haryana and Tamil Nadu, bureaucrats had been made chairs of these Committees, and in Madhya Pradesh, ministers had been put in charge of them – in violation of the amendment's spirit (Datta, 2003).

A study conducted by Participatory Research in Asia (PRIA) on 'urban governance' highlights the fact that DPC in Himachal Pradesh is a weak link in the planning process in the state. It is due to (a) lack of an organic *linkage* between Panchayat, Panchayat Samiti, Zilla Panchayats and ULBs regarding plan preparation and implementation and (b) paucity of funds, and foremost, the lack of strong political and administrative will to make them work. In Chhattisgarh, the DPC is unfortunately not yet functional though it has been constituted in all the districts. The state government, in contravention of its own rules, constituted DPCs in 2005 in all districts by nominating all members instead of holding elections. The DPC is chaired by state ministers, which is another major problem. This ensures that the DPC works only as an arm of the state government and is incapable of independent functioning (Occasional Paper Series, 2008, p. 35).

Members in such Committees are liable to be dominated by the minister. No decision can be taken in such a Committee which is against the policy of the state government. In fact, in Chhattisgarh, the DPC is emerging as a non-participatory arm of the state administration, which is quite contrary to the role envisaged for the local body by the Constitution (Occasional Paper Series, 2008, p. 35). The need of the hour is that the DPCs should be made effective and the district plan prepared by the PRIs and municipalities should be approved by the state government without any change. It is also desirable that the DPC may issue guidelines to the lower level units in regard to their annual action plan and consolidated five year plan. The situation is much less encouraging as far as the MPCs are concerned.

Another problem area of ULBs is the participation of SCs/STs, (OBCs) or Other Backward Classes and women in these bodies. The very presence of large numbers of poor people in local councils, mainly on account of seat reservations, is a very significant development in the local political landscape of most parts of India where they were previously excluded from public life and political participation (Robinson, 2005, p. 17). Women have come in their own ways. They are participating in protests and rallies against low wages, faulty implementation of schemes and so on. Thus, things are not as bleak as depicted by some of the problems we have discussed here. There are many positives and the picture is looking up.

CONCLUSION

Decentralization is no magic wand as the experience indicates. The success or failure of decentralization hinges upon the nature of the institutions created, the extent of power and finances delegated, the pattern of power distribution among groups in the region and the participation of civil society. On the basis of the above analysis, it can be said that decentralization has firmly been established both in rural and urban areas. Local democracy has been deepened, political participation broadened and representation diversified as a result of the 73rd and 74th Constitutional Amendment Acts. The decentralization process has now given RLBs and ULBs an opportunity to assume greater responsibility for rural and urban management. The new system of decentralized governance has provided an element of continuity and enlarged the participatory process at the grassroots level. The states have taken certain measures to transfer functions and devolve funds upon the local bodies.

Despite this, the local bodies at the grassroots level are faced with the insurmountable task of addressing the problem of governance. The experience brings to the fore the need to address the challenges faced by the local bodies to meet the desired standards of governance. In this process, the state has a vital role to play, so that the right kind of system of governance is established at the grassroots level. In operationalizing the Panchayat and Municipal Acts, the Centre has a vital role to play in providing support for building of local institutions, legal framework and in creating an enabling environment for people to participate and take advantage of opportunities. The need of the hour is positive intervention by the State through policies for human resource development and institutional development to further strengthen the process of decentralization. Besides, in the era of globalization, the central as well as the state governments will have to provide critical support to local institutions in terms of infrastructure and institution building, as globalization will definitely have its impact on the village life. Transparency, accountability, effective planning and efficient delivery of goods and services can go a long way in improving the decentralization pattern in India.

Preparatory Questions

- Define the term decentralization and discuss its various approaches.
- Discuss the nature and significance of decentralization.
- Examine the administrative and functional dimensions of decentralization.
- Critically examine the 73rd Constitutional Amendment Act, 1993.
- Write an essay on rural and urban local governance.
- Examine decentralization in the context of 74th Constitutional Amendment Act.

REFERENCES

Occasional Paper Series No. 4. (2008) *Democratic Decentralization of Urban Governance*. New Delhi: PRIA.

Arora, R. K. and Goyal, R. (1995) *Indian Public Administration*. New Delhi: Wishwa Prakashan.

Awasthi, A. and Maheshwari, S. R. (1980) *Public Administration*. Agra: Lakshmi Narain Agarwal.

Aziz, A. (2007) 'The Decentralization Experience in Karnataka: How Clientelism and Accountability Work: A Case Study of West Bengal' in Singh, S. and Sharma, P. K. (eds.). *Decentralization Institutions and Politics in Rural India*. New Delhi: Oxford University Press.

Chakraborty, B. and Chand, P. (2012) *Public Administration in a Globalizing World*. New Delhi Sage Publications.

Chaubey, P. K. (2004) *Urban Local Bodies in India*. New Delhi: Indian Institute of Public Administration.

Datta, P. (2003) 'Panchayati Raj.' *Frontline*. 19 July–1 August.

Fesler, J. W. (1965) 'Approaches to the Understanding of Decentralization.' *Journal of Politics*. XXVII(3).

Gupta, D. N. (2004) *Decentralization Need for Reforms*. New Delhi: Concept Publishing Company.

Jain, S. P. (2003) 'Decentralization in India: An Appraisal' in Mishra, S. N. et al. (eds.). *Public Governance and Decentralization*. Vol. II. New Delhi: Mittal.

Jayal, N. G. (2006) 'Engendering Local Democracy: The Impact of Quotas for Women in India's Panchayats.' *Democratization*. 13(1).

Kothari, R. (1988) *State Against Democracy: In Search of Human Governance*. New Delhi: Ajanta.

Kueck, G. W., Mathur, S. C. and Schindler, K. (1998) *Federalism and Decentralization*. New Delhi: Konrad Adenaver Foundation.

Manor, J. (2010) 'Local Governance. Jayal, N. G. and Mehta, B. P. (eds.).' *The Oxford Companion to Politics in India*. New Delhi: Oxford University Press.

Mathew, G. (2007) 'Decentralization and Local Governance: How Clientelism and Accountability Work: A Case Study of West Bengal' in Singh, S. and Sharma, P. K. (eds.). *Decentralization Institutions and Politics in Rural India*. New Delhi: Oxford University Press.

Mathur, K. (2013) *Panchayati Raj*. New Delhi: Oxford University Press.

Mishra, S. N. (1981) *Rural Development and Panchayati Raj*. New Delhi: Mittal Publications.

Mishra, S. N. (2005) 'The 73rd Constitution Amendment and the Local Resource Base: A Critical Appraisal' in Chahar, S. S. (ed.). *Governance at Grassroots Level in India*. New Delhi: Kanishka.

Mishra, S. N. and Sweta, M. (2002) *Decentralized Governance*. New Delhi: Shipra Publications.

Mishra, S. N. (1989) *New Horizons in Rural Development Administration*. New Delhi: Mittal Publications.

Mishra, S. (1994) *Democratic Decentralization in India*. New Delhi: Mittal Publications.

Mishra, S. (2003) 'Decentralization: Concept, Characteristics and Constraints' in Alka Dhameja, A. (ed.). *Contemporary Debates in Public Administration*. New Delhi: Prentice Hall of India.

Mishra, S. (2006) 'Understanding Decentralization in Contemporary Settings' in *Decentralisation and Local Governance*. MPA-016, IGNOU Course Material.

Pfiffner, J. M. and Sherwood, F. P. (1960) *Administrative Organization*. Englewood-Cliffs (NJ): Prentice Hall.

Rajiv Gandhi Foundation. (2000) *Status Report on Panchayati Raj in India – Task Force on Panchayati Raj*. New Delhi. Rajiv 'Gandhi Foundation.'

Robinson, M. (2005) 'A Decade of Panchayati Raj Reforms: The Challenge of Democratic Decentralization in India' in Jain, L. C. (ed.). *Decentralization and Local Governance*. New Delhi: Orient Longman.

Rondinelli, D. A. and Cheema, S. G. (1983) 'Implementing Decentralization Policies: An Introduction' in Rondinelli, D. A. and Cheema, G. S. (eds.). *Decentralization and Development Policy Implementation in Developing Countries*. US: Sage.

Sarkar, Siuli (2010) Public Administration in India. New Delhi. PHI.

Sharma, R. (2007) 'Kerala's Decentralization The Ideal in Practice' in Singh, S. and Sharma, P. K. (eds.). *Decentralization Institutions and Politics in Rural India*. New Delhi: Oxford University Press.

Smith, B. C. (1985) *Decentralization: The Territorial Dimension of the State*. London: George Allen and Unwin.

Vittal, C. P. (1998) 'Devolution of Powers and Functions to Panchayati Raj Institutions.' *Kurukshetra*. 26(7).

White, L. D. (1958) *Introduction to the Study of Public Administration*. 4th ed. New York: Macmillan.

Chapter Twenty

Nature of Financial Administration

Uma Medury and Sweta Mishra

LEARNING OBJECTIVES

After completing this chapter, you should be able to:

- Explain the nature of financial administration
- Describe the importance and types of budget
- Discuss the phases of Indian budgetary system
- Examine the steps involved in budget preparation enactment and execution; and
- Analyse the role of audit and Parliamentary Committees in exercising control over Indian financial administration

INTRODUCTION

Administration and finance are related to each other in the same way as are fuel and engine. Just as the engine cannot run without fuel, similarly administration cannot work without finance. For the administration to run smoothly and to carry out its objectives, finance becomes very important. In the absence of a proper finance mechanism, development goals and welfare of the people cannot be achieved, especially in developing countries. Insufficient financial resources severely impact the implementation of government programmes. Government initiatives cannot be completed in the absence of sufficient funds, as a consequence of which the entire administrative system could come to a halt. Hence, finance is the lifeline of administration. This chapter will try to explain the concept of financial administration in some detail. As budget is the backbone of financial administration, the chapter would specifically focus on the meaning, nature and significance of the budget. It will endeavour to describe various types of budget, keeping in view participatory budget, green budget and gender budget among others. The chapter will also outline the budgetary process in Parliament, underlining the distinct role of audit and Parliamentary Committees.

DEFINING FINANCIAL ADMINISTRATION

Financial administration is that set of activities, which is related to making funds available to the various departments and ministries of the government so that they can carry forward their goals and objectives in an efficient, effective and economical manner. It consists of those operations that aim to make funds available for governmental activities and ensure lawful and efficient use of these funds (Sharma and Sadana, 1998, p. 518). It means making the funds available and using them in the best possible way, so as to achieve the set goals and objectives. It involves facilitating the funds in such a manner that the people are not burdened and at the same time development programmes and policies also do not suffer. In other words, it means that the government functions in such a manner that it does not put extra burden on the people and neither do development programmes and policies suffer from lack of funds.

Financial administration relates to the system which generates, regulates and distributes the monetary resources needed for the sustenance and growth of an organization. In this respect, it has been observed, financial administration is similar to the circulatory system in complex living organisms (Thavraj, 1978, p. 1). It involves planning of public expenditure and revenues, making funds available for the governmental activities and ensuring the lawful and efficient use of these funds (Bhattacharya, 2011, p. 364). Its scope is expanding day by day to encompass within its fold many dynamic aspects and processes such as financing, planning, collecting, budgeting, resource mobilization and its investment, appropriating, controlling and expending public money for public welfare as also proper accounting and auditing of that money. It also includes auditing income, expenditures, receipts and disbursements and accounting for funds needed to be expended on public services (Sarkar, 2010, p. 256). In short, financial administration has assumed a multifaceted role in order to achieve maximum welfare of the people by eliminating unwanted expenditure and ensuring the optimum use of available resources and funds.

MEANING OF BUDGET

The word budget has been derived from the French word, 'bougette', which means a sack or a pouch, which carries the financial papers. In the contemporary context, it refers not to the sack, but to the financial papers. It means the financial papers outlining the financial details for a financial year. It is a statement containing a forecast of revenue and expenditure as also the plan of action of the government for a period of time. It is a statement which spells out the objectives and goals designed by the government for the coming year. It is a forecast and an estimate of all the public receipts and expenses and an authorization to incur them and to collect them (Bhattacharya, 2011, p. 366). It is a plan of action; it reflects and manifests the programme of the chief executive for the ensuing financial year. It is much more than a mere statement of revenue and expenditure of the government (Awasthi and Maheshwari, 1987, p. 447).

Budget is planned by career officials; assembled, coordinated and standardized by a budget agency; submitted to the political overseers for approval and relayed to the legislature for concurrence and official execution supervised by the budget agency. The central position of the budget agency enables it to perform economic-policy functions, budget planning, purchasing, taxation, accounting, efficiency audit and personnel control in a super housekeeping organization (Caiden, 1971, p. 189). In other words, it is a reflection of what government intends to do in a year.

IMPORTANCE OF BUDGET

Budget is one of the main tools of financial administration. In the absence of a budget, financial administration cannot move ahead. It is the heart of management and as such becomes a powerful tool for achieving coordination in administration. Budgeting gives an opportunity to evaluate the various policies and programmes of the government and in this way one gets an idea as to those policies and programmes that are not required and should be discontinued. Budget, thus, helps in eliminating all kinds of duplication and wastage.

Budget is important for bringing about socioeconomic change in the society. Through the budget, the government takes care of every section of the society. By introducing new policies and programmes and earmarking funds for the same, the government tries to bring about socioeconomic change in the society. It promotes economic growth of the country by imposing heavy taxation upon articles of consumption and also encouraging investment. It also taxes the rich and in this way it tries to reduce socioeconomic inequalities. It covers the entire social life of the citizens. The budgetary policy of the government is directed towards those policies and programmes through which the government aims to ameliorate poverty, provide employment opportunities, uplift the status of the weaker sections of the society, provide educational and health facilities as also take care of maldistribution of wealth. In this way, budget becomes a medium through which socioeconomic change can be brought in the society.

Budget is important also because it is a tool of legislative control. It means that no tax can be collected without the prior approval and authorization of the legislature and similarly no expenditure can be incurred without the legislature's prior approval. Thus, by having a control over the public purse, legislature controls the executive. The executive becomes answerable to the legislature for spending as well as for the collection of taxes.

In short, we see that budget is very important for bringing about socioeconomic change in the society, for controlling the executive and also as a powerful tool of coordination as also eliminating waste and duplication. In the words of Awasthi and Maheshwari (1987, p. 451), the budget is many things 'to an economist, it is a device of influencing the country's economy; to the politician a device for defending or criticizing the government programmes; to an administrator a framework for communication and coordination as well as for exercising administrative discipline throughout the administrative structure'.

The major actors in the budgetary process in India are the Parliament, Parliamentary Committees, executive, ministry of finance and Comptroller and Auditor General (CAG) of India. Audit is in the form of appropriation audit, through which the CAG ensures that it is an (i) audit from the point of view of accountancy and classification, (ii) audit from the point of view of authority, (iii) audit of appropriation and finance accounts and (iv) audit from the point of view of propriety (Chakraborty and Chand, 2012, pp. 424, 425, 435).

TYPES OF BUDGET/BUDGETARY INNOVATIONS

After discussing the concept of budget, in the succeeding pages an attempt is made to present a brief account of the different types of budget.

Traditional or Line–Item Budget

Line–item, as the name suggests, is that budget in which in each line an item and its cost is marked. In line–item budget, resources are allocated on the basis of the cost of each item. In this type of budget, the focus is on itemized classification of expenditure. The entire expenditure in this type of budget is presented through a series of Demands for Grants. It focuses more on the cost aspects rather than the results. It only indicates what the government buys and not what it does. It focuses only on inputs and not outputs. It does not provide any adequate link between the financial outlays and the physical targets. The performance of the line items cannot be measured in this type of budget. Line–item budget is used as a control mechanism for the financial operations of the government. In other words, through line–item budget, greater fiscal accountability can be ensured.

Performance Budget

Performance budgeting is a system of presentation of public expenditure in terms of functions, programmes, performance units and so on. It focuses both on inputs and outputs. It provides a link between the financial outlays and the physical targets. It is a system by operations and programmes, and 'links performance levels' of those operations and programmes 'with specific budget amounts' (Henry, 2008, p. 222). Hence, the performance of the programme becomes important in performance budgeting. The emphasis here is on accomplishment rather than on the means of accomplishment. In other words, it shifts the emphasis from the means of achievement to the achievement itself, from what the government buys and acquires to the service it renders.

The main purpose of performance budget is to clearly define the objectives and the tasks, the means of achieving them and the estimated cost of the performance. It measures progress towards long-term objectives as given in the plan. As a result of the performance measurement, a department's future allocation is decided. If a department's performance does not exceed the objectives, it will receive less money and if it exceeds, then the department gets more money. Thus, budgets no longer are merely a means of controlling expenditures; they also are a way to fulfil public purposes (Henry, 2010, p. 222).

Different types of budgets/budgeting are as follows:

- Traditional/Line–item
- Performance
- Planning–Programming
- Zero–Base
- Gender
- Green

Planning–Programming Budgeting

Planning–programming budgeting (PPB) is a system which is concerned not only with inputs and outputs but also with effects and alternatives. It emerged as a reaction to the unscientific and disjointed planning in preparing the budget. PPB evaluates policy by dividing it into separate programmes and quantifying their gains and losses (Singh, 2002, p. 199). This system of budgeting focuses on cost–benefit analysis and also improves the efficiency and effectiveness of government. It systematically weighs the cost of a project against the amount of benefit in terms of money or material saved or earned that an agency or department can expect in return. It is, perhaps, the single most comprehensively rational system of budgeting as it brings about cost savings in the expenditure of the government and offers greater flexibility because they allow any combination of expenditures that will achieve a programme's objectives and yield the greatest benefits for the cost involved.

Zero–Based Budgeting

Zero-Based Budgeting (ZBB) is a system of budgeting in which the organization reassesses its actions from top to bottom, from a hypothetical zero base. It means starting from the scratch. It is a budgetary innovation of the early 1970s and was used/applied for the first time by Peter A. Phyrr in 1970. Later Jimmy Carter, US President, applied it to the federal government in 1977. In ZBB, each function, whether it is part of the previous year's programme or part of the new programme, should be explained and justified in its comprehensive totality and not part by part every year. ZBB is a budgetary system in which each decision unit is identified, each decision unit within a decision package is analysed, all decision packages to develop the appropriations request are evaluated and ranked and finally, a detailed operating budget that reflects those decision packages approved in the budget appropriations are prepared (Henry, 2010, p. 226).

> Participatory Budget
>
> It involves a process of democratic deliberation and decision making in which people decide the budgetary allocations of municipal or public budget. Through mutual consent and deliberation, the civic priorities are identified and budgetary allocations are made. Participatory budgeting was experimented for the first time in Porte Alegre in Brazil. It was a part of various reformist, innovative programmes undertaken by the local administration to lessen socioeconomic inequalities in Brazilian society.
>
> In India, Bangalore was the first city to implement along these lines with the efforts of a local NGO. This campaign resulted in citizens' budget priorities being approved in over 20 per cent of the city's wards. In 2006, it was also initiated in the Pune municipal corporation. The recent initiative of Delhi government termed AAP's Janta Ka Budget is considered an exercise in participatory budgeting. Mohalla Sabhas are conducted in each of the assembly constituency and through deliberation and voting by the residents of the area, civic projects to be taken up on priority in state budget are in a way decided

Gender Budget

Gender budget means gender-sensitive and gender-responsive budget. It is a tool that can be used to ensure that the aggregate national or departmental budget is gender sensitive. The main aim of gender budget is to achieve gender-just allocations and outcomes in all sectors and ministries. It is a system of budgeting which incorporates a gender perspective at different stages of budgeting, that is, planning, policy formulation, assessment of needs of target groups, allocation of resources, implementation, impact assessment and reprioritization of resources (Chakrabarty and Chand, 2012, p. 420).

Gender budgeting is a tool through which the needs and priorities of women can be identified. It can also be used to address issues such as increased feminization of poverty; exploitation of women in low paid, arduous, insecure jobs; persistently high infant mortality rate, maternal mortality rate, morbidity, anaemia and malnutrition due to lack of access to nutrition and quality healthcare (Mehta, 2007, p. 221). Apart from this, it should be used for correcting gender gaps in education, wage differentials between men and women, violence against women, trafficking of women, bias in the female–male ratio, lack of access to water/drinking water, statistical invisibility of women's work and providing access to work (Mehta, 2007, p. 221). In other words, gender budgeting means that the budget should be prepared in such a way that it takes care of the needs of women, which have been neglected for so long. There need not be a separate budget for women but a gender-centric budget.

Green Budget

The latest innovation in the field of budgeting is green budget. Due to air, water and soil pollution, various environmental problems such as climate change, melting of glaciers, soil erosion and global warming are on the increase globally. These changes have a detrimental effect on all life on earth. As a result, there has been an increased focus on climate change and environment management over the past few years across the globe, and India is no exception to this.

The budget for the year 2011–2012, made a positive dent towards environmental issues and their rectification. The then finance minister, Mr Pranab Mukherjee, while presenting the 2011–2012 budget, stressed the importance of protection and regeneration of forests and allocated 60 million rupees, which was of great social, ecological and economic value. There was around a 4 per cent increase in the budget allocation for the Ministry of Environment and Forests as compared with 2010–2011, that is, from 220 million to 230 million rupees.

Green budget means adding 'green' component to the budget. It means a budget which is socially just and ecologically sustainable. It focuses on the environmental considerations in the budgetary allocations, shifting subsidies, allocating more funds for clean and renewable energy systems and shifting focus on ecological agriculture. Green budget can help meet the environmental challenges of climate change, develop or clean energy resources and sustain nation's lands, water and other natural resources.

It can be said that since the earliest concept of line–item budget, we have moved on to newer concepts in budgeting, keeping in view the contemporary demands. These new concepts or innovations in budgeting help in addressing the emerging socioeconomic and environmental challenges. The traditional or the line–item budget focussed on itemized budget highlighting the inputs only and was a tool of control. The performance budget moved one step further to include inputs as well as outputs. Budgeting was done on the basis of functions, programmes, performance, activities, projects, etc. The PPB included not only inputs and outputs but also their effects and alternatives. In ZBB, the focus was on explaining and justifying each function in totality and not in parts. Gender budget emphasizes a gender-just, gender-sensitive and gender-centric budget. Finally, green budget focuses on environment-sensitive or environment friendly budget. Thus, the innovations are an attempt to improve budgeting and to bring about socioeconomic change in the society through them.

BUDGETARY SYSTEM IN INDIAN FINANCIAL ADMINISTRATION

The annual financial statement or the statement of estimated receipts and expenditure of the government of India pertaining to each financial year is known as the budget. The budget is presented to Lok Sabha in two parts, namely, the railway budget that deals with railway finance and the general budget that provides an overall financial position of the Government of India, excluding the railways.

There are certain procedures laid down by the Indian Constitution under Article 112, relating to the government budget. These include the following procedures:

- The President shall, in respect of every financial year, cause to be laid before both the houses of Parliament a statement of the estimated receipts and expenditure of the Government of India for that year. The budget is presented by the Finance Minister, generally by the end of February every year.
- The statement indicates the receipts and payments of the government in three parts in which the accounts are kept –Consolidated Fund, Contingency Fund and Public Account.
- The estimates of expenditure indicate the following:
  (a) Amount of money needed to meet the expenditure charged on the Consolidated Fund of India.
  (b) Amount of money required to meet other expenditure to be met out of the Consolidated Fund of India.

Consolidated Fund of India

It constitutes all revenues received by the government, loans raised by it and loan recoveries. All expenditure of the government is incurred from the Consolidated Fund and no amount can be withdrawn from the fund without the approval of the Parliament

Contingency Fund

It is the fund placed at the disposal of the President of India and the money from it is used to meet unforeseen expenditure, for example, natural calamities

Public Account

This comprises funds which do not belong to the government and which have to be paid back at some point of time to the persons and authorities who deposited the money. This includes transactions relating to Provident Fund, small savings and other deposits. There is no requirement of parliamentary authorization for payments from this account

PHASES IN PREPARATION OF BUDGET

The budget preparation and consolidation has the following stages:

- Preparation and consolidation of preliminary estimates by the disbursing officers (heads of ministries/departments)
- Scrutiny of budget estimates by the department controlling officers
- Scrutiny of the revised estimates by the Accountant General and administrative department
- Scrutiny and consolidation of estimates by the Ministry of Finance
- Approval by the Cabinet

Budget Enactment in Parliament

The enactment of the budget in Parliament is done through certain phases as indicated below:

- The general budget is presented by the Finance Minister in the Lok Sabha on the last working day of February. The Finance Minister makes the budget speech and generally part A of it deals with the general economic survey of the country and part B encompasses taxation proposals, in the form of Finance Bill for the ensuing financial year.

- No discussion on the budget takes place on the day that it is presented in the Parliament.
- The budget discussion is done in two parts – the general discussion followed by detailed discussion and voting on the Demands for Grants. Once the budget is presented to the Parliament by the Finance Minister, the time for general discussion is allotted by the speaker. During these, the budget as a whole or any issue relating it is discussed. No cut motion can be moved. After the general discussion, the House is adjourned for a fixed period.
- During this period, the Demands for Grants of all the ministries/departments are first considered by the departmental standing committees which submit the report to the House.
- The House then proceeds to the discussion and voting on Demand for Grants, ministry-wise. At this stage, cut motions are moved to reduce any Demand for Grants but no amendments can be made to a motion seeking to reduce any demand. These are generally tabled by the members of the opposition.
- On the last of the allotted days for the discussion and voting on Demands for Grants, the speaker puts every question necessary to dispose of all the outstanding matters relating to the Demands for Grants. This is called *guillotine.* This implies concluding the discussion on Demands for Grants.
- The whole process of budget enactment in Parliament generally extends beyond the financial year. Therefore, a Constitutional provision empowers the Lok Sabha to provide grant in advance to the government for its various activities till the voting of Demands for Grants and passing of the Appropriation and Finance Bills. As a result, Vote on Account is passed by the Lok Sabha for a sum equivalent to one sixth of the estimated expenditure for the entire year under various Demands for Grants.
- Once the Demands for Grants are passed by the Lok Sabha, a bill to provide for the appropriation out of the Consolidated Fund of India of all moneys required to meet the grants and expenditure charged on the Consolidated Fund of India is introduced, considered and passed.
- The Finance Bill which contains all taxation proposals is also considered and passed by the Parliament.

Listed below is useful information on Cut Motions:

- These are Motions that are moved by the members of Parliament in Lok Sabha to reduce the amounts of Demands for Grants
- There are three types of Cut Motions
- Disapproval of Policy Cut: This is proposed by a member to express disapproval against a specific Demand for Grant. It reflects resentment against a particular policy. This motion is moved by requesting to reduce the Demand for Grant to one rupee
- Economy Cut: This is made to recommend reduction in the amount of Demand for Grant
- Token Cut: It is moved to reduce any Demand for Grant by a nominal amount. It is done to highlight any specific grievance pertaining to a policy or programme of the government

Execution of the Budget

The execution of the budget is the responsibility of the executive government. It involves the collection of taxes and other revenues, maintenance of accounts and audit. The enactment of Appropriation

Act initiates the process of budget execution. The Finance Ministry intimates the ministries/departments about their respective budgetary allocations. The controlling officers deliberate and allocate the money to the disbursing officers who in turn delegate to the pay and accounts officers.

The Department of Revenue in the Ministry of Finance is entrusted with the responsibility of collection of direct and indirect taxes. This control is exercised through the Central Board of Direct Taxes and Central Board of Excise and Customs.

The maintenance of accounts and auditing are two important stages in budget execution. Initially, both these were combined under one authority. In 1976, the Indian Civil Accounts Service was set up headed by the Controller General of Accounts (CGA) after the separation of the auditing and accounting functions in the ministries. The Ministries of Posts, Defence and Railways have their own accounting systems while the CGA is entrusted with the responsibility of administering the accounting system of other ministries of the government. It performs the functions of laying down accounting procedures and consolidation of annual and monthly accounts of the Government of India.

- The Central Board of Direct Taxes is entrusted with the task of policy and planning of direct taxes. It administers direct taxes laws through the income tax department
- The Central Board of Excise and Customs is responsible for the formulation and implementation of policies concerning customs and central excise duties

Audit

This is an important component of financial administration. Audit is a key tool to ensure financial control over the executive by ascertaining the proper spending of the money apportioned by the legislature. In public organizations in India, two types of audit, namely internal and external, are conducted. Internal audit is done by the concerned organization's accounting professionals or at times by independent auditors. The objective of this is to examine financial records, evaluate internal controls and bring out any lapses to ensure financial discipline.

The external audit is done by the CAG of India who is entrusted by the Constitution of India with the responsibility of the audit of accounts of the Union and states. The CAG is to audit and report on the following:

- Expenditure from the Consolidated Fund of India and of each state as to whether such expenditure has been in accordance with the law.
- Expenditure from the Contingency Fund and the public account of the Union and of the states.
- Trading, manufacturing and profit and loss accounts kept by any department of the Union or a state.

Types of audit conducted by CAG are of the following three types:

- Financial audit to ensure that the financial statements made are correct and inclusive in all respects and are presented with adequate disclosures
- Compliance audit to see whether the appropriate Constitutional provisions, laws, rules and regulations made under various orders and instructions issued by the competent authority are being complied with
- Performance audit to assess the extent to which an activity, programme or organization operates economically, efficiently and effectively

PARLIAMENTARY CONTROL OVER PUBLIC EXPENDITURE

The Indian Parliament exercises its control over financial matters in addition to the conduct of audit by the CAG, question hour and debates and also through Parliamentary Committees. These Committees comprising members of Parliament ensure supervision and accountability.

These are of two types, namely, ad hoc and standing committees. The former are constituted for specific purposes. The latter are set up every year or periodically. There are three financial standing committees namely, Public Accounts Committee, Estimates Committee and Committee on Public Undertakings.

Public Accounts Committee

This comprises 22 members, 15 from Lok Sabha and 7 from Rajya Sabha. It is entrusted with the functions of examining the following:

- Whether the money shown in the accounts as having been disbursed were legally available and applicable to the purposes for which they have been allotted.
- The expenditure conforms to the authority that governs it.
- Every reappropriation has been made properly in accordance with the rules.
- Examine the statement of accounts of state corporations, trading and manufacturing schemes and projects, and autonomous and semi-autonomous bodies.

Estimates Committee

It is constituted only from Lok Sabha and has 30 members. Its functions are as follows:

- Report any improvements, reforms brought about in the organization.
- Suggest suitable measures to improve economy and efficiency in administration.
- Examine whether the money is well laid down within the limits of policy implied in the estimates.
- Suggest the form in which the estimates shall be presented to the Parliament.

Committee on Public Accounts

It has 22 members, 15 from Lok Sabha and 7 from Rajya Sabha. It:

- Scrutinizes the reports and accounts of government owned companies and reports of CAG on the public sector undertakings.
- Exercises such other functions allotted by the speaker.

Budgeting and financial control are the two important components of Indian financial administration. The Ministry of Finance plays a key role in formulation and implementation of the country's economic policies. The monetary and fiscal policies are the mechanisms used by the government and the Reserve Bank of India to foster economic planning.

- Monetary policy is formulated by the Reserve Bank of India to control the supply and availability of money and in determining the rate of interest to ensure the economic growth and stability. It attempts to achieve a balance between the demand and supply of money
- Fiscal policy is laid down by the government and encompasses various measures pertaining to taxes, savings, public debt and any other related expenditure. The policy reflects the taxation and expenditure decisions of the government

CONCLUSION

Financial administration is a complex process that encompasses several activities in ensuring proper utilization of public money. The system works towards ensuring generation, regulation and distribution of monetary resources needed for the growth and sustenance of organizations. In public organizations it assumes greater significance as the limited financial resources are to be utilized towards realizing national goals. This calls for giving primacy to public interest, political direction, stability and simplicity in system, and efficient and effective control through accountability systems.

Preparatory Questions

- Explain the nature of financial administration.
- Highlight the significance of budget.
- What is line–item budget?
- List the steps involved in zero–based budgeting.
- Explain the concept of participatory budget.
- Bring out the features of green budget.
- Discuss the various phases of enactment of budget in Parliament.
- Explain the various types of cut motions.
- What are the different types of audit conducted by CAG?

REFERENCES

Awasthi, A. and Maheshwari, S. R. (1987) *Public Administration*. Agra: Laxmi Narain Agarwal.

Bhattacharya, M. (2011) *New Horizons of Public Administration*. 6th ed. New Delhi: Jawahar Publishers & Distributors.

Caiden, G. (1971) *Dynamics of Public Administration*. US: Dryden Press.

Chakraborty Bidyut and Prakash Chand, (2012) *Public Administration in a Globalization World*. New Delhi: Sage India.

Henry, N. (2010) *Public Administration and Public Affairs*. New Delhi: Pearson Education.

Mahajan, S. K. and Anupama, P. M. (2014) *Financial Administration in India*. New Delhi: PHI.

Mehta, A. K. (2006) *Gender Budgeting*. New Delhi: UNIFEM and IIPA.

Sarkar, S. (2010) *Public Administration in India*. New Delhi: PHI.

Sharma, M. P. and Sadana, B. L. (1998) *Theory and Practice of Public Administration*. New Delhi: Kitab Mahal.

Singh Amita, (2002) *Public Administration: Roots and Wings*. New Delhi: Galgotia.

Thavraj, M. J. K. (1978) *Financial Management of Government*. New Delhi: Sultan Chand.

Chapter Twenty One

Understanding Good Governance

Anil Dutta Mishra

LEARNING OBJECTIVES

After completing this chapter, you should be able to:

- Elaborate the concepts of governance and good governance
- Discuss the different perspectives of good governance
- Identify the key benchmarks of good governance
- Describe the good governance initiatives in India; and
- Make a critical appraisal of the concept of 'good governance'

INTRODUCTION

An administrative culture, as reiterated many a time, mediates among individuals, groups and communities and needs to be continuously strengthened, especially, if contemporary society, administration and government have to be made more meaningful and socially productive. This concern is now being addressed through 'good governance'. The expression has become a buzzword in contemporary discourse on public administration globally. Good governance is considered to be an essential ingredient for economic development and social upliftment of poor and marginalized sections of society.

In the 1980s, the issues of governance started receiving serious attention from researchers, policy makers and the international development community. Governance not only came to occupy centre stage in the development discourse, but also came to be considered as a crucial element to be incorporated in the development strategy. It is not that the issue was never a part of administrative dialogue; it just gained prominence in the Liberalization, Privatization and Globalization (LPG) context. In fact, governance has always been a pertinent issue. In the Indian tradition too, 'governance' is not an alien or new concept. The essence of governance has always been a strict code of conduct, a sense of duty, a service to subjects, and a willingness to sacrifice for the sake of upholding moral values, fair play and justice.

One can find the elements and essence of good governance in *Ramayana, Bhagavad-Gita and Shanti-Parva of Mahabharata as well as Kautilya's Arthashastra.* Even during the freedom struggle, *swaraj* and good governance were treated synonymously. After independence, we adopted the Constitution, which enshrined the aspirations and ideals of the freedom struggle and set out to achieve the objectives of equality, freedom and social justice; in essence, the goals of 'good governance'.

Our Constitution provides for certain fundamental rights to citizens to ensure governmental accountability. It also includes Directive Principles of State Policy as a moral obligation on the government towards citizens. Good governance would certainly mean that all Fundamental Rights are ensured to all the citizens and that various policies of the government are not only in conformity with the Directive Principles, but also implemented in the right spirit. The government determines policy, based on which it sets up various goals and targets for implementation. The questions to ponder are why good governance? Are not all governance strategies good? Are we not under some type of effective governance always? Also, why has the terminology changed from 'governance' to good governance?

This chapter tries to answer these questions by discussing the concepts of governance and good governance. It focuses on different perspectives of good governance and stresses the need to understand the broad definition of good governance that talks of bringing into its purview the government, the citizens, the voluntary or non-governmental agencies and private organizations.

CONCEPT OF GOVERNANCE

Before we talk of good governance, the concept of governance needs to be understood. The formal study of governance has a long history. In the Western civilization, its origins lie in ancient Greece and Greek political theory. Plato is credited with developing the concept of 'philosopher king' as the ideal ruler. The 'father' of the comparative study of government, Aristotle, was perhaps the first political theorist to deal with the term 'governance', when he classified political organizations by indicating the manner in which they were ruled – a kind of numerical count of rule by one – dictatorship, by a few – autocracy, or by many – democracy (Sinclair, 1962, p. 18).

According to Pierre and Peters (2000), the term 'governance' was first used in France in the 14th century, where it meant 'a seat of government'. The World Bank seems to have reinvented it in its Report on sub-Sahara Africa in 1989. The World Bank implied that governance is the exercise of political power to manage a nation's affairs. The current rebirth of 'governance' can be attributed to the macroeconomic policy reforms initiated through the Structural Adjustment Programmes (SAPs) of the early 1980s. The SAPs were intended to give a boost to development through sound economic policy making. The outcome was not as successful as was initially expected. In addition, the social impact was much more negative than anticipated.

Yet, the end of the cold war seemed to suggest that there was only one ideology with a moral stature – the adoption of pluralist democracy and free market economy. In simplest terms, it implied that governance relates to the effective management of the political and economic affairs of a country at all levels; guaranteeing its territorial integrity and securing the safety and efficiency of its organizations as well as safety and overall welfare of its people.

At the turn of the century, five mega global trends had an impact on the structure, functions and the process of governance: (i) strategies for redesigning the State; (ii) methods for managing rapid and rampant change; (iii) accounting for widening and broadening leadership from all segments of society; (iv) impact of technology and innovation and (v) innovative and specific mega trends. These five factors are *changing* the ways the public administrative systems in developing countries are functioning and in effect, these factors should be instrumental in pioneering the reorganization and reform efforts (Rahman, 2001, p. 231).

One of the first international organizations to use the term 'governance' was the World Bank in 1992. It defined it as having three distinct aspects:

- The form of a political regime (parliamentary or presidential, military or civilian and authoritarian or democratic)
- The processes by which authority is exercised in the management of a country's economic and social resources
- The capacity of governments to design, formulate and implement policies and, in general, to discharge governmental functions

Ever since the 1990s, significant efforts are being made to identify partners who, along with governments, can support and lead the path of economic development and social justice. The term 'governance' means different things to different people. It has a range of meanings, from the act or manner of governing, office or power, which make it synonymous with government, to being virtuous or wise in one's general behaviour. After the Peace of Westphalia in 1648 (*origin of sovereignty is attributed to it*), the term became fully synonymous with government.

Hyden (1992) defines 'governance' as 'conscious management of regime structures with the express aim of increasing their legitimacy among the public'. According to him, the study of governance involves identification of conditions that facilitate sound management and effective problem-solving strategy.

As per Hyden (1992), study of governance can be elaborated in the form of the following three main empirical dimensions:

1. Citizens' influence and oversight characterized by the following:
   a. Degree of political participation
   b. Means of preference aggregation
   c. Methods of public accountability
2. Responsive and responsible leadership characterized by the following:
   a. Degree of respect for the civic public realm
   b. Level of openness in public policy making
   c. Extent of adherence to the rule of law
3. Social reciprocities characterized by the following:
   a. Degree of political equality
   b. Degree of inter-group tolerance
   c. Degree of inclusiveness in associational membership

The Ford Foundation drew the attention to good governance, as a result of apparent inability of governments in the developing societies to regulate and control their activity. Accordingly, it advocates that governments must be checked and controlled by an active, articulate and organized citizenry. The main assumption is that the quality of governmental activity is promoted when there is consent and voluntary compliance of the people, stressing its *normative* quality as a framework for political and administrative systems worldwide.

It is in this spirit that the term 'good governance' has found favour with those engaged in policy processes. The term describes *how* public institutions conduct public affairs and manage public resources. While governance refers to a political *system*, whether democratic or not, good governance constitutes the systems and processes through which they achieve their goals and compare ineffective economies or political bodies with those that are viable.

In recent times, 'Good governance is associated with efficient and effective administration or governance in a democratic framework. The term, however, does *not* enjoy uniformity of meaning. For example, international organizations like the World Bank associate good governance primarily with capacity building and the exercise of political power needed for efficient and effective management of concrete national programmes, whether the political system is *democratic* or not' (Bratton and Donald, 1992, pp. 264–265).

Similarly, for scholars such as Dunn, 'Good governance implies a high level of organizational effectiveness without any choice as to its *ideological* premise' (cited in Buijtenhuijs and Rijinierse, 1993, p. 35). Good governance has been described as being equivalent to purposive and development-oriented administration, which is committed to improvement in quality of life of the mass of the people without being necessarily democratic (Jeffreis, 1992, pp. 207–226).

For yet another group of scholars, good governance implies the rule of law, safeguarding of human rights, presence of honest and efficient government, accountability, transparency, predictability and openness. Good governance and administrative reforms became a part of the broad package of the reforms, which were being promoted. The links between governance and development were made in a number of publications from the late 1980s such as the *World Bank Report on Governance and Development* 1992 and the *World Bank Report on the State in a Changing World* 1997 (Joseph, 2000).

Good governance espouses freedom of information, a strong legal system and efficient administration, backed by political mobilization of the disadvantaged through movements or political parties. Good governance is more than mere sound and efficient public administration. It is a process dedicated to the achievement of three major objectives in the present day world enshrined in the proclamation of the Social Development Summit 1995: (a) alleviation of poverty, (b) creation of productive employment and (c) social integration (Shelley, 2001, p. 166). For practical reasons, many use good governance and governance interchangeably.

Following the definitions given by the World Bank and the United Nations Development Programme (UNDP), there are three different, *albeit* interconnected, spheres of governance: (a) political, (b) economic and (c) administrative. Governance relates to a country or society as a *whole* (UNESCO, World Bank). It is about processes (UNESCO), as well as institutions and mechanisms (UNDP, World Bank). Governance is the exercise of power and authority (UNDP, World Bank) in pursuit of a society's present and future welfare (UNESCO) and derived from the interests of the citizens (UNDP, UNESCO) (cited in Cheema, 2001, p. 516).

KEY ELEMENTS OF GOOD GOVERNANCE

The phrase 'good governance' is epitomized by the World Bank (1997) in its recent literature as predictable, open and enlightened policy making, a bureaucracy imbued with a professional ethos, acting in furtherance of public good, rule of law, transparent processes and a strong civil society participating in public affairs. Poor governance, on the other hand, is characterized by arbitrary policy making, unaccountable bureaucracies, unenforced or unjust legal systems, abuse of executive power, unengaged civil society and widespread corruption. Good governance fosters a strong State, capable of sustained economic and social development and institutional growth. Poor governance undermines all efforts to improve policy making and to create durable institutions. Let us now reflect on the *key features* of good governance.

According to the United Nations Centre for Human Settlements (UNCHS), there are *five* key elements that outline a workable and fair mode of governance. They imply the need for fiscal responsibility and sound management of national and local resources. They require building and utilizing the capacity for analysis and formulation of sound social and economic policies. They describe governance as a partnership between the public and private sectors, government and private citizens and management and labour. These are as follows:

1. Equity (sustainability, gender equality and intergenerational equity).
2. Effectiveness (efficiency, subsidiarity and strategic vision).
3. Accountability (transparency, rule of law and responsiveness).
4. Participation (citizenship, consensus orientation and civic engagement).
5. Security (conflict resolution, human security and environmental safety).

Many other scholars/reports have spoken of varied elements of good governance. Succinctly, we may talk of the following as the key *benchmarks* of good governance:

- *Accountability*: First and foremost, good governance requires *accountability* by public officials, both elected political leaders and civil servants. Their public functions must serve the community at large. Legitimacy, vital for accountable governance, emphasizes the need for a system of governance, which operates with the consent of the governed and thus provides the means to give or withhold their consent.

- Accountability involves the *existence of a mechanism*, which ensures that both politicians and officials are answerable for their actions and use of public resources and performance. Decision makers in government, private sector and civil society organizations are accountable to the public as well as to institutional stakeholders. This accountability differs depending on the nature of organization and whether the decision is internal or external to an organization.
- *Transparency*: Good governance also requires *transparency* in public procedures, processes, investment decisions, contracts and appointment. In fact, transparency is a precondition to accountability. It is not sufficient that information is simply made available; it must also be reliable and presented in useful and understandable ways to facilitate accountability. Openness and transparency emphasize the need for public access to quality information and making public all the transactions in which public interest is involved.
- Transparency is built on the *free flow of information*. Processes, institutions and information are directly accessible to those concerned with them and enough information needs to be provided to understand and monitor them. Good governance demands transparent administration by not only letting the decision-making criterion and the programme design open to the public but also involving them in policy processes. The right to information has become the need of the hour as corruption and malpractices have become an undeniable reality in the administration (Ahammed, 1999, pp. 59–60).
- *Participation*: Widespread *participation* in public policies and regulations (*and even in the operation of markets*) is an ingredient of good governance. Major public choices demand wide scale participation and debate involving not just ethical governmental agencies but also accountable Non-Governmental Organizations (NGOs). The main objective of good governance, since it relates to participation, is to encourage political leadership to reflect and promote ideals of good citizenship such as informed opinion, compassion and fairness.
- Participation envisages participation of the entire society in governance and decision making through change in their subsidiary roles and direct involvement in areas hitherto kept exclusively in the public domain. This is also possible through *legitimate intermediate institutions* that represent their interests. Such broad participation is also built on freedom of association and speech as well as capacities to participate constructively. Good governance depends on the cooperation and involvement of a large number of citizens and organizations. These requirements are considered not only essential for good governance but are important for sustainable human development (Minocha, 1997, p. 3).
- *Rule of law*: Good governance is built on the *rule of law*. Modern societies, especially those in cities, are extremely complex. Those that remain organized and prosperous do so because rules and expectations closely correlate to how political procedures and markets function. Legal frameworks should be fair and enforced impartially, particularly the laws on human rights and laws for the disadvantaged.
- *Predictability*: Public and private institutions, such as government agencies and markets, must have some measure of *predictability*. The rule of law helps to protect against erratic and uneven

enforcement as well as the whims of public officials. However, the process of making and changing public rules and expectations must also be predictable (UNCHS, 1996). A few more *benchmarks* can be added to this core list. These are as follows:

- *Competence*: Competence demonstrates the capacity to create effective policy and decision-making processes in order to achieve the efficient delivery of goods and services, which involve public interest (Kumar, 2001, p. 248).
- *Consensus orientation*: Good governance mediates differing interests to reach a broad consensus on what is in the best interests of the stakeholders and, where possible, on policies and procedures in a sustainable and practical manner.
- *Equity*: Good governance should provide equal opportunities for its stakeholders to maintain, enhance, or generally improve the wellbeing of all in society.
- *Effectiveness and efficiency*: Good governance has to promote effective and efficient organizations engaged in delivery of goods and services. This is possible if governance strategies are put to use in a judicious manner aiming at goal maximization and cost minimization processes. The institutions of governance should attempt to produce results that meet targeted goals, while making the best use of resources.
- *Strategic vision*: Leaders and the public have a broad and long-term perspective on good governance and human development. There is also an understanding of the historical, cultural and social complexities in which that perspective is grounded.

The policy documents of UNDP further state that 'It needs to be recognized that these core characteristics are mutually reinforcing and cannot stand alone' (Mehta, 2001, pp. 322–324).

Key benchmarks of good governance are as follows:

- Participation
- Legitimacy
- Competence
- Transparency
- Accountability
- Predictability
- Consensus orientation
- Equity
- Effectiveness and efficiency
- Strategic vision

Good governance, thus, 'encompasses a wide range of issues from concerns about efficient government, including accountability and transparency, to concerns about human rights, social cohesion, equity (gender, poor), democracy, participation, corruption, military expenditures, countries in crises, and, last but not the least, political thought, culture and discourse' (Cheema, 2001, p. 517).

NATURE OF GOOD GOVERNANCE

The objective of good governance in India was voiced by Pandit Jawaharlal Nehru in his soul-stirring speech at the dawn of India's independence on 15th August 1947. It got reflected in his sentiments on 'ending of poverty and ignorance and disease and inequality of opportunity'. Mahatma Gandhi also prescribed a set of stiff yardsticks for judging the efficacy of public policies in a system of good governance. He said, 'Will it restore to him (*the poorest and the weakest man*) control over his own life and destiny? In other words, will it lead to *Swaraj* for the hungry and spiritually starving millions'?

However, despite the vision of our national leaders on good governance and its translation into Constitutional provisions, the Indian State has somewhat failed in its responsibilities towards its citizens over the last 60 odd years. Good governance in India is still unfulfilled as the machinery that works with full transparency of operation and is fully accountable is somewhat wanting on many counts.

Good governance involves people who are entrusted with the responsibility to govern the systems, which they put in place. This implies maximum good of maximum people. It is not a one-time effort but a continuous struggle. To protect the right of the governed, to meet their needs and fulfil their aspirations is by any yardstick an enormous task and requires herculean efforts. After centuries of experimentation including that of Soviet Union, it is largely accepted that the democratic form is by far the most suitable means for achieving the objective of good governance. However, if such governments have enormous powers to deliver effective governance, they also have equal opportunities and temptations to misuse such powers.

The phenomenal growth in the pervasiveness of governmental institutions and the points of interface with the common person have resulted in corresponding growth in the opportunities to do good or mischief. Therefore, in today's context with the advanced state of technology, particularly information technology, large-scale global interaction, enormous powers enjoyed by government agencies and equally great expectations of people, the most challenging task is how to minimize the mischief by those involved in the governing process and how to make them do maximum good, that is, to provide good governance (Tiwari, 2000, pp. 104–105).

The UNDP workshop on 'Governance for Sustainable Human Development' 1994, identified certain characteristics of good governance and these are as follows:

- Participation
- Responsiveness to people
- Development of resources and methods of governance
- Mobilization of resources for social purposes
- Operation by rule of law
- Enabling and facilitative environment
- Promotion of equity and equality
- Regulation rather than control
- Service orientation
- Sustainability
- Acceptability to people
- Promotion of gender balance
- Accountability (cited in Sobhan, 1998).

There is a need to pay attention to the mechanisms and modalities followed by governments to determine public policies and it is equally important to critically examine whether the policies are being efficiently and honestly implemented by the concerned government agencies and organizations. It also needs to be seen whether, and to what extent, the governments have established meaningful linkages with various elements of civil society, which can support the concerns of governance (Vohra, 2000, p. 169).

The attainment of the objectives of good governance would require political, economic, executive and judicial authority to be exercised in a manner, which ensures that the people are enabled to enjoy their rights, discharge their obligations and resolve their disputes within the parameters of the Constitution and the rule of law. The failures of the legislatures, the communalization and criminalization of politics, brutalization of society, endemic corruption and the chronic ineffectiveness of governments have impacted on the very credibility of governance. The consequential cynicism among the citizenry is the most disturbing development and, if allowed to continue, is bound to adversely affect the growth of stable and productive societies and may even endanger the future of democracy (Vohra, 2000, p. 175).

The entire spectrum of public services, from village level upwards, has the responsibility of carrying out duties with promptness, efficiency and honesty. Critical consequences have arisen on account of the failures of the administrative systems and structures to efficiently implement and deliver even the poverty alleviation programmes on time.

Good governance aims at the following:

- Improving the quality of life of citizens
- Enhancing the effectiveness and efficiency of administration
- Establishing the legitimacy and credibility of institutions
- Securing freedom of information and expression
- Providing citizen-friendly administration
- Ensuring transparency and accountability
- Using information technology to improve citizen–government interface
- Improving the productivity of organizations
- Promoting organizational pluralism – State, market and civil society organizations for governance

Many initiatives to increase accountability are in the offing. Citizens' charters have been introduced in states such as Andhra Pradesh and Karnataka. In order to make direct interactions between citizens and government and service providers possible, a number of methods are being introduced such as *websites* providing information on governmental policies, *ministerial portals and ministers' e-mails.* To improve efficiency in public administration, strategies such as introducing profitability criteria, 'contracting out' functions of governments to NGOs or private agencies or sharing them, decentralization of levels of administration, marketing and the like have been adopted as part of the post-welfare State reorganization in many countries. Similar measures are now being tried out in India (Vohra, 2000).

Administration should take the role of 'working with the people' *instead* of a traditional role of 'helping the people' in nation building. The need for devolution of social and political power from the highly powerful central government to lower echelons of government is also recognized. India has already given Constitutional status to the third tier of government, that is, panchayati raj institutions and urban local bodies (Hassan, 2000, p. 185).

Good governance initiatives in India include the following:

- Citizens' charters
- Avenues for redressal of citizens' grievances
- Use of information technology
- Right to information
- People's participation
- Lokpal and Lokayukta

We will not go into details on the good governance initiatives in this chapter, as other chapters in this volume deal with them in detail. The empowerment of the people has to be the *keystone* for change in future. A reorganization of the ownership of national resources that would help in fulfilling the basic needs of the poorer sections of the population is also essential to facilitate good governance.

GOOD GOVERNANCE: A CRITICAL APPRAISAL

The 'good governance' agenda identifies many desirable governance goals for developing countries but their implementation and outcomes have *not* been very satisfactory. As Mushtaq Khan (2010) avers, 'one reason could be that the good governance framework *confuses* means and ends and ignores very significant historical facts about growth pattern in developing countries. Its position as the dominant consensus sets poor countries unachievable agendas, creating dissatisfaction, and takes the attention away from achievable and critical governance agendas'.

The legacy of 'one size fits all' does not end with good governance. A uniform agenda is still being imposed by the developed world in the form of benchmarks, strategies and outcomes. The concept and strategy of 'governance' has been a subject of critical debate. George H. Fredrickson (2007) has challenged the validity and usefulness of the concept on the following five fundamental grounds:

- The concept of 'governance' is fashionable and most favourite of academics. It appears to be a *rehash* of old academic debates under a new name. As fashion changes, the utility of concept of governance could diminish over time.
- The concept is *imprecise*, complicated and broad and connotes several meanings. The term 'governance' is said to lack a precise meaning.
- The concept of governance is laden with *values*. Some approaches to governance as public administration reflect anti-bureaucratic and anti-government sentiments, limited government and so on. Some models are contextual, based on Constitutional, legal, organizational and political influences as well as imperatives. All these broaden the study and in the process, it makes it un-public administration like.
- Scholars, specially referring to governance in Europe, claim that it is primarily about change and reforms but the underlying value of governance is not primarily about change but about *order*.
- Governance is often centred on non-state in situations – both non-profit and for-profit contractors, NGOs and inter-governmental organizations. It diminishes the capacity of the core State executive to steer. In the hollow State, conditions of State are reversed; the State is steered by its governance partners. It is the States and their sub-jurisdictions that deal with problems of poverty, justice and race (cited in Medury, 2010, p. 202).

Fredrickson opines that the 'governance' approach to the study of public administration lays emphasis on theory and research, explains change and reform rather than functioning of State, regional and global institutions. In addition, governance theorists attempt to provide a 'general theory' that will provide an explanation for the past and a means to predict the future. Generally, no such simple pattern has been observed. According to Fredrickson, although 'governance is a serious challenge, it does not render the concept useless. Governance even with its weakness is the most useful and available concept for describing the powerful forces currently at work in the world' (cited in Medury, 2010, p. 202).

Among the major reasons for such gross failures is that the public services have been politicized. Functionaries who conform to systems, procedures and the rule of law are harassed, unceremoniously transferred, marginalized, punished without adequate bases and virtually eliminated. Promotions and appointments are made *not* on the basis of proven competence, experience, seniority and integrity but on considerations of political affiliation, caste, community and pliability. The end result is that the public services have degenerated, become unaccountable and dishonest and are consequently unable to provide leadership and initiatives (Vohra, 2000, p. 175).

Another problem has arisen due to the fact that democracy is being viewed as a component of good governance in the thinking of lending agencies and donor governments. Democracy and development and good governance are now considered to be *interrelated* goals, each supporting the other (Joseph, 2000, p. 1012). Looked at in holistic terms, the balance between onslaught of the market and good governance is not very easy to establish because the inherent democratic values of good governance clash with non-altruistic concerns of the market. Nevertheless, a right chord can be struck, as per Kiggundu (2004), if the following are promoted:

- Improvement in public security, economic management and public administration.
- Shared system of values through core public and private sector institutions.
- Development of civil society and indigenous executive, legislative, judicial and administrative institutions.
- Good governance, democratic development and an effective capacity for development.

CONCLUSION

Governance has many dimensions and no single solution can eliminate all forms of bad governance or misgovernance. The good governance agenda advocates freedom of information, a strong legal system and efficient administration to help the underprivileged claim equality, but these have been most successful when backed up by strong political mobilization through social movements or political parties with a clear-cut vision.

In the present context, good governance is a reform strategy and also an initiative to strengthen the institutions with the objective of making the government more accountable, more open, more transparent and more democratic. To talk of good governance means bringing about goodness in all the three sectors: government, civil society and corporate world, including transnational corporations. Good governance has been observed to be a tryst with trust, a commitment of the people for the people, a social contract for the greatest good and the collective conscience of the community.

The success of any administrative system depends on the vigilance of citizens. The interface of administration and citizens has put the administration into a very dominant position. Without effective public accountability, the governance strategies could have very serious consequences. How to increase public accountability and make the administration responsive is the main challenge of good governance. If we really want to see good governance operational on the ground, we have to avoid the following seven *social sins* which Mahatma Gandhi advocated before independence:

Politics without principles
Wealth without work
Pleasure without conscience
Knowledge without character
Commerce without morality
Science without humanity
Worship without sacrifice

This chapter, has discussed the indispensability of governance to government; more so good governance in the same hue. It has described the key parameters of good governance and critically examined their relevance and import.

Preparatory Questions

- What do you mean by good governance?
- Describe the major features of good governance.
- Elucidate the steps taken by the government to safeguard good governance in India.
- Discuss the various tools of ensuring good governance.

REFERENCES

Ahammed, M. A. (1999) 'Good Governance through Transparency'. *Management in Government.* XXXI(3).

Bandyopadhyay, D. (1996) 'Administration, Decentralization and Good Governance'. *Economic and Political Weekly.* XXXI(48).

Bratton, M. and Donald, R. (1992) 'The Institutional Bases of Governance in Africa' in Hyden, G. and Bratton, M. (eds.). *Governance and Politics in Africa*. London: Lynne Rienner Publishers.

Buijtenhuijs, R. and Rijinierse, E. (1993) *Democratization in Sub- Sahara Africa* (1989–92)*: An Overview of the Literature.* Leiden: Africa Study Centre.

Cheema, G. S. (2001) 'A Governance Approach to Development: New Role for Development Co-operation' in Hye, A. D. (ed.). *Governance: South Asian Perspectives*. New Delhi: Manohar. p. 516.

Etounga, M. A. (1993) 'Democratization and Good Governance in Africa.' (Summary of a Lecture Presented at the Good Governance Lectures). The Hague: Ministry of Foreign Affairs.

Hassan, M. (2000) 'The Agenda For Good Governance in a Globalised World'. *South Asian Survey.* 7.

Hyden, G. (1992) 'Governance and the Study of Politics' in Hyden, G. and Bratton, M. (eds.). *Governance and Politics in Africa*. 'London: Lynne Rienner Publishers'.

Jeffreis, R. (1997) 'Unborn Population Attitudes Towards The Economic Recovery Programme and PNDC Government in Ghana'. *Journal of African Affairs*. 91.

Joseph, S. (2001) 'Democratic Good Governance: New Agenda for Change'. *Economic and Political Weekly*. 36(12).

Khan, M. (2010) 'The illusory lure of "Good Governance" and the Hard Realities of Growth in Poor Countries'. *Seminar* at Danish Institute for International Studies (DIIS), 24th June.

Khosla, I. P. (2000) 'Governance and Difference'. *South Asian Survey*. 7(2).

Kiggundu, (2004) *cited in* Jabbra, J. G. and Dwivedi, O. P. 'Globalization, Governance and Administrative Culture'. *International Journal of Public Administration*. 27(13).

Fredericksion, H. G. (2007) 'Whatever happened to Public Administration' Governance, Governance Everywhere. The oxford Handbook of Public Management (eds.) Ewan Ferlie and Christopher Pollitt, USA, Oxford.

Kulshreshtha, A. (2000) 'Good Governance and Audit' in Mathur, B. P. (ed.). *Public Audit, Good Governance and Accountability.* New Delhi: Institute of Public Auditors of India.

Kumar, G. M. R. (2001) 'Local Government for Good Governance: Experience in Andhra Pradesh' in Hye, H. A. (ed.). *Governance: South Asian Perspectives*. New Delhi: Manohar. pp. 516–248.

LaPorte, R. Jr. (2001) 'Governance and Public Administration' in Hye, H. A. (ed.). *Governance: South Asian Perspectives*. New Delhi: Manohar. p. 18.

Medury, U. (2010) *Public Administration in the Globalization Era: The New Public Management Perspective.* New Delhi: Orient Blackswan.

Mehta, D. (2001) 'Urban Governance: Lessons from Asia' in Hye, H. A. (ed.). *Governance: South Asian Perspectives.* New Delhi: Manohar. pp. 322–324.

Minocha, O. P. (1997) 'Good Governance: Concept and Operational Issues'. *Management in Government.* XXIX(3).

Nayyar, D. (2004) 'Alleviating poverty: Role of Good Governance and Constitutional Reform'. *Economic and Political Weekly.*

Overseas Development Administration (1993) 'Overseas Development Administration (ODA) Report.' *Taking Account of Good Government*. London.

Pierre, J. and Peters, B. G. (2003) *cited in* Bovaird, T. and Loffler, E. (eds.). *Public Management and Governance.* London: Routledge.

Pierre, J. and Peters, B. G. (200) 'Governance, Politics and the State, London St Martin.'

Rahman, S. (2001) 'Governance and Local Government System' in Hye, H. A. (ed.). *Governance: South Asian Perspectives*. New Delhi: Manohar. p. 516.

Shelley, M. R. (2001) 'Governance and Administration: Challenge of New Millennium' in Hye, H. A. (ed.). *Governance: South Asian Perspectives*. New Delhi: Manohar. p. 516.

Sinclair, T. A. (1962) *Aristotle: The Politics*. Baltimore (MA): Penguin Books.

Sobhan, R. (ed.) (1998) *Towards a Theory of Governance and Development Learning from East Asia*. Dhaka: The Bangladesh University Press.

Tiwari, A. C. (2000) 'Good Governance and Audit' in Mathur, B. P. (ed.). *Public Audit, Good Governance and Accountability.* New Delhi: Institute of Public Auditors of India. pp. 104–105.

UNCHS. (1996) 'An Urbanizing World: Global Report on Human Settlements.' *United Nations Centre for Human Settlements* (*HABITAT*). New York: Oxford.

UNESCO. (1997) UNESCO Report. *Capacity Building for Governance*. Paris.

UNDP. (1994) UNDP Report. *Governance for Sustainable Human Development.* New York.

UNDP. (1995) UNDP Report. *Public Sector Management, Governance and Sustainable Human Development.* New York.

UNDP. (1997) UNDP Reports. *Governance for Sustainable Growth and Equity; Governance for Sustainable Human Development; Participatory Urban Governance; Public–Private Partnerships for the Urban Environment; Reconceptualizing Governance.*

Vohra, N. N. (2000) 'Cooperating for Good Governance in South Asia.' *South Asian Survey*. 7(2). p. 169.

World Bank. (1992) World Bank Report. *Governance and Development.* Washington, DC: The International Bank for Reconstruction and Development. Pierre Jon and Guy Peters (2000) Governance, Politics and the State, London St Martin.

World Bank (1994) World Bank Report. *Governance, The World Bank Experience*. Washington, DC.

World Bank (1994) World Bank Report. *The World Bank and Participation*. Washington, DC.

World Bank (1997) World Bank Report. *The State in a Changing World.* Washington, DC.

Chapter Twenty Two

Forms of Public Accountability

Vaishali Narula

LEARNING OBJECTIVES

After completing this chapter, you should be able to:

- Provide a conceptual framework of accountability
- Understand the changing nature of accountability in the contemporary times
- Describe the importance of Accountability
- Explain the important measures of ensuring various forms of accountability
- Bring forth the different initiatives towards accountability in India; and
- Discuss the role of agencies/institutions working towards redressal of grievances

INTRODUCTION

Accountability is instrumental in making governance effective through bettering or improving service delivery and governmental answerability. In recent times, citizens' empowerment has become an essential component or dimension in enforcing accountability. This dimension has been invoked through innumerable reform measures. It has been realized that any initiative towards social, political or economic reforms requires building up of the State's capacities, encouraging participation of civil society and strengthening the synergy between the State and civil society. This is envisaged through a transparent system that allows for answerability to public conduct. This is why accountability becomes so pertinent, as it is a way or method of building transparency in administrative systems.

To understand the concept of accountability, it is important to understand the working of our democratic framework. India, as a democracy, functions on the pillars of legislature, executive, judiciary and civil society. The Constitution in its 'basic structure' through Fundamental Rights (*Article* 14 and *Article* 32) and Fundamental Duties empowers the citizens to demand accountability of governmental agencies.

The Constitution of India envisages the Parliament and the bureaucracy as the pillars of political stability, economic building and social strengthening. The bureaucracy is also described as the steel frame of the country, as it helps in its political and economic sustenance. However, the bureaucracy, instead of being receptive to the people's needs, has been allegedly working for its self-aggrandizing benefits and also for the interests of its political masters. The central reason behind this is the structure of bureaucracy, which has not been able to extricate itself from the colonial mindset. As a result, the administrative system revolves around an *ideal framework* of rules and principles that has led to non-fulfilment of goals. The adherence to rules and principles in bureaucratic systems are the characteristics of dogmatism and formalism (*Weber's Ideal Bureaucracy*), which have made the administrative system very rigid, closed, inflexible, inefficient and ineffective.

Thus, a nexus between the politicians and the bureaucrats has emerged, which has begun to work for their own interests. The administrative system has come to revolve around secrecy, red- tapism, rigidity and formalism. Therefore, a need is being felt to *build* integrity in the administrative system with accountability, transparency and openness. This chapter will attempt to understand accountability as a concept. It will discuss its nature, types and dimensions. Along with this, an effort will be made to understand certain pertinent questions related to why democracies desire accountability and what has led to increasing demand of accountability. Is it lack of effective institutions? Is it absence of effective implementation? Is it non-existence of effective agencies for redressal of grievances, or is it some other issue? This chapter will also examine the mechanisms to ensure accountability in India. It will look into the reasons behind inadequacy of strategies to ensure accountability.

MEANING OF ACCOUNTABILITY

Accountability is a way forward towards setting goals. It is differently understood across disciplines. Accountability is *interchangeably* used with concepts of answerability and responsibility. It is described as explaining and justifying what has been done, what is currently being done and what is being planned. It is therefore about giving information on the available resources and regular conduct of evaluation exercises to determine if the goals are being met.

Accountability, in the process of governance, is commonly associated with the following:

- Bureaucratic answerability
- Political responsibility
- Economic conscientiousness

Accountability is also defined as answerability for performance or the obligation to report to others. It is to explain, to justify and to answer questions about *how* resources have been used and to *what* extent. With respect to this, it can be said that accountability is a constraint on *arbitrary* use of power. It strengthens the legitimacy of institutions, which meet the *obligation* to report their activities to appropriate group of authorities. Accountability is a form of *introspection* by institutions to examine their operations and at the same time have a *critical review* from outside.

Accountability can be described as a *force* on external behaviour to ensure that its compliance with specific policies and directives stands firm. In traditional public administration, accountability was confined to *bureaucratic answerability*. Contemporary administration attempts to make accountability *broader*, bringing in its ambit accountability of legislature, executive, judiciary as well as non-state actors.

The traditional model of administration was unconsciously oriented towards the following:

- Rationality
- Centralization
- Rigid hierarchical structures

In classical democratic theory, 'the line of accountability is fairly straightforward'. It shows that the people elect their representatives who make policies on their behalf. The executive is entrusted to carry out these policies and is answerable to the political representatives. The present day administration does not work on this *dichotomy* of policy maker and executor. Even the political executive is involved in implementation by setting its guidelines. The permanent executive too is involved in policy making by playing an important advisory and data bank role (Bhattacharya, 2001). In this complex scenario, accountability is an intricate process involving many actors and processes.

CHANGING NATURE OF ACCOUNTABILITY

Accountability as a concept cannot be described in a single definition, as it would render the concept meaningless. In the political context, the conception of accountability is tied to beliefs about the nature of a just government, the role of the citizenry in setting policy and the *interaction* between elected officials and career civil servants. Thus, the operative definition of accountability is to ascertain performance. Accountability accounts for the relationship between bureaucracy, leaders, community and society. It can also be described as the relationship between the 'source of control' and the 'degree of control'. Therefore, accountability *encompasses* different dimensions based on its value emphasis, that is, it could be hierarchical, legal, professional and political.

The *paradigmatic move* in the ideological framework of neo-liberalism and public choice (about which you have read in the earlier chapters of this volume) has led to a shift in the functioning of our democratic State. The last three decades have witnessed integration of elements such as performance and quality in the governance of State with emphasis on accountability. The *accountability panacea* is driven by market needs, managerialism and individual choice. It calls for downsizing and delayering of the government with active participation of citizens.

The debate on accountability actually got a new impetus from the *New Public Management or NPM reforms* across the world. The focus on entrepreneurial government reoriented the administration towards performance, productivity and efficiency. It led to keeping an account of resources and their utilization. Therefore, accountability is answerability for public officials' behaviour or actions. The *essence* of accountability is based on the following:

- Implementation of laws without delay.
- Changing the nature of policies as needed for socioeconomic development.
- Citizens' participation.
- Performance orientation.

Hence, the nature of accountability, with the contemporary focus on NPM, has reoriented itself from a closed to an open system, sharing of information and redressal of grievances. Therefore, the administration is no more under the umbrella of permanence and absence of answerability. NPM has brought in an accent on delayering, productivity, job specificity and performance accountability (5th Pay Commission, 1997). NPM lays emphasis on quality of the government as against the size and imagines a more responsive, policy-competent and citizen-friendly incarnation in policy framework.

The *shift* towards the neo-liberal framework has led to a restructuring of the government and developing an upward and downward link; with the civil society putting premium on performance for greater accountability. The idea of 're-inventing government' (Osborne and Gabeler, 1992) emphasized a result-oriented, customer-driven and decentralized government. Therefore, the search for speedy decisions with institutional integrity led to envisaging accountability as an essential component of democracy. It is essential to understand, however, that the dimensions of accountability cannot be restricted to efficiency, performance and effectiveness because responsibility, ethics, values and culture are *also* an integral part of accountability. Reforms of any kind need to encompass regulations, social services and exchange rate policy. Therefore, reforms are about capability and effectiveness.

The nature of accountability in public administration can be understood as a cause and effect of the *shift* from government to governance. 'Governance', in its broad sense, refers to 'a concept that goes beyond the traditional notion of government to focus on the relationships between leaders, public institutions and citizens, including the processes by which they make and implement decisions (Transparency International, 2008). The practice of 'good governance' contains certain *core* characteristics that promote equity and accountability as well as minimize opportunities for corruption. Good governance covers a range of practices, including respect for the rule of law, enhanced disclosure and greater participation. In broad terms, good governance also implies sustainable systems, both for policy processes and outcomes.

Accountability is *central* to the idea of good governance. The ascendency of the concept of good governance can be traced to the *World Bank Report* of 1989, which emphasized on structural adjustment and redefinition of the role of the State. The State reflected the ascendance of neo-liberal ideology in neo-economic theory and public choice framework. A large number of States were unable to implement their welfare policies due to inflexible and non-participatory bureaucratic framework. Consequently, social spending started getting reduced and reliance on the market increased to meet the demands of the citizens for which alternative strategies were devised.

These developments led to a shift from the traditional Weberian model of bureaucracy to a more flexible and open system of governance. Indian bureaucracy is considered to have many Weberian characteristics, administered by political turbulence, secrecy and commitment. Thus, the quest for good governance led to drawing up of institutions beyond the government and made a case for *autonomous self-governing institutions* with the capacity to get things done.

The roots of the administrative reforms can be traced to Thatcherism; that is, the Margret Thatcher administration in the UK and the Reaganomics (Ronald Reagon's economic policies) in the US in the 1980s under the spell of neo-liberal politico-economic thinking. The period witnessed the collapse of the Soviet Union, which led to a transition to the new politico-administrative system. This brought in a unique victory for liberalism and democracy. This led to demand for reforms in administration with rolling back of the State and downsizing of the bureaucracy (you have already read about it in the chapter 14 on NPM). There was a demand for people's voice and active participation of civil society. The Reagan administration worked towards encouraging entrepreneurship and installing limits to the growth of social spending.

The Reagan and Thatcher administration worked towards administrative reforms in the core State functions. The objective centred around building of State's capacity. The focus of the States was to cut the size of State bureaucracy, while simultaneously making the government more efficient and more responsive to citizens. Therefore, the governmental reform movement concentrated on building of State's capacity and fighting corruption.

In reforming public bureaucracy, we need to put emphasis on accountability, competence, sharing of information and control of corruption. Transparency is an essential component of accountability. It has the potential to stem out corrupt practices and provide precision to government policies. It facilitates better assessment of government's performance. Transparency is but one mechanism to secure accountability; there are other methods such as openness of the system, access to information and responsiveness towards people, through which governments and public officials can still be held accountable. The challenge is to minimize corruption and transcend towards a more transparent and accountable system of governance.

Jabbra and Dwivedi (1988) categorize accountability into the following types:

- Organizational/Administrative
- Legal
- Professional
- Political
- Moral

Besides the nature of accountability, it is important to understand the various dimensions of accountability. This raises questions such as what makes an organization accountable? Does an organization follow procedures or does it have an open-ended way of functioning with reviewable and non-reviewable procedures? There are five dimensions of accountability, namely, transparency, liability, controllability, responsibility and responsiveness. These categories are not mutually exclusive, that is, organizations may be accountable in more than one sense. Indeed, the first two kinds of accountability (transparency and liability) can be thought of as *foundations* and the other three are the *supporting* notions of accountability.

TYPES OF ACCOUNTABILITY

Accountability is the 'driving force' that generates responsible and performance-oriented administration. Accountability has a substantive and a procedural role in administration. Thus, on one hand, it regulates through rules and principles and on the other hand, ensures effectiveness and achievement of goals. The Indian Constitution lays down the basic structure under which it defines the power and responsibility of the organs of the government. It regulates the relationship between people, administration and different organs of the government. This can be understood through the different measures, methods and means by which accountability is sought in our legislature, executive and judiciary. Let us try to understand the different types of responsibilities first.

Organizational Accountability

It literally means adherence to laws and rules as promulgated by the organization from time to time. Every organization has its own system to ensure accountability, be it organizational/departmental enquiries, punitive career advancement policies, hierarchical answerability to immediate bosses, service conduct rules, etc. We can divide organizational accountability into fiscal accountability (lacunae in financial transactions), process accountability (presence of irregularities in various institutions) and programme accountability (effectiveness of initiatives and not just their implementation). Professional accountability is also a part of this; as has been observed, every professional organization entails exhibition of high standards of work and qualitative performance of assigned work (Sabarwal, 2013).

Political Accountability

Political accountability connotes accountability of the government to its people/citizens. It comprises accountability of the legislature and the executive, as they are *both* responsible for effective implementation of their policies and fulfilment of basic needs of the people that their policies reflect. In the Indian democracy, the legislature comprises representatives of the people. The administration is made responsible to the elected representatives and people are the most important constituent of a democracy.

Kettle and Fesler (2005) point out that 'bureaucratic accountability has to be seen from *two* standpoints. *One* is accountability in terms of answerability for whatever the bureaucracy does or does not do and the *second* is ethical behaviour. Bureaucracy has a responsibility towards the people for whom it enforces programmes, not just to the political masters who assign them to enforce these programmes'. The legislature, on the other hand, has been given powers by the Constitution by which it is able to keep an effective check on malpractices in administration, and answerability is sought through the following methods:

Question hour: The first hour of everyday sitting shall be available for asking and answering questions. Every member has the right to ask questions irrespective of their party affiliations. The objective is to seek answerability of the administration.

Zero hour: This Parliamentary discussion has been in use since 1962. Ministers such as Krishna Menon had to resign due to heated debate on accountability of public enterprises in the Parliament. These discussions brought forth the administrative failure on several fronts.

Control by committees: The committee system helps to investigate the policies by administration. Committees such as Public Accounts Committee, Estimates Committee, Standing Committee and the Committee of Public Undertakings have been responsible in exposing major scandals from animal husbandry scam that has led to conviction of Laloo Prasad Yadav to discussing the contours of *Lokpal* Bill and passing it subsequently.

Appropriation Act and Parliamentary audit: This is the exercise which helps to exert financial control on administration's demand for money. The administrators are answerable to the Comptroller and Auditor General (CAG) to look into the overall action and explanation.

Ombudsman: It is the institution for ordinary citizens to enable to file a complaint against unfair administration and seek remedial action. It has its origin in the Scandinavian countries. In India, there is a provision for minister for public grievance or *Lokayukta* at the state level and a *Lokpal* at the Centre (you will read more about them in chapter 26 in this volume).

Different types of accountability are as follows:

- Political: Question hour, zero hour, control by committees, ombudsman-type institutions
- Organizational: Departmental inquiries, service conduct rules, system of hierarchy, superior-subordinate relationship, fiscal accountability, monitoring
- Judicial: Judicial review, Public Interest Litigation (PIL), writs and suits

Judicial Accountability

Judicial accountability is sought through judicial review, statutory appeals, and writs and suits against the government:

Judicial review: The judiciary has the power to *interpret* the Constitution to protect the rights of the citizens. Article 32 of the Constitution empowers the Supreme Court, and Article 226 empowers the High Court to protect the Fundamental Rights of the people. Further, Articles 136 and 130 *confer* reviewing power of the administrative action and petition against government servants, respectively.

Public Interest Litigation (*PIL*): It is because of the efforts of Justice P. N. Bhagwati and Justice V. R. Krishna Iyer who made justice available to the commoner that we have PIL today. It has brought administration at the doorstep of answerability. PIL means penetration of power to the grassroots. From safeguarding human rights to espousing environment protection to dealing with the issues of child labour or maladministration, all matters lie under the purview of PIL. The Supreme Court of India extended this method of access to justice to simple writing, which could be treated as official proof to reprimind the erring officials.

Writs and Suits: The Constitutional Writs are the effective judicial remedies for the enforcement of Fundamental Rights. These Constitutional Writs, under Articles 32 and 226, help in restoration of Fundamental Rights. These Writs are *habeas corpus* (against unlawful detention), *mandamus* (against any official authority to perform their specific duties), *certiorari* (commanding to present records of matter), *prohibition* (preventing action in the lower court) and *quo warranto* (questioning the legality of a claim to an office).

WHY ACCOUNTABILITY?

Accountability in public administration is not about technical questions of designing control procedures and institutions, it is a question of democracy. It places the following four requirements on public administration:

- Make laws work as envisioned, without delay and wastage.
- Exercise lawful and sensible administrative discretion.
- Recommend new policies and propose changes in existing policies.
- Enhance citizens' confidence in the administrative institutions of government (Bhattacharya, 2001).

If we review the purpose of accountability, three issues assume importance, (a) controlling abuse of bureaucratic power and discretion, (b) bureaucracy has to ensure that policy enforcement is as per standards and quality, and (c) a system that could facilitate continuous improvement in governance (Bhattacharya, 2001). Accountability provides legitimacy to public officials and public organizations. It ensures responsiveness, transparency and effectiveness. It fights corruption and is a mechanism for achieving accountable governance. Accountability is a prerequisite for democracy, equality and individual freedom.

> Transparency International India's Corruption Study, 2008 carried out to measure the extent of bribes paid by the rural below poverty line (BPL) households to avail the eleven basic (e.g. PDS, hospitals, school education, electricity, water supply) and need-based services (e.g. land records, housing, forest, NREGS, banking and police). The findings revealed that the total bribe amount paid by the BPL households in a year was Rs 883 crore. This, however, did not include operational irregularities or corruption not involving rural citizens directly.

Democracy and accountability go hand in hand. Democracy leads to higher participation in decision making. It supports human rights and facilitates the mechanism to monitor and curtail corruption. Democracy is concerned with protecting individual rights and checking abuse of power. It ensures accountability of those holding power and prevents tyranny of State power. In turn, accountability is posited as an obvious means in the search for justice and democracy, equating it with the achievement of generating ethics and a more efficient and an effective system of governance.

The prevalence of corruption and the general lack of accountability in the most mature democracies indicate that benefits of democracy are not fructifying to the extent they should be. There are myriad problems which underlie the working of a democratic system, of which corruption is the most prominent one. The democratic systems strive towards social welfare but are confronted with limitations such as *inefficient* and *ineffective leadership*. They severely curtail social and political rights, are prone to corruption and maladministration and retard social and economic growth. It is this confrontation which has led to the demand for effective accountability.

It has been the World Bank's policy to find out ways of increasing 'exit' and 'voice' at the design stage of service delivery projects. This involves the commitment of both government and society at large. We have the government and governmental agencies functioning in a global environment, with competition from private operators. There are large corporations on the scene that are organizing not only their commercial activities but also their lobbying activities and self-regulation at a global level to protect their transnational activities. Then there are the non-governmental organizations which are expanding fast. The changed scenario posits more pressure on democracy and accountability.

As per Mohit Bhattacharya (2001), the ends of accountability or characteristics that are reflective of accountability are as follows:

- Legitimacy
- Moral conduct
- Responsiveness
- Openness/transparency
- Optimal resource mobilization
- Efficiency and effectiveness

INITIATIVES TOWARDS ACCOUNTABILITY

The demand for answerability and responsiveness has gathered momentum in democracies across the world. The need for accountability has arisen due to lack of transparency, decentralization and loss of legitimacy of the legislature. Despite Constitutional provisions which have ascribed the organs of government to strengthen the framework of democracy, there are several *lacunae* in the process of governance. The obstacles to effective, transparent and impartial governance are as follows:

- Corruption.
- Centralization of power.
- Lack of effective institutions for redressal of grievances.
- Lack of participation of people.

The bureaucracy has for long been weaving around itself the cocoon of secrecy, hierarchy, mindless adherence to rules and status. It has been described as a 'doer' and not an 'enabler'. The administration has been embedded in red-tapism and confidentiality. The people need to evolve from the attitude that the 'government would do it for them'. There is a need to push down the administration to the people and involve people in both planning and implementation. We need an administrative system which is pragmatic, flexible, dynamic and capable of prompt ad hoc decisions without worrying too much about protocol and procedures.

The period of 1990s saw an emerging nexus among bureaucrats, politicians and muscle power. The nexus led to the corrosion of administration and the process of governance. With thoroughly crumbling credibility, it was imperative to redefine the roles and responsibilities of bureaucracy and bring about reforms, which would have an interface with the people. The Indian response to these obstacles was outlined in Chief Secretaries' Conference of 1996, as it reiterated the need for a more 'effective and responsive administration'.

In view of these gaps, as we mentioned earlier, the *Fifth Pay Commission* (1997) recommended the downsizing of government, and called for transparency, openness, and contractualism. The Commission further recommended the repeal of the Official Secrets Act and emphasized sharing of information, which gradually paved the path for the 'Right to Information' (RTI) Act. As a part of Civil Service Reforms, the Commission insisted on the formation of 'efficient machinery for the redressal of grievances', which would readily be accessible, speedy and easy to operate. Thus, deriving from the experiences of ombudsman in Finland (1919), Denmark (1954) and Norway (1955), the *Lokpal* at the Centre and *Lokayukta* at the state level were sought to be established. Drawing upon the examples of Canada and the UK, Citizen's Charters defining the rights of citizens/customers were mooted.

The *ninth five year plan* reiterated the need for people's participation for enhancing policy performance. It emphasized people's participation, as it would make policies more cost effective and protect democracy against totalitarianism and statism. The *Approach Paper* to the twelfth Five Year Plan echoes the same view. It emphasizes that much needs to be done by the centre and the states to reduce the *discretionary* powers of administration and ensure greater accountability and transparency.

A few *seminal* judgements in the area of strengthening accountability have been brought about in recent times. Sengupta (2013) mentions the first few as follows:

1. Incarcerated persons cannot contest elections.
2. Election Commission is to provide 'none of the above' option on electronic voting machines.
3. A convicted member of the Legislative Assembly will be immediately disqualified on conviction, irrespective of appeals.
4. The Supreme Court has made it clear that civil servants must refrain from acting on oral instructions of political bosses, except in certain exceptional circumstances. They have to ensure that the orders are given in writing before they are carried out (Venkatesan, 2013).
5. On October 30, 2013, the Supreme Court of India, considering a PIL by several retired senior civil servants, ruled in favour of greater order and transparency in transfers and posting. It directed the formation of a Civil Services Board of senior civil servants to decide on transfers and postings and a fixed tenure for postings (Narayan, 2013).

These developments could go a long way in strengthening legislative accountability.

AGENCIES/INSTITUTIONS FOR REDRESSAL OF GRIEVANCES IN INDIA

The Planning Commission in its *National Human Development Report* (2002) describes corruption as the most endemic disease in India. In the era of liberalization, there is an emphasis on the rolling back of the State. However, there is an essential need to build institutions, which would be vested with the power of ensuring accountable and transparent functioning of governments. Caiden (1969) describes administrative reform as an 'artificial inducement of administrative transformation against resistance'. India has made various attempts towards reforms through its redressal agencies and institutions.

The institutions to hold public officials and administration accountable are as follows:

- CAG
- Central Vigilance Commission (CVC)
- Lokpal and Lokayuktas
- Citizens' Charters
- Social Audit
- Parliamentary Committees
- RTI Act

The Comptroller and Auditor General

The CAG is a Constitutional body. It is the guardian of the public purse and it is the duty of CAG to see that only authorized expenditure is made out of the Consolidated Fund of India. The office of CAG carries out its duties in an autonomous manner and is independent of any kind of executive control. The CAG presents its Report to the Parliament through the Public Accounts Committee. It ensures that the money shown in the accounts is utilized for the prescribed purpose and the expenditure conforms to the authority which governs it.

The Central Vigilance Commission

The CVC was established in 1964 on the recommendations of the Santhanam Committee Report. It was to play an advisory role. The CVC was given a statutory status after the enactment of the law in the Parliament in 2003. The CVC works through the preventive and participative means of combating corruption. It is conceived as the apex vigilance institution, free of control from any executive authority, monitoring all vigilance activity. Therefore, it is a body for reviewing and keeping vigilance over all organizations but it does not take any action against them.

Lokpal and Lokayukta

These institutions have their origin in the office of the *ombudsman* which originated in Sweden in 1716. Since then it has been a grievance redressal device/mechanism in all Scandinavian countries. The idea behind it is to have a user-friendly office in which the citizens could enter without any fear or threat. An ombudsman is generally considered as a person who is commissioned to protect citizens against any possible maladministration.

As a response to the mounting levels of corruption in India, the *Administrative Reforms Commission* (ARC; 1966) recommended the Constitution of two independent bodies at the Centre and state levels to enquire into complaints against government officials. The body at the Centre, *Lokpal,* is supposed to look into the complaints of ministers at the Centre. The authority at the state level, *Lokayukta,* is to look into complaints at the state level (we will not go into more details here as you will read about it in chapter 26 on Redressal of Grievances and Right to Information in this volume).

Odisha (earlier Orissa) was the first state to create the institution of the *Lokayukta,* followed by Maharashtra (1972), Rajasthan (1973), Bihar (1974), UP (1975), Karnataka (1979), Madhya Pradesh (1981), Andhra Pradesh (1983), Gujarat (1986) and Punjab (1995). The National Capital Territory of Delhi announced its Lokayukta in 1997. The states have adopted the Lokayukta as per a framework, which suits their cultural and social needs. The institution is a mode of redressal of grievances of the people in cases of non-observance of norms of integrity and conduct by public functionaries. Thus, it addresses the grievances related to corruption, maladministration or misuse of power.

However, there are many states which have not yet joined the ombudsman movement. They are satisfied with their variations in the conventional models that they are following. Kerala has created a three-member Commission under *Kerala Public Member Corruption* (Investigation and Inquiries Commission) set up in 1984. All its members are appointed by the governor on the advice of the chief minister, the chief justice and the leader of the opposition. However, the demand for uniformity in Lokayuktas' functioning across the states is still alive and so is the question of keeping its appointment out of political purview. The issue of *Lokpal* has been resolved for now as it has been passed in December 2013.

The dimensions of accountability are as follows:

- Standards of accountability (what)
- Agents of accountability (whom)
- Means of accountability (how) (Bhattacharya, 2001)

CITIZENS' CHARTERS

This is a *non-agency* devise for people's participation. The concept was first initiated in Britain when the conservative government of John Major issued a white paper in the form of Citizens' Charter in 1991. It is a concept based on government–citizen relationship. The idea of the Charter is to build efficiency and effectiveness of public service. Many government departments have been brought under its purview since its inception. Since citizens are at the centre of the Charter, it insists on the following *key* elements to fulfil its aims:

Standards: Setting, monitoring and publication of standards of service that the user can expect.

Information and openness: Full and accurate information readily available in a simple language. This would include those who are involved in the delivery.

Choice and consultation: Public sector should provide choice wherever available, in consultation with those for whom the service is being made available.

Courtesy and helpfulness: Helpful service from those involved in service.

Putting things right: The Charter has to ensure that the services are provided within the norms, else they need an apology.

Value for money: It is about efficient and effective delivery with maximum utilization of resources.

As is evident, the norms of the Citizens' Charter are a reiteration of the norms which are integral to the *foundation* of accountability of public administration and which had got eroded due to various socio-political circumstances. The Ministry of Personnel and Public Grievances has instructed all departments to construct a Charter for a citizen-friendly administration. The Charter is a definite step towards citizen-friendly, open, transparent, sensitive and accountable administration. In India, as on September 2009, as many as 131 Citizens' Charters were formulated by the central government ministries/departments/organizations and about 800 by various agencies of 24 state governments and administration of union territories. The number of Charters is also increasing every year. These Charters are open to public scrutiny.

The *Second ARC* (2005) recommended wide-range consultations with the civil society in the formulation of Citizens' Charters and their periodic evaluation, redress mechanisms in the case of default, holding officers accountable for results and so on. The Commission was of the opinion that the Citizens' Charter cannot be an end in itself; it is rather a means to an end – a tool to ensure that the citizen is always at the heart of any service delivery mechanism. The second ARC recommended a *Seven Step Model* for citizen centricity. The seven steps are as follows:

- Define all services which are provided and identify clients.
- Set standards and norms for each service.

- Develop capability to meet the set standards.
- Perform to achieve standards.
- Monitor performance against the set standards.
- Evaluate the impact through an independent mechanism.
- Continuous improvement based on monitoring and evaluation of results.

Right to Information

RTI mandates timely response to citizens' requests for government information. It is an initiative taken by the Department of Personnel and Training and the Ministry of Personnel, Public Grievances and Pensions to provide a gateway to citizens for quick search of information. The RTI Act, 2005 is an Act of Parliament that provides for setting out the practical regime of RTI for citizens. Information disclosure in India was hitherto restricted by the Official Secrets Act, 1923 and various other special laws, which the new RTI Act now relaxes (we will not go into more details as it is discussed in chapter 26 on Redressal of Grievances and Right to Information in this volume).

Just to refresh your memory, the RTI Act empowers every citizen to do the following:

- Ask any questions from the government or seek any information.
- Take copies of any governmental documents.
- Inspect any governmental documents.
- Inspect any governmental works.
- Take samples of materials of any governmental work.

RTI legislation endorses a *two-way* information sharing, proactive dissemination and reactive disclosure of information. This constructive engagement between public authorities and citizens, which addresses the response and voice aspects of governance, makes RTI an important social accountability tool. It empowers the citizens by giving them legal rights to access government information.

Social Audit

The concept of social audit has gained significance with the enactment of the 73rd Constitutional Amendment related to panchayati raj institutions. Social audit is an innovative mechanism for ensuring public accountability. It scrutinizes the efficacy of any public utility within a social relevance framework. It is a process that enables an organization to assess and demonstrate the social, economic and environmental benefits of its programmes and their impact on various stakeholders including the public. While financial audit ensures that money has been spent properly, social audit assesses that expenditure has made a difference to the wellbeing of the community. Social audit evaluates the performance of an organization based on its core community values and its impact on different social groups.

Thus, we can say that accountability is *vital* to the functioning of liberal democracy. It helps to keep a check on the powers of the government and keeps the public informed. The concentration of power at the Centre has led to maladministration and delay in work. The malpractices have led to increased corruption. The Santhanam Committee on the Prevention of Corruption in 1962 stated that 'any action or failure to take action in the performance of duty by the government servant for some advantage is corruption'. Initiatives to combat corruption have been few and far between due to lack of political will and the absence of ethics and integrity in administration.

There is a strong need to strengthen the ethical values in public administration. The United Nations Development Programme (2002) *initiatives* are anchored towards governance issues and have emphasized accountability and transparency. They have further laid focus through their *Programme on Accountability and Transparency* on the following:

- Participation of stakeholders in policy dialogue and an international agenda for the redressal of issues and concerns.
- Building up comprehensive anti-corruption reforms and strategies.
- Creating partnership at global, national and regional levels for strategic interventions.

CONCLUSION

Accountability is a complex issue involving participation of multiple actors to contest it. The role of civil society in preventing corruption has made a tremendous impact in seeking remedy for public grievances and enforcing accountability. It has led to the use of pressure tactics by the citizenry on the government for redressal of grievances and at the same time to ensure transparency and access to information. The role of social activists such as Anna Hazare needs a special mention in revolutionizing the society towards zero tolerance or non-acceptability of corruption. His 'India against Corruption' movement has led to the formation of the Aam Aadmi Party (AAP) under Arvind Kejriwal., which is now ruling in Delhi since their huge victory in 2015 elections.

However, we still have a long way to go. Corruption will remain one of the greatest obstacles in the efficient delivery of goods and resources. The continued stress on administrative mechanisms such as ombudsman, quasi-judicial vigilance commissioners and inspector generals are potentially valuable but are not enough. We do not need agencies as structures of accountability but as a means of attaining accountability with people's participation and strengthening of democracy to build an effective and efficient system of administration, at micro and macro levels.

It is pertinent to state that a transparency and information model does not, in itself, lead to accountability. Transparency demands clarity of procedures to achieve results. Active participation from all segments of society can cumulatively work towards questioning arbitrary decision making with respect to State-dominated economic policies in the era of liberalization and work towards a participatory and effective accountable system.

Preparatory Questions

- Define accountability and examine its different forms.
- Critically examine the changing nature of accountability.
- Bring out the relationship between accountability and responsive democratic system.
- Analyse the roal of various agencies for the redressal of grievances in India.

REFERENCES

Bhattacharya, M. (2001) *New Horizons of Public Administration*. New Delhi: Jawahar.

Burke, J. P. (1986) *Bureaucratic Responsibility*. Baltimore (MD): Johns Hopkins University Press.

Caiden, G. (1969) 'Development Administration and Administrative Reform.' *International Social Science Journal*. 2(1). p. 8.

Caiden, G. E. (1988) 'The Problem of Ensuring the Public Accountability of Public Officials' in Jabbra, J. G. and Dwivedi, O. P. (eds.). *Public Service Accountability: A Comparative Perspective*. West Hartford (CT): Kumarian Press. pp. 17–38.

Dreze, J. and Amartya Sen. (1989) *India: Development and Participation*. New York: OUP.

Jabbra, J. G. and Dwivedi, O. P. (1988) 'Introduction: Public Service Responsibility and Accountability' in Jabbra, J. G. and Dwivedi, O. P. (eds.). *Public Service Accountability: A Comparative Perspective*. West Hartford (CT): Kumarian Press. pp. 17–38,.

Fukuyama, F. (1992) *The End of History and the Last Man*. New York: Free Press.

Gandhi, R. (1988) 'Responsive Administration, Speech at Coimbatore', cited in *Times of India*.

Gopinath, G. R. (2013) 'Bring the CBI under the Lokpal.' *The Hindu*, November 18.

Government of India. (1997) *The Fifth Central Pay Commission Report*. Vol. 1. New Delhi: Government of India.

India governance.gov.in/RTI. (Accessed 20th June, 2015)

Haque, M. S. (2000) 'Significance of Accountability under the New Approach to Public Governance.' *International Review of Administrative Sciences*. 66(4). 599–617.

Kettle, D. F. and Fesler, J. W. (2005) *The Politics of Administrative Process*. Washington, DC: CQ Press.

Narayan, S. (2013) 'A Question of Accountability.' *The Hindu*, November 15.

Lewis, N. (1993) 'The Citizens' Charter and Next Steps: A New Way of Governing?' *Political Quarterly*. 64(3). pp. 316–326.

Osborne, D. and Gabeler, T. (1992) *Reinventing Government: How the Entrepreneurial Spirit is Transforming the Public Sector: From Schoolhouse to State House, City Hall to the Pentagon*. New Delhi: Prentice Hall of India.

Sabarwal, M. (ed.) (2013) *Public Administration in South Asia: India, Bangladesh, and Pakistan*. US: CRC Press.

Sen.A. (1975) *Poverty and Famines: An Essay on Entitlement and Deprivation*. New York: OUP.

Sengupta, A. (2013) 'Activist Verdicts.' *Frontline*, November.1.

Singh, A. (2002) *Public Administration: Roots and Wings*. New Delhi: Galgotia Publishing Company.

Transparency International India. (2008) *India Corruption Study*. New Delhi: Transparency International India.

UNDP. (2002) 'National Human Development Report.' *Deepening Democracy in a Fragmented World*. New York: OUP.

Venkatesan, S. (2013) 'Oral Instructions undermine Accountability: Supreme Court.' *The Hindu*, November 1.

World Bank. (1989) 'World Bank Report.' *World Development Report*. New York: OUP.

World Bank. (1997) 'World Bank Report.' *The State in a Changing World*. Washington, DC.

Chapter Twenty Three

Role of Non-Governmental Organizations

Poornima M.

LEARNING OBJECTIVES

After completing this chapter, you should be able to:

- Define Non-Governmental Organization(NGOs)
- Enumerate the characteristics of NGOs
- Provide a historical context of NGOs
- Discuss the nature and types of NGOs
- Debate upon the varied roles of NGOs in the globalization scenario; and
- Evaluate the functioning of NGOs by focusing on their advantages and limitations

INTRODUCTION

Public administration in contemporary times is not only concerned with the activities of the government or public organizations, but also encompasses a wide range of activities of various players, namely, Non-governmental Organizations (NGOs), private corporations, associations and even pressure groups, which in a way directly or indirectly influence governmental activities and public programmes. Public administration of today, apart from influencing the activities of government agencies and NGOs, also gets influenced by these organizations.

Thus, in recent times, especially after much debate on the role of the State as a 'steerer or rower', focus has been on the *enabling* role of the State, in which private organizations and NGOs become the fore players. NGOs have gained much prominence in recent years. Although the concerns of NGOs majorly centred around the welfare and development of the masses earlier, in present times, NGOs are *also* playing a predominant role in influencing the administration and public policies of the government. In this chapter, we will examine the role of NGOs in public administration, underlining their meaning, nature and evolution. We will also explore the relevance of NGOs in the backdrop of the changing role of public administration.

ROLE OF NON-GOVERNMENTAL ORGANIZATIONS

NGOs have become a buzzword in recent times, and the significance of NGOs in meeting the diverse needs of the society is being acknowledged all over the world. The NGOs have emerged from among the plural institutions and have become important agents of civil society. They play a very important role in development work and also in delivery of services. They work with the grassroots movements, make efforts in partnership with the government, make people aware of their rights and responsibilities and thereby try to empower them.

NGOs are categorized in different forms according to the nature of work taken up by them and also as per the purposes they espouse and financial support they receive. Some NGOs are *charitable* or voluntary, established for the sake of delivering a key set of services to the people. These NGOs are structured around their objectives. There are other types of NGOs, which are *advocacy* organizations or mutual benefit organizations, which particularly stick to a specific cause and lobby for the same and aim at producing benefits, primarily for their members (Denhardt and Denhardt, 2006, p. 49).

Apart from advocacy and service delivery, NGOs are also involved in activities such as emergency response, democracy building, livelihood generation, conflict resolution, human rights awareness, environmental activism and policy analysis (Lewis and Kanji, 2009, p. 1). NGOs operate at all levels, namely, international, national and local and they tend to take a different shape and form in different countries.

An NGO is normally *characterized* as an independent organization that is neither run by government nor driven by the profit motive such as private sector businesses. Yet, there are some NGOs that receive high levels of government funding and possess some of the characteristics of bureaucracies, while others resemble highly professionalized private organizations with strong corporate identities (Lewis and Kanji, 2009, p. 3).

Public administration practitioners in recent times prefer the involvement of NGOs the most in *delivering* public services or in *implementing* the policies of the government, as they are looked at as flexible organizations in comparison to the government. Moreover, NGOs are also preferred, for the reason that they can experiment with new programmes, responding more rapidly and readily to the new needs of the society (Pynes and Arndt, 2001).

Often, NGOs and civil society are equated with each other. However, NGOs and civil society are not the same (you have already read about civil society in chapter 15 of this volume). Civil society covers a wider spectrum, which encompasses an extensive array of institutions such as citizens' groups, mass movements, action groups, political groups, trade associations, women's organizations, non-commercial organizations, community-based organizations, NGOs and so on.

The components and organization of civil society is again a matter of contention and an unresolved debate. We can, however, include NGOs as an important part of the civil society as they play a pertinent and sometimes leading role in *activating* citizens' participation in socioeconomic development and politics and *also* in shaping or influencing policy (Ghaus-Pasha, 2007). Indeed, NGOs contribute towards strengthening of the civil society and play important roles as 'incubators' of civil society's ideas and values. That is, NGOs help in fostering civil society values such as participation, cooperation, trust and internal democracy (Lewis and Kanji, 2009).

There is no *universal* definition of NGOs. The UN definition of NGOs states that 'NGOs are any non-profit, voluntary citizens' groups that are organized at a local, national and international level. They are task-oriented as well as driven by persons with a common interest. Further, NGOs perform a variety of service and humanitarian functions, bring citizens' concerns to governments, advocate and monitor policies and encourage political participation through provision of information. Some are organized around the specific issues, such as human rights, environment and health. They provide analysis and expertise, serve as early warning mechanisms and help monitor and implement international agreement' (Henderson, 2001).

In common terminology, NGOs are defined as 'organizations, concerned with the promotion of social, political or economic change and they are primarily engaged in work relating to the areas of development or humanitarian work at local, national and international levels' (Lewis and Kanji, 2009). According to Vakil (1997), 'NGOs are self-governing, private, not-for-profit organizations that are geared to improving the quality of life for disadvantaged people'.

In India, the NGOs are registered under the Societies Registration Act, 1861. The organizations that come under this Act are not expected to make profit on their activities and they are considered as non-governmental

NGOs are called by different names in different countries. Even within the same country, they are called by different names based on their nature of work. The different terminologies used for NGOs are not because of a wide *variation* in the activities played by them but because of the influence of different cultures and context of different regions in which the ideas of NGOs have emerged. 'Voluntary' or 'charity' organizations are the common terms used for NGOs in the UK, where there is a long history of *philanthropy* and voluntarism. In the US, NGOs are called as non-profit organizations, where citizens' organizations are rewarded with fiscal benefits if they show that they are *not* commercial, profit-making entities and work for the public good. Lewis (2007) has developed diversity of acronyms for NGOs.

CHARACTERISTICS OF NGOs

It has been observed that NGOs have five characteristic features, which help in *differentiating* them from other kinds of organizations. The key characteristics are as follows:

- NGOs are *formal* in structure and have regular meetings of office bearers. It means they have some organizational permanence.
- NGOs are *private,* as they are institutionally separate or autonomous from government, although a few such NGOs receive support from the government.
- NGOs are *non-profit distributing* agencies, as the financial surplus of NGOs does not accrue to owners or directors.
- NGOs are *self-governing,* as they are able to control and manage their own affairs.
- Finally, NGOs are *voluntary* in nature, which implies that though NGOs do not have voluntary staff as such, there is at least some degree of voluntary participation in the conduct or management of NGOs (Salamon and Anheier, 1999; Lewis and Kanji, 2009, p. 10).

Characteristics of NGOs are as follows:

- Private or autonomous in complexion
- Non-profit oriented
- Self-governing
- Voluntary in nature
- Bear a systematic structure

EVOLUTION AND GROWTH OF NGOs

When we trace the evolution of NGOs, we find that NGOs are not a recent phenomenon. The idea or seeds of NGOs were sown in the form of philanthropy way back, the intention behind which was to serve the community, rather than one's own family. Later, philanthropy took a different turn and serving the needs of the society came to be openly acknowledged. It happened because religious organizations considered such needs of the society that were unattended or least noticed by others.

In the colonial era, NGOs emerged in the form of 'voluntary associations', which attempted to bring about improvements in the field of education, health service provision, women's rights, agricultural development, etc. Despite the existence of NGOs since time immemorial in various forms, the present form of NGOs gained shape only after 1970s. The emergence of NGOs can be *collated* with the different phases of development approach. In the first phase, the development approach was more about *development for the people*, where the State had the supreme role and the interventions towards development were more top down. This phase can be equated with the first generation role of NGOs, where priority of NGOs was on meeting the immediate needs of people, by way of undertaking relief and welfare work. State was predominant in this phase with minimum role of NGOs.

The second phase in late 1960s created the *sectoral approach* to development, in which various programmes were developed by the government for the development of the people. This approach stressed the value of decentralizing authority to lower levels of government organization in order to enhance the management of the sectoral programmes. The main idea of this approach was *development of the people.* In this phase, the approach of NGOs was more towards building small-scale and self-reliant local development initiatives and State-promoted non-governmental initiatives to some extent.

The third phase of development was oriented towards *policy approach*, which was developed by the end of 1970s. Under this approach, the challenge was no longer on how to administer or manage development; it was more on identifying the incentives that may facilitate it. The role of market and private and voluntary organizations were recognized in working with people to realize their aspirations. NGOs were able to do *with* the people what the government had failed to do *for* the people. The perception of development under this approach was an exercise carried out by the people. Thus, in the third generation/phase, there was a strong focus on *sustainability*. The role of NGOs became quite vibrant, influencing the wider institutional and policy context through advocacy. Towards late 1980s, NGOs gained greater prominence under the assumption that they can bring fresh solutions to complex and long-standing development problems.

The following steps mark the evolution of NGOs in India:

- First phase – development for the people through top-down strategies
- Second phase – sectoral approach to development with focus on decentralization and self-reliant local development
- Third phase – policy approach with focus on incentives facilitating development
- Fourth phase – people constitute the principal force of development, with bottom-up approach

The fourth phase of development was more oriented towards *bottom-up approach*. It was realized that development is not only about the projects, programmes or policies but also about politics. It was recognized in the 1990s that people must be given the right incentives and opportunities, not only in the economic but also in the political arena. People constitute the principal force of development and must have the chance to create institutions and organizations that respond to their needs and priorities. Development in this stage was regarded as something done *by the people*. Thus, in the fourth generation, NGOs became more closely linked to wider social movements and combined local action with activities at national or global levels. These initiatives aimed at long-term structural change (Hyden and Court, 2006; Lewis and Kanji, 2009).

The analysis of *historical context* of NGOs in India too reflects a similar scenario. Even in our country, voluntarism originated as pure philanthropy or charity and this was the core concern of NGOs in historical times. In the colonial era, the activities of NGOs were more reformist rather than philanthropic in nature. The concern during this phase was on creating social awakening and in eradicating the evils that were deep seated in the Indian society in the form of sati, child marriage and dowry. Sen (1992) highlights the *distinctive* factors of this phase, such as the influence of Christian missionaries, the growth of reformist middle classes in many areas of the country and the influential ideas of Mahatma Gandhi, who placed the concept of voluntary action at the centre of his vision of development for the country. In the initial phase after independence, the legacy of the Gandhian era influenced voluntary action to fulfil the unfinished tasks undertaken before independence.

After independence, the social welfare and developmental responsibilities, which were the main responsibilities of voluntary sector, *shifted* to the government sector. Thus, the activities of NGOs during this phase were quite dormant as the *State took the lead* in meeting the welfare of the people. However, after 1970s, the critical role of NGOs in meeting the needs and demands of the people was recognized. For the first time, the role of NGOs was recognized in the *Seventh Five Year Plan* by the Government of India, and nearly Rs 1500 million was earmarked for NGOs to carry out the socioeconomic activities. Towards 1990s, NGOs became vibrant in India and were considered *equal partners* in meeting the objectives of the State. The involvement of NGOs today is seen not only in implementation of government programmes, but also in the process of formulation of government policies.

NATURE AND TYPES OF NGOs

From time to time in India, especially in the past few decades, an evident unrest has been observed in the community for better *access to basic services, economic and social rights.* People from different strata of society are vociferously raising their voice against injustice, inequality and apathy. Earlier protests were more in the form of peasants' movements, trade unions strikes and demonstrations by cooperatives; now they revolve around social issues such as inflation, price rise, identity-based struggles, women's safety and recently the Jan Lokpal Bill.

Emergence of every such protest/movement has a close link with NGOs. Either many NGOs come together in these struggles or new NGOs are born out of such movements. In the 1970s, there were movements oriented towards *empowerment of women* in India. As an outcome of such women's movements, many NGOs sprang up in India in order to protect the rights of women. A good example of such NGOs is the Self-Employed Women's Association or SEWA, founded by Ela Bhatt in Ahmedabad. The main goal of SEWA is to address the problems faced by women such as domestic harassment, low earnings, educational constraints and family health. The overall goal is to support women in building financial sustenance. The activities of SEWA are spread across various states, besides Gujarat (Lewis and Kanji, 2009; www.sewa.org).

The 1980s witnessed protests against dowry deaths and violence against women. NGOs that emerged out of such protests were 'Saheli', a Women's Resource Centre and Forum against Oppression of Women (Goswami and Bandyopadhyay, 2012). In the aftermath of 'Nirbhaya gang rape' in New Delhi in December 2012, a countrywide call was made for protection of women. The protests attracted the participation of many NGOs, students, political associations, etc., across the country. Many NGOs working for the protection and safety of women filed complaints. The Delhi police had a series of interactions with various NGOs such as Centre for Social Research, Jagori, Centre for Equality and Inclusion, Action India, etc., that work for the safety and empowerment of women. Inputs were given by various NGOs, which were used to revise the Delhi police standing orders on safety of women in order to come up with an action plan to enhance the safety of women (National Legal Research Desk, 2013).

The anti-corruption movement (*India against Corruption*) of 2011 is one such social movement that kindled a spark in the common people to campaign against corruption in India. The basic demand raised by social activists, led by Anna Hazare, was the enactment of the long-pending Lokpal Bill against corruption. The movement is considered to be a milestone in the Indian history forcing the government to accept civil society's demand to have a say in drafting the stringent anti-corruption law, the Lokpal Bill (Goswami and Bandyopadhyay, 2012). The movement culminated into a political party called the Aam Aadmi Party or AAP. The party created a stir by bagging 28 seats in Delhi's legislative assembly in its debut elections of December 2013, and 67 seats in February 2015. After assuming office, it is now actively formulating policies and strategies to combat corruption.

Mazdoor Kisan Shakti Sangathan (MKSS) is another such movement that has been instrumental in the enactment of Right to Information Act in 2005 (chapter 26 on 'Redressal of Grievances' will discuss it in detail). In the area of environmental protection too, the role of NGOs is noteworthy. For example, the NGO, Greenpeace, has made a significant impact on protection of environment. It has, through its strategies, influenced environmental policies, thereby reducing environmental degradation. Greenpeace International has been formed as an umbrella organization to unify the work of Greenpeace campaigners around the world including India (Susanto, 2007). Earlier environmental protests such as the Chipko movement, silent valley protests and save the tiger have been noteworthy in the area of environmental protection.

Parameters that decide the nature of NGOs are as follows:

- Sources of funding
- Purpose/target group
- Organization/structure
- Functions/activities
- Motivation/ideology
- Religious affinity
- Area of operation
- Size
- Legal status

In terms of structure too, NGOs are *heterogeneous* in nature. NGOs range from small to large, formal to informal, bureaucratic to flexible. Sometimes, NGOs are structured based on the *funding* they receive and from whom they receive it. NGOs are also classified based on the *purpose* or issue dealt by them. Lewis and Kanji (2009) assert that some may be well resourced and affluent, whereas others may be leading a 'hand-to-mouth' existence, struggling to survive from one year to the next.

There are NGOs with highly professional staff, while others rely heavily on volunteers and supporters. In terms of values, NGOs are driven by a range of *motivations*. There are secular NGOs as well as an increasing number of faith-based, radical and paternalistic organizations. A single NGO may also combine several of these different elements at any given time. Some of the organizations directly deliver services to the poor people while others organize people in helping themselves and building their capabilities. Among these NGOs, there are some who involve themselves in replicating the policies and programmes of the government and other such organizations innovate and demonstrate new programmes themselves (Kanal, 2011). Although some clarity on typology of NGOs exists, the accurate number of NGOs that are in operation is difficult to ascertain.

The nature or type of NGOs is actually determined by certain parameters such as legal status, source of inspiration, structure, size, area of operation and functional diversity. On these bases, we can identify NGOs/Voluntary Organizations (VOs), societies, foundations, cooperatives, citizens' groups and so on. Voluntary Action Network India (VANI) has prepared a list of NGOs/VOs with their parameters and examples (*see* VANI, 2001).

ROLE OF NGOs IN PUBLIC ADMINISTRATION

In his book 'The Spirit of Public Administration' George Frederickson (1997) states that 'the public in public administration manifests itself in many ways and 'government' is an important manifestation of the public, but it is just one aspect of it'. The modern public administration is a network of vertical and horizontal linkages among organization of all types – governmental, non-governmental and quasi-governmental, and the NGOs play a significant role.

L. D. White commented that 'the study of public administration needs to be related to the broad generalizations of political theory concerned with such matters as justice, liberty, obedience, and the role of the State in human affairs' (White, 1948, p. 10; Denhardt and Denhardt, 2006, p. 2). If this aspect is considered to be the core concern of public administration, then it can be said that the NGOs have a close relation with the subject matter of public administration, as aspects such as justice, liberty and accountability are carried out in practice by the NGOs and the activities of the State are supplemented by NGOs in modern times by way of its tasks such as advocacy and service delivery.

Although NGOs have been in existence for a long time, the role of NGOs in public administration has emerged as an area of concern only in recent decades, especially in the era of globalization. Today, we can witness a *shift* in the way governance takes place. Gone are the times when governance accorded the State or government the status of being the sole operator of policy process and delivery of goods and services. The rigid hierarchy which has been the guiding factor of classical public administration has been slashed down, paving the way for closer relationship with various players of the society, especially the private sector and Civil Society Organizations (CSOs).

Globalization has impacted governance of today. The State is not the sole player but one of the many players. The State has started playing a steering role and is supposed to just facilitate the role of other actors, be it private players, NGOs, non-profit bodies, etc. Various new developments have given rise to different types of CSOs that are beginning to influence policy decisions. The examples of SEWA, MKSS, Lokpal Bill and environmental initiatives that we have read in this chapter show how public policy process of public administration has been influenced by the NGOs and social movements. In fact, the constitution of Justice Verma Committee, as a consequence of Nirbhaya gang rape in New Delhi (in December 2012) case to recommend amendments to the criminal law, for providing quicker trial and enhanced punishment to criminals accused of committing sexual assault against women, is a fit instance of NGOs and public policy process interface.

In this chapter, we have used NGOs in the wider sense and included protests and movements along with them. They are all different in structure and role, though their goals are more or less the same. However, we will not go into the details on the distinction over here. It is sufficient to understand that in the globalization, public value and multiple-role player context, NGOs will continue to play a significant role in public administration.

At the global level, the relationship between public policy process and NGOs may vary from nation to nation. Though, by and large, NGOs play a complementary and supplementary role to governance processes and public administration, there are instances where the relationship is more intense. The role of the NGOs, as we mentioned earlier, can be classified on the basis of activities undertaken/facilitated by them. Based on such classification, the tasks of the NGOs are numerous; they could be advocates, educators, monitors, whistle blowers, mediators, lobbyists, activists or mobilizers and protectors of human rights (Sooryamoorthy and Gangrade, 2001). They also play an important role in the public policy process. Let us see how.

Policy making: Public policy making is an important aspect of public administration and involves the task of analysing the existing policies and their impact. It also attempts to assess the possible effects of different courses of action and suggest new directions for public policy. Denhardt and Denhardt (2006) assert that public policy is simply what an agency or an entire network of public, private and NGOs decides to do or not to do. In the task of policy making, NGOs play a crucial role, which is called upon to develop, implement and evaluate government programmes and policies. Since NGOs have a better rapport with the local communities, they are in a better position to understand the needs of the community and inform the public about the policies and programmes of the government and at the same time, provide feedback to the State in order to facilitate changes in the existing policies.

Policy implementation: The role of NGOs in policy implementation is in their involvement in the delivery of health care, education, micro finance, human rights, emergency relief, etc. Moreover, since NGOs are involved in developmental activities and directly work with the people, they can provide important inputs to the policy-making process. Further, the grassroots experience that the NGOs possess can serve as the basis for improving policies. As watchdogs, they can also apply pressure on the government to ensure that appropriate policies are enacted and implemented. With regard to policy implementation, NGOs can monitor the application of laws, and where compatible with community interests, design programmes that complement rather than undermine or contradict government policies (Ghaus-Pasha, 2007).

Service delivery: The role of service delivery by NGOs is either executed out of interest as part of their mission or at times, contracted out by the government for providing the same to the community. However, the service delivery role of the NGOs is not without scepticism and not all NGOs are efficient in prompt delivery of services. There are instances where service provision by NGOs is characterized by problems of quality control, limited sustainability, poor coordination and general amateurism.

Catalyst: As a catalyst, NGOs inspire, contribute or facilitate improved thinking and action to promote change. It may include grassroots organizing and group formation, gender and empowerment work, lobbying and advocacy work, undertaking and disseminating research and attempts to influence wider policy processes through innovation and policy entrepreneurship (Lewis and Kanji, 2009).

Advocacy: The advocacy role of the NGOs gained prominence only after the 1990s. It is viewed as an important strategy for improving the effectiveness and impact of development work by NGOs and as a potential strategy for 'scaling-up' successful ideas and interventions. By playing the advocacy role, unaddressed problems of the society are brought to public attention by the NGOs in order to protect basic human rights and thus give voice to a wide range of political, environmental and social concerns (Ghaus-Pasha, 2007).

Innovation: Innovation is the special quality of NGOs for which reason the involvement of such players are usually preferred by the State. That is, an ability to innovate is often claimed as a special quality, or even as an area of comparative advantage, of NGOs over other kinds of organizations, especially government agencies. 'The small size of the NGOs, their enormous flexibility, immense adaptability, desire to experiment and provide new problem-solving ideas gives them the strength to experiment new ideas, which are replicated by the State at a larger level, based on their outcome'. One example of such small innovative experiment of NGOs that got scaled up to perform a larger role is the case of the *Grameen Bank* of Bangladesh.

Watchdog/ Whistleblower: Another key role that NGOs play is that of a watchdog, in monitoring the policies and programmes of the government. By being a whistle blower, NGOs are able to keep a track of such policies that remain unimplemented or poorly implemented. This helps in making a quick review of such policies and taking measures for future directions.

Partner: As a third sector in the governance system of today, NGOs also reflect the role of a partner in which multiple players of State, market and CSOs are involved in delivering services or other programmes or projects. Such a partnership arrangement helps in making proper use of scarce resources and in sharing the roles and responsibilities as well as the risks. Instances of such examples can be found in the education for all programme the '*Sarva Shiksha Abhiyan*', where NGOs are active partners of the government. The purpose is to identify school drop-outs and put them on a bridge course. The object is to mainstream such children into regular schools.

Functions of NGOs are as follows:

- Policy making
- Policy implementation
- Watchdog
- Advocacy
- Catalyst
- Service delivery
- Innovation
- Partnership

NGOs: AN EVALUATION

In recent years, it can be seen that important tasks of implementing public policies and service delivery are shifting to other organizations and very often, to the NGOs. The main reason for such involvement of NGOs is that they appear to be in a better position than the government in certain aspects because of their operational advantages. However, the analysis of the role and activities of NGOs gives a *mixed* picture, as not all NGOs are completely good or completely bad. NGOs are usually preferred for the benefits attached with them such as proximity to people, integrity, flexibility and dedication.

At the same time, the involvement of NGOs in governmental tasks is also feared for reasons such as lack of coordination, inadequate managerial skills and lack of accountability. However, it can be stated that even though a few NGOs do not turn out to be genuine, a number of them play a crucial role in impacting the government programmes and policies, either through direct delivery of services or through pressure and persuasiveness. In the World Summit for Social Development Programme of Action, held at Vietnam in 1998, it was expressed that 'NGOs should continue their advocacy and dialogue with donors to promote greater accountability and better targeting of basic social services for the poor' (Henderson, 2001). This reiterates the importance of the role of NGOs.

NGOs have many advantages and some of them are as follows:

- Flexible
- Innovative
- Non-formal
- Smaller in size
- Non-bureaucratic
- Participatory
- Bottom-up

The *comparative* advantages of NGOs are as follows:

- NGOs are found to be in a better position than the government in aspects such as *flexibility* in operation and scope for innovation, unlike the government whose operation is limited by rigid hierarchy, red tapism and lengthy procedures.

- The *small size* of the NGOs is an advantage, as they can work more efficiently at the micro level and it becomes easy for the NGOs to devise strategies to achieve the goal by experimenting with innovative ideas. Innovations in community health, basic education, indigenous medicine, micro finance and appropriate credit systems that benefit the poor all have had wider repercussions for the society at large (Sooryamoorthy and Gangrade, 2001).
- NGOs are less rule-bound, non-bureaucratic, *non-formal*, cost-effective as well as easily accessible and flexible in their structure and operations.
- Easy availability of funds makes the NGOs *financially sound*, which helps them to concentrate on activities towards their goals.
- NGOs use participatory, bottom up, grassroots processes of project implementation; they help empower poor people to gain control of their lives and they work with and strengthen local institutions.

However, working with NGOs may at the same time lead to other types of *challenges*, which are as follows:

- One of the major challenges of NGOs is the issue of *transparency* and accountability. For example, when government programmes are run directly by the government, responsibility for their success lies squarely with the government agency. However, when such programmes are actually delivered by the NGOs, traditional mechanisms for control and accountability may not work. Maintaining a proper concern for democratic values such as equity and responsiveness may, in the long run, prove more difficult. For instance, in the context of Bangladesh, concerns are raised about a 'franchise State' in which key services are increasingly being delegated to local NGOs with unclear lines of accountability to citizens (Lewis and Kanji, 2009).
- Sometimes, the funding from external agencies acts as a major challenge. Many NGOs just become the 'implementing agency of the donors'. They merely act as *contractors* to their tailor-made programmes. Sometimes, funds from foreign agencies are irregular and NGOs get adversely affected. A primary weakness of NGOs is to rely too much on a single source of support or to not look beyond the next grant cycle for their funding.
- Financial *constraints* limit the scale and functioning of CSOs, significantly impairing their ability to deliver and maintain services.
- Other obstacles of NGOs include, uncertain financing and *erratic regulation*, lack of coordination, and fragmentation into small and often rival operations. Additionally, NGOs frequently lack managerial skills.

Disadvantages of NGOs are as follows:

- Uncertain funding
- Erratic regulations
- Donors' control
- Lack of coordination
- Reliance on single source of support
- Inadequate transparency
- Lack of accountability

CONCLUSION

Although NGOs in modern times are severely criticized, the transitional and developmental role played by NGOs in various aspects of development cannot be ignored. The comparative advantages of NGOs only seem to outnumber the drawbacks of such an involvement. There was a time in the evolution of NGOs, when they were regarded as flawless. However, with their increasing involvement in varied governance tasks, we need to be realistic on what can be and cannot be actually done by NGOs, in order to optimally utilize their potential.

NGOs remain a prominent face of civil society. They are significantly engaged in strengthening the civil society by actively engaging in advocacy, empowerment and capacity building activities. They thereby influence public policies by pressuring them to meet the demands of society. In the context of public administration, NGOs play a transformative role. They, on the one hand, help in making the State responsive, accountable, efficient and effective; and on the other, assist in capacitating the citizens to participate in the development process of their country. This chapter discussed some of these concerns and underlined the crucial role played by NGOs in the areas of social justice, empowerment of women, environment and sustainable existence.

Preparatory Questions

- Describe the characteristics of NGOs.
- Write a note on the evolution of NGOs.
- Discuss the parameters that determine the nature and types of NGOs.
- What, in your view, is the role of NGOs in public administration?
- Examine the advantages and disadvantages of NGOs.

REFERENCES

Adair, A. (1999) *Code of Conduct for NGOs: A Necessary Reform.* London: Institute of Economic Affairs.

Blumenthal, W. M. (1983) 'Candid Reflections of a Businessman in Washington' in Perry, J. L. and Kraemer, K. L. (eds.). *Public Management.* Palo Alto (CA): Mayfield Publishing. pp. 30–31.

Chandhoke, N. (2007) 'Civil Society.' *Development in Practice.* 17(4). pp. 607–614.

Denhardt, R. B and Denhardt, J. V. (2006) *Public Administration: An Action Orientation.* 5th ed. Belmont (CA): Thomson Wadsworth.

Frederickson, H. (1997) *The Spirit of Public Administration.* San Francisco (CA): Jossey-Bass.

Ghaus-Pasha, A. (2007) 'Role of Civil Society Organizations in Governance' in Rondinelli, D. A. (ed.). *Public Administration and Democratic Governance: Governments Serving Citizens.* New York: United Nations. pp. 203–225.

Goodsell, C. T. (2006) 'A New Vision for Public Administration.' *Public Administration Review.* 66(4). pp. 623–635.

Goswami, D. and Bandyopadhyay, K. (2012) *The Anti-Corruption Movement in India.* New Delhi: PRIA.

Hamdan, F. (2007) 'The Green Movement 20 Years after the Brundtland Report. Sustainability Plus? Global Challenges 20 Years after the Brundtland Report,' *Seminar Presentation.* European Foundation Centre, Madrid, June 3.

Henderson, K. M. (2001) 'NGOs and Grass-Roots Organizations in Developing Countries' in Kuotsai. T. L (ed.). *Handbook of Public Management Practice and Reform,* New York: Marcel Dekker. pp. 619–636.

Howell, J. and Pearce, J. (2001) *Civil Society and Development: A Critical Exploration.* Boulder (CO): Lynne Reinner Publishers.

Hyden, G. and Court, J. (2006) 'Governance and Development: Trying to Sort out the Basics in Poverty, Inequality and Access to Justice for the Poor in South Asia,' *Conference Paper.* New Delhi: Centre for the Study of Law and Governance, JNU.

Kanal, S. A. (2011) 'Disaster Resilience through Right Based and Capability Perspectives of NGOs: A Case Study of 2004 Tsunami in Nagapattinam.' *Dynamics of Public Administration.* 28(2). pp. 215–237.

Kooiman, J. (2003) *Governing as Governance.* London: Sage.

Katorobo, J. (2007) 'Decentralization and Local Autonomy for Participatory Democracy' in Rondinelli, D. A. (ed.). *Public Administration and Democratic Governance: Governments Serving Citizens.* New York: United Nations. pp. 238–267.

Lewis, D. (2003) 'Management of Non-governmental Development Organizations: Towards a Composite Approach.' *Public Management Review.* 5(3). pp. 325–344.

Lewis, D. (2007) *The Management of Non-Governmental Development Organizations.* 2nd ed. London: Routledge.

Lewis, D. and Kanji, N. (2009) *Non-Governmental Organizations and Development.* London: Routledge.

Light, P. C. (2000) *Making Nonprofits Work: A Report on the Tides of Nonprofit Management Reform.* Washington, DC: Brookings Institutions.

Lipsky, M. and Smith, S. R. (1990) 'Nonprofit Organizations, Government and the Welfare State.' *Political Science Quarterly.* pp. 625–648.

Nations, U. (2007) *Public Administration and Democratic Governance: Governments Serving Citizens.* New York: United Nations-Department of Economic and Social Affairs.

Pynes, J. E and Arndt, L. M. 'The Impact of the New Public Management on NonProfit Organizations' in Liou, K. T. (ed.). *Handbook of Public Management Practice and Reform.* New York: Marcel Dekker. pp. 573–588.

Rizvi, G. (2007) 'Reinventing Government: Putting Democracy and Social Justice back into the Discourse' in Rondinelli, D. A. (ed.). *Public Administration and Democratic Governance: Governments Serving Citizen.* New York: United Nations. pp. 78–115.

Salamon, L. (1987) 'Partners in Public Service: The Scope and Theory of Government-Nonprofit Relations' in Powell, W. (ed.). *The NonProfit Sector: A Research Handbook.* New Haven: Yale University Press. pp. 99–117.

Salamon, L. and Anheier, H. (1999) 'The Third Sector in the Third World.' *International Perspectives on Voluntary Action: Reshaping the Third Sector.* London: Earthscan.

Sen, S. (1992) 'Non-profit Organizations in India: Historical Development and Common Patterns.' *Voluntas.* 3(2). pp. 175–193.

Susanto, S. R. (2007) 'The Transformation of Greenpeace Strategy in the 1990s: From Civil Disobedience to Moderate Movement.' *Global and Strategic.* 1(2). pp. 186–205.

Smith, B. and A. (2000) *The Complete Guide to Nonprofit Management.* New York: New Wiley & Sons.

Sooryamoorthy, R. and Gangrade, K. D. (2001) *NGOs in India: A Cross-Sectional Study* New Delhi: Rawat Publications.

Streeten, P. (1997) 'Non-governmental Organizations and Development.' *Annals of the American Academy of Political and Social Science–Issue on the Role of NGOs: Charity and Empowerment.* 554. pp. 193–210.

Tandon, R. and Mohanty, R. (2000) *Civil Society and Governance: A Research Study in India.* New Delhi: PRIA.

Thampi, G. K. and Balakrishnan, S. (2002) 'Public Policy and Civil Society: Ambiguities and Possibilities.' *Public Affairs Centre.* pp. 1–7.

Thomas, A. (1992) 'NGOs and Limits to Empowerment' in Wuyts, M., Mackintosh, M. and Hewitt, T. (eds.). *Development Action and Public Policy.* Oxford: Oxford University Press.

VANI. (2001) *Voluntarism and Government: Policy, Programme and Assistance.* New Delhi: Voluntary Action Network India.

Vakil, A. (1997) 'Confronting the Classification Problem: Toward a Taxonomy of NGOs.' *World Development.* 25(12). pp. 2057–71.

Walters, J. (2000) 'The Welfare Bonanza.' *Governing.* 13(4). pp. 34–36.

White, L. D. (1948) *The Study of Public Administration.* New York: Macmillan.

Websites:

Bagci, C. (2008) *Historical evolution of NGOs: NGO proliferation in the post-cold war era.* [Online] Available from: http://www.turkishweekly.net/print.asp?type=2&id=222.

National Legal Research Desk. Nirbhaya rape case verdict. Available from: www.nlrd.org. [Accessed: 5th November 2013].

Chapter Twenty Four

Concept of Corporate Governance

Roopinder Oberoi

LEARNING OBJECTIVES

After completing this chapter, you should be able to:

- Give a conceptual framework of corporate governance
- Understand the various perspectives on corporate governance
- Make a case for effective corporate governance as an instrument of growth and development
- Enlist the principals of corporate governance
- Describe the models of corporate governance
- Examine corporate governance initiatives at the international level
- Elaborate the measures towards better corporate governance in India; and
- Examine the challenges to corporate governance reforms

INTRODUCTION

The subject of corporate governance leapt to global business limelight from relative obscurity after a string of collapses of high profile companies. Enron, the Houston, WorldCom – the telecom behemoth – and Satyam shocked the business world with the scale of their unethical and illegal operations. Corporate governance has taken centre stage even in the developing world with the recent spate of corporate scandals in developing economies. The recent financial crisis has been a particularly strong wake-up call because it has adversely affected employment, consumer spending, pensions, the finances of national and local governments worldwide and the global economy. It has brought to fore the pertinence of governance in corporates, the need for due ethical procedure and accountability.

Corporate governance is perhaps one of the most important differentiators of a business that has an impact on the profitability, growth and even sustainability of business. It is a multi-level and multi-tiered process that is distilled from an organization's culture, its policies, values and ethics, especially emanating from the people running the business and the way it deals with various stakeholders. Creating value that is not only profitable to the business but sustainable in the long-term interests of all stakeholders *necessarily* means that businesses have to run with a high degree of ethical conduct and good governance, where compliance is not only in letter but also in spirit.

At the macro level, it is now well established that good corporate governance and economic development of a country are intrinsically interlinked. Effective corporate governance systems promote the development of strong financial systems irrespective of whether they are largely bank-based or market-based, which, in turn, have an encouraging impact on economic growth and investment inflows. If also provides a trickledown effect of prosperity. There are several channels through which this causality works. Poor corporate governance obstructs the creation and development of opportunities, as lack of transparency and accountability deters new firms to pool in money into a system with weak governance practices and institutions.

Corporate governance has also been a fundamental field of query within the finance discipline for decades. Economist Adam Smith had documented the predicament over two centuries ago and since then there has been an ongoing contest about whether the Anglo-Saxon market model of corporate governance is superior to the bank-based models of Germany and Japan.

Before examining these issues pertaining to corporate governance, it is important to define the concept of corporate governance. The vast sum of literature accessible on the subject ensures that there exist innumerable definitions of corporate governance. To get a reasonable outlook on the subject, it is practical to give a narrow as well as a broad explanation of corporate governance. This chapter tries to explain the concept of corporate governance and examine its pertinence and effectiveness. The constituents, principles and models of corporate governance are put forth to grapple with the growth and development of the concept at the national and international levels. It also juxtaposes it with the good governance framework to explain its immediate context.

DEFINING CORPORATE GOVERNANCE: NARROW AND BROAD VIEWS

The origin of the term governance is from 'gubernate', which implies 'to steer'. Corporate governance would then simply denote 'to steer an organization in the desired direction'. The liability to steer lies with the board of directors/governing board. The term 'corporate' is derived from the Latin term 'corpus', which means a 'body'. Governance means to administer the course and system positioned for fulfilling stakeholder anticipation. When united, corporate governance has been defined as a set of systems, procedures, policies, practices, standards established by a business and sustained by the different stakeholders in an open and transparent manner.

Corporate governance codes do not often explicitly define what corporate governance is. Most codes of best practice deal with corporate governance as a concept and explain its importance without defining its meaning. Yet, the way corporate governance is defined may affect the scope and content of a code. Perhaps the most famous definition of corporate governance was provided in 1992 by Sir Adrian Cadbury in the Report on Financial Aspects of Corporate Governance in the UK: 'Corporate Governance is the system by which companies are directed and controlled' (Cadbury Committee Report, 1992).

The phrase 'corporate governance' illustrates 'the framework of rules, relationships, systems and processes within and by which authority is exercised and controlled within corporations. It encompasses the mechanisms by which companies, and those in control, are held to account'. (ASX Corporate Governance Council, 2014). Corporate governance has been defined as 'the structure and the functioning of corporate policies' (Eells, 1960) and as 'the mechanism by which corporations and managers are governed' (Holmstrom and Kaplan, 2001). Corporate governance includes both internal and external governance mechanisms. Internal mechanisms address issues such as how the board of directors, board committees and executive compensation contracts are used to align the interests between shareholders and managers. External mechanisms deal with the market forces for corporate control, such as takeover offers and proxy contests. In practice, the four principles of good corporate governance are: transparency, accountability, responsibility and fairness.

In his survey paper, Denis (2001) summarizes the literature on corporate governance and points out that it is frequently believed that corporate governance problems are associated with the separation of ownership and control in modern corporations. Shareholders own stocks and are owners, but do not have direct and thorough control over their firms. They entrust control of the corporation to management. The foremost advantage of assigning routine operations to management is professional management. Nonetheless, the altered incentives between managers and shareholders can set in motion agency problems, specifically; managers may not work in the best interests of shareholders but may work towards their own interests. Denis (2001) argues that the 'inconsistency of interest' may take the form of managerial shirking, managerial consumption of perquisites, managements' desire to remain in power, managerial risk aversion, and misuse of free cash flow. According to Jensen and Meckling (1976), agency costs include (i) costs incurred by the agent to bond him with the principle, (ii) costs incurred by the principle to monitor the agent and (iii) residual loss resulting from the agent's pursuance of non-value-maximizing behaviours.

Most lately, the efforts of worldwide reforms and initiatives introducing improvement of monitoring standards as well as the globalization process based on increased capital mobility, flexibility and market transparency has drawn added attentiveness to corporate governance practices. The corporate governance practices have, of late, assumed importance for ensuring business flexibility, market transparency, corporate ethics and maintaining the monitoring standards. This has also been necessitated due to rise in corporate scandals at the global level.

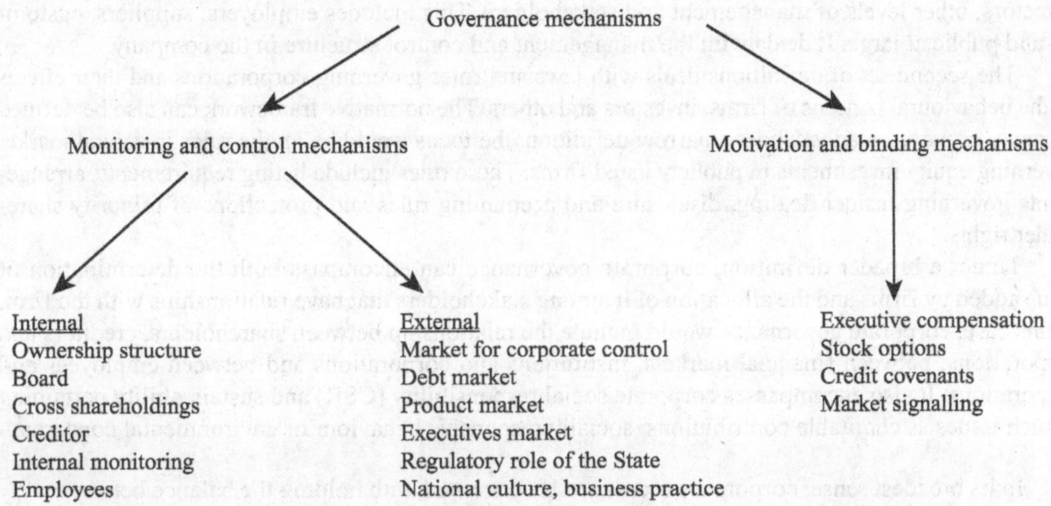

FIGURE 24.1 Governance mechanisms.

Source: Wolf (1999, p. 17).

The corporate governance outline consists of (1) unequivocal and implied contracts between the company and the stakeholders for allotment of responsibilities, rights and rewards, (2) procedures for reconciling the sometimes conflicting interests of stakeholders in accordance with their duties, privileges and roles and (3) procedures for proper supervision, control and information flows to serve as a system of checks and balances (http://www.businessdictionary.com).

DIFFERENTIATING NARROW AND BROAD VIEW ON CORPORATE GOVERNANCE

Corporate governance literature categorizes corporate governance into two factions. The first category focuses on the actual behaviour of corporations – their performance, efficiency, growth, financial structure and treatment of shareholders and other stakeholders. The second category concerns itself with the normative framework, that is, the rules under which firms operate. These rules originate from diverse sources as the legal system, the judicial system, financial markets and labour markets (Cadbury, 2003). 'The term "corporate governance" is susceptible both to broad and narrow definitions. In fact, many of the codes do not even attempt to articulate what is encompassed by the term. The crucial point is that corporate governance is a conception, rather than an individual apparatus. It includes debate on the appropriate management and control structures of a company. Further it includes the rules relating to the power relations between owners, the Board of Directors, management and, last but not least, the stakeholders such as employees, suppliers, customers and the public at large' (Fernando, 2006).

The first set of definitions covers corporate governance issues within the firm itself. These issues embrace such themes as how the board of directors operates, the role of executive compensation in determining firm performance, the correlation between labour policies and firm performance and the position of multiple shareholders. Corporate governance is a broad framework encompassing the mechanisms, processes of governance and establishes the relations between the owners, Board of

Directors, other levels of management and stakeholders. This includes employers, suppliers, customers and public at large. It deals with the management and control structure in the company.

The second set of definitions deals with laws and rules governing corporations and their effects on the behavioural patterns of firms, investors and others. The normative framework can also be defined narrowly or more broadly. Under a narrow definition, the focus would be on the rules in capital market governing equity investments in publicly listed firms. These rules include listing requirements, arrangements governing insider dealing, disclosure and accounting rules and protections of minority shareholder rights.

Under a broader definition, corporate governance can encompass both the determination of value added by firms and the allocation of it among stakeholders that have relationships with the firm. In this case, corporate governance would include the relationship between shareholders, creditors and corporations; between financial markets, institutions and corporations and between employees and corporations. It also encompasses corporate social responsibility (CSR) and sustain ability pertaining to such issues as charitable contributions, socially responsive behaviour or environmental concerns.

> In its broadest sense, corporate governance is concerned with holding the balance between economic and social goals and between individual and community goals. The governance framework is there to encourage the efficient use of resources and equally to require accountability for the stewardship of those resources. The aim is to align as nearly as possible the interest of individuals, of corporations and of society.
>
> Cadbury (2003)

Corporate governance is a broad and amorphous concept. Corporate governance is also a relatively recent concept (Organization for Economic Co-operation and Development (OECD), 1999, 2004; Cadbury 2003). Corporate governance codes do not often explicitly define what corporate governance is. Most codes of best practice deal with corporate governance as a concept and explain its importance without defining its meaning. Yet, the way corporate governance is *defined* may affect the scope and content of the codes. Perhaps the most commonly cited definition of corporate governance was provided in 1992 by Sir Adrian Cadbury in the Report on Financial Aspects of Corporate Governance in the UK: 'Corporate Governance is the system by which companies are directed and controlled'.

Here, corporate governance is defined as a set of mechanisms through which firms operate when ownership is separated from management. 'One size does not fit all' and other definitions of corporate governance may also be used. Regardless of whether a broad or a narrow definition of corporate governance is chosen, it is important that the fundamental values of transparency, accountability, fairness and responsibility be respected in order for firms to build and sustain the confidence of investors, stakeholders and society as a whole.

Corporations, it has been observed in the *Securities and Exchange Board of India (SEBI) Consultative Paper of 2003*, pool capital from a large investor base, both in the domestic and in the international capital markets. In this context, investment is ultimately an *act of faith* in the ability of a corporation's management. When an investor invests money in a corporation, she or he expects the board and the management to act as trustees and ensure the safety of the capital and also earn a rate of return that is higher than the cost of capital. In this regard, investors expect management to act in their best interests at all times and adopt good corporate governance practices (IEDC, 2006).

Narayana Murthy Committee (2003) has described corporate governance as the acceptance by management of the inalienable rights of shareholders as the true owners of the corporation and of their own role as trustees on behalf of the shareholders. It is about commitment to values, about ethical business conduct and about making a distinction between personal and corporate funds in the management of a company (cited in Fernando, 2006).

PERTINENCE OF CORPORATE GOVERNANCE

As a result of globalization and the increasing complexity of business operations, there is a greater reliance on the private sector, especially private corporations, as the engine of growth in both developed and developing countries. Corporations are legal entities created by societies because they are an efficient form of organization and society benefits from their existence. Corporations contribute to economic growth and development, which in turn leads to improved standards of living as well as the alleviation of poverty.

Gregory and Simms (1999) observe that 'the quality of corporate governance is important since it has a direct impact on:

- Efficiency with which a corporation employs assets
- Ability to attract low-cost capital
- Capacity to meet the expectations of society
- Overall performance

According to Global Corporate Governance Forum (2005), corporate governance has taken significance because of following developments:

- The private, market-based investment process – underpinned by good corporate governance – is now much more important for most economies than it used to be. Privatization has raised corporate governance issues in sectors that were previously in the hands of the State. Firms have turned to public markets to seek capital, and mutual societies and partnerships have converted themselves into publicly listed corporations.
- Technological progress, liberalization and opening up of financial markets, trade liberalization, and other structural reforms – notably, price deregulation and the removal of restrictions on products and ownership – have all made the allocation of capital among competing purposes, within and across countries, more complex. So has the monitoring of the use of capital. This complexity makes good governance more important – but also more difficult.
- The mobilization of capital is increasingly one step removed from the principal/owner, given the increasing size of firms and the growing role of financial intermediaries. The role of institutional investors is also growing in many countries.
- This increased delegation of investment has raised the need for good corporate governance arrangements.
- Deregulation and reform have reshaped the local and global financial landscape. Longstanding institutional arrangements for corporate governance are being replaced with new institutional arrangements, and in the meantime, inconsistencies and gaps have emerged.
- International financial integration has increased as have trade and investment flows. This has led to many cross-border issues in corporate governance, including occasional clashes of differing corporate governance cultures.

How does corporate governance matter for growth and development?
Contemporary literature has *identified* several channels through which corporate governance affects growth and development:

- Increased access to external financing by firms can lead, in turn, to larger investment, higher growth and greater employment creation.
- Lowering of the cost of capital and associated higher firm valuation makes more investments attractive to investors, also leading to growth and more employment.
- Better operational performance through better allocation of resources and better management results in more general wealth creation.
- Good corporate governance can be associated with a reduced risk of financial crises, which is particularly important given that financial crises can have large economic and social costs.
- Good corporate governance can mean better relationships with all stakeholders, which in turn improve social and labour relationships, help to address such issues as environmental protection and can help further reduce poverty and inequality.

All these channels matter for growth, employment, poverty alleviation and well-being more generally. Empirical evidence using various techniques has documented these relationships at the level of the country, the sector, the individual firm and from investor perspectives (Coles et al., 2007).

WHAT CONSTITUTES GOOD CORPORATE GOVERNANCE?

Good corporate governance is the broader view of corporate governance that focuses on the relationship between a company and a broad range of other stakeholders. It is based on the satisfaction of all kinds of stakeholders, CSR and ethics. Good corporate governance is about how an organization is managed. It is about commitment to values, ethical business conduct and exercise of powers as these are closely connected. The question is – can corporate governance achieve excellence without good governance in the long term?

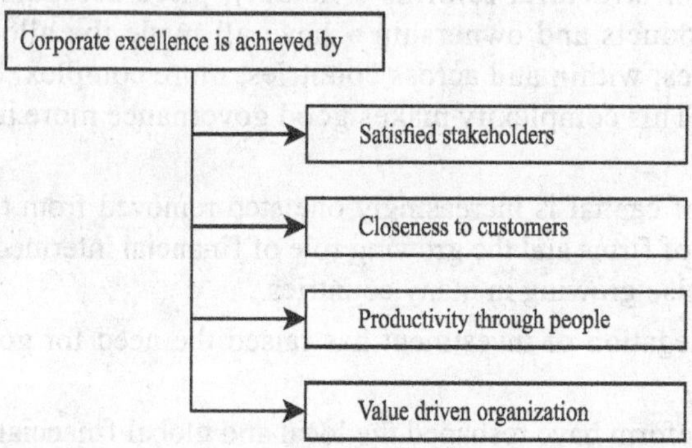

Deloitte and Touche (2013) in their webcast titled 'Framing the Future of Corporate Governance' explored the challenges of enterprise-wide corporate governance and the role of an effective framework in establishing an appropriate governance programme. The framework offers an end-to-end view of corporate governance. It forms the basis for the tools that help boards and executives identify opportunities to improve effectiveness and efficiency. A framework helps define the role of the board and management, delineates duties and helps prevent duplicated efforts and the overlooking of critical issues. It can also assist with the execution of the board's core processes by providing structure to policies and tools (e.g. annual calendar, meeting agendas, committee charters and guidelines). This allows the board to focus on the right issues and properly prioritize its limited time and resources. In addition, a framework provides the board with a structured way to collaborate with management on specific issues the company faces with minimal risk of confusion and loss of productivity. Lastly, a framework can help clarify each board committee's roles in fulfilling the board's objectives from a governance perspective.

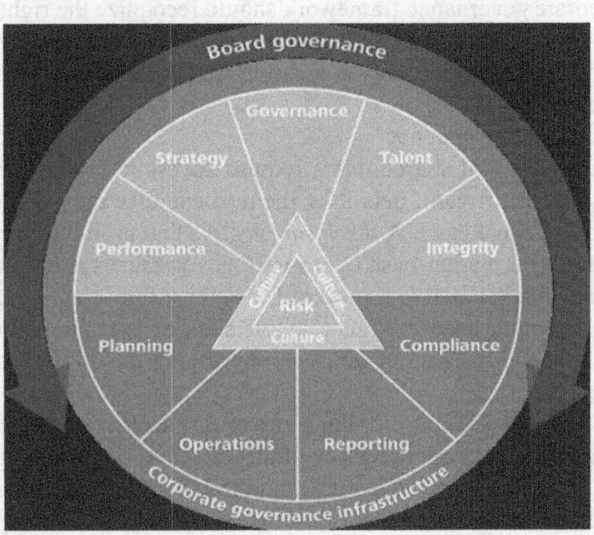

Source: Deloitte and Touche LLP: Framing the Future of Corporate Governance.

With the public ever more attentive of social and environmental issues, corporate governance entails an explicit engagement with ethical matters via CSR and with issues of good corporate governance. Defining corporate governance, both in terms of how it is done and who is affected by it or has input into it, is therefore crucial for the financial and social survival of the modern global business.

PRINCIPLES OF CORPORATE GOVERNANCE

To move towards convergence, the standard principles of corporate governance that have been internationally accepted are generally applied to assess company's corporate governance.

The six principles of corporate governance are as follows:

1. 'Ensuring the basis for an effective corporate governance framework'
   The corporate governance framework should promote transparent and efficient markets, be consistent with the rule of law and clearly articulate the division of responsibilities among different supervisory, regulatory and enforcement authorities (OECD, 2004).

2. 'The rights of shareholders and key ownership functions'
   Shareholders or equity investors who entrust to invest their funds have certain rights. They have the right to claim of profit, to influence on the company's decision making by participating in meeting or voting and to be informed reliably about the company.
3. 'The equitable treatment of shareholders'
   This principle emphasizes fair treatment to all shareholders and especially provides effective protection for the minority shareholder. Therefore, there is no expropriation of minority shareholders by managers or controlling shareholders. Shareholders are able to initiate legal and administrative proceedings when their rights are violated. This principle also prohibits insider trading and self-dealing practices.
4. 'The role of stakeholders in corporate governance'
   The corporate governance framework should recognize the rights of stakeholders established by law or through mutual agreements and encourage active co-operation between corporations and stakeholders in creating wealth and jobs and in sustaining financially sound enterprises.
5. 'Disclosure and transparency'
   Actual and potential shareholders require access to regular, reliable and comparable information in sufficient detail for them to exercise their ownership rights on a fully informed and equal basis. A *disclosure regime* that promotes transparency is thus a pivotal feature of a market-based corporate governance system. It underpins confidence in the stock market, and is a powerful tool for influencing the behaviour of companies and for protecting investor rights. Insufficient or ambiguous information will hamper the ability of the markets to function, increasing the cost of capital and discouraging investment.

   In the course of developing a strong disclosure regime, the channels, timing and procedures for disseminating corporate information can be just as important as the content of the information itself. Material information needs to reach the market and the concerned authorities in a cost-effective, easily accessible, predictable and timely fashion.
6. 'The responsibilities of the board'.
   This principle, regardless of board structure types, indicates that the board is professionally responsible for monitoring managerial performance and providing an adequate return for shareholders, while avoiding conflicts of interest and maintaining to the balance of competing demands. OECD also suggests that the board be able to exercise objective and independent judgements.

	Examples of detailed principles
Rights of shareholders	• Sufficient and timely information on general meetings and on issues to be decided at the meetings • Equal effect should be given to votes cast in person or in absentia • Anti-takeover devices should not be used to shield management and the board from accountability

Equitable treatment of shareholders	• Equitable treatment of all shareholders, including minority and foreign shareholders • All shareholders should have the opportunity to obtain effective redress for violation of their rights
Role of Stakeholders	• Recognize the right of stakeholders as established by law or through mutual agreements • Active cooperation between corporations and stakeholders in creating wealth, jobs and the sustainability of financially sound enterprises
Disclosure and transparency	• Timely and accurate disclosure is made on all material matters regarding the corporation • Annual audit conducted by an independent, competent and qualified auditor
Responsibilities of the board	• Ensure the strategic guidance of the company by the board • Effective monitoring of management by the board • Board should treat all shareholders fairly and take into account interests of stakeholders

At the international level, most efforts to improve corporate governance practices have, for obvious reasons, focussed on developing non-binding and principles-based common standards. The development of international corporate governance standards is led primarily by multilateral and regional organizations such as the *OECD* and *the Commonwealth Association of Corporate Governance.*

These standards can successfully serve as benchmarks and models for national codes and regulations. Many countries such as the Republic of Korea, Russia, India and Zambia, have used the OECD *Principles of Corporate Governance* as the starting point of their national codes. International standards and guidelines have primarily targeted listed companies, although many of these governance recommendations are expected to benefit a wider range of firms. Building on the need to address the concerns of specific sectors, international standards have also been developed to provide guidelines to institutional investors and, more recently, to State-owned enterprises (Cadbury, 2003).

Six principles of corporate governance:

- Consistency between efficient market and the rule of law
- Providing reliable information to shareholders
- Equitable treatment of shareholders
- Recognition of rights of stakeholders, disclosure and transparency
- Encouraging disclosures regime for transparency
- Professional responsibility of board for monitoring managerial performance

MODELS OF CORPORATE GOVERNANCE

The belief that the purpose of the modern corporation is to maximize shareholder value, along with typical capital market and ownership features has been associated with the 'Anglo-Saxon' agency model of the corporation. This contrasts the '*German* (and *Japanese*) conception of the company as a social institution'. In making this distinction, commentators have mostly focussed on the extent and nature of the separation of ownership and control.

Principal–Agent Model

Principal–Agent Theory is based on the relationship between the principal who assigns duties and responsibilities to other people termed as agent. This is expressed in the form of a contract, whereby the agent agrees to provide a service for the principal for an approved amount of compensation

The *Anglo-Saxon* model is characterized by a clear separation between management control and shareholder ownership and hence is described as an 'outsider' system of corporate governance. It is contrasted with the 'insider' system, thought to be more descriptive of European and Japanese corporate forms. Shareholder primacy is embodied in the finance view of corporate governance, which is a special instance of the *principal–agent theory approach* in economic theory (this approach is discussed in detail in chapter 14 on 'Concept of New Public Management' in this volume).

In corporate governance framework, there is separation of ownership from management. This is done with a view to balance the objectives of management with that of shareholders. The control and monitoring mechanism adopted by the management is to ensure shareholder wealth maximization.

While companies are encouraged to *foster* long-term relationships with stakeholders by taking their interests into account, there is no concomitant pressure to build into corporate governance, structures and processes that would ensure company accountability towards stakeholder groups. It is frequently argued that attempts to *mediate* stakeholder claims may obscure performance evaluation and therefore facilitate discretionary behaviour by management.

It is argued that the new high technology world has significantly reduced the opportunity, ability and motivation of consumers to engage in rational decision making. Therefore, the development of loyal, inclusive *stakeholder relationships*, rather than the production of a better product at a lower price, will be the most important determinant of commercial viability and business success. The main intention of the stakeholders' concept as theory is to affirm and show that the company, together with its executive board, is responsible not only for shareholders, but also for individuals or groups that have a stake in the actions and decisions of such organization. The theory implies understanding the company as a social institution in which distinct groups with rights and demands participate.

With reference to manageability of company, *stakeholder theory* implies searching for a balance among the distinct company interest groups – shareholders, workers, clients, suppliers, banks, subsidiaries, local communities, pressure groups and the like – that are part of the executive board. Furthermore, the executive board should also look for participation of those individuals and groups – either directly or by means of representatives – that are somehow linked to the aims of the organization.

CORPORATE GOVERNANCE AT THE INTERNATIONAL LEVEL

The last decade has also seen a flurry of regulations introduced across different countries aimed at improving corporate governance practices in organizations; however, the results from such regulatory changes have been mixed. There are several reports and recommendations of the international committees/associations and so on, on the development of appropriate framework for promoting good corporate governance standards, codes and practices to be followed globally.

These recommendations and principles have been *mainly* focussed on company structure, financial and non-financial disclosures, compliance with codes of corporate governance, competitive remuneration policy, shareholders' rights and responsibilities, financial reporting and internal controls, etc. All these efforts at the international level, in turn, help to bring favourable changes in the operating systems of board of directors, companies' management and administration; as well as improve the complexion of relationship between supervisory and executive bodies.

The several milestone reports on corporate governance at the international level are as follows:

- Cadbury Committee Report – The Financial Aspects of Corporate Governance (1992)
- Greenbury Committee Report on Directors' Remuneration (1995)
- Hampel Committee Report on Corporate Governance (1998)
- The Combined Code, Principles of Good Governance and Code of Best Practice, London Stock Exchange (1998)
- CalPERS' Global Principles of Accountable Corporate Governance (1999)
- Blue Ribbon Report (1999)
- King Committee on Corporate Governance (2002)
- Sarbanes Oxley Act (2002)
- Higgs Report: Review of the Role and Effectiveness of Non-executive Directors (2003)
- The Combined Code on Corporate Governance (2003)
- ASX Corporate Governance Council Report (2003)
- OECD Principles of Corporate Governance (2004)
- The Combined Code on Corporate Governance (2006)
- UNCTAD Guidance on Good Practices in Corporate Governance Disclosure (2006)
- The Combined Code on Corporate Governance (2008)
- Walker Review of Corporate Governance of UK Banking Industry (2009)
- UK Corporate Governance Code (Revised) (2012)

CORPORATE GOVERNANCE: DEVELOPMENTS IN INDIA

At the time of independence in 1947, India had functioning stock markets, an active manufacturing sector, a fairly developed banking sector and also a comparatively well-developed British-derived convention of corporate practices. From 1947 through 1991, the Indian government pursued markedly socialist policies when the State nationalized most banks and became the principal provider of both debt and equity capital for private firms.

The government agencies that provided capital to private firms were evaluated on the basis of the amount of capital invested rather than on their returns on investment. Competition, especially foreign, was suppressed. Private providers of debt and equity capital faced serious obstacles in exercising oversight over managers due to long delays in judicial proceedings and difficulty in enforcing claims in bankruptcy.

Public equity offerings could be made only at government-set prices. Public companies in India were only required to comply with limited governance and disclosure standards enumerated in the Companies Act of 1956, the Listing Agreement, and the accounting standards set forth by the Institute of Chartered Accountants of India. Faced with a fiscal crisis in 1991, the Indian Government responded by enacting a series of reforms aimed at general economic liberalization. *SEBI* – India's securities market regulator – was formed in1992, and by the mid-1990s, the Indian economy was growing steadily and Indian firms had begun to seek equity capital to finance expansion into the market spaces created by liberalization and the growth of outsourcing.

Weaknesses in corporate governance structures within companies and banks were cited as reasons for excessive risk taking, skewed incentive compensation for senior managers and the predominance of a board culture that values short-term gains over sustained, long-term performance. However, 'these crises are manifestations of several structural reasons why corporate governance has become more important for economic development and a more significant policy issue in many countries' (Stiglitz, 2010). In India, the need for capital, among other things, led to corporate governance reform and many major corporate governance initiatives were launched since the mid-1990s; most of these initiatives were focussed on improving the somewhat rudimentary governance climate prevalent in corporate India, at that time.

1. *Codifying Good Governance Norms in India*

In April 1998, India produced one of the first substantial codes of *best practice in corporate governance* in Asia. It was published not by a governmental body, a securities regulator or a stock exchange, but by the Confederation of Indian Industries (CII), the country's industrial body. The following year, the government appointed a committee under the leadership of Kumar Mangalam Birla, Chairman, Aditya Birla Group, to draft India's first *national code* on corporate governance for listed companies. Many of the committee's recommendations were mandatory, closely aligned to international best practices at the time and set higher governance standards for listed companies than most other jurisdictions in Asia. The Indian Code of Corporate Governance, approved by SEBI in early 2000, was implemented in stages over the following two years and led to changes in stock exchange listing rules, notably the new Clause 49 in the Listing Agreement.

It requires that companies have, among other things, audit committees, a minimum number of independent directors and chief executive officer and chief financial officer certification of financial statements and internal controls. Initially, the reforms applied only to larger firms; they reached smaller public firms after a several-years lag (*SEBI, Clause 49 of Listing Agreement,* cited in Black and Khanna, 2007). Further, reforms have been made over the past decade to modernize both Company Law and securities regulations. The Companies Act, 1956 has been amended several times, in areas such as postal ballots and audit committees, while committees were appointed in 2002 and 2004 to recommend improvements. The latest committee, on Company Law, chaired by Dr J. J. Irani, was charged with undertaking a comprehensive review of the 1956 Act and its recommendations led to a rewrite of the law and a new Companies Bill, 2013.

In the area of securities regulation, SEBI has made numerous changes in recent years including: revising and strengthening Clause 49 in relation to independent directors and audit committees; revising Clause 41 of the Listing Agreement on interim and annual financial results and amending other listing rules to protect the interests of minority shareholders, for example, in mergers and acquisitions. Not surprisingly, the *Satyam* fraud of late 2008 led to renewed reform efforts by Indian authorities and regulators. SEBI brought out new rules in February 2009 requiring greater disclosure by promoters (i.e., controlling shareholders) of their shareholdings and any pledging of shares to third parties. In November 2009, SEBI announced that it would be making some further changes to the Listing Agreement, including required listed companies to produce half yearly balance sheets.

2. *Corporate Governance Voluntary Guidelines 2009*

Though the corporate governance efforts in India have been spearheaded by SEBI over the last decade, the more recent steps have been taken by the Ministry of Corporate Affairs (MCA). The Companies Bill, 2013, does contain several aspects of corporate governance, which have hitherto been the mainstay of Clause 49. This represents a trend towards legislating on corporate governance rather than leaving it to the domain of the Listing Agreement. It also signifies a shift in corporate governance administration from SEBI, which oversees the implementation of Clause 49, towards the MCA, which administers the Companies Act.

In December 2009, the MCA published a new set of 'Corporate Governance Voluntary Guidelines 2009', designed to encourage companies to adopt better practices in the running of boards and board committees, the appointment and rotation of external auditors and creating a whistle blowing mechanism. They provide for a set of good practices, which may be voluntarily adopted by the public companies. Private companies, particularly the bigger ones, may also like to adopt these guidelines. The guidelines are recommendatory in nature.

Although some leading Indian companies deserve credit for actively pursuing high standards of governance, including producing examples of world-class corporate disclosure, there is still a fair degree of complacency towards corporate governance and the rights of minority shareholders.

In March 2012, MCA constituted a committee under the chairmanship of Mr Adi Godrej to formulate policy document on corporate governance. In September 2012, the committee submitted its document, specifying 17 guiding principles on corporate governance.

Companies Bill, 2013

The new Companies Bill 2013 received the president's assent on August 29, 2013. The new Companies Bill replaces the six-decade-old regulations of Companies Act, 1956, that governed companies. The Companies Bill 2013 provides for modifying the rules and regulations that earlier governed the companies in the country. It focuses on the social welfare and protection of investors against fraud. It aims to bring transparency in the working of the company.

Some of the key highlights on the Companies Bill 2013 are as follows:

- Introduction of concept of 'one person company.'
- Inclusion of e-governance in all processes.
- Mandatory transfer of 2 per cent of average net profit of preceding three years for CSR.
- Compulsory internal audit for different class of companies.
- The tenure of appointment of auditors at Annual General Meeting of company, extended to five years, instead of annual appointment/retirement (other than government company).
- In case of listed companies, one third of total no of directors to be 'independent directors.'
- Manager or managing director or chief executive officer, whole time director, chief financial officer and company secretary as key 'managerial personnel.'
- Prohibition of insider trading of securities.
- The maximum number of members for private company increased to 200 from 50.
- Annual ratification of appointment of auditors.
- Appointment of at least one woman director in the company.
- Redefinition of the term 'subsidiary', 'control' and associate 'company.'
- Statutory status to be conferred upon the Serious Fraud Investigation Office.

Many committees were set up to deliberate and evolve consensus about the regulatory parameters needed for the Indian market and companies. Some of the landmark committees which laid the foundation for Indian corporate governance landscape are listed in Table 24.1.

Table 24.1 Landmark Committees of Indian Corporate Governance

April 1998	CII released Code of Corporate Governance
May 1999	SEBI announced the formation of Kumar Mangalam Birla Committee to propose reforms in corporate governance
February 2000	Clause 49 of Listing Agreement introduced
August 2002	Naresh Chandra Committee on Corporate Audit and Governance
February 2003	Narayana Murthy Committee – 1 (SEBI)
August 2003	SEBI amended Listing Agreement and strengthened the criteria of independent directors
November 2003	Narayana Murthy Committee – 11 (SEBI)
October 2004	SEBI withdrew the amendment and introduced a revised Listing Agreement
January 2006	Clause 49 of the Listing Agreement
March 2007	Revised changes proposed to Clause 49
December 2009	Government introduced Corporate Governance Voluntary Guidelines
August 2013	Companies Bill 2013 replaced the six-decade-old regulations of Companies Act, 1956

Source: SEBI.

CONCLUSION

The foremost challenges to corporate governance reforms in India are as follows:

- Control of the dominant shareholder(s).
- Deficiency of inducement for companies to put into practice corporate governance reform measures (no direct correlation between implementing expensive governance systems and corresponding returns).
- Immature external monitoring systems.
- Deficiency of genuine independent directors.
- Feeble regulatory oversight including multiplicity of regulators.

Corporate governance restructuring in India presently rests at an exciting intersection. The upcoming expansion of the next generation reforms and their implementation during the contemporary decade will hinge on how valuable they are for the Indian business scenario.

To sum up, the emerging consensus on good corporate governance seeks to address the following areas:

- Building sustainable value.
- Conduct of achieving the firm's goals.
- Increasing shareholders' satisfaction.
- Providing proficient and effective management.
- Increasing reliability.

- Guaranteeing efficient risk management.
- Making available an early warning structure against all risk.
- Providing for certain an approachable and answerable corporation.
- Unfolding the role of a firm's units.
- Developing control and internal auditing.
- Maintaining a balance between economic and social benefit.
- Ensuring professional use of resources.
- Controlling performance.
- Allocating responsibility fairly.
- Producing all essential information for stakeholders.
- Keeping the board autonomous from management.
- Facilitating sustainable performance.

In conclusion, it can be said that corporations face different problems at different times; dynamic problems need dynamic solutions. The past three decades have witnessed the dynamic nature of both governance problems and solutions. Sometimes internal governance mechanisms are in a controlling position, whereas at other times external governance mechanisms are dominant. The array of agencies involved in managing the regulatory and legal framework of corporate governance has expanded. In addition, effective governance mechanisms may differ from firm to firm and country to country. Therefore, governance issues present a never-ending challenge to corporations, regulators and scholars. However, many of the problems can be avoided or mitigated if the involved parties collaborate to find solutions ahead of time. This chapter has attempted to describe some of these issues.

Preparatory Questions

- Describe the relevance of corporate governance for growth and development.
- What constitutes good corporate governance?
- Discuss the landmark committees of Indian corporate governance and their contribution in establishing regulatory framework for corporates.
- Examine the nature and purpose of corporate governance in the present era of liberalization and globalization.
- List out the important features of corporate governance in the Companies Act 2013.
- Discuss the models of corporate governance.

REFERENCES

ACGA. (2010) *White Paper on Corporate Governance in India.* Hong Kong: Asian Corporate Governance Association (ACGA).

Alchian, A. and Demsetz, H. (1972) 'Production, Information Costs and Economic Organization.' *The American Economic Review.* 62. pp. 777–795.

Aras, G. and Crowther, D. (2010) *A Handbook of Corporate Governance and Social Responsibility*. London: Gower Publishing Limited.

Berle, A. A. and Means, G. C. (1932) *The Modern Corporation and Private Property*. New York: The Macmillan Corporation.

Bessire, D., Chatelin, C. and Onnée, S., (2010) 'cited in Güler Aras and David Crowther', *A Handbook of Corporate Governance and Social Responsibility*. London: Gower Publishing Limited.

Black, B. S. and Khanna, S. V. (2007) 'Can Corporate Governance Reforms increase firm Market Values? Event Study Evidence from India.' *Journal of Empirical Legal Studies*. 4. pp. 749–96.

Bushman, R. M. and Smith, A. J. (2001) 'Financial Accounting Information and Corporate Governance.' *Journal of Accounting and Economics*. 32. pp. 237–333.

Cadbury Committee Report. (1992) *Financial Aspects of Corporate Governance* London: Gee and Co.

Cadbury, A. (2003) *Foreword to Corporate Governance and Development*. Global Corporate Governance Forum, Focus 1. Washington DC: World Bank.

Coase, R. H. (1937) 'The Nature of the Firm.' *Economica*. IV(16). pp. 386–405.

Confederation of Indian Industry (CII). (2009) *Report of the CII Taskforce on Corporate Governance*, Chaired by Mr. Naresh Chandra.

Denis, D. K. (2001) 'Twenty Five Years of Corporate Governance Research and Counting.' *Review of Financial Economics*. 10. pp. 191–211.

Eells, R. (1960) *The Meaning of Modern Business: An Introduction to Philosophy of Large Corporate Enterprise*. New York: Columbia University Press.

Fernando, A. C. (2006) *Corporate Governance, Principles, Policies and Practices*. New Delhi: Pearson.

Global Corporate Governance Forum. (2005) 'Developing Corporate Governance Codes of Best Practice.' Vol. 1. *User Guide*. Washington, DC: World Bank.

Gregory, H. J. and Simms, M. E. (1999) 'Corporate Governance-What is it, Why it Matters.' at 9th *Anti-corruption Conference*. Durban, South Africa.

Holmstrom, B., and Kaplan, S. (2001) 'Corporate Governance and Merger Activity in the United States: Making sense of the 1980s and 1990s.' *Journal of Economic Perspectives* 15(2). pp. 121–144.

Jensen, M. C. and Meckling, W. H. (1976) 'Theory of the Firm: Managerial Behaviour Agency Costs and Ownership Structure.' *Journal of Financial Economics*. 3(4). pp. 305–60.

Keasey K., Thompson, S. and Wright, M. (1997) 'Introduction: The Corporate Governance Problem - Competing Diagnoses and Solutions' in Keasey, K., Thompson, S. and Wright, M. (eds.). *Corporate Governance: Economic, Management, and Financial Issues*. Oxford: Oxford University Press.

Mayer, F. (1997) 'Corporate Governance, Competition, and Performance in Enterprise and Community: New Directions' in Deakin, S. and Hughes, A (eds.). *Corporate Governance*. Oxford: Blackwell Publishers.

Ministry of Corporate Affairs. (2009) *Corporate Governance Voluntary Guidelines*. Government of India. New Delhi.

National Foundation for Corporate Governance. (2004) *Discussion Paper: Corporate Governance in India: Theory and Practice*. National Foundation for Corporate Governance.

National Foundation for Corporate Governance. (2012) *Discussion Paper: Corporate Governance in India: Theory and Practice*. Government of India.

OECD. (1999) *Report of the Task Force on Corporate Governance, Principles of Corporate Governance*.

Patterson Report. (2001) *The Link between Corporate Governance and Performance*.

Shaw, H. (2010), 'cited in Güler Aras and David Crowther', *A Handbook of Corporate Governance and Social Responsibility*. London: Gower Publishing Limited.

Shleifer, A. and Vishny, R. W. (1997) 'A Survey of Corporate Governance.' *Journal of Finance*. 52. pp. 737–83.

Solomon, J. and Solomon, A. (2004) *Corporate Governance and Accountability*. New York: John Wiley & Sons, Chichester Publishing Co.

Stiglitz, J. E. (2010) *Free Fall*. New York: W. W. Norton & Company.

Wolf, J. B. (1999) *The Effects of Agency Problems on the Financial Behaviour, Performance and Efficiency of German Industrial Stock Corporations*. Peter lang International Academic Publishers, Berlin.

Websites:

ASX Corporate Governance Council. (2014) 'Corporate Governance Principles and Recommendations.' 3rd ed. ASX Corporate Governance Council. Available from: www.asx.com.au/.../cgc-principles-and-recommendations-3rd-edn.pdf

Coles, J. L., Lemmon, M. L. and Meschke, F. (2007) 'Structural Models and Endogeneity in Corporate Finance: The Link between Managerial Ownership and Corporate Performance.' Available from: http://ssrn.com/abstract=423510. (Accessed Oct 10, 2013)

Consultative paper on review of corporate governance norms in India, Securities and Exchange Board of India. Available from: www.sebi.gov.in/cms/sebi_data/attachdocs/1357290354602.pdf. (Accessed November 15, 2013).

Deloitte and Touche. (2013) 'Framing the future of corporate governance – deloitte Governance Framework.' Available from: www.deloitte.com/.../US_AERS_Governance_%20Framework_102412. (Accessed Nov, 2013)

Confederation of Indian Industries, Desirable Corporate Governance-A Code – (CII). Available from: www.ciionline.org. (Accessed June, 2014)

Discussion paper on corporate governance in India: Theory and practice: National foundation for corporate governance. Availble from: www.nfcgindia.org/library/cgitp.pdf. (Accessed March 2014)

OECD. (2004) 'Principles of Corporate Governance.' Available from: http://www.oecd.org/corporate/oecdprinciplesofcorporategovernance.htm. (Accessed March 2014)

OECD. (2004) 'Principles of Corporate Governance.' Available from: www.oecd.org/dataoecd/32/18/31557724.pdf. (Accessed March 2014)

OECD. (2012) '*Related Party Transactions and Minority Shareholder Rights*.' OECD Publishing: doi: 10.1787/9789264168008-en France. (Accessed March 2014)

SEBI. (2012) 'Consultative Paper on Review of Corporate Governance Norms in India.' Available from: www.sebi.gov.in/cms/sebi_data/attachdocs/1357290354602.pdf. (Accessed March 2014)

Chapter Twenty Five

Significance of e-Governance

Sanghamitra Nath

LEARNING OBJECTIVES

After completing this chapter, you should be able to:

- Trace the evolution of e-governance in India
- Explain the concept of e-governance
- Describe the elements of e-governance
- Discuss the role of e-governance in effective public service delivery
- Identify the hurdles in e-governance
- Analyse the e-governance initiatives in India; and
- Elucidate the challenges to e-governance

INTRODUCTION

e-Governance is a new concept for those in public administration or bureaucracy, as well as for those who are the ultimate recipients of the evolved means of governance. Simply put, e-governance refers to the use of Information, Communication and Technology (ICT) for country-wide or state-wise governance. It endeavours towards attenuating corruption, delays and inefficiencies in delivery of public services to beneficiaries. In doing so, it aims to bring government services to the beneficiaries (citizens, businesses, interest groups and other agencies of government) in a transparent, speedy, easy and efficient way.

The transition of governance into ICT came with the Second Administrative Reforms Commission. Under Mr Veerappa Moily, former Chairperson, and Mr P. I. Suvrathan, former Additional Secretary, the Commission and its 11th Report on Reforms emphasized on 'Promoting e-Governance: The SMART Way Forward'. The ICT-based governance opened new economic opportunities, brought transparency in private–public transactions, insights into outsourcing processes and accountable administration. It introduced a minimal guarantee against arbitrary exchanges and government procurements and some form of standardization of procedures. This chapter attempts to describe the role of e-governance in public services delivery. It traces the evolution of e-governance in India through various initiations and examines the hurdles in its accessibility and reach.

HISTORY OF e-GOVERNANCE IN INDIA

Over the years, the bureaucracy has become not only an inevitable component of the government but also an obstacle for the governed. For the government, the bureaucracy helps in the discharge of myriad public services. Through the agency of bureaucracy, the government makes public utilities available to people at large. At the same time, beneficiaries often face innumerable problems when they approach government offices or bureaucracy such as complexity of procedure, lack of access to relevant functionary with respect to an issue, absence of transparency in decision making, uncertainty about time required for processing a case, slow and inefficient working and non-communication of decisions even after they are made (Rawal, 2007).

The disappointment of beneficiaries has prompted the government to improvize service delivery through improved governance. At the same time, it has been felt that digital opportunities should be created as an integral part of development discourse which addresses 'core' development challenges. This concern has brought ICT to the attention of the Government of India (GoI). In 1976, the National Informatics Centre (NIC) was established through the Electronics Commission under the then Prime Minister Indira Gandhi (Prasad, 2012).

The NIC received external stimulus from a United Nation Development Programme (UNDP) project and by 1977, it became fully functional. It emerged as the 'prime builder' of e-governance through networking and computer applications in various organs of the government at the central, state and district levels, and as the promoter of digital opportunities for sustainable development. Through its NIC network or 'NICNET', NIC developed institutional linkages with all the ministries/departments of the central government, 35 State governments/union territories and about 625 district administrations of India. By facilitating improved government services, wider transparency, decentralized planning and management, it helped to bring about better efficiency and accountability to citizens of the country. At present, it is responsible for the 'informatics-led-development' programme of the government which includes setting up of ICT infrastructure, implementation of national and state level e-governance projects, products and services, consultancy to the government departments, research and development and capacity building.

Thus, 'smart governance captured the soul of governance which aspired for institutional reform without inculcating the demeanour to displace vested interests in pre-existing forms and structures' (Rossel and Finger, 2007). In 1985, the then Prime Minister Rajiv Gandhi decided to accelerate the use of ICT whereby the role of NIC increased prominently. In May 1998, National Task Force on Information Technology (IT) and Software Development was set up under the leadership of the deputy chairperson of Planning Commission. The Task Force submitted three reports in June 1998, August 1998 and March 1999, which strongly recommended the creation of an appropriate investment climate. It also noted that the computerized information systems till then merely displayed existing rules and procedures of the government and failed to serve the interests of people.

The Working Group on Citizen–IT interface made several recommendations, some of them are as follows:

- To create government-wide electronic infrastructure to simplify service delivery, reduce duplication and improve the level and speed of service to the public
- To encourage the establishment of internet service providers
- The government and the private sector to collaborate to put in place electronic fund transfer system
- Re-engineering of the existing government processes and procedures to bring about transparency reduce bureaucratic controls, increase efficiency and productivity and reduce cost of service delivery

In 2000, the IT Act was passed by the Atal Bihari Vajpayee-led government. The Act was subsequently amended in 2008. Most importantly, the erstwhile fragmented initiatives of e-governance were unified under the common vision and strategy 'National e-Governance Plan (NeGP)' in 2006 (Prasad, 2012). The vision statement of NeGP states the primary purpose of the e-governance initiative in the country. Through extensive infrastructure connecting even the remotest of villages and large-scale digitization of records, NeGP intends to bring public services at the doorstep of citizens, through common service delivery outlets, and ensure efficiency, transparency, and reliability of such services at affordable costs to realize the basic needs of the common person' through easy and reliable access over the internet. The NeGP as approved by the government, had 27 Mission Mode Projects (MMPs) and eight components as on May 18, 2006. Five years later, four more projects were added to it which covered areas such as health, education, public distribution system and posts and the final list included 31 MMPs (http:/deity.gov.in/content/national-e-governance-plan).

However, the government approval of NeGP did not guarantee financial approval(s) of all MMPs and components therein. Some of the noteworthy core infrastructure components to promote e-governance in a holistic manner are State Data Centres, State Wide Area Networks, Common Services Centres (CSCs) and middleware gateways, that is, National e-Governance Service Delivery Gateway, State e-Governance Service Delivery Gateway and Mobile e-Governance Service Delivery Gateway. Of late, the concept of cloud computing (provision of pay–for–use computing data/applications) has garnered interest in India and abroad. The government started a framework for authentication via e-Pramaan and G-I cloud to avail of the benefits of cloud computing in e-governance in India (http:/deity.gov.in/content/national-e-governance-plan).

CONCEPT OF e-GOVERNANCE

The underlying intention behind the ICT-based governance is to facilitate the process of 'governing. Governance is a dynamic process. It is always evolving; there is no end to governance and no perfect governance. The bureaucracy has been the representative of the government, be it the Centre or the states, for decades. There is no absolute definition of governance. Generally, it may be said to be a 'system of directing and controlling the actions, affairs, policies and functions of a political unit, organization or nation' (Sumanjeet, 2006). The UNDP defined governance as 'the exercise of economic, political and administrative authority to manage a country's affairs at all levels comprising the mechanisms, processes and institutions through which that authority is directed'. The World Bank also gave certain parameters of governance, which included six indicators (Rawal, 2007).

In the view of the World Bank, following are the parameters of governance:

- Voice and accountability
- Political stability/Non-violence
- Government effectiveness
- Regulatory quality
- Rule of law
- Control of corruption

Governance demarcates loci for interaction among private sector, civil society and the State. The process of governance brings together all three entities, thereby enabling articulation of their interests, rights and obligations, and mediation of their differences. Under the influence of ICT, these interactions transform into the phenomena of 'e-Governance' (Saxena, 2005). The beginning of globalization in India witnessed a concomitant push in public reforms. These reforms were centred on ICT which eventually paved the way for e-governance in the country.

e-Governance has been understood as digital governance to improve the system of governance that is in place and thus provide better services to the citizens. The application of electronic means in the interaction between government and citizens (G2C) and government and business (G2B) as well as in internal government operations (G2G) to simplify and improve democratic government and business aspects of governance (Saxena, 2005), and to improve the efficiency or effectiveness of the executive function of government including the delivery of public services (Sumanjeet, 2006).

Electronic-governance is composed of five elements. These are as follows:

Computer: Includes all the hardware and software requirements of government
Connectivity: Includes all the information carrier system, bandwidth and more
Content: Information that is exchanged between the 'consumers' of the system
Consumer: Entire human and human substitute systems that access and use the 'content' in the e-Governance system
Confidence building: Measures that help the citizens to develop confidence in e-governance and encourage them to take to e-transformation (Saxena, 2005)

In short, e-governance represents the initiatives of the government to harness ICT for its myriad participants, from government to business and citizens. To be more precise, the government has delineated three models of e-governance for the country. In this way, the government aims to reach out to citizens and business or non-governmental organizations and other branches of the government. The citizen-centric model emphasizes on joint initiatives by government and private organizations such as e-seva in land records, license, passport, income certificate, caste certificate, permanent account number (PAN), public grievance registration, marriage certificates, railway reservation and more, wherein the revenues are remitted from sale of government data or services. The Tarahocit or Franchisee or Kiosk model caters to profit-making sectors as well as non-profit sectors with income tax payment, Value Added Tax (VAT), corporation tax, registration of a new company, customers declarations, police inquiry of employees and more. Finally, the public-oriented models serve government organizations such as NIC, CMC, C-DAC, State Electronic Corporations and more, all of which are initiated and funded by the government. It helps the government ministries, departments and agencies in collection of tax, water charges, professional taxes etc. (Sumanjeet, 2006).

As evident from the above-mentioned models, the concept of e-governance has been derived from a purely functionalist perspective. A crucial difference between tradition and modernity is the speed at which communication, transfer of money or goods or services and other kinds of work may be achieved. Simply put, modernity is distinguished by speed and efficiency. The underlying motive of efficiency is to achieve as much as possible in the least amount of time or attain returns on input as fast as possible, of course, without compromising on quality or effectiveness. In this regard, ICTs have been indispensable and they have been increasingly recognized for their contribution to fast, reliable and easy accomplishment of tasks. The GoI, like in the advanced West, incorporated ICTs into governance in order to create the image of a modern bureaucracy and to indicate a shift from traditional methods of bureaucratic work. ICTs, thereby, not only symbolized an evolved bureaucracy but also an improved one.

ICT stresses on the following:

- Delivery of essential services to citizens closer to home
- Eliminating touts and undesirable practices such as delays, harassment and unnecessary documents
- Enhancing productivity and efficiency of administrative functions
- Ensuring transparency and right to information in governmental activities
- Enhancing access to information and communication across large distance
- Creating healthy relationship between government, citizens and private bodies and encouraging their participation in 'governance'
- Encouraging direct participation of citizens in government policy-making process and development efforts
- Enhancing citizen empowerment and democratization
- Creating a business-friendly environment
- Improving agriculture productivity
- Eliminating poverty
- Improving the overall quality of life of the common person

A modern bureaucracy governed and performed physically as well as virtually. The benefits of modern bureaucracy in the form of e-governance helped to bridge the gap between citizens and information and services, provided opportunities for online trade and net banking and reduced time and paperwork. By bringing technology in governance, e-governance encouraged confidence building among citizens, private entities and the government machinery by creating avenues for quick approvals and clearances, easy monitoring and tracking of files, market expansion and organized job creation, which left a positive impact on the macro economy (Sumanjeet, 2006). As a Corollary, the advantages stemming from e-governance contributed to good governance. Good governance embodied an administration that was corruption free, transparent, responsive, accountable and moral (Saxena, 2005). However, it would be too naive to assume that technology would cure governance of all its ills.

Miscellaneous Hurdles in e-Governance

There is a host of other obstacles impeding the next-level e-governance revolution in India. According to Sumanjeet (2006), these are as follows:

- No clear roadmap with measurable milestones on e-governance
- Poor management of knowledge and human resources
- Lack of large scale computerization
- Capability in use of local language in the IT sector
- Inadequate and inappropriate IT infrastructure
- Lack of standardization in data encoding, application logic, user interfaces, etc.
- Lack of baseline data and availability of information needed for decision making
- Lack of coherent government policies
- Government unwilling to commit funding
- Corruption, inefficiency and incompetence present in public services and welfare/development projects
- Low funding from the GoI and International Funding Organization
- Lack of co-ordination between different service agencies
- Non-compatibility between IT projects and business processes
- Brain drain of IT professionals from our country

The government should try to overcome the above-mentioned deficiencies in a timely manner. For efficient, cost-effective, convenient services to citizens and businesses, greater citizen access to public information and accountability in delivery of services to citizens, e-governance is a noteworthy step.

INITIATIVES OF e-GOVERNANCE IN INDIA

The Department of Electronics and Information Technology (DeitY), under the Ministry of Communications and IT, GoI, launched the CSC. Approved in May 2006, the CSC, a commitment of the National Common Minimum Programme, is a strategic cornerstone of the NeGP to introduce e-governance on a massive scale. The aim of CSC is to provide high-quality and cost-effective video, voice and data content and services as well as education, health, telemedicine, entertainment as well as other private services as part of e-governance. The CSC guidelines envisage a wide variety of content and services in the following areas:

- Agriculture services (agriculture, horticulture, sericulture, animal husbandry, fisheries, veterinary).
- Education and training services (school, college, vocational education, employment, etc.).
- Health services (telemedicine, health check-ups, medicines).
- Rural banking and insurance services (micro-credit, loans, insurance).
- Entertainment services (movies, television).
- Utility services (bill payments, online bookings).
- Commercial services (Desktop Publishing (DTP), printing, internet browsing, village-level BPO).

A significant component of CSC is its outreach in rural areas. It offers web-enabled e-governance services such as application forms, certificates and utility payments (electricity, telephone and water bills). Furthermore, it creates a platform for the private sector and NGOs to play an active role in implementation of the CSC scheme. In the process, the private sector and NGOs become partners with the GoI in rural development of India. The resulting Public Private Partnership (PPP) model of the CSC scheme envisions a 3-tier structure consisting of the following:

- CSC operator (called Village Level Entrepreneur or VLE).
- Service Centre Agency (SCA) responsible for a division of 500–1000 CSCs.
- State Designated Agency (SDA) identified by the state government, responsible for managing the implementation in the entire state.

The CSC has also developed online monitoring tools as part of monitoring solutions. These are CSC SMART Solution (http://www.cscsmart.in), CSC Online Monitoring Solution, CSC Online Dashboard (http://www.csclive.in/dashboard) and CSC Connect (http://www.csclive.in/cscconnect). Some of the functions of these solutions are providing unique identification of a CSC based on geography, maintaining a centralized database of CSCs, tracking online registration status of CSCs and enabling recording of BSNL connectivity status at each of the CSCs (http://deity.gov.in/content/common-services-centres). Besides the national initiatives on e-Governance, there are many state-level e-programmes geared towards responsive governance. Some of the e-governance projects are Akshaya, Gyandoot, Digital Saksharta Abhiyaan and e-Passport Seva (http://www.egovindia.org/egovportals.htm).

Akshaya Initiative

During the 1990s, the United Nations ranked the state of Kerala at par with the developed West on several social parameters. The Nobel laureate, Amartya Sen, has attributed the achievements to the wide reach of education in Kerala. The educated population in Kerala has availed of ICT services to further economic development. However, it was found that a vast majority were not aware of the benefits of ICT services and were deprived of access and usage of this technology. Keeping in view the widening digital divide, the Akshaya project envisioned to remove the digital disparities by empowering the less privileged sections of society with ICT tools. Even the heads of the 3-tier panchayat system realized the potential of ICT and partnered with the state government with plan proposals to bring ICT to every household. The state government, on its part, constituted a State IT Mission (http://www.akshaya.kerala.gov.in/index.php/background).

The Kerala IT Mission stood for the following objectives:

- Transparency in administration
- Speed in administration
- Responding to the needs of people at the grassroots level
- Making ICT applicable at the grassroots level to facilitate social engineering for development

The overall agenda of the State government was meant to improve living standards with the application of ICTs in all spheres of life. The task force on IT recommended that the state government adopt administrative reforms based on computerization, high visibility and penetrable citizen-centric projects. Discussions with many stakeholders led to the conclusion that e-literacy was necessary and its implementation required a 2-pronged approach – firstly, computer facilities should be provided in the rural areas and secondly, education to citizens for fruitful utilization of those facilities must be stressed upon. It was decided that a user-friendly content or courseware would be most useful to educate citizens on ICT. The Akshaya-e-Kendra was established as an ICT access point, one for every 1000 families living in two or three municipal or panchayat wards (http://www.akshaya.kerala.gov.in/index.php/background).

The Project was responsible for rendering new government-to-citizens (G2C) and business-to-citizens (B2C) services. It brought about e-ticketing, e-consignment and e-payment. Through e-learning programmes such as Intel Learning, Learn English, Arabic Tutor, Internet for Masses, Medical Transcription and e-Vidhya, people had better job prospects and could work competently.

The Project's biggest accomplishment was 'Entegramam', an online community portal in Malayalam created and maintained by citizens of each village, providing detailed information of the panchayat, a catalogue of 'useful services', history of land, governance, information on public services, and locally relevant news and announcements. Entegramam, a bilingual G2C initiative, was funded by UNESCO.

Gyandoot

The Gyandoot Project was started in 2000 in the Dhar district of Malwa region in western Madhya Pradesh. Through an Intranet network, computers in 21 major centres in five blocks of the district were connected. While the Intranet network was named Gyandoot, the computers established in gram panchayats were called Soochanalayas. All the Soochanalayas are fitted with telephone line connectivity and electric connection. The zilla panchayat procures computer hardware and gives it to the gram panchayat which, in turn, hands it over to the Soochak. The Soochak is the operator of the Soochanalaya. He is a locally trained youth from the same village who runs the Soochanalaya commercially as a means of livelihood for himself. Thus, the Soochak is an entrepreneur and not an employee of the state government. The Soochaks are trained at the zilla panchayat for seven days in three stages at their own expenses by computer operators of District Rural Development Agency (DRDA). They are trained in computer maintenance and numeric data entry skills. After the training, the Soochaks are selected interactively by the gram panchayat along with representatives from the zilla panchayat. Only the best trainees are selected as Soochaks, to run the Soochanalaya at their own cost and also pay 10% of their income as commission to the zilla panchayat for maintenance of the net. There is a Soochana Kosh, that is, a remote access server housed in the computer room in the zilla panchayat.

Beginning from November 1999, the Project Gyandoot was conceptualized as a top-down bureaucratic endeavour. The basic idea was borrowed from the 'wired villages' project of Warna in Kolhapur district of Maharashtra, where a cluster of villages were connected via a computer network. The supporting software was developed and implemented on time. As a result, the project took off in less than two months. The Project Gyandoot has been entitled 'A mass based information technology revolution', where the total outlay of Rs 25 lakhs was borne by panchayats. Gyandoot is a very cost-effective system which serves not only the specific 21 villages but also the surrounding 25–30 villages. The Soochanalayas are located in the buildings of gram panchayats, situated either at block headquarters or prominent 'haat' or 'bazaar' places or prominent villages on major roads. The Gyandoot network offers information on a wide range of needs of villagers and co-operatives and covers over half a million villagers living in 311 gram panchayats and over 600 villages (http://www.dhar.nic.in/GYANDOOT.htm).

Digital Saksharta Abhiyaan

The Haryana government has proposed to launch the Information Technology Mass Literacy Scheme called 'Digital Saksharta Abhiyaan' in concurrence with the objective of 'Digital Haryana'. The Electronics and Information Technology Department of the state said that the programme would be rolled out through the CSCs to impart training to 1.10 lac people in five selected blocks, that is, one person from every eligible household to make them digitally literate. In the first phase, the training would be geared towards making the person IT literate and adept in computer operations such as sending and receiving emails and surfing the internet for information. In the second phase, the trainees would learn about the various G2C and B2C services. Around 50% of the trainees would be selected from SC/ST/BPL categories. The primary objective is to attain 100% digital literacy within the marked out blocks.

e-Passport Seva

The Ministry of External Affairs launched the Passport Seva Project in May 2010. The passport is an essential document to travel out of the country for work, business, education, leisure, medical or other purposes. With increasing globalization and a flourishing economy, there has been an equally increasing demand for passport-related services. Estimates show that the passport demand has been growing at 10% per annum. Thus, the Ministry of External Affairs, in a PPP with Tata Consultancy Services, has started a simple, efficient and transparent process for passport delivery and related services. The sovereign and fiduciary functions such as verification, granting and issuing of passport; ownership and strategic control of core assets including data or information have been retained with the ministry. The ministry integrates with the state police for physical verification of the applicants' credentials and India Post for passport delivery.

Under the NeGP, the Passport Seva Project is one of the largest MMPs of the GoI. The project effectively uses ICT to transform the entire process of citizen service delivery countrywide through a networked environment integrating Passport Seva Kendras (PSKs), Passport Offices and external stakeholders involved in the process such as police, India Security Press and India Post. A Tier III Data Centre and an active–active Data Recovery Centre have been set up with 24×7 operations with built-in interoperability to exchange information with other government departments. At present, there are 39 passport issuance authorities and 77 State-of-the-art PSKs and 18 Passport Seva Laghu Kendras are coming up.

The Passport Seva Project won the National Award for e-Governance (Gold Award) for outstanding performance in citizen-centric service delivery. At the 18th National Conference on e-Governance held at Gandhinagar, Gujarat, on 30 January 2015, Smt. Anandiben Patel, Hon'ble Chief Minister of Gujarat handed over the award in recognition of the Project's qualitative and quantitative use of ICT for enhanced citizen-centric service. Till date, the new system has processed over 22 million applications. More than 50,000 applications are processed daily and the online portal http://passportindia.gov.in receives over 20 million hits per day. The huge number of passport applications made India the third largest passport issuing country in the world after China and the US.

NEW DEVELOPMENTS IN e-GOVERNANCE: THE SHIFT IN INTERNET PROTOCOL VERSIONS

India has planned to shift gradually from IPv4 to IPv6 this year to overcome the approaching exhaustion of IPv4 addresses. The abbreviation IPv stands for Internet Protocol version. With the growing need for more internet addresses in the world as well as new consumers and devices (mobile phones and tablet PCs) getting connected to web every day, the current protocol IPv4 is being depleted of IP addresses. The IPv6 will replace the existing IPv4 for which the government has proposed a task force that will look into IPv6-related issues on priority basis. The proposed task force will be headed by the telecom secretary who will be responsible for taking strategic policy decisions. The task force will meet every four months to provide vision, mission, strategic plan and national directions for IPv6 implementation in India. It will examine the impact of exhaustion of IPv4 address from the standpoints of infrastructure providers, equipment vendors, system integrators and service providers. In the long term, all the activities of the task force will be over taken by the Indian IPv6 Centre for Innovation (Sengupta and Julka, 2011).

The Number Resource Organization oversees the allocation of IP addresses at the global level. In February 2011, it announced that its store of unallocated IPv4 address space was fully depleted. Soon after, the Asia Pacific Network Information Centre (APNIC), the internet registry that oversees the allocation of web address resources for the region including India, planned to conserve the remaining stock of IPv4 address resources allotted to this region much ahead of time. The APNIC boasts of over 3000 account holders. Paul Wilson, Director General APNIC, argued that the demand for new address would be met sparingly to ensure the remaining IPv4 address space lasted longer even as the world transitioned to IPv6.

The IPv4 is an old number-based address system that enables devices to communicate with one another on the Internet. IPv6, with 128-bit addresses, can support more IP addresses than the 32-bit IPv4. The IPv6 standard can support as many as 3.4×10^{38} IP addresses enabling several devices connected to the web with a unique IP address. The APNIC authorized the Indian Registry for Internet Names and Numbers (IRINN) to begin issuing IPv6 addresses in the country. The IRINN set the initial price of IPv6 addresses at Rs 21,999. Rajesh Charia, President of the Internet Service Providers Association of India, said that IPv6 addresses would prove to be cheaper than IPv4 for companies but the government would need to put in place new equipment and devices that were compatible with IPv6.

There are many advantages in IPv6 that are not available in IPv4. For example, IPv6 simplifies aspects of address assignment (Stateless address auto configuration), network renumbering and router announcements when internet connectivity providers change. The standardization of IPv6 subnet size by fixing the size of the host identifier portion of an address to 64 bits helps an automatic mechanism for forming the host identifier from link-layer media addressing information (MAC address). The IPv6 architecture also has a built-in network security. However, IPv6 necessitates creation of a parallel independent network. It does not implement interoperability features with IPv4 and exchanging traffic between the two networks requires special translator gateways. In modern computer operating systems, there is a provision of dual-protocol software for transparent access to both networks either natively or using a tunnelling protocol such as 6to4, 6in4 or Teredo 'transition technology'.

CHALLENGES BEFORE e-GOVERNANCE

Compared with the US, China, Canada and many other developed and developing countries, India lags behind in e-governance. Despite immense scope for the growth of e-governance, it has not reached its optimum potential for a variety of reasons. According to Saxena (2005, pp. 317–324), these hurdles are as follows:

Administrative Hurdles

Uneven development of e-governance initiatives: Based on a survey conducted by NASSCOM among 10 key states, it was found that the southern states of Andhra Pradesh, Karnataka and Tamil Nadu did exceptionally well in implementing projects of e-governance, whereas Kerala, Gujarat, Maharashtra, Madhya Pradesh, West Bengal and Rajasthan were trying to catch up. The remaining states were yet to begin the process of implementing e-governance. Furthermore, it came to light that a mere 1% of the bureaucracy had been computerized even after 20 years of e-governance in India.

- *Inflexibility of bureaucracy*: The reluctance to use ICT for government offices has led to a huge failure in proliferation of e-governance. Government servants with a conventional mindset are accustomed to manual mode of work. This impedes e-governance implementation.
- *Absence of sufficient infrastructure*: Owing to lack of infrastructure such as internet connectivity, public access infrastructure, uninterrupted power supply and so on, e-governance will not be realized.
- *Top down model of Indian bureaucracy*: The entire planning and design of e-governance system has been done with a top driven policy mindset. Bottom-up, demand-driven development objectives, in addition to the usual top-down, supply-driven objectives would prove more effective. The exclusive top-down model of the bureaucracy inhibited the expression and appreciation of the real needs of final recipients of e- governance.

Social Hurdles

Digital divide: It is defined as the disparity between haves and have-nots of computers and the internet. The disparity in digital access spans across age, gender, regions, language, income and more. However, the most neglected have been people with low income (particularly those below the poverty line), rural backgrounds (especially remote villages with negligible electricity) and women. Due to lack of access to ICT, they have been deprived of the benefits of digitalization and good governance.

Lack of content in local languages: Most of the content in government websites as well as the content in keyboard is in English. There is an implicit assumption that recipients of e-governance will know this foreign language and decipher the benefits described in this language construction. English education in India is not as widespread as one would like to believe. There seems to be a pervasive attitude of 'taking for granted' that English would easily be the link language between suppliers and recipients of e-governance when almost 70% of India's population live in villages and are deprived of English literacy. Even those in the urban centres suffer from the same deprivation. Naturally, this language barrier precludes people from taking part in e-governance.

The exclusive emphasis on English limits the role of ICTs in e-governance. There is less outreach since translation software is as yet in the nascent stage. The Department of Information Technology started a web-based translation facility in October 2008 to help Indians translate from English to regional languages. The facility allowed for machine translation of six Indian languages from English and bi-directional translation of nine Indian languages. It also included 'cross lingual information access' wherein net search results were available in Hindi, English and one of the six regional languages. This translation facility would enable internet users to overcome their linguistic limitations and access web content in several languages (Prasad, 2012).

Gender Divide: Women face a serious digital barrier due to this gender role. India represents a staunchly patriarchal society where women's education, career opportunities and well-being are highly constrained. Given the widespread son preference, women get discriminatory treatment and access to life chances. A huge proportion of women, without basic literacy, cannot access ICT services to take advantages of e-governance. They face constraints in entering public kiosks or internet cafés mostly run or used by men and in many social and cultural groups women are not allowed to visit these places alone. The marginalization of women in technological education not only creates a lack of awareness but also keeps them out of production of IT, whether as internet content providers, programmers, designers, inventors or fixers of computers as well as from decision making on structures in IT in our country.

CONCLUSION

The degree of e-governance development in the country is dependent on the collective national and local capital supplying IT services. It also relies on informal social and human capital creating a demand for e-governance. The supply side calls for public officials and citizens to be able to access the internet which is contingent upon the country's modern resources and political openness.

Governance is a domain of politicians and administrators for public-sector decision making. By introducing technology in governance, the pace for organizational innovations and processes of change has been set. It has been observed that ICT has not only brought about transformation in the public sector performance but also overcome problems of democracy such as distribution of public services and pubic resources. When technology meets governance, it builds professional bureaucracy skilled in analytics, data management and organizational decision making. This would curb politicization of bureaucracy as well as technological determinism. This chapter examined some of these issuses.

Preparatory Questions

- How is bureaucracy a boon as well as a bane for people?
- What do you understand by e-governance?
- What are the five elements of e-governance?

- List the different e-governance initiatives in India.
- Discuss the advantages of e-Passport Seva.
- Examine the challenges in e-governance.

REFERENCES

Singh, A. (2002) 'Digital Opportunities for All: Report Card.' 28th G8 Summit Kananaskis, Canada June 26-27.

Prasad, K. (2012) 'e-Governance policy for modernizing government through digital democracy in India'. Journal of Information Policy. 2. pp. 183–203.

Rawal, K. L. (2007) 'e-Governance in India: Initiatives and Issues by R. P Sinha'. *Indian Journal of Industrial Relations*. 42(4). Trade Unions And Civil Society: Papers Submitted for IIRA Asian Regional Congress. pp. 757–761.

Pierre, R. and Finger, M. (2007) *Proceeding of the First International Conference on Theory and Prachice of electronic governance*. New York. ACM.

Saxena, A. (2005) 'e-Governance and Good Governance: The Indian context.' *The Indian Journal of Political Science*. 66(2). pp. 313–328.

Sengupta, D. and Julka, H. (2011) 'Lack IPV6 networks may lead to IPV4 Black markting'. *Economic Times*. June 8.

Sumanjeet, (2006) 'e-Governance: An Overview in the Indian Context'. *The Indian Journal of Political Science*. 67(4). pp. 857–866.

Websites:

Available from: http://deity.gov.in/content/national-e-governance-plan (Accessed Dec 2014)

Available from: http://www.akshaya.kerala.gov.in/index.php/history (Accessed Nov 2014)

Available from: http://www.akshaya.kerala.gov.in/index.php/e-literacy (Accessed Nov 2014)

Available from: http://www.akshaya.kerala.gov.in/index.php/platform-for-services (Accessed Nov 2014)

Available from: http://www.akshaya.kerala.gov.in/index.php/educational-programs (Accessed Nov 2014)

Available from: http://www.akshaya.kerala.gov.in/index.php/entegramam (Accessed Oct 2014)

Available from: http://www.dhar.nic.in/GYANDOOT.htm (Accessed Oct 2014)

Available from: http://passportindia.gov.in/AppOnlineProject/online/knowPassportSeva (Accessed Nov 2014)

Chapter Twenty Six

Redressal of Grievances and Right to Information

Sweta Mishra

LEARNING OBJECTIVES

After completing this chapter, you should be able to:

- Describe the machinery for redressal of citizens' grievances
- Discuss the significance of Right to Information (RTI) as one of the important grievance redressal machanisms
- Provide important provisions of RTI Act; and
- Analyse the accountability tools for RTI

INTRODUCTION

Administration is an integral part of citizens and vice versa; the two are completely intertwined. The basic aim of administration is the welfare of people, that is, providing them the basic amenities of life, such as, education, health, electricity, employment opportunities, safe drinking water, better infrastructure and so on. The success of any administrative system depends on the efficient and effective delivery of these services to the citizens.

The administration on its own cannot deliver effective goods and services to citizens. It needs their support and cooperation. In other words, citizens should become active participants in the process of service delivery and should cooperate with administration. In fact, in the contemporary context, the powers and functions of the State have increased manifold and the scope of administration has widened. It plays a very important role in the socioeconomic development of the country and in this process, has acquired immense discretionary powers and prerogatives.

It is generally felt that in the exercise of vast administrative powers, there is always scope for malpractices, corruption and harassment of the citizens. It is being increasingly realized that the existing mechanism for the redressal of citizens' grievances is inadequate to safeguard the citizens against the arbitrary use and misuse of power by the administrators and the public authorities. This realization has attracted many to revisit the Scandinavian office of ombudsman, especially in the democratic countries. This chapter attempts to discuss the various initiatives with regard to the grievance redressal mechanism in general and Right to Information (RTI) in particular.

MACHINERY FOR THE REDRESSAL OF CITIZENS' GRIEVANCES

According to Robson (1956), 'The achievement of good relations between the government and the public is a matter which does not by any means depend solely on the conduct of the civil servants and politicians. It depends equally on the attitude of citizens, groups, corporations, associations of all kinds and, indeed, of all unofficial bodies to public authorities. If we want public servants to behave well towards us, we must behave well towards them'.

This 1950s observation holds true even today. In a democracy, proper machinery for the redressal of citizens' grievances becomes imperative. It is the citizens who elect their representatives and give them the power to govern, and in return they expect them to work for people's welfare. If the public authorities do not produce results as per the needs and aspirations of citizens and start misusing the power, the whole purpose of democracy is defeated. In such a situation, there is a need for a machinery through which citizens can get their grievances ventilated.

According to Chambers Dictionary, grievance means 'a ground of complaint; a condition felt to be oppressive or wrongful'. A grievance may arise due to the *non-fulfilment* of certain demands and expectations on the part of the public authorities. A grievance, thus, needs to be *redressed*. Keeping this in mind, a number of countries all over the world have made a number of provisions to this effect and India is no exception.

OMBUDSMAN: THE SCANDINAVIAN INSTITUTION

Ombudsman is the earliest democratic institution for the redressal of public grievances. It was first established in Sweden in 1809 and later in Finland in1919, Denmark in 1955, Norway and New Zealand in 1962 and the UK in 1967. It is a device for controlling not only the ever growing powers of bureaucracy but also an effective agency for redressal of citizens' grievances. It is effective in taking necessary corrective measures against cases of maladministration or wilful neglect on the part of the administrators (Jain, 1976, p. 359).

Ombudsman, originally a Swedish word, refers to 'an officer appointed by the legislature to handle complaints against administrative and judicial action' (Rowat, 1968, pp. 7–36). It refers to a person who acts as a representative of another person. An ombudsman is generally considered as a person who is commissioned to protect citizens against any possible maladministration. The important features of the ombudsman are as follows:

- S/he is an officer of the legislature and not of the executive. S/he is appointed by the legislature and is free to report back to it at any time.
- S/he is a protector of the rights of the citizens. S/he also supervises administration on the day-to-day functioning of the governments.
- S/he is an impartial investigator and is politically independent even of the legislature. Her/his office is provided for in the Constitution, and once s/he has begun the investigation of a case, the legislators do not and cannot intervene.
- S/he has the power to investigate on her/his own initiative on the basis of information s/he might acquire from inspections, press reports or other sources.
- Conduct investigations informally. In investigating complaints, the ombudsman has free access to all the files of the administration and s/he can demand explanations from the official authorities concerned. Administrative tribunals and courts, on the other hand, are bound by formal rules in hearing cases and have more limited powers of inspection.
- Handle appeals against administrative decisions through methods that are – unlike those of the courts – direct, informal, speedy and cheap. In order to initiate on appeal, all that is required is that the complainant should write a letter (Rowat, 1968, pp. 7–36).

After the success of ombudsman in Scandinavian as well as in the Commonwealth countries, a number of countries all over the world have created ombudsman-like institutions with different nomenclatures and functions. This institution has attracted considerable attention in India too.

GRIEVANCE REDRESSAL MECHANISM IN INDIA

After Independence, many measures were initiated by the government for the redressal of citizens' grievances. At the national level, there are primarily *two* nodal agencies which look into the grievances of the citizens. These agencies are (i) Department of Administrative Reforms and Public Grievances, Ministry of Personnel, Public Grievances and Pensions and (ii) Directorate of Public Grievances, Cabinet Secretariat. Apart from these two nodal agencies of grievance redressal, there are some other institutions. Let us discuss them:

The Central Vigilance Commission

The Central Vigilance Commission (CVC) was set up in 1964, as a follow-up of the recommendations of the Santhanam Committee, by the executive resolution of the Government of India. It is a non-statutory body. It falls within the jurisdiction of the Ministry of Personnel. It is headed by a Central Vigilance Commissioner, who is appointed by the President of India for a period of six years or till the age of 65 years, whichever is earlier. S/he cannot be removed or suspended from office except in the manner provided for the removal or suspension of the chairperson of the UPSC.

After retirement, the Central Vigilance Commissioner cannot accept any further employment under the central or state governments. In addition to the Commissioner, the commission has a number of functionaries such as secretary, officer on special duty, chief technical commissioner, commissioners for departmental enquiries, undersecretaries and technical commissioners. The jurisdiction of the Commission covers all employees in public undertakings, corporate bodies and other institutions working under the central government, the Delhi Metropolitan Council and New Delhi Municipal Committees. The scope of the CVC's authority is as follows:

- It deals with cases in which a public servant is suspected or alleged to have acted in a corrupt way or for an improper purpose.
- It asks for reports from agencies in order to control and supervise them and make an overall vigilance on them.
- It can take over under its direct control complaints for further action. Such action may be either (a) to ask the Central Bureau of Investigation, the principal investigating agency of the union government, to register a regular case and investigate it or (b) to enlist it for enquiry by the Central Bureau of Investigation or the agency concerned.
- It may initiate review of procedures and practices of investigation in so far as they maintain integrity in administration.

The Santhanam Committee on Prevention of Corruption also made detailed recommendations with regard to strengthening of the vigilance organization in each ministry/department in order to make it more effective. The secretary of the department has the primary responsibility for the maintenance of integrity and efficiency in his organization. In each ministry/department, an officer designated as Chief Vigilance Officer (CVO) is entrusted with the vigilance work. S/he acts as a link between the CVC and the ministries/departments. Another officer, designated as Vigilance Officer (VO), is attached to the subordinate offices and public sector undertakings. The CVO coordinates the work of the VOs of his/her ministry/department. The CVC coordinates and monitors the vigilance work of various ministries. The CVC is also empowered to ask for reports, returns or statements from all ministries/departments in order to have a general check and supervision over them to minimize corruption. Apart from this, the CVC can also take over any case under its direct control.

In each state, there is a State Vigilance Commission (SVC). There is also a Special Police Establishment (SPE) to deal with cases of corruption in both the state government offices and state public undertakings. The SVC is headed by a commissioner whose status is at least that of a High Court judge. He is appointed for a term of five years. Besides, there is a commissioner for departmental inquiries, whose function is to conduct such inquiries under charges of corruption. The SVC presents an annual report to the state government and the same is placed before the state legislature. The SVC performs similar functions as that of a CVC. At the district level, there is a District Vigilance Officer (DVO), who is appointed by the district collector from among the gazetted officers. Thus, there has emerged a *web* of vigilance agencies in the country. These agencies are responsible for ensuring accountability of government servants through the vigilance mechanism.

Lokpal and Lokayukta

The first Administrative Reforms Commission (ARC), constituted in 1966, gave priority to the problem of redressal of citizens' grievances and recommended the creation of an ombudsman-type institution in order to remove the sense of injustice from the minds of adversely affected citizens and also to instil public confidence in the efficiency of the administrative machinery (Jain, 1976, p. 376). After a careful examination of the difficulties in adopting the Scandinavian institution in India, the Commission felt that it was desirable and possible to establish independent authorities for the redressal of citizens' grievances. The ARC recommended the establishment of two special authorities designated as Lokpal and Lokayukta. The *Lokpal* was intended to deal with the complaints against administrative acts of ministers and secretaries to the government at the central and state levels and the *Lokayuktas* in every state, dealing with complaints against administrative acts of specified top officials.

The Lokpal and the Lokayuktas were to be independent of the executive as well as the legislature and the judiciary. The investigations and proceedings were to be conducted in private and were to be informal in character. Their appointment, as far as possible, was to be non-political. Their proceedings were not to be subject to judicial interference. The ARC, based on these features, recommended that a draft bill be introduced in the Parliament for establishing these two institutions with regard to Lokpal and Lokayukta. The recommendations of the ARC were accepted by the Government of India, and accordingly in May, 1968 a Bill named *Lokpal and Lokayukta Bill*, 1968 was introduced in the Lok Sabha. It was passed by the Lok Sabha on August 20, 1968 and was then sent to the Rajya Sabha for consideration. However, the Bill could not be passed as the Lok Sabha was dissolved in December 1970.

The Bill was once again introduced in the Lok Sabha in 1971, but could not be passed. Since then several attempts have been made till date to establish these institutions but due to various reasons the Bill could not be passed. However, upon failure of the Lokpal Bill, some of the states have initiated the Lokayukta Bill. Odisha was the first state to pass the Lokayukta Act and create the institution of Lokayukta in 1970.

After this, many states have followed suit and created the institution of Lokayukta – Maharashtra in 1972, Rajasthan in 1973, Bihar in 1974, UP in 1975, Karnataka in 1979, Madhya Pradesh in 1981, Andhra Pradesh in 1983, Gujarat in 1986, Punjab in 1995 and so on. These states have constituted the Lokayuktas to investigate the allegations or grievances arising out of the conduct of public servants including political executives, legislators, officers of the state government, local bodies, public enterprises and other instruments of the government.

In most states, the tenure of the Lokayukta is five years or till he attains the age of 65 years, whichever is earlier with no provision for reappointment. As far the structure of the Lokayukta is concerned, there are some *variations* in the different states. The Lokayukta is usually responsible to the legislature of the state. The Lokayuktas have the power to start investigations at their own initiative and can call for relevant files or documents from the state government if necessary for their investigation.

The functions of the Lokayuktas are as follows:

- Lokayukta can accept and investigate any complaint involving allegation or grievance against administration from any citizen, without making the facts and information public
- While examining the validity of the complaint, the Lokayukta acts like a civil court
- Lokayukta, on investigation, has to make a recommendation to the state legislature in the form of a written report
- Lokayukta must inform the complainant about the corrective measures, if any, taken by the state legislature

The working of the Lokayuktas in different states clearly shows that though the Lokayuktas have been vested with the above-mentioned powers, they are not *allowed* to exercise these powers in a proper manner. They hardly get the support from the state's political leadership in performing these functions. Instead of supporting it, the leadership always interferes and does not allow the Lokayuktas to function in an independent and impartial manner, possibly for fear of being *exposed*. As no party is free of corruption, Lokayuktas may not be able to address the issue of corruption effectively (Jain, 1976, p. 396).

The Lokayuktas are mostly surrounded by controversies and have suffered as a result of the apathy of the state governments. This is quite evident from the fact that in Andhra Pradesh, the then governor Kumudben Joshi did not endorse the nomination for the office of Lokayukta made by the then Chief Minister N. T. Rama Rao, leading to the abolition of the institution for a while. Another example can also be quoted over here. In Odisha, Chief Minister J. B. Patnaik's reluctance held up the appointment of Lokayukta for as many as four years. In 1992, investigations against some ministers of the Biju Patnaik government were taken up by the Lokayukta but ultimately the institution itself was abolished (Sarkar, 2010, p. 298).

Similarly in Maharashtra, when investigations by the Lokayukta revealed that two ministers of the state government were guilty of malpractice, the report was regarded to be a politically motivated one. In case of Bihar, the Lokayukta was virtually forced to close a case on the conduct of a minister because the state government did not provide a report for almost eight years (Sarkar, 2010, p. 298.). There are many such *instances* which go to show that the Lokayuktas are being constantly obstructed in performance of their functions.

These examples present a negative picture of the working of the Lokayukta as an institution. However, there are some glaring examples when the Lokayukta has come forward and tried to weed out corruption prevailing in the various state institutions; but such examples are few and far between. In 2010 in Karnataka, the Lokayukta, Mr Santosh Hegde, had exposed major irregularities in mines in Bellary, including those owned by Obulapuram Mining Company and by the prominent politicians, who were then ministers in the government of Karnataka. The Lokayukta's report uncovered major violations and systemic corruption in iron ore mining in Bellary. It recommended banning all exports of iron ore and limiting iron ore production for captive production of iron and steel.

In another example, Delhi's Lokayukta, Justice Manmohan Sarin, acting on the complaint filed by Dr Harsh Vardhan against incumbent Chief Minister Smt. Sheila Dixit ruled that regularization of colonies in 2008 by the Delhi government was done for political mileage (Grover, 2013). Keeping in view the importance of the institutions of Lokpal and Lokayukta and the non-willingness on the part of the political leaders to pass the Lokpal Bill and establish the above institutions, there was a *Jan Andolan* in our country in 2011, led by social activist, Anna Hazare and his team to get this Bill passed. This did fructify and the Lokpal Bill has been passed in January 2014. More such independent and adequately powerful vigilance bodies need to be established in order to prevent or control high-level corruption in government institutions (Sarkar, 2010, p. 305).

In whatever manner the institutions of Lokpal and Lokayukta are created in future, one thing must be kept in mind, as suggested by the ARC in its Interim Report on Problems of Redress of Citizens' Grievances, in the following words: 'the setting up of these authorities is not the complete answer to the problem of redressal of citizens' grievances. They only provide the ultimate set-up for such redressal, it is not available through the normal departmental or governmental machinery and do not absolve the department from fulfilling its obligations to the citizens for administering its affairs without generating, as far as possible, any legitimate sense of grievance' (ARC Report, 1966, p. 426). The enactment of the RTI Act is a welcome step in this direction.

RIGHT TO INFORMATION ACT

RTI has emerged as a prominent concern in the field of public administration and is regarded as one of the most important social innovations of this century in the field of grievance redressal mechanism. It has become an important area of discussion in the present times. It continues to be advocated as a pertinent component of policy packages to *improve* governance in developing countries. In fact, it has become an important instrument through which openness, transparency and accountability can be brought about in the governance process and citizens' grievances redressed. It also strengthens the foundations of grassroots democracy through people's participation in local governance and development activities. In other words, RTI is a basic necessity of good governance.

RTI has been derived from the Universal Declaration of Human Rights (UDHR) 1948. According to Article 19 of UDHR, 'everyone has the right to freedom of opinion and expression without any interference and to seek information, receive and impart ideas through any media regardless of frontiers'. It is a fundamental human right and the touchstone for all freedoms to which UN is consecrated (UN General Assembly Resolution, 1946). Sweden was the first country to provide this freedom to its citizens way back in 1766. This freedom was part of the Freedom of the Press Act. It was incorporated as a reaction towards excessive administrative secrecy as also press censorship.

However, the other countries adopted it quite late. It was in the last decade of the 20th century and beginning of 21st century that many countries made provisions for this freedom. In 1951, Finland enacted a law providing for the Freedom of Information (FOI). Denmark and Norway followed suit in 1970. The US enacted the Act in 1966 and later on amended it in 1974. The Act provides the individuals a right to *access* information and in case the information is not provided, the government has to justify the reason for *not* providing the information.

Countries such as Austria, France and the Netherlands made such provisions during the 1970s, whereas Australia, Canada and New Zealand enacted the FOI Act during the early 1980s. Britain, since the very beginning, believed in maintaining secrecy. It had the Official Secrets Act, which was put aside when the FOI Act was enacted there in 2000 and amended in 2005. The British Act provides for public access to all types of 'recorded' information held by the government departments, local authorities and other public bodies. Robin Bell and Helen Watchirs in their paper 'Freedom of Information: The Commonwealth Experience' (1988), agree on some common features of FOI in developed countries.

Features of FOI in developed countries are as follows:

- Legal right of access to government records without a demonstrated need to know
- Specific exemptions to protect natural security, personal privacy, law enforcement and the like
- Where access is refused, a right of appeal lies independent of government officials (Bell and Watchirs, 1988, p. 297)

THE INDIAN SCENARIO

In India, the disclosure of government information is governed by a law which was enacted during the British rule. This law was the Official Secrets Act of 1889, which was amended in 1923. This Act secures information related to security of the State, sovereignty of the country and friendly relations with foreign States and contains provisions which prohibit disclosure of non-classified information.

The right to FOI is not explicitly provided for in the Indian Constitution. However, Article 19(1)(a) of the Constitution, which confers the Right to Freedom of Speech and Expression, includes RTI when read with Article 19 of UDHR. Even the Supreme Court of India interprets this right as part of Article 19(1)(a). The Supreme Court, way back in 1975, expressed this proposition in a landmark judgement in the State of UP vs. Raj Narain case (Chadah, 2006, pp. 5–6).

Since this judgement, the Supreme Court has time and again talked about giving right to FOI to the citizens so that they can express their informed opinion on the functioning of the government as well as the public institutions and can also get their grievances redressed. Apart from this, there has been political commitment too with regard to the citizens' RTI. In 1977, the Janata Party promised an open government and declared that it would not misuse the intelligence services and governmental authority for 'personal and partisan ends' (Guha Roy, 2003, p. 313). After coming to power in 1977, the then Prime Minister, Shri Morarji Desai, constituted a working group, which was supposed to modify the Official Secrets Act to facilitate greater flow of information to the public; however, the working group did not suggest any change in the Act.

The second attempt in this direction was made in 1989 in the wake the people's frustration towards the Congress government headed by Shri Rajiv Gandhi. The Government was not ready to disclose information relating to Bofors and other deals (Guha Roy, 1990, p. 493). The National Front, in its election manifesto, talked about its commitment to 'open government and declared in very clear terms that it would guarantee the citizen's RTI through Constitutional provisions. After coming to power, the National Front government headed by Shri V. P. Singh promised to amend the Official Secrets Act in order to make the functioning more transparent as also to provide for RTI in the Constitution. However, this commitment died a premature death, as the government collapsed before completing its term.

As a result of these efforts, the demand for RTI got intensified and took the shape of mass movement. Subsequently, the National Democratic Alliance government introduced the FOI Bill, 2000 in the Parliament. The Bill was finally passed in 2002. Meanwhile, some of the state governments successfully enacted the RTI laws. These states were Tamil Nadu (1997), Goa (1997), Rajasthan (2000), Karnataka (2000), Delhi (2001), Maharashtra (2002), Madhya Pradesh (2003), Assam (2002) and Jammu and Kashmir (2004). The Maharashtra and Delhi state level enactments are considered to have been most widely used. However, the Tamil Nadu Act has imposed several restrictions on the application of the Right.

PROVISIONS OF RIGHT TO INFORMATION ACT, 2005

The doomed FOI Act led to sustained pressure for a better national RTI enactment. Accordingly, the RTI Bill, 2005 was enacted by the United Progressive Alliance government. The Act came fully into force on October 13, 2005. The Act provides to the citizens of India access to records of the central and state governments. As per the Provisions of the Act, any citizen (including the citizens within Jammu and Kashmir) may request information from a public authority, which is required to reply expeditiously or within thirty days. As per the Act, every public authority is required to computerize their records for wide dissemination and to proactively publish certain categories of information so that the citizens need minimum recourse to request for information formally.

The Act applies to all states and union territories of India, except Jammu and Kashmir (RTI Act, Section 1(1)), as it is covered under a state law. It includes within its ambit all the Constitutional authorities, Including the legislature, executive and judiciary – both at the central and state levels – Panchayati raj institutions and the local bodies. It also applies to those bodies or authorities which are owned or controlled or substantially financed by the government. Even those NGOs, which are substantially financed, directly or indirectly, by the government, are in the purview of the Act. The Act, however, does not apply to the private sector.

DEFINITION OF RIGHT TO INFORMATION

A person seeking information may submit a request in writing or through electronic form to the Public Information Officer (PIO) of the concerned office (RTI Act, Section 6(i)). The application shall be accompanied with the prescribed fee of Rs 10. The particulars of the information required must be specified in the application. The reply is to be given within 30 days of receipt of the application or the request can be rejected for reasons as specified under the Act (RTI Act, Section 7). However, if life or liberty of any person is involved, the PIO is expected to reply within 48 hours. The Act also talks about the role of the government in order to make the Act functional (RTI Act, Section 26). The Act enjoins the central and the state governments to initiate necessary steps to achieve the following:

- Develop educational programmes for the public, especially disadvantaged communities on RTI.
- Encourage the public authorities to participate in the development and organization of such programmes.
- Promote timely dissemination of accurate information to the public.
- Train officers and develop training materials.
- Compile and disseminate a user guide for the public in the respective official language.
- Provide public names, designations, postal addresses and contact details of PIOs and other information such as notices regarding fees to be paid and remedies available in law if request is rejected.

RTI Act, Section 2(j) specifies that citizens have a right to the following:

- Request any information (as defined)
- Take copies of documents
- Inspect documents, works and records
- Take certified samples of materials of work
- Obtain information in form of printouts, tapes, CDs, DVDs, or in any other electronic mode

SIGNIFICANCE OF RTI

Emphasizing the importance of the RTI for achieving good governance and also as a grievance redressal mechanism, the *First Report of the Second ARC* has made the following observations:

- Without good governance, no amount of developmental schemes can bring improvements in the quality of life of the citizens.
- Good governance has four elements – transparency, accountability, predictability and participation. Transparency refers to availability of information to the general public and clarity about functioning of governmental institutions.

RTI opens up government's records to public scrutiny, thereby arming citizens with a vital tool to inform them about what the government does and how effectively; thereby making the government more accountable. Transparency in government organizations makes them function more objectively, thereby enhancing predictability. Information about functioning of government also enables citizens to participate in the governance process effectively. In a fundamental sense, RTI is a basic necessity of good governance (Government of India, 2006, p. 1).

The RTI, if implemented properly, would ensure greater accountability and transparency in governance. It will not only check corruption, secrecy and bureaucratic apathy towards citizens but will also give to the citizens their rightful due. Its effective implementation will create an environment of vigilance which will help promote functioning of a more participatory democracy (Goel, 2007, p. 549).

In a system reeking with corruption and becoming increasingly insensitive to the problems of the disadvantaged citizenry, RTI has shown promise of empowering citizens to ensure accountability and act as an enforcer of good governance (Gandhi, 2009). The RTI Act is a torch-bearer that can lead to more open, accountable, responsive and people-friendly governance.

Elements of good governance needed for RTI to be effective are as follows:

- Transparency
- Predictability
- Accountability
- Participation
- Efficiency

The RTI is a unique and unprecedented effort in strengthening grassroots democracy in India. It is regarded as one of the most important cornerstones of *participatory* democracy because public access to information instils a spirit of accountability and transparency in governance. It is a mechanism through which transparency and accountability is strengthened at every step of the delivery chain, by creating platforms for citizens so that they can articulate their voice and directly engage themselves with the State. The RTI is seen as a corrective instrument, which takes care of the accountability principle.

RTI IN PRACTICE AT THE GRASSROOTS LEVEL

The RTI movement at the grassroots level was initiated by a people's organization called Mazdoor Kisan Shakti Sangathan (MKSS) in Rajasthan under the leadership of Ms. Aruna Roy. However, social activists such as Anna Hazare, Nirmala Deshpande and Pankaj Rai have also contributed in their own way and tried to sensitize the rural masses towards their rights and privileges. MKSS is a registered society set up in 1990 to fight corruption related to departmentally implemented Public Works Programme. RTI supported struggles of rural workers on issue of non-payment of full minimum wages. It also raised issues such as fabricated muster rolls in the works implemented by gram panchayats under *Jawahar Rojgar Yojana*, a centrally sponsored scheme.

The mode of public hearings initiated by MKSS commences with the gathering of people in a village by beat of drums and then a demand for all documents related to works undertaken with public funds. In Rajasthan, the MKSS has organized as a popular movement and demanded information from the panchayats about the quantum of public funds that was available and the manner in which it was spent. By organizing *jan sunvai* or public hearings, they have compelled the panchayat leaders and government officials to account for the development expenditure (Ghosh, 2005, p. 269).

The sarpanches in several villages have paid up the recoveries demanded by the people and *jan-sunvais* have been highly effective in mobilizing villages on the issues of transparency and accountability (Background Paper, 1999, p. 29). By mid-1994, the MKSS was able to mobilize the rural people in formulating a specific demand for copies of financial records of expenditure incurred in the panchayats (Ghosh, 2005 p. 261). The demand for transparency, accountability and redressal through social audit came into being in this manner.

Through the creation of a digitized monitoring system, on-site muster roll verification, proactive disclosure of all records and regular social audits, RTI can be realized (Mishra, 2009, p. 697). In order to realize this, the state governments have come up with different tools. For example, some governments have entered into strategic partnerships with Civil Society Organizations (CSOs) to develop accountability tools. In other parts of the country, one-time mass social audits have been conducted, while others have seen the proliferation of networks of CSOs that have come together to conduct audits, create report cards and monitor the implementation of the Act (Aiyer and Samji, 2012, p. 232).

The following are the accountability tools for RTI:

- Digitized Monitoring System
- On-site Muster Roll Verification
- Proactive Disclosure of Records
- Regular Social Audits
- Vigilant Evaluation System
- Participation of CSOs

The use and importance of RTI at the grassroots level is visible in the Mahatma Gandhi National Rural Employment Guarantee Act (MNREGA), 2005. According to the MNREGA guidelines, all levels of government should maintain proper records containing information on inputs, processes, outputs and outcomes related to MNREGA. In order to ensure that this information is proactively disclosed and made available to the citizens, the MNREGA guidelines stipulate that all information be displayed to the public through display boards and paintings on the walls of the panchayat offices. Apart from this, there is a provision that all the MNREGA accounts and their summaries at the gram panchayat level should be made publicly available for scrutiny (Aiyer and Samji, 2012, p. 235).

For the successful implementation of the RTI, vigilant monitoring, transparency and accountability as well as active participation of the civil society and people is important. In some states, unique partnerships between governments and CSOs have been established. The Andhra Pradesh government, in 2006, embarked on a process to *institutionalize* social audits for all MNREGA programmes in the State. The government collaborated with CSOs and built up a 35-member team which could facilitate and manage the audit process. During the audit, details of government expenditure on MNREGA are verified, assets developed are assessed and information on MNREGA is shared with village communities. The audit ends with a public meeting, where the findings of audit are shared in the presence of local government officials and politicians (Aiyer and Samji, 2012, p. 236).

The government–civil society partnership is also visible in Rajasthan. In November 2007, the Rajasthan government collaborated with the Rozgar *Avam Soochna Ka Adhikar Abhiyaan*, to develop a decentralized worksite management system. The purpose of this *Abhiyaan* has been to create a pool of trained worksite managers that take daily measurements of worksites and determine daily output. The key emphasis is on transparency (Aiyer and Samji, 2012, p. 237).

The above analysis reveals that the RTI at the grassroots level is being implemented through social audits of MNREGA. Although the analysis reveals the success of social audits and in turn success of RTI, there are examples which suggest that the implementation of MNREGA has not been done in a genuinely democratic and decentralized manner. There are instances where correct information has not been provided when sought for. In Manipur, information was sought relating to the beneficiaries of *Indira Awas Yojana*, repairing of a culvert and holding of a panchayat meeting in respect of Bijoy Govinda gram panchayat in Imphal's west district. According to N. Memi, the information provided by the Rural Development and Panchayati Raj Department was tampered, misleading and incorrect (Panchayati Raj Update, Sept. 2008, pp. 3–4).

There are cases of fraud and glaring irregularities in the implementation of MNREGA schemes. The Comptroller and Auditor General (CAG) has noted such irregularities in the case of Karnataka (Panchayati Raj Update, July 2008, p. 6). A sample survey conducted by the Delhi-based Centre for Environment and Food Security in Madhya Pradesh points to a Rs 2100 crore scam in the implementation of schemes. According to the survey, only 25% of scheme funds have been actually spent on providing for the poor and remaining 75% have been siphoned off through fake muster rolls and job cards (Panchayati Raj Update, July 2008, p. 6).

In Delhi, a voluntary organization called *Parivartan* has been quite successful in facilitating the use of RTI in addressing their grievances, getting the pending works done by government departments and also inspecting government works. It is helping the poor people in getting ration cards or receiving their ration quota on Antodaya card under the public distribution system by exercising the RTI (Guha Roy, 2006, p. 15).

Finally, the media has also been playing an effective role in furthering the flow, authenticity and quality of information. The media has to become a responsible and an active participant in increasing awareness among people, lending a voice to the voiceless and generating debate on the use and misuse of RTI and exposing corrupt practices of the government without any fear or favour (Mishra, 2009, p. 701).

> Right to information in words of Veerappa Moily, Chairperson of Second ARC has been seen 'as the key to strengthening participatory democracy and ushering in people-centred governance; access to information can empower the poor and the weaker sections of the society to demand and get information about public policies and actions, thereby leading to their welfare. Therefore, RTI has also been said to be the life blood of democracy'. (Government of India, 2006, p. 1)

CONCLUSION

Thus, we can say that systematic implementation of redressal measures can have a direct impact on the citizens in the sense that they can keep a check on the functioning of the local bodies by asking for information on any works related to the panchayats. The experience gained from the experiment of *jan sunvais* (public hearings) in Rajasthan is a proof that the citizens can no longer be misled or the misutilized. This is a very positive impact of RTI. It is hoped that in near future, the local institutions will reconcile the ethical values with democratic values through participatory and accountable governance processes. The success of RTI depends on the harmonious relationship between the citizens and the administrators. Administration should function in a humane and responsive manner and citizens should meaningfully cooperate with the administrators.

RTI is not only an effective instrument of ensuring decentralized governance by way of citizens' participation but also an effective instrument through which the citizens can get their grievances redressed. Citizens are using this mechanism on a regular basis and pressurizing the government to provide for relevant information with regard to their queries/grievances. In this way, they are getting their grievances redressed to some extent. Citizens' grievances against the administration are on the increase and at the same time, concerted efforts are being made by the government to reduce the growing discontent. This chapter has specifically highlighted the importance of FOI, the various grievance redressal mechanisms, enactment of RTI Act and the Lokpal Bill.

Preparatory Questions

- Critically examine the role of CVC.
- In what way has RTI brought administration closer to the people?
- 'RTI is a means of ensuring good governance'. Comment.
- Discuss the various grievance redressal machineries in India.
- Write a note on Lokpal and Lokayuktas.
- Write an essay on the passage of 'RTI' in India.

REFERENCES

Background Paper (1999) *Background Paper for Seminar on Accountability of Local Bodies and DRDAs*. National Academy of Audit and Accounts, Shimla, 15th and 16th September.

Bell, R. and Watchirs, H. (1998) 'Freedom of Information: The Commonwealth Experience'. *Australian Journal of Public Administration*. XLVII(4).

Chadah, S. (2006) 'Right to Information Regime in India: A Critical Appraisal'. *The Indian Journal of Public Administration*. LII(1).

Chakrabarty, B. and Chand, P. (2012) *Public Administration in a Globalizing World*. New Delhi: Sage.

Ghosh, B. (2005) 'Accountability of Panchayats: Ends and Means' in L. C. (ed.). *Decentralization and Local Governance*. New Delhi: Orient Longman.

Government of India. (1966) 'Administrative Reforms Commission'. *Interim Report on Problem of Redress of Citizens' Grievances*. New Delhi: Government of India.

Government of India. (2006) 'Second Administrative Reforms Commission'. *First Report on Right to Information: Master Key to Good Governance*. Para 1.1.1.

Grover, N. (2013) Colony Goel, S. L. (2007) 'Right to Information and Administrative Reforms'. *The Indian Journal of Public Administration*. LIII(3).

Jain, R. B. (1976) *Contemporary Issues in Indian Administration*. New Delhi: Vishal Publications.

Mishra, S. (2009) 'Right to Information and Decentralized Governance'. *The Indian Journal of Public Administration*. LV(3).

Panchayati Raj Update. (2008) *Institute of Social Sciences*. XV(7).

Robson, W. A. (ed.) (1956) *The Civil Service in Britain and France.* Hogarth Press London.

Rowat, D. C. (1968) 'The Spread of the Ombudsman Idea' in Anderson, S. V. (ed.). *Ombudsman for American Government.* Englewood Cliffs (NJ): Prentice Hall.

Roy, J. G. (1990) 'Open Government and Administrative Culture in India'. *The Indian Journal of Public Administration.* 36(3).

Roy, J. G. (2003) 'Right to Information: A Key to Accountable and Transparent Administration' in Dhameja, A. (ed.). *Contemporary Debates in Public Administration.* New Delhi: Prentice Hall of India.

Roy, J. G. (2006) *Right to Information Initiatives and Impact, Occasional Paper.* New Delhi: Indian Institute of Public Administration.

RTI Act (2005) Section 1(1), Section 2(j), Section 6(i), Section 7 and Section 26.

Sarkar, S. (2010) *Public Administration in India.* New Delhi: PHI.

UN General Assembly Resolution (1946) 59(1), 65th Plenary Meeting, December 14.

Websites:

(2013) Regularization: Delhi Lokayukta Slams Dikshit's Poll Gimmick. *Firstpost* November 5. Available from: www.firstpost.com

Aiyer, Y. and Samji, S. (2012) 'Guaranteeing Good Governance: Understanding the Effectiveness of Accountability Mechanisms' in NREGA. *The National Rural Employment Guarantee Act Design, Process and Impact,* NREGA Knowledge Network. Available from: indiagovernance.gov.in/files/strengtheningpublicaccountability (Accessed 16th August 2014)

Available from: en.wikipedia.org/wiki/N_Santosh_Hedge (Accessed 17th September 2014)

Gandhi, S. (2009) 'Right to Information – A Tool to Improve the Governance of India.' Available from: http://www.bcasonline.org (Accessed 18th October 2014)

Chapter Twenty Seven

Social Welfare Administration and Protection of Weaker Sections

Sachin Chowdhry

LEARNING OBJECTIVES

After completing this chapter, you should be able to:

- Define a Welfare State
- Provide a conceptual framework of social welfare
- Reflect upon the various welfare measures under Five Year Plans in India
- Discuss the important protective measures for the disadvantaged sections
- Describe the key components of development strategy for weaker sections; and
- Explain the administrative arrangements for ensuring effective social welfare administration

INTRODUCTION

Social welfare is based on the ideas that 'social justice is the first virtue of social institutions' and that democratic governing principles should ensure equitable distribution of resources and benefits of development among population. Social welfare can be discussed at two levels – at the level of the individual and also at more collective forms of well-being, such as that of a whole community or nation. The dictionary meaning of social welfare is 'organized public or private social services for the assistance of disadvantaged groups'. Here it is important to understand that social welfare has broader connotations than the terms such as 'social service', 'social work' or 'social security'. In fact, it includes all three and much more.

This chapter attempts to explain the meaning of social welfare. It underlines the evolution of the term and examines the nature of welfare administration in India, with special reference to social welfare measures through Five Year Plans. The welfare strategies towards weaker sections are also discussed in detail. These sections include scheduled castes (SCs), scheduled tribes (STs), women, children, people with disabilities, minorities and backward classes in general. For clarity and better understanding of the concept of welfare, we have divided the chapter into five separate sections, each dealing with a different aspect of welfare. Let us first try to comprehend the concept of social welfare.

CONCEPT OF SOCIAL WELFARE

The term social welfare can be traced back to written sources from the 14th century but has a much older oral tradition. However, some scholars have pointed out that the term originated in the Beveridge Report of the UK. The State, in its welfare functions, focuses on the socioeconomic development of weaker sections of the society. Such welfare functions are performed both by the government and non-governmental organizations/voluntary agencies. Although both public and private agencies are involved in the process, it is people's well-being through State intervention that impacts a larger population. All countries in the world have varying degrees of such functions, which is why they are also called welfare States.

> The Report of the Inter-Departmental Committee on Social Insurance and Allied Services, known commonly as the Beveridge Report, was an influential document in paving the way for the welfare State in the UK. It was chaired by William Beveridge. Five 'giant evils' such as squalor, ignorance, want, idleness and disease were identified in the Report and widespread reforms were proposed.

To some, a welfare State is synonymous with the concept of the State and embraces the whole political and economic organization, as it does in Scandinavian countries. To others, a welfare State is built upon a limited number of social programmes, the aim of which can be to alleviate poverty, protect groups of citizens from certain difficult situations, compensate for loss of income, care for the rights of the citizens, raise quality of life in society, distribute income more evenly or solve social problems in general (Kildal, 2003).

> Encyclopaedia Britannica defines 'welfare State' as a 'system of laws and institutions through which a government attempts to protect and promote the economic and social welfare of its citizens usually based on various forms of social insurance against vulnerabilities'. The Encyclopaedia of Social Sciences defines it as 'the institutional outcome of the assumption by a society of legal and therefore formal and explicit responsibility for the basic well-being of its members'

The conceptualization of welfare State materialized into social programmes for the population at large and for groups in need, and the term welfare State was used to describe these activities. As the social programmes expanded, they became an integrated part of other societal and economic activities, the content of the State changed and today it is difficult to separate welfare State activities from other State activities. Intervention strategies vary from country to country, even if the challenges are similar. In fact, 'States conform to specific societal values' (Leibfried and Obinger, 2001). However, the nature of public arrangements or institutional responses indicates some common ideals and values across the world.

Whether described as an 'institutional redistributive model' (Titmuss, 1958) or a 'social democratic Welfare State regime' (Esping-Andersen, 1990), one of the most distinctive traits of welfare policies is that public benefits are instituted as social rights to high-level benefits. Most of these policies are generally categorical, related to politically defined needs arising in different phases of life such as old age, sickness and unemployment, or disadvantaged sections of the society or in other words, different vulnerabilities. The following section deals with the nature of welfare administration in India.

WELFARE ADMINISTRATION IN INDIA

Gearing up to the demands of joblessness, old-age vulnerabilities, inadequate health services and so on, the Indian State too has responded to the contemporary challenges in an operative manner. The Constitution itself has *several* provisions to bring disadvantaged sections into the mainstream. The fact is that the scope of welfare activities of the State has increased over the years. The *response* may not be of the type of what we find in the Scandinavian countries; however, given the challenges that the Indian State faces, it is noteworthy. Some of the challenges, such as backwardness of certain communities, had historical roots but some arose in the years ahead, way after independence, because of the socioeconomic conditions of the people and resource constraints.

Economic liberalization under globalization in the past two decades has also impacted the State response. The 'neo-liberalism' *discourse* brought the manner of intervention into scrutiny. There has been serious *debate* in recent times as to what should be the role of the State, that is, whether the State should focus on creating the enabling environment and invest more in social sectors or continue pumping subsidies into various programmes.

There are scholars who advocate reducing the scope of direct intervention, based on the findings; like for every rupee that reaches a beneficiary, the cost for the State is three rupees. Analysis of interventions during various Plan periods gives sufficient indications that the scope of welfare activities has increased over the years. The strategy has been twin-fold – *protective* and *developmental*. Several Constitutional and statutory provisions have been laid down for the protection of weaker sections and many developmental programmes have been designed for direct and indirect benefits of the target groups.

SOCIAL WELFARE IN FIVE YEAR PLANS

The *First Five Year Plan* sought to deepen the unity of the people and harness it for economic development and cultural achievement through social welfare.

The First Five Year Plan mentioned that 'the object of social welfare is the attainment of social health, which implies the realization of such objectives as adequate living standards, the assurance of social justice, opportunities for cultural development through individual and group self-expressions, and re-adjustment of human relations leading to social harmony. A comprehensive concept of living standards will include the satisfaction of basic needs such as food, clothing and shelter as well as normal satisfactions of family life, enjoyment of physical and mental health, opportunities for the expression of skills and recreational abilities, and active and pleasurable social participation'

The First Plan used terms such as 'social service' and 'social work', which implied that the strategy was to extend preventive *cum* curative *cum* rehabilitative services to meet the special needs of the vulnerable groups. These vulnerable groups, it identified, were *women, children, youth, family and under-privileged groups*. It emphasized that 'the central government, the various state governments and local self-governing bodies, each in its own sphere, have to ensure that they have at least the minimum administrative machinery for dealing with social problems'. Alongside, the *importance* of role of private voluntary agencies was also accepted. The regional communities were proposed to be supported by the state.

As part of the First Plan, the central government set up a *Central Social Welfare Board* with the object especially of assisting voluntary agencies in organizing welfare programmes for women and children and the handicapped groups. The board collaborated with State governments and organized State Social Welfare Boards throughout the country. In the *Second Five Year Plan*, proposals were made for provision of *social and moral hygiene and after-care services* by establishing a large number of homes and shelters, education, training and employment and the provision of social and cultural amenities for the physically and mentally handicapped; youth camps and labour service for students to encourage youth participation in constructive national activities; and for juvenile delinquency, vagrancy or beggary and probation.

In this Plan, the suggestion was made that funds available with endowments and trusts may be an important method of supplementing resources, which states and private agencies could raise for social welfare. However, it was observed that despite getting substantial sums for promoting social welfare activities, many trusts became *inactive* later on and that their income was not spent for the purposes originally intended. As a result, unproductive investments occurred.

In the *Third Five Year Plan*, the state governments and the voluntary organizations were associated closely in drawing up the proposals. While providing services, effort was directed in particular towards sections of the community which needed *special care and protection*. The object was to replace individual haphazard relief and charity by organized and sustained activity for education, welfare and rehabilitation with the general support of the community. The resources provided were utilized both for expanding the existing services and for assisting voluntary organizations to continue their activities. To this extent, development of new services tended to be limited.

A review of the development of welfare services showed certain weaknesses such as inadequate attention being paid to the needs of destitute children. Absence of counselling or advisory services, lack of statistical data, deficiencies in management and supervision at the field level and absence of proper coordination between the Central Social Welfare Board and state departments of Social Welfare were noted to be the other *limitations*. Even the expenditure remained much lower than the Plan outlay. The *Fourth Five Year Plan* proposed to organize and expand programmes for the prevention and treatment of *juvenile delinquency, probation, suppression of immoral traffic of women and girls, social and moral hygiene and eradication of beggary.*

The Fourth Five Year Plan proposed to establish statistical cells in the Central and State Departments of Social Welfare and the Central and State Social Welfare Advisory Boards to overcome the problem of absence of statistics and lack of information about the performance of different schemes.

The *Fifth Five Year Plan* gave major thrust to the expansion of *preventive and developmental programmes*. Many innovative programmes were designed.

During the Fifth Five Year Plan period, child welfare was given the highest priority. The scheme Integrated Child Development Services (ICDS) was launched to ensure healthy growth and development of children and reduce infant and maternal mortality rates. Tribal Sub-Plan approach was adopted to focus on welfare measures for tribal population. The Plan proposed to strengthen the linkages of social welfare programmes with economic programmes, which had not fully materialized.

The *Sixth Five Year Plan* stressed that 'areas which were most backward and prone to the handicaps or social disorders should be identified. In these areas, the *most needy families should be identified specially* among the landless agricultural labour, scheduled castes, scheduled tribes and other sections'.

The Sixth Plan proposed to give preference to preventive and developmental services over institutional care, as the latter was very costly and could substitute family care only in exceptional cases. The programmes such as *National Rural Employment Programme* and the beneficiary-oriented *Integrated Rural Development Programme* were expected to contribute substantially in this regard, besides agriculture, animal husbandry, irrigation and other economic activities.

The Sixth Five Year Plan stated that 'social planning should be an integral part of economic planning, and every economic project would build into its study and costs, the social problems and their solutions. While developing infrastructural facilities under major sectors such as power, transport, industries and irrigation, their benefit to the weakest should be specially noted and correctives provided for where necessary'.

The *Seventh Five Year Plan* continued the same strategy as in the Sixth Plan. It noted that welfare services expanded considerably during the previous Plans, particularly in the areas of children and women's welfare. Besides, a variety of programmes for the economically weaker sections were introduced by different ministries at the centre and also by the state governments.

So it emphasized the need for *strengthening the administrative machinery for project identification, formulation and implementation*, particularly at the state level, taking into account the programme content and coverage. As a long-term strategy, it sought the expansion of employment opportunities and stabilization of income, especially among the vulnerable population groups to combat malnutrition and under-nourishment.

The strategy in the *Eighth Five Year Plan* was to ensure that the benefits of development from different sectors did not bypass women. Special programmes were implemented to complement the general development programmes. It sought to ensure that the *targets set for women beneficiaries were reached in the existing poverty alleviation programmes* such as Integrated Rural Development Programme, *Training Rural Youth for Self-Employment and Jawaharlal Rozgar Yojana*. The scheme of *Development of Women and Children in Rural Areas* was proposed to be strengthened. In the programmes of agricultural production, emphasis was on implementation of land reforms, restructuring of agrarian institutions and promotion of rural industries. Child development programmes were also accorded high priority.

The *Ninth Five Year Plan* proposed to prepare a *National Charter for Social Justice* to ensure all-round development of the disadvantaged sections of the society. Thus, approach to social welfare in the Ninth Plan was distinct from the earlier Plans, as it proposed to adopt the following *three-fold* strategy, specific to each individual group: (a) empowering the persons with disabilities; (b) reforming the social deviants and (c) caring for the other disadvantaged. Older persons were included in the strategy as a focussed group.

At the *field* level, the Panchayati Raj Institutions and the Urban Local Bodies were proposed to be actively involved along with the voluntary sector and the community in implementing, coordinating and supervising/monitoring the welfare programmes. Upholding the spirit of 'co-operative federalism', the Ninth Plan sought *more involvement and co-operation from the states/UTs in respect of social welfare/social defence* programmes whose responsibility mainly rested with the State sector.

The *Tenth Five Year Plan* focussed on the agenda of *inclusive approach*. The policy of integrating welfare activities with the developmental programmes continued. This period was contextualized by the broad economic and administrative reforms. So, welfarism was seen from that angle. *Gender budgeting* was also emphasized and included in allocation for programmes.

The *Eleventh Five Year Plan* gave a special impetus to several programmes aimed at *building rural and urban infrastructure* and providing basic services with the objective of *increasing inclusiveness* and reducing poverty. Some of the important programmes which sought to help the welfare of various groups were National Rural Employment Guarantee Scheme, Indira Aawas Yojana, National Rural Health Mission, Pradhan Mantri Gram Sadak Yojana, ICDS, mid-day meals, Jawaharlal Nehru National Urban Renewal Mission, Sarva Shiksha Abhiyan, etc.

The approach paper to the *Twelfth Five Year Plan* emphasizes inclusiveness. At the same time, it accepts that 'the progress towards inclusiveness is more difficult to assess, because inclusiveness is a multidimensional concept'. The paper recognizes the challenges and accepts that along with new policies and government programmes, there is need to bring *institutional and attitudinal changes,* though they may take time.

The Twelfth Five Year Plan acknowledges that the 'inclusive growth should result in lower incidence of poverty, broad-based and significant improvement in health outcomes, universal access for children to school, increased access to higher education and improved standards of education, including skill development. It should also be reflected in better opportunities for both wage employment and livelihood, and in improvement in provision of basic amenities like water, electricity, roads, sanitation and housing'. It reiterates the commitment to the needs of the SC/ST and other backward classes (OBCs) population, as well as women and children. Minorities and other excluded groups too have been focussed upon to bring them into the mainstream.

PROTECTIVE MEASURES FOR DISADVANTAGED SECTIONS

Besides the thrust on social welfare in the Five Year Plans, the Constitution of India guarantees protection from social *injustice and all forms of exploitation* (Art. 46). It guarantees equality before law (Art. 14), and enjoins upon the State not to discriminate against any citizen on grounds of caste (Art. 15 (1)). Untouchability stands abolished and its practice in any form is forbidden (Art. 17). The Constitution mandates that no citizen shall, on grounds only of caste or race, be subjected to any disability and restriction (Art. 15 (2)).

It empowers the State to make provisions for reservation in educational institutions (Art. 15 (4) and (5)), and in appointments for posts in favour of SCs (Art. 16 (4), 16 (4A), 16 (4B) and Art. 335). Reservation of seats for SCs in the Lok Sabha is provided under Article 330, in the state assemblies under Article 332 and in the local self-governments bodies under Articles 243D and 340T. In addition to the above, the parliament has enacted the Untouchability (Offences) Act, 1955, renamed as

Protection of Civil Rights Act, in 1976. To check and deter atrocities against the SCs and STs, the Scheduled Castes and the Scheduled Tribes (Prevention of Atrocities) Act, 1989 has also been enacted.

The Scheduled Tribes and other Traditional Forest Dwellers (Recognition of Forest Rights) Act, 2006 provides for the right to cultivate forest land to the extent under occupation (subject to a ceiling of 4 hectares); the right to own, collect, use and dispose of minor forest produce; rights inside forests which are traditional and customary, for example, grazing. Women and children have been the priority target groups since the beginning. Of late, increasing crimes against women have led to many legislations such as Dowry Prohibition Act, 1961, Dowry Prohibition (Maintenance of Lists of Presents to the Bride and Bridegroom) Rules 1985 (*see* Box 27.1).

There are many Acts for protecting the children such as The Guardian and Wards Act, 1890, The Immoral Traffic (Prevention) Act, 1956, The Young Persons (Harmful Publications) Act, 1956, The Child Labour (Prohibition and Regulation) Act, 1986, The Pre-Conception and Pre-Natal Diagnostic Techniques (Prohibition of Sex Selection) Act, 1994, The Infant Milk Substitutes, Feeding Bottles and Infant Foods (Regulation of Production, Supply and Distribution) Act, 1992 and its Amendment Act in 2003.

The Prohibition of Child Marriage Act, 2006 was enacted repealing the Child Marriage Restraint Act of 1929. These Acts are primary laws relating to welfare of children (*below* 18 *years of age*) in need of care and protection. The *National Commission for Protection of Child Rights*, a statutory body, was set up in March 2007 under the Commissions for Protection of Child Rights Act, 2005 to ensure that all laws, policies, programmes and administrative mechanisms are in consonance with the child rights perspective, as enshrined in the Constitution of India and also the UN Convention on the Rights of the Child.

Box 27.1 Major Constitutional Acts for the Disadvantaged Sections

- Untouchability (Offences) Act 1955, later renamed as Protection of Civil Rights Act in 1976
- Dowry Prohibition Act, 1961
- Indecent Representation of Women (Protection) Act, 1986
- Child Labour Protection Regulation Act, 1986
- Mental Health Act, 1987
- The Commission of Sati (Protection) Act, 1987
- National Commission for Women Act, 1990
- Persons with Disabilities (Equal Opportunities, Protection of Rights and Full Participation) Act, 1995
- National Trust for Welfare of Persons with Autism, Cerebral Palsy, Mental Retardation and Multiple Disability Act, 1999
- The Juvenile Justice (Care and Protection of Children) Act, 2000
- Protection of Women from Domestic Violence Act, 2005
- The Commission for Protection of Child Rights Act, 2005
- The Prohibition of Child Marriage Act, 2006

Though the Constitution does not make *specific* provisions for OBCs, it empowers the State to make provisions for reservation in appointments or posts in favour of any backward class of citizens which, in the opinion of the State, is not adequately represented in the Services under the State (Art. 16 (4)). In pursuance of the Supreme Court judgement, *Indira Sawhney and Others* versus *Union of India* (1992), the *National Commission for Backward Classes* was set up on 14 August 1993 under the National Commission for Backward Classes Act, 1993, which facilitated 27% reservation in services in the government of India and public sector undertakings.

The State is directed to provide relief and help to the disabled and the unemployable, vide Entry 9 in List II of the Seventh Schedule. Article 41 lays down that the State shall, within the limits of its economic capacity and development, make effective provisions for securing the right to work, to education and to public assistance in cases of unemployment, old age, sickness and disablement. Additionally, there are specific legislations specifically directed towards the protection, welfare, rehabilitation and development of people with disabilities (*see* Box 27.1).

In addition to the legal framework, a comprehensive *National Policy for Persons with Disabilities* had been announced in February 2006. The United Nations Convention on the Rights of People with Disabilities (UNCRPD) was ratified by India in October 2007. It enjoins upon India to ensure that all the rights enshrined in the Constitution, the current legislations, as well as UNCRPD, are speedily and effectively operationalized.

Similarly, measures have been taken for protecting and promoting language, religion and culture of the minorities, as well as making special efforts for their socioeconomic development and mainstreaming. As per the provisions under the National Commission of Minorities Act, 1992, five religious communities including Muslims, Christians, Sikhs, Buddhists and Zoroastrians (*Parsis*) have been notified as minorities.

DEVELOPMENT STRATEGY FOR WEAKER SECTIONS

State intervention in welfare activities and the scope of such activities has increased manifold by including more and more disadvantaged groups over the years. The response appears to be dynamic as a lot many protective measures have been taken in the recent past. Similarly, linking of various developmental activities with the benefits for the weaker sections has led to increased investments and expenditures in the welfare activities.

Development of Scheduled Tribes (STs)

The tribal communities differ in their socioeconomic levels, educational attainments and cultural milieus. This has affected the implementation of development programmes for many years. Funding for the tribal development programme was only 1% of the total Plan outlay in the First Plan. The Second Plan saw 0.60% of total Plan outlay committed to such programmes. It reduced to 0.10% in the Third Plan and was only 0.50% in the Fourth Plan. Incidentally, many of the development activities such as construction of dams, mines, industries and roads were located on tribal lands but did not benefit the tribals. This led to adoption of Tribal Sub-Plan (TSP) approach in the Fifth Five Year Plan (Taradutt, 2001).

> The TSP approach is credited to Prof. S. C. Dube, who was the chairperson of the expert committee set by Ministry of Education and Social Welfare in 1972. Initially, the strategy involved 18 states and UTs. Today the number has increased to 21 states and UTs. Arunanchal Pradesh, Meghalaya, Mizoram and Nagaland do not have this approach as more than 80% population in these states is tribal and hence the entire Plan of these states is for tribals

Integrated Tribal Development Projects (ITDPs) were constituted in tribal majority blocks. The objective of the programmes was to benefit majority of tribal population, as more than 50% of the population in these blocks was tribal. Later on, in the Sixth Plan, those smaller pockets also became part of TSP approach where the tribal population was 50% or more and which were not covered by ITDPs. These pockets were termed as *Modified Area Development Approach* (MADA). The clusters and dispersed tribal groups were also included in the approach later on. Thus today TSP areas include the scheduled areas and non-scheduled areas as well.

Each ITDP/ITDA, MADA cluster formulates a project report for its area every year, conducts assessment and then tailors the programmes accordingly. It is an important focal point of the approach. These project reports in aggregate form the part of TSP of the concerned state. In order to provide focussed attention to the survival, protection and development of 75 identified *Primitive Tribal Groups*, a special scheme was launched in 1998–1999 to provide tribe specific services and support including, *inter alia*, housing, land, agricultural inputs, cattle rearing, health, nutritional services and income generating programmes.

As per the guidelines, the flow of funds to TSP out of the total State Plan outlay should not be less than the proportion of the ST population in the respective state. Special Central Assistance (SCA) is also given by the centre for TSP. It covers the tribal population living below the poverty line. The SCA to TSP is to be utilized as a gap filler to the schemes being taken up out of the TSP funds.

Funds are also granted under Article 275 (1) for promoting the welfare of STs. The National Scheduled Tribes Finance and Development Corporation (NSTFDC) was set up in 2001 to support various income and employment generating activities through loans, marketing support, training, and so on. Special focus is accorded to women beneficiaries under programmes, which facilitate income generating activities through women's Self-help Groups (SHGs).

The State ST Development Corporations, which function as channelling agencies in identifying eligible beneficiaries and extending financial and other assistance to them, are also supported by NSTFDC. The Tribal Cooperative Marketing Development Federation of India Ltd. provides marketing assistance and remunerative prices to STs for collection of Minor Forest Produce (MFPs), and surplus agricultural produce to protect them from exploitative private traders and middlemen.

Development of Scheduled Castes (SCs)

The government adopted the strategy of having a separate development Plan called the Special Component Plan for the SCs in 1978. It was similar to TSP approach. It has recently been renamed the *Scheduled Caste Sub-Plan* (SCSP). All central ministries/departments are expected to formulate SCSP and ensure that the flow of funds to SCSP in their Plans is at least in proportion with the SC population of the country. At present, 17 central ministries/departments have done so. Similarly, 27 States/UTs are implementing SCSP through different mechanisms. However, one *shortcoming* has been noticed in this.

The state governments generally divide their resources into 'divisible' and 'non-divisible' components and earmark funds for SCs only from the divisible pool. As a result, the actual funds flowing directly to SCSP from the total state Plan become much less than the proportion of SC population to the total population of the state. Under *Special Central Assistance to Special Component Plan*, cent per cent assistance is given as additive to SCSP of the states/UTs on the basis of certain criteria such as SC population of the states/UTs and relative backwardness of the States/UTs percentage to enable them to cross the poverty line.

The Tenth Plan adopted a multipronged approach for the socioeconomic development of the SCs: social empowerment through educational development; economic empowerment through income and employment enhancing avenues; protection through effective implementation of protective legislations and eradication of occupations such as manual scavenging and holistic development through earmarking of funds proportionate to the population.

The other programmes include scholarships programmes; providing coaching facilities to students to prepare them for various competitive examinations being conducted by Union Public Service

Commission, State Public Service Commissions, banks and so on and hostel facilities to both boys and girls for pursuing education from middle level onwards.

The scheme of grant-in aid to the Scheduled Castes Development Corporations (SCDCs) was introduced in 1978–1979. The SCDCs finance employment-oriented schemes cover the following:

- Agriculture and allied activities including minor irrigation
- Small-scale industry
- Transport
- Trade and service sector

The National Scheduled Castes Finance and Development Corporation (NSFDC) established in 1989, provides financial and other support to beneficiaries for taking up various income generating activities. The *National Safai Karamcharis Finance and Development Corporation* was established in 1997 to provide financial support to the safai karamcharis (scavengers) to take up various income-generating activities. SCDCs also finance projects by dovetailing the loan component from NSFDC/Banks.

The main guidelines for SCSP and TSP are as follows:

- Earmarking of funds for SCSP and TSP from the total state Plan outlay should at least be proportionate to the SC and ST population of the State/UT
- Making the Social Welfare/Tribal Welfare Department the nodal department for formulation and implementation of SCSP and TSP
- Placing the funds earmarked for SCSP and TSP at the disposal of the Principal Secretary/Secretary, Social Welfare/Tribal Welfare, who will work as Planning Secretary and have exclusive authority for the reallocation of funds to other line departments for SC and ST development schemes
- Backing the SCSP and TSP earmarked funds by 100% budget provision, sanctions and timely release of funds to the line departments and implementing agencies
- Including only those schemes under SCSP and TSP that ensure direct benefits to individuals or families belonging to SCs or STs
- Preparing a detailed SCSP and TSP document with physical and financial targets against each scheme with the objective of bridging the gap between the rest of the population and the SCs and STs within 10 years
- Ensuring that the other line departments cooperate in the proper implementation of the SCSP and TSP schemes allocated to them and put up the schemes to the nodal departments for sanction and release of funds
- Preventing the diversion and lapse of funds allocated to SCSP and TSP in the annual Plans. SCSP and TSP should not be allowed to be changed at revised estimate stage by the planning commission
- Carrying forward the lapsed/unutilized SCSP and TSP amount to the next annual Plan of the state/UT as an additional fund for SCSP and TSP
- Ensuring that the Centrally Sponsored Scheme (CSS) and SCA Schemes of the Centre have a SCSP and TSP component in them as per the proportion of SCs and STs in the states/UTs
  Central Ministries/Departments
- Earmarking of funds by every central ministry/department towards SCSP and TSP should be as per the proportion of SC and ST population in the country. Non-earmarking of SCSP and TSP funds by the ministry/department will result in non-approval of their annual Plan
- SCSP and TSP funds should be non-divertible
- Implementing SCSP and TSP schemes and programmes through a newly created dedicated SCSP and TSP unit
- Ensuring the accrual of benefits of schemes to SCs and STs
- Strictly following of the guidelines issued to central ministries/departments

Source: Eleventh Five Year Plan.

Development of Women and Child Welfare

Empowered women living with dignity and contributing as equal partners in development in an environment free from violence and discrimination and, well-nurtured children with full opportunities for growth and development in a safe and protective environment are ideals for any society. The efforts of government have been geared towards this over the various Plan periods.

The programmes for women have evolved over the years from a purely 'welfare-oriented' approach to the 'development' approach to 'empowerment' module and now recognize women as agents of change. In the First Plan, the idea was that adequate services needed to be promoted for women welfare so that they may fulfil their legitimate role in the family and the community, which continued till almost the Fifth Plan. From the Sixth Plan, there has been a *thrust* on health, education and employment of women. In the Eighth Plan, 'empowerment' of women was recognized and accepted as a distinct strategy. The Ninth Plan adopted the 'Women's Component Plan' that made it obligatory on both the central and state governments to ensure that not less than 30% of the funds/benefits are earmarked in all the women-related sectors. It envisaged participation of women in the planning process and the promotion of SHGs.

The Tenth Plan recognized the *importance* of gender budgeting by stating that 'the two effective concepts of Women Component Plan and Gender Budgeting should be tied up to play a complementary role to each other'. The Eleventh Plan recognized gender as a *crosscutting theme* across all sectors and sought to reinforce the commitment to gender budgeting and specifically stated that gender equity requires adequate provisions to be made in policies and schemes across ministries and departments.

There has been a plethora of schemes for women since the beginning. Some of these deserve mention. The scheme of *Hostel for Working Women* envisages provision of safe and affordable hostel accommodation to working women and for women being trained for employment. The scheme of *Short Stay Home* for women and girls was introduced to prevent women from exploitation and to support their survival and rehabilitation in 1969. A similar scheme *Swadhar – A Scheme for Women in Difficult Circumstances* was launched by the Department in 2001–2002.

Support to Training and Employment Programme for Women was launched in 1986–1987, to ensure sustainable employment and income generation for marginalized and asset-less rural and urban women across the country. The National Credit Fund for Women known as *Rashtriya Mahila Kosh* was set up by the Government of India in 1993 as a national-level organization to meet the credit needs of poor and asset-less women in the informal sector.

Credit is provided to the poor women beneficiaries through *intermediary micro-financing organizations* working at grassroots level such as NGOs, women federations, co-operatives, not for profit companies and other voluntary/civil society organizations for livelihood and income generation activities, housing, micro-enterprises, etc.

In 1998, the ministry formulated a National Plan of Action to Combat Trafficking and Commercial Sexual Exploitation of Women and Children. *'Ujjawala'*, a comprehensive scheme to combat trafficking was launched by the ministry in December, 2007 and is being implemented mainly through NGOs. The scheme has *five* components – prevention, rescue, rehabilitation, reintegration and repatriation of trafficked victims.

Indira Gandhi *Matritva Sahyog Yojana* was introduced in October 2010 to facilitate a better enabling environment by providing cash incentives for improved health and nutrition of pregnant and nursing mothers. 'Rajiv Gandhi Scheme for Empowerment of Adolescent Girls

(AGs) – *Sabla'* was introduced in 2010 in 200 selected districts using the ICDS platform by replacing the Nutrition Programme for Adolescent Girls and *Kishori Shakti Yojana* (KSY). In the non-*Sabla* districts, KSY continues as before. It provides nutrition in the form of take home ration or hot cooked meal for 11–14 years who are out of school and to all AGs (out of school and in school girls) between 14–18 years. In the non-nutrition component, the out of school AGs (11–18 years) are being provided health check-up and referral services, nutrition and health education, counselling/guidance on family welfare, adolescent reproductive sexual health, child care practices and life skill education and accessing public services and 16–18 year old AGs are also being given vocational training.

National Mission for Empowerment of Women was launched in March 2010. The Mission was operationalized during 2011–2012, with the setting up of a full-fledged mission directorate and a National Resource Centre for Women within the nodal ministry. The ICDS scheme, one of the oldest programmes, focuses on early childhood development. It is the foremost symbol of the country's commitment to its children and nursing mothers as a response to the challenge of providing preschool non-formal education on one hand and breaking the vicious cycle of malnutrition, morbidity, reduced learning capacity and mortality on the other. The beneficiaries under the scheme are children in the age group 0–6 years, pregnant women and lactating mothers.

The *Integrated Child Protection Scheme* (*ICPS*) was launched in 2009–2010, under which financial and technical support is provided to the state governments/UT administrations. ICPS brings several existing child protection programmes under one umbrella, with improved norms. These include (i) A Programme for Juvenile Justice; (ii) An Integrated Programme for Street Children and (iii) Scheme for Assistance to Homes (*Shishu Greh*) to promote in-country adoption.

India's commitment towards prevention of trafficking

- Article 23 of the Constitution of India prohibits trafficking in human beings and beggars
- 'Immoral Traffic (Prevention) Act, 1956' lays down provisions for stringent punishment to the perpetrators of the crime
- Indian Penal Code also has provisions for preventing crimes related to trafficking
- India has ratified the following:
  (a) UN Convention against Transnational Organized Crime with its Protocol to Prevent, Suppress and Punish Trafficking in Persons especially Women and Children
  (b) SAARC Convention on Preventing and Combating Trafficking of Women and Children in Prostitution
  (c) Convention on the Elimination of All Forms of Discrimination against Women
  (d) Convention on the Rights of the Child

Development of Other Backward Classes

Specific programmes for the development of OBCs were initiated from the Eighth Plan. *The National Backward Classes Finance and Development Corporation* (NBCFDC) was set up in 1992 to promote self-employment projects among the OBCs living below the poverty line. During the Ninth Five Year Plan period, programmes such as pre-matric and post-matric scholarship schemes and construction of hostels and pre-examination coaching centres for OBCs were introduced. The Pre-examination Coaching Scheme for OBCs was merged with the umbrella Coaching and Allied Scheme for Weaker Sections including SCs, OBCs and minorities from September 2001.

The NBCFDC provides financial assistance through state channelling agencies nominated by the state governments/UTs. It assists a wide range of income generating activities, which include agricultural and allied activities, artisan and traditional occupations, small-scale and tiny industry, small business, etc. Entrepreneurs with annual income less than double the poverty line are eligible for concessional finance.

Development of Persons with Disabilities

From the Ninth Plan, there was a slight shift from a welfare-based approach for the disabled to a *rights-based* approach. The Persons with Disabilities Act, 1995 and the National Trust for Welfare of Persons with Autism, Cerebral Palsy, Mental Retardation and Multiple Disability Act, 1999, cover a wide range of activities, which include issuance of disability certificates and prevention and early detection of disabilities; promoting the integration of disabled students in mainstream schools and removal of architectural barriers from schools, colleges, and universities; providing incentives to private sector employers to ensure that persons with disabilities constitute at least 5% of their workforce and framing a scheme for payment of an unemployment allowance to those disabled people who have been registered with a special employment exchange for over two years but could not be placed in any gainful employment.

Under the Disabilities Act, 3% reservation in employment is being provided to the disabled people. Industrial Training Institutes provide 3% reservation in seats for persons with disabilities. The *Swarnajayanti Gram Swarojgar Yojana*, *Indira Awaas Yojana*, *National Rural Employment Guarantee Act* and *Sampoorna Grameen Rozgar Yojana* provide for 3% reservation/benefits to disabled people. The National Handicapped and Finance Development Corporation provides loans on concessional terms to self-employed persons with disabilities. Aids and appliances are provided to the disabled under the Scheme of Assistance to Disabled Persons for Purchase/Fitting of Aids/Appliances.

The National Policy for Persons with Disabilities, adopted in 2006, focuses primarily on prevention of disability, early detection and appropriate interventions, physical and economic rehabilitation measures, inclusive education, employment in the public as well as private sector and self-employment, creation of a barrier-free environment and development of rehabilitation professionals.

Development of Minorities

Till the Seventh Five Year Plan, minorities continued to get the developmental benefits along with OBCs. In 1983, the Prime Minister's 15-Point Programme was launched to provide a sense of security to minority communities and ensure their rapid socioeconomic development. This programme was based on a *3-pronged* approach: (a) to tackle the situation arising out of communal riots; (b) to ensure adequate representation of the minority communities in employment under the central and state governments as well as PSUs and (c) other measures, such as ensuring flow of benefits to the minority communities under various development programmes, maintenance and development of religious places, *Wakf* properties and redressal of grievances of the minorities. In 1989, an autonomous, non-political, non-profit organization – the *Maulana Azad Education Foundation* – was set up to promote education among educationally backward Muslims, especially girls.

During the Eighth Plan, two exclusive schemes were introduced for their educational and economic development. In 1994, the *National Minorities Development and Finance Corporation* was set up. The Ninth Plan saw a new scheme for *pre-examination coaching* for weaker sections. It assisted voluntary organizations to run coaching centres for minorities for various competitive and professional examinations. It was later merged with the similar scheme for SCs in 2001, and renamed *Coaching and Allied Scheme for Weaker Sections* including SCs, OBCs and minorities.

The Prime Minister's *new 15-Point Programme* launched in 2006 aimed at making certain that benefits of various schemes/programmes flow equitably to the minorities. For this, it quantifies a certain portion of development projects to be established in areas with a concentration of minorities. It stipulates that wherever possible, 15% of targets and outlays under various schemes be earmarked for the minorities. All central ministries/departments, State governments/UT administration have been advised to implement this new programme. Five central ministries – human resource development, labour and employment, housing and urban poverty alleviation, rural development and women and child development – have been given responsibilities in their respective areas.

As many pockets with substantial minority populations continued to lack adequate physical and social infrastructure, the Eleventh Plan proposed to adopt an area-based approach. It was mentioned that concerted efforts were needed to ensure that universally available services under ICDS, *National Rural Health Mission* and so on, reach the localities where the minority communities live.

To ensure comprehensive development through a multi-sectoral approach, 90 minority concentration districts, covering 34% of the minority population in the country, have been identified on the basis of either human development indicators or basic amenities indicators.

Linguistic minorities living in relative social and economic backwardness and in need of preservation of their culture and language were also proposed to be paid special attention in the Eleventh Plan.

Welfare of Senior Citizens

India has the second largest population of older (60+) persons in the world. The number of older persons in the population is expected to increase from 71 million in 2001 to 173 million in 2026. To bring about a qualitative improvement in the services to older persons, the scheme of Assistance to Voluntary Organizations for Welfare of the Aged was revised in 1998 to make it very flexible. The new scheme – *An Integrated Programme for Older Persons* was designed to meet diverse needs of the aged, including reinforcement and strengthening of family and awareness generation on issues related to the aged.

The eight basic principles of the UNCRPD are as follows:

- Respect for inherent dignity, individual autonomy including the freedom to make one's own choices and independence of persons with disabilities
- Non-discrimination
- Full and effective participation and inclusion in society
- Respect for difference and acceptance of disabled people as part of human diversity and humanity
- Equality of opportunity
- Accessibility
- Equality between men and women
- Respect for the evolving capacities of children with disabilities and respect for their right to preserve their identities

The government announced a *National Policy for Older Persons* in January 1999. The principal areas of intervention envisaged by the policy include financial security; healthcare and nutrition; shelter/housing; education, training and information; protection for life and property; provision of appropriate concessions, rebates and discounts to older persons; a welfare fund and a national council for older persons. To translate the policy into action and ensure equitable coverage, cost-effective operation and better convergence of programmes, emphasis has been laid on utilizing available institutions, government/semi-government machinery, panchayati raj institutions and local bodies.

The scheme, *Integrated Programme for Older Persons,* was revised in 2008 to include new projects such as maintenance of respite care homes and continuous care homes, running of multi-service centres for older persons, running of day care centres for Alzheimer's/dementia patients, physiotherapy clinics for older persons, training of caregivers, etc.

ADMINISTRATIVE ARRANGEMENTS

Welfare activities are administered through cooperative efforts of the central ministries and the state government departments. The administrative machinery at the Centre for implementing the various social welfare programmes continued without much of a change till 1985.

National Level

The Ministry of Welfare was formed on September 25, 1985 by transferring subjects relating to welfare of SCs, STs, minorities and OBCs from the Ministry of Home Affairs, and the welfare of the disabled and programmes of social defence from the erstwhile Ministry of Social and Women's Welfare. Work relating to *Wakfs* was transferred from the Ministry of Law to the Ministry of Welfare in January 1986.

The *Department of Women and Child Development* was set up in the year 1985 as a part of the Ministry of Human Resource Development to give the much needed impetus to the holistic development of women and children. With effect from January 30, 2006, the Department has been upgraded to a ministry, with the nodal responsibility to advance the rights and concerns of women and children.

The name of the Ministry of Welfare was changed to the *Ministry of Social Justice and Empowerment* (MSJE) in May 1998. The ministry is the nodal ministry to oversee the interests of the SCs, OBCs, disabled and older persons. Although the primary responsibility for promotion of interests of the SCs rests with all the central ministries in the area of their operations and the state governments, the ministry complements their efforts by way of interventions in critical sectors through specifically tailored schemes.

Further, in October 1999, the Tribal Development Division was moved out to form a separate Ministry of Tribal Affairs and it is the nodal ministry for overall policy, Planning and coordination of programmes of development for the STs. Till the end of 2005–2006, the MSJE continued to be the implementing agency for programmes for educational development and economic empowerment of minorities. In January 2007, the Minorities Division along with Wakf Unit was moved out of the ministry and formed as a separate ministry to ensure a more *focussed* approach towards issues relating to the minorities.

In light of the specialized nature of the subject, a separate *Department of Disability Affairs* was created in May 2012 within the MSJE. So now there are *two* departments – Department of Social Justice and Empowerment, and Department of Disability Affairs. It facilitates empowerment of the persons with disabilities. The *Social Defence Bureau* of the ministry caters to the requirements of drug addicts and offenders and the aged and a host of others who need special care, protection and support. The bureau plays the role of a *catalyst* and has promoted voluntary action. The State governments, autonomous bodies, NGOs and even the corporate world are also involved in formulating and implementing the policies. The programmes of these ministries play a supplementary and complementary role to the other general developmental programmes in the sectors of health, education, rural development, etc. For their programmes, the respective line ministries become the nodal ministries. All these efforts are directed to ensure that these vulnerable groups are empowered, both economically and socially, and thus become equal partners in development.

State Level

At the state levels, while majority of the state governments have exclusive departments/directorates of social welfare, a few states still continue to handle the social welfare programme in a scattered way. As these state departments/directorates are *not* equipped adequately with technical manpower, they need to be strengthened with professionally trained persons to ensure formulation of need-based programmes and their effective implementation. The states, normally, adhere to guidelines issued by the government of India. All the programmes from various ministries at the central level require each State to have adequate administrative machinery. In each state, there is a nodal ministry, which looks after the affairs of respective central ministry.

District Level

District level officers of various line departments are nodal officers at the district level. However, the overall coordination is looked after by the district collector/magistrate. He is expected to conduct monthly meetings of each department every month. The Ninth Plan proposed to involve the panchayati raj institutions and the local bodies actively, along with the voluntary sector and the community in implementing, coordinating and supervising/monitoring the welfare programmes.

CONCLUSION

Evaluation of various policies and programmes over the years at various stages by several agencies reveals that despite the best intentions, there have been shortcomings in addressing the concerns of the disadvantaged groups. There have been reports of administrative inadequacies, leakages in programmes, apathy of concerned agencies and many types of lapses in identification procedures. The situation is worsened by the fact that quite often, the concerned agencies are not able to utilize even the funds that are available for the schemes, that is, financial targets are not achieved. Sometimes, political apathy has affected the implementation. For example, often the administrative ministries are created or merged due to political expediency. Targeting has been often affected by political considerations.

However, with increased public awareness, rising aspirations and restructured access to information and resources, we can expect the future to be brighter for the weaker sections. This chapter has tried to provide a comprehensive account of welfare measures in India through the Five Year Plans as well as governmental schemes and programmes.

Preparatory Questions

- Define welfare State and describe its characteristics.
- Discuss the various provisions for protection against discrimination of women in the Indian Constitution.
- What are the similarities and dissimilarities between TSP and SCSP?

- List the various welfare provisions in different Five Year Plans.
- Discuss the administrative arrangements for welfare administration in India.
- Critically analyse the provisions for welfare of minorities.

REFERENCES

Esping–Andersen, G. (1990) *The Three Worlds of Welfare Capitalism.* Cambridge: Polity Press.

Government of India. (1956–2012) *Planning Commission. Five Year Plans (First to Eleventh).* Government of India.

Government of India. (2011–2012) *Ministry of Women and Child Development. Annual Report.* Government of India.

Government of India. (2011–2012) *Ministry of Tribal Affairs.* Annual Report. Government of India.

Government of India. (2011–2012) *Ministry of Social Justice and Empowerment.* Annual Report. Government of India.

Government of India. (2013) 'Planning Commission.' *Approach Paper to Twelfth Five Year Plan.* Government of India.

Kildal, N. (2003) 'The Welfare State: Three Normative Tensions'. *Working Paper 9*, Stein Rokkan Centre for Social Studies, Bergen University Research Foundation.

Leibfried, S. and *Obinger*, H. (2001) 'Welfare State Futures: An Introduction' in *Leibfried, S.* (ed.). *Welfare: State Futures.* Cambridge: Cambridge University.

Taradutt, (2001) *Tribal Development in India: with Special Reference to Orissa.* New Delhi: Gyan Publication House.

Titmuss, R. M. (1958) 'The Social Division of Welfare'. *Essays on the Welfare State.* London: Allen & Unwin.

Bibliography

Sweta Mishra

GOVERNMENT DOCUMENTS

Administrative Reforms Commission. (1966) *Interim Report on Problem of Redress of Citizens' Grievances*. New Delhi.

Government of India. Planning Commission. (1953) *Gorwala, A. D. Report on Public Administration*. New Delhi: Government of India.

Government of India. Planning Commission. (1956–2012) *Five Year Plans* (*First to Eleventh*). Government of India. New Delhi.

Government of India. (1997) *The Fifth Central Pay Commission Report*. Vol. 1. New Delhi.

Government of India. Second Administrative Reforms Commission. (2006) *First Report on Right to Information: Master Key to Good Governance*. Para 1.1.1. New Delhi.

Government of India. Ministry of Corporate Affairs. (2009) *Corporate Governance Voluntary Guidelines*. New Delhi.

Government of India. Ministry of Social Justice and Empowerment. (2011–12) *Annual Report*. New Delhi.

Government of India. Ministry of Tribal Affairs. (2011–12) *Annual Report*. New Delhi.

Government of India. Ministry of Women and Child Development. (2011–12) *Annual Report*. New Delhi.

Government of India, Planning Commission. (2013) *Approach Paper to Twelfth Five Year Plan*.

National Commission to Review the Working of the Constitution. (2001) *Review of the Working of the Constitutional Provisions for Decentralization* (*Panchayats*). New Delhi: Consultation Paper.

Second ARC. (2006) *Right to Information: Master Key to Good Governance*. Second ARC, Government of India. New Delhi.

BOOKS

S. Benhabib, *et. al* (1993) Overseas Development Administration (ODA) Report. *Taking Account of Good Government*. London.

(1994) *The Polity Reader in Gender Studies*. Cambridge, UK: Polity Press.

(1994) UNDP Report. *Governance for Sustainable Human Development*. New York.

(1995) UNDP Report. *Public Sector Management, Governance and Sustainable Human Development*. New York.

(1997) UNDP Reports. *Governance for Sustainable Growth and Equity; Governance for Sustainable Human Development; Participatory Urban Governance; Public-Private Partnerships for the Urban Environment; Reconceptualizing Governance.* New York

(1997) UNESCO Report. *Capacity Building for Governance*. Paris.

(1999) *OECD Report of the Task Force on Corporate Governance. Principles of Corporate Governance.*

(2006) *Indian Economy Documents Compendium (IEDC)*. New Delhi: Academic Foundation.

(2008) *Occasional Paper Series No. 4 Democratic Decentralization of Urban Governance*. New Delhi: PRIA.

Abel, C. F. (2004) *Evolutionary Critical Theory and its Role in Public Affairs*. New York: M. E. Sharpe.

Adair, A. (1999) *Code of Conduct for NGOs: A Necessary Reform*. London: Institute of Economic Affairs.

Adiseshaiah, M. (1986) *The Why, What and Whither of the Public Sector Enterprise*. New Delhi: Lancer International.

Agarwal, M. D. (1987) *Studies in Zero-Base Budgeting*. Jaipur: Jaipur Research' Development Association.

Agarwal, R. C. (1961) *State Enterprises in India*. Allahabad: Chaitanya Publishing House.

Agarwal, U. C. (ed.) (2004) *Public Administration: Vision and Reality*. New Delhi: Indian Institute of Public Administration.

Aggarwal, N. D. and Mathur, B. L. (1983) *Public Enterprises in India*. Jaipur: Ramesh Book Depot.

Ahrens, J., Caspers, R. and Weingarth, J. (eds.) (2011) *Good Governance in 21st Century: Conflict, Institutional Change and Development in the Era of Globalization*. UK: Edward Elgar.

Ahuja, K. and Ojha, A. K. (2008) *Governance and Reforms*. Jaipur: Aalekh Publication.

Albrow, M. (1970) *Bureaucracy*. London: Macmillan.

Anderson, J. E. (1975) *Public Policy Making*. New Delhi: Thomas Nelson and Sons Ltd.

Anheir, K. H. *et al.* (2001) *Introducing Global Society*. London, UK: LSE Global Governance.

Appleby, P. H. (1952) *Morality and Administration in Democratic Government*. Baton Rouges (LA): State Univ. Press.

Arora, R. K. (1972) *Comparative Public Administration: An Ecological Perspective*. New Delhi: Associated Publishing House. p. 10.

Arora, R. K. (ed.) (1974) *Administrative Change in India*. Jaipur: Aalekh Publishers.

Arora, R. K. et al. (eds.) (1978) *The Indian Administrative System—Essays in Honour of Ziauddin Khan*. New Delhi: Associated Publishing House.

Arora, R. K. (ed.) (1984) *Administrative Theory*. New Delhi: Indian Institute of Public Administration.

Arora, R. K. (ed.) (1979) *People's Participation in Development Process: Essays in Honour of B. Mehta*. Jaipur: The HCM State Institute of Public Administration.

Arora, R. K. (ed.) (1979) *Perspectives in Administrative Theory*. New Delhi: Associated Publishing House.

Arora, R. K. and Kukar, J. C. (1979) *Training and Administrative Development*. Jaipur: HCM State Institute of Public Administration.

Arora, R. K. and Goyal, R. (1995) *Indian Public Administration*. New Delhi: Wishwa Prakashan.

Arora, R. K. (2003) 'Riggs' Administrative Ecology' in Chakraborty, B. and Bhattacharya, M. (eds.). *Public Administration: A Reader*. New Delhi: Oxford.

Arora, R. K. (2004) 'Public Administration: Resilience and Rejuvination' in Arora, R. K. (ed.). *Public Administration: Fresh Perspectives*. Jaipur: Aalekh.

Asian Corporate Governance Association. (January, 2010) *White Paper on Corporate Governance in India*. Hong Kong: Asian Corporate Governance Association (ACGA).

Awasthi, A. and Maheshwari, S. R. (1980) *Public Administration*. Agra: Lakshmi Narain Agarwal.

Aziz, A. (2007) 'The Decentralization Experience in Karnataka: How Clientelism and Accountability Work: A Case Study of West Bengal' in Singh, S. and Sharma, P. K. (eds.). *Decentralization Institutions and Politics in Rural India*. New Delhi: Oxford University Press.

Bailey, S. K. (1986) 'Objectives of Theory of Public Administration' in Charles–Worth, J. C. (ed.). *Theory and Practice of Public Administration: Scope, Objectives and Methods*. Philadelphia: American Academy of Political and Social Science.

Baisya, K. N. (1986) *Financial Administration in India*. Bombay: Himalaya.
Baker, R. J. S. (1972) *Administrative Theory and Public Administration*. London: Hutchinson University Library.
Baksh, R. S. (1986) *Politicians, Bureaucrats and Development Process*. New Delhi: Radiant Publishers.
Barbara, A. (1999) *Politics and Feminism*. Oxford, UK: Blackwell Publishers.
Barnard, C. (1938) *The Functions of the Executive*. Cambridge (MA): Harvard University Press.
Barnard, C. (1956) *Organization and Management: Selected Papers*. Massachusetts: Harvard University Press.
Barthwal, C. P. (ed.) (2003) *Good Governance in India*. New Delhi: Deep and Deep.
Barzelay, M. (1992) *Breaking through Bureaucracy*. Berkeley (CA): University of CA Press.
Barzelay, M. (2000) *The New Public Management: Improving Research and Policy Dialogue*. Berkeley (CA): University of California Press.
Barzelay, M. (1993) *The New Public Management*. US: Russel Sage.
Basu, P. K. (1982) *Public Enterprises: Policy, Performance and Professionalization*. New Delhi: Allied Publishers.
Basu, R. (1990) *Public Administration: Concepts and Theories*. 2nd revised ed. New Delhi: Sterling Publication Pvt. Ltd.
Batley, R. (1999) *The Role of Government in Adjusting Economies: An Overview of Findings*. Birmingham: International Development Department.
Bava, N. (1984) *People's Participation in Development Administration in India*. New Delhi: Uppal Publishing Co.
Baviskar, B. S. and Mathew, G. (eds.) (2009) *Inclusion and Exclusion in Local Governance: Field Studies from Rural India*. New Delhi: Sage.
Beetham, D. (1974) *Max Weber and the Theory of Modern Politics*. London: George Allen and Unwin.
Bell, D. (1976) *The Coming of Post-Industrial Society*. New York: Basic Books.
Bendix, R. (1962) *Max Weber: An Intellectual Portrait*. Garden City (NY).
Berle, A. A. and Means, G. C. (1932) *The Modern Corporation and Private Property*. New York: The Macmillan Corporation.
Bertalanffy, L. V. (1999) 'General Systems Theory Foundation, Development, Applications' in Ray, S. N. (ed.). *Modern Comparative Politics: Approaches Methods and Issues*. New Delhi: Prentice Hall of India Private Ltd.
Beteille, A. (2000) *Antimonies of Society: Essays on Ideologies and Institutions*. New Delhi: Oxford University Press.
Bhambri, C. P. (1971) *Bureaucracy and Politics in India*. Bombay: Vikas Publications.
Bhambri, C. P. (1972) *Administrators in a Changing Society*. Delhi: National Publishing House.
Bhambri, C. P. (1973) *Public Administration in India* Delhi: Vikas.
Bhatnagar, S. C. (2008) I-Government: Building a SMART Administration for India's States in Chakraborty, B. and Bhattacharya, M. (eds.). *The Governance Discourse: A Reader*. New Delhi: Oxford University Press.
Bhatnagar, S. (2003) *Administrative Corruption: How Does E-government Help? Global Corruption Report*. New York: Transparency International.
Bhattacharya, M. (1996) *Public Administration and Planning*. Calcutta: World Press Pvt. Ltd.
Bhattacharya, M. (1999) *New Horizons of Public Administration*. New Delhi: Jawahar Publishing.
Bhattacharya, M. (1979) *Bureaucracy and Development Administration*. New Delhi: Uppal.
Bhattacharya, A. (1984) *Recruitment Rules and Civil Services*. New Delhi: Prachi Prakashan.
Bhattacharya, M. (2002) *Social Theory and Development Administration*. 3rd ed. New Delhi: Jawahar.
Bhattacharya, M. (2003) 'Bureaucracy and Politics in India' in Chakraborty, B. and Bhattacharya, M. (eds.). *Public Administration: A Reader*. New Delhi: Oxford University Press.
Bhattacharya, M. (1997) Restructuring Public Administration. New Delhi: Jawahar Publishers.
Biju, M. R. (2007) *Goods Governance and Administrative Practices*. New Delhi: Mittal.
Blau, P. M. and Meyer, M. W. (1987) *Bureaucracy in Modern Society*. New York: Random House.
Blau, P. (1956) *Bureaucracy in Modern Society*. New York: Free Press.
Blumenthal, W. M. (1983) 'Candid Reflections of a Businessman in Washington' in Perry, J. L. and Kraemer, K. L. (eds.). *Public Management*. Palo Alto (CA): Mayfield Publishing.
Bodley, J. H. (2002) *The Power of Scale: A Global History Approach*. New York: M. E. Sharpe.

Box, R. C. (ed.) (2007) *Democracy and Public Administration*. New Delhi: Prentice-Hall of India.

Boyne, G. and Ashworth, R. (2010) *Organizing Government.* Vol. I. London: Sage.

Bratton, M. and Donald, R. (1992) 'The Institutional Bases of Governance in Africa' in Hyden, G. and Bratton, M. (eds.). *Governance and Politics in Africa*. London: Lynne Rienner Publishers.

Brautigam, D. (1991) *Governance and Economy: A Review, Working Papers Policy and Review Departments*. The World Bank. Washington D.C.

Brinkerhoff, D. W. and Coston, J. M. (2004), cited in Jain, R. B. (1999), 'Sustainable Development through Good Governance in India Challenges and Strategies' in Geden, M. M. and Haque, S. (eds.). *Handbook of Development Policy Studies*. New York: Marcel Dekker.

Brush, L. D. (2003) *Gender and Governance*. US: Alta Mira Press.

Buijtenhuijs, R. and Rijinierse, E. (1993) *Democratization in Sub-Sahara Africa* (1989–92)*: An Overview of the Literature*. Leiden: Africa Study Centre.

Burke, J. P. (1986) *Bureaucratic Responsibility*. Baltimore (MD): Johns Hopkins University Press.

Burkhead, J. (1956) *Government Budgeting*. New Delhi: Wiley and Sons Inc.

Burns, T. E. and Stalker, G. M. (1961) *The Management of Innovation.* Urbana (IL): Univ. of Illinois.

Bystydzienski, J. M. (ed.) (1992) *Women Transforming Politics; Worldwide Strategies for Empowerment*. Indianapolis (IN): Indiana University Press.

Cadbury Committee Report. (1992) *Financial Aspects of Corporate Governance*. London: Gee & Co.

Cadbury, A. (2003) *Foreword to Corporate Governance and Development.* Global Corporate Governance Forum, Focus 1. Washington, DC: World Bank.

Caiden, G. E. (1971) *Dynamics of Public Administration*. US: Dryden Press.

Caiden, G. (1976) *Indian Administration*. 2nd ed. London: Allen and Unwin Ltd.

Caiden, G. (1982) *Public Administration*. 2nd ed. Pacific Palisades (CA): Palisades Publishers.

Campo, S. S. and Sundaram P. S. A. (eds.) (2004) *To Serve and To Preserve: Improving Public Administration in a Competitive World.* Manila: Asian Development Bank.

Chakraborty, B. and Bhattacharya, M. (eds.) (2003) *Public Administration A Reader.* New Delhi: Oxford University Press.

Chakraborty, B. and Bhattacharya, M. (eds.) (2008) *The Governance Discourse: A Reader*. New Delhi: Oxford University Press.

Chakraborty, B. and Chand, P. (2012) *Public Administration in a Globalising World*. New Delhi: Sage.

Chakraborty, B. (2007) *Reinventing Public Administration: The Indian Experience*. New Delhi: Orient Longman.

Chandler, R. C. and Plano, J. C. (1982) *The Public Administration Dictionary*. New York: John Wiley and Sons.

Chandoke, N. (1995) *State and Civil Society: Explorations in Political Theory*. New Delhi: Sage.

Chapman, B. (1959) *The Profession of Government*. London: Allen and Unwin.

Chatterji, S. K. (1981) *Development Administration*. Delhi: Surjeet.

Chaturvedi, T. N. (ed.) (1984) *Administrative Accountability*. New Delhi: Indian Institute of Public Administration.

Chaubey, P. K. (2004) *Urban Local Bodies in India*. New Delhi: Indian Institute of Public Administration.

Cheema, G. S. and Rondinelli, D. A. (eds.) (1983) *Decentralization and Development: Policy Implementation in Developing Countries*. Beverly Hills (CA): Sage.

Cheema, G. S. (2001) 'A Governance Approach to Development: New Role for Development Co-operation' in Hye, H. A. (ed.). *Governance: South Asian Perspectives*. New Delhi: Manohar.

Chettur, S. K. (1962) *The Steel Frame of India and I: Life in the Civil Service*. Bombay: Asia Publishing House.

Cheung, A. and Scott, I. (2003) *Governance and Public Sector Reforms in Asia: Paradigms, Paradoxes and Dilemmas*. New York: Routledge.

Chilcote, R. H. (2000) *The Political Economy of Imperialism: Critical Appraisals*. Maryland: Rowman and Littlefield.

Chopra, R. N. (1983) *Public Sector in India: Its Performance, Profitability, and Industrial Relations*. New Delhi: Intellectual Publishing House.

Christensen, T. and Laegreid, P. (2011) *Ashgate Research Companion to New Public Management*. Ashgate Publishing House.

Christensen, T. and Laegrid, P. (2001) *New Public Management: The Transformation of Ideas and Practice*. Aldershot: Ashgate.

Clarke, M. (ed.) (1983) *Corruption, Causes, Consequences and Controls*. London: Frances Pinter.

Clegg, S., Kornberger, M. and Pitsis, T. (2005) *Managing and Organizations: An Introduction to Theory and Practice*. Thousand Oaks (CA): Sage.

Cohen, J. L. and Arato, A. (1994) *Civil Society and Political Theory*. US: MIT Press.

Confederation of Indian Industry (CII) (2009) *Report of the Task Force on Corporate Governance Chairperson Naresh Chandra*. New Delhi

Confederation of Indian Industry (CII). (1998) *Desirable Corporate Governance: A Code*. New Delhi

Corson, J. and Harris, J. (1967) *Public Administration in Modern Society*. London: McGraw-Hill.

Cox III, R. W., Susan, J. B. and Morgan, B. N. (2005) *Public Administration in Theory and Practice*. 2nd ed. New Delhi: Pearson.

Craig, D. and Porter, D. (2006) *Development beyond Neoliberalism? Governance, Poverty Reduction and Political Economy*. New York: Routledge.

Crozier, M. (1964) *The Bureaucratic Phenomenon*. Chicago (IL) University of Chicago Press.

Daneke G. A. (1994) 'A Science of Public Administration' in White, J. D. and Adams, G. B. (eds.). *Research in Public Administration: Reflections on Theory and Practice*. UK: Sage.

Das, S. K. (1998) *Civil Service Reform and Structural Adjustment*. New Delhi: Oxford University Press.

Datta, A. (ed.) (1984) *Local Government*. New Delhi: Indian Institute of Public Administration.

Dayal, I. et al. (1976) *Dynamics of Formulating Policy in Government of India: Machinery for Policy Development*. Delhi: Concept Publishing Company.

DeHoog, R. H. (2000) 'Bureaupathology' in Shafritz, J. M. (ed.). *Defining Public Administration-Selections from the International Encyclopedia of Public Policy and Administration*. Colorado: Westview Press (Indian reprint: Jaipur/New Delhi: Rawat Publications).

Denhardt J. V. and Denhardt, R. B. (2007) *New Public Service*. New York: M. E. Sharpe.

Denhardt, R. B. (1985) 2008 *Theories of Public Administration*. Patrick, Australia: Thomson Dunleavy.

Denhardt, R. B. (1991) *Public Administration: An Action Orientation Brooks*. Pacific Grove (CA): Cole Publishing Company.

Denter, B. and Rose, L. E. (2005) *Comparing Local Governance: Trends and Developments*. New York: Palgrave Macmillan.

Desouza, P. R. (2002) 'Decentralization and Local Government: The "Second Wave" of Democracy in India' in Hasan, Z., Sridharan, E. and Sudarshan, R. (eds.). *India's Living Constitution: Ideas, Practices, Controversies*. Delhi: Permanent Black.

Dey, P. K. (1989) *Public Policy and System*. New Delhi: Pearson.

Dhameja, A. (ed.) (2003) *Contemporary Debates in Public Administration*. New Delhi: Prentice-Hall of India.

Dhameja, A. (2003) 'Role of Ethics in Public Administration' in Arora, A. K. and Saxena, T. Jaipur: Aalekh.

Dhameja, A. (2010) 'Introduction' in Dhameja, A. (ed.). *Contemporary Debates in Public Administration*. 3rd ed. New Delhi: Prentice-Hall of India.

Dimock, M. E. and Dimock, G. O. (1969) *Public Administration*. New York: Holt, Rinehart and Winston.

Dixit, M., Chaturvedi, J. and Syed, I. H. (2003) *Public Administration*. Lucknow: New Royal Book.

Downs, A. (1967) *Inside Bureaucracy*. Boston (MA): Little, Brown & Company.

Dror, Y. (1974) *Public Policy Making Reexamined*. San Francisco (CA): Leonard Hill Books.

Dubashi, P. R. (1985) *Essays in Public Administration*. New Delhi: NBO Publishers.

Dubashi, P. R. (1987) *Essays in Development Administration*. New Delhi: Archives.

Duna, P. K. (1991) *Public Administration and the State*. New Delhi: Concept.

Dunleavy, P. (1991) *Democracy, Bureaucracy, and Public Choice: Economic Explanations in Political Science*. New York: Harvester Wheatsheaf.

Dunleavy, P. (1991) 'Democracy, Bureaucracy and Public Choice' in Hughes, O. (ed.). *Public Management and Administration: An Introduction*. 2nd ed. Macmillan Basingstoke.

Dunn, W. N. and Fozouni, B. (1976) *Towards a Critical Administrative Theory*. Beverly Hills (CA): Sage Publications, London.

Dunsire, A. (1973) *Administration: The Word and the Science*. London: Martin Robertson and Co. Ltd.

Dwivedi, O. P. and Jain, R. B. (1985) *India's Administrative State*. New Delhi: Gitanjali.

Dye, T. R. (1987) *Understanding Public Policy*. 6th ed. Englewood-Cliffs (NJ): Prentice Hall.

Dye, T. R. (2004) *Understanding Public Policy*. 3rd ed. New Delhi: Pearson Education.

Easton, D. (1965/1994) 'A Framework for Political Analysis' in Chilcote, R. H. (ed.). *Theories of Comparative Politics: The Search for a Paradigm Reconsidered*. 2nd ed. US: Westview Press.

Emerson, K and Murchie, P. (2011) 'Collaborative Governance and Climate Change: Opportunities for Public Administration' in O'Leary, R., Van Slyke, D. M. and Kim, S. (eds.). *The Future of Public Administration around the World: The Minnowbrook Perspective*. Washington, DC: Georgetown University Press.

Esping-Andersen, G. (1990) *The Three Worlds of Welfare Capitalism*. Cambridge (MA): Polity Press.

Etounga, M. A. (1993) *Democratisation and Good Governance in Africa* (*Summary of a Lecture Presented at the Good Governance Lectures*). The Hague: Ministry of Foreign Affairs.

Etzioni, A. (1964) *Modern Organizations*. New Jersey: Prentice Hall.

Farazmand, A. (ed.) (1991) *Handbook of Comparative and Development Administration*. New York: Marcel Dekker.

Farazmand, A. and Pinkowski, J. (eds.) (2006) *Handbook of Globalization, Governance, and Public Administration* London and New York: Taylor & Francis.

Farazmand, A. (1994) 'The New World Order and Global Public Administration: A Critical Essay' in Garcia, J. C. et al. (eds.). *Public Administration in the Global Village*. West Port (CT): Praeger.

Fayol, H. (1949) *General and Industrial Management*. London: Pitman (originally written and published in 1916 in French).

Fayol, H. (1973) 'The Administrative Theory of the State' in Gulick, L. and Urwick, L. (eds.). *Papers in the Science of Administration*. New York: Columbia University Press.

Fernando, A. C. (2006) *Corporate Governance, Principles, Policies and Practices*. New Delhi: Pearson.

Frederickson, H. G. and Smith, K. B. (2003) *The Public Administration Theory Primer*. Boulder (CO): Westview Press.

Frederickson, H. G. (1980) *New Public Administration*. Alabama: The University of Alabama Press.

Frederickson, H. (1997) *The Spirit of Public Administration*. San Francisco (CA): Jossey-Bass.

Freedman, J. (2001) *Feminism*. Buckingham, UK: Open University Press.

Fried, R. C. (1990) 'Comparative Public Administration: The Search for Theories' in Noami B. L. and Wildavsky, A. (eds.). *Public Administration: The State of the Discipline*. Chatham House Publication. London

Friedlander, W. A. (1967) *Introduction to Social Welfare*. New Delhi: Prentice-Hall of India.

Fry, B. (1989) *Mastering Public Administration*. Chatham (NJ): Chatham House Publishers.

Fukuyama, F. (1992) *The End of History and the Last Man*. New York: Free Press.

Gant, G. F. (1979) *Development Administration: Concepts, Goals, Methods*. London: The University of Wisconsin Press.

Gaus, J. M. (1974) *Reflections on Public Administration*. Alabama: University of Alabama Press.

Gaus, J. M., White, L. D. and Dimock, M. E. (1936) *The Frontiers of Public Administration*. Chicago (IL): University of Chicago Press.

Gerston, L. N. (1974) *Public Policy Making: Process and Principles*. Armonk (NY): M. E. Sharpe.

Gerth, H. and Mills, C. (eds.) (1976) *From Max Weber*. New York: Oxford Univ. Press.

Ghaus-Pasha, A. (2007) 'Role of Civil Society Organizations in Governance' in Rondinelli, D. A. (ed.). *Public Administration and Democratic Governance: Governments Serving Citizens*. United Nations. New York.

Ghosh, B. (2005) 'Accountability of Panchayats: Ends and Means' in L. C. (ed.). *Decentralization and Local Governance*. New Delhi: Orient Longman.

Giddens, A. (1958) 'Introduction' in Parsons, T. (trans.) and Weber, M. (eds.). *The Protestant Ethic and the Spirit of Capitalism*, (1–12(b)). New York: Charles Scribner's Sons.

Gilligan, C. (1982) *A Different Voice*. US: Harvard University Press.

Gladden, E. N. (1952) *An Introduction to Public Administration*. 2nd ed. London: Staples Press.

Global Corporate Governance Forum. (2005) *Developing Corporate Governance Codes of Best Practice. User Guide.* Washington, DC: World Bank.

Goel, S. L. (2010) *Social Welfare Administration* (*Vol.* 2, *Social Justice and Empowerment*). New Delhi: Deep and Deep Publications.

Golembiewski, R. T. (1977) *Public Administration as a Developing Discipline: Perspectives on Past and Present*. New York: Marcel Dekker.

Golembiewski, R. T. (1995) *Practical Public Management*. New York: Marcel Dekker.

Goodnow, F. and J. Rohr. (2003) *Politics and Administration*. New Brunswick (NJ): Transaction.

Goodnow, F. J. (1900) *Politics and Administration*. New York: Macmillan.

Goodsell, C. (2003) *The Case for Bureaucracy*. 4th ed. Washington, DC: CQ Press.

Goodsell, C. T. (1990) 'Public Administration and Public Interest' in Wamsley, G. L., Bacher, R. N. et al. (eds.). *Refounding Public Administration*. London: Sage.

Gormley, W. (1989) *Taming the Bureaucracy.* Princeton (NJ): Princeton University Press.

Gore, A. L. (1993) *From Red Tape to Results: Creating a Government that Works Better and Costs Less. The Report of the National Performance Review* 1. Washington, DC. Diane Publishing

Goswami, D. and Bandyopadhyay, K. (2012) *The Anti-Corruption Movement in India*. New Delhi: PRIA.

Gramsci, A. (1971) *Selections from the Prison Notebooks*. New York: International Publishers.

Gregory, H. J. and Simms, M. E. (1999) 'Corporate Governance-What is it, Why it Matters' in 9th*Anti-corruption Conference, Durban, South Africa.*

Gross, B. M. (1964) *The Managing of Organization: The Administrative Struggle.* Vol. 1. New York: The Free Press.

Gulick, L. and Urwick, L. (eds.) (1973) *Papers on the Science of Administration*. New York: Columbia University Press.

Gupta, B. N. (1976) *Government Budgeting, with Special Reference to India.* Bombay: Bombay Publishing House.

Gupta, B. B. (1975) *Problems of Indian Administration.* Allahabad: Chugh Publications.

Gupta, D. N. (2004) *Decentralization: Need for Reforms*. New Delhi: Concept Publishing Company.

Gurthrie, D. M. (2003) *Engaged Governance: An Institutional Approach to Government-Civil Society Engagement.* Background Paper for United Nations Department of Economic and Social Affairs, Interregional workshop on 'Engaged Governance, Colombo, Sri Lanka, 9–11 December, 2003.

Habermas, J. (1971) *Toward a Rational Society*. Boston (MA): Beacon Press.

Habermas, J. (1983) *Theory of Communicative Action*. Vol. 1. Cambridge (MA): MIT Press.

Handa, K. L (ed.) (1986) *Financial Administration*. New Delhi: Indian Institute of Public Administration.

Handa, K. L. (1979) *Programme and Performance Budgeting*. New Delhi: Uppal Publishing House.

Haragopal, G. (1980) *Administrative Leadership and Rural Development in India*. New Delhi: Light and Life.

Hayek, F. (1994) *The Road to Serfdom*. Chicago (IL): University of Chicago Press.

Heady, F. and Stokes, S. L. (ed.) (1962) *Papers in Comparative Public Administration*. Ann Arbor (MI): Michigan Institute of Public Administration, The University of Michigan.

Heady, F. (1996) *Public Administration: A Comparative Perspective*. Englewood-Cliffs (NJ): Prentice-Hall.

Hegel, G. F. W. (1991) *Philosophy of Right, (Edited by Allen W. Wood)*. Cambridge (MA): Cambridge University Press.

Held, D. et al. (2005) *Debating Globalization*. Cambridge (MA): Polity Press.

Held, D. (2002) 'Cosmopolitanism: Ideas, Realities and Deficits' in Held, D. and McGrew, A. (eds.). *Governing Globalization*. Cambridge (MA): Polity.

Henderson, K. M. (2001) 'NGOs and Grass-Roots Organizations in Developing Countries' in *Handbook of Public Management Practice and Reform*. New York: Marcel Dekker.

Henry, N. (2007) *Public Administration and Public Affairs*. 10th ed. New Delhi: Prentice-Hall of India.

Heper, M. (1987) *The State and Public Bureaucracies*. Westport (CT): Greenwood.

Heydebrand, W. V. (1973) *Comparative Organizations: The Result of Empirical Research*. New Jersey: Prentice Hall.

Holzer, M. and Schwester, R. W. (2011) *Public Administration: An Introduction*. New Delhi: PHI Learning.

Hooja, R. and Arora, R. K. (eds.) *Administrative Theories: Approaches, Concepts, and Thinkers in Public Administration*. Jaipur/New Delhi: Rawat Publications. 2007

Howell, J. and Pearce, J. (2001) *Civil Society and Development: A Critical Exploration*. Boulder (CO): Lynne Reinner Publishers.

Hughes, O. E. (1998) *Management and Administration: An Introduction*. 3rd ed. Basingstoke: Macmillan.

Hummel, R. (2007) *The Bureaucratic Experience: The Post-modern Challenge*. 5th ed. Library of Congress Cataloging-in-Publication Data.

Hyden, G. and Court, J. (2006) 'Governance and Development: Trying to Sort out the Basics' in *Poverty, Inequality and Access to Justice for the Poor in South Asia, Conference Paper*. New Delhi: Centre for the Study of Law and *Governance*, JNU.

Jain, R. B. (1976) *Contemporary Issues in Indian Administration*. Delhi: Vishal.

Jain, R. B. (ed.) (1983) *Public Services in a Democratic Context*. New Delhi: Indian Institute of Public Administration.

Jain, R. B. (ed.) (1980) *District Administration*. New Delhi: Indian Institute of Public Administration.

Jain, R. B. (ed.) (1981) *Panchayati Raj*. New Delhi: Indian Institute of Public Administration.

Jain, R. B. (ed.) (2004) *Corruption Free Sustainable Development: Challenges and Strategies for Good Governance*. New Delhi: Mittal.

Jain, R. B. (2002) *Public Administration in India: 21st Century Challenge for Good Governance*. New Delhi: Deep and Deep.

Jain, S. P. (2003) 'Decentralization in India: An Appraisal' in Mishra, S. N. et al. (eds.). *Public Governance and Decentralization*. Vol. II. New Delhi: Mittal.

Jann, W. (2007) 'Public Administration Under Pressure: The Search for New Forms of Public Governance' in Bertucci, G. and Rosenbaum, A. (eds.). *Implementing the Millennium Development Goals: Challenges and Responses for Public Administration.* New York: The United Nations Committee of Experts on Public Administration. New York. UN.pp16-28

Jayal, N. G. (2003) 'The Governance Agenda: Making Democratic Development Dispensable' in Chakraborty, B. and Bhattacharya, M. *Public Administration: A Reader*. New Delhi: Oxford.

Jayal, N. G. and Pai, S. (2001) *Democratic Governance in India*. New Delhi: Sage.

Jayal, N. G. (2007) *Local Governance in India: Decentralization and Beyond*. New Delhi: Oxford University Press.

Jean, D. and Sen, A. (1989) *India: Development and Participation*. New York: OUP.

Jha, S. N. and Mathur, P. C. (eds.) (1999) *Decentralization and Local Politics*. New Delhi: Sage.

Joshi, P. L. (1987) *Zero-Base Budgeting Technology in India*. Bombay: Dhruv and Deep.

Katz. S. M. (1970) 'A System Approach to Development Administration' in Riggs, F. W. (ed.). *Frontiers of Development Administration*. Durham (NC): Duke University Press.

Kaushik, S. L. and Sahni, P. (eds.) (1983) *Public Administration in India: Emerging Trends*. Allahabad: Kitab Mahal.

Kaushik, S. (ed.) (1984) *Public Administration: An Alternative Perspective*. New Delhi: Ajanta Publications.

Keasey, K., Thompson, S. and Wright, M. (1997) 'Introduction: The Corporate Governance Problem — Competing Diagnoses and Solutions' in Keasey, K., Thompson, S. and Wright, M. (eds.). *Corporate Governance: Economic, Management, and Financial Issues*. Oxford: Oxford University Press.

Keraudran, P. and Vicrlo, H. V. (1998) 'Theories of Public Management Reform and Their Practical Implications' in Verheijen, T. and Coombes, D. (eds.). *Innovations in Public Management: Perspectives from East and West Europe*. Cheltenham: Edward Elgar.

Kettle, D. F. and Fesler, J. W. (2005) *The Politics of Administrative Process*. Washington, DC: CQ Press.

Kildal, N. (2003) *The Welfare State: Three Normative Tensions*. Working Paper 9, Stein Rokkan Centre for Social Studies, Bergen University Research Foundation.

Kim, S. et al. (2011) 'The Legacy of Minnobrook' in O'Leary R., Van Slyke, D. M. and Kim, S. (eds.). *The Future of Public Administration around the World: The Minnowbrook Perspective*. Washington, DC: Georgetown University Press.

Kingsley, D. J. (1944) *Representative Bureaucracy: An Interpretation of the British Civil Service*. Yellow Springs (OH): The Antioch Press.

Kooiman, J. (2003) *Governing as Governance*. London: Sage.

Korten, D. C. and Camer, G. (1984) 'Planning Frameworks for People-centred Development' in Korten, D. C. and Klans, R. (eds.). *People-Centred Development: Contributions Towards Theory and Planning Frameworks*. Connecticut: Kumarian Press.

Korten, D. C. (1984) 'Rural Development Programming: The Learning Process Approach' in Korten, D. C. and Klans, R. (eds.). *People-Centred Development: Contributions Towards Theory and Planning Frameworks*. Connecticut: Kumarian Press.

Kothari, R. (1988) *State Against Democracy: in Search of Human Governance*. New Delhi: Ajanta.

Kothari, S. and Roy, R. (1969) *Relations Between Politicians and Administrators at the District Level*. New Delhi: Indian Institute of Public Administration.

Kousoulas, G. D. (2003) 'On Government and Politics' in Ray, S. N. (ed.). *Modern Comparative Politics: Approaches Methods and Issues*. Prentice Hall of India Pvt. Ltd., New Delhi.

Kruse, A. (1960) *Administration of Social Welfare Agencies* (*Social Work Year Book*). New York: National Association of Social Work.

Kueck, G. W., Mathur, S. C. and Schindler, K. (1998) *Federalism and Decentralization*. New Delhi: Konrad Adenaver Foundation.

Kulshreshtha, A. (2000) 'Good Governance and Audit' in Mathur, B. P. (ed.). *Public Audit, Good Governance and Accountability*. New Delhi: Institute of Public Auditors of India.

Kumar, G. (2006) *Local Democracy in India: Interpreting Decentralization*. New Delhi: Sage.

Kunkle, J. H. (1970) *Society and Economic Growth*. London: Oxford University Press.

Landau, M. (1962) 'The Concept of Decision-Making in the 'Field' of Public Administration' in Malick, S. and Van Ness, E. H. (eds.). *Concepts and Issues in Administrative Behaviour*. Englewood-Cliffs (NJ): Prentice-Hall.

Landau, M. (1970) 'Development Administration and Decision Theory' in Weidner, E. W. (ed.). *Development Administration in Asia*. Durham Duke University Press.

Lane, J. E. (2000) *New Public Management*. London: Routledge.

Lassman, P. and Speirs, R. (eds.) (1994) *Weber: Political Writings*. Cambridge: Cambridge University Press.

Leibfried, S. and Obinger, H. (2011) 'Welfare State Futures: An Introduction' in Leibfried, S. (ed.). *Welfare: State Futures*. Cambridge: Cambridge University.

Lerner, G. (1984) 'The Rise of Feminist Consciousness' in Bender, E. M., Burk, B. and Walker, N. (eds.). *All of Us Are Present*. Columbia (MO): James Madison Wood Research Institute, Stephen's College.

Levine, H. M. (1988) *Public Administration Debated*. Englewood-Cliffs (NJ): Prentice Hall.

Lewis, D. and Kanji, N. (2009) *Non-Governmental Organizations and Development*. London: Routledge.

Lewis, D. (2007) *The Management of Non-Governmental Development Organizations*. 2nd ed. London: Routledge.

Light, P. C. (2000) *Making Nonprofits Work: A Report on the Tides of Non-profit Management Reform*. Washington, DC: Brookings Institutions.

Likert, R. (1961) *New Patterns of Management*. New York: McGraw Hill.

Long, N. E. (1962) *The Polity*. Chicago (IL): Rand Mc-Nally.

Lowi, T. J. (1979) *The End of Liberalism: The Second Republic of United States*. New York: W. W. Norton and Company.

Lyer, L. E. Jr., Heinrich, C. J. and Hill, C. J. (2001) *Improving Governance: A New Logic for Empirical Research*. Washington, DC: Georgetown University Press.

Maddick, H. (1970) *Panchayati Raj: A Study of Rural Local Government in India*. London: Longman Group, Ltd.

Maheshwari, S. R. (1971) *Local Government in India*. New Delhi: Orient Longman.

Maheshwari, S. R. (1979) *Indian Administration*. 3rd ed. New Delhi: Orient Longman.

Maheshwari, S. R. (2000) *Public Administration in India*. New Delhi: Macmillan.

Mallin, C. A. (2007) *Corporate Governance*. 2nd ed. New Delhi: Oxford University Press.

Manohar, K. et al. (1991) *Administrative Theory: Trends and Perspectives*. Warangal: Book Bird Publisher.

Manor, J. (2010) 'Local Governance' in Jayal, N. G. and Mehta, P. B. (eds.). *The Oxford Companion to Politics in India*. New Delhi: Oxford University Press.

Mansukhani, H. L. (1979) *Corruption and Public Servants*. New Delhi: Vikas.

Maor, M. and Lane, J. E. (eds.) (1999) *Comparative Public Administration*. Vol. II. Dartmouth Brookfield, US: Ashgate.

March, J. G. and Simon, H. A. (1958) *Organizations*. New York: John Wiley and Sons.

Marini, F. (ed.) (1971) *Toward a New Public Administration: The Minnowbrook Perspective*. Scranton: Chandler Publishing Company.

Marx, F. M. (1957) *The Administrative State: An Introduction to Bureaucracy*. Chicago (IL): University of Chicago Press.

Marx, K. (1971) *On the Jewish Question* (*Karl* Marx, Early Texts, Edited and Translated by David McLellan). England: Oxford.

Mathew, G. (2007) 'Decentralization and Local Governance: How Clientelism and Accountability Work: A Case Study of West Bengal' in Singh, S. and Sharma, P. K. (eds.). *Decentralization Institutions and Politics in Rural India*. New Delhi: Oxford University Press.

Mathur, K. (1986) *A Survey of Research in Public Administration,* 1970–9. New Delhi: Concept.

Mathur, K. (2013) *Panchayati Raj*. New Delhi: Oxford University Press.

Mayer, F. (1997) 'Corporate Governance, Competition, and Performance in Enterprise and Community: New Directions' in Deakin, S. and Hughes, A. (eds.). *Corporate Governance*. Oxford: Blackwell Publishers.

Mayo, E. (1933) *The Human Problems of an Industrial Civilization*. Boston (MA): Harvard Business School.

Mayo, E. (1945) *The Social Problems of an Industrial Civilization*. London: Routledge and Kegan Paul.

Mayo, E. (1947) *The Political Problem of Industrial Civilization*. Boston (MA): Harvard Business School.

Mc Swite, O. C. (1997) *Legitimacy in Public Administration: A Discourse Analysis, Advances in Public Administration*. U.S: Portland State University.

Willey, M. and Minogue, M. (2000) *The Internationalization of Public Management: Reinventing the Third World State*. UK: Edward Elgar.

McCurdy, H. E. (1977) *Public Administration: A Synthesis*, Sydney: Cummings Publishing Company.

Mcginnis, M. D. and Ostrom, E. (1996) 'Design Principles for Local and Global Commons' in *International Political Economy and International Institutions*. Vol. 2. UK: Edward Elgar.

Medury, U. (2010) *Public Administration in the Globalization Era: The New Public Management Perspective*. New Delhi: Orient BlackSwan.

Meenakshisundaram, S. S. (1999) 'Decentralization in Developing Countries' in Jha, S. N. and Mathur, P. C. (eds.). *Decentralization and Local Politics*. New Delhi: Sage.

Merton, R. (1952) *Bureaucratic Structure and Personality: A Reader in Bureaucracy*. New York: Free Press.

Merton, R. (1949) 'Bureaucratic Structure and Personality' in Merton, R. (ed.). *Social Theory and Social Structure*. New York: Free Press of Glencoe.

Michalski, W., Miller, R. and Stevens, B. (2001) 'Governance in the 21st Century: Power in the Global Knowledge Economy and Society' (Governance in the 21st Century: Future Studies). Paris OECD.

Mises, L. V. (1944) 'Bureaucracy.' New Haven (CT): Yale University Press.

Mills, C. W. (1959) *The Power Elite*. New York: Oxford University Press.

Mishra, S. N. and Swetha, M. (2002) *Decentralized Governance*. New Delhi: Shipra Publications.

Mishra, S. N. (1981) *Rural Development and Panchayati Raj*. New Delhi: Mittal Publications.

Mishra, S. N. (1989) *New Horizons in Rural Development Administration*. New Delhi: Mittal Publications.

Mishra, S. N. (2005) 'The 73rd Constitution Amendment and the Local Resource Base: A Critical Appraisal' in Chahar, S. S. (ed.). *Governance at Grass roots Level in India*. New Delhi: Kanishka.

Mishra, S. (2012) *Citizen-Centric Public Systems*. New Delhi: Pearson.

Mishra, S. (2012) *Managing State Governments*. New Delhi: Pearson.

Mishra, S. (2003) 'Decentralization: Concept, Characteristics and Constraints' in Dhameja, A. (ed.). *Contemporary Debates in Public Administration*. New Delhi: Prentice Hall of India.

Molitor, A. (1959) *The University Teaching of Social Sciences: Public Administration*. Paris: UNESCO.

Montgomery, J. D. and Siffin, W. (eds.) (1966) *Approaches to Development: Politics, Administration and Change*. New York: McGraw-Hill.

Montiero, J. B. (1966) *Corruption: Control of Maladministration*. Bombay: Manaktalas.

Mookerji, R. K. (1919) *Local Government in Ancient India*. Oxford: Clarendon Press.

Moore, M. (1995) *Creating Public Value: Strategic Management in Government*. Cambridge: Harvard University Press.

Morrow, W. L. (1975) *Public Administration: Politics and Political System*. New York: Random House.

Nabatchi, T. (2011) 'Why Public Administration Should Take Deliberative Democracy Seriously' in O'Leary, R., Van Slyke, D. M. and Kim, S. (eds.). *The Future of Public Administration around the World: The Minnowbrook Perspective*. Washington, DC: Georgetown University Press.

Naidu, S. P., Apparao, J. and Mallikarjunayya, G. (1986) *Elements of Modern Public Administration*. New Delhi: S. Chand and Co.

Narain, I. et al. (1970) *Panchayati Raj Administration: Old Controls and New Chain*. New Delhi: Indian Institute of Public Administration.

National Academy of Audit and Accounts. (1999) *Background Paper for Seminar on Accountability of Local Bodies and DRDAs*. National Academy of Audit and Accounts. Shimla, 15th and 16th September.

National Foundation for Corporate Governance. (September, 2004) *Discussion Paper: Corporate Governance in India: Theory and Practice*. National Foundation for Corporate Governance. CII New Delhi

Newman, J. (2001) *Modernizing Governance: New Labour Policy and Society*. London: Sage.

Nigro, F. A. (1965/1971) *Modern Public Administration*. 2nd ed. New York: Harper International Edition.

O'Leary, R., Van Slyke, D. M. and Kim, S. (eds.) (2011) *The Future of Public Administration around the World: The Minnowbrook Perspective*. Washington, DC: Georgetown University Press.

Osborne, D. and Gaebler, T. (1992) *Reinventing Government: How the Entrepreneurial Spirit is Transforming the Public Sector*. London: Plume.

Osmani, M. (2012) *Developing a Conceptual Framework for Evaluating Post-NPM Public Sector Transformation Doctoral Symposium*. London: Brunel Business School.

Ostrom, V. (1974) *The Intellectual crisis in American Public Administration*. Tuscaloosa and London: University of Alabama press.

Palanithurai, G. (2005) 'Development Roles Reversed: People's Initiative and Government's Participation' in Jain, L. C. (ed.). *Decentralization and Local Governance*. New Delhi: Orient Longman.

Panandikar, P. V. A. (ed.) (1974) *Development Administration in India*. Delhi: Macmillan.

Panandikar, P. V. A. and Bishnoi, R. N. and Sharma, O. P. (1983) *Development Bureaucracy*. New Delhi: Oxford & 1BH.

Panandikar, P. V. A. and Kshirasagar, S. S. (1968) *Civil Service and Development Administration*. New Delhi: Indian Institute of Public Administration.

Panandikar, P. V. A. and Kshirasagar, S. S. (1978) *Bureaucracy and Development Administration*. New Delhi: *Centre for Policy Research*.

Panandikar, P. V. A. (1977) *Towards a Theory of Development Administration, Centre for Policy Research*. New Delhi:.

Panandiker, V. A. P. and Kshirsagar, S. S. (1978) 'Bureaucratic Adaptation to Development Administration' in Sharma, S. K. (ed.). *Dynamics of Development: An International Perspective*. New Delhi: Concept.

Pardo, T. A., Gil-Garcia, J. R. and Luna-Reyes, L. F. (2011) 'Collaborative Governance and Cross-boundary Information Sharing: Envisioning a Networked and IT-enabled Public Administration' in O'Leary, R.Van Slyke, D. M. and Kim, S. (eds.). *The Future of Public Administration around the World: The Minnowbrook Perspective*. Washington, DC: Georgetown University Press.

Parker, S. R. et al. (1967) *The Sociology of Industry*. London: George Allen and Unwin.

Pateman, C. 'Feminist Critique of Public/Private Dichotomy' in Squires, J. (ed.). *Gender in Political Theory*. Cambridge, UK: Polity Press.

Pelczynski, Z. A. (ed.) (1984) *The State and Civil Society: Studies in Hegel's Political Philosophy*. Cambridge CUP Archive.

Peters, B. G. and Pierre, J. (2003) *Handbook of Public Administration*. London: Sage.

Peters, B. G. (1996) *American Public Policy: Promise and Performance*. 4th ed. New Jersey: Chathan House.

Peters, B. G. (1996) 'Models of Governance for the 1990s' in Kettl, D. F. and Milward, H. B. (eds.). *The State of Public Management*. Baltimore (MD): The Johns Hopkins University Press.

Peters, G. (1988) *Comparing Public Bureaucracies*. Tuscaloosa (AL): University of AL Press.

Pfiffner, J. M. and Sherwood, F. P. (1960) *Administrative Organization*. Englewood-Cliffs (NJ): Prentice Hall.

Pfiffner, J. and Presthus, R. (1953) *Public Administration*. New York: Ronald Press.

Pierre, J. and Peters, B. G. (2003) in Bovaird, T. and Loffler, E. (eds.). *Public Management and Governance*. London: Routledge.

Pollitt, C. and Bouckaert, G. (2004) *Public Management Reform: A Comparative Analysis*. 2nd ed. Oxford: Oxford University Press.

Pradhan, G. (2005) 'Civil Service Reforms in Independent India' in Chakraborty, B. and Bhattacharya, M. (eds.). *Administrative Change and Innovation: A Reader*. New Delhi: Oxford University Press.

Prasad, K. (2006) *Indian Administration: Politics, Policies and Prospects*. New Delhi: Pearson Longman.

Prasad, R. D., Prasad,V. S. and Satyanarayana, P. (2001) *Administrative Thinkers*. New Delhi: Sterling Publishers Pvt. Ltd.

Presthus, R. (1975) *Public Administration*. New York: The Ronald Press Company.

Puri, K. K. (1985) *Public Administration: Indian Spectrum*. Allahabad: Kitab Mahal.

Pyhrr, P. (1973) *Zero-Base Budgeting*. New York: John Wiley and Sons, Inc.

Pynes, J. E. and Arndt, L. M. (2001) 'The Impact of the New Public Management on Nonprofit Organizations' in Liou, K. T. (ed.). *Handbook of Public Management Practice and Reform*. New York: Marcel Dekker.

Rabin, J. and Bowman, J. (eds.) (1984) *Politics and Administration*. New York: Marcel Dekker.

Rabin, J., Hildreth, B. W. and Miller, G. J. (eds.) (2007) *Handbook of Public Administration*. 3rd ed. London, New York.

Rajiv Gandhi Foundation (March 2000) *Status Report on Panchayati Raj in India — Task Force on Panchayati Raj*. New Delhi: Rajiv Gandhi Foundation.

Raju, R. S. (2003) 'Principles and Practices of Corporate Governance' in Dhameja, A (ed.). *Contemporary Debates in Public Administration*. New Delhi: Prentice-Hall of India.

Ramachandran, P. (1996) *Public Administration in India*. New Delhi: National Book Trust.

Ray, S. N. (1996) *Modern Comparative Politics Approaches, Methods and Issues*. New Delhi: Prentice Hall of India.

Redford, E. S. (1958) *Ideal and Practice in Public Administration*. Alabama: Univ. of Alabama Press.

Rhienstein, M. (1954) *Max Weber on Law in Economy and Society*. New York: Simon and Shuster.

Rhodes, R. A. W. (1999) 'Governance and Public Administration' in Pierre, J. (ed.). *Debating Governance.* Oxford: Oxford University Press.

Rhodes, R. A. W. (2010) 'The New Governance: Governing without Government' in Boyne, G. and Ashworth, R. (eds.). *Organizing Government.* Vol. I. London: Sage.

Riggs, F. (1994) 'Global Forces and the Discipline of Public Administration' in Garcia-Zamor, J. and Khator, R. (eds.). *Public Administration in the Global Village*. Westport (CT): Praeger, 1994.

Riggs, F. (1994) 'Bureaucracy: A Profound Perplexity for Presidentialism' in Farazmand, A. (ed.) *Handbook on Bureaucracy*. New York: Marcel Dekker.

Riggs, F. W. (ed.) (1971) *Frontiers of Development Administration*. Durham (NC): Duke University Press.

Riggs, F. W. (1962) *The Ecology of Public Administration*. Bombay: Asia Publishing House.

Riggs, F. W. (1964) *Administration in Developing Countries: Theory of the Prismatic Society*. Houghton Mifflin Company.

Robinson, M. (2005) 'A Decade of Panchayati Raj Reforms: The Challenge of Democratic Decentralization in India' in Jain, L. C. (ed.). *Decentralization and Local Governance*. New Delhi: Orient Longman.

William, A. R. (ed.) (1956) *The Civil Service in Britain and France*. Hogarth Press. London.

Roethlisberger, F. J. and Dickson, W. J. (1964) *Management and the Worker: An Account of a Research Programme Conducted by the Western Electric Company, Hawthorne Works*, Chicago (Paperback edition). Harvard: Harvard Univ. Press.

Rohr, J. A. (1990) 'The Constitutional Case for Public Administration' in Wamsley, G. L. et al., (eds.). *Refounding Public Administration*. London: Sage.

Rondinelli, D. A., Nellis, J. R. and Cheema, G. S. (1984) *Decentralization in Developing Countries*. Washington, DC: World Bank.

Rondinelli, D. A. and Cheema, G. S. (1983) 'Implementing Decentralization Policies: An Introduction' in Rondinelli, D. A. and Cheema, G. S. (eds.). *Decentralization and Development Policy Implementation in Developing Countries*. US: Sage.

Rosenau, J. E. (1992) 'Governance, Order and Change in World Politics' in Rosenau, J. E. and Ernst-Otto Czempiel, E. O. (eds.). *Governance Without Government: Order and Change in World Politics*. Cambridge: Cambridge University Press.

Rosenbloom, D. H. and Kravchuk, R. S. (2002) *Public Administration: Understanding Management, Politics and Law in the Public Sector*. 5th ed. New York: McGraw Hill.

Rosenbloom, D. (1983) *Public Administration and Law: Bench v. Bureau in the United States*. New York: Marcel Dekker, Inc.

Rourke, F. (1984) *Bureaucracy, Politics, and Public Policy*. New York: HarperCollins.

Rowat, D. C. (1968) 'The Spread of the Ombudsman Idea' in Stanley V. A. (ed.). *Ombudsman for American Government*. Englewood-Cliffs (NJ): Prentice Hall.

Rowbotham, S. (1973) *Hidden from History*. London: Pluto Press.

Rowley, C. and Schneider, F. (2004) 'Principal Agent Relationships in the Theory of Bureaucracy' in C.Rowley and F.Schneider (eds.). *The Encyclopedia of Public Choice*. Vol. II. New York: Springer.

Roy, G. J. (2003) 'Right to Information: A Key to Accountable and Transparent Administration' in Dhameja, A. (ed.). *Contemporary Debates in Public Administration*. New Delhi: Prentice Hall of India.

Ruthnaswamy, M. (1953) *Principles and Practice of Public Administration*. Allahabad: Central Book Depot.

Sabarwal, M. (ed.) (2013) *Public Administration in South Asia*. Bangladesh and Pakistan: CRS Press.

Sachdeva, D. R. (2010) *Social Welfare Administration in India*. New Delhi: Kitab Mahal.

Sachdeva, D. R. and Dua, B. D. (1969) *Studies in Indian Administration*. Allahabad: Kitab Mahal.

Sadasivan, T. N. (1984) *Citizen and Administration*. New Delhi: Indian Institute of Public Administration.

Sahni, P. and Etakula, V. (2010) *Administrative Theory*. New Delhi: PHI Learning.

Sahni, P. and Kaushik S. L. (1983) *Public Administration in India: Emerging Trends*. Allahabad: Kitab Mahal.

Salamon, L. and Anheier, H. 'The Third Sector in the Third World' in *International Perspectives on Voluntary Action: Reshaping the Third Sector*. London: Earthscan.

Salamon, L. (1987) 'Partners in Public Service: The Scope and Theory of Government-Nonprofit Relations' in Powell, W. (ed.). *The NonProfit Sector: A Research Handbook*. New Haven (CT): Yale University Press.

Sapru, R. K. (1996) *Theories of Administration*. New Delhi: S. Chand and Co. Ltd.

Sapru, R. K. (2010) *Public Policy: Art and Craft of Policy Analysis*. New Delhi: PHI Learning Private Limited.

Sarkar, S. (2010) *Public Administration in India*. New Delhi: PHI.

Sayles L. R. (1958) *Behaviour of Industrial Work Groups*. (Retrieved by Hendry A. Landsberger) McGraw Hill.

Schuchter, W. (1981) *The Rise of Western Rationalism: Max Weber's Developmental History (trans.)*. Berkeley (CA): University of California Press.

Self, P. (1972) *Administrative Theories and Politics: An Enquiry into the Structure and Processes of Modern Government*. London: Allen & Unwin.

Sen, A. (1975) *Poverty and Famines: An Essay on Entitlement and Deprivation*. New York: OUP.

Sharan, P. (1978) *Public Administration in India*. Meerut: Meenakshi.

Sharkansky, I. (1978) *Public Administration and Policy Making*. Bosten Houghton Mifflin Harcourt.

Sharma, B. R. (1986) *Administrative Stress*. New Delhi: Indian Institute of Public Administration.

Sharma, M. P. (1958) *Public Administration in Theory and Practice*. Bombay: Kitab Mahal.

Sharma, P. K. and Devasher, M. (2007) 'Right to Information in India: Legislation and Beyond' in Singh, S. and Sharma, P. K. (eds.). *Decentralization: Institutions and Politics in Rural India*. New Delhi: Oxford University Press.

Sharma, R. D. (1987) *Development Administration in a Changing Society*. New Delhi: National Book Organization.

Sharma, R. (2007) 'Kerala's Decentralization The Ideal in Practice' in Singh, S. and Sharma, P. K. (eds.). *Decentralization Institutions and Politics in Rural India*. New Delhi: Oxford University Press.

Sharma, V. K. and Kumar, A. (2011) 'Corporate Governance in India: Some Thoughts' in Mokta, M., Chauhan, S. S., Mahajan, S. and Agnihotri, S. (eds.). *Challenges in Governance*. New Delhi: Anamica Publishers.

Shils, E. A. and Finch, H. A. (eds.) (1949) *The Methodology of the Social Sciences*. New York: Free Press.

Siffin, W. J. (ed.) (1957) *Toward a Comparative Study of Public Administration*. Bloomington (IN): Indiana University Press.

Simon, H. A., Smithburg, D. W. and Thompson, V. A. (1950) *Public Administration*. New York: Knopf.

Simon, H. A. (1961) *Administrative Behaviour: A Study of Decision-making Processes in Administrative Organization*. 2nd ed. New York: Macmillan.

Singh, A. (ed.) (2005) 'Introduction: Exploring Dimensions of Sustainability in Administrative Reforms' in Singh, A. *Administrative Reforms: Towards Sustainable Practices*. New Delhi: Sage.

Singh, A. (2002) *Public Administration: Roots and Wings*. New Delhi: Galgotia Publishing.

Singh, B. (1996) *Decentralization, Panchayati Raj and District Planning*. New Delhi: Atlantic Publisher and Distributers.

Singh, B. P. and Singh, S. P. (eds.) (1982) *Dimensions of Development Administration in India*. Patna: Swarna.

Singh, H. and Sachdeva, P. (2005) *Administrative Theory*. Allahabad: Kitab Mahal.

Singh, H. (1997) *Administrative Theory*. Allahabad: Kitab Mahal.

Singh, K. (2009) *Rural Development: Principle, Policies and Management*. 3rd ed. New Delhi: Sage.

Singh, S. and Sharma, P. K. (eds.) (2007) *Decentralization: Institutions and Politics in Rural India*. New Delhi: Oxford University Press.

Singh, S. (2009) *Reforms in Governance: Six Decades of Administrative Reforms*. New Delhi: Indian Institute of Public Administration.

Smith, B. C. (1985) *Decentralization: The Territorial Dimension of the State*. London: George Allen and Unwin.

Sobhan, R. (ed.) (1998) *Towards a Theory of Governance and Development Learning from East Asia*. Dhaka: The Bangladesh University Press.

Solomon, J. and Solomon, A. (2004) *Corporate Governance and Accountability*. New York: John Wiley & Sons, Chichester Publishing Co.

Sooryamoorthy, R. and Gangrade, K. D. (2001) *NGOs in India: A Cross-Sectional Study*. New Delhi: Rawat Publications.

Stewart, D. W. (1990) 'Women in Public Administration' in Lynn, N. B. and Wildavsky, A. (eds.). *Public Administration: The State of the Discipline*. New Delhi: Westview Press.

Stillman, R. J. (2000) *Public Administration: Concepts and Cases*. Boston (MA): Houghton Mifflin Company.

Stivers, C. (ed.) (2001) *Democracy, Bureaucracy and Study of Administration*. Boulder (CO): West view Press.

Stivers, C. (2002) *Gender Images in Public Administration; Legitimacy and the Administrative State*. London: Sage Publications.

Stone, D. C. (1963) 'Government Machinery Necessary for Development' in Kreisberg, M. (ed.). *Public Administration in Developing Countries* in Proceedings of an International Conference held in Bogotá, Brookings Institution. Columbia, April 15–21.

Streeten, P. (1997) 'Non-governmental Organizations and Development' in *Annals of the American Academy of Political and Social Science – Issue on the Role of NGOs: Charity and Empowerment*. Vol. 554. NO.1.

Subramaniam, V. (1990) *Public Administration in the Third World: An International Handbook*. Westport (CT): Greenwood Press.

Swetha, M. (1994) *Democratic Decentralization in India*. New Delhi: Mittal Publications.

Swetha, M. (2006) 'Understanding Decentralization in Contemporary Settings' in *Decentralization and Local Governance*. MPA-016, IGNOU Course Material.

Swerdlow, I. (1963) *Development Administration: Concepts and Problems*. New York: Syracuse University Press.

Talbot, C. (2004) 'Paradoxes of Human Nature and Public Management Reform' in Jabes, J. (ed.). *The Role of Public Administration in Alleviating Poverty and Improving Governance* in Selected Papers from Launching Conference of the Network of Asia-Pacific Schools and Institutions of Public Administration and Governance (NEPSIPAG), Asia Development Bank, Kuala Lumpur.

Tandon, R. and Mohanty, R. (2000) *Civil Society and Governance: A Research Study in India*. New Delhi: PRIA.

Taradutt, (2001) *Tribal Development in India: with Special Reference to Orissa*, New Delhi: Gyan Publication House.

Taylor, F. W. (1947) *The Principles of Scientific Management*. New York: Harper and Row.

Thavaraj, M. J. K. (1987) *Financial Administration of India*. 2nd ed. New Delhi: Sultan Chand and Sons.

Thomas, A. (1992) 'NGOs and Limits to Empowerment' in Wuyts, M. M. and T. Hewitt (eds.). *Development Action and Public Policy*. Oxford: Oxford University Press.

Thompson, J. D. (1959) *Comparative Studies in Administration*. Pittsburgh (PA): University of Administrative Science Centre.

Titmuss, R. M. (1958) 'The Social Division of Welfare' in *Essays on the Welfare State*. London: Allen & Unwin.

Transparency International India. (2008) *India Corruption Study*. New Delhi.

Tullock, G. (1965) *The Politics of Bureaucracy*. Washington, DC: *Public Affairs Press*.

Tullock, G. (1967) *The Politics of Bureaucracy*. New York: Sage.

Tummala, K. K. (1962) *Elements of Public Administration*. Tenali: Kaviraja Publishers.

Turner, M. and Hume, D. (1997) *Governance, Administration and Development: Making the State Work*. London: Macmillan.

UN General Assembly Resolution 59(1), 65th Plenary Meeting, December 14, 1946.

UNCHS. (1996) *An Urbanizing World: Global Report on Human Settlements*. United Nations Centre for Human Settlements (HABITAT). New York: Oxford.

UNDP. (2002) 'National Human Development Report.' *Deepening Democracy in a Fragmented World*. New York: OUP.

UNESCO. (1982) *Public Administration and Management: Problems of Adaptation in Different Socio-Cultural Contexts*. Paris: UNESCO.

United Nations Development Programme. (1997) Reconceptualizing Governance, Discussion Paper 2. New York.

United Nations Document. (1995) 'Rethinking Public Administration: An Overview.' Government and Public Administration Branch, Division of Public and Development Management, Department of Economic and Social Affairs.

United Nations-Department of Economic and Social Affairs. (2007) *Public Adminsitration and Democratic Governance: Governments Serving Citizens*. New York: United Nations-Department of Economic and Social Affairs.

Vadilal, D. (ed.) (1969) *The Public Sector in India: A Survey*. Bombay: Vora & Co.

Van Slyke, D. M., O'Leary, R. and Kim, S. 'Challenges and Opportunities, Crosscutting Themes, and Thoughts on the Future of Public Administration' in O'Leary, R. Van Slyke, D. M. and Kim, S. (eds.). *The Future of Public Administration around the World: The Minnowbrook Perspective*. Washington, DC: Georgetown University Press.

VANI. (2001) *Voluntarism and Government: Policy, Programme and Assistance*. New Delhi: Voluntary Action Network India.

Varma, R. S. (1973) *Bureaucracy in India*. Bhopal: Progress Publishers.

Vepa, R. K. (1978) *Change and Challenge in Indian Administration*. New Delhi: Manohar.

Verma, S. P. (ed.) (1984) *Development Administration*. New Delhi: Indian Institute of Public Administration.

Waldo, D. (1948) *The Administrative State*. New York: Ronald Press.

Waldo, D. (ed.) (1971) *Public Administration in a Time of Turbulence*. Scranton: Chandler Publishing Company.

Waldo, D. (ed.) (1970) *Temporal Dimensions of Development Administration*. Durham (NC): Duke University Press.

Waldo, D. (1955) *The Study of Public Administration*. Garden City (NY).

Waldo, D. (1981) *The Enterprise of Public Administration: A Summary View*. Novato (CA): Chandler and Sharp Publishers, Inc.

Waldo, D. (1948) *The Administrative State: A Study of the Political Theory of American Public Administration*. New York: Ronald Press.

Wamsley, G. L. (1996) 'Introduction' in Wamsley, G. L. et al. (eds.). *Refounding Democratic Public Administration: Modern Paradoxes, Post-modern Challenges*. London: Sage.

Wamsley, G. L., Wolf, J. et al., (eds.) (1996) *Refounding Democratic Public Administration: Modern Paradoxes, Post-modern Challenges*. London: Sage.

Wamsley, G. L., Bacher, R. N. et al. (1996) 'Agency Perspective' in Wamsley, G. L. et al. (eds.). *Refounding Democratic Public Administration: Modern Paradoxes, Post-modern Challenges*. London: Sage.

Weber, J. A. (2003) 'Understanding the Dimensions of Uncertainty' in Public Administration. Dhameja, A. (ed.). *Contemporary Debates in Public Administration*. New Delhi: PHI.

Weber, M. (1972) 'Wirtschaft und Gesellschaft: Grundriss der verstehenden Soziologie [Economy and Society: Handbook of Interpretative Sociology].' 5th ed. Tubingen, Germany.

Weber, M. (1978) *Economy and Society*. Berkeley (CA): University of California Press.

Weber, M. (1946) 'Bureaucracy' in Gerth, H. H. and Mills, C. W. (eds.). *From Max Weber: Essays in Modern Society*. Oxford: Oxford University Press.

Weber, M. (1946) *Essays in Sociology*. Oxford: Oxford University Press.

Weber, M. (1949) 'Objectivity in Social Science and Social Policy' in Shils, E. A. and Finch, H. A. (eds. and trans.) *The Methodology of the Social Sciences*. New York: Free Press.

Weber, M. (1992) 'The Protestant Ethic and the Spirit of Capitalism' in. Parsons, T. (trans.) and Giddens, A. (intro). London: Routledge.

Weber, M. (1994) 'The Nations State and Economic Policy (Freiburg Address)' in Lassman, P. and Speirs, R. (ed. and trans.). *Weber: Political Writings*. P. Lassman and R. Speirs (ed. and trans.), Cambridge: Cambridge University Press.

Weber, M. (1997) *The Protestant Ethic and the Spirit of Capitalism*. London: Routledge.

Weidner, E. W. (1970) 'Development and Innovational Roles' in Weidner, E. W. (ed.). *Development Administration in Asia*. Durham (NC): Duke University Press.

Weimer, D. L. and A. R. Vining. (1996) 'Economics' in Kettl, D. F. and Milward, H. B. (eds.). *The State of Public Management*. Baltimore/London: The Johns Hopkins University Press.

White, G. L. (1987) *Creating Opportunities for Change*. Bouldner (CO): Lynne Reiner.

White, J. D. and Adams, G. B. (1994) 'Making Sense with Diversity: The Conttext of Research, Theory and Knowledge Development in Public Administration' in White, J. D. and Adams, G. B. (eds.). *Research in Public Administration: Reflections in Theory and Practice*. UK: Sage.

White, L. D. (1955) *Introduction to the Study of Public Administration*. New York: Crowell-Collier and Macmillan.

William, N. (1971) *Bureaucracy and Representative Government*. New York: Aldine Atherton.

Willoughby, W. F. (1972) *Principles of Public Administration: With Special Reference to the National and State Governments of the United States*. Baltimore (MD): Johns Hopkins Press.

Wilson, J. Q. *Bureaucracy, What Government Agencies Do and Why They Do It*. 1st ed. New York: Basic Books.

Wilson, W. (1953) 'The Study of Administration' in Waldo, D. (ed.). *Ideas and Issues in Public Administration*. New York: McGraw-Hill.

Wolff, R. (2012) 'In Capitalist Crisis, Rediscovering Marx' in Marcello, M. (ed.). *Marx for Today*. London: Routledge.

World Bank. (1989) *Sub-Saharan Africa: From Crisis to Sustainable Growth—A Long-term Perspective Study*. Washington, DC: World Bank.

World Bank. (1992) *The World Bank in Governance: The World Bank Experience*. Washington, DC: World Bank.

World Bank. (1992) *World Development Report*. Washington, DC: Oxford University Press, New York.

World Bank. (1994) World Bank Report. *Governance, The World Bank Experience*. Washington, DC.

World Bank. (1994) World Bank Report. *The World Bank and Participation*. Washington, DC.

World Bank. (1997) World Bank Report. *The State in a Changing World*. Washington, DC.

World Bank. (April, 1992) World Bank Report. *Governance and Development*. Washington, DC: The International Bank for Reconstruction and Development.

World Bank. (1989) *World Development Report*. New York: OUP.

World Bank. (1989) *The Bank and the Heavily Indebted Middle-Income Countries*. Washington, DC: World Bank.

Wesley, B. et al. (1975) *The Sociology of the Third World*. Cambridge: Cambridge University Press.

ARTICLES

(2009) Right to Information: Present Status and Issues. *Special Issue of Indian Journal of Public Administration*. LV(3).

(2011) Controlling Corruption in India: Various Aproaches and their Efficacy. *Special Issue of Indian Journal of Public Administration*. LVII(3).

(2013) Ethical Governance and Society. *Special Issue of Indian Journal of Public Administration*. LIX(3).

Ahammed, M. A. (1999) Good Governance through Transparency. *Management in Government*. XXXI(3).

Alchian, A. and Demsetz, H. (1972) Production, Information Costs and Economic Organization. *The American Economic Review*. 62.

Andrew, C. and Goldsmith, M. (1988) From Local Government to Local Governance: And beyond? *International Political Science Review*. 19(2).

Appu, B. S. (March 1986) The Decline of the Indian Bureaucracy. *Man and Development*. 8.

Argyris, C. (1973) Some Limits of Rational Man Organizations Theory. *Public Administrative Review*. 33(3).

Arora, R. K. and Ferreros, A. (1972) A Dimensional Approach to the Ecology in Public Bureaucracies — an addendum to John Forward. *Indian Journal of Public Administration*. XVIII(2).

Bagai, A. (2009) Development Administration: Temporal and Spatial Dimensions. *Indian Journal of Public Administration*. LV(1).

Bagchi, A. (1972) Civil Service Neutrality: Concept and Practice. *Academy of Administration*. 17(2).

Bailey, M. T. (1989) Minnowbrook II: An End or a New Beginning. *Public Administration Review*. 49(2)

Banarjee, A. M. (1963) Fifteen Years of Administrative Reforms — an overview. *IPA*. IX(3).

Bandyopadhyay, D. (1996) Administration, Decentralization and Good Governance. *Economic and Political Weekly*. XXXI(48).

Bell, R. and Watchirs, H. (1998) Freedom of Information: The Common Wealth Experience. *Australian Journal of Public Administration*. XLVII(4).

Bhambri, C. P. (1970– 1971) Should India have a Committed Bureaucracy? *Indian Political Science Review*. V(1).

Bhambri, C. P. (1971) Public Corporations in India: Autonomy Versus Control. *Political Science Review*. 10(1–2).

Bhattacharaya, M. (1998) Conceptualizing Good Governance. *Indian Journal of Public Administration*. XLIV(3).

Bjur, W. and Caiden, G. (1978) Reforming Institutional Bureaucracies. *Institutional Review of Administrative Sciences*. XXIV.

Black, B. S. and Vikramaditya Khanna, S. V. (2007) Can Corporate Governance Reforms Increase Firm Market Values? Event Study Evidence from India. *Journal of Empirical Legal Studies*. 4.

Borins, S. (1995) The New Public Management is here to Stay. *Canadian Public Administration*. 38(1).

Braibanti, R. (1962) Reflections on Bureaucratic Corruption. *Public Administration* (*London*). 40(4).

Burnier, D. L. (1993) Reinventing Government from a Feminist Perspective: Feminist Theory and Administrative Reality. *Feminist Teacher*.

Butani, K. N. (1969) Personnel Administration: A Muffled Cry for Change by the Administrative Reforms Commission. *Indian Journal of Public Administration*. XV(1).

Butcher, T. (1995) The Major Government and White Hall: The Civil Service at the Crossroads. *Teaching Public Administration*. Vol 15, No.1, 19–31

Caiden, G. (1969) Development Administration and Administrative Reform. *International Social Science Journal*. 2(1).

Carey, A. (1967) The Hawthorne Studies as Radical Criticism. *American Sociological Review*. 32(3).

Chadah, S. (2006) Right to Information Regime in India: A Critical Appraisal. *Indian Journal of Public Administration*. LII(1).

Chakravarthy, N. S. (1990) Management and Administration in India — Impact of Vigilance Machinery. *Indian Journal of Public Administration*. XXXVI(4).

Chandhoke, N. (2007) Civil Society. *Development in Practice*. 17(4).

Chandra, B. (1969) Personnel Administration: Time for Action. *Indian Journal of Public Administration*. XV(2). Volume 28, Issue 4

Chapman, B. (1950) A Development in French Regional Administration. *Public Administration* (*London*).

Chaturvedi, M. K. (1971) Commitment in Civil Service. *Indian Journal of Public Administration*. XVII(1).

Chaturvedi, T. N. (1972) Role of Training in Administration. *Prasasnika*. 1(4).

Christensen, T. (2012) Post-NPM and Changing Public Governance. *Meiji Journal of Political Science and Economics*. (12).

Clark, D. (2000) Citizen's Charter and Public Service Reform in France and Britain. *Government and Opposition*. 35(2).

Dahl, R. A. (1974) The Science of Public Administration: Three Problems, a Brief, Incisive Critique of "Orthodoxy". *Public Administration Review*. 7. Vol 20 No.15 19 July–1August

Dasappa, H. C. (1961) Parliamentary Control and Accountability of Public Undertakings. *IPA*. VII(2).

Dash, S. C. (1970–1971) Should India have a Committed Bureaucracy? *Indian Political Science Review*. Vol 5. NO (1).

Datta, P. (2003) Panchayati Raj. *Frontline*. Vol.20, No.15, 19 July-1 August

Datta, S. K. (1963) New Training Programmes for Central and State Government Employees. *Indian Journal of Public Administration*. IX(3).

Dave, P. K. (1965) The Collector, Today and Tomorrow. *IPA*. XI(3).
Davy, T. J. (1962) Public Administration as a Field of Study in the United States. *International Review of Administrative Sciences*. 28.
Grazia, A. D. (1960) The Science and Values of Administration. *Administrative Science Quarterly*. 5.
Denhardt, R. B. and Perkins, J. (1976) The Coming Death of Administrative Man. *Public Administration Review*. 36(4).
Dubashi, P. R. (1969) ARC Report on Personnel Administration: Faulty Superstructure on False Premise. *Indian Journal of Public Administration*. XV(4).
Dubashi, P. R. and Ramaiah, K. (1987) The Role of the Cabinet Secretariat. *Management in Government*. XVIII(4).
Dubashi, P. R. (1984) Role of Bureaucracy in Development. *Administrator.* 29(1 & 2).
Dubashi, P. R. (1971) Committed Bureaucracy. *Indian Journal of Public Administration*. XVII(1).
Dubashi, P. R. (1970) Administrative Reforms of Public Sector Undertaking. *The Modern Review*. CXXVII(5).
Dubey, S. N. (1972) Organizational Analysis of Panchayati Raj Institutions in India. *Indian Journal of Public Administration*. XVIII(2).
Dutta, A. (1986) Reforming the Budgetary practice: From Industrial to Zero-Base Budgeting. *Lok Udyog*. 19(1).
Dutta, P. K. (1990) Democratizing Rural Administration: The West Bengal Experience. *Indian Journal of Administrative Science*. 1(1).
Dwivedi, O. P. (1989) Administrative Heritage, Morality and Challenges in the Sub-Continent since the British Raj. *Public Administration and Development*. 9.
Dwivedi, O. P. (1997). Development Administration: An Overview. *Indian Journal of Public Administration*. XLIII(3).
England, R. E. and Morgan, D. (1988) The Two Faces of Privatization. *PAR*. 48(6).
Epstein, L. D. (1950) Political Sterilization of Civil Servants: The United States and great britain. *PAR*. X(4).
Farazmand, A. Development and Comparative Public Administration: Past, Present and Future. *Public Administration Quarterly*. 20(3).
Farazmand, A. (1999) Globalization and Public Administration. *Public Administration Review*. 59(6).
Fesler, J. W. (1965) Approaches to the Understanding of Decentralization. *Journal of Politics*. XXVII(3).
Finer, S. E. (1956) The Individual Responsibility of Ministers. *Public Administration (London)*. 34. Vol. 49 No. 2, June 1998 Pg 210–233
Flyvbjerg, B. (1998) Habermas and Foucault: Thinkers for Civil Society? *British Journal of Sociology.* Vol 49 No. 2, June 1998 Pg 210–233
Frederickson, G. H. (1989) Minnowbrook II: Changing Epochs of Public Administration. *Public Administration Review*. March/Appril Vol 49 No. 2, P.95
Frederickson, G. H. (1996) Comparing the Reinventing Government Movement with the New Public Administration. *Public Administration Review*. 56(3).
Fry, W. L. (1976) The maligned F. W. Taylor: A Reply to his Many Critics. *Conceptual Notes in The Academy of Management Review*. 1(3).
Galbraith, J. K. (1961) Public Administration and Public Corporation. *Indian Journal of Public Administration*. (4).
Gandhi, R. (1988) Responsive Administration. Speech at Coimbatore, cited in Times of India.
Ghuman, B. S. (2001) New Public Management: Theory and Practice. *Indian Journal of Public Administration*. XLVII(4).
Goodsell, C. T. (2006) A New Vision for Public Administration. *Public Administration Review*. 66(4).
Gopinath, G. R. (2013) Bring the CBI Under the Lokpal. *The Hindu*. November 18.
Gordon, M. R. (1971) Civil Servants, Politicians and Parties. *Comparative Politics*. IV(1).
Graham, P. (2001) Civil Society Ttheory and Euro-Nationalism. *Studies in Social and Political Thought*. (4).
Roy, J. G. (1990) Open Government and Administrative Culture in India. *Indian Journal of Public Administration*. 36(3).
Guy, M. E. (1989) Minnowbrook II Conclusions. *Public Administration Review*.

Haldipur, R. N. (1977) On Debureaucratizing Bureaucracy. *Indian Journal of Public Administration*. XXIII(3).

Haque, S. M. (2000) Significance of Accountability Under the New Approach to Public Governance. *International Review of Administrative Sciences*. 66(4).

Haque, S. M. (1998) Legitimation Crisis: A Challenge for Public Service in the Next Century. *International Review of Administrative Sciences*. 64.

Harris, N. (2003) Globalization and the Management of Indian Cities. *Economic and Political Weekly*. 38(25).

Hassan, M. (2000) The Agenda for Good Governance in a Globalized world. *South Asian Survey*. 7.

Heady, F. (1959) Bureaucratic Theory and Comparative Administration. *Administrative Science Quarterly*. 3(4).

Hill, L. (1991) Who Governs the Administrative State: A Bureaucratic-Centered Image of Government. *Journal of Public Administration Research and Theory*. 1(3).

Hood, C. (1991) A Public Management for all Seasons? *Public Administration*. 69(1).

Iyer, R. R. (2004) The Meaning of Good Governance. *Indian Journal of Public Administration*. 50(1).

Jackson, R. H. (1996) An Analysis of the Comparative Public Administration Movement Canadian Public Administration. *Journal of the Institute of Public Administration of Canada*. IX(1).

Jayal, N. G. (2006) Engendering Local Democracy: The Impact of Quotas for Women in India's Panchayats. *Democratization*. 13(1).

Jha, S. N. (1979) Representative Bureaucracy: An Indicator of Political Development. *Indian Journal of Public Administration*. XXV(2). pp. 324–333.

Joseph, S. (2001). Democratic Good Governance: New Agenda for Change. *Economic and Political Weekly*. 36(12).

Jreisat, J. E. (1975) Synthesis and Relevance of Comparative Public Administration. *Public Administration Review*.

Jreisat, J. (2004) Governance in a Globalized World. *International Journal of Public Administration*. 27(13–14).

Jun, J. S. (1976) Renewing the Study of Comparative Administration. *Public Administration Review*. 36.

Juneja, S. V. S. (1973) Panchayati Raj — a Survey. *Indian Journal of Public Administration*. XIX(1).

Kanal, S. A. (2011) Disaster Resilience through right Based and Capability Perspectives of NGOs: A Case Study of 2004 Tsunami in Nagapattinam. *Dynamics of Public Administration*. 28(2).

Kapoor, J. C. (2000) IT and Good Governance. *Indian Journal of Public Administration*. XLVI(3).

Khosla, I. P. (2000). Governance and Difference. *South Asian Survey*. 7(2).

Kirlin, J. J. (1996) The Big Question in a Democracy *Public Administration Review*. Vol 56, 416–423.

Kumar, S. (2000) Civil Society in Society. *Economic and Political Weekly*. 35(31).

Lauth, T. P. (1978) Zero-base Budgeting in Georgia State Government: Myth and Reality. *Public Administration Review*. 38(5).

Leftwich, A. (1993) Governance, Democracy and Development in the Third world. *Third World Quarterly*. 14(3).

Lewis, D. (2003) Management of Non-governmental Development Organizations: Towards a Composite Approach. *Public Management Review*. 5(3).

Leys, C. (1956) What is the Problem about Corruption? *Journal of Modern African Studies*. III(2).

Lindblom, C. E. (1959) The Science of Muddling through. *Public Administration Review*. 19(2).

Ling, T. (2002) Delivering Joined-up Government in the UK: Dimensions, Issues and Problems. *Public Administration*. 80(4).

Lipsky, M. and Smith, S. R. (1990) Nonprofit Organizations, Government and the Welfare State. *Political Science Quarterly*. 104, No.4 (625–48)

Long, N. E. (1952) Bureaucracy and Constitutionalism. *APSR*. XLVI(3).

Mahajan, G. (1999) Civil Society and its Avatars: What happened to Freedom and Democracy? *Economic and Political Weekly*.

Mathai, P. G. (1988) Budget Making: A Byzantine Exercise. *India Today*. 15 March, 15.

Mathur, K. (1971) A Committed Bureaucracy for India — Notes towards Evolving a model. *Political Science Review*. X(1 & 2).

Meier, J. K. and O'Toole, L. J. (2006) Political Control Versus Bureaucratic Values: Reframing the Debate. *Public Administration Review*. 66(2).

Minocha, O. P. (1998) Good Governance: New Public Management Perspective. *Indian Journal of Public Administration*. XLIV(3).

Mishra, A. D. (2011) Gandhian Perspective on Corruption. *Indian Journal of Public Administration*. LVII(3).

Mishra, A. D. (2013) Gandhian Perspective on Ethical Governance and Society. *Indian Journal of Public Administration*. LIX(3).

Mishra, S. N. and Mishra, S. (1998) Good Governance, People's Participation and NGO's. *Indian Journal of Public Administration*. 44(3).

Mishra, S. (1997) Women and 73rd Constitutional Amendment act: A Critical Appraisal. *Social Action*. 47(1).

Mishra, S. (2009) Right to Information and Decentralised Governance. *Indian Journal of Public Administration*. LV(3).

Mishra, S. (2002) Empowerment of Women in Urban Local Bodies: An Assessment. *Nagarlok*. XXXIV(4).

Molitor, A. (1961) Public Administration Towards the Future. *International Review of Administrative Sciences*. 27.

Moore, L. E. (1947) Current Issues in Industrial Sociology. *American Sociological Review*. 12(6).

Mosher, F. C. (1956) Research in Public Administration: Some Notes and Suggestions. *Public Administration Review*. 16.

Moynihan, D. P. and Thomas, J. C. (2013) Citizen, Customer Partner: Rethinking the Place of the Public in Public Management. *Public Administration Review*. 73(6).

Muttalib, M. A. (1976) Committed Bureaucracy or Positions of Confidence? *Administrative Change*. 4(1).

Narayan, S. (2013) A Question of Accountability. *The Hindu*, November 15.

Nayyar, D. (2000) Alleviating Poverty: Role of Good Governance and Constitutional Reform. *Economic and Political Weekly*.

Nigam, S. S. (1960) Equality and the Representation of the Scheduled Classes in Parliament. *Journal of the Indian Law Institute*. 2.

Lewis, N. (1993) The Citizens' Charter and Next Steps: A New Way of Governing? *Political Quarterly*. 64(3).

Osborne, S. P. (2006) The New Public Governance. *Public Management Review (Editorial)*. 8(3).

Pathak, A. (2009) Government Interference and Management Problems of Public Sector Firms. *Annals of Public and Cooperative Economy*. 40(3).

Peters, B. G. (2011) Theoretical Debates in Public Administration in the Past 50 Years. *HKJU-CCPA*. 11.

Pollitt, C. (1995) Justification by Works or by Faith? Evaluating the New Public Management. *Evaluation*. 12.

Prasad, A. (1960) The Theory and Practice of the Public Corporation in a Democracy. *Indian Journal of Public Administration*. VI(1).

Premchand, A. (1967) Towards a Functional Budget. *Economic and Political Weekly*. (2).

Puranik, S. N. (1978) The Problem of Autonomy and Control in Public Enterprises an India. *Indian Journal of Public Administration*. XXIV(4).

Raghavulu, C. V. and Narayan, E. A. (1991) Reforms in Panchayati Raj: A Convocative Analysis of Andhra Pradesh, Karnataka and West Bengal. *Indian Journal of Public Administration*. XXXVII(I).

Rai, H. (1965) Institution of District Collector. *Indian Journal of Public Administration*. XI(3).

Rapheali, N. (October 1970) The Civil Servants as Gatekeepers. *Personnel Review*. XXXI.

Ray, A. (1987) New Panchayati System in Karnataka. *Economic and Political Weekly*. XXII(7).

Rhodes, R. A. W. (1994) The Hallowing Out of the State: The Changing Nature of Public Service in Britain. *The Political Quarterly*. 65(2).

Riggs, F. (1993) Fragility of the Third world's Regimes. *International Social Science Review*. No. 136.

Riggs, F. W. (1962) Trends in Comparative Study of Public Administration. *International Review of Administrative Sciences*. 281(1), Cited in Jun, J. S. (1976) Renewing the Study of Comparative Administration: Some Reflections on the Current Possibilities. *Public Administration Review*. (36).

Riggs, F. W. (1976) The Group and the Movement: Notes on Comparative and Development Administration. *Public Administration Review*.

Riggs, F. (1987) The Interdependence of Politics and Administration, *Philippine Journal of Public Administration*. XXXI(4).

William A. R. (1961) The Present State of Teaching and Research in Public Administration. *Public Administration*. 39.
Rosenbloom, D. H. (1983) Public Administrative Theory and the Separation of Powers. *PAR*. 43(3).
Rosenbloom, D. H. (1981) Federal Equal Employment Opportunity: Is the Polarization Worth the Preference? *Southern Review of Public Administration*. 5(1).
Rosenbloom, D. (January–December, 2013) Public Administration Theory and Separation of Powers. *Administrative Change*. XL, No. 2 and XLI(1).
Roy, A. and Dey, N. (2002) Fighting for the Right to know in India. *Development Dialogu*. 1.
Roy, A., Singh, S. and Dey, N. (2006) A Fight for 'Right to Know' *Yojana*. 50.
Roy, B. (1996) Right to Information Profile of a Grass Root Struggle. *Mainstream*. 34(23).
Roy, D. F. (1952) Quota Restrictions and Gold-bricking in a Machine Shop. *American Journal of Sociology*. 57.
Sainath, P. (2006) Privatization: Come hell or high water. *The Hindu*. March, 22.
Sayre, W. S. (1958) Premises of Public Administration: Past and Emerging. *Public Administration Review*. 18.
Schick, A. (1966) The Road to PPB: The Stages of Budget Reform. *PAR*. 26(4).
Scott, W. G. (1961) Organization Theory: An Overview and an Appraisal. *Journal of the Academy of Management*. 4(1).
Selznick, P. (1943) An Approach to a Theory of Bureaucracy. *American Sociological Review*. 8(1).
Sen, S. (1992) Non-profit Organizations in India: Historical Development and Common patterns. *Voluntas*. 3(2).
Sengupta, A. (2013) Activist Verdicts. *Frontline*. November 1.
Sethi, J. D. (1983) Bureaucracy and Accountability. *Indian Journal of Public Administration*. XXIX(3).
Shils, E. (1960) Political Development in the New States. *Comparative Studies in Society and History*. 2(3).
Shivaraman, B. (1971) Generalists and the Specialists in Administration. *Indian Journal of Public Administration*. XVII(3).
Shleifer, A. and Vishny, R. W. (1997) A Survey of Corporate Governance. *Journal of Finance*. 52
Sigelman, L. (1972) Do Modern Bureaucracies Dominate Underdeveloped Politics a Test of the Imbalance Theories. *APSR*. LXVI(2).
Simon, H. (1973) Organizational Man: Rational or Self-actualisation. *Public Administration Review*. 33(4).
Singh, S. and Singh, M. (2006) Changing Governance Forever. *Yojana*. 50.
Svara, J. H. (2001) The Myth of the Dichotomy: Complementarity of Politics and Administration in the Past and Future of Public Administration. *Public Administration Review*. 61.
Tahmasebi, R. and Seyyed, M. M. M. (2011) Politics-Administration Dichotomy: A Century debate. *Administratie Si Management Public*. 17.
Thavaraj, M. J. K. (1984) Performance Budgeting in India — an Evaluation. *Indian Journal of Public Administration*. XXX(1).
Tummala, K. K. (1981) Higher Civil Service in India: 'Commitment' or 'Establishment'?. *Politics, Administration and Change*. VI(2).
Vakil, A. (1997) Confronting the Classification Problem: Toward a Taxonomy of NGOs. *World Development*. 25(12).
Vittal, C. P. (1998) Devolution of Powers and Functions to Panchayati raj Institutions. *Kurekshetra*. 26(7).
Vohra, N. N. (2000) Cooperating for Good Governance in South Asia. *South Asian Survey*. 7(2).
Waldo, D. (1965) The Administrative State Revisited. *Public Administration Review*. 25(1).
Walters, J. (2000) The Welfare Bonanza. *Governing*. Volume 13 No.4.
Williams, D. W. (2009) Reinventing the Proverbs of Government. *Indian Journal of Public Administration*. Vol. 15, No. 3.
Wilson, W. (1887) The Study of Administration. *Political Science Quarterly*. II(I).
Wood, E. M. (1990) The Uses and Abuses of' Civil Society. *Socialist Register*. 26(26).
Zhiyong, L. and Rosenbloom, D. H. (1992) Editorial: Public Administration in Transition. *Public Administration Review*. 52(6).

Index

B

C

M

N

O

P

U

V

W

Z